Chronicles of Lake Champlain

Journeys in War and Peace

Preface by Arthur B. Cohn
Director, Lake Champlain Maritime Museum

Also by Russell P. Bellico

Sails and Steam in the Mountains:
A Maritime and Military History of
Lake George and Lake Champlain

Chronicles of Lake George:
Journeys in War and Peace

Chronicles of Lake Champlain

Journeys in War and Peace

Russell P. Bellico

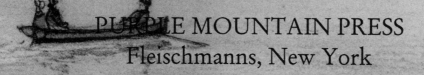

PURPLE MOUNTAIN PRESS
Fleischmanns, New York

To my son Bill

First Edition 1999
published by
Purple Mountain Press, Ltd.
1060 Main Street, P.O. Box E3
Fleischmanns, New York 12430-0378
914-254-4062, 914-254-4476 (fax)
Purple@catskill.net   http://www.catskill.net/purple

Library of Congress Cataloging-in-Publication Data

Bellico, Russell P. (Russell Paul), 1943-
    Chronicles of Lake Champlain : journeys in war and peace / Russell
P. Bellico. -- 1st ed.
      p.   cm.
    Includes bibliographical references and index.
      ISBN 0-916346-71-4 (acid-free paper). -- ISBN 0-916346-70-6 (pbk. :
acid-free paper)
    1. Champlain, Lake, Region--History Sources. I. Title.
F127.C6B45   1999
974.7'54- -dc21   99-23978
                                                                         CIP

Manufactured in the United States of America. Printed on acid-free paper.
    1 2 3 4 5 6 7 8 9

Front cover and title page: "Village of Essex N.Y." by E. Whitefield (1846).
New York State Museum, Albany, New York

Back cover: "Battle of Plattsburgh Bay," lithograph, *American Naval Broadsides.*
E. Newbold Smith Collection, Independence Seaport Museum, Philadelphia, Pennsylvania

Contents

Acknowledgments   7
Preface   11
Introduction   15

Part I   **Passage in the Wilderness**

    1.   Samuel de Champlain 1609   21
    2.   Peter Kalm 1749   45

Part II   **The French and Indian War**

    3.   Louis-Joseph de Montcalm 1758   73
    4.   Jeffery Amherst 1759   101
    5.   Robert Rogers 1760   143

Part III   **Settlement**

    6.   William Gilliland 1765   171

Part IV   **The American Revolution**

    7.   Jocelyn Feltham 1775   187
    8.   Bayze Wells 1776   205
    9.   Enos Hitchcock 1777   239

Part V   **Temporary Peace**

    10. Isaac Weld 1796   273

Part VI   **War of 1812**

    11. Thomas Macdonough 1814   295

Part VII   **The Northern Tour**

    12. Tyrone Power 1835   329
    13. Benjamin Clapp Butler 1873   349
    14. Augusta Brown 1895   373
    15. Seneca Ray Stoddard 1915   401

Index   431

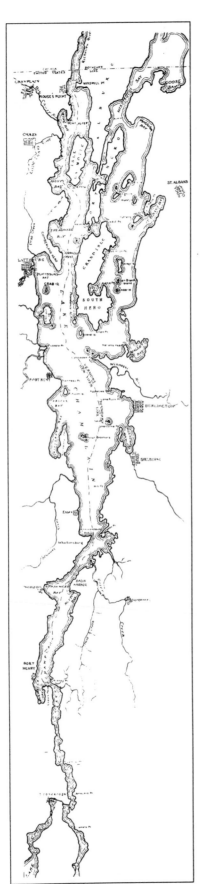

Lake Champlain. From *Life of Commodore Thomas Macdonough* by Rodney Macdonough (1909).

Acknowledgments

MANY INSTITUTIONS AND INDIVIDUALS have contributed to the research and final production of this book. I wish to thank Drs. Allen B. Ballard and Dan S. White of the State University of New York at Albany for their efforts in securing my appointment as a Visiting Scholar in History in 1997, which among other benefits, provided me with access to the university's microfilm collection of the Colonial Office Records, Public Record Office (London) and the Horatio Gates Papers. My semester in Albany also afforded me access to the New York State Library and Archives. The dedicated staffs at the state library and archives were especially helpful in ferreting out obscure documents, early maps, and a wide variety of published sources. I am very grateful to Craig Williams, senior curator (history) at the New York State Museum, for his untiring aid in locating historical materials and facilitating the use of illustrations.

I am deeply appreciative for the research assistance provided by a number of individuals: Christopher D. Fox, Curator of Collections at Fort Ticonderoga / Thompson-Pell Research Center; Karen Stites Campbell, reference specialist in Special Collections at the Bailey / Howe Memorial Library at the University of Vermont; J. Kevin Graffagnino, former Special Collections librarian at UVM; Janet Letteron of the Hadley-Luzerne Historical Society; Jerold Pepper, librarian at the Adirondack Museum; Martha H. Smart, reference assistant at the Connecticut Historical Society; Edward Vermue, Special Collections librarian at the Penfield Library at SUNY Oswego; and Albert W. Fowler, archivist, and Bruce Cole, reference librarian, at the Crandall Library. The helpful staffs of many libraries assisted me in locating materials relating to Lake Champlain: the Huntington Library (San Marino, CA.), the University of Massachusetts Library at Amherst, the Amherst College Library, the Mount Holyoke College Library, the Smith College Library, the Benjamin F. Feinberg Library at SUNY Plattsburgh, the

Plattsburgh Public Library, Boston Public Library, the National Archives in Washington, D. C., the National Archives of Canada in Ottawa, the Starr Library at Middlebury College, the Bixby Library in Vergennes and the Sherman Library in Port Henry. I am also very appreciative of the research materials supplied by individuals: Joseph W. Zarzynski, Gary S. Zaboly, Scott Padeni, Timothy J. Todish, Sibyl Blake Selkirk, Warder H. Cadbury, and George A. Bray III.

Recognition is gratefully acknowledged to many institutions and people who assisted in securing illustrations: Mahlon and Gina Teachout, Gary S. Zaboly, Timothy J. Todish, L. F. Tantillo, Craig Williams (New York State Museum), Dick Andress (New York State Archives), Arthur B. Cohn (Lake Champlain Maritime Museum), Kevin J. Crisman (Texas A&M University), Christopher D. Fox (Fort Ticonderoga), William Farrar (Crown Point State Historic Site), Richard K. Dean (Dean's Photography), Paul Carnahan (Vermont Historical Society), Jim Meehan (Adirondack Museum), Tracy N. Meehan (Adirondack Museum), Robyn Woodworth (Shelburne Museum), Nicole Wells (The New-York Historical Society), Jackie Spafford (Royal Ontario Museum), Beverly C. Olmsted (New York State Historical Association), Linda Best (Mead Art Museum, Amherst College), David Manning (Naval Historical Foundation, Washington, D.C.), Michael F. Angelo (Independence Seaport Museum), and the staffs of the National Archives of Canada, Library of Congress, and the Beaverbrook Art Gallery.

I am especially indebted to several individuals at Westfield State College who carefully developed and printed photographs for the book: the late John Morytko, former director of photographic services; David Harris-Fried, director of photographic services; and Carla Lemnah Warner, photography consultant. I will be forever grateful to Helen Lent, former administrative assistant at the college, and Barbara Rock, a work study student, who earnestly and laboriously transcribed my drafts onto a word processor and accommodated my endless revisions. Danielle Bramucci, an administrative assistant at Westfield State College, was extremely supportive in making my final corrections and handling communications with libraries, historical societies, and art galleries. Two skilled reference librarians at the Westfield State College Library, Jennifer Hanna and Ralph Wagner, provided help in locating obscure research materials. Two retired English professors from the college, Drs. Wallace Goldstein and Frank Salvidio, patiently read the manuscript and suggested many changes which improved the readability of the text. Acknowledgment is gratefully due Dr. Ruth Ohayon of the Department of Foreign Languages who translated French sources.

Nicholas Westbrook, executive director of Fort Ticonderoga and one of the most knowledgeable historians specializing in early American history of the Northeast, graciously volunteered to proofread the chapters covering the seventeenth and eighteenth centuries. His incisive comments and suggestions were instrumental in enriching the manuscript. A special thank you is due Arthur B. Cohn, director of the Lake Champlain Maritime Museum and an expert on the lake's maritime heritage, who generously agreed to write a preface to the book. I am also thankful to Dr. James C. Dawson at the State University of New York at Plattsburgh for his suggestions on the geology of Lake Champlain and Jim Shaughnessy of Troy, New York, for checking the accuracy of the section of the text dealing with railroads. The encouragement of Joseph W. Zarzynski, executive director of Bateaux Below,

Inc., and that of my colleagues on the board of directors was very much appreciated. Recognition is also due to the divers who patiently posed for my underwater photographs of Lake Champlain shipwrecks over many years: Richard A. Bellico, Frank Canosa, Joseph W. Zarzynski, Dan B. Couture, Jack Sullivan, and Robert Benway. Thanks are also due to Captain Dan B. Couture (Marine Explorers) for his excellent scuba diving charters to the many shipwrecks of Lake Champlain.

I would like to give a special acknowledgment to my publishers, Wray and Loni Rominger, for their continued encouragement during the writing stage of this project and their effort in producing this book. Their unwavering commitment to the publication of regional history will be appreciated by many generations of readers to come and will provide a lasting legacy.

I am deeply grateful for the understanding and support of my wife Jane and son Bill, who also made sacrifices while I spent endless hours in my study or at libraries working on this project. I relied heavily on my wife's sound advice and proofreading as the manuscript progressed over a three-year period. Finally, I would especially recognize my brother, Richard A. Bellico, who accompanied me on my diving adventures to Lake Champlain 30 years ago in search of Benedict Arnold's lost gunboat. These early trips kindled my interest in further exploring the history of the lake. Although ostensibly an eon ago, these first exciting expeditions to Lake Champlain seem to have occurred only yesterday, and like a fine wine, the memories improve with age.

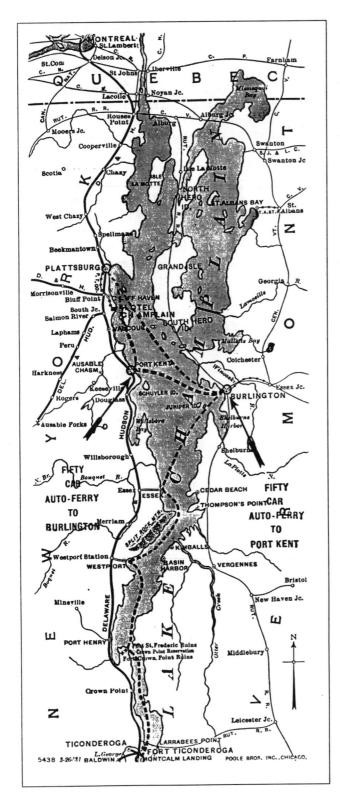

The Champlain Transporta-
tion Company's 1931 map
showing steamboat routes.
(Author's collection)

Preface

by Arthur B. Cohn

Lake Champlain: A Great Lake

LAKE CHAMPLAIN was undoubtedly better known to eighteenth and nineteenth century travelers than it is today. By benefit of its north-south orientation, location, and evolving world events, the lake was then one of North America's great arteries of military conquest and commercial fortune.

When the "Great Lake" debate broke out across the country in 1997, most Americans scoffed at the idea that a place they had never heard about should consider itself "great." Sadly, heated discussion among citizens revealed an almost total lack of knowledge about the origins of their country. Few Americans could locate Lake Champlain on a map, much less explain its military connections to such figures as the Marquis de Montcalm, Jeffery Amherst, Benedict Arnold, Horatio Gates, John Burgoyne, or Thomas Macdonough. Indeed, few people are aware that for most of the nineteenth century, Lake Champlain served as one of the nation's most dynamic commercial corridors. Those of us who study and value our region's historical legacy wish to share these special stories with a wider audience. We are kindred spirits in the desire to "exploit" the region's rich lessons of war, peace, commerce, and technology to gain a better understanding of society.

Russ Bellico has been a student and teacher of the Lake Champlain-Lake George corridor for more than three decades. He loves the region, recognizes its contributions to our present-day society and is eager to share it with new generations. In *Chronicles of Lake Champlain*, Bellico evokes the voices of people who recorded their observations at various moments in time. Through the use of journalists' personal experiences, Bellico captures the texture of each period.

The last two decades have seen enormous changes in the perception of the region's historical importance. When I began working at the lake as a professional diver in the early 1970s, few realized its historic or archaeological significance. But there were some: Ferry Captain Merritt Carpenter, Vermont state archivist John Williams, historian J. Robert Maguire and writer Ralph Nading Hill. The work of these individuals helped stimulate Russ Bellico, Peter Barranco, Kevin Crisman, Dennis Lewis, me and others to carry the quest for knowledge about the Champlain Valley into the next century. We all hope that some readers of this book may in turn join the next generation of chroniclers.

For me, interest was fueled by the wealth of shipwrecks and other submerged archaeological resources lying on the lake's bottom and waiting to be discovered. The *Phoenix* (1815), the oldest surviving steamboat hull in the world; the Burlington Bay Horse Ferry (ca.1825), the only known surviving example of marine horse-powered technology; the *Boscawen* (1759), one of Jeffery Amherst's sloops-of-war; the Revolutionary War "Great Bridge," remarkably built on the ice by American forces during the winter of 1777; the American brig *Eagle* (1814) and the British brig *Linnet* (1814), along with two other survivors of the War of 1812; the *General Butler* (1862), which led to our awareness of the existence of sailing canal boats, have all been located and documented over the past two decades. Just last year one of Benedict Arnold's gunboats (similar to the one on which Lieutenant Bayze Wells served) was discovered sitting upright on the lake bottom with its bow cannon still in place and its mast still standing. As the number of shipwreck sites grew, it appeared that Lake Champlain contained the best preserved collection of wooden ships in North America.

These wooden "time capsules" provide a new and extraordinary window through which the past can be viewed. They are a special legacy which our generation has just begun to value, attempt to manage, and preserve for future generations. Our studies have now included vessels upon which each of the contributing voices in the *Chronicles* might have traveled.

Today, places where history was made are now historic places. Over the past decade renewed interest in Champlain Valley history has led to a string of new historic sites being developed that provide access to selected chapters of the story. Venerable Fort Ticonderoga now has a new historic site neighbor across the lake at Mount Independence; Crown Point now shares its narrow passage with the historic site at Chimney Point. New interpretive centers in the communities of Whitehall and Port Henry, New York, have counterparts in Vermont's Lake Champlain Maritime Museum and the Ethan Allen Homestead. It is fair to say that the interest in the region's history, which peaked during the 1909 Tercentenary Celebration and then waned through the middle of the century, is being renewed and refreshed. Efforts are currently underway to organize Champlain Valley historic sites into a "Heritage Corridor," making the collection of sites more accessible to the public. Perhaps interest in the region's history will build again and culminate as we observe the 400th anniversary of Champlain's arrival in the not-to-distant year of 2009.

These are exciting times for America and for the region. As the nation moves into the next millennium, where will it find the touchstones of its origin and character? Where can we locate a more accessible chronology of the evolution from the world of Native Americans, military contests, canals and commerce? The Lake Champlain chronology leads us to our recreational present and challenges us to be caretakers of the environmental and cultural legacy of this special place. What better laboratory for a new generation of citizens to gain a perspective on the interrelationship of history, archaeology, economics, art, and the environment?

Russ Bellico's *Chronicles of Lake Champlain* combines the best of historical source material to bring this special place to the reader and visitor and, in so doing, reminds us why Lake Champlain is historically the nation's first Great Lake.

Arthur B. Cohn is the director of the Lake Champlain Maritime Museum, dedicated to preserving and sharing the historical legacy of the Champlain Valley through exhibits, curricula, films, archaeological fieldwork, research, and conservation.

"A Map of the British Empire in America" by Henry Popple (1733). From *The French Occupation of the Champlain Valley from 1609 to 1759.*

Introduction

W hether during military campaigns, commercial treks, or tourist excursions, travelers to Lake Champlain always remembered the grand scenery of the lake. Journeying on a Lake Champlain steamboat during the late nineteenth century, J. Arbuthnot Wilson, a tourist from Great Britain, was surprised by the breadth and beauty of the waterway: "Before us spreads a vast sea, with a limitless horizon to [the] southward—you might suppose it a branch of the Atlantic, or a great open fiord [fjord] on the coasts of Norway."[1] Writing a few years later, William H. H. Murray ("Adirondack" Murray) stated that after having viewed "most of the localities of the continent noted for their beauty, I can but declare that I know no other spot which for loveliness of appearance, majesty of scenery, and varied resources of entertainment can compare with Lake Champlain."[2]

The scenery of Lake Champlain is the product of multiple geological forces beginning over a billion years ago. Geologists' understanding of the origins of the lake basin have resulted from studies of various rock formations in the region. The Grenville rocks of the present-day Adirondack Mountains were formed about 1200 million years ago as a result of mountain-building activity which metamorphosed older igneous rocks into schists, marbles, quartzites, and gneiss. Thereafter, perhaps from 640 to 450 million years ago, the region was flooded by the Cambrian Sea, depositing sandstones and limestones in the area. This marine advance was irregular, causing erosion of some of the sediments during periods when the sea occasionally retreated. Two hundred million years later, additional mountain-building, particularly in New England, created faults which moved huge blocks of earth from east to west, further defining the eastern section of the Champlain basin. Somewhat less than a million years ago, the first of several great glaciers of the Pleistocene period began creeping across North America, gouging out the modern-day Champlain depression. Reaching as far as present-day New Jersey, the last of the great glaciers finally retreated from the Champlain Valley about 12,000 years ago. As this glacier receded, bare bedrock was exposed in many areas and debris, once encased in the ice, was spread unevenly over the valley. Salt water from the Atlantic Ocean was then able to flow into the depression left by the ice, forming the Champlain Sea inhabited by marine life forms, including whales. But without the weight of the ice, the Champlain Valley slowly rebounded and the contours of the modern-day lake were circumscribed. The inflow of the water from the north reversed direction and gradually formed a freshwater lake.

Aside from the Great Lakes, Lake Champlain is today the largest natural body of deep freshwater in the United States, encompassing 435 square miles of surface water, 71 islands, and 587 miles of shoreline. The lake, ninety percent of which is fed by tributaries, spans 120 miles from Whitehall to its outlet in the Richelieu River in Quebec and reaches a maximum width of 12 miles and a depth of 400 feet.

The first people to inhabit the Lake Champlain Valley were Paleoindians whose hunting camps have been discovered by archaeologists in present-day East Highgate, Vermont, and in other locations on the eastern side of Lake Champlain. Available scientific evidence suggests that the Paleoindians entered this area about 9300 B.C.[3] Paleoindian artifacts, including fluted points and stone scrapers, have also been found on the western shore of Lake Champlain at Crown Point.[4] The Paleoindians most likely moved into the Champlain Valley from the south, hunting large animals such as caribou or perhaps marine mammals living in the Champlain Sea. With the changeover to a freshwater lake and a concomitant reduction in the number of large animal species in the region, the mobile Paleoindians moved on.[5] By approximately 3500 B.C., new peoples, who subsisted by hunting, fishing, and gathering, arrived in the Champlain Valley.[6] Linked to an archaeological site on Otter Creek, the Vergennes Archaic peoples may in fact be the ancestors of the western Abenakis.[7] Although hunting-fishing-gathering tasks dominated the lives of native peoples in the subsequent Woodland period (1000 B.C.-1600 A.D.), additional activities associated with this era included hide processing, woodworking, burial ceremonialism, trade, and the making of pottery, smoking pipes, and copper tools.[8] The most extensive sites of occupation in the Champlain Valley during the Middle Woodland period include eight acres on the banks of the Winooski River and another dozen locations from Missisquoi Bay to East Creek in Vermont.

Prior to European migration to North America, the Algonquin peoples would come to dominate the North Atlantic coastal areas as well as the interior of the Northeast. The Iroquois, who had gradually migrated northward into New York, would eventually challenge the Algonquin presence in eastern New York, including that of the Mahicans (Mohicans).[9] In 1600 the western Abenakis (Algonquin Confederacy), whose ancestors can be traced to the late Woodland peoples, inhabited the eastern side of Lake Champlain.[10] By then Lake Champlain represented the boundary between the Algonquin and Iroquois peoples. However, the hunting ground of the Mohawks of the Iroquois Confederacy (Five Nations) extended along Lake Champlain and as far north as the St. Lawrence River. The continuing encroachment by the Iroquois would ultimately lead to a violent confrontation at the lake. At the time of Samuel de Champlain's 1609 voyage on Lake Champlain, the Mohawks had so usurped the Algonquins in the region that Champlain referred to the Richelieu River as "the river of the Iroquois."[11] (Although Native Americans had occupied the shoreline of Lake Champlain for thousands of years, the elaborate Tercentenary celebration of 1909 commemorated Samuel de Champlain as the "discoverer of Lake Champlain."[12])

Champlain's battle with the Mohawks at Lake Champlain in 1609 proved to be the first of many battles fought for control of the vital waterway. From the late seventeenth century to the end of the War of 1812, the Champlain Valley witnessed a continual struggle for control of its strategic water route as part of the larger political and military contest for the continent. The military campaigns at Lake Champlain and Lake George were widely reported in North American and European newspapers of the day, making place names at the lakes common knowledge.

Following the wars, the ruins of the forts often evoked strong feelings in travelers to the region. For nineteenth century American tourists on the Northern Tour, the observation of the ruins of the forts, as well as the scenes where the great naval engagements had occurred, elicited a sense of national pride and identity. Stories relating to these historic sites were told early in the nineteenth century by proud local citizens. Even visitors from the British Isles took note of the military accounts. Writing in Plattsburgh in 1819, Scottish traveler Frances Wright remarked that "the shores of this beautiful lake are classic ground to the American and perhaps to all those who love liberty and triumph in the struggles for it. For myself, I have listened with much interest to the various stories attached to the different villages and ruined forts that line these waters. The Americans, rich and poor, gentlemen and mechanics, have all the particulars of their short but eventful history treasured in their minds, with an accuracy which, at first, cannot fail to surprise a foreigner."[13]

Visits to the ruins of America's past were never forgotten by excursionists. During a stop at Fort Ticonderoga in the summer of 1835, Nathaniel Hawthorne sat down in "one of the roofless barracks. . .[and] closed [his] eyes on Ticonderoga in ruins, and cast a dream-like glance over pictures of the past, and scenes of which this spot had been the theatre."[14] Fifty years later William H. H. Murray recounted a similar experience at Ticonderoga: "One summer night I visited the most historic of all historic places, this most romantic of all our ruins, and watched the night out seated upon its crumbled walls or wandering along its mounded ramparts. . .I confess that night and its emotions remain after a quarter of a century of time as clearly and impressively engraved on my memory as the features of my mother's face."[15]

Public interest in the history of Lake Champlain was sustained during the nineteenth and early twentieth centuries by a series of guidebooks which combined lengthy historical accounts with descriptions of the majestic scenery and picturesque communities along the lake. As travel grew in popularity during this period, newer steamboats offered ever more luxurious accommodations. A rise in commercial traffic on Lake Champlain at the same time was related to access to the lake via the Champlain and Chambly Canals, making canal boats, including sloop- and schooner-rigged vessels, common sights on the lake. However, by the late nineteenth century, railroads would have a significant negative impact on lake traffic; in the twentieth century automobiles would eventually supplant the grand steamboats in carrying tourists.

The fame of Lake Champlain mounted in the late nineteenth century with a succession of popular books by such authors as Peter S. Palmer, Benjamin C. Butler, and William H. H. Murray. The tempo continued in the twentieth century with the works of Walter Hill Crockett, W. Max Reid, Wallace E. Lamb, Frederic F. Van DeWater, Harrison Bird, Ralph Nading Hill, and others. These writers provided the inspiration and foundation for continued research by new generations of authors delving into the vibrant history of the lake. The story of Lake Champlain will never be finished for new archival resources will be uncovered and archaeologically significant shipwrecks will continue to be found at the bottom of the lake. In recent years the use of side-scan sonar has led to the discovery of numerous important vessels from both the military and commercial eras at Lake Champlain, renewing public interest in the history of the lake.

Today the Lake Champlain Maritime Museum has provided the leadership in the interpretation of underwater cultural resources, the conservation and exhibition of significant Lake Champlain maritime artifacts, and the supervision of Lake Champlain's Underwater Historic Preserves. The discovery of Benedict Arnold's last gunboat in 1997 by the LCMM represents the most important find since the gunboat *Philadelphia* was located in 1935. Similarly, the site interpretation and exhibits at Fort Ticonderoga, Crown Point State Historic Site, Mount Independence State Historic Site, Clinton County Historical Museum, Skenesborough Museum, Ticonderoga Historical Society, Fort Lennox, Fort Chambly, and many other historic sites play a vital role in preserving the heritage of the Champlain Valley.

Chronicles of Lake Champlain is a collection of firsthand diaries, journals, reports, and guidebooks which illustrates the changing epochs in the history of the lake. From tumultuous war periods to the tranquil era of tourist excursions, Lake Champlain has made an indelible impression on visitors. By relying on the words of eyewitnesses, readers garner an intimate glimpse into the historic events as they unfolded during the wars; later in the book they are exposed to descriptions of long forgotten scenes of bustling communities and commercial trade along the lake. The introductions that accompany the words of each participant allow readers to comprehend the transitions at the lake that occurred in the intervals between periods covered in succeeding chapters of the book.

The serene vistas of Lake Champlain today are in stark contrast to the landscape during the turbulent war eras of the eighteenth and nineteenth centuries. Where thousands of brave but apprehensive soldiers once had prepared for the onslaught of battle, tourists disembark from their air-conditioned vehicles to view the over-grown remains of moldering earthworks of long-abandoned forts. Charter boats with protruding fishing poles have replaced powerful sailing warships, bristling with cannon. Where intrepid Rangers engaged in dangerous winter forays through the densely-forested mountainsides, modern hunters calmly wander through the radiant autumn woodlands along Lake Champlain. Sleek fiberglass pleasure boats have supplanted the plain wooden canal boats once loaded with resources to supply a growing nation. But the chronicles of the most historic water route in North America will not be forgotten by today's disciples of American history.

NOTES

1. J. Arbuthnot Wilson, *Belgravia: An Illustrated London Magazine*, October 1883, 416.
2. W. H. H. Murray, *Lake Champlain and Its Shores* (Boston: DeWolfe, Friske & Co., 1890), 3.
3. William A. Haviland and Marjory W. Power, *The Original Vermonters: Native Inhabitants Past and Present* (Hanover, N. H.: University Press of New England, 1981), 31. The date of 9300 B.C. represents an uncorrected radiocarbon date which may be written with lowercase letters (b.c.). See page 15.
4. William A. Ritchie, *The Archaeology of New York State*, rev. ed. (Fleischmanns, N. Y.: Purple Mountain Press, 1994), 19-22.
5. Haviland and Power, 89.
6. Ibid., 59, 86; Ritchie, 31, 84-89.
7. Haviland and Power, 89.
8. Ibid., 129, 131, 91; Ritchie, 179-80, 185; Two intact pots found at the bottom of Lake Champlain are believed to be from the Woodland period. See "Ancient pot found in Champlain," *The Post-Star* (Glens Falls), 28 May 1997; Dennis M. Lewis, "An Intact Prehistoric Ceramic Pot from Cumberland Bay, Lake Champlain," *Bulletin of the New York State Archaeological Association* 107 (Spring 1994): 25.
9. Haviland and Power, 199; Shirley W. Dunn, *The Mohicans and Their Land 1609-1730* (Fleischmanns, N. Y.: Purple Mountain Press, 1994), 91-92; Dean R. Snow, *The Iroquois* (Cambridge, MA.: Blackwell Publishers, Inc., 1994), 19-21; Denys Delâge, *Bitter Feast: Amerindians and Europeans in Northeastern North America, 1600-64*, trans. Jane Brierley (Vancouver: University of British Columbia Press, 1993), 104, 122-23.
10. Haviland and Power, 150, 199.
11. H. P. Biggar, ed., *The Works of Samuel De Champlain* (Toronto: The Champlain Society, 1925), Volume 2, 76.
12. Henry Wayland Hill, *The Champlain Tercentenary: First Report of the New York Lake Champlain Tercentenary Commission*, 2d. ed. (Albany: J. B. Lyon Company, State Printers, 1913), 1.
13. Frances Wright, *Views of Society and Manners in America*, ed. Paul R. Baker (Cambridge, MA.: The Belnap Press of Harvard University Press, 1963), 149.
14. Nathaniel Hawthorne, "A Visit to Ticonderoga 100 Years Ago," *The Bulletin of the Fort Ticonderoga Museum* 4 (January 1936): 14-15.
15. Murray, 85.

Samuel de Champlain Memorial Lighthouse at Crown Point, dedicated on July 5, 1912.
(Photo by the author)

Part I: Passage in the Wilderness

1. Samuel de Champlain 1609

SAMUEL DE CHAMPLAIN, explorer, geographer, ethnographer, and colonizer, left an indelible mark on the New World. As the founder of New France, his influence on the eventual political configuration of North America has implications for the present. While we have learned a great deal about the geography and native peoples of North America from Champlain's writings, details of Champlain's personal life remain somewhat elusive. Nevertheless, Champlain's narration of the sights and events along Lake Champlain in 1609 provides the first documentation by a European of the lake that would subsequently become the focus of rival political entities for the next two hundred years.

Champlain was born c.1570 in Brouage, France, a Huguenot seaport noted for its salt industry. Little is known about his parents except for Champlain's notation "of the late Anthoine de Complain, in his lifetime Captain in the Navy, and of Dame Margueritte Le Roy" that he listed on his marriage contract of 1610.[1] In the 1590s Champlain served as a quartermaster in the French army of King Henry IV. A civil and religious war in France escalated when King Phillip II of Spain dispatched troops to France to aid the Catholic Holy League which opposed the succession of Henry IV, a Huguenot, to the throne. Armies crisscrossed northwest France (Brittany) before the war ended in 1598. Consistent with Champlain's later adventures, the young sergeant emerged from the war unscathed.

Making his way to the south coast of Brittany, Champlain met his uncle, "Guillaume Hellaine or Allène, known as le capitaine provencal," who was preparing to repatriate Spanish troops.[2] As a guest on his uncle's ship, the 500-ton *Saint Julian*, Champlain sailed for Cadiz, Spain, on September 9, 1598. The *Saint Julian* was later chartered for Spain's annual voyage to America. After four months in Spain, the *Saint Julian*, with Champlain aboard, set sail early in 1599 for the New

World. During the trip Champlain observed the Lesser Antilles, Puerto Rico, Cuba, the Cayman Islands, Vera Cruz (Mexico), and made an inland journey to Mexico City. Following a month in Mexico, Champlain embarked on a voyage aboard a small sailing vessel to the Isthmus of Panama. Although Champlain has been credited with having the first thoughts on the possibility of a canal, the idea had been considered 60 years earlier.[3] During the expedition to the West Indies, Champlain had the adeptness to make friends with the native population, a capability that would later prove useful in his North American forays.

In 1603 Aymar de Chaste, holder of a new trade monopoly from the king, invited Champlain on an expedition to the St. Lawrence River Valley. Earlier attempts at colonization on the St. Lawrence in 1541-1542 by Jacques Cartier and Jean-François de la Roque (Sieur de Roberval) in 1541-1543 had failed, leaving the region open to independent fur traders centered in Tadoussac at the mouth of the Saguenay River (northeast of present-day Quebec). Although the king had granted monopoly privileges to a series of trading companies in return for establishing a permanent trading post, independent fur traders successfully lobbied for the revocation of any monopolies. An attempt by Pierre Chauvin in 1600 to initiate a permanent colony at Tadoussac failed after a bitter winter.

Samuel de Champlain sailed to Canada in 1603 on board the 120-ton *La Bonne Renommée*, commanded by François Pont-Gravé. He landed at Tadoussac, following a treacherous two-month voyage which involved avoiding numerous icebergs in the North Atlantic. Soon after his arrival, Champlain participated in a feast with the Algonquin Indians which included consuming "the flesh of moose, which is like beef, with that of bear, seal, and beaver. . .with great quantities of wild fowl. . . They were celebrating this triumph for a victory they had won over the Iroquois."[4] Champlain was intrigued by the assonance of Algonquin speech but would never learn their language and depended on interpreters even after several decades of travel and residence in Canada.

On June 18, 1603, Champlain and Pont-Gravé began an expedition further west on the St. Lawrence River aboard a 12-ton pinnace, a small sailing galley transported from France in frames and assembled at Tadoussac. Passing present-day Quebec City and Trois-Rivières, Champlain and Pont-Gravé briefly surveyed the Richelieu River. Sailing as far as today's Montreal, the explorers encountered rapids which Champlain named Sault Saint-Louis (La Chine Rapids). By questioning the Native Americans, Champlain was able to sketch a remarkable delineation of the western portion of the St. Lawrence River, Niagara Falls, and the Great Lakes. Through these lakes, Champlain believed that a passage to an Asian sea might exist, an idea that would frustrate him, as well as many explorers to follow. On July 11 Champlain and Pont-Gravé returned to Tadoussac, where they prepared for their voyage back to France. After trading for furs with Native Americans, the explorers departed for home, reaching France in September 1603. Champlain delivered a map to the king and without delay published a 36-page account of the venture entitled *Des Sauvages, ou, Voyage de Samuel Champlain*. While the book was quite factual, Champlain conformed to the expectations of the period for unusual tales from the New World by repeating the legend of the "Gougou," which the Native Americans had told to him. The "Gougou," according to Champlain's sources, "had the form of a woman, but very terrible, and of such size that they told me the top of the masts of our vessel would not reach to [her] waist."[5] Not only did the "Gougou" diet on the Native Americans, but the beast carried them off in a great pocket and made "horrible noises."[6] The preposterous tale undoubtedly helped sell the book.

Following the death of de Chaste, King Henry IV and his council awarded Pierre du Gua, Sieur de Monts, the monopoly for the fur trade and jurisdiction over North America from the 40th to the 46th parallel (present-day Philadelphia to Cape Breton). De Monts, an old ally of the king and a merchant who had earlier invested in de Chaste's voyage, recruited 120 artisans, carpenters, masons, and soldiers and chartered François Pont-Gravé's ship *La Bonne Renommée* and two other vessels for the voyage to New France. Solicited by de Monts, Champlain was directed by the king to record the expedition. Although Champlain did not have an official title on the voyage, he functioned as a geographer. By early May 1604, the crew of *La Bonne Renommée*, de Monts' flagship, observed Sable Island. After eight more days, the flagship landed at Cape La Have (near present-day Halifax, Nova Scotia). On May 19, while waiting for Pont-Gravé's ship to catch up, Champlain was dispatched by de Monts in an eight-ton pinnace with a crew of ten to explore the region to the south in search of an interim base for settlement. In a three-week period, Champlain surveyed present-day Yarmouth and the shoreline of the Bay of Fundy. After Champlain returned, de Monts sailed *La Bonne Renommée* to Annapolis Basin and later crossed the Bay of Fundy, viewing the St. John River. Shortly thereafter, de Monts established a temporary settlement on Sainte-Croix Island, a five-acre isle in the St. Croix River, situated along the border of present-day Maine and New Brunswick. The choice of an island for the settlement was probably related to defense. Prefabricated buildings, including doors, windows, and furniture, had been transported from France. Battling black flies and mosquitoes in June, de Monts' men quickly assembled barracks, housing for de Monts, a 50-foot storehouse, chapel, kitchen, grain mill, and several other houses.

Samuel de Champlain's map of Sainte-Croix Island in 1604.
From *Les Voyages du Sieur de Champlain* (1613).

On September 2, 1604, Champlain embarked with 12 men and two Indians aboard a second pinnace to further explore the region and search for a site for a permanent settlement. Covering 150 miles in a period of one month, he produced impressive maps of Maine's shoreline. Many geographic features named by Champlain in 1604, including Mount Desert Island (L'Isle des Monts-déserts), have been retained to this day. Champlain reached Penobscot Bay before turning back for the Sainte-Croix base. While de Monts and 78 men prepared for the winter at their island village, Pont-Gravé sailed for France with the two large ships (the third had been sent to Tadoussac, Quebec, at the beginning of the voyage). A fierce winter, coupled with short supplies, proved catastrophic for the colonists, especially when a dreadful outbreak of scurvy took its toll. Champlain recorded that the men had "superfluous and driveling flesh. . .teeth became very loose. . .[and] could not rise nor move. . .so that out of seventy-nine, who composed our party, thirty-five died and more than twenty were on the point of death."[7]

When Pont-Gravé failed to return with fresh supplies by mid-May, de Monts readied his survivors to abandon Sainte-Croix. A month later, before the two pinnaces and their crews were to sail for the Gulf of St. Lawrence in an attempt to find fishermen who would take them back to France, a shallop (sailing/rowing long boat) from Pont-Gravé's ship arrived at the island. With the security of renewed provisions, de Monts and Champlain, with 20 seamen and the Micmac sachem Panounias, set out a few days later on the larger of the two pinnaces to search for a more suitable site for a colony. The party explored the rest of Maine's coastline, journeyed northward along the Back River and reached present-day Wiscasset, Merrymeeting Bay, and finally sailed south on the Kennebec River. The pinnace was later anchored at the mouth of the Saco River where Champlain inspected a palisaded Native American agricultural community. De Monts and Champlain forged ahead to present-day Boston Harbor, meeting more Native Americans. The explorers then landed in Plymouth Harbor, again observing Indians (Aptucxets) and later sailed around Cape Cod, mooring in Nauset Harbor (south of present-day Eastham). Running low on provisions and after a brief skirmish with the Nauset Indians, de Monts and Champlain departed for Sainte-Croix on July 25, 1605. The accurate maps produced by Champlain, as a result of this expedition, deservedly led to his recognition as the "first cartographer of New England."[8]

Without finding an acceptable place for a permanent settlement, de Monts decided to move the village at Sainte-Croix to a northern harbor on Nova Scotia in the Annapolis Basin. Protected by surrounding hills, Port-Royal (Annapolis-Royal today) would prove a better location for a winter colony than Sainte-Croix. De Monts returned to France, leaving Pont-Gravé and approximately 45 men at the village. Only three men who had survived the disastrous winter at Sainte-Croix resolved to stay at Port-Royal; the rest returned to France. Champlain remained "hoping to have an opportunity to make some new explorations towards Florida."[9] Although the winter of 1605-1606 was relatively mild compared to the previous year, scurvy recurred, leaving 12 men dead. The next spring, Champlain and Pont-Gravé set out for another voyage of exploration, but two mishaps prevented the pinnace from leaving the Bay of Fundy. When no supply ship appeared by mid-July, Pont-Gravé and Champlain loaded the two pinnaces and sailed for Cape Breton to locate fishing boats from France. While passing the southeastern tip of

Nova Scotia on July 24, however, the crews met de Monts' secretary aboard a shallop with the news of the resupply of Port-Royal. By the time the shallop and two pinnaces reached Port-Royal, Jean de Biencourt de Poutrincourt, the new governor of Port-Royal, had moored the 120-ton *Jonas* in the harbor.

Champlain's drawing of the Port-Royal habitation (1606-1607) on Nova Scotia.
From *Les Voyages du Sieur de Champlain* (1613).

Seeking a warmer site for a settlement, Poutrincourt and Champlain embarked on a voyage of discovery the next month aboard a recently-constructed pinnace. Instead of heading directly for unexplored areas, however, Poutrincourt wished to observe the Maine coast himself—a region that Champlain had already documented. Nearly a month later, the voyagers reached Cape Cod, spending two weeks at Stage Harbor (present-day Chatham). A deadly attack by Nauset Indians on a contingent of Poutrincourt's men ended their stay at Cape Cod. After observing what was probably Martha's Vineyard, the French voyagers returned to Stage Harbor for revenge, but more men were lost to the Nauset warriors. With less than half their supplies remaining, Poutrincourt and Champlain turned back to Port-Royal, arriving there on November 14, 1606.

Mild weather during the winter of 1606-1607, combined with ample provisions, allowed for a relatively pleasant season. On May 24, 1607, a pinnace from the ship *Jonas* arrived with the news that de Monts' trading monopoly in North America had been cancelled. The end of the monopoly privilege resulted from the influence of competing fur traders and higher fur prices which had brought objections from

French hatters. The departure of the *Jonas* for France was delayed to permit fur and fish trading. Before the *Jonas* departed for France on September 3, 1607, Champlain had more time to explore the coast of Cape Breton Island. Champlain's explorations resulted in a detailed set of maps of the Atlantic coastline from Cape Breton Island to Cape Cod.

Upon arriving in France in October 1607, Champlain presented Sieur de Monts with his charts and a description of New France. De Monts was understandably disheartened over his losses in the Canadian enterprise, but Champlain was able to propose a new strategy. France's North Atlantic settlements, in Champlain's opinion, were a lost cause, lacking minerals, furs, interior waterways, or an outlet to the South Sea. He persuaded de Monts to support a trading post and colony at Quebec. Shortly thereafter, de Monts and Champlain convinced King Henry IV to restore the monopoly. The monopoly, however, was granted for only one year in return for a permanent colony in Canada.

Champlain was designated a lieutenant of de Monts, and three ships were outfitted for the voyage: *Le Levrier*, under the command of Pont-Gravé; *Le Don de Dieu*, under Champlain's control; and a third ship (not identified) that sailed to Acadian waters. When Champlain reached Tadoussac on the St. Lawrence River on June 3, 1608, he found Pont-Gravé wounded aboard *Le Levrier*. Pont-Gravé had arrived earlier at Tadoussac and immediately confronted the Basque fur traders, presenting his royal letters granting the fur-trading monopoly. The Basques refused to end their illicit trade and attacked the crew of *Le Levrier*, wounding Pont-Gravé and disarming his ship. After a lengthy discussion with the Basque captain, Champlain concluded a truce with the rival fur traders, leaving a final settlement of the dispute over fur trading rights to the French courts.

While carpenters worked to assemble a 12-ton sailing pinnace from pre-cut frames, Champlain traveled northwest of Tadoussac on the Saguenay River, learning more about present-day Hudson Bay from Native Americans. Returning to Tadoussac, Champlain departed on the last day of June aboard the new pinnace, arriving at Quebec on July 3, 1608.* Champlain had searched "for a place suitable for our settlement, but I could find none more convenient or better situated than the point of Quebec, so called by the savages, which was covered with nut trees."[12] His workmen promptly began felling butternut trees, sawing planks, and digging foundations for the "habitation." The settlement would eventually consist of three two-story buildings surrounded on all sides by a stockaded wall and moat.

As the "habitation" was under construction, Champlain had to deal with a sinister plot to assassinate him and turn the new settlement over to the Basque fur traders and Spaniards who were then at Tadoussac. Jean Duval, a locksmith and survivor of the 1606 attack on Cape Cod by the Nauset Indians, was the instigator of the conspiracy against Champlain. After the captain of the supply pinnace from Tadoussac was alerted to the plot by one of the conspirators with a guilty conscience, Champlain was quickly informed of Duval's plan. Champlain devised a scheme which enticed Duval and the other traitors aboard the pinnace for a wine party where they were quickly seized. The conspirators were tried and condemned to

---

*The name Quebec appeared first on the 1601 Levasseur map and was used two years later by Champlain in his work *Des Sauvages*. The term was derived from the Micmac word "Kebec," which signified the narrows of a river.[10] Similarly, the Algonquin word "Quebeio" or "Quelibec" meant "a narrowing or contracting."[11]

death with Jean Duval, "hung at Quebec, and his head put on the end of a pike, to be set up in the most conspicuous place on our fort."[13] Three others were also sentenced to death, but were sent back to France, their fate placed in the hands of Sieur de Monts.

On September 18, 1608, Pont-Gravé sailed for France with the three prisoners. Champlain remained at Quebec to supervise the work on the "habitation" and later explored nearby St. Charles River where he found the remains of Jacques Cartier's fort of 1535-1536 at a distance of two or three miles from the mouth of the St. Charles River. Champlain had first scrutinized the site during his 1603 voyage to New France and in 1608 described "remains of what seems to have been a chimney, the foundation. . .large pieces of hewn, worm-eaten timber, and some three or four cannon-balls."[14]

Replica of *Le Don de Dieu* built for the 1909 Tercentenary.
Samuel de Champlain had sailed on the original ship from France to Canada in 1608.
From *The Champlain Tercentenary* by Henry Wayland Hill (1909).

The brutal winter of 1608-1609 took a severe toll on the French settlement and the Montagnais Indians living nearby. Having little success hunting game and with their supply of smoked eel exhausted, the Montagnais were forced to eat their dogs and the animal skins that they had used for clothing. Champlain recorded that the Montagnais were mere "skeletons, most of them being unable to stand. . .I ordered bread and beans to be given them."[15] The French colonists at Quebec did not have sufficient provisions to prevent the Montagnais from starving, and only spring and abundant shad in the St. Lawrence ended their cruel predicament. For Champlain and his men, the winter was just as cruel—only eight of the 24 men survived. Some died of dysentery, while ten died of scurvy. Although Champlain was touched by scurvy, the indefatigable explorer survived.

Early in June 1609, Pont-Gravé's future son-in-law, Sieur des Marais, reached Quebec with the news that Pont-Gravé had arrived at Tadoussac. Within a few days, Champlain met with Pont-Gravé at Tadoussac and convinced him to support plans for exploration further westward with their Native American allies. On June 18 Champlain and his men boarded a shallop to begin a journey westward through the lush virgin scenery of the St. Lawrence River. Champlain met several hundred Algonquins, Hurons, and Montagnais camped near the island of St. Eloi where their leaders, "Iroquet" and "Ochasteguin," reminded the French explorer that "ten moons ago" he had promised "that Pont-Gravé and I wished to help them against their enemies [the Iroquois]. With these they had long been at war, on account of many cruelties practised against their tribe."[16] Champlain's Indian allies asked to see the French settlement at Quebec with which Champlain readily agreed and pronounced that "I had no other intention than to make war" on their enemies.[17] Champlain's decision to join the war party was partially based on his desire to observe new territory which might otherwise be inaccessible without Native American guides. Champlain's support would also solidify the French trading relationship with the Indians.

On June 28, 1609, after five or six days of dancing and feasting at Quebec, Champlain and Pont-Gravé set forth in two shallops along with the Native Americans in canoes. Three days later Pont-Gravé turned back for Quebec, leaving Champlain and 11 men to push forward with the expedition against the Iroquois. By July 11 the party reached the mouth of the Richelieu River, where they camped. Before embarking on the campaign, some of the Indians returned to their villages. The remaining party of 60 Algonquins, Hurons, and Montagnais in 24 canoes accompanied Champlain's shallop south on the Richelieu River. Upon reaching the rapids at Chambly, Champlain realized that the assurances of the Indians for an uncomplicated passage on the River of the Iroquois (Richelieu River) was in error. While the Indians carried the canoes and baggage around the rapids, Champlain sent Sieur des Marais back to Quebec with the shallop and continued southward with only two of his men. Champlain's trip provides the first description by a European of the scenery, wildlife, fish, and geography of Lake Champlain. As Champlain and his war party approached Iroquois territory, they traveled only at night to avoid discovery. On the evening of July 29, 1609, Champlain's band encountered Mohawk warriors of the Iroquois nation on the lake near the end of a "cape" on the western shore, later identified as present-day Ticonderoga. Both Indian parties hurled insults at one another and agreed to a battle at daylight. The ensuing battle, described by Champlain in detail in his journal, has long been debated by historians as a link to the collision course of the French and the Six Nations in subsequent years.[18] After the battle, Champlain was forever recognized by his Native American allies for his bravery and for keeping his promises. On the other hand, if the engagement with the Mohawks had not occurred, Champlain may have proceeded through Lake George and explored the Hudson River, perhaps beating Henry Hudson as the European discoverer of the waterway. But if Champlain hadn't agreed to the war party, the Native Americans would never have guided him into the southern Champlain Valley. The battle also introduced Native Americans to the the use of firearms. Henceforth, Indians would barter with Europeans for these powerful weapons.

Samuel de Champlain's detailed drawing of the battle has provided a legacy of information on this important event. The famous illustration, published in his *Les Voyages du Sieur de Champlain* (1613), however, has a few shortcomings. The Indians are shown without their costumes or accoutrements since drawing Native American dress may have been beyond Champlain's artistic ability and the style of the day (ie., artist Théodore de Bry) usually showed Native Americans naked to distinguish them from Europeans. In addition, Champlain's illustration shows Native American canoes resembling French bateaux and the foliage includes a few palm trees. Because the engraver of Champlain's drawing may have modeled the finished product after de Bry's 1590s illustrations, Champlain's original depiction may have been modified (e.g., palm for willow trees).[19]

Samuel de Champlain's original drawing of the battle with the Iroquois.
(National Archives of Canada)

Champlain sailed for France on September 5, 1609, and subsequently presented souvenirs of his adventures in North America to King Henry IV, including a skull of a huge Lake Champlain garpike. Although de Monts' fur monopoly was not extended by the king, de Monts managed a partnership with merchants to assist in financing another voyage to New France. Champlain returned to Quebec on April 28, 1610, where 60 Montagnais were waiting for him to accompany them on the warpath against the Iroquois. Shortly thereafter, on June 19, 1610, Champlain, along with the Montagnais, joined the Hurons and Algonquins already at the mouth of the Richelieu River (present-day Sorel). Champlain spearheaded an attack on the Iroquois barricade, erected a short distance from the mouth of the river. Although an Iroquois arrow split his earlobe and lodged in his neck, Champlain and his allies successfully stormed the fort, killing and capturing the defenders. This would be Champlain's last victory over the Iroquois.

After learning of the assassination of King Henry IV, Champlain departed for France in August 1610. In late December, Champlain, then about 40 years old, entered into a marriage contract with 12-year-old Hélène Boullé. Because of the age of the bride, the marriage contract postponed the consummation of the marriage for two years, but Champlain immediately received 4,500 livres of a 6,000-livre dowry.

In a little over two months, Champlain once again sailed for New France. While traveling to present-day Montreal, he named a nearby island Sainte-Hélène for his young wife and later shot the treacherous rapids (La Chine) in a canoe. After returning to France, Champlain was named lieutenant to the viceroy of New France by King Louis XIII. In 1613 Champlain's most important work was published, *Les Voyages du Sieur de Champlain*, which exhibited the best maps to date of Canada, including more than a dozen harbor charts, numerous drawings, and his fascinating journal of events in New France. Over his lifetime, Champlain would make 23 voyages across the North Atlantic. Champlain's explorations of New France included the search for an elusive "Northwest Passage" to the Orient, which led him to the waters of Lake Huron, Lake Ontario, Lake Oneida, the Ottawa River and numerous other rivers. He was also involved in another attack on an Iroquois fort (Onondaga) in October 1615, in which he was wounded and defeated.

At the age of 22, Hélène made her first trip to New France with Champlain in the spring of 1620. Henceforth Champlain's time was dedicated to the administration of New France; his explorations of the New World had come to an end. Champlain and Hélène returned to France on August 21, 1624. Hélène would never return to Canada; Champlain, however, resumed his duties in New France in 1626, remaining there until 1629. In 1629 Champlain was elevated to the de facto governor of New France under Cardinal Armand Jean du Plessis Richelieu. But in July of the same year Champlain was forced to surrender Quebec to English invaders. Returning to France from England in December 1629, Champlain urged the king to press England for the reestablishment of New France, which finally occurred in 1632. Champlain, however, was not reappointed to command New France until the next year. He made his last voyage to Quebec in 1633. Two years later in October, Champlain suffered a paralyzing stroke and never left his bed again. On Christmas Day 1635, the "Father of New France" died. Champlain would never know that a council in Paris, under the leadership of Cardinal de Richelieu, had designated someone else as the governor of New France for the coming year. Hélène de Champlain, after her husband's death, joined an Ursuline convent, where she died in 1654.

During his lifetime Samuel de Champlain received little in the way of official recognition or title from the French monarchy. By the nineteenth century, Champlain's work was finally recognized and the title "The Father of New France" came into use. Champlain's deference toward Native Americans allowed French Canada to grow in relative peace. As historian Samuel Eliot Morison noted, "perhaps more important for Canada in the long run. . .was his policy of making friends with the

Indians, respecting their customs and prejudices, and treating them with wisdom and justice."[20]

Unfortunately, no true likeness of Champlain has been found. None of the existing portraits of Champlain are authentic representations--Perhaps the vague drawing that Champlain drew of himself at the 1609 battle at Lake Champlain provides the closest idea of his looks. Undoubtedly, he had a rugged constitution, for he survived many harsh winters in North America during which even younger men succumbed to scurvy and other diseases. Champlain displayed boundless energy, seemingly unaffected by the piercing cold, near starvation, and constant adversity of an uncharted wilderness. He was a steadfast adventurer: brave, unyieldingly honest, never disgruntled in the face of hardship, and loyal to his friends, king, and church.

Detail of Champlain's map of New France (1632) showing Lake Champlain.
From *The Documentary History of the State of New-York* by E. B. O'Callaghan.

Voyages of Samuel de Champlain[21]

A large number of islands of various sizes where there are many butternut trees and vines and beautiful meadows with much game-birds and beasts-which go from the mainland to these islands.* More fish are caught there than in any other part of the river we had visited. From these islands we went to the mouth of the river of the Iroquois [Richelieu], where we stayed two days and refreshed ourselves with choice game, birds, and fish which the Indians** gave us. Here there broke out amongst them some difference of opinion regarding the war, the result of which was that only a part of them decided to come with me, whilst the rest went back to their own country, with their wives and the goods they had bartered.

Setting out from the mouth of that river, which is some four or five hundred yards wide and very beautiful, and proceeding southward we reached a place in latitude 45°, twenty-two or twenty-three leagues*** from the Three Rivers. The whole of this river from its mouth to the first rapid, a distance of fifteen leagues, is very level and bordered with woods, as are all the other places mentioned above, and with the same varieties of wood. There are nine or ten beautiful islands as far as the first rapid of the river of the Iroquois, and these are about a league or a league and a half long and covered with oaks and butternuts. The river is in places nearly half a league wide and full of fish. We did not find anywhere less than four feet of water. The approach to the rapid is a sort of lake [Chambly Basin] into which the water flows down, and it is about three leagues in circumference. Near by are meadows where no Indians live, by reason of the wars. At the rapids there is very little water, but it flows with great swiftness, and there are many rocks and boulders, so that the Indians cannot go up by water; but on the way back they run them very nicely. All this region is very level and full of forests, vines and butternut trees. No Christians but ourselves had ever penetrated to this place; and we had difficulty enough in getting up the river by rowing.

As soon as we reached the rapids, Des Marais, La Routte and myself, with five men, went ashore to see whether we could pass this spot, and walked about a league and a half without seeing how this could be done. There was only the river running with great swiftness, and on either side many very dangerous stones, and little water. The rapid is perhaps six hundred yards wide. Seeing that it was impossible to cut down the trees and make a road with the few men I had, I resolved, by common consent, to do something different from what we had originally intended when we trusted to the assurances of the Indians that the way was easy, for, as I have stated, we found the contrary to be true, and this was the reason of our return to our shallop, where I had left some men to guard it, and to inform the Indians, when they arrived, that we had gone to explore the banks alongside the rapid.

*These islands are in Lac St. Pierre, a section of the St. Lawrence River.

**Champlain, like other French writers of the period, referred to the natives of North America as "les sauvages" by which he meant "uncivilized." He did, however, use the term "les Indians" for the natives of Spanish America.[22]

***A French league is two and one-half miles.

†Champlain reached the rapids at Chambly with Pont-Gravé's future son-in-law, Sieur des Marais (Glaude Godet), and the shallop's pilot, La Routte, who was one of the survivors of the brutal winter of 1608-1609 at Quebec.

Romanticized painting of Samuel de Champlain's 1609 voyage to Lake Champlain.
(National Archives of Canada)

Having seen what we wished of this place we met on our way back with some Indians who were coming to examine it as we had done, and they told us that all their companions had arrived at our shallop. There we found them quite pleased and satisfied because we had gone in this way without a guide, trusting only to the reports which they had several times made to us.

Having returned and realizing the small prospect there was of getting our shallop past the rapid, I was distressed, and I was particularly sorry to return without seeing a very large lake [Lake Champlain], filled with beautiful islands, and a large, beautiful region near the lake, where they had represented to me their enemies lived. Having thought it over well, I decided to proceed thither in order to carry out my promise and also to fulfil my desire. And I embarked with the Indians in their canoes and took with me two men who were eager to go.* Having laid my plan before Des Marais and the other men in the shallop, I requested Des Marais to return to our settlement with the rest of our men, in the hope that shortly, by God's grace, I should see them again.

Thereupon, I went and conferred with the Indian chiefs and made them understand how they had told us the contrary of what I had seen at the rapids, that is to say, that it was impossible to pass them with the shallop: yet that this would not prevent me from assisting them as I had promised. This information troubled them greatly, and they wished to change their plan, but I told them and urged upon them to persist in their first design, and that with two others I would go on the war-path with them in their canoes; for I wished to show them that for myself I would not fail to keep my word to them, even if I went alone. And I told them that

*The two volunteers may have been named Chavin and Dupont.[23]

this time I should not force any of my companions to embark, and should take with me only two whom I had found eager to go.

They were quite satisfied with what I told them, and were glad to learn the resolution I had taken, persisting in their promise to show me fine things.

I set out then from the rapid of the river of the Iroquois on the second of July.* All the Indians began to carry their canoes, arms and baggage about half a league by land, to avoid the swiftness and force of the rapid. This they soon accomplished.

Then they put all the canoes into the water and two men with their baggage into each; but they made one of the men of each canoe go by land some three leagues which is about the length of the rapids, but the water is here less impetuous than at the entrance, except in certain places where rocks block the river, which is only some three or four hundred yards wide. After we had passed the rapids, which was not without difficulty, all the Indians who had gone overland, by a rather pleasant path through level country, although there were many trees, again got into their canoes. The men whom I had with me also went by land, but I went by water in a canoe. The Indians held a review of all their people and there were sixty men in twenty-four canoes. After holding the review we kept on our way as far as an island [Ile Ste. Thérèse], three leagues long, which was covered with the most beautiful pines I had ever seen. There the Indians hunted and took some game. Continuing some three leagues farther, we encamped to take rest during the following night.

Immediately each began, some to cut down trees, others to strip bark from the trees to cover their wigwams in which to take shelter, others to fell big trees for a barricade on the bank of the river round their wigwams. They know how to do this so quickly that after less than two hours work, five hundred of their enemies would have had difficulty in driving them out, without losing many men. They do not barricade the river bank where their boats are drawn up, in order to embark in case of need. After their wigwams had been set up, according to their custom each time they camp, they sent three canoes with nine good men, to reconnoitre two or three leagues ahead, whether they could perceive anything; and afterwards these retired. All night long they rely upon the explorations of these scouts, and it is a very bad custom; for sometimes they are surprised in their sleep by their enemies, who club them before they have time to rise and defend themselves. Realizing this, I pointed out to them the mistake they were making and said that they ought to keep watch as they had seen us do every night, and have men posted to listen and see whether they might perceive anything, and not live as they were doing like silly creatures. They told me that they could not stay awake, and that they worked enough during the day when hunting. Besides when they go to war they divide their men into three troops, that is, one troop for hunting, scattered in various directions, another troop which forms the bulk of their men is always under arms, and the other troop of scouts to reconnoitre along the rivers and see whether there is any mark or sign to show where their enemies or their friends have gone. This they know by certain marks by which the chiefs of one nation designate those of another, notifying one another from time to time of any variations of these. In this way they recognize whether enemies or friends have passed that way. The hunters never hunt in advance of the main body, nor. . .the scouts, in order not to give alarm, or to cause confusion, but only when these have retired and in a direction from which they do not expect

---

*This date was probably July 12.[24]

the enemy. They go on in this way until they are within two or three days march of their enemy, when they proceed stealthily by night, all in a body, except the scouts. In the day time they retire into the thick of the woods, where they rest without any straggling, or making a noise, or making a fire even for the purpose of cooking. And this they do so as not to be noticed, if by chance their enemy should pass that way. The only light they make is for the purpose of smoking which is almost nothing. They eat baked Indian meal, steeped in water, which becomes like porridge. They keep these meal cakes for their needs, when they are near the enemy or when they are retiring after an attack; for then they do not waste time in hunting but retire quickly.

Each time they encamp they have their Pilotois or Ostemoy [medicine men], who are people who play the part of wizards, in whom these tribes have confidence. One of these wizards will set up a tent, surround it with small trees, and cover it with his beaver-skin. When it is made, he gets inside so that he is completely hidden; then he seizes one of the poles of his tent and shakes it whilst he mumbles between his teeth certain words, with which he declares he is invoking the devil, who appears to him in the form of a stone and tells him whether his friends will come upon their enemies and kill many of them. This Pilotois will lie flat on the ground, without moving, merely speaking to the devil, and suddenly he will rise to his feet, speaking and writhing so that he is all in a perspiration, although stark naked. The whole tribe will be about the tent sitting on their buttocks like monkeys. They often told me that the shaking of the tent which I saw, was caused by the devil and not by the man inside, although I saw the contrary; for, as I have said above, it was the Pilotois who would seize one of the poles of the tent, and make it move in this way. They told me also that I should see fire coming out of the top, but I never saw any. These scamps also counterfeit a loud, distinct voice, and speak a language unknown to the other Indians. And when they speak in an old man's voice, the rest think that the devil is speaking, and is telling them what is going to happen in their war, and what they must do.

Yet out of a hundred words all these scoundrels, who pretend to be wizards, do not speak two that are true, and go on deceiving these poor people to get things from them, as do many others in this world who resemble these gentry. I often pointed out to them that what they did was pure folly, and that they ought not to believe in such things.

Having learned from their wizards what is to happen to them, the chiefs take sticks a foot long, one for each man, and indicate by others somewhat longer, their leaders. Then they go into the wood[s], and level off a place five or six feet square, where the headman, as sergeant-major, arranges all these sticks as to him seems best. Then he calls all his companions, who approach fully armed, and he shows them the rank and order which they are to observe when they fight with the enemy. This all these Indians regard attentively, and notice the figure made with these sticks by their chief. And afterwards they retire from that place and begin to arrange themselves in the order in which they have seen these sticks. Then they mix themselves up and again put themselves in proper order, repeating this two or three times, and go back to their camp, without any need of a sergeant to make them keep their ranks, which they are quite able to maintain without getting into confusion. Such is the method they observe on the war-path.

We departed on the following day, pursuing our way up the river as far as the entrance to the lake. In it are many beautiful low islands covered with very fine woods and meadows with much wild fowl and animals to hunt, such as stags, fallow deer, fawns, roebucks, bears, and other kinds of animals which come from the mainland to these islands. We caught there a great many of them. There are also many beavers, both in that river and in several small streams which fall into it. This region although pleasant is not inhabited by Indians, on account of their wars; for they withdraw from the rivers as far as they can into the interior, in order not to be easily surprised.

On the following day we entered the lake which is some 80 or 100 leagues in length;* in which I saw four beautiful islands about ten, twelve and fifteen leagues in length, which, like the Iroquois river, were formerly inhabited by Indians: but have been abandoned, since they have been at war with one another.** There are also several rivers flowing into the lake, on whose banks are many fine trees of the same varieties we have in France, with many of the finest vines I had seen anywhere. There are many chestnut trees which I had only seen on the shore of this lake, in which there is also a great abundance of many species of fish. Amongst others there is one called by the natives Chaousarou, which is of various lengths; but the largest of them, as these tribes have told me, are from eight to ten feet long. I have seen some five feet long, which were as big as my thigh, and had a head as large as my two fists, with a snout two feet and a half long, and a double row of very sharp, dangerous teeth. Its body has a good deal the shape of the pike; but it is protected by scales of a silvery gray color and so strong that a dagger could not pierce them. The end of its snout is like a pig's. This fish makes war on all the other fish which are in these lakes and rivers. And, according to what these tribes have told me, it shows marvelous ingenuity in that, when it wishes to catch birds, it goes in amongst the rushes or reeds which lie along the shores of the lake in several places, and puts its snout out of the water without moving. The result is that when the birds come and light on its snout, mistaking it for a stump of wood, the fish is so cunning that, shutting its half-open mouth, it pulls them by their feet under the water. The natives gave me the head of one of them, a thing they prize highly, saying that when they have a headache, they bleed themselves with the teeth of this fish at the spot where the pain is and it eases them at once.***

Continuing our way along this lake in a westerly direction and viewing the country, I saw towards the east very high mountains on the tops of which there was snow.† I enquired of the natives whether these parts were inhabited. They said they were, and by the Iroquois, and that in those parts there were beautiful valleys and fields rich in corn such as I have eaten in that country, along with other products in abundance. And they said that the lake went close to the mountains, which, as I judged, might be some twenty-five leagues away from us. Towards the south I saw

*Lake Champlain measures 120 miles from the Richelieu River to Whitehall, New York.

**The four islands may have been Isle La Motte, North Hero, Grand Isle, and Valcour Island.

***This section of his journal has been misinterpreted by some who have suggested that Champlain observed the illusive Lake Champlain monster.[25] It is clear from this passage that Champlain had viewed a five-foot garpike. Upon his return to France, Champlain presented the skull of a Lake Champlain garpike to King Henry IV.

†Champlain may have observed reflections of rock outcroppings on distant mountaintops.

others which were not less lofty than the first mentioned, but there was no snow on these. The Indians told me that it was there that we were to meet their enemies, that the mountains were thickly populated, and that we had to pass a rapid which I saw afterwards. Thence they said we had to enter another lake which is some nine or ten leagues in length, and that on reaching the end of it we had to go by land some two leagues and cross a river which descends to the coast of Norumbega, adjoining that of Florida.* They could go there in their canoes in two days, as I learned afterwards from some prisoners we took, who conversed with me very particularly regarding all they knew, with the help of some Algonquin interpreters who knew the Iroquois language.

Now as we began to get within two or three days journey of the home of their enemy, we proceeded only by night, and during the day we rested. Nevertheless, they kept up their usual superstitious ceremonies in order to know what was to happen to them in their undertakings, and often would come and ask me whether I had had dreams and had seen their enemies. I would tell them that I had not, but nevertheless continued to inspire them with courage and good hope. When night came on, we set off on our way until the next morning. Then we retired into the thick woods where we spent the rest of the day. Towards ten or eleven o'clock, after walking around our camp, I went to take a rest, and while asleep I dreamed that I saw in the lake near a mountain our enemies, the Iroquois, drowning before our eyes. I wanted to succor [help] them, but our Indian allies said to me that we should let them all perish; for they were bad men. When I awoke they did not fail to ask me as usual whether I had dreamed anything. I told them what I had seen in my dream. This gave them such confidence that they no longer had any doubt as to the good fortune awaiting them.

Evening having come, we embarked in our canoes in order to proceed on our way, and as we were paddling along very quietly, and without making any noise, about ten o'clock at night on the twenty-ninth of the month [July], at the extremity of a cape which projects into the lake on the west side,** we met the Iroquois on the war-path. Both they and we began to utter loud shouts and each got his arms ready. We drew out into the lake and the Iroquois landed and arranged all their canoes near one another. Then they began to fell trees with the poor axes which they sometimes win in war, or with stone axes; and they barricaded themselves well.

Our Indians all night long also kept their canoes close to one another and tied to poles in order not to get separated, but to fight all together in case of need. We

*The rapid was the lower falls in the La Chute River which empties into Lake Champlain from Lake George at Ticonderoga. The La Chute River would have had to be bypassed to enter Lake George, and from there a 13-mile land portage would be required to reach the Hudson River. Norumbega was originally an Algonquin word that was used by both French and English explorers in the sixteenth century in referring to the area between Nova Scotia and Cape Cod.[26]

**The location of the "cape" where Champlain encountered the Iroquois has been the subject of some controversy over the years. While a few researchers believed that the area was Crown Point, most of the circumstantial evidence points to the Ticonderoga peninsula.[27] Champlain observed the "rapid" (falls at Ticonderoga) and spent three hours after the battle with his Indian allies while they celebrated their victory before departing northward. Given the limited time frame and 15-mile distance by water from Crown Point to the falls at Ticonderoga, it seems more logical that the "rapid" would have been close to the site of the engagement with the Iroquois. There is also archaeological evidence that the Ticonderoga promontory had once been a Native American campsite.

were on the water within bow shot of their barricades. And when they were armed, and everything in order, they sent two canoes which they had separated from the rest, to learn from their enemies whether they wished to fight, and these replied that they had no other desire, but that for the moment nothing could be seen and that it was necessary to wait for daylight in order to distinguish one another. They said that as soon as the sun should rise, they would attack us, and to this our Indians agreed. Meanwhile the whole night was spent in dances and songs on both sides, with many insults and other remarks, such as the lack of courage of our side, how little we could resist or do against them, and that when daylight came our people would learn all this to their ruin. Our side too was not lacking in retort, telling the enemy that they would see such deeds of arms as they had never seen, and a great deal of other talk, such as is usual at the siege of a city. Having sung, danced, and flung words at one another for some time, when daylight came, my companions and I were still hidden, lest the enemy should see us, getting our fire-arms ready as best we could, being however still separated, each in a canoe of the Montagnais Indians. After we were armed with light weapons, we took, each of us, an arquebus and went ashore.* I saw the enemy come out of their barricade to the number of two hundred, in appearance strong, robust men. They came slowly to meet us with a gravity and calm which I admired; and at their head were three chiefs. Our Indians likewise advanced in similar order, and told me that those who had the three big plumes were the chiefs,** and that there were only these three, whom you could recognize by these plumes, which were larger than those of their companions; and I was to do what I could to kill them. I promised them to do all in my power, and told them that I was very sorry they could not understand me, so that I might direct their method of attacking the enemy, all of whom undoubtedly we should thus defeat; but that there was no help for it, and that I was very glad to show them, as soon as the engagement began, the courage and readiness which were in me.

As soon as we landed, our Indians began to run some two hundred yards towards their enemies, who stood firm and had not yet noticed my white companions who went off into the woods with some Indians. Our Indians began to call to me with loud cries; and to make way for me they divided into two groups, and put me ahead some twenty yards, and I marched on until I was within some thirty yards of the enemy, who as soon as they caught sight of me halted and gazed at me and I at them. When I saw them make a move to draw their bows upon us, I took aim with my arquebus and shot straight at one of the three chiefs, and with this shot two fell to the ground and one of their companions was wounded who died thereof a little later. I had put four bullets into my arquebus. As soon as our people saw this shot so favorable for them, they began to shout so loudly that one could not have heard it thunder, and meanwhile the arrows flew thick on both sides. The Iroquois were much astonished that two men should have been killed so quickly, although they

---

*The "arquebus" was a short-muzzle-loading matchlock weapon of Spanish origin. The lightweight firearm was discharged when the trigger depressed a forked holder with a lit match or fuse, known as a serpentine, which ignited the powder in the flash pan, setting off the load in the barrel.[28] In preparation for the battle, Champlain also donned a half-suit of armor consisting of a breastplate, flaring tassets (thigh protectors), back plate, burgonet (open-faced helmet), and a swept-hilted sword on a waist belt.[29]

**Champlain was probably describing Iroquois war captains, not chiefs, since the latter would have worn horns and would not have been participating directly in battle.[30]

"The Arquebusier" of the seventeenth century by J. B. Madou (1860).
(Print, author's collection)

were provided with shields made of cotton thread woven together and wood, which were proof against their arrows.* This frightened them greatly. As I was reloading my arquebus, one of my companions fired a shot from within the woods,** which astonished them again so much that, seeing their chiefs dead, they lost courage and took to flight, abandoning the field and their fort, and fleeing into the depth of the forest, whither I pursued them and laid low still more of them. Our Indians also killed several and took ten or twelve prisoners. The remainder fled with the wounded. Of our Indians fifteen or sixteen were wounded with arrows, but these were quickly healed.

After we had gained the victory, our Indians wasted time in taking a large quantity of Indian corn and meal belonging to the enemy, as well as their shields, which they had left behind, the better to run. Having feasted, danced, and sung, we three hours later set off for home with the prisoners. The place where this attack took place is in 43° and some minutes of latitude, and was named Lake Champlain.

Having gone about eight leagues, the Indians, towards evening, took one of the prisoners to whom they made a harangue on the cruelties which he and his friends without any restraint had practised upon them, and that similarly he should resign himself to receive as much, and they ordered him to sing, if he had the heart. He did so but it was a very sad song to hear.

Meanwhile our Indians kindled a fire, and when it was well lighted, each took a brand and burned this poor wretch a little at a time in order to make him suffer the greater torment. Sometimes they would leave off, throwing water on his back. Then they tore out his nails and applied fire to the ends of his fingers and to his membrum virile. Afterwards they scalped him and caused a certain kind of gum to drip very hot upon the crown of his head.*** Then they pierced his arms near the wrists and with sticks pulled and tore out his sinews by main force, and when they saw they could not get them out, they cut them off. This poor wretch uttered strange cries, and I felt pity at seeing him treated in this way. Still he bore it so firmly that sometimes one would have said he felt scarcely any pain. They begged me repeatedly to take fire and do like them. I pointed out to them that we did not commit such cruelties, but that we killed people outright, and that if they wished me to shoot him with the arquebus, I should be glad to do so. They said no; for he would not feel any pain. I went away from them as if angry at seeing them practice so much cruelty on his body. When they saw that I was not pleased, they called me back and told me to give him a shot with the arquebus. I did so, without his perceiving anything, and with one shot caused him to escape all the tortures he would have suffered rather than see him brutally treated. When he was dead, they were not satisfied; they opened his body and threw his bowels into the lake. Afterwards they

---

*Defensive shields were apparently used widely by Native Americans. Gabriel Sagard, a missionary lay brother who traveled in Canada in 1623-1624, noted that the Huron carried large shields as well as "armour and cuirass," protecting the chest, back, and legs.[31] In a later period Father Joseph Lafitau recorded that the Iroquois used breastplates and round shields of cedar wood overlaid with thongs of hide.[32]

**Champlain's drawing from *Les Voyages* shows both of his French companions firing from the woods.

***Whether scalping among Native Americans was prevalent before European exploration has been the subject of much debate. However, Donnaconna, a Huron chief, showed scalps to Jacques Cartier in October 1535 at present-day Quebec City.[33] During the next century Europeans offered bounties to Native Americans for scalps of their enemies.[34]

Top: Romanticized drawing of Champlain's 1609 battle with the Iroquois.
From *Story of America in Pictures* by Allan C. Collins (1953).
Above: Champlain's original drawing showing his failed attack on the
Onondaga fort in 1615. (New York State Library)

cut off his head, arms and legs, which they scattered about; but they kept the scalp, which they had flayed [stripped of skin], as they did with those of all the others whom they had killed in their attack. They did another awful thing, which was to cut his heart into several pieces and to give it to a brother of the dead man to eat and to others of his companions who were prisoners. These took it and put it into their mouths, but would not swallow it. Some of the Algonquin Indians who were guarding the prisoners made them spit it out and threw it into the water. That is how these people act with regard to those whom they capture in war. And it would be better for them to die fighting, and be killed at once, as many do, rather than to fall into the hands of their enemies. When this execution was over, we set out upon our return with the rest of the prisoners, who went along continually singing, without other expectation than to be tortured like him of whom we have spoken. When we arrived at the [Chambly] rapids of the river of the Iroquois [Richelieu], the Algonquins returned into their own country and the Ochateguins [Huron] also with some of the prisoners, all much pleased at what had taken place in the war, and because I had gone with them willingly. So we all separated with great protestations of mutual friendship, and they asked me if I would not go to their country, and aid them continually like a brother. I promised them I would.

I came back with the Montagnais. After I had questioned the prisoners regarding their country and its characteristics, we packed our baggage for our return. This we accomplished with such speed that every day we made twenty-five or thirty leagues in their canoes, which was their usual rate. When we reached the mouth of the river of the Iroquois there were some of the Indians who dreamed that their enemies were pursuing them. This dream made them at once shift their camp, although the weather that night was bad on account of wind and rain; and they went and spent the whole night in the high bulrushes which are in lake St. Peter, for fear of their enemies. Two days later we arrived at our settlement [Quebec], where I ordered bread and peas to be given to them; and also some beads for which they asked me, to decorate the scalps of their enemies, which they carry in their festivities on returning home. On the following day I went with them in their canoes to Tadoussac to see their ceremonies. Approaching the shore each took a stick, on the end of which they hung the scalps of their slain enemies with some beads, singing mean-while all together. And when all were ready, the women stripped themselves quite naked, and jumped into the water, swimming to the canoes to receive the scalps of their enemies which were at the end of long sticks in the bow of their canoes, in order later to hang them round their necks, as if they had been precious chains. And then they sang and danced. Some days afterwards they made me a present of one of these scalps as if it had been some very valuable thing, and of a pair of shields belonging to their enemies, for me to keep to show to the king. And to please them I promised to do so.

NOTES

1. *Dictionary of Canadian Biography* (Toronto: University of Toronto Press, 1966), Volume 1, 186.
2. Samuel Eliot Morison, *Samuel de Champlain: Father of New France* (Boston: Little, Brown and Company, 1972), 18; Edwin Asa Dix, *Champlain: The Founder of New France* (New York: D. Apple-

ton and Company, 1903), 16; Morris Bishop, *Champlain: The Life of Fortitude* (New York: Alfred A. Knopf, 1948), 12.

3. Bishop, 21.
4. Ibid., 42; See also Kenneth M. Morrison, *The Embattled Northeast* (Berkeley: University of California Press, 1984), 21.
5. Edward Gaylord Bourne, ed., *The Voyages and Explorations of Samuel de Champlain* (New York: Allerton Book Co., 1922), Volume 2, 227.
6. Ibid., 228.
7. W.L. Grant, ed., *Voyages of Samuel De Champlain 1604-1618* (1907; reprint ed., New York: Barnes & Noble, Inc., 1946), 53.
8. *Dictionary of Canadian Biography*, 189.
9. Grant, 79.
10. Morison, *Champlain*, 102.
11. Francis Parkman, *France and England in North America* (Boston: Little, Brown, and Company, 1891), Part First, 329.
12. N. E. Dionne, *Champlain* (Toronto: University of Toronto Press, 1963), 41.
13. Grant, 136.
14. Ibid., 137; See also Samuel Eliot Morison, *The Great Explorers: The European Discovery of America* (New York: Oxford University Press, 1978), 239-41.
15. H.P. Biggar, ed., *The Works of Samuel De Champlain* (Toronto: The Champlain Society, 1925), Volume 2, 54-55.
16. Ibid., 69; See also Edwin Asa Dix, *Champlain: The Founder of New France* (New York: D. Appleton and Company, 1903), 107.
17. Biggar, 71.
18. Bishop, 152; Dionne, 49; Dix, 114; Morison, *Champlain*, 111; Parkman, 337; Ralph Flenley, *Samuel De Champlain: Founder of New France* (Toronto: The Macmillan Company of Canada, Limited, 1924), 36; Henry Dwight Sedgwick, Jr., *Samuel De Champlain* (Boston: Hougton Mifflin and Company, 1902), 26-27.
19. Morison, *Champlain*, 110-11; Gordon M. Sayre, *Les Sauvages Américains: Representations of Native Americans in French and English Colonial Literature* (Chapel Hill: The University of North Carolina Press, 1997), 55-56,77; See also John Wagner, "Au Plaisir," *Adirondack Life*, January/February 1988, 55; Champlain also incorrectly suggested that the canoes were made of oak rather than elm. See Parkman, 348; Wagner, 55; Hallie E. Bond, *Boats and Boating in the Adirondacks* (Blue Mountain Lake, N.Y.: The Adirondack Museum, 1995), 23-24.
20. Morison, *Champlain*, 226.
21. Biggar, 76-107; See also Samuel de Champlain, *Les Voyages du Sieur de Champlain* (1613; reprint ed. Ann Arbor, MI: University Microfilms, Inc., 1966), 218-33.
22. Morison, *Champlain*, 23.
23. Guy Omeron Coolidge, *The French Occupation of the Champlain Valley from 1609 to 1759*, 2nd ed. (1938; reprint ed., Mamaroneck, N.Y.: Harbor Hill Books, 1989), 10.
24. Biggar, 82.
25. Majorie L. Porter, "The Champlain Monster," *Vermont Life*, Summer 1970, 47; "The Champ of Champlain," *Time*, March 30, 1981, 30; Roger Houston, "Finding Champ," *Offshore*, April 1988, 109; For an excellent overview of the history of Champ sightings see Joseph W. Zarzynski, *Champ-Beyond the Legend* (Wilton, N.Y.: M-Z Information, 1988).
26. Morison, *Champlain*, 280.
27. Coolidge, 12; Bishop, 354.
28. Harold L. Peterson, *Arms and Armor in Colonial America 1526-1783* (New York: Bramhall House, 1956), 14; Morison, 282.
29. Peterson, 133, 77.
30. Wagner, 55.
31. Gabriel Sagard, *The Long Journey into the Country of Hurons*, ed. by George M. Wrong (1939; reprint ed., New York: Greenwood Press, 1968), 154.
32. Parkman, 350.
33. Morison, *The Great Explorers*, 241; See also Parkman, 351; Sagard, 159.
34. Ian K. Steele, *Warpaths* (New York: Oxford University Press, 1994), 131.

Portrait of Peter Kalm at the age of 48. J. G. Geitel (1764).
(National Museum, Finland)

2 Peter Kalm 1749

SWEDISH PROFESSOR PETER KALM, a young naturalist and economist, provided
the first scientific description of Lake Champlain. In July 1749 and later in October,
on the return leg of his journey to Canada, Kalm depicted Native American life and
detailed the scenery, plant life, geology, and wildlife along the inland sea. Not only
was Kalm impressed by the panorama of Lake Champlain, he also commented on
the quality of water which "was very clean, extremely clear and of excellent taste."[1]
His North American journey occurred at a crucial point in history—just after King
George's War (1744-1748) and before the French and Indian War (1755-1763). Kalm's
journal includes many references to the tense military and political climate between
France and England, as well as a delineation of the French fortification at Crown
Point.

In the years following Samuel de Champlain's expedition into Iroquois territory
and prior to Kalm's arrival in North America, the rivalry between the Iroquois and
the French colonizers intensified in the Champlain Valley. New France, dependent
on the lucrative fur trade with the Hurons, discouraged any trade between the
Hurons and Iroquois which might divert business from Quebec to the Dutch
settlement at Fort Orange (Albany). New France's relations with Native Americans
remained a delicate balancing act during the seventeenth century. Jesuit missionaries,
while spreading Christianity, were thought to strengthen New France's influence
with Native Americans. Ironically, the Jesuits may have had the opposite effect,
decimating the Huron population by unwittingly introducing European diseases.[2]
The missionaries themselves were often placed in perilous situations. Father Isaac
Jogues, the most famous Jesuit missionary, was taken captive in Canada by an
Iroquois war party in 1642 and transported through Lake Champlain to their villages
on the Mohawk River.[3] Despite torture suffered during his 1642-1643 captivity,

Jogues agreed to return to the Mohawk villages as a peace ambassador in 1646. On his journey to the Indian settlements, he traveled south on Lake Champlain and Lake George, naming the latter Lac du Saint-Sacrement. After caterpillars had ruined the villager's grain crop along the Mohawk River, Jogues was blamed for the problem and decapitated late in 1646.

The rivalry between European powers for control of North America dominated a good part of the seventeenth century. In 1629 English invaders forced Samuel de Champlain to surrender Quebec; the region did not return to French control until 1632. After 12 years of intermittent warfare, the English seized the Dutch colony of Fort Orange in 1664. Nine years later the Dutch recaptured their colony, but by 1675 the English had permanently eliminated Dutch official presence in North America. With the end of the Dutch colony and the rebirth of interest in the economic prospects of North America by France in the 1660s, the stage was set for the inevitable confrontation between England and France.

The collision course between the rival colonial powers was prompted by a series of Iroquois raids on Canadian settlements in the 1660s. The danger of Iroquois attacks convinced the French to rebuild Fort Richelieu at the mouth of the Richelieu River, build new fortifications in the region, and deploy a regiment of seasoned Carignan-Salières regulars in New France. In December 1665 a peace treaty was concluded between New France and the Iroquois, but the Mohawks failed to take part in the agreement. In the next month the governor-general of New France, Daniel de Courcelles, led a raid to destroy the Iroquois villages along the Mohawk River. The expedition failed, and French leaders in Canada continued with plans to eliminate the Mohawk threat. During the summer of 1666 Captain de la Motte (Pierre de Saint-Paul, Sieur de la Motte-Lussière) and his regiment of regulars were dispatched to an island at the northern end of Lake Champlain (present-day Isle La Motte) to begin construction of a fort. A peace overture by representatives of the Five Iroquois Nations occurred that summer, but new Mohawk incursions precipitated a 1,300-man French expedition in early fall. Traversing Lake Champlain and Lake George on their way southward, the raiders destroyed four Iroquois villages on the Mohawk River, inducing the Iroquois to offer peace the following spring.

Relative peace lasted for nearly two decades, but new English land grants, sporadic skirmishes with the Iroquois,and the belief that the English were covertly trying to renew Iroquois wars against the French generated a proposal in 1688 by the governor of New France to build a fort at the end of Lake Champlain. According to contemporary French maps, this terminology (end of the lake) referred to Crown Point.[4] On August 1, 1689, upon the outbreak of King William's War (1689-1697), 1,300 Iroquois warriors attacked the village of La Chine near Montreal, largely to avenge a French attack on the Seneca Nation two years earlier. In response, a 210-man French expedition, which included 96 Native American allies, was dispatched on a raid against Fort Orange, but instead attacked and burned the village of Schenectady on February 9, 1690. In late March the governor of New York sent Captain Jacobus de Warm and a small party to establish an advance post near Crown Point. De Warm chose Chimney Point on the east side of the lake for a "little stone fort."[5]

By the summer, plans for a major offensive by English colonists against New France were well underway. One expedition under Major General Fitzjohn Win-

French burning of the village of Schenectady on February 9, 1690.
(National Archives of Canada)

throp of Connecticut was slated to invade Canada through Lake Champlain while a second force under Sir William Phips was dispatched to seize Quebec City via the St. Lawrence River. Winthrop's army reached the southern end of Lake Champlain near present-day Whitehall, but a shortage of boats and supplies ended the campaign on August 15, 1690.[6] However, a party of militia and Mohawks under Captain John Schuyler (grandfather of Revolutionary War General Philip Schuyler) assailed La Prairie near Montreal. After a cannon duel with Quebec City's shore batteries and the landing of 2,000 soldiers, Sir William Phips withdrew his ill-prepared force from the St. Lawrence River and returned with his fleet to Boston. The war ended with the Treaty of Ryswick in 1697. In 1701 the Five Iroquois Nations concluded a peace treaty with New France and England, creating a de facto buffer between English and French colonists. In reality the presence of the Iroquois had thwarted French penetration of New York during the seventeenth century.

The fragile peace was only temporary since the War of Spanish Succession in Europe engulfed North America in the conflict known as Queen Anne's War (1702-1713). In 1703 French and Indian raids against English settlements began in present-day Maine. The most devastating attack occurred when a French and Indian war party destroyed Deerfield, Massachusetts, in February 1704, which resulted in the deaths of 47 villagers and the capture of 112. English plans for a two-pronged campaign against New France in 1709, a strategy similar to that of 1690, were again thwarted. An army under the command of Colonel Francis Nicholson reached Wood Creek at the southern end of Lake Champlain in the summer of 1709, but

"Defense of Quebec" from attack in 1690 by English forces led by Sir William Phips.
(National Archives of Canada)

"Stockade fort 1731 at Chimney Point [Point à la Chevelure]."
Drawing by Len Tantillo.
(Crown Point State Historic Site)

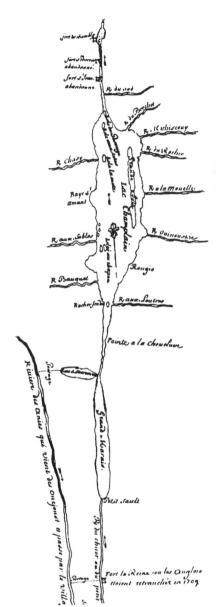

Theyanoquin or King Hendrick (also known as Tee Yee Neen Ho Ga Row) was one of four Native American sachems who met with Queen Anne in 1710. Hendrick was killed while fighting French forces at the Battle of Lake George in 1755. Painting by John Verelst.
(National Archives of Canada)

"Carte du Lac Champlain avec les Rivières." An early eighteenth-century French map of Lake Champlain.
(Map collection, National Archives of Canada)

the expedition was later abandoned when English warships that had been scheduled for an attack on Quebec City were redirected to Lisbon, Portugal.

Two years later the same basic plan was again put into action. In 1711, 2,000 troops with 600 bateaux under Lieutenant General Francis Nicholson were to invade Canada through Lake Champlain via Lake George. Some of Nicholson's advance units reached Lake George in September when news that a massive English fleet under Admiral Hovendon Walker had withdrawn from the St. Lawrence River following a calamitous navigation accident that destroyed eight transports and two supply vessels. Nicholson once again abandoned his campaign, burned the recently-rebuilt Fort Anne, and returned to Albany with his troops. The Treaty of Utrecht ended the war in 1713, leaving the boundary between New York and New France at Split Rock on Lake Champlain. The treaty also recognized the Iroquois Five Nations as allies of Great Britain. Three years earlier several Mohawk chiefs had accompanied Peter Schuyler to England, helping to improve relations between the Iroquois and Great Britain.

Relative peace prevailed in the Champlain Valley following the Treaty of Utrecht, but the rival powers, England and France, maintained a vigilant eye on the region. In 1730, following reports that English colonists had journeyed to Lake Champlain to trade with Native Americans, the governor of New France ordered French soldiers to eject the intruders. Later that year the governor recommended to the king of France that a fort be constructed at Crown Point to block the English incursions and for use as a base to harass their settlements.[7] In 1731 French workmen and soldiers built a small stockaded fort at "Point à la Chevelure"; three years later a more substantial stone fort was begun on the west side of the lake at Crown Point. Fort St. Frédéric, named for Jean-Frédéric Phélypeaux, Comte de Maurepas, a minister of France, was nearly finished by 1737 but underwent further enlargement in subsequent years.

King George's War (1744-1748), known in Europe as the War of the Austrian Succession, renewed the open conflict between France and Great Britain. Using Fort St. Frédéric as a base during the war, the French and their Native American allies attacked Saratoga, Fort Massachusetts, Fort Number Four (New Hampshire), and other English settlements in the region. Reverend John Norton, the chaplain at Fort Massachusetts who was captured when the garrison surrendered, described Fort St. Frédéric on August 28, 1746, as "an irregular form, having five sides to it; the

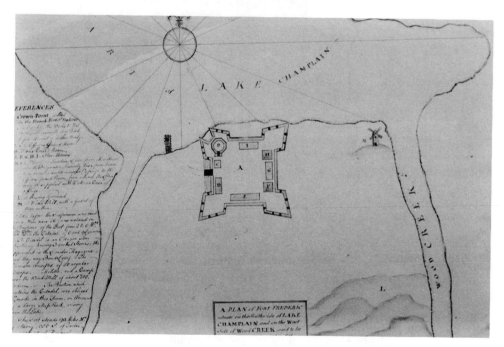

English drawing of Fort St. Frédéric at Crown Point.
(Crown Collection, New York State Library)

ramparts twenty feet thick, the breast work two feet and half; the whole about twenty feet high. There were twenty-one or twenty-two guns upon the wall. . . The citadel an octagon built three [four] stories high, fifty or sixty feet diameter, built with stone laid in lime, the wall six or seven feet thick."[8] Governor William Shirley of Massachusetts called for an expedition against Fort St. Frédéric during King George's War, but a successful campaign in 1745 against the French fortress of Louisbourg on Cape Breton Island prevented any large-scale military activity in the Lake Champlain region. Fort St. Frédéric remained a major French base in North America when the Treaty of Aix-la-Chapelle ended the war in 1748. Shortly thereafter, Peter Kalm, our journal keeper, viewed the sites of the conflict and visited Fort St. Frédéric.

Peter Kalm has been recognized as the most celebrated foreign traveler in America during the mid-eighteenth century. Born in Sweden in 1716, Peter (Pehr) Kalm was the son of Gabriel Kalm, a clergyman from Finland, and Catherine Kalm, the daughter of a merchant whose ancestors were of Scottish descent. Six weeks after Peter's birth, his father died and his mother and Peter settled in Voyri, Finland. Upon entering Turku (Abo) University (Finland) in 1735, Peter Kalm concentrated his studies in the field of theology, but by the time he began his academic career at the University of Uppsala (Sweden) in 1740, his interests had turned to the natural sciences. In the early 1740s Kalm began his regional travels and became enamored with the idea of a natural science expedition to distant countries. Under his professors' tutelage at Uppsala University, Kalm's philosophical outlook embraced utilitarianism, by which everything was judged on its usefulness to the national welfare. These views were strongly influenced by his academic mentors, Baron Sten Carl Bielke and Carl Linnaeus. At the time, the ideological foundation of the Swedish Academy of Sciences was predicated upon a combination of natural sciences and economics, allowing the "adapatation of natural sciences to the creation of wealth."[9] Swedish economists of this period studied ways to take advantage of natural products to enhance economic growth.

After writing several technical reports, Kalm was elected to the Swedish Academy of Sciences in 1745. Following a recommendation by the chancellor of Turku University to create the first professorship in economics, Kalm received the appointment to his old alma mater in 1747. His selection was linked to plans for a North American expedition in search of plants that would enhance the growth of the national economy, an expedition under consideration by the Swedish Academy of Sciences since 1744. Kalm would later view North America, not as a dedicated purist of nature's beauty, but with an eye to adapting nature to the benefits of an economic society.

Kalm sailed from Sweden on November 30, 1747, but the very next day a fierce storm nearly destroyed his ship, forcing Kalm to spend two months in Grömstad, Norway, while the vessel underwent repairs.* Kalm was accompanied on the expedition by Lars Jungström, a faithful servant and knowledgeable gardener. After finally arriving in London on February 6, 1748, Kalm and Jungström were compelled to remain in England as ship captains marked time until the end of the War of the Austrian Succession and made arrangements to form a convoy to lessen the

---

*Kalm's dates, based on a calendar that was discontinued in 1752, are earlier than those of a modern calendar. The date of departure would have been December 11, 1747, on a post-1752 calendar.

danger from privateers. The delay allowed Kalm time to meet English scientists and study the agricultural methods of the country. At long last, Kalm and Jungström departed for America aboard the ship *Mary Gally* on August 5, 1748. Ideal weather conditions made the ship's passage unusually rapid, and Kalm reached the port of Philadelphia on September 15, 1748.

Kalm's first business in America was to present letters of introduction from two influential Londoners to Benjamin Franklin, who had an established name with the European scientific community. Kalm cultivated a close friendship with Franklin, who introduced the new visitor to his prominent friends during the fall and winter months. During the fall of 1748 Kalm traveled through Pennsylvania, New Jersey, and Delaware to New York City. Kalm decided to spend more time in the middle colonies than the original expedition design had envisioned, but the Swedish Academy of Sciences advised him to carry out the initial plan to examine and collect plants and seeds from the northern latitudes, whose climate was comparable to that of Sweden.[10]

Kalm and Jungström left New York City on June 10, 1749, bound for Albany aboard a sailing vessel on the first leg of the expedition to Canada. Kalm arrived in Albany early on the morning of June 13 and spent the next nine days making observations about the people and vegetation there. His negative characterization of the inhabitants of Albany included comments about "avarice, selfishness and immeasurable love of money," and he accused the residents of trading "with the very Indians who murdered the inhabitants of New England [during King George's War]" by purchasing "articles such as silver spoons, bowls, cups, etc. of which the Indians robbed the houses in New England. . .though the names of the owners were engraved on many of them."[11] His opinion of the residents of Albany, however, may have been related to his jaundiced attitude toward the Dutch in general, who earlier had competed with Sweden for overseas markets.

Late on June 21, 1749, Kalm, Jungström and two assistants, including William Printup (Printop) as an interpreter, departed from Albany in a canoe since the preferred vessel, a bateau, was not available.* For help with the route to Lake Champlain and the procurement of guides, Kalm had the advice of William Johnson, the most notable colonial mediator with the Iroquois.[13] The journey would take the party through a dangerous war-torn frontier where, only ten miles from Albany, the travelers observed burned-out houses in which settlers had returned to live "under a few boards which they propped up against each other."[14] At Saratoga Kalm noted that the fort had been burned by the English in 1747 because they were not "able to defend themselves in it against the attacks of the French and their Indians."[15]

As a result of low water and other difficulties, Kalm and his party abandoned their heavy canoe (probably at present-day Fort Miller) before reaching the "Great Carrying Place," located on a bend in the Hudson River. On June 26 Kalm arrived at the traditional portage site and scrutinized the overgrown remnants of Fort Nicholson, built in 1709, and the ruins of John Lydius' trading post which had been burned by the French and Indians in 1745. The next day the travelers reached the

---

*Kalm described an Albany-made canoe as "a single piece of wood, hollowed out: they are sharp on both ends" and made of white pine and often tarred and painted. The bateau was "made of boards of white pine; the bottom is flat. . .sharp at both ends, and somewhat higher towards the end than in the middle. They have seats in them, and are rowed as common boats."[12]

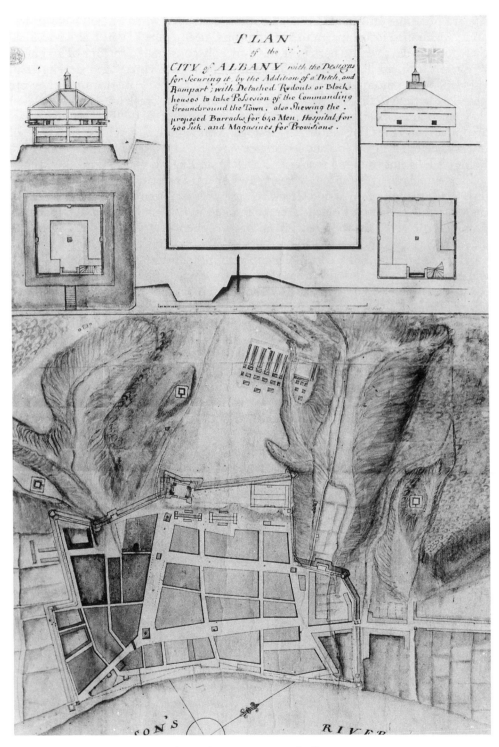

Eighteenth-century map of Albany.
(Crown Collection, New York State Library)

site of Fort Anne on Wood Creek, an outpost destroyed when Francis Nicholson's army abandoned its campaign in 1711 during Queen Anne's War. Kalm remained there for two days while a bark boat was hurriedly constructed and one of his guides recovered from an illness. Like others who would later visit Wood Creek, Kalm "never saw the mosquitoes more plentiful in any part of America than they are here."[16] On June 29 the group proceeded north on Wood Creek until nightfall when they encountered a French sergeant and five soldiers from Fort St. Frédéric, accompanying three Englishmen to Saratoga. Although the French sergeant warned of the danger from six Indians seeking revenge for the deaths of their comrades, Kalm decided not to take his advice to wait at an English village until the French soldiers could escort Kalm and his party to Fort St. Frédéric. The bark boat was of little use at that point on Wood Creek because trees had been deliberately cut across the waterway earlier by French forces to impede an English invasion of Canada, so Kalm left the vessel for the Frenchmen. In turn, the soldiers allowed Kalm to take one of their bark canoes that had been pulled ashore six miles to the north.

The first part of Kalm's Lake Champlain journal begins, in this text, on July 1 and ends when he arrives at Fort St. Jean on the Richelieu River late on July 21. It is a remarkable early description of Lake Champlain and the French presence at Crown Point. Kalm remained in Canada until October 14. Because French authorities denied him permission to travel to Forts Frontenac and Niagara, Kalm returned to New York via the Richelieu River. He traveled through Lake Champlain and Lac St. Sacrement (Lake George) to the Hudson River, finally reaching Philadelphia on November 21, 1749. Kalm's travels continued during 1750 when he observed Niagara Falls, sending a detailed description to Benjamin Franklin. In 1750 Kalm married the widow of Reverend Johan Sandin (born Anna Magaretha Sjöman) of the Swedish parish of Racoon, New Jersey. Kalm departed for Europe on February 13, 1751, never traveling to America again.

When Kalm returned to Turku University in August 1751, there was no tilled plot available to sow seeds or plant the roots taken from North America. The following spring the university granted Kalm a house on a nearby island with a tract of land suitable for his plantings. The first seeds were sown there in 1752 and additional plantings followed in 1757 at the new university garden at Turku. Only a small number of the North American plants proved suitable for the Finnish/Swedish climate, however. Kalm's lectures on his plants, travels, and ideas continued to attract students and were influential in deepening interest in the cultivation of gardens. Kalm's observations of North America were published in Stockholm in three separate volumes over a period of eight years (1753-1761). Shortly thereafter, German, English, and Dutch translations were printed. The following version of his journal, the first American edition of Kalm's work, was edited by Adolph B. Benson and published in 1937. Some nonessential passages have been omitted from the following text.

Peter Kalm's Travels in North America[17]

July the 1st, 1749. At daybreak we got up, and rowed a good while before we got to the place where we left the true course.* The country which we passed was the poorest and most disagreeable imaginable. We saw nothing but a row of amazingly high mountains covered with woods, steep and rough on their sides, so that we found it difficult to get to an open place in order to land and boil our dinner. In many places the ground, which was very smooth, was under water, and looked like the sections of our Swedish morasses which are being drained; for this reason the Dutch in Albany call these parts the "Drowned Lands." Some of the mountains run from S.S.W. to N.N.E., and along the river** they form perpendicular shores, and are full of rocks of different sizes. The river flows for several miles from south to north.

"Lake Champlain near Benson" by D. Johnson, engraved by Robert Hinshelwood.
(Print, author's collection)

The wind blew from the north all day, and made it very hard work for us to travel on, though we all rowed as hard as we could, for what little we had left of our provisions was eaten to-day at breakfast. The river was frequently an English mile and more broad, then it became narrow again, and so on alternately; but upon the whole it kept a good breadth, and was surrounded on both sides by high mountains.

*Kalm's party made a wrong turn the preceding day and rowed 12 miles out of their way, probably on the Poultney River.

**During the eighteenth century the southern section of Lake Champlain was often referred to as a river or as Wood Creek.

Approaching Fort St. Frédéric. About six o'clock in the evening we arrived at a point of land about twelve English miles from Fort St. Frédéric. Behind this point the river is converted into a spacious bay, and as the wind still kept blowing pretty strong from the north, it was impossible for us to proceed, since we were extremely tired. We were therefore obliged to pass the night here, in spite of the remonstrances of our hungry stomachs.*

It is to be attributed to the peculiar grace of God towards us that we met the above-mentioned Frenchmen on our journey, and that they gave us leave to take one of their bark boats. It hardly happens once in three years that the French take this route to Albany; for they commonly pass over Lake St. Sacrement, or, as the English call it, Lake George, which is the nearer and better way, and everybody wondered why they took this troublesome one.** If we had not gotten their large, strong boat, and had been obliged to keep the one we had made, we would in all probability have been very ill off; for to venture upon the great bay during the least wind with so wretched a vessel, would have been a great piece of temerity, and we should have been in danger of starving if we had waited for a calm. For being without fire-arms, and these wildernesses having but few quadrupeds [four-legged animals], we would have been obliged to subsist upon frogs and snakes, which (especially the latter) abound in these parts. I can never think of this journey, without reverently acknowledging the peculiar care and providence of the merciful Creator.

July the 2nd. At Crown Point. Early this morning we set out on our journey again, it being moonlight and calm, and we feared lest the wind should change and become unfavorable to us if we stopped any longer. We all rowed as hard as possible, and happily arrived about eight in the morning at Fort St. Frédéric, which the English call Crown Point. Monsieur Lusignan, the governor, received us very politely.*** He was about fifty years old, well acquainted with polite literature, and had made several journeys into this country, by which he had acquired an exact knowledge of several things relative to it.

July the 5th. Indian Revenge. While we were at dinner we heard several times a repeated, disagreeable, bloodcurdling outcry, some distance from the fort, in the river Woodcreek: Mr. Lusignan, the commander, told us this cry was ominous, because he could conclude from it that the Indians, whom we escaped near Fort Anne, had completed their design of avenging the death of one of their brethren upon the English, and that their shouts showed that they had killed an Englishman. As soon as I came to the window, I saw their boat, with a long pole at the front, at the extremity of which they had put a bloody human scalp. As soon as they had landed, we heard that they, being six in number, had continued their journey (from the place where we saw marks of their passing the night) till they had gotten within the English boundaries, where they found a man and his son employed in harvesting.

---

*The travelers spent the night on the Ticonderoga peninsula.

**Lake St. Sacrement was renamed Lake George in 1755 by Major General William Johnson in honor of King George II of Great Britain. The name Lake George was added to the 1770 translation of Kalm's original work.

***Captain Paul-Louis Dazemard de Lusignan (1691-1764) had served at Fort Niagara (N.Y.), Fort Saint Joseph (Mich.), and Baiedes-Puants (Wis.) before becoming the commandant at Fort St. Frédéric. During the French and Indian War he was variously assigned to Forts St. Frédéric, Carillon, Isle-aux-Noix, St. Jean, and Chambly.[18]

They crept on towards this man and shot him dead. This happened near the very village where the English, two years before, killed the brother of one of these Indians, who had then gone out to attack them. According to their custom they cut off the scalp of the dead man and took it with them, together with his clothes and his son, who was about nine years old. As soon as they came within a mile of Fort St. Frédéric, they put the scalp on a pole in the fore part of the boat, and shouted as a sign of their success. They were dressed in shirts, as usual, but some of them had put on the dead man's clothes; one his coat, the other his breeches, another his hat, etc. Their faces were painted with vermilion, with which their shirts were marked across the shoulders. Most of them had great rings in their ears, which seemed to be a great inconvenience to them, as they were obliged to hold them when they leaped or did anything which required a violent motion. Some of them had girdles of the skins of rattlesnakes, with the rattles on them; the son of the murdered man had nothing but his shirt, breeches and cap, and the Indians had marked his shoulders with red. When they got on shore they took hold of the pole on which the scalp was put, and danced and sung at the same time. Their object of taking the boy was to carry him to their tent, to bring him up instead of their dead brother, and afterwards to marry him to one of their relations so that he might become one of them. Notwithstanding they had perpetrated this act of violence in time of peace, contrary to the command of the governor in Montreal, and to the advice of the governor of St. Frédéric, the latter could not at present deny them provisions and whatever they wanted for their journey, because he did not think it advisable to exasperate them; but when they came to Montreal, the governor called them to account for this action, and took the boy from them, whom he afterwards sent to his relations.* Mr. Lusignan asked them what they would have done to me and my companions, if they had met us in the wilderness. They replied that as it was their chief intention to take their revenge on the Englishmen in the village where their brother had been killed, they would have let us alone. But it would have depended on the humor they were in when we first came in sight. However, the commander and all the Frenchmen said that what had happened to me was infinitely safer and better.

July the 6th. Veterans' Cottages. The soldiers who had been paid off after the war [King George's War 1744-1748] had built houses round the fort on the grounds allotted to them; but most of these habitations were no more than wretched cottages, no better than those in the most wretched places of Sweden. There was that difference, however, that the inhabitants here were rarely oppressed by hunger, and could eat good and pure wheat bread. The huts which they had erected consisted of boards, standing perpendicularly close to each other. The roofs were of wood too. The crevices were stopped up with clay to keep the room warm. The floor was usually clay, or a black limestone, which is common here. The hearth was built of the same stone, except the place where the fire was to burn, which was made of gray stones, which for the greatest part consisted of particles of quartz. In some hearths

*Six Ottawas, Nipissings, and Abenakis had killed and scalped a provincial sergeant who had been plowing a field near Fort Number Four, located near the Connecticut River in Charlestown, New Hampshire. Their action was in retaliation for the death of a fellow warrior killed during an unsuccessful siege of the fort several years earlier. The nine-year-old captive was Enos Stevens, son of Captain Phineas Stevens. The elder Stevens had been appointed by Governor William Shirley of Massachusetts as an emissary to New France to seek the release of New England prisoners. Young Enos was freed in Montreal prior to his father's first pilgrimage to Canada.[19]

the stones quite close to the fireplace were of limestone. However, I was assured that there was no danger of fire, especially if the stones which were most exposed to the heat were of a large size. Dampers had never been used here and the people had no glass in their windows.

July the 10th. Boats. The boats which are here used, are of three kinds. 1. Bark boats, made of the bark of trees, with ribs of wood; 2. Canoes, consisting of a single piece of wood, hollowed out, which I have already described. These are here made of the white fir, and of different sizes. They are not propelled by rowing but by paddling, by which method not half the strength can be applied which is used in rowing. A single man might, I think, row as fast as two of them could paddle. 3. The third kind of boats are bateaux. They are always made very large here, and used for large cargoes. They are flat-bottomed, and the bottom is made of red, but more commonly of white oak which shows better resistance when it runs against a stone than other wood. The sides are made of white fir, because oak would make the bateau too heavy.* They make plenty of tar and pitch here.

A Soldier's Rations. The soldiery enjoy such advantages here as they are not allowed in any part of the world. Those who formed the garrison of this place had a very plentiful allowance from their government. They get every day a pound and a half of wheat bread, which is almost more than they can eat. They likewise get plenty of peas, bacon, and salt or dried meat. Sometimes they kill oxen and other cattle, the flesh of which is distributed among the soldiers. All the officers kept cows, at the expense of the king, and the milk they gave was more than sufficient to supply them. The soldiers had each a small garden outside the fort, which they were allowed to attend and to plant in it whatever they liked. Some of them had built summer-houses in them and planted all kinds of vegetables. The governor told me that it was a general custom to allow the soldiers a plot of ground for kitchen gardens, at. . .the French forts hereabouts as were not situated near great towns, from whence they could be supplied. In time of peace the soldiers have very little guard duty when at the fort; and as the lake close by was full of fish, and the woods abounded with birds and animals, those amongst them who chose to be diligent could live extremely well and like a lord in regard to food. Each soldier got a new coat every two years; but annually, a waistcoat, cap, hat, breeches, cravat, two pair of stockings, two pair of shoes, and as much wood as he had occasion for in winter. They likewise got five sols [French coin] apiece every day, which is augmented to thirty sols when they have any particular labor for the king. When this is considered it is not surprising to find the men are very healthy, well fed, strong and lively here. When a soldier falls sick he is brought to the hospital, where the king provides him with a bed, food, medicine, and people to take care of and serve him. When some of them asked leave to be absent for a day or two to go away it was generally granted them if circumstances would permit, and they enjoyed as usual their share of provisions and money, but were obliged to get some of their comrades to mount guard for them as often as it came to their turns, for which they gave them an equivalent. The governor and officers were duly honored by the soldiers; however, the soldiers and officers often spoke together as comrades, without any ceremonies, and with a very becoming freedom. The soldiers who are sent hither from France commonly serve till they are forty or fifty years old, after which they are honorably discharged and

---

*British and provincial bateaux were also constructed with oak bottoms and sides of pine boards.[20]

allowed to settle upon and cultivate a piece of ground. But if they have agreed on their arrival to serve no longer than a certain number of years, they are dismissed at the expiration of their term. Those who are born here commonly agree to serve the crown during six, eight, or ten years, after which they are [honorably] discharged and settle down as farmers in the country. The king presents each discharged soldier with a piece of land, being commonly 40 arpents* long and but three broad, if the soil be of equal goodness throughout; but they get somewhat more, if it be poorer. As soon as a soldier settles to cultivate such a piece of land, he is at first assisted by the king, who supplies him, his wife and children with provisions during the first three or four years. The king likewise gives him a cow and the most necessary instruments for agriculture. Some soldiers are sent to assist him in building a house, for which the king pays them. These are of great help to a poor man who begins to keep house, and it seems that in a country where the troops are so highly, distinguished by royal favor, the king cannot be at a loss for soldiers. For the better cultivation and population of Canada, a plan was proposed some years ago for sending three hundred men over from France every year, by which means the old soldiers might always be retired, marry and settle in the country. The land which was allotted to the soldiers about this place, was very good, consisting throughout of a deep mould, mixed with clay.**

July the 16th. West of Lake Champlain. This morning I crossed Lake Champlain [Bulwagga Bay] to the high mountain on the western side, in order to examine the plants and other curiosities there. From the top of the rocks, a little distance from Fort St. Frédéric, a row of very high mountains [Adirondack Mountains] appear on the western shore of Lake Champlain, extending from south to north. On the eastern side of this lake is another chain of high mountains [Green Mountains], running in the same direction. Those on the eastern side are not close to the lake, being about ten or twelve miles from it. The country between them is low and flat, and covered with woods, which likewise clothe the mountains, except in such places as the fires, which destroy the forest here, have reached and burnt them down. These mountains have generally steep sides, but sometimes they are found gradually sloping. We crossed the lake [Bulwagga Bay] in a canoe, which could only contain three persons, and as soon as we landed we walked from the shore to the top of one of the mountains. Their sides are very steep, and covered with earth, and some great rocks lay on them. All the mountains are covered with trees, but in some places the forests have been destroyed by fire. After a great deal of trouble we reached the top of one of the mountains, which was covered with a dusty mould. It was not one of the highest, and some of those which were at a greater distance were much higher, but we had no time to go to them, for the wind increased and our boat was but a little one. We found no curious plants or anything remarkable there.

When we returned to the shore we found the wind had risen to such an intensity that we did not venture to cross the lake in our boat, and for that reason I left a man to bring it back, as soon as the wind had subsided and we walked round the bay, which was a distance of about seven English miles. I was followed by my servant,

---

*One arpent was 175-198 feet long, depending on the locality and the period of time.

**In 1750 Captain Benjamin Stoddard reported French settlers on both sides of the lake at Crown Point: "there are fourteen farms on it, and great encouragement given by the king for that purpose, and I was informed that by the next fall, several more families were coming there to settle."[21]

and for want of a road we kept close to the shore, where we passed over mountains and sharp stones, through thick forests and deep marshes, all of which were known to be inhabited by [numerous] rattlesnakes, of which we happily saw none at all. The shore is full of stones in some places, and covered with large angulated rocks, which are sometimes roundish [on] their edges as if worn off. Now and then we came upon a small sandy spot, covered with gray, but chiefly with the fine red sand which I have before mentioned; and the black iron sand likewise occurred sometimes. We found stones of red mica of a fine texture on the mountains. Occasionally these mountains with the trees on them stood perpendicular at the waterside, but in some places the shore was marshy.

The mountains near the shore are amazingly high and large, consisting of compact gray rock, which does not lie in strata as the limestone. Its chief constituent parts are a gray quartz and a dark mica. This rock reached down to the water in places where the mountains stood close to the shore, but where they were a short distance from it there were strata of gray and black limestone, which reached to the water side, and which I never have seen covered with gray rocks.

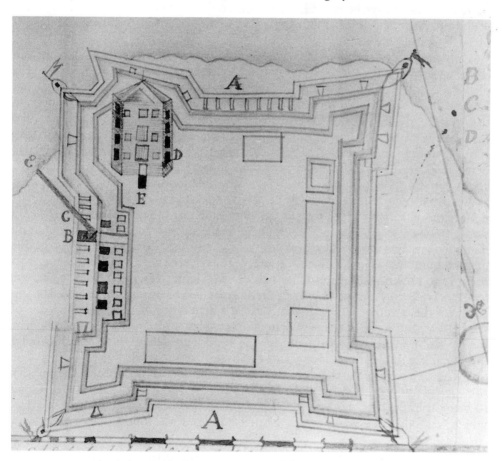

Detail of English drawing of Fort St. Frédéric based on scouting reports.
(Crown Collection, New York State Library)

July the 17th. The intermitting fever sometimes appears amongst the people here, and venereal disease is common. The Indians are likewise infected with it; many of them have had it, and some still have it; but they are possessed of an infallible art of curing it. There are examples of Frenchmen and Indians, infected all through the body with this disease, who have been "radically" and perfectly cured by the Indians within five or six months. The French have not been able to find out this remedy, though they know that the Indians employ no mercury, but that their chief remedies are roots, which are unknown to the French. I afterwards heard what these plants [Lobelia plant] were and gave an account of them to the Royal Swedish Academy of Sciences.

July the 19th. At Crown Point. Fort St. Frédéric is a fortification on the southern extremity of Lake Champlain, situated on a neck of land, between that lake and the river, which arises from the union of the river Woodcreek [southern Lake Champlain] and Lake St. Sacrement. The breadth of this river is here about a good musketshot. The English call this fortress Crown Point, but its French name is derived from the French secretary of state, Frédéric Maurepas, in whose hands the direction and management of the French court of admiralty was at the time of the erection of this fort. It is to be observed that the government of Canada is subjected to the court of admiralty in France, and the governor-general is always chosen from that court. As most places in Canada bear the names of saints, custom has made it necessary to prefix the word Saint to the name of the fortress. The fort is built on a rock, consisting of black lime or slate, as mentioned before. It is nearly square, has high, thick walls made of the same limestone, of which there is a quarry about half a mile from the fort. On the eastern part of the fort, is a high tower, which is proof against bombshells, provided with very thick and substantial walls, and well stored with cannon from the bottom almost to the very top; and the governor lives in the tower.* On one side of the fort is a pretty little church, and on the other side, houses of stone for the officers and soldiers. There are sharp rocks on all sides towards the land, beyond a cannon shot from the fort, and among them are some which are as high as the walls of the fort and very near them.

The Englishmen insist that this fort is built on their territory and that the boundary between the French and English colonies in this locality lies between Fort

---

*In 1749 Captain Phineas Stevens described the citadel at Fort St. Frédéric as "four stories high, each story contains four convenient rooms; the partitions are walls of stone of great thickness; each story arched over with stone of great thickness, for its twenty-four large stone steps from one story to another; each room has one very large window, three or four feet wide, seven or eight high. The commandant lives in the third story, where there are two such windows. In his room, I saw 110 small arms, 50 of them fixed with bayonets, and about 50 pairs of pistols. I had not opportunity to discover the number of cannon in the fort and citadel. . . I would here further note, there are eighteen houses near Crown Point, some on each side of the water, but not all inhabited at present."[22] A year later Captain Benjamin Stoddard recorded the following description: "This fort is built of stone the walls of a considerable height and thickness, and has twenty pieces of cannon and swivels, mounted on the ramparts and bastions, the largest of which is six pounders, and but a few of them. . . At the entrance to the fort is a dry ditch, eighteen or twenty foot square and a draw bridge, there is a subterraneous passage under this draw bridge to the lake which I apprehend is to be made use of in time of need to bring water to the fort, as the well they have in it affords them but very little. In the north[east] corner of the fort stands the citadel; it is a stone building eight square, four story high each turned with arches, mounts twenty pieces of cannon and swivels, the largest six pounders, four of which are in the first story and are useless until the walls of the fort are beat down. The walls of the citadel are about ten foot thick the roof high and very tant covered with shingles."[23]

St. Jean and the Prairie de la Madeleine; on the other hand, the French maintain that the boundary runs through the woods, between Lake St. Sacrement and Fort Nicholson [site of Fort Edward after 1755].

The soil about Fort St. Frédéric is said to be very fertile, on both sides of the river, and before the last war a great many French families, especially old soldiers, settled there, but the king obliged them to go into Canada, or to settle close to the fort, and sleep in it at night. A great number of them returned at this time, and it was thought that about forty or fifty families would go to settle here this autumn. Within one or two musketshots to the east of the fort, is a windmill, built of stone with very thick walls, and most of the flour which is needed to supply the fort is ground here. This windmill is so constructed as to serve the purpose of a redoubt, and at the top of it are four or five small pieces of cannon. During the last war [King George's War 1744-1748], a number of soldiers was quartered in this mill, because they could from there look a great way up the river [lake], and observe whether the English boats approached, which could not be done from the fort itself. This was a matter of great consequence, as the English might (if this guard had not been placed here) have gone in their little boats close under the western shore of the river, and then the hills would have prevented their being seen from the fort. Therefore the fort ought to have been built on the spot where the mill stands,* and all those who come to see it, are immediately struck with the absurdity of its location. If it had been erected in the place of the mill, it would have commanded the river, and prevented the approach of the enemy; and a small ditch cut through the loose limestone, from the river (which comes out of the Lake St. Sacrement) to Lake Champlain, would have surrounded the fort with flowing water, because it would have been situated at the extremity of the neck of land. In that case the fort would always have been sufficiently supplied with fresh water, and at a distance from the high rocks which surround it in its present situation. We prepared to-day to leave this place, having waited several days for the arrival of the boat, which plies constantly all summer between the [F]ort Saint Jean and Fort St. Frédéric.** During our stay here, we had received many favors. The governor of the fort, Mr. [Captain Paul-Louis Dazemard de] Lusignan, a man of learning and of great politeness, heaped kindness upon us, and treated us with as much civility as if we had been his relations. I had the honor of eating at his table during my stay here, and my servant was allowed to eat with his. We had our rooms, etc. to ourselves, and at our departure the governor supplied us with ample provisions for our journey to Fort Saint Jean. In short he did us more favors than we could have expected from our own countrymen, and the officers were likewise particularly obliging to us.***

---

*After the capture of Fort St. Frédéric by British forces under Major General Jeffery Amherst in 1759, a small fort (Grenadier Redoubt) was built on the site of the windmill. In 1858 a 55-foot-high lighthouse was constructed on the peninsula which was rebuilt as the Samuel de Champlain Memorial Light in 1911-1912.

**This 45-ton ship was built in 1742 by the Corbin brothers of Quebec. The vessel, probably named the *St. Frédéric*, was commanded by Joseph Payant St. Onge and made regular trips between Fort St. Frédéric and Fort St. Jean well into the 1750s.[24]

***The hospitality may have been a complementary gesture since French scientists were always treated as guests of the Swedish government while in the latter country.[25] Kalm's reception at Fort St. Frédéric may have also been influenced by his passport, which had been issued by "His Most Christian Majesty the King of France" and had been acquired in London by the former Swedish minister to France.[26]

On Lake Champlain. About eleven o'clock in the morning we set out with a fair wind. On both sides of the lake are high chains of mountains, with the difference which I have before observed, that on the eastern shore is a low piece of ground covered with a forest, extending between nine to twelve English miles, after which the mountains begin [Green Mountains], and the country beyond them belongs to New England. This chain consists of high mountains, which are to be considered as the boundaries between the French and English possessions in these parts of North America. On the western shore of the lake, the mountains reach to the waterside. The lake at first is but a French mile broad, but keeps increasing in size afterwards. The country is inhabited within a French mile of the fort, but after that it is covered with a thick forest. At a distance of about ten French miles from Fort St. Frédéric, the lake is four such miles broad, and we perceived some islands in it. The captain of the boat said there were some of considerable size. He assured me that the lake was in most parts so deep that a line of two hundred yards could not fathom it, and close to the shore, where a chain of mountains generally runs across the country, it frequently has a depth of eighty fathoms.* Fourteen French miles from Fort St. Frédéric we saw four large islands in the lake, which is here about six French miles

Four Brothers Islands.
(Photo by Richard K. Dean)

---

*Lake Champlain reaches a maximum depth of 400 feet just north of Split Rock Point and Thompson's Point which Kalm passed on July 19.

broad.* This day the sky was cloudy, and the clouds, which were very low, seemed to surround several high mountains near the lake with a fog. From many mountains the fog rose, as the smoke of a charcoal kiln. Now and then we saw a little river which emptied into the lake. The country behind the high mountains, on the western side of the lake, is, as I am told, covered for many miles with tall forests, intersected by many rivers and brooks with marshes and small lakes, and is very suitable for habitations. The shores are sometimes rocky and sometimes sandy here. Towards night the mountains decreased gradually. The lake was very clear, and we observed neither rocks nor shallows in it. Late last night the wind abated, and we anchored close to the shore, and spent one night here.

July the 20th. This morning we proceeded with a fair wind. The place where we passed the night was more than half way to Fort Saint Jean, for the distance of that place from Fort St. Frédéric, across Lake Champlain, is computed to be forty-one French miles. That lake is here about six English miles in breadth. The mountains were now out of sight, and the country low, plain and covered with trees. The shores were sandy, and the lake appeared now from four to six miles broad. It was really broader but the islands made it appear narrower.

Indians. We often saw Indians in bark boats, close to the shore, which was, however, not inhabited, for the Indians came here only to catch sturgeons, wherewith this lake abounds, and which we often saw leaping up into the air. These Indians lead a very singular life. At one time of the year they live on the small store of corn, beans, and melons, which they have planted; during another period, or about this time, their food is fish, without bread or any other meat; and another season they eat nothing but game, such as stags, roes, beavers, etc., which they shoot in the woods and rivers. They, however, enjoy long life, perfect health, and are more able to undergo hardships than other people. They sing and dance, are joyful, and always content, and would not for a great deal exchange their manner of life for that which is preferred in Europe.

When we were yet ten French miles from Fort Saint Jean, we saw some houses on the western side of the lake, in which the French had lived before the last war, and which they then abandoned, as it was by no means safe. They now returned to them again. These were the first houses and settlements which we saw after we had left those about Fort St. Frédéric.**

An Old Fort. There formerly was a wooden fort or redoubt on the eastern side of the lake, near the waterside, and the place where it stood was shown to me; at present it is quite overgrown with trees.*** The French built it to prevent the incursions of the Indians over this lake, and I was assured that many Frenchmen had been slain in these places. At the same time the Canadians told me that they numbered four women to one man in Canada, because annually several Frenchmen were killed on their expeditions which they undertook for the sake of trading with the Indians.

*Kalm observed the Four Brothers Islands, east of the Willsboro peninsula, which were also known as the Four Winds Islands/Les Isles au Quatre Vents in the eighteenth century.

**These dwellings, built before 1744, may have been at the mouth of the Chazy River. In 1752 Sieur Jean-Antoine Bedout became proprietor of the land.[27]

***The ruins of Fort St. Anne, built of logs in 1666 on Isle La Motte, would still have been clearly visible in Kalm's time.

A windmill, built of stone, stood on the east side of the lake on a projecting piece of ground.* Some Frenchmen lived near it; but they left it when the war broke out, and have not yet come back to it. From this mill to Fort Saint Jean they considered it eight French miles. The English, with their Indians, had burnt the houses here several times, but the mill remained unhurt.

The boat in which we went to Saint Jean was the first that was built here, and employed on Lake Champlain, for formerly they made use of bateaux to send provisions over the lake. The Captain was a Frenchman born in this country.** He had built it in order to find out the true course, between Fort Saint Jean and Fort Saint Frédéric. Opposite the windmill the lake was about three fathoms deep, but it grew more and more shallow, the nearer it came to Fort Saint Jean.

We now perceived houses on the shore again. The captain had otter skins in the cabin, which in color and species were just like the European ones. Otters are said to be very abundant in Canada.

Below the afore-mentioned windmill, the breadth of the lake is about a musket-shot, and it looks more like a river than a lake.*** The country on both sides is low and flat, and covered with deciduous trees. We saw at first a few scattered cottages along the shore, but a little further on, the country was uninhabited without interruption. The lake was here from six to ten feet deep, and had several islands. During the whole course of this voyage, the direction of the lake was always directly from S. S.W. to N.N.E.

The lake was now so shallow in several places that we were obliged to trace the way for the boat by sounding the depth with branches of trees. In other places opposite it was sometimes two fathoms deep.

In the evening, about sunset, we arrived at Fort Saint Jean, or St. John, having had a continual change of rain, sunshine, wind and calm all afternoon.

July the 21st. Fort St. John [St. Jean] is a wooden fort, which the French built in 1748 on the western shore of the mouth of Lake Champlain, close to the waterside. It was intended to protect the country round about it, which they were then going to people, and to serve as a magazine for provisions and ammunition, which were usually sent from Montreal to Fort St. Frédéric; because they might go in boats from here to the last mentioned place, which is impossible lower down, as about two gunshots further there is a shallow place full of stones and very rapid water in the river, over which they can pass only in bateaux or flat vessels. Formerly Fort Chambly, which lies four French miles lower, was the magazine of provisions; but since they were forced first to send them hither in bateaux, and then from here in boats, and the route to Fort Chambly† from Montreal being by land, and round about, this fort was erected. It has a low location and lies on a sandy soil, and the country about it is likewise low, flat and covered with woods. The fort is square and includes the space of one arpent square. In each of the two corners which look

---

*The windmill was probably on Windmill Point, lying across the lake from present-day Rouses Point.

**Joseph Payant St. Onge, captain of the *St. Frédéric*, commanded the schooner *La Vigilante* during the French and Indian War.

***At this point Kalm's party was sailing on the Richelieu River.

†Travelers had to transport boats and gear around the Richelieu Rapids at Fort Chambly, several miles to the north of Fort St. Jean. In 1665 Fort Chambly was only a wooden stockade, but a stone fortification was ordered built on the site in 1709.

towards the lake is a wooden building, four stories high, the foundation of which is of stone to the height of about a fathom and a half. In these buildings which are polyangular, are holes for cannon and lesser fire-arms. In each of the two other corners towards the country is only a little wooden house, two stories high. These buildings are intended for the habitation of the soldiers and for the better defense of the place. Between these houses there are poles, two fathoms and a half high, sharpened at the top and driven into the ground close to one another. They are made of the *thuya* [aborvitae] tree, which is here considered the best wood for withstanding rot, and is much preferable to fir in that point. Lower down the palisades are double, one row within the other. For the convenience of the soldiers, a broad elevated platform of more than two yards in height is made in the inside of the fort all along the palisades, with a balustrade. On this platform the soldiers stand and fire through the holes upon the enemy, without being exposed to their fire.

Kalm's Return Journey On Lake Champlain

October the 14th [1749]. At seven o'clock in the morning we set out [from Fort St. Jean] in the name of the Lord in a canoe which was quite small and rather heavily loaded. Three natives accompanied us in a similar boat. There was a gentle wind, but it was directly against us.

We saw American natives frequently on both sides of the river on which we were paddling. They had their quarters for the night on the shore, as it was the season when they were out hunting deer.

We stopped for the night a little south of the windmill, still on the western side of the lake. They reckoned that it was about ten leagues (thirty English miles) from this place to St. Jean.

Three native women also came in their canoe and took shelter for the night next to us. They had no man with them, yet each of them had a gun, for they had set out to shoot ducks. One was married, the other two were said to be single. They were Abenaquis [Abenaki] Indians. The native who accompanied us during the whole journey was an Iroquois Indian. It is singular that an Abenaquis and an Iroquois rarely take lodgings together, yet they now and then intermarry. The women who had come hither had their funnel-shaped caps, trimmed on the outside with white glass beads. They also had on the French women's waists and jackets which I had never before seen natives wearing. Their evening meal consisted of corn and native Iroquois beans boiled together.

October the 15th. At daybreak in the morning we continued our journey; the weather was a little cool. The shores were everywhere lined with black stones.

In the evening we put up for the night just north of Rivière au Sable [Ausable River]. This river is clearly indicated on the map, but has been given no name. It is on the western side of the lake, right opposite Isle Valcour. It is said to have received its name from the fact that along the shore lies a long sand bar of about six feet in height, with the lake on the eastern side and low-lying morasses and land on the western. A great many black ducks which the French called outards were swimming outside of this bar.

October the 16th. We continued on our journey in the morning, but as the weather was against us, with a stiff wind blowing and our small boat heavily loaded, we neither dared nor could proceed. After rowing about a league we were compelled to seek the shore and wait until the weather changed or the wind spent itself. We found a haven at the mouth of a small stream, which it was said was a tributary of the same river [lower mouth of Ausable River] on whose banks we had camped at night. The entire shore was sandy; some of the sand had the same characteristics as desert sand, namely that it was swirled about by the wind. The monkey flower (*Mimulus*) grew in moist places on the banks of the river. The seeds were ripe and had partly fallen from the pods.

In the afternoon the wind came up and we continued our journey. As the wind increased and our boat began to leak badly we did not dare to sail any farther, but were compelled to seek a haven at a place opposite the Isle au Chapon [Schuyler Island] on the western side of the lake.

Description of Shore. The shore here as well as in many other places consisted entirely of rounded stones of varied composition. I do not know whether there had been more water in this lake formerly than now. I shall describe how the lake appears. Next to the water the shore is largely filled with rounded stones as just mentioned, either of the complex variety or the black limestone. The shore rises gradually up to six fathoms from the edge of the water, where there is ordinarily a rather steep bank of earth of about two to four fathoms height. The land above is usually level and free from rocks. This is how it appears at least in most places. Here and there are small steep cliffs of bed rock next to the water; in other places there are large rocks at the water's edge, then a high and steep bank of earth with round stones in it, and above it high mountains. Again there are sand banks which are next to the water, and often back of them is marshy land. Once in a while there are gentle, sloping sandy shores with a somewhat steep sandhill about thirty-six to sixty feet from the water's edge, above which the country is level. Occasionally the shore is so low and marshy that it is impossible to walk upon it without sinking down into the mud. This then, in brief, is the description of this lake's shoreline. Frequently there is a high bank next to the water, and back of it lowlands, level and large in area. On nearly all sides of the lake, a little distance away, are large and rather high mountains nearly all overgrown with forests, and it is these mountains they hold responsible for the uncertain weather and the gales. I saw no visible indications that the water had decreased in the lake. It might have been possible, judging from the higher rocks which were three to five feet higher than the present water-line, but I am of the opinion that condition might have obtained during the spring after a winter with much snow.

October the 17th. A Storm. At sunrise in the morning we continued our journey with the wind against us, though it was not yet very strong. About eight o'clock when we were almost opposite the Isle de Quatre Vents [Four Brothers Islands], the wind changed and became northeast, which was the best wind for us. We hoisted our sail and proceeded [on our journey], but our good fortune did not last long. The wind became steady, but it increased so that the waves began to be rather high. We found it wisest to seek the shore, and it was just in the nick of time, as before we reached land the wind had become so strong that we had to furl our sail, for fear that it might shatter our fragile boat. It looked rather bad for us to begin with, inasmuch as the shore nearest us was full of stones and so steep that we could not make a landing without endangering our lives. We were certain that even if we saved our lives, all that we had brought with us would be lost or spoiled. We were compelled, therefore, in spite of great danger, to row around a peninsula in order to get behind it into quiet waters. The waves were terribly high and the wind came in squalls, as it had done daily since we came to this lake. But God be praised! we got ashore safe and sound. May the Lord calm the winds so that we may soon get away from here! The place where we are now is in the inlet, which is formed by the promontory we rowed around and an extended cliff. From this cliff it is said to be six French miles to Fort St. Frédéric. It was 11 A. M. when we reached land.

Rocks embellished with peculiar markings were found about on the shore. I call them embellished from the fact that the water had eaten into them and had made figures just as if someone had carved a lot of foreign characters upon the whole rock. I have found here several such rocks. If one of these were carried far up into the forests to some little hillock [small hill] and left there, some European, on coming to that place, would believe that it were a grave and that the symbols on the rock were a foreign and unknown script which the people who had come here in earlier times had made use of, and that it contained the life history of the one who was buried there. The rock was composed of a gray, closely grained sandstone mixed with a limestone of the same grain and color. Within were seen stripes of dark gray pyrites [iron disulfide]. Perhaps the same pyrites had covered the outside, and either the air, sun, water or rain had caused erosion and in some way had formed these characters.

We also found cockroaches in the place where we were resting. When we had made a fire by the side of an old decayed stump on the shore, a large number of these insects came creeping out of it driven out of their winter quarters by the fire and smoke. The French neither recognized them nor knew their name.

In Lake Champlain I did not see anything that was new to me, neither plants nor anything else floating in it. The water was very clean, extremely clear and of excellent taste with the exception of some places near the shore where some brook in the neighborhood emptied into the lake. Here the water tasted musty and somewhat swampy. Generally there were on both sides of this lake great stretches of level lowlands, which some day when they are populated and cultivated will make a glorious country, because the soil is so fertile. The greater part of the land about the lake has already been donated by the King to certain families of the gentry; consult my map.* The land about Fort St. Frédéric is said to belong to the King still, although it is to a great extent inhabited. On the eastern side of the lake are seen in the distance high mountains which separate Canada from New England.—The Abenaquis [Abenaki] Indians who wander about in these woods on the border are the Englishman's worst enemy.—They reckoned forty leagues (about 120 miles) from Fort St. Frédéric to Fort Chamblais [Chambly]. Fort St. Jean is four leagues this side of Fort Chamblais. The low-lying fields about the lake were said to be marshy.

How the Natives Paint Designs on Their Bodies. I have related before that the Indians paint various designs on their bodies and that these are put on in such a way that they remain as long as the natives live. When they wish to paint some figures

*This map was not in Kalm's original work.

on the body, they draw first with a piece of charcoal the design which they desire to have painted. Then they take a needle, made somewhat like a fleam [scalpel], dip it into the prepared dye and with it prick or puncture the skin along the lines of the design previously made with the charcoal. They dip the needle into the dye between every puncture; thus the color is left between the skin and flesh [tattoo]. When the wound has healed, the color remains and can never be obliterated.

October the 18th. A storm continued throughout the day and prevented us from making any headway. We had to stay on that account in a place where there was no hunting because of the absence of animals.

In the afternoon the storm abated somewhat and people began to venture forth on the lake. We saw first a few natives sail by us, and shortly thereafter the two English boats with the Englishmen on board who had escorted home the French prisoners captured in the last war with the English. This made me indignant, as I had left three days before they reached Montreal. But the treacherous weather made my journey to begin with a slow one, and now we had put our boat in such an inlet that the weather prevented our leaving it. We were compelled to remain until toward evening when the gale moderated and we eventually got away from there.

Finally we left there in the evening and rowed far into the night until we came within six miles of Fort St. Frédéric. On some parts of the shore the rocks were perpendicular and in others they sloped slightly. In still other places where the rocks consisted of the black stone the water had worn away the rock at the base so that the upper part extended over the water. I paid particular attention this evening to the rocks and noticed that the height of the water in this lake at this time could not be more than three to four feet higher than at present, since the water had worn smooth a horizontal band at the latter height. From this it was possible to see how high the water rose when at its greatest height. Above this line the rocks were overgrown with lichens [fungi/algae plants], and every where were trees, especially arbor vitae and pines.

In many places the rocks on the shore were composed of black limestone which generally lay like slate in strata. In some places these did not lie horizontally but sloped, so that the southern part was lower and the northern higher, or they appeared as if they had been placed there during a south wind. In one place the black stone had separated into thin flag-stones, like a slate shingle, but as they had been exposed to the air for some time they could not be used for roof covering. Monsieur de la Galissonnière showed me in Quebec pieces which had been taken from this place.*

In the evening we stopped for the night on the shore of the lake; the night was rather cold.

October the 19th. We continued our journey from the place where we had passed the night. The sky was now almost entirely overcast and it looked as if snow might fall. It was quite cold. At 9:30 A. M. we arrived at Fort St. Frédéric. Before we reached the shore the soldiers accompanying me gave their customary salute with their muskets after which called *vive le roi* [long live the king]! As soon as I reached the shore and stepped out of the boat, they gave a salute of five or six guns from the

*Rolland-Michel Barrin, Marquis de la Gallissonnière (1693-1756), was a French naval officer and governor-general of Canada from 1747 to 1749. Kalm was very impressed by his knowledge of natural history.[28]

fortress in my honor, and all the officers together with the barefooted monk, Père Hippolite, came toward me on the shore and conducted me up to the commandant who was now Monsieur Herbin, as Monsieur Lusignan, who was in command this summer when I first came here, had now been released from his post.* I was received here with all possible good will and graciousness. As the Englishmen who had come hither yesterday afternoon and had left here this morning had taken away with them a large part of the bread supply, there was not enough left for my four men and myself for our whole journey. I was forced to postpone my departure to the following day, until fresh bread had been baked, which was indeed better for us. The officers here fared very well, for not only were all bodies of water full of ducks and game which now flew over in large numbers, preparing themselves for their fall migration, but it was also the season when the natives staged their hunt for roe deer in the large neighboring wastes and woodlands, whence they very frequently came to the fortress with fresh meat to be exchanged for gunpowder, bullets, shot, bread and anything else they needed.

October the 20th. Collecting the Seeds of the Sugar Maple. In the morning when everything was ready we continued our journey. I went a little ahead down the country road in order to gather seeds from the sugar maple. Some of them had fallen from the trees. My men rowed along the bay which extends up to the Woodcreek. The commander, Monsieur Herbin, and the other officers followed me part of the way along the road and when I was a short distance outside of the fort I was honored with a salute of from five to six guns which were fired at the fort for my sake. When I had said farewell to the officers, I walked quickly to the last Canadian farm on this side. It was about three miles south of the fort. I stopped there until 2 P.M. to gather the seeds of the sugar maple which had fallen and were lying on the ground.**

Notes

1. Adolph B. Benson, ed., *Peter Kalm's Travels in North America* (New York: Wilson-Erickson, Inc., 1937), Volume 2, 575.
2. Ian K. Steele, *Warpaths: Invasions of North America* (New York: Oxford University Press, 1994), 70; Francis Jennings, *The Ambiguous Iroquois Empire* (New York: W. W. Norton & Company, 1984), 88-89.
3. For Father Jogue's own account see Isaac Jogues, "Of the Captivity of Father Jogues, of the Society of Jesus, Among the Mohawks, in 1642 and 1643," *Collections of the New-York Historical Society* 3 (2nd Series) (1857): 173-207.
4. Guy Omeron Coolidge, *The French Occupation of the Champlain Valley from 1609 to 1759*, 2nd ed. (1938; reprint ed., Mamaroneck, N.Y.: Harbor Hill Books, 1989), 53; A small wooden fort may have been built by the French during the fall of 1666 at Ticonderoga "close to the falls which separate the two bodies of water." See Roger R. P. Dechame, "The First Fort at Fort Ticonderoga," *The Bulletin of the Fort Ticonderoga Museum* 15 (Winter 1988): 11.

*Father Hippolyte Collet (Cober), a Recollect priest, had been the chaplain at Fort St. Frédéric from 1747 to 1754. Frederic-Louis Herbin (1677-1754), the leader of the expedition against Saratoga in 1747, commanded Fort St. Frédéric from late 1749 to 1751. Paul-Louis Dazemard Lusignan, holder of a seigniory (land grant) near Missisquoi Bay, resumed his command of the fort in 1751 and continued at that post until 1759.[29]

**On October 21, 1749, Kalm began a four-day journey through Lake George, then called Lac du Saint-Sacrement.

5. Coolidge, 59.
6. For Winthrop's journal of the expedition see E. B. O'Callaghan, ed., *Documents Relative to the Colonial History of the State of New-York* (Albany: Weed, Parsons and Company, 1854), Volume 4, 193-96.
7. Peter S. Palmer, *History of Lake Champlain*, 4th ed. (1886; reprint ed., Fleischmanns, N.Y.: Purple Mountain Press, 1992), 56.
8. Samuel G. Drake, *A Particular History of the Five Years French and Indian War* (1870; reprint ed., Bowie, MD: Heritage Books, Inc., 1995), 268; Arthur Latham Perry, *Origins in Williamstown*, 3rd ed. (Williamstown, MA: Arthur Latham Perry, 1900), 169-70.
9. Martti Kerkkonen, *Peter Kalm's North American Journey* (Helsinki, Finland: The Finnish Historical Society, 1959), 33.
10. Ibid., 93.
11. Benson, 1:344-45.
12. Ibid., 1:333.
13. James Sullivan, ed., *The Papers of Sir William Johnson* (Albany: The University of the State of New York, 1921), Volume 1, 228.
14. Benson, 1:355.
15. Ibid., 1:358; This was the second fort at Saratoga. See Perry, 161-63.
16. Benson, 1:365.
17. Ibid., 1:372-80, 2:381-98, 561-81; Kalm's complete journal has been reprinted in one volume. Adolph B. Benson, ed., *Peter Kalm's Travels in North America* (1937; reprint ed., New York: Dover Publications, Inc., 1966).
18. *Dictionary of Canadian Biography*, Volume 3 (Toronto: University of Toronto Press, 1974), 168-69.
19. Ian K. Steele, *Betrayals: Fort William Henry & the Massacre* (New York: Oxford University Press, 1990), 8, 10; Colin G. Calloway, *North Country Captives* (Hanover, N.H.: University Press of New England, 1992), 22; M. Crespel, a member of the French clergy who lived at Fort St. Frédéric and Pointe à la Chevelure from November 1735 to September 1736, suggested that Indians would "cut off [an enemy's] scalp which they carry on a pole, as a proof that they have defeated their enemies. This custom gave a name to the place [Scalping Point] as in a battle at this point many Indians were scalped." Crespel also described conditions during the winter of 1735-1736: "the house in which we lodged was not finished. . .Most of our soldiers were affected with scurvy, and we had all such disorders in our eyes, that we were even fearful we should lose our sight. Our food was not better than our lodging. We found little to eat near the post but a few partridges." M.Crespel, *Travels in North America* (London: Sampson Low, 1797), 41-45.
20. John Gardner, "Bateau 'Reconstructed' from Remains, Drawing," *National Fisherman*, August 1967, 8-A; Hallie E. Bond, *Boats and Boating in the Adirondacks* (Blue Mountain Lake, N.Y: The Adirondack Museum/Syracuse University Press, 1995), 32-33.
21. *Proceedings of the New York State Historical Association* 10 (1911): 113.
22. Phineas Stevens, "Journal of Capt. Phineas Stevens to and from Canada-1749," *Collections of the New Hampshire Historical Society* 5 (1837): 204.
23. *Proceedings*, 112.
24. John C. Huden, "The Admiral of Lake Champlain," *Vermont History* 30 (January 1962): 67.
25. Benson, 2:393.
26. Kerkkonen, 104.
27. Palmer, 52-53; Coolidge, 110-11.
28. Benson, 1:374, 2:504.
29. Coolidge, 144, 152, 187, 194, 88, 207.

Painting of Louis-Joseph de Montcalm by Natoire.
(Fort Ticonderoga Museum)

Part II: The French and Indian War

3. Louis-Joseph de Montcalm 1758

T HE MARQUIS DE MONTCALM, the most celebrated French general of the French and Indian War, left an indelible imprint on the history of the Lake George-Lake Champlain valleys. As field commander of the army battalions in New France, he has been lauded for his victories in North America from 1756 through 1758 and mourned upon his tragic death on the Plains of Abraham in 1759. Despite his earlier triumphs, some historians deem him responsible for the loss of French Canada.[1]

Louis-Joseph de Montcalm was born on February 28, 1712, at his family's ancestral chateau of Candiac, near Nimes, France. His father, Louis-Daniel de Montcalm, served as a lieutenant colonel in the French infantry, and his mother, Marie Thérèse de Castellane, was a woman of strong character who would have considerable influence over her son throughout his life. Unlike his younger brother, Montcalm was a disappointing student under the private tutelage of Louis Dumas. But while continuing his education with his tutor, Montcalm was commissioned an ensign in his father's regiment in 1727 at the age of 15. Two years later he was elevated to captain in the same regiment, probably through a purchase of rank. His active service, however, did not begin until 1732. The following year, during the War of the Polish Succession (1733-1735), Montcalm received his first taste of battle with a French expeditionary force under Maréchal de Saxe. During the course of the siege and capture of Philippburg in 1738, Montcalm witnessed the death of Maréchal Duke of Berwick, one of the greatest military strategists of his time. With the death of his father in 1735, Montcalm returned to the chateau of Candiac as head of the family. The next year he married Angélique-Louise Talon de Boulay, the daughter of an army colonel, and eventually they had ten children, six of whom survived childhood. In 1741, during the War of the Austrian Succession (1740-1748), Montcalm served as an aide-de-camp to the Marquis de La Fare. After capturing

Prague the following spring, the French army was besieged and forced to retreat. Despite being wounded, Montcalm exhibited remarkable courage during the retreat. In March 1743 Montcalm was promoted to colonel of the regiment of Aurerrois, which he would subsequently lead in three campaigns in Italy. During a battle at Piacenza, Italy, Montcalm was severely wounded with "five sabre cuts" and taken prisoner by the Austrians.[2] Paroled to France after recovering from his injuries, he was elevated to the rank of brigadier in 1747 by King Louis XV. Following his release from parole as a result of an exchange of prisoners, Montcalm returned to the Italian campaign where he was once again wounded in battle. When the Treaty of Aix-la-Chapelle in 1748 ended the war, Montcalm remained in the peacetime army, receiving a pension in 1753.

Montcalm's real opportunity for fame occurred during the French and Indian War (1755-1763). With the capture of Jean-Armand Dieskau (Baron de Dieskau), the commander of French troops in North America, at the Battle of Lake George on September 8, 1755, Montcalm was appointed as his replacement and promoted to the rank of major general. Prior to his official appointment, Montcalm's wife opposed the North American assignment, but his mother encouraged her son to take advantage of the chance for distinction.

On April 3, 1756, Major General Montcalm and his staff sailed for Canada aboard the frigate *Licorne*, reaching the St. Lawrence River five weeks later. In North America Montcalm faced a daunting task: a year earlier at a conference of English colonial governors, plans had been approved to forcibly expel the French from Forts Duquesne, Niagara, St. Frédéric, and Beauséjour (Nova Scotia). Although the British and provincial troops under Major General Edward Braddock were defeated in the campaign against Fort Duquesne and the English expeditions against Niagara and St. Frédéric stalled in 1755, the smaller population and armed forces available to New France made prospects for future French victories bleak.

Before the ultimate collapse of the French empire in America, Montcalm would lead the French army to a series of stunning victories which would check the English advance. The French strategy during the early part of the war was largely a response to the detailed British plans found among Edward Braddock's papers, which had been taken during the 1755 battle. As a countermove to the British designs against Forts Frontenac and Niagara, Pierre de Rigaud de Vaudreuil de Cavagnial, the governor-general of New France, formulated a strategy to capture the English stronghold at Oswego, consisting of Forts Ontario, Oswego, and George at the mouth of the Oswego River on Lake Ontario. With 20 cannon and 3,500 men, Montcalm prepared to lay siege to Fort Ontario on the east side of the Oswego River. Before the French bombardment began, British and provincial forces abandoned the fort and moved to Fort Oswego. On August 14, 1756, following a short cannonading and the death of the British commander, Lieutenant Colonel James F. Mercer, the garrison surrendered to the French invaders. The French victors captured 1,700 prisoners, two brigs, one schooner, one sloop, a large number of bateaux, 121 pieces of artillery, several chests of money and a large amount of provisions.[3] As French troops demolished the three forts, Montcalm readied for a possible attack by British soldiers under Colonel Daniel Webb. But upon hearing the news of the British surrender, Webb quickly retreated southward, burning

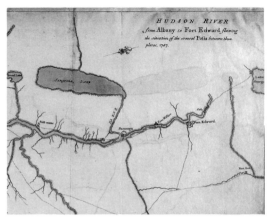

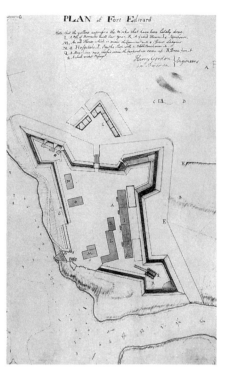

Clockwise from above: Map of the posts along the Hudson River in 1757. (Henry E. Huntington Library)

Plan of Fort Edward. (Crown Collection, New York State Library)

Fort William Henry and Entrenched Camp 1757. (Crown Collection, New York State Library)

One of the British sloops built in 1756 at the entrance to the Narrows of Lake George. (Crown Collection, New York State Library)

"Siege of Fort William Henry 1757." From *The Passing of New France* by William Wood.

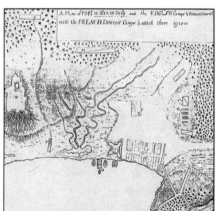

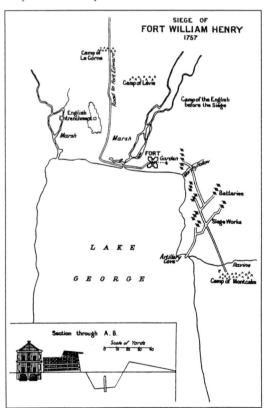

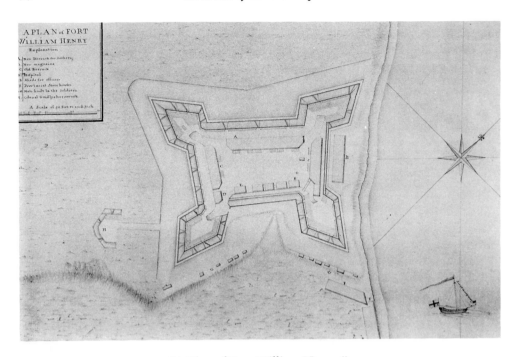

"A Plan of Fort William Henry."
(Crown Collection, New York State Library)

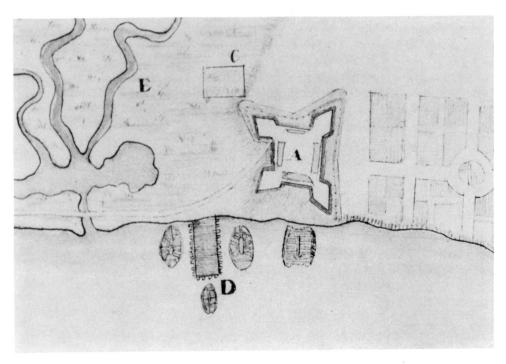

Detail of plan of Fort William Henry 1757.
(Crown Collection, New York State Library)

several newly-constructed forts at the Great Carrying Place (near present-day Rome, New York).

After the Oswego conquest, strained relations between Montcalm and Governor-General Vaudreuil became more conspicuous. Montcalm was subordinate to the governor-general, who had ultimate command of the army in New France. While Vaudreiul firmly believed in guerrilla raids to isolate English frontier forts and settlements, Montcalm embraced traditional European military tactics. Disagreement, intrigue, and criticism by both men undermined a consistent French military strategy in North America. The outright antagonism between the two leaders resulted from Montcalm's belief that Vaudreuil had claimed too much credit for himself and the Canadians after the success of the Oswego operation.

Pierre de Rigaud de Vaudreuil de Cavagnial (1698-1778), governor-general of New France. Painting by Henri Beau. (National Archives of Canada)

Early in 1757 Governor-General Vaudreuil prepared a scheme to destroy Fort William Henry at Lake George. Although Montcalm suggested "burning, at least, the outer parts of the fort with 800 men" under the leadership of a regular officer, Vaudreuil instead authorized a force of 1,600 men commanded by his younger brother, François-Pierre de Rigaud de Vaudreuil, who had led the successful raid against Fort Massachusetts in 1746.[4] In March 1757 Rigaud and his troops spent more than a week in the cold during a vain attempt to burn Fort William Henry. The winter raid, however, did succeed in destroying all of the fort's outer buildings, several hundred bateaux, and a number of larger vessels.* After the invaders retreated

---

*The vessels were sloops built in 1756 by provincial troops under British supervision. In October Dr. Ammi Ruhamah Cutter, a surgeon attached to a New Hampshire regiment, noted that "the fleet consists of 1 sloop about 40 tons, 2 smaller 20 tons each, another sloop on ye ways ready to launch of

to Fort Carillon, British and provincial troops discovered the charred remains of the French scaling ladders and their dead soldiers, "thrust into a Hole, made in the Ice."[8]

When a large number of British and provincial troops were sent to attack the French fortress of Louisbourg on Cape Breton Island during the summer of 1757, Governor Vaudreuil decided "to take advantage of the absence of the best troops [and]. . .lay seige to Fort William [Henry]."[9] Using Fort Carillon as the base of operations, Montcalm assembled a force of 3,081 regulars, 188 artillerymen, 2,946 Canadian militia, and 1,806 Native Americans, representing 40 Indian nations.[10] A short time before Montcalm's expedition was to depart, Colonel John Parker with his New Jersey regiment was sent "to attack the advance guard at Ticonderoga," but was instead assaulted by a party of French and Indians at Sabbath Day Point.[11] Only 60-70 provincials out of the 350-man unit escaped the ambush.

On July 27, 1757, at a grand council of Native Americans at Ticonderoga, Kisensik, the noted Nipissing chief, thanked the Indian nations of the west "for having come to help us defend our lands against the English who wish to usurp them."[12] In response, Montcalm reassured the assembled multitude that "the great King has without doubt sent me to protect and defend you."[13] Only a handful of interpreters was available to translate Montcalm's message; in some cases French officers could communicate only indirectly with their allies through other Native Americans. While many Indians sought to forestall future English expansion, others were there for plunder and retaliation.[14]

On August 1 Montcalm's army departed from Ticonderoga in 250 bateaux and 31 artillery rafts, the latter fashioned by laying a platform on two bateaux. Earlier in the day Montcalm's Native American allies had embarked in 150 canoes; two days earlier 2,488 French soldiers and Indians had set out on foot along an old Mohawk trail west of Lake George. After stopping briefly at present-day Bolton Landing, the French army landed on the western shore of the lake, several miles north of Fort William Henry. The siege of the fort by Montcalm's forces lasted nearly one week. With no hope of reinforcements from Fort Edward, the battered 2,300-man garrison at the fort and adjacent entrenched camp finally surrendered on August 9.[15] The next day, as the British and provincial troops began their march to Fort Edward, the Indians plundered the line of evacuees, "taking the Officers Swords Hats Watches Fuzees Cloaths and Shirts leaving [them] quite naked."[16] According to Captain Jean Nicholas Desandrouins, a French engineer, the Indians "killed their prisoners by hitting them on their heads rather than abandoning them; a great number dragged them to their small boats [canoes] and escaped" before "the spectacle of this butchery" ended.[17] The "massacre" was similar to an incident that had occurred one year earlier after the Oswego victory in which approximately 30 wounded prisoners had been butchered. The earlier episode was overlooked by the French officers, and the Indians also learned that English prisoners could be ransomed to the French.

ye bigness of [the] former."[5] A month earlier General John Winslow, in command of the provincial troops at Lake George, reported "One Sloop with two Six pounders, One Seven Inch Mort[a]r and Eight Swivels fifty men, One Sloop four Swivels forty men, one Ditto two Swivels and thirty five men."[6] Although French sources indicated that four large vessels were burned in the March 1757 raid, two sloops apparently escaped destruction since they were moored at Fort William Henry during the summer of 1757.[7]

Early in 1758 William Pitt, the British secretary of state, formulated plans for a three-theater offensive against Fortress Louisbourg, Fort Duquesne, and Fort Carillon. Orders from England envisioned an expedition against Carillon by 20,000 provincial troops and 5,000-6,000 British regulars. The great logistical problems involved in equipping and deploying such a huge army on a northern lake delayed the campaign against the French fort, allowing the garrison time to mount a defense.[18] The expedition to Ticonderoga was led by Major General James Abercromby, the 52-year-old commander in chief of British forces in North America. After an unremarkable military career in Europe, Abercromby had served two years in North America without holding an autonomous position before elevation to commander in chief. The field command of the campaign was delegated to 34-year-old Brigadier George Augustus Howe, a popular leader who had adopted many new techniques suitable to fighting in the American wilderness. In early July 1758, 6,367 British regulars and 9,024 provincial troops assembled at the southern end of Lake George, representing the largest military expedition to date in North America. The army, buoyed with optimism, departed for Ticonderoga on July 5 in 900 bateaux, 135 whaleboats, rafts for artillery and horses, and three small radeaux or floating batteries.[19] Dr. James Searing, a 19-year-old regimental surgeon, observed "the great spirit of the troops" as the bateaux, organized in four columns, slowly advanced northward, accompanied by "fine Musick," according to another eyewitness, Samuel Fisher.[20] The flotilla stopped at Sabbath Day Point where Sergeant Seth Tinkham, who was with a Massachusetts regiment, noted "several men's bones lay there" from the ambush of Colonel John Parker's detachment one year earlier.[21] After lighting campfires to mislead French scouts, the army renewed its journey northward by 11 P.M., reaching the end of the lake the next morning. French soldiers briefly fired on the British invaders at the northern landing and set a blockhouse ablaze before fleeing. After disembarking, the British and provincial armies were delayed as the result of an unfortunate encounter with a French scouting party. Because it was believed that the French would defend the bridge over the La Chute River, near the sawmill, Major General Abercromby and Brigadier Howe decided to outflank the French army by taking a roundabout route. Traveling through the densely-forested western shoreline along the outlet from Lake George, troops led by Majors Robert Rogers and Israel Putnam and Brigadier Howe stumbled upon a 350-man French scouting detachment. Although approximately 150 French prisoners were taken, Howe was killed in the action. Late in the day British and provincial troops accidentally fired on one another and remained scattered in the woods overnight.

Montcalm had reached Fort Carillon on June 30 to prepare a defense. With an army only one-fifth the size of the British forces, Montcalm was in a precarious position. As the 15,000-man British and provincial army assembled at Lake George, Montcalm received exaggerated reports of a 20,000-25,000-man enemy force.[22] Complicating matters for Montcalm, Governor-General Vaudreuil had divided French forces by sending a diversionary army of 1,600 men under Brigadier General François de Lévis to the Mohawk Valley.

Since Fort Carillon was never designed to hold all of the French troops, Montcalm inspected the area surrounding the fort on July 1 with engineers Nicolas Sarrebource de Pontleroy and Jean-Nicolas Desandrouins and other officers in order to choose a site for a defensive position. The next day the parameters for a protective breastwork were initially marked out on the high ground between the fort and the outlet from Lake George. After reports arrived on July 6 of British bateaux on Lake George, engineers Pontleroy and Desandrouins were dispatched to make the final measurements for the breastwork. Late that same day Colonel François-Charles de Bourlamaque's troops destroyed the bridge at the sawmill and joined Montcalm's main force. On July 7 nearly 3,000 soldiers and officers worked frantically to complete the breastwork along a one-third-mile-long stretch of land that followed the sinuosity of the hillside. The wall was constructed by piling logs and tree trunks horizontally one upon another with earth packed between. Topped with sandbags, the breastwork was set in a flanking arrangement with an abatis of felled trees with sharpened branches strewn for 200-300 feet before the wall. At 7:30 on the evening of July 7, 300 reinforcements from the Levis expedition arrived with Captain Pierre Pouchot, a career officer in the Bearn Regiment. Later that night, Chevalier de Levis arrived with more troops, bringing the total French army on the field of battle to 3,526 men.[23] The delay in the British advance caused by the July 6 skirmish provided crucial time for Montcalm to prepare his works on the "Heights of Carillon."

On July 7 Abercromby sent Colonel John Bradstreet to secure the bridge across the La Chute River. Finding the crossing destroyed, provincial carpenters rebuilt the structure by nightfall. Early the next morning Abercromby sent a junior engineer, Lieutenant Matthew Clerk (also spelled Clark) and several other officers to assess the French breastwork. Although there was some disagreement among the officers over the strength of the wall, Abercromby accepted Clerk's opinion that it was a weakly-constructed wall "which we might easily get to and push down with our shoulders."[24] Colonel James Montresor, the chief engineer, was ill at the time; and Major William Eyre, a senior engineering officer, was not employed as the result of a dispute with Abercromby over Eyre's relinquishing control of the 44th regiment. "I was told if I did not give Up the Command of ye Reg^t I must have nothing to do with [the engineering]," Eyre later wrote.[25] Eyre chose to lead the 44th Regiment and consequently never evaluated the strength of Montcalm's defenses. Relying on the exaggerated numbers of expected reinforcements culled from French prisoners and the belief that an attack could be made before the French had time to finish their entrenchment, Ab-

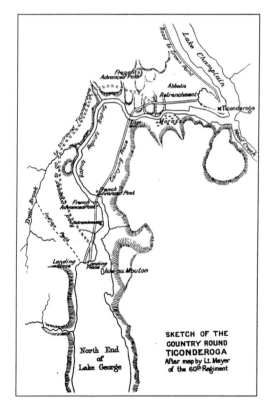

SKETCH OF THE
COUNTRY ROUND
TICONDEROGA
After map by Lt. Meyer
of the 60th Regiment

North End
of
Lake George

Sketch of the northern end of Lake George and Ticonderoga 1758. From *The Passing of New France* by William Wood.

ercromby decided upon an immediate attack on Montcalm's breastwork.

As the army began its frontal assault on the French outworks, several regiments of provincial troops began moving the artillery from the Lake George landing site to the sawmill. According to Lemuel Lyon, a provincial recruit, his regiment "got near the Mil[l]s and we had orders to leave the Artiller[y] the[r]e."[27] At the same time provincial carpenters completed two hastily-built floating batteries on the La Chute River. The gun platforms, mounting four field pieces, proved worthless since cannon fire from Fort Carillon quickly forced them back. Prior to the first action of the day, Sir William Johnson's Native American allies rendered ineffective musket fire from present-day Mount Defiance.

In contrast to the lack of strong leadership in the British ranks, Montcalm was able to solidify the resolve of the French army against the expected British onslaught. The night before the battle he gathered his troops and carefully explained his directions for the defense of the rudimentary barricade. Montcalm admonished his officers to "let the soldiers fire at will and urge them to adjust their aim well," according to Captain Jean-Nicolas Desandrouins.[28] While Montcalm was steadfast in front of his troops, he was understandably worried about facing an overwhelming British army. Captain Pierre Pouchot recorded that Montcalm was "rather irresolute all that morning [July 8]. He did not know whether to resist the enemy attack or to withdraw to St. Frédéric [and make a stand there]."[29] Nevertheless, by the time the fighting began Montcalm was ready and his army unwavering in its resolve. On the right or northernmost section of the breastwork, the regiments of La Reine, Béarn, and Guyenne were led by Brigadier General Lévis; on the left Colonel Bourlamaque had charge of the La Sarre and Languedoc; in the center Montcalm commanded the Royal Roussillon and one battalion of the Berry, while another of the latter battalion manned Fort Carillon.

At approximately 12:30 the British army formed into four columns and began an attack at different points along the breastwork, according to French sources, but the offensive lacked coordination.[30] With the death of Brigadier Howe on July 6, no one assumed the duties of field commander. Brigadier Thomas Gage, the highest ranking officer under Abercromby, failed to take responsibility for tactical control of the disorganized army. Subsequent military service would more clearly reveal his shortcomings as a field commander.

Abercromby came to the battlefield after the attack had already begun and only exerted loose control over his troops. Montcalm, on the other hand, removed his outer uniform and vigorously directed his soldiers on the front lines. Five or six deadly charges occurred during the battle. Colonel Louis Antoine de Bougainville, Montcalm's aide-de-camp, recorded that the Scottish Highlanders "returned unceasingly to the attack, without becoming discouraged or broken."[31] To the horror of the valiant English troops, the French breastwork was a formidable structure, constructed of "logs, well fitted together, with slits left open between them at a proper height, for loopholes—and made so high as to come above their heads," and the felled trees before the wall made the breastwork "almost inaccessible."[32] Many of the provincial soldiers described the day-long carnage, including Lieutenant Archelaus Fuller from Middleton, Massachusetts, who observed that "de[a]d men and wounded lay on the groun[d], the wounded having some of [their] legs. . .arms and other lim[b]s broken, others shot thr[ough] the bod[y] lay in blood and the earth tremb[led]."[33] Benjamin Jewett with the Connecticut militia wrote that the British regulars were in such "plain sight that ye French cut them down amazin."[34]

Late in the day Captain Jean d'Anglais de Bassignac "attached his handerkerchief, which was red, to the end of his musket & used it to signal," but the British troops mistook it as a gesture of surrender and advanced to the breastwork until Captain Pouchot ordered a "volley, shooting down two or three hundred of them."[35] Twenty-two-year-old Abel Spicer from Connecticut noted the flag "deception" in his diary, as well as the French soldiers' trick of setting "their hats just above the top of the breast work."[36] At six o'clock the British launched their final assault. An hour later the defeated army, having suffered 1,944 killed or wounded, retreated.[37] The deadly French fire can be explained by Captain Desandrouins' calculation that each French soldier "fired 70 to 80 shots" in the course of the clash.[38] Given the fortified position of Montcalm's army, it was remarkable that the British forces managed to inflict several hundred casualties upon the French with only musket fire. The high number may have resulted from the close-range firing after the penetration of the abatis by the Highlanders and regulars as well as the volume of "continual fireing" for hours by British and provincial troops.[39]

When the battle ended, the English soldiers retreated to their hurriedly-constructed breastwork near the sawmill and later to Lake George. Abner Barrows, an enlistee from Middleboro, Massachusetts, was appalled to "see the Slain how thick th[e]y Lay on the Ground when our men Retreated," a scene noted by many others, including Abel Spicer, who remarked that the dead and wounded filled the "roads. . . so full that a man could hardly walk without treading on them."[40] Unnerved by the disastrous defeat, some units of the army departed for the southern end of Lake George during the night. Most, however, including Abercromby's principal forces, embarked the next morning. Captain Charles Lee of the 44th Regiment of Foot shortly thereafter vehemently criticized Abercromby's leadership for failing to utilize the cannon which would "have occur'd to any blockhead who was not absolutely so far sunk in Idiotism as to be oblig'd to wear a bib and bells. So far, his behaviour cou'd only be call'd stupid, ridiculous & absurd; but the subsequent part was dishonorable and infamous & had some strong symptoms of cowardice" since the troops were "eager" to fight again, but Abercromby retreated in "so much hurry precipitation and confusion as to give it entirely the air of flight. . .thirteen thousand men. . .r[a]n away from three thousand."[41]

On the evening of July 8 Captain David Waterbury of Connecticut was sent with a 500-man party to a point of land along the Lake George shoreline to prevent a French ambush of the departing British troops. His orders were to remain there until relieved by another party. Unknown to Waterbury, most of his men left during the night. After one soldier, sent in the morning by Waterbury to the sawmill area failed to return, another was dispatched and later reported that most of the army had departed and were two or three miles away.* Waterbury's remaining troops found "some battoos Left and we took them and pus[h]of[f] after the Rest of the army," reaching the southern end of the lake at eight o'clock at night.[42]

---

*This would not be the last time that Waterbury would be left behind. During the American Revolution, Waterbury served as second in command to Benedict Arnold at the Battle of Valcour Island on Lake Champlain. Commanding the row galley *Washington*, Waterbury was captured near Split Rock on October 13, 1776, as other American vessels fled "and left me in the rear, to fall into enemy's hands."[43]

In contrast to the disorder and panic that seized the British army after the engagement, Montcalm "had wine and beer conveyed to the field of battle, to refresh the troops" and "passed in front of all the battalions [accompanied by Chevalier de Lévis] and expressed how pleased they felt at their conduct."[44] The French army remained under arms on the battlefield during the night, awaiting a renewed attack by the British the next day. Despite the exhaustion of battle, French troops labored during the night to perfect their breastwork in preparation for a resumption of fighting. The following day the army continued to toil on its entrenchment and began the grisly task of burying the dead on both sides. At dawn on July 10 Montcalm dispatched Lévis with eight grenadier companies to investigate the enemy position. Lévis discovered "wounded, provisions, shoes left in miry places, remains of barges [bateaux] and burned pontoons [rafts]."[45] The next day François-Pierre de Vaudreuil, brother of the governor-general of New France, arrived at Carillon with approximately 3,000 Canadian militia and Native Americans, three days too late to have assisted Montcalm's troops during the British assault.

Soon after the victory at Carillon, Pierre de Rigaud de Vaudreuil, the governor-general, issued orders to Montcalm to undertake additional offensive actions against British forces. Montcalm largely ignored the directives, as he had a year earlier when Governor Vandreuil had pressured him to destroy Fort Edward after the destruction of Fort William Henry. The smoldering conflict between the two French leaders erupted in 1758, following Vaudreuil's communique to France which lauded the Canadians for their efforts during the July 8 battle, but denigrated the regulars as well as Montcalm's leadership. Montcalm quickly responded with accusations against Vaudreuil and criticism of the Canadian militia.

Bow of 1758 radeau *Land Tortoise* in 107 feet of water.
The vessel was designated a National Historic Landmark in 1998.
(Photo by the author)

The Lake George-Lake Champlain theater of war remained stalemated for the rest of 1758. While British and provincial officers contemplated a renewed expedition against Carillon in 1758, the chief accomplishment of the forces at Lake George involved the construction of a number of war vessels, including the sloop *Earl of Halifax*, the seven-sided radeau *Land Tortoise*, another smaller radeau, and two row galleys. The fighting in the region continued during the summer of 1758 with two large-scale French raids on English outposts between Fort Edward and Lake George and a third engagement near Wood Creek, involving Joseph Marin de La Malgue's French force and 530 troops under Robert Rogers and Israel Putnam.

By August 17 most of the Canadian militia had returned home, leaving 3,193 effective troops at Carillon. Four days later Montcalm consecrated a roughly hewn cross at the site of the French breastwork with the inscribed words, "Christian! It was not Montcalm and his prudence, Nor these felled trees, the heroes, their exploits, Which dashed the hopes of the bewildered English; It is the hand of thy God, conqueror on this cross."[46] The victory, however, was an anomaly. Following the French loss at Louisbourg and Fort Frontenac (Kingston, Ontario), Montcalm was briefly recalled to Canada. Still anticipating a major attack on Carillon, Montcalm returned on September 16 after a ten-day absence. Additional defensive works to strengthen Forts Carillon and St. Frédéric were completed during the fall of 1758. After news of the British abandonment of Lake George, Montcalm and his army departed in early November from Carillon. The weather, however, hampered his return to Canada, according to Montcalm: "We met with a gale on Lake Champlain which scattered our fleet of boats like those of St. Cloud. This was followed by a cold which made us abandon a great many boats on the ice."[47]

The dispute between Governor Vaudreuil and Montcalm persisted into 1759. Vaudreuil was in total disagreement with Montcalm's recommendation to relinquish the Ohio Valley and the peripheral forts on Lake Ontario and Lake Champlain. The only point of agreement between the two men was Vaudreuil's support of Montcalm's request for recall to France. Montcalm also recommended the cessation of guerilla tactics by the Canadians and the adoption of a traditional European military strategy. Montcalm's aide, Bougainville, and André Doreil, the financial commissary of wars, were sent to France with letters to the council of ministers. In an effort to demonstrate the vulnerability of New France, Bougainville painted a gloomy picture of France's position in North America. Bougainville also presented a strategy which would involve a French invasion of North Carolina. The council of ministers dismissed the idea of a military expedition to North Carolina but otherwise supported Montcalm's assessment of New France over Vaudreuil's views. In the end, the ministers decided to concentrate France's efforts in Europe, sending minimal reinforcements and supplies to Canada. Montcalm's petition for recall was turned down, but his promotion to lieutenant general provided a rank higher than that of a colonial governor, thus insuring his supreme command over all military forces in New France.[48]

By May, Bougainville returned to Quebec with 20 supply ships and several hundred reinforcements. Early the next month a British fleet arrived at Quebec loaded with 9,000 troops under the command of Major General (local rank) James Wolfe, a 32-year-old career officer who had distinguished himself at Louisbourg a year earlier. Although Montcalm had recommended batteries along the river one

"View of the Taking of Quebec," September 13, 1759.
After a drawing by Captain Hervey Smith.
(Print, author's collection)

year before, Vaudreuil, and to a lesser extent Montcalm himself, were overconfident that British warships would be unable to navigate the narrow, tricky river channel to Quebec. French fireships that were sent against the British fleet failed, as did an attack on Wolfe's land position on the opposite shore. Stricken with illness, Wolfe vacillated during the summer before launching a bold pre-dawn offensive on September 13. More than 4,000 British soldiers ascended the cliffs leading to the Plains of Abraham, less than a mile from Quebec City. Totally surprised by the maneuver, Montcalm initially did not believe the reports of British soldiers on the Plains. Upon reaching the site, Montcalm counted the regiments himself and observed the Highlanders forming the center, a déjà vu of Ticonderoga. Montcalm mustered nearly the same number of troops as the British on the field of battle, but the French force incorporated a large number of green militia. Fearing that any delay would allow Wolfe's army to entrench on the Plains, Montcalm prepared for an immediate attack. Although Colonel Bougainville's 3,000 troops were only a few hours away, Montcalm, following a council with his officers, decided not to wait for reinforcements. Mounting a large dark horse and brandishing his sword, Montcalm fearlessly led his French regulars and Canadian militia against the British position. Shortly thereafter, the French force was cut down by two devastating, double-shotted volleys from Wolfe's regiments. The onslaught of the French army was quickly broken. Leading a grenadier advance, Wolfe was wounded twice; a third bullet ripped into his chest, mortally wounding the young general. As Montcalm tried to rally his vanquished army, two successive wounds ended his efforts.

Two soldiers held Montcalm on his horse as he entered Quebec City through the St. Louis Gate. At five o'clock the next morning, the 47-year-old general died. In the disorder of the French defeat, a proper coffin for Montcalm could not be located. That evening a crude box holding his remains was buried in a shell crater under the floor of the Ursuline chapel (present-day Ursulines Museum, 12 rue Donnacona). A few days later Jean-Baptiste-Nicolas-Roch de Ramezay, the commander of the Quebec garrison, surrendered the city to the British. The end of the French empire in North America was now inevitable; total capitulation would follow a year later. Although historians have long debated Montcalm's role in the fall of New France, he died heroically at the head of his troops in defense of the French colony.

The following report of Montcalm, relating the 1758 French victory at Carillon, was written on July 20, 1758, to Marshal Louis-Charles-Auguste Fouquet de Belle-Isle, the minister of war. The account was at least partially written by Montcalm's aide-de-camp, Louis Antoine de Bougainville, whose journal closely parallels this document. This report is a version of one sent earlier to Governor-General Vaudreuil.

Death of Montcalm. Detail of painting by Vateau.
(National Archives of Canada)

Account of the Victory Won by the Royal Troops at Carillon on the 8th Day of July, 1758[49]

The Marquis de Vaudreuil, uncertain of the movements of the enemy, had thought necessary at the beginning of this campaign to distribute his forces. He had appointed the Chevalier de Levis* to execute a secret expedition with a picked detachment, of which 400 men were chosen from the land troops. The rest of these troops were sent by order of the Marquis de Montcalm to defend the border of the Lake Saint Sacrement [Lake George]. The Marquis de Montcalm arrived at Carillon the 30th of June. The report of prisoners made a few days before left him no doubt that the enemy had gathered, near the ruins of Fort William Henry, an army of 20,000 to 25,000 men and that their intention was to advance immediately upon him.**

He imparted at once this news to the Marquis de Vaudreuil and did not hesitate to take an advanced position which would deceive the enemy, retard his movement and give time for the Colonial help to arrive. In consequence, le Sieur de Bourlamaque*** was ordered to take possession of the portage at the head of Lake Saint Sacrement, with the battalions of the Queen's, of the Guyenne and of the Bearn Regiments. The Marquis de Montcalm, with those of the Sarre, of the Royal Roussillon, of the Languedoc Regiments and the 1st battalion of the Berry,† occupied personally the two banks of the [La] Chute River, thus named because in that spot the Lake Saint Sacrement, narrowed by the mountains pours its bubbling waters into the St. Frederic River [southern basin of Lake Champlain] and Lake

---

*François de Lévis began his career as a second lieutenant in the Régiment de la Marine in 1735. He was promoted to captain during the War of Polish Succession (1733-1735) and later served in Italy at the time of the War of the Austrian Succession (1740-1748). When Montcalm was sent to lead New France's army in North America in 1756, Lévis was appointed second in command with the rank of brigadier general. After playing a key role in the successful siege of Fort William Henry in 1757, Lévis was given command in June 1758 of 1,600 men, including 400 French regulars, by Governor-General Vaudreuil to proceed to the Iroquois villages along the Mohawk River to persuade the Mohawks to enlist in a joint assault on nearby provincial settlements. However, when news of the immediacy of the attack on Carillon reached Canada, Levis was reassigned to defend the Lake Champlain fort. Montcalm was critical of Vaudreuil's strategy which divided the limited number of French troops. Vaudreuil responded with the excuse that "no provisions having arrived from France, he was unable to defend that frontier [Carillon] except by a diversion" to the Mohawk Valley.[50]

**Although British plans had called for 20,000 to 25,000 soldiers for the expedition, Abercromby assembled 15,391 troops at the southern end of Lake George in early July 1758.[51] While Montcalm used the higher figure in his correspondence, other contemporary French sources more accurately estimated Abercromby's army at 14,000.[52]

***François-Charles de Bourlamaque (1716-1764) began his military career in 1739, rising to the rank of captain before his service in the War of the Austrian Succession. Appointed third in command in North America and promoted to colonel, Bourlamaque sailed for Quebec in April 1756. He managed the sieges of Oswego in 1756 and Fort William Henry the following year, and was assigned to lead the troops on the left wing or southern section of the breastwork at Carillon in 1758. Bourlamaque served to the end of the war in North America and in 1763 was appointed governor of Guadeloupe, where he died the next year.

†Some modern translations use *i* in place of *y* for some words; Berri for Berry and Guienne for Guyenne.

Champlain. The 2nd Berry battalion took charge of the defense and service at the Fort of Carillon.

The Marquis de Montcalm made the Sieurs de Pontleroy and Desandrouins, Engineers,* reconnoitre and determine a site for a fortified position which could cover this fort; and as we had only a few Canadians and only 15 savages, he took from the French battalions two troops of Volunteers, the command of which was given to the Sieur Bernard, captain in the Bearn Regiment and Duprat, captain in the Sarre Regiment.

In the evening of the 5th, scouts which we had on the Lake Saint Sacrement, informed us that they had seen a large number of barges [bateaux] which might be and were, in fact, the vanguard of the enemy's army. At once the order was given to the troops of the portage and the Chute camps to take their armaments, to spend the night at the bivouac, and to clear the equipages. The Volunteers of Duprat were sent to take position on a creek called the Bernetz which, flowing between the mountains that cover this part of the country, runs into the Chute River.** The enemy could pass around us by the back of these mountains. It was essential to be aware of such a movement. 350 men under the command of the Sieur Trepezec, captain in the Bearn Regiment, were detached to take a position between the Pelee Mountains [Rogers Rock/Cooks Mountain] and the left bank of the Lake Saint Sacrement and the Volunteers of Bernard occupied another post intermediary between the Pelee Mountains and the Portage camps. Measures were taken also to throw a light [keep an eye] on a possible disembarkment which the enemy might make on the right bank of the lake.

The 6th. At four o'clock in the morning, the vanguard of the opponent's army was located in sight of the portage. At once the Marquis de Montcalm sent orders to the Sieurs de Pontleroy and Desandrouins to lay out, in front of Carillon on the ground already marked, trenches and abattis and to the 2nd Battalion of Berry to work at them with its ensigns.

The enemy began to disembark at nine o'clock; the Sieur de Bourlamaque retreated then in their presence with the 3rd battalion from the portage and in the

---

*Nicolas Sarrebource Maladre de Pontleroy (1717-1802) joined the engineer corps in 1736, later serving during the War of the Austrian Succession. Promoted to captain in 1745, he was later awarded the prestigious Cross of Saint-Louis for his war service. Following a successful stint as an engineer at Fortress Louisbourg (1755-1757), Pontleroy was appointed chief engineer in New France in 1757 instead of Michel Chartier de Lotbinière, who had supervised the original construction of Fort Carillon and was Governor Vaudreuil's favored candidate for the position. After the 1758 battle of Carillon, Pontleroy, with the help of engineer Desandrouins, made improvements in the outer defenses of the fort. Pontleroy was promoted to lieutenant colonel in October 1758 and served to the end of the war in North America. Remaining in the engineering service, he was elevated to major general in 1780, five years before retirement. Pontleroy lived until 1802.

Jean-Nicolas Desandrouins (1729-1792) entered the army as a lieutenant in 1746 during the War of the Austrian Succession. After graduating from a military engineering school in 1752, Desandrouins served in France before promotion to captain and assignment to Canada in 1756. His engineering skills were instrumental in the French victory during the sieges of Oswego and Fort William Henry. Desandrouins was awarded the Cross of Saint-Louis for his contribution to the French success at Carillon in 1758. He remained in North America until the end of the war and served for another 31 years as an engineer in the French army, including an assignment as the commander of engineers for Rochambeau's army during the American Revolution.

**Bernetz Creek had been named in 1756 for Chevalier de Bernetz, a lieutenant colonel and commander of a Royal Roussillon battalion.[53] The creek, known today as Trout Brook, lies mainly on the west side of Route 9N and empties into the La Chute River in Ticonderoga.

best of order. He joined the Marquis de Montcalm who was waiting for him, formed for battle, on the heights at the right bank of the Chute, with the Roussillon Regiment and the first Berry Battalion; these five battalions passed the river, destroyed the bridge and combined with the Sarre and Languedoc Regiments occupied the heights which edge the left bank. This retreat would have been carried out without the loss of a single man, if the detachment of the Sieur de Trepezec had not lost its way. Abandoned by the few savages that acted as guides, it strayed in those wood-covered mountains and came, after walking 12 hours, upon an English column bound for the Chute River. Of this detachment 6 officers and about 150 soldiers were killed or made prisoners. They defended themselves a long time but they had to retreat before a superior force. The English made an important loss in the person of Lord Howe, quarter-master general of their army and Colonel of one of the Regiments of old England.*

At six o'clock in the evening, the Sieur Duprat, having announced that the enemy were heading towards the Bernetz Creek with pioneers [provincial troops and Rangers] and that their plan was evidently to throw a bridge over it, the Marquis de Montcalm sent the order to retreat and started his own retreat towards the heights of Carillon, where he arrived at Sunset. That same evening a portion of the opponent's regular troops and Rangers occupied the two banks of the Chute River, going towards the Bernetz Creek and entrenching there. The rest of their army occupied the place of disembarkment and the portage, and entrenched there also.**

The 7th. The French army was all employed working at the abattis which had been started the day before by the 2nd Berry Battalion. The officers were setting the example and the flags were hoisted—the plan of the defense had been laid out on the heights, 650 fathoms from the Carillon fort.***

On the left side it was backed up by an embankment 80 fathoms away from the Chute River, the top of which was capped by a wall. This wall was flanked by a gap

---

*George Augustus Howe (1725-1758) was a colonel of the 55th Regiment of Foot with the local rank of brigadier. The rank of brigadier was synonymous with brigadier general in original accounts.[54]

Troops under Brigadier Howe and Majors Robert Rogers and Israel Putnam advanced along the western shore of the La Chute River in order to outflank the French army at the sawmill in Ticonderoga. The advance party, however, was hampered by a lack of Indian guides and the diversion of 600 Rangers to the Louisbourg expedition. Late on the afternoon of July 6 Captain Trepezec's 350-man detachment accidently encountered the English troops in the densely-wooded terrain. The first shots of the French scouting party ripped into Howe's chest, killing him instantly. The death of the British field commander was a crucial setback for the expedition and a heart-felt loss for the whole army. "A Brave and Bold Commander, that worthy man, my Lord Howe, who is lamented by us all, and whose Death calls for our Revenge," wrote 20-year-old Rufus Putnam of Massachusetts.[55] Howe had earned the respect of the provincials and was noted for "forming his regular troops to the method of bush-fighting. . .ordered all the coats of his regiment to be cut short. . .forbid. . .his officers all superfluous baggage" and also cut his own hair as an example.[56] Although 148 French prisoners were taken in the skirmish, the British expedition faltered after Howe's death. The initiative of the British army was further weakened when two groups of soldiers from the original Howe/Rogers/Putnam detachment accidently fired on one another and "Remain[e]d all night in the woods."[57]

**On July 6 provincial troops began building breastworks and a bridge across Lake George at the northern landing (probably near the present-day natural stone dam).[58] The next day provincial carpenters were sent to the sawmill on the La Chute River to build another bridge and more breastworks.[59]

***Montcalm's measurement would place the French breastwork about three-quarters of a mile from the fort. However, a modern calculation of the distance is less than half a mile.

back of which 6 cannon were to be placed to fire at it as well as to the river. On the right it was also backed by an embankment the slope of which was not as steep as the one on the left; the plain between this hill and the Lake Saint Sacrement River was bordered by a branch of the trenches and also by a battery of 4 cannon which were only placed there the day after the battle.* Also the guns of the Fort were pointed toward this plain as well as at any other disembarkment which might be effected on the left.

The Center followed the sinuosities of the ground, keeping the top of the heights, and all the parts flanked one another reciprocally. Several, to tell the truth, were hit there, as well as on the right and on the left by a cross of fire of the enemy, but it was because we didn't have time to put up traverses. That kind of defence was made by tree trunks put one on top of the other, and had in front of it fallen trees the branches of which, cut and sharpened, gave the effect of a chevaux de frise [obstacle with projecting wooden spikes].

Between 6 and 8 o'clock in the evening the piquets of our troops, detached by order of the Chevalier de Levis arrived at the camp and the Chevalier de Levis himself went there at night.

Left: Major General James Abercromby. Oil painting by Allan Ramsay (1760).
(Private Collection, Fort Ticonderoga Museum)
Right: Painting of Louis-Joseph de Montcalm.
(National Archives of Canada)

*There is little evidence that any cannon (except swivel guns) were mounted at Montcalm's main breastwork during the battle. Batteries were mounted at the French breastwork after the battle on July 8. One French document, printed in December 1758, noted "six cannon. . .posted behind this opening," but the report was a second-hand account; Desandrouins later mentioned two batteries, one of four cannon on the right plain near the Canadians and a second of six pieces by the water.[60] Several provincial diaries mention cannon firing from the French breastwork during the battle, but the writers were not at the front lines.[61] Veteran Alexander Colden, who participated in the assault, only listed "small arms, Wall pieces [swivel cannon], and muskets" at the entrenchment.[62]

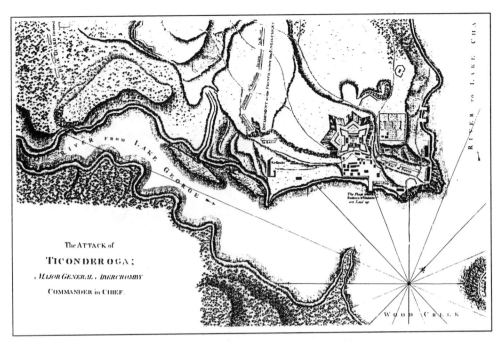

"The Attack of Ticonderoga" showing Fort Carillon in 1758.
From The History of the Late War in North-America by Thomas Mante (1772).

All day our Volunteers fired against the Rangers of the enemy. General Abercrombie with the main part of the militia and the balance made up of regular troops, advanced up to the falls. He had sent there several barges [bateaux] and pontoons [floating batteries] mounted with two guns each. These troops built also on the same day, several trenches, one in front of the other, of which the nearest one to our abattis was hardly a cannon range away. We spent the night at the Bivouac along side the trenches.

The 8th. At dawn, we beat the drums, so as to let all the troops know their posts for the defense of the entrenchment, following the above arrangement, which was about that in which they worked. The army was composed at the right of battalions of Queen's, La Sarre, Royal Roussillon, Languedoc and Guyenne Regiments and two Berry and the one battalion of the Bearn Regiment and also of 450 Canadians or Marines which brought the total amount to 3,000 fighting men.*

At the left of the line they posted the Sarre and the Languedoc battalions and the two piquets that had arrived the day before. The volunteers of Bernard and Duprat were guarding the gap on the Chute River.

The Center was occupied by the first Berry Battalion, by one Royal Roussillon and by the rest of the piquets of the Chevalier de Levis.

Battalions of the Queen's, the Bearn and the Guyenne defended the right and in the plain between the embankment of this right [flank] and the Saint Frederic River they had posted the Colonial troops and the Canadians, defended also by

*Other translations of Montcalm's same report had 3,600 French troops present. The journal of Colonel Louis Antoine de Bougainville listed a total of 3,526 men; Montcalm's journal recorded 3,506.[63]

British troops assaulting Montcalm's breastwork in 1758. Painting by
Frederic Remington. From *Harper's New Monthly Magazine*, November 1897.

abattis.* On the whole front of the line each battalion had back of itself a company
of Grenadiers and a piquet in reserve to support their battalion and also to be able
to move where they might be needed. The Chevalier de Levis took charge of the
right, the Sieur Bourlamaque of the left, the Marquis de Montcalm kept the center
for himself.

This arrangement, fixed and known, the troops at once fell back to work; some
of them got busy improving the abattis, the rest erecting the two batteries mentioned
above and a redoubt to protect the right.

That day in the morning, Colonel Johnson joined the English army with 300
savages of the Five Nations with "Tchactas," the Wolf, and Captain Jacob with 140
more. Soon after we saw them, as well as some Rangers, standing on a mountain
opposite Carillon on the other side of the Chute River. They even discharged much
musketry which interrupted the work. We did not bother answering them.**

*Some historians have maintained that Abercromby's army could have outflanked the French
breastworks on the northern boundary where a gap existed and only 400 Canadians were stationed.[64]
Others have suggested that Abercromby could have starved Montcalm's troops into submission since
the French army had only five days' provisions. Although an officer with Abercromby recorded that
the English expedition had "five days provisions per man," Abercromby's letter of June 29, 1758, to
William Pitt noted that some of the bateaux would "carry 22 men with 30 Days Provisions."[65] With
easy access to supplies from the staging area at Lake George, Abercromby's force would have had
enough supplies to outlast the French regiments at Carillon.

**Sir William Johnson, the Superintendent of the Six Nations and victor at the Battle of Lake George,
was pressured by Abercromby to muster a substantial force of Native Americans for the expedition
against Carillon. More than 400 warriors, including Captain Jacobs, a Mohegan known as
Cheekaunkun or King Ben, were stationed on present-day Mount Defiance, then known as Rattlesnake

At half past twelve, the English army debouched upon us. The company of Grenadiers, the Volunteers and the advanced guards retreated in good order and joined the line again. At the same movement and at a given signal all the troops took their posts.

The left was attacked first by two columns, one of which was trying to turn the trenches and found itself under the fire of the Sarre Regiment, the other directed its efforts on a salient between the Languedoc and the Berry battalions. The center, where the Royal Roussillon was, was attacked almost at the same time by a third column; a fourth attacked the right between the Bearn and the Queen's battalion. All these columns were intermingled with their Rangers and their best riflemen, covered by the trees, kept up a murderous fire.

At the beginning of the fight, several barges and pontoons coming from the Chute advanced in sight of Carillon. The steadiness of the volunteers of Bernard and Duprat, supported by the Sieur [Captain] de Poulharies at the head of a company of Grenadiers and of a piquet of the Royal Roussillon with a few cannon shots fired from the fort made them retreat.*

These different attacks were almost all in the afternoon and almost everywhere of the greatest intensity.

As the Canadians and the Colonial Troops had not been attacked they directed their fire upon the column which was attacking our right and which from time to time was within their reach.** This column made up of English Grenadiers and of Scotch Highlanders combined to charge repeatedly for three hours without either being rebuked or broken up and several were killed at only fifteen feet from our abattis.***

At about five o'clock, the column which had attacked vigorously the Royal Roussillon, threw itself back on the salient defended by the Regiment of Guyenne and by the left wing of the Bearn; the column which had attacked the right wing drew back also, so that the danger became urgent in those parts. The Chevalier de Levis moved there with a few troops of the right [wing] at which the enemy was only shooting. The Marquis de Montcalm hastened there also with some of the reserves and the enemy met a resistance which slowed up, at last, their ardor.

Hill. Dr. Caleb Rea, a 30-year-old regimental surgeon from Massachusetts, noted that "Sir Jo[h]nson & his party, the Mohawks, as soon as Landed formed a Circle, and their Chiefs made a fine harangue. . . [e]ncouraging his men on ye present enterprise."[66] Daniel Shute, a chaplain from Massachusetts who was not actually present at the battle, later noted that Johnson suggested to him that he had encouraged Abercromby to continue the campaign against Carillon: "Heard myself, Gen Johnson declare to God, that when Ab[e]cromby mentioned to him his intention to retreat to W. Henry, he earnestly dissuaded him from it."[67]

*Provincial carpenter Benjamin Glasier noted on July 8 that he "went to work to build two flo[a]ting Bat[t]erys. . .got four Cann[on] on the Bat[t]erys and went Down the Lake so n[ear] the forte that they fir[ed] the Cann[on] on them. . .and w[e]re [o]bliged to Return Back."[68] Rufus Putnam from Massachusetts reported "some Field pieces went down the River toward the Fort, on Floating Batteries which our men builded below the Falls."[69] The vessels were also described as "two radeaux that were to carry two six pound cannons each."[70]

**Although Montcalm had praised the Canadian troops in his July 9 letter to Governor Vaudreuil, he omitted the favorable remarks in his July 25 report.[71] This omission infuriated Vaudreuil, who in turn criticized Montcalm's handling of the defense of Carillon and requested the general's recall to France.[72]

***The August 1758 issue of *The Scots Magazine* printed a letter from a lieutenant in the late Lord Howe's regiment which described the Highlanders' attack on the French breastwork: "They actually mounted the enemy's intrenchments. . .they appeared like roaring lions breaking from their chains."[73]

The left was still standing up against the firing of two columns which were endeavoring to break through that part. The Sieur de Bourlamaque had been dangerously wounded there at about 4 o'clock and the Sieur de Senezeraque and de Privat, Lieutenant Colonels of the Sarre and the Languedoc Regiments were taking his place and giving the best of orders.* The Marquis de Montcalm rushed there several times and took pains to have help sent there in all critical moments.

At 6 o'clock the two columns on the right gave up attacking the Guyenne battalions and made one more attempt against the Royal Roussillon and Berry. At last, after a last effort to the left, at 7 o'clock, the Enemy retreated, protected by the shooting of the Rangers, which kept on until night. They abandoned on the battle-field their dead and some of their wounded.**

The darkness of the night, the exhaustion and small number of our troops, the strength of the enemy which, in spite of its defeat, was still in numbers superior to us, the nature of these woods in which one could not, without the assistance of the savages, start out against an army which must have had from 400 to 500 of them, several trenches built in echelon from the battlefield up to their camp; those are the obstacles that prevented us following the enemy in its retreat.*** We even thought that they would attempt to take their revenge and we worked all night to escape attack from the neighboring heights by traverses, to improve the Canadian abattis, and to finish the batteries of the left and of the right [flanks] which had been begun in the morning.

The 9th. Our Volunteers having informed the Marquis de Montcalm that the post of the Chute and of the portage seemed abandoned, he gave orders to the Chevalier de Levis to go the next day at day break with the Grenadiers, the Volunteers and the Canadians to reconnoitre what had become of the enemy.

The Chevalier de Levis advanced beyond the portage. He found everywhere the vestige of a hurried flight, wounded, supplies, abandoned equipage, debris of barges

---

*François-Charles de Bourlamaque recovered from his shoulder wound at Ticonderoga. The following year he was promoted to brigadier general and commanded an army at Isle-aux-Noix after the evacuation of Forts Carillon and St. Frédéric. In 1760 Bourlamaque was wounded again at the Battle of Sainte-Foy near Quebec and later was with General François de Lévis when the French army surrendered at Montreal.

Etienne-Guillaume de Senezergues de la Rodde (1707-1759) would receive a fatal wound on the Plains of Abraham at Quebec City during the epic battle between Montcalm's and Wolfe's forces on September 13, 1759.

**Abner Barrows, a 25-year-old recruit from Massachusetts, observed the hasty British retreat: "I fear a great many Wounded men fell Into the hands of our Enemy & the Slain all Lay on the spot."[74] Around midnight, according to Garrett Albertson, who served with the Jersey Blues, the French "were out plundering our dead and wounded, with candles and lanterns."[75] On July 24 Montcalm sent a letter to Abercromby, disclosing that 70 British wounded had been found on the field of battle the next morning but "the delay of a night has been fatal to the wounded who remained there. . .the majority of them have died; 34 remain who have been fit to be conveyed with our own to Montreal."[76] The dead were buried in shallow graves on the battlefield. Eighteen years later during the American Revolution, Colonel Anthony Wayne referred to the terrain as a "place of Skulls—they are so plenty here that our people for want of Other Vessels drink out of them whilst the soldiers make tent pins of the shin and thigh bones of Abercrumbies men."[77]

***Montcalm probably included this passage to blunt any criticism by Governor-General Vaudreuil, regarding his failure to pursue the defeated British army. Actually, British and provincial troops expected the French to pursue them. During the retreat Joseph Nichols, a Massachusetts enlistee, heard that "the Enemy was coming to fall upon us" causing "Confusion" as the men rushed to the bateaux on Lake George: "The Cry of Enemy made our People Cry out & made Sad Lamentations."[78]

[bateaux] and charred pontoons [rafts]; unquestionable proof of the great loss which the enemy had made.* We estimate it at about 4,000 men killed or wounded.** Were we to believe some of them, and judge by the promptitude of their retreat, it would be still more considerable. They have lost several officers and generals, Lord Howe, Sir Spitall, Major General Commander in Chief of the forces of New York,*** and several others.

The savages of the Five Nations [with William Johnson] remained as spectators at the tail of the column; they were waiting probably to declare themselves after the result of a fight which, to the English, did not seem doubtful.

The orders which were published in their colonies for the levying and the upkeep of this army, announces the general invasion of Canada and the same statements are made in all the commissions of their officers and militia.† We must do them justice in saying that they attacked us with the most ardent tenacity. It is not ordinary that trenches have stood 7 hours' attack at a stretch and almost without respite.

We owe this victory to the good manoeuvres of our generals before and during the action and to the extraordinary, unbelievable gallantry of our troops. All the officers of the army behaved in a way that each one of them deserves special praise. We have had about 350 men killed and wounded, 38 of which were officers.‡

---

*Captain Pierre Pouchot reported that the British had "abandoned 700 quarts of flour [approximately 70 tons], after smashing some of the containers. We found in the mire of the road leading to the Falls more than 500 pairs of shoes complete with buckles."[79] Joseph Smith of Groton, Connecticut, remarked that his unit "stove to p[ieces] about 150 barr[e]ls of flo[u]r" before departing.[80]

**Abercromby's report to Secretary of State William Pitt listed 1,944 killed or wounded: "464 regulars killed, 29 missing, 1117 wounded; and 87 provincials killed, 8 missing, and 239 wounded."[81] Many of the wounded men later succumbed to their injuries.

***Montcalm was in error here. He was referring to Captain John Spittal (Spital) of the 47th Foot, who acted as a brigade major in the expedition against Carillon. His name was not on the list of British officers killed or wounded at Ticonderoga.[82] Regarding the New York forces, Montcalm may have been making a reference to one of two people: Colonel Bartholomew Le Roux, who was wounded in the battle, or the adjutant, Lieutenant Mauncey, who was killed.

†British plans for the 1758 campaign called for the mobilization of 20,000 provincial troops (only about half that amount was actually raised); the immense logistical problems raising and outfitting such a large force compromised the timing and effectiveness of the Abercromby expedition.[83]

‡Louis Antoine de Bougainville recorded 44 officers and "nearly" 400 men killed or wounded, while Jean-Nicolas Desandrouins casualty list included 33 officers and 340 soldiers.[84]

Notes

1. *Dictionary of Canadian Biography*, Volume 3 (Toronto: University of Toronto Press, 1974), 468.
2. Abbé H. R. Casgrain, *Wolfe and Montcalm* (1905; reprint ed., Toronto: University of Toronto Press, 1964), 7; Francis Parkman, *Montcalm and Wolfe* (1884; reprint ed., New York: Atheneum, 1984), 209.
3. Pierre Pouchot, *Memoir Upon the Late War in North America Between the French and English, 1755-60*, trans. Michael Cardy and ed. Brian Leigh Dunnigan (Youngstown, N.Y.: Old Fort Niagara Association, Inc., 1994), 104; Louis Antoine de Bougainville, *Adventures in the Wilderness: The American Journals of Louis Antoine de Bougainville 1756-1760*, trans. and ed. Edward P. Hamilton (Norman, OK: University of Oklahoma Press, 1964), 26; E. B. O'Callaghan, ed., *Documents Relative to the Colonial History of the State of New-York* (Albany: Weed, Parsons and Company, 1858), Volume 10, 468-69; Casgrain, 34-35; *Dictionary of Canadian Biography*, 3: 459.
4. O'Callaghan, 551.
5. Ammi Ruhamah Cutter, "Dr. A.R. Cutter's Journal of his Military Experience, 1756-1758," in *A History of the Cutter Family of New England*, by William Richard Cutter (Boston: David Clapp & Son, 1871), 66; See also Stanley M. Gifford, *Fort William Henry: A History* (Lake George, N.Y.: Fort William Henry Museum, 1955), 32; William Hervey, *Journals of Hon. William Hervey* (Bury St. Edmund's: Paul & Mathew Butter Market, 1906), 38.
6. Winslow recorded sighting a French vessel (probably a large bateau)at the northern end of the lake, "built after the manner of a Row Galley." John Winslow to Lord Loudoun, September 5, 1756, Loudoun Papers, LO 1710, Huntington Library, San Marino, California; Cutter described the French vessel as a "Shallop," Cutter, 65; Lieutenant Colonel Ralph Burton described the British fleet at Fort William Henry in 1756 as "two small Sloops of about Twenty Tons each, have four Swivels mounted on each, One Sloop of 30 Tons. . .another of the same size to be launched. . . Two large Scows, and one a Building." Public Record Office, London, Colonial Office 5/47, University Publications of America microfilm reel 2, frame 23.
7. Bougainville, 97; O'Callaghan, 542, 545; James Montresor, "Journal of Col. James Montresor," *Collections of the New-York Historical Society* 14 (1881): 37; PRO, CO 5/48, UP microfilm reel 2, frame 546.
8. PRO, CO 5/48, UP microfilm reel 2, frame 364.
9. Bougainville, 119.
10. O'Callaghan, 606-7; Bougainville, 153; See also Louis-Joseph de Montcalm, *Journal Du Marquis De Montcalm Durant Ses Campagnes En Canada De 1756 à 1759*, ed. H.-R. Casgrain (Quebec: Imprimerie De L.-J. Demers & Frère, 1895), 268-69.
11. "Extract of a letter from a Gentlemen at Fort William-Henry. . . July 26, 1757," *The London Magazine* (September 1757): p.n.a.; O'Callaghan, 734; See also "Detailed Statement of Operations at Ticonderoga, 1758," *Pennsylvania Archives*, ed. Samuel Hazard (Philadelphia: Joseph Severns & Co., 1853), Volume 3, 472; Bougainville, 138, 140, 142; PRO, CO 5/48, UP microfilm reel 2, frames 545-46.
12. Bougainville, 146.
13. Ibid., 147.
14. Ian K. Steele, *Warpaths: Invasions of North America* (New York: Oxford University Press, 1994), 203.
15. Joseph Frye, "Joseph Frye's Journal and Map of the Siege of Fort William Henry, 1757," ed. by James L. Kochan, *The Bulletin of the Fort Ticonderoga Museum* 15 (1993): 352-53; See also Joseph Frye, "A Journal of the Attack of Fort William Henry," Parkman Papers 42: 147, Massachusetts Historical Society, Boston; Bougainville, 169-70; While Lieutenant Colonel George Monro, the defeated British commander, brought accusations against General Daniel Webb for his conduct during the siege of Fort William Henry, he was also negative in regard to the conduct of some provincial regiments. "The Provincials in the Fort, behav'd scandalously, when they were to fire Over the Parap[e]t, they lay down upon their faces and fir'd str[a]ight up in the Air. I sent orders. . .to take the first Man that behav'd in that Manner, And hang him over the Wall to be shot at by the Enemy." George Monro Memorandum, November 1, 1757, Loudoun Papers, LO 5309, Huntington Library.

16. "A Journal Kept During the Siege of Fort William Henry, August 1757," *Proceedings of the American Philosophical Society* 37 (1898): 150; See also Russell P. Bellico, *Chronicles of Lake George: Journeys in War and Peace* (Fleischmanns, N.Y.: Purple Mountain Press, 1995), 73; Earlier, when troops evacuated Fort William Henry, Captain William Arbuthnot witnessed "the French Indians Kill the sick and Wounded. . .in View of the French Officers who did not attempt to hinder or prevent it." Loudoun Papers, LO4660, Huntington Library.

17. Jean-Nicolas Desandrouins, *Le Maréchal De Camp Desandrouins 1729-1792*, ed. L'Abbé Gabriel (Verdun: Imprimerie Renvé-Lallemant, 1887), 109-10; Casgrain, 50; Jonathan Carver, a private in a Massachusetts regiment, observed that "men, women, and children were dispatched in the most wanton and cruel manner, and immediately scalped. Many of these savages drank the blood of their victims." Jonathan Carver, *Travels Through the Interior Parts of North America in the Years 1766, 1767 and 1768* (1778; reprint ed., Minneapolis: Ross & Haines, Inc; 1956), 319; See also "Samuel Angell to Governor William Greene, August 14, 1757," *The Historical Magazine* 8 (November 1870): 259; William Arbuthnot, Affidavit concerning the murders [massacre] by the French Indians at FWH, Loudoun Papers, LO 4660, Huntington Library.

18. M. John Cardwell, "The British Expedition Against Fort Ticonderoga in 1758," (M.A. thesis, The University of New Brunswick, 1990), 143.

19. *Boston Gazette and Country Journal*, 20 November 1758; See also William Sweat, "Captain William Sweat's Personal Diary of the Expedition Against Ticonderoga," *The Essex Institute Historical Collections* 93 (1957): 42; James Searing, "The Battle of Ticonderoga, 1758," *Proceedings of the New-York Historical Society* 5 (1874): 113; Melancthon Taylor Woolsey, *Letters of Melancthon Taylor Woolsey* (Champlain, N.Y.: Moorsfield Press, 1927), 12; *New-York Mercury*, 24 July 1758; Garrett Albertson, "A Short Account of the Life and Travels and Adventures of Garrett Albertson, Sr.," *The Bulletin of the Fort Ticonderoga Museum* 4 (July 1936): 44; See also Abercromby Papers, AB 436, Huntington Library; The idea for building platforms upon bateaux may have come from the observation of French rafts in 1757. See Webb to Earl of Loudoun, September 2, 1757, Loudoun Papers, LO 4385, Huntington Library.

20. Searing, 113; Samuel Fisher, "Diary of Operations Around Lake George, 1758," MS, Library of Congress; See also General Orders for the attack on Ticonderoga, Abercromby Papers, AB 407, Huntington Library; Nathan Whiting, *Orderly Book of Colonel Nathan Whiting: Second Connecticut Regiment at Lake George 1758* (Hartford: Connecticut State Library, 1940), 34.

21. Seth Tinkham, "The Diary of Seth Tinkham," in *History of Plymouth County, Massachusetts*, by D. Hamilton Hurd (Philadelphia: J.W. Lewis & Co., 1884), 996; See also "Detailed Statement of Operations," 472.

22. O'Callaghan, 737; Bougainville, 228; Pouchot, 138.

23. Bougainville, 231; See also Montcalm, 398.

24. Hervey, 50; Joshua Loring wrote that the French lines were "reported to be a Slight Breast worke of Logs. . .so weakly bound together that it would be easy to push them down by the Light Infantry."Joshua Loring, Chatham Papers, PRO 30/8/96, fol. 98; See also Thomas Mante, *The History of the Late War in North-America* (1772; reprint ed., New York: Research Reprints, n.d.), 147;Although Clerk's signature was spelled with an e, both William Hervey and Thomas Mante used the spelling Clark for the engineer; "Return of the names of the Officers of the Several Regiments. . .killed or wounded near Ticonderoga" also spelled the name Clark. Abercromby Papers, AB 425, Huntington Library.

25. Stanley Pargellis, ed., *Military Affairs in North America 1748-1765* (1936; reprint ed., New York: Archon Books, 1969), 420.

26. "Extract of a Letter from Major General Abercromby to the Right Hon. Mr. Secretary Pitt, dated at Camp, at Lake George, July 12, 1758," *The London Magazine* (August 1758): 427.

27. Lemuel Lyon, "Military Journal for 1758," in *The Military Journals of Two Private Soldiers, 1758-1775*, by Abraham Tomlinson (1854; reprint ed., New York: Books for Libraries Press, 1970), 22; See also Lawrence Henry Gipson, *The Great War for the Empire: The Victorious Years 1758-1760* (New York: Alfred A. Knopf, 1949), Volume 7, 229.

28. Desandrouins, 171; Cardwell, 101.

29. Pouchot, 145.

30. O'Callaghan, 743; Bougainville, 232; Pouchot, 146; Pargellis, 421; Captain Charles Lee of the 44th Regiment later lamented "that no General was heard of, no Aid de Camps seen, no instructions receiv'd; but every officer left at the head of his division, company, or squad, to fall a sacri-

fice to his own behaviour and the stupidity of his commander." Charles Lee, "Narrative—Enclosed in Letter of September 16th 1758," *Collections of the New-York Historical Society (1871): 12-13*; See original in the Fort Ticonderoga Thompson-Pell Research Center.

31. Bougainville, 233.
32. Searing, 116, 115; See also Montcalm, 395; Abercromby Papers, AB 437, Huntington Library.
33. Archelaus Fuller, "The Journal of Archelaus Fuller May-Nov. 1758," *The Bulletin of the Fort Ticonderoga Museum* 13 (December 1970): 11; See also Archelaus Fuller, "Journal of Col. Archelaus Fuller of Middleton, Mass., in the Expedition Against Ticonderoga in 1758," *Historical Collections of the Essex Institute* 46 (1910): 214.
34. Benjamin Jewett, "The Diary of Benjamin Jewett–1758," *National Magazine* 17 (1892-93): 63.
35. Pouchot, 147-48.
36. Abel Spicer, "Diary of Abel Spicer," in *History of the Descendants of Peter Spicer*, comp. by Susan Meech and Susan Billings Meech (Boston: F.H. Gilson, 1911), 395; See also Bellico, 101.
37. "Extract of a Letter from Major General Abercromby to the Right Honourable Mr. Secretary Pitt, dated at Camp, at Lake George, July 12, 1758," *The Universal Magazine* (August 1758): 97.
38. Desandrouins, 186; See also Alexander Colden, "Eye-Witnesses' Accounts of the British Repulse at Ticonderoga," *The Canadian Historical Review* 2 (December 1921): 362.
39. Joseph Smith, "Journal of Joseph Smith, of Groton," *Connecticut Society of Colonial Wars Proceedings* 1 (1896): 307; See also Cardwell, 115-20.
40. Abner Barrows, "Diary of Abner Barrows," in *History of the Town of Middleboro*, by Thomas Weston (New York: Houghton Mifflin, 1906), 97; Spicer 407; See also Peter Pond, "Experiences in Early Wars in America," *The Journal of American History* 1 (1907): 91.
41. Lee, 13-14; Captain Joshua Loring commented that "everybody was Eager for renewing the Attack the Next Morning as the Strength of the Enemy was well known to us." However, "At Nine in the Evening the[re] was Orders give to all the Regiments. . .to March Immediately to the place where the Boats Lay, and Embark their Troops as Fast as Possible. . .no Men ever received any Orders with more surpriz[e] nor executed them with more Reluctancy. . .thinking the[re] must have been some Mistake in the Orders." Loring, fol. 99.
42. David Waterbury, "Personal Roster and Diary of Captain David Waterbury in the Lake George Campaign 1758," typed transcript, 9, 10, Fort Ticonderoga Thompson-Pell Research Center.
43. Peter Force, ed., *American Archives, Fifth Series* (Washington, D.C.: M. St. Clair Clarke and Peter Force, 1851), Volume 2, 1224.
44. O'Callaghan, 724.
45. Bougainville, 235; See also François de Lévis, *Journal Des Champagnes Du Chevalier De Lévis En Canada De 1756 à 1760* (Montreal: C.O. Beauchemin & Fils, 1889), 139; Pouchot, 150; O'Callaghan, 725, 797; Montcalm, 402.
46. Bougainville, 264.
47. Arthur G. Doughty, ed., *Report of the Public Archives for the Year 1929* (Ottawa: F.A. Acland, 1930), 78.
48. *Dictionary of Canadian Biography*, Volume 3, 463-64; See also Parkman, 406-7.
49. Courtesy Fort Ticonderoga Museum. Reprinted from *The Bulletin of the Fort Ticonderoga Museum* 2 (July 1930): 69-76; See also O'Callaghan, 737-41, 788-800; Doughty, 102-6.
50. O'Callaghan, 788; See also 754, 768, 787.
51. "Extract of a Letter from Major General Abercromby to the Right Honourable Mr. Secretary Pitt, dated at Camp at Lake George, July 12, 1758," *The Universal Magazine* (August 1758): 96; See also Mante, 145; Abercromby Papers, AB 44(a), Huntington Library.
52. O'Callaghan, 814.
53. Pouchot, 143, 346.
54. Howe was listed as a brigadier general on the "Return of the names. . .killed or wounded near Ticonderoga," Abercromby Papers, AB425, Huntington Library; Major General Jeffery Amherst interchanged the rank of brigadier and brigadier general in his 1759 journal. J. Clarence Webster, ed., *The Journal of Jeffery Amherst* (Toronto: The Ryerson Press, 1931), 147.
55. E. C. Dawes, ed., *Journal of Gen. Rufus Putnam 1757-1760* (Albany: Joel Munsell's Sons, 1886), 68; General Abercromby wrote that "Howe was universally beloved and respected throughout the Army," Public Record Office, London, 272, War Office 34/30, fol. 22.
56. *The Scots Magazine* (September 1758): 442; See also [Ann Grant] *Memoirs of an American Lady* (1808; reprint ed., New York: Research Reprints, Inc., 1970), Volume 2, 66-70.

57. Melancthon Woolsey, *Letters of Melancthon Woolsey* (Champlain, N.Y.: Moorsfield Press, 1927), 15; See also Joseph Nichols, "Joseph Nichols Military Journal 1758-59," HM 89, 20, Huntington Library; Albertson, 44-45; Abercromby to DeLancy, July 18, 1758, Abercromby Papers, AB 445, Huntington Library; Loring, fol. 97.

58. Benjamin Glasier, "French and Indian War Diary of Benjamin Glasier of Ipswich 1758-1760," *The Essex Institute of Historical Collections* 86(1950): 76.

59. Ibid.; See also Barrows, 96; Spicer, 407; Salah Barnard, "Journal of Major Salah Barnard," MS Fort Ticonderoga Thompson-Pell Research Center; Henry Champion, "The Journal of Colonel Henry Champion," in *Champion Genealogy*, by Francis Bacon Trowbridge (New Haven, CT.: F. B. Trowbridge, 1891), 419.

60. O'Callaghan, 742; Desandrouins, 167; See also Montcalm, 395.

61. Caleb Rea, "The Journal of Dr. Caleb Rea, Written During the Expedition Against Ticonderoga in 1758," *The Essex Institute of Historical Collections* 18 (1881): 105; Seth Tinkham, 997.

62. Colden, 362.

63. O'Callaghan, 739; Doughty, 104; Bougainville, 231; Montcalm, 398.

64. *Dictionary of Canadian Biography*, Volume 3, 462.

65. "Extract of a letter from an officer at Lake George, dated July 11," *The Scots Magazine* 20 (August 1758): 439; Abercromby Papers, AB 397, Huntington Library.

66. Rea, 104.

67. Daniel Shute, "A Journal of the Rev. Daniel Shute, D.D., Chaplain in the Expedition to Canada in 1758," *Historical Collections of the Essex Institute* 12 (April 1874): 137-38.

68. Glasier, 76; See also Montcalm, 399.

69. Putnam, 69; See also Spicer, 394.

70. "Detailed Statement of Operations at Ticonderoga, 1758," *Pennsylvania Archives*, ed. by Samuel Hazard (Philadelphia: Joseph Severns & Co., 1853), Volume 3, 472.

71. O'Callaghan, 749.

72. Ibid., 780-83.

73. "Extract of a letter from a lieutenant in Howe's regiment, dated Lake George, July 10," *The Scots Magazine* 20(August 1758): 439.

74. Barrows, 97.

75. Albertson, 47.

76. O'Callaghan, 775.

77. Charles J. Stille, *Major-General Anthony Wayne and the Pennsylvania Line in the Continental Army* (Philadelphia: J.B. Lippincott Company, 1893), 37.

78. Nichols, 24.

79. Pouchot, 150.

80. Joseph Smith, "Journal of Joseph Smith of Groton," *Connecticut Society of Colonial Wars Proceedings* 1(1896): 307; See also Lemuel Lyon, "Military Journal for 1758,"in *The Military Journals of Two Private Soldiers, 1758-1775*, by Abraham Tomlinson (1854; reprint ed., New York: Books for Libraries Press, 1970), 23.

81. *The London Magazine* (August 1758): 427; *The Universal Magazine* (August 1758): 97; Abercromby to DeLancey, July 18, 1758, Abercromby Papers, AB 445, Huntington Library; See also Abercromby Papers, AB 436.

82. O'Callaghan, 728-32; See also PRO 272, WO 34/30, fol. 23.

83. Abercromby Circular Letter to Northern Governors, March 15, 1758, Abercromby Papers, AB 44(2), Huntington Library. For an excellent examination of the political and operational problems that plagued the Abercromby campaign see M. John Cardwell, "Mismanagement: The 1758 British Expedition Against Carillon," *The Bulletin of the Fort Ticonderoga Museum* 15(1992): 237-91.

84. Bougainville, 236; Desandrouins, 185-86; See also Montcalm, 403-5.

Major General Jeffery Amherst. Oil on canvas by Joseph Blackburn (1758).
(Mead Art Museum, Amherst College)

4. Jeffery Amherst 1759

JEFFERY AMHERST first visited the region in October 1758 after marching five battalions from Boston to Albany to supplement Abercromby's forces in preparation for a renewed attack on Fort Carillon. Late on October 5 Amherst reached the British and provincial camp at Lake George. The next day Amherst met with Abercromby and his officers and decided against another attack in 1758, mainly because of the lateness of the season and the strengthening of the breastwork and other defenses at Fort Carillon by Montcalm's army. Amherst, however, would return the following year as the British commander in chief and succeed in the capture of Forts Carillon and St. Frédéric. He would leave a lasting impression on the countryside by ordering the construction of a series of forts to protect the frontier against the French army and their Native American allies. Plans for his largest fort began the day he arrived at Crown Point in 1759: "I ordered the Engineer to reconnoitre the best place for erecting a Fort that I may set about it [as] soon as possible. This is a great Post gained, secures entirely all the country behind it. . .and country about it is better than anything I have seen."[1]

Amherst was born in Kent, England, in the parish of Sevenoaks on January 29, 1717, to Jeffery Amherst, a successful attorney, and Elizabeth Kerrill Amherst. The Amherst family's roots can be traced to 1215 with a continuous progression of well-respected lawyers, politicians, and clergymen. Young Jeffery Amherst was raised with two older siblings, Sackville and Elizabeth, and two younger brothers, John and William, both of whom would also make the military their career. Jeffery Amherst's formal education was brief; just before turning twelve years old he was appointed a page at Knole Castle. It had once been owned by King Henry VIII, was bestowed to Queen Elizabeth and later conferred to her cousin Thomas Sackville, the Duke of Dorset and Lord-Lieutenant of Ireland. Perhaps because of this association with power and class, Amherst's ambitions were kindled. In 1731 Lionel Cranfield Sackville, Amherst's benefactor, obtained a commission as a cornet for the young page in Colonel John Ligonier's cavalry regiment.[2] However, the facts relating to Amherst's military career in the 1730s are subject to differing accounts.[3] In 1739 Major General Ligonier notified Amherst that a lieutenant's commission was available through a purchase of rank; the funds for the promotion were forthcoming from Amherst's father.

During the War of the Austrian Succession (1740-1748), Amherst became an aide-de-camp to General Ligonier, at the time one of the most competent officers in the British military. Amherst's baptism of fire came in 1743 during the battle at Dettingen (Germany), in which Ligonier and other officers led their army to victory over the French forces. Several other young officers, who would later participate in the battles in North America, also saw action with Amherst at Dettingen, including Robert Monckton, George Townshend, and James Wolfe. It was during this period that Amherst began a journal of daily occurrences, noting effective strategies and problems. In 1745 at the Battle of Fontenoy in Flanders, the lack of coordination of command became apparent when the British army under the leadership of William Augustus, the Duke of Cumberland and son of King George II, was turned back. British forces were again defeated the next year at Roucoux. Amherst's career, however, continued to advance with a promotion to captain in the First Foot Guards (equivalent to lieutenant colonel of the line) in December 1745 and two years later with an appointment as an aide-de-camp to the Duke of Cumberland, then the commander in chief of the allied forces in Europe. Coincidently, Lord George Augustus Howe, who would later be killed in the battle at Ticonderoga in 1758, was another aide-de-camp to Cumberland at this time. At the Battle of Laffeldt in the summer of 1747 General Ligonier was captured and once more the British and their allies were overwhelmed by the French. This battle directly led to the end of the war and the Treaty of Aix-la-Chapelle was signed in early 1748. Amherst emerged from the war with a wealth of military experience and important connections; both would serve him well during the Seven Years' War.

On May 3, 1753, Amherst married thirty-one-year-old Jane Daylson, his second cousin. For a short while the newlyweds were content with their life together in a London apartment, but a strain in the relationship developed after Jane moved to Amherst's family homestead, Brook's Place, while Amherst remained in London. Years of separation during Amherst's military assignments clearly took a toll on the marriage; his unanswered letters to his wife were the result of resentment following her seclusion at Brook's Place. During the 1760s Amherst's illegitimate son, born in 1752, was sent to live with Jane Amherst, an arrangement which had an undetermined impact on the marriage.

The renewal of the conflict between England and France would ultimately bring Amherst to the zenith of his military career. Beginning in North America as the French and Indian War, the hostilities would soon engulf Europe in the Seven Years' War (1756-1763). Amherst was sent to Germany in 1756 to supervise the commissariat of 8,000 Hessian troops in British service. Upon his return to England, Amherst was commissioned a colonel of the 15th Regiment of Foot. Early the next year he was dispatched to Germany where he again witnessed the defeat of an army led by the Duke of Cumberland.

In October 1757 after the Duke of Cumberland had resigned, William Pitt, the secretary of state, selected General John Ligonier, Amherst's old patron, as the commander in chief of British forces. Ligonier's duties included recommending appointments for the North American campaigns. Unhappy with the failure of the Earl of Loudoun (John Campbell) to capture Fortress Louisbourg in 1757, Ligonier was determined to appoint someone who would accomplish the task. Ligonier selected Amherst, his trusted aide-de-camp from the last war. Amherst's appointment as a major general and commander in chief of the Louisbourg expedition won the approval of the cabinet and King George II in late December. The sudden elevation from colonel to major general came as a complete surprise to Amherst, especially since he had never held an independent position of command.

On March 16, 1758, Amherst sailed for North America aboard the H.M.S. *Dublin*. After 11 weeks at sea the *Dublin* finally neared the harbor of Halifax on May 28, just in time to meet Admiral Edward Boscawen leaving the harbor with 157 naval and transport ships bound for Louisbourg. Boscawen's departure fulfilled Pitt's and Ligonier's instructions to sail before the end of the month. Without time to relax on dry land, Amherst immediately transferred to the flagship *Namur*. On June 2 the British fleet anchored in Gabarus Bay, southwest of Louisbourg. This was the same place where the New England fleet had anchored on May 11, 1745, when preparing for an assault on Louisbourg. Championed by Governor William Shirley of Massachusetts, the militias of New England forced the capitulation of the fortress on June 26, 1745, only to have the stronghold returned to France by the terms of the Treaty Aix-la-Chapelle in 1748.

Although opposed by French sharpshooters, British and provincial troops made a successful amphibious landing at Freshwater Cove in Gabarus Bay on June 8, 1758. After several hours the French defenders abandoned their post. Methodically, Amherst proceeded with traditional siege operations on the west flank of Louisbourg. In addition, Amherst sent Brigadier James Wolfe with 1,200 men to seize Lighthouse Point on the eastern shore of the harbor, approximately a mile from Louisbourg. With the capture of this strategic point, Wolfe was able to establish a battery to shell the French men-of-war and an island in the harbor. Following the silencing of the French island battery, Wolfe's energy was devoted to the main artillery offensive on the town. After an unrelenting bombardment which resulted in fires inside the fortress, Chevalier de Drucour, the governor to Louisbourg, agreed to Amherst's terms of capitulation on July 27, 1758.

Amherst and other officers, including Brigadier Wolfe, had hoped to capture Quebec after the fall of Louisbourg, but Admiral Boscawen maintained that an expedition to Quebec was not possible given the time constraints, and Major General James Abercromby's defeat at Ticonderoga forced a rethinking of the strategy. Abercromby's official letter requesting reinforcements at Lake George did not arrive at Amherst's camp until August 12.[4] Reinforcement, however, was temporarily delayed by arrangements to send over 5,000 French prisoners to Europe aboard five men-of-war and ten transport vessels.

Five battalions departed for Boston aboard transports on August 27 and 28 for the first leg of a journey to reinforce Abercromby's men at Lake George. Amherst embarked on August 30 on the H.M.S. *Captain*, commanded by his brother John Amherst; the passage to Boston would require two weeks. The celebration of the

Louisbourg victory by the local citizenry was renewed once Amherst reached Boston: "The troops remained encamped on the Common of Boston where Thousands of People came to see them and would give them Liquor and make the men Drunk in Spite of All that could be done."[5] Amherst and his troops marched from Boston on September 16, reaching Albany on October 3. The next day Amherst immediately set out for Lake George, receiving orders at Stillwater from Abercromby to hold his troops at Albany. Amherst arrived at Abercromby's camp late on October 5. The next day Amherst met with Abercromby and other officers, concluding that "there was no probability of attempting anything against Ticonderoga" at that late date.[6] A formal inspection of the camp followed as "the whole Army Paraded without arms before their respective parts of the Lines, when Generals Amh[e]rst Abercromb[y]. . .past round ye whole Incampment to take a View, and as they pass'd by. . .Officers walked in Procession after."[7]

Amherst thereafter returned to Halifax, Nova Scotia, where he received dispatches from New York containing letters from Secretary of State William Pitt with congratulations on the Louisbourg expedition and an appointment to the position of commander in chief of all British and provincial forces in North America, replacing James Abercromby who was recalled to England. Jeffery Amherst made his way to New York City for winter quarters but stopped again in Boston to visit and discuss plans with Thomas Pownall, governor of Massachusetts. In an effort to further solidify a cooperative relationship with colonial governments, Amherst also paid visits to the governors of Rhode Island and Connecticut.

William Pitt's orders for the 1759 campaigns included an expedition under James Wolfe to capture Quebec, an invasion of Canada by Amherst after taking Forts Carillon and St. Frédéric, and the seizure of Fort Niagara. Despite major funding delays from the colonies and England, Amherst succeeded remarkably in planning and organizing logistical support for the 1759 campaigns. Although Pitt had asked colonial governors to provide 20,000 troops for 1759, enlistments fell short of the intended number. Amherst reached Albany at the beginning of May, the approximate time for the rendezvous of the army, only to find that the provincial troops had not yet arrived. By the end of the month, most of the troops had finally reached the staging area. In total, Amherst had mobilized more than 16,000 provincial and regular troops, including 5,000 soldiers destined for the Fort Niagara expedition under Brigadier John Prideaux. While in Albany, Amherst began making plans for the Lake Champlain campaign, calling on his naval commander, Captain Joshua Loring, to build "Two Brigs [and]. . .Two Snows, capable of Mounting Eighteen Six Pounders."[8]

Amherst departed from Albany on the morning of June 3, arriving at Fort Edward three days later. While at the Fort Edward camp, Amherst supervised the repair of the military road to Lake George and the building of a series of outposts and stockaded forts along the route as way stations for transporting supplies and to discourage French ambushes that had plagued the area the previous year. The fortified outposts included the Four-Mile Post located closest to Fort Edward; Fort Amherst south of Halfway Brook (in present-day Glens Falls); Halfway Brook Post, built in 1758 and rebuilt in 1759, positioned just north of Halfway Brook; Fort William, approximately three miles south of Lake George; and Fort Gage (built in 1758), situated only one mile south of the lake.[9]

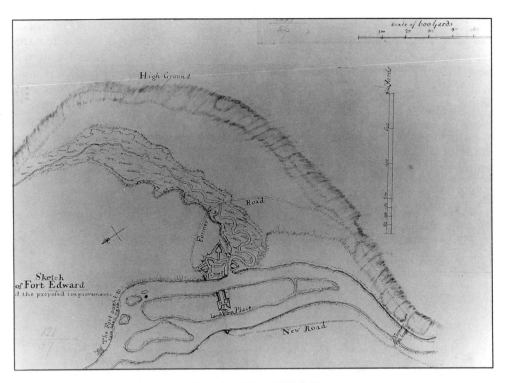

"Sketch of Fort Edward"
(Crown Collection, New York State Library)

Early on the morning of June 21, Amherst marched his army in two formal columns to Lake George, taking precautions against a French attack. The next day, following an earlier directive from William Pitt, Amherst "went with Col. [James] Montresor and fixed on the ground for building a fort."[10] Engineer Montresor, with input from Colonel William Eyre, further refined the plan of Fort George prior to laying the foundation on July 2.

Before Amherst's army could proceed to Ticonderoga, his men needed to retrieve vessels that had been "sunk in Different Parts of the Lake [in 1758]. . .200 Batteaus, 3 Rowe Gallys, 1 Large Luggade Boat, [and] the Sloop," according to Captain Joshua Loring.[11] Without the protection of a fort at Lake George, Abercromby's troops were forced to sink their vessels to safeguard them from French raiding parties during the winter. The sloop *Earl of Halifax*, measuring "51 Feet Keel," would require ten days to be raised and dragged to the shoreline.[12] Loring was not able to locate the seven-sided radeau *Land Tortoise* ("Large Luggade Boat") which rested in 107 feet of water.* The 52-foot vessel, built under the supervision of Major Thomas Ord in 1758, had been "planked up higher than a man's Head Shelving in or arching inwards to defend ye men's Bodys & Heads with Port-Holes

---

*Using side-scan sonar, an archaeological team led by Joseph Zarzynski discovered the radeau *Land Tortoise* at the bottom of Lake George in June 1990. During the next two years, the oldest intact warship in North America underwent a full archaeological survey under the direction of Dr. D. K. Abbass. The vessel is presently a New York State Submerged Heritage Preserve and has been designated a National Historic Landmark.

for ye Cannon."[13] Because all of the vessels were not recovered from the bottom of the lake, Amherst's carpenters hurriedly constructed additional vessels for the expedition to Carillon.* Major Thomas Ord again supervised the construction of a large radeau, the two-masted *Invincible*, later armed with "four 24 pounders, and four 12 pounders."[18] On July 5 provincial carpenters launched the vessel *Snow Shoe*, which subsequently carried men, ammunition, and "waggoneers. . . with 70 horses."[19] In addition, a "Flat bottomed English boat with a [brass] three-Pounder mounted as a swivel" in her bow had been transported from the Hudson River overland to Lake George.[20] Lastly, rafts "were made by building a stage on three battoes" to transport the artillery mounted on carriages.[21]

Detail of "A Perspective View of Lake George [and] Plan of Ticonderoga" in 1759 showing the sloop *Earl of Halifax*. Drawing by Captain-Lieutenant Henry Skinner, published in the November 1759 issue of *The Universal Magazine*. (Library of Congress)

By six o'clock on the morning of July 21, 1759, the armada of bateaux and assorted vessels began its departure for Ticonderoga. The huge flotilla was organized into four double columns with the English flat-bottomed boat and 43 whaleboats in the lead. Two row galleys accompanied the outer columns; the radeau *Invincible* headed another column of rafts, supply bateaux, and the *Snow Shoe*; the sloop *Halifax* followed at the rear of the entire fleet.[22] Despite rain and wind which hampered the

---

*Whether an additional row galley was built in 1759 remains uncertain. It is not clear how many row galleys were raised from the lake floor in 1759. Only two row galleys accompanied Amherst's flotilla to Ticonderoga.[15] A reading of Henry Skinner's journal (July 7, 14, 16), however, suggests that three "proes" or row galleys were at Lake George in July 1759. Lemuel Wood noted on July 26 that "3 Rogalleys [were] Drawn out of Lake George. . .and Put into Lake Champlain."[16] One contemporary source implies that a row galley was built in 1759 at Lake George: "An iron eighteen-pounder was mounted to-day, in the stern of a new-built proe."[17]

progress of the expedition, Amherst's army reached present-day Hague by eight o'clock in the evening.[23] The following morning the troops landed at Ticonderoga on the eastern shoreline of the lake. An advance party of Rangers and light infantry promptly marched to the sawmills on the La Chute River where a brief skirmish ensued with 300 Indians and some grenadiers under Brigadier General François-Charles de Bourlamaque.

The next day Amherst learned that the French army had fled northward in sloops and bateaux. Observing Amherst's determined advance, Bourlamaque evacuated his main force of 2,600 regulars, Canadian militia, and several hundred Indians from Carillon to Fort St. Frédéric, relying on a small force at the fort under Captain Louis-Philippe Le Dossu d'Hébécourt to delay the British advance. The British regulars approached Montcalm's infamous breastwork cautiously, sending several men forward to check on the enemy. With the realization that the log wall had been abandoned, the British troops "rushed on and took Posession of th[eir] Bre[a]st work ye French fir[e]d with th[eir] Cannon from ye fort."[24] William Amherst, Jeffery's younger brother who served as an aide-de-camp, remarked that "it is the luckiest thing that could have happened, the enemy not destroying their lines."[25] With the protection of the French breastwork, a siege of the fort would move more expeditiously.

Amherst's batteries were slated to open fire on the morning of July 27, but the evening before, a deserter informed him that the French garrison had departed and the fort would soon explode. At the same time, Amherst sent Rangers under Robert

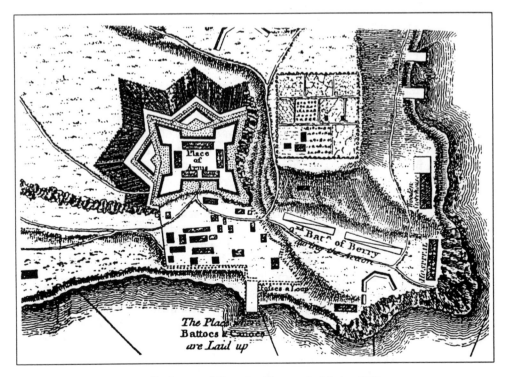

Detail of map of Fort Carillon and vicinity 1758.
From *The History of the Late War in North-America* by Thomas Mante (1772).

Rogers and Colonel William Haviland with the light infantry in the English flat-bottomed boat and whaleboats to capture the French evacuees. At 11 o'clock at night a loud explosion in the fort illuminated the summer sky and shook the ground a quarter mile away at the breastwork—the blast also reverberated as far as the landing at Lake George. At one o'clock in the morning some of the troops entered the fort in an effort to put out the fire. The next day Amherst "ordered all the camp kettles to be taken down to the Fort, to endeavour to extinguish the fire."[26] As the fort continued to burn, William Amherst remarked in his journal that "this ground is one of the prettiest situations I have seen in America; exceeds everything in strength & is in every respect a most considerable acquisition to us."[27] The fire continued to flare up as late as July 31 at which time Amherst decided that he would repair the fort along the lines of the French design.

On August 5 Amherst dispatched a letter to Secretary of State William Pitt, outlining his plans for "the fort of Ticonderoga," noting that only "one bastion [out of four], and part of two curt[a]ins [walls connecting two bastions], demolished. . . The casements are good; the walls of the burnt barracks are not damaged. Eleven good ovens have helped us greatly."[28] While provincial soldiers were struck by the design of the fort at Ticonderoga which had stone walls "about 24 feet high" and "large barracks built the whole length of the fort with stone and lime 2 stories high," John Hurlbut was impressed by the French garden: "cabbage is very plent[iful] and all sorts of greens. They had a fine garden large [enough] to give the whole army a mess."[29]

Cognizant that the French fleet on Lake Champlain would thwart British control, Amherst had directed Captain Joshua Loring on July 27 to repair the French sawmill for use in building a brig. The immediate need, however, involved providing enough vessels to transport men and equipment to Crown Point. By August 4, Loring had assembled a small fleet on Lake Champlain, including two radeaux built at Ticonderoga, armed with "six 12 pounders in yr sides and one 24 in ye bow four ro[w] galleys yt carry one 18 in each of yr bows one flat boat and one six pounder and four bayboats with swiv[e]lls."[30] The English flat-bottomed boat and "3 Ro[w]gal[l]eys [had been] Drawn out of Lake George" and relaunched in Lake Champlain, according to Lemuel Wood.[31] On August 1 Amherst had learned that the French had vacated Fort St. Frédéric; three days later an assortment of vessels brought the British and provincial army to Crown Point.

Because Brigadier General Bourlamaque had blown up the citadel of Fort St. Frédéric, Amherst immediately began the task of selecting the site for a new fort. Over the next few weeks as many as 1,600 men labored on the new fortification at Crown Point. On August 25 James Henderson, a provincial recruit from Massachusetts, recorded a description of the new fort under construction at Crown Point with "walls being 23 feet Thick being made with very large Timbers there will be a Magaz[ine] in the Inside of the walls which will be 20 feet thick there is 5 Bastions in said Fort so that it will be invincible almost When Finished."[32] In addition to the fort, soldiers worked on several redoubts at Crown Point; others toiled at rebuilding the fort at Ticonderoga, constructing Fort George, laying out several new roads, and completing a major road to the Connecticut River.

As a result of frequent breakdowns at the sawmill and the construction of a wharf, progress on the new brig at Ticonderoga had been slow. After a French deserter provided detailed information regarding the composition of the French fleet, Amherst met with Major Thomas Ord and Captain Joshua Loring, who jointly decided that a radeau armed with six 24-pound cannon was the most expedient method of enlarging the British squadron. Ord would build the radeau at Crown Point along the same lines as the *Land Tortoise* and *Invincible*. On August 31 Loring wrote a letter to Amherst with the news that the "Brig [was] Safe into the water" after a launch the previous evening.[33] The positive news, however, was short-lived since a scouting report from Sergeant Major Joseph Hopkins, along with information from three French prisoners, revealed that a new French sloop had been launched at Isle-aux-Noix. Amherst quickly embarked on two courses of action: the first strategy involved sending a raiding party to attempt to burn the French vessel, and the second to build a 16-gun sloop.

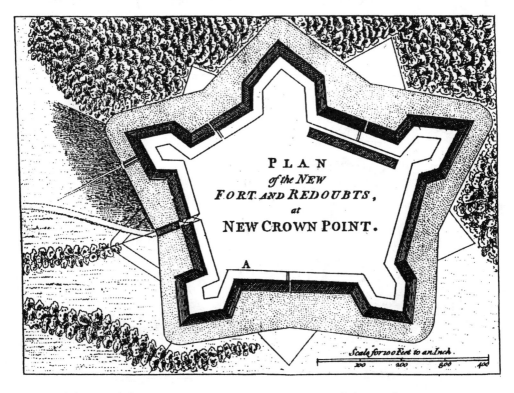

Plan of the British fort at Crown Point 1759. From *A Set of Plans and Forts in America: Reduced from Actual Surveys* by Mary Ann Rocque (1765).

On September 29 Ord launched the 84-foot radeau *Ligonier* which the *Boston Gazette* described as 300 tons "and contriv'd so that tis impossible for the Enemy to board her: She rows with 40 oars. . .and has 2 large Masts, and square Sails with running Rigging; so that in short no Ship can lay along Side of her."[34] As Loring pushed to complete the sloop, both he and Amherst endeavored to find seamen and cannon for the new vessels.[35] As the season advanced, Amherst grew impatient and pondered mounting the expedition "without waiting for the Sloop."[36] On October

10, 1759, Captain Loring sailed the 155-ton brig *Duke of Cumberland,* mounting twenty 6-pound and 4-pound cannon and 20 swivel guns, into Crown Point. The next day Lieutenant Alexander Grant brought the 80-foot sloop *Boscawen,* mounting sixteen 6-pound and 4-pound cannon and 22 swivels, to Crown Point.

Without delay, Amherst departed for Canada aboard the radeau *Ligonier* on the afternoon of October 11, 1759, the very same day that the *Boscawen* had arrived at Crown Point. The fleet was organized in four columns with the *Ligonier* at the head of the bateaux armada. The sloop *Boscawen* and brig *Duke of Cumberland* sailed after the main body of vessels had set forth, but quickly passed Amherst's fleet. Samuel Merriman, a sergeant from Northfield, Massachusetts, in Timothy Ruggles' regiment, observed the departure of 5,500 regulars and described the secondary vessels as "two arke [radeaux] which mounted 1-24 pounder each & some mort[a]rs & [several boats] & three Ro[w]ga[l]leys which mounted on[e] 18 pounder each & some mort[a]rs besides some 6 & 8 pounders & pr[etty] many swi[vel]s."[37] Amherst's expeditionary force was primarily composed of regulars; the provincial troops were assigned to work on the fort and other projects.

The sloop *Boscawen* and brig *Duke of Cumberland* under sail.
Drawing by Kevin J. Crisman. (Lake Champlain Maritime Museum)

During the night Loring and Grant, aboard the *Duke of Cumberland* and *Boscawen,* inadvertently passed the three French sloops near Four Brothers Islands, reaching the vicinity of Grand Isle where they observed the French schooner *La Vigilante.* Joseph Payant St. Onge, the commander of the 70-ton schooner, sailed his vessel through the shoal waters of Bixby and Young Island (Sister Islands), adjacent to South Hero Island. The British commander, unfamiliar with the north-

Remains of Amherst's brig *Duke of Cumberland* raised at Ticonderoga in 1909 and erroneously identified as a Revolutionary War vessel. (Postcard, author's collection)

Remains of the brig *Duke of Cumberland* at Ticonderoga in the late twentieth century.
(Photo by the author)

ern lake, was drawn into a trap and grounded on the shoal, allowing St. Onge with *La Vigilante* to escape. After extricating his vessels, Loring observed the three French sloops (also called xebecs), *La Musquelongy* (The Muskellunge), *La Brochette* (The Pike), and *L'Esturgeon* (The Sturgeon), attempting to return to Isle-aux-Noix. Without hesitation, Loring, with a favorable wind, pursued his adversaries. Since the eight-gun sloops were no match for the larger British vessels, Joannis-Galand d'Olabaratz, the French commander, fled southward to Cumberland Bay, tacking to a position along the shoreline near present-day Cliff Haven. Perceiving that his escape was blocked, d'Olabaratz, after a council with his officers, scuttled the three vessels.

Earlier, Amherst and his men had rowed all night (October 11/12). In the darkness soldiers from the Highlander regiment in bateaux became separated from the main bateaux fleet after they had mistakenly followed a light in the *Duke of Cumberland* instead of the *Ligonier*. More than a dozen men and Ensign MacKay (also spelled McKoy) had been captured after a skirmish with sailors and marines from the French sloops. Amherst's crews struggled against an adverse wind on October 12; by nightfall the flotilla pulled "into a bay on the western shore. . .[and Amherst] ordered the rangers on an island."[38] While Corlaer Bay and Schuyler Island appear to be logical candidates for the site, the name of Ligonier Bay appears in some of the original sources.[39] As a result of intense stormy weather, Amherst was forced to remain in the bay until October 18; the next day he visited the site of the scuttled French sloops. With news of the British victory at Quebec and the probable movement of the remaining French army toward Montreal, Amherst recognized that his army could now be outnumbered by fresh reinforcements sent to Isle-aux-Noix. By then it was also apparent that the season was too far advanced for a campaign and thus orders were given to return to Crown Point. Over the next month all three sloops would be salvaged. *La Musquelongy*, which had been run onshore, was repaired by October 18, while the *La Brochette* and *L'Esturgeon* were raised from the shallow water, arriving at Crown Point on November 16.

At the end of November Amherst departed for winter quarters in New York City; when the Hudson River froze at Albany, he walked for six days to New York City. Amherst was appointed Governor of Virginia by King George II in late 1759. Since Amherst wished to return to England as soon as peace was established, he acceded to the honor with assurances that he would not have to live in Virginia. The position, which carried an ample stipend, was purely nominal; the work would be done by the lieutenant governor.

Although Amherst's army did not reach Canada in 1759, British and provincial forces had taken both French forts on Lake Champlain and achieved naval control of the lake. British victories at Fort Niagara and Quebec City further reduced New France's ability to survive. With confidence in Amherst's ability, Secretary Pitt's instructions for 1760 were simply to take Canada: "It is His Majesty's Pleasure that You do attempt the Invasion of Canada. . . Accordingly as You shall from your Knowledge of the Countries through which the War is to be Carried."[40] Amherst's plans for the campaign involved a three-pronged invasion: a pincer movement, whereby Brigadier (local rank) James Murray would move his Troops east from Quebec to Montreal while Brigadier (local rank) William Haviland would sail with his army north on Lake Champlain, capturing Isle-aux-Noix and St. Jean before reaching Montreal. Amherst with the largest army would take the most difficult route to Montreal from Lake Ontario along the St. Lawrence River. The plan worked in near synchronization as 17,000 British troops converged on the remaining French soldiers in Montreal. On September 8, 1760, Governor-General Pierre de Rigaud de Vaudreuil signed the articles of surrender of New France.

While Amherst refused the surrendering French army the "honors of war" because of the "infamous part the troops of France had acted in exciting the savages to perpetuate the most horrid and unheard of barbarities," he was far more generous in his treatment of the inhabitants of New France.[41] Amherst allowed free exercise of the Catholic Religion, recognized the laws and customs of Canada, and ended the feudal-like judicial authority of manorial lords, but allowed land owners to retain their holdings. Amherst's handling of the Canadians would later be the basis for the liberal Quebec Act of 1774 which would preempt Canadian support for the American Revolution.

"The Humanity of General Amherst" (1760), illustrating Amherst's charity toward the French-Canadian noncombatants. Oil on canvas by Francis Hayman.
(Beaverbrook Art Gallery, Fredericton, New Brunswick)

Amherst's itinerary on his return trip to New York City in 1760 included a visit to the fortification at Isle-aux-Noix which he ordered demolished, a repetition of what had occurred at Louisbourg. After a two-week visit at Crown Point to check the ongoing construction, Amherst made an inspection of Forts Ticonderoga and George. Upon reaching New York City, Amherst was treated to a cannon salute and a hero's welcome from the mayor and other dignitaries. Earlier celebrations had been held throughout the colonies when news of Amherst's victory had reached local communities. Bostonians held a parade, then a dinner at Faneuil Hall, followed by fireworks and the firing of 63 cannon.

Aerial view of Amherst's fort at Crown Point.
(Photo by the author)

Amherst remained in America, settling into the role of a defacto governor-general of British North America. His determination to finish his grand fort at Crown Point continued into 1762 with the assignment of 3,025 provincial soldier-laborers to the project.[42] For the next few years, however, a number of trouble spots required his attention. Early in 1761 Secretary of State William Pitt shifted his focus to the Caribbean which required Amherst to organize expeditions against the French possessions of Dominica, Martinique, and St. Lucia. After Britain declared war on Spain in January 1762, Amherst reassigned some of his troops to the siege of Havana. At the same time a French attack on St. John's, Newfoundland, required Amherst to send his brother, Colonel William Amherst, and 1,500 soldiers to expel the invaders.

Amherst's position in America necessitated an attempt to prohibit colonial trade with Britain's enemies, particularly with the French and Spanish islands in the Caribbean. Although the British government had suggested the idea of an embargo on colonial trade, Amherst had adroitly avoided a confrontation with colonial governments. With mounting pressure from home, Amherst was compelled to implement a general embargo on colonial exports in the spring of 1762. Although he quickly eliminated the restrictions, the precedent had sown the seeds of discontent with British rule in America.

Peace in Europe, ending the Seven Years' War in 1763, brought a cessation of hostilities in the New World. However, Amherst's plans to return home were short-circuited by problems with Native Americans. Although Sir William Johnson had argued for a continuation of generous gifts and supplies to the Indians, Amherst reduced the outlays based on the expense and his own negative feelings toward Indians which lingered from the French and Indian War. Johnson maintained that providing gifts to the Indians was "infinitely cheaper and much more effectual than keeping of a large body of regular troops in their several countries."[43] More importantly, Native Americans were unhappy with the failure of Britain to live up to commitments and treaties, the lack of compensation for use of Indian land for military purposes, and the inability to restrict English colonists from lands assigned to Indians.

The lightly garrisoned forts on the western frontier were easy targets for the Ottawa chief, Pontiac. Although Pontiac had early successes at the outbreak of hostilities in May 1763, within a few months Colonel Henry Bouquet had quelled the uprising. After Amherst persuaded a French commander to write a circular letter to Indian chiefs that informed them of the peace between France and England, Pontiac's ambitions were terminated. One incident, however, stands out in the campaign. In a letter to Bouquet, Amherst suggested spreading smallpox among Native Americans. Bouquet endorsed the idea, suggesting that blankets could be infected with the disease and transferred to the Indians.[44]

On November 10, 1763, after five years of service in North America, Amherst embarked for home aboard the sloop-of-war *Weasel*. Writing to his close friend Colonel William Eyre, Amherst announced: "I have no thought of returning to America."[45] When he reached London, there was little celebration for the hero who had delivered New France to England. He was knighted in person, however, by King George III, an honor that had actually been conferred upon Amherst two years earlier while he was in America. Amherst had written to William Pitt beforehand, expressing his desire to decline the honor, but Pitt never informed the king. His return home was a sad disappointment. By then his wife was completely demented, dying several months after his homecoming. With his eldest brother's death, Amherst inherited the dilapidated family estate, Brook's Place, which he demolished and replaced with a new house nearby. In 1767 Amherst, then 50 years old, married 47-year-old Elizabeth Cary, daughter of General George Cary.

In 1768 Amherst was pressured to move to Virginia or resign his governorship of the colony and accept an annuity. Offended by the government's handling of the affair, Amherst, then a lieutenant general, resigned his army commission. A storm of controversy followed, generating public support for Amherst. After a brief time, he was reappointed to the army with higher remuneration. Two years later Amherst accepted the governorship of the Island of Guernsey, a titular appointment once held by his earlier patron, Sir John Ligonier. In 1772 Amherst was made a lieutenant general of Ordnance which included a seat on the Privy Council; he was then the defacto chief military leader in England.

Following the French and Indian War, parcels of land in North America were granted to officers for their service. After several preferred tracts of land were taken, Amherst was granted 20,000 acres in the Adirondacks. Because the land was considered worthless, the title was allowed to lapse. In 1769 Amherst began an

Elizabeth Cary Amherst, Jeffery Amherst's second wife. Detail of oil on canvas
by Sir Joshua Reynolds (ca. 1767). (Mead Art Museum, Amherst College)

application for a large land grant of forfeited Jesuit land in Canada. The matter was
never settled, resulting in the substitution of an annuity that was posthumously
granted to his heirs.

During the American Revolution Amherst twice refused the request of King
George III to take charge of the British army in America. His unwillingness to return
to North America, however, had nothing to do with support for the colonial
rebellion; his refusal was for personal reasons and perhaps related to the uncertain
prospects for British success against the American rebels. Early in 1782, as a result
of the losses in America and a subsequent turnover of leadership in the British
government, Amherst was dismissed from the commander in chief position in Great
Britain (appointed 1778) and as the Lieutenant General of the Ordnance. Amherst,
however, was not out of favor with George III, who appointed him to head the
Second Troop of Life Guards, responsible for the security of the king. When a new
war with France broke out in 1793, Amherst was again made commander in chief.
Two years later, at the age of 76, he stepped down but in 1796 received his last honor,
a promotion to field marshall. In failing health, Amherst retired to his home and

Lord Jeffery Amherst. Oil on canvas by Thomas Gainsborough (ca. 1785).
(Mead Art Museum, Amherst College)

died on August 3, 1797. He was interred in the family vault beside his two brothers, John and William.*

Although not as dashing as some other contemporary generals, Amherst had a laudable military career during the French and Indian War, characterized by unbroken successes. Amherst left nothing to chance; his methodical, careful management of campaigns resulted in few casualties, no setbacks and ultimate victory in North America. Perhaps Colonel Nathan Whiting from Connecticut best summed up Amherst's career in a letter written prior to the 1759 expedition against Fort Carillon: "the General appears to me to be cool and very clever and every thing Looks with a favorable Aspect."[46]

The following journal from July 21, 1759, to October 21, 1759, is a condensed version of his original account, omitting some of the routine entries and those dealing with military activities in other sectors.

---

*Admiral John Amherst had died in 1778. Amherst's younger brother, General William Amherst, had died in 1781, leaving a daughter, 12-year-old Elizabeth and a son William Pitt Amherst, age eight. Since the children's mother had also passed away, Amherst adopted the children. Jeffery Amherst's illegitimate son, who had lived with his first wife at Brook's Place in the 1760s, made a career in the army, eventually rising to the rank of major general.

The Journal of Jeffery Amherst 1759[47]

[July] 21st. The General [reveille/drum call to assemble] at Lake George]at two in the morning. Two ten Inch Mortars sunk last night and the wharf gave way.* I got everything embarked as fast as possible after a great many changes of boats I was obliged to make. I could not have gone if I had waited for all the Artillery to set out, so left Br. Gage** to see all off & the sloop to bring up. The Rear got all under way about nine and the wind being fair we got through the narrows and I advanced the Heads of the Columns as far as I could without being seen from the Enemys Post and there I stop[p]ed that the whole might come up.*** Ordered the Corps under Col Haviland† to lead as soon as possible in the morning. Br. Gage & Major Ord‡ came up at night. [Colonel Archibald] Montgomerys 150 men [77th Highlanders] arrived at Fort George. Great deal of rain in the day & some wind at night that made it impossible to keep the Columns quite well together.

22nd. At day break the whole got into the order of Rowing & after giving a proper time to Col Haviland to advance we put forward. As the Enemy had no Party at the place called the advanced Guard & that Col Haviland was to cut off the

---

*Apparently, provision was made to raise the artillery since Colonel James Montresor at Fort George noted on September 22 that "four men came here to. . .dive for the Ten mortar."[48]

**Thomas Gage (1719-1787) served as an aide-de-camp to the Earl of Albemarle during the War of the Austrian Succession. Promoted to Lieutenant Colonel of the 44th Regiment of Foot in 1751, Gage led the advance troops in the disastrous 1755 Braddock expedition and served as second in command in the 1758 Abercromby campaign following Lord Howe's death. After failing to capture the French post of La Galette (near Ogdensburg, N.Y.) in 1759, Gage was relegated to direct the rear guard in Amherst's drive to Montreal in 1760. Nevertheless, he was promoted to major general in 1761 and two years later succeeded Amherst as commander in chief in North America. Gage ordered the seizure of rebel stores at Concord on April 19, 1775, precipitating the American Revolution. He was recalled to England later in the year and subsequently promoted to full general in 1782. Gage died at his home in Portland, England, on April 2, 1787.

***Although a few contemporary sources suggest that Amherst's fleet stopped for the night at Sabbath Day Point, the troops remained in their boats overnight further north in Hague.[49] Samuel Merriman recorded that the flotilla had sailed "as far as ye second Narrows by ye great smooth rock [present-day Rogers Rock]"; Henry True and Constantine Hardy both noted a distance of only a few miles to the Ticonderoga landing site.[50]

†William Haviland (1718-1784) was commissioned an ensign in 1739, rising to the rank of lieutenant colonel in the 27th Regiment of Foot in 1752. During the winter of 1757-1758, Haviland commanded Fort Edward and participated in Abercromby's failed expedition to Ticonderoga the following summer. In 1760 he led a force of 3,400 men against the French fort at Isle-Aux-Noix on the Richelieu River. Haviland later participated in the military expeditions to Martinique and Havana, winning a promotion to major general in 1762. Following his advancement to lieutenant general in 1772, he served on Amherst's staff in England during the American Revolution. Haviland died in England in 1784, a year after promotion to general.

‡Thomas Ord had been appointed a captain in the Royal Artillery in 1746. Held in high regard by William Augustus, the Duke of Cumberland, Ord was chosen to direct the artillery under Major General Edward Braddock in 1755. Ord commanded the artillery in the expedition to Fort Carillon under Major General James Abercromby in 1758 and supervised construction of the radeau *Land Tortoise* at Lake George the same year. Promoted to major, Ord again commanded the artillery in Amherst's 1759 campaign and oversaw construction of the radeaux *Invincible* and *Ligonier*. In 1759 he was elevated to the rank of lieutenant colonel and became a colonel-commandant of the 4th Battalion of the Royal Artillery in America in 1771. Ord was granted 5,000 acres of land in Newcomb, New York (Essex County), for his service in America. He died in 1777.

Retreat of any Partys that might be out. I landed the light Infantry of Gages to the Right and [General Phineas] Lymans [1st Connecticut Regiment] being the first of the left Column to the left as flankers, as far as the water would carry them. Landed and marched forward covering [Colonel Peter] Schuylers [Jersey Blues] & [Colonel Timothy] Ruggles Regts [Massachusetts Regiment] who cleared the Road, which must have cost them a good deal of trouble to have laid the timber across. A Report from [Lieutenant]Col [Francis] Grant the Enemy had attacked our advanced Partys. I ordered Post to be taken on the rising grounds beyond the saw mills & that the Army was ready to sustain it & marched on accordingly. I had the Carpenters immediately repair the bridge and brought up two twelve- and two six-Pounders as soon as I got the Road cleared, which the Provincials did vastly well. The Party of the Enemy disputed the ground but a little while afterwards continued firing at a great distance. We took two Prisoners killed three or four men, had one man only killed and wounded. I lay on my Arms the night, threw up a Post at the Landing Place, another at the Saw Mills & a third to keep possession of the commanding ground. A little firing in the night. I had ordered the Army to be ready to march at day break & intended to march by the rising Grounds strait to Lake Champlain, but the Cannon the Enemy had seen me bring over the Sawmills, I imagine, determined them not to dispute the Lines but to march off and leave a Garrison to defend the Place, for as soon as it cleared.

23rd. in the morning the Officers commanding Posts opposite to Ticonderoga reported to me all their tents struck and that the whole was gone off in the Sloops and batteaus.* I marched as I had before intended but as my intelligence was very sure I proceeded over the broken ground to the Lines instead of marching across and taking Posts to advance in a full Front. On some of the light Infantry appearing the Garrison began to cannonade but the Lines covered the march of the Columns and I put the Lines in my Front, taking Possession of some of the advantageous Ground within, opening communications & throwing up a banquet [defensive embankment or berm] for the Regts to defend the Lines against any Sortie the Garrison could make and I employed as many men as I had tools for to cover themselves within the Lines. The Army lay on their Arms. The Disposition was the two Brigades of English at the Lines, Rangers, light Infantry of Regts & Gages & Grenadiers with three Batt[alion]s of Provincials covering the Rear. Those Batt[alion]s at the landing Place to guard Artillery Provisions Batteaus &c. Two opposite Ticonderoga, one at the Post at the Saw mills, two on the Communication from the Sawmills to this. They threw Shells and cannonaded from the Fort all day and most part of the night with no effect. I sent for the tents but could get so few up that the Army lay on their Arms all night. Made a Banquet[te], kept the Picquets[pickets] under Arms, ordered Col Haviland to take an advanced Post by the Lakeside.

24th. The Garrison burnt all their outhouses on the Lake side of the Fort, strip[ped] off the shingles from their buildings & kept a continual fire of cannon

---

*After surveying British siege preparations, Brigadier General François-Charles de Bourlamaque moved his 2,600-man army to Fort St. Frédéric, leaving a token garrison of 400 men under the command of Captain Louis-Philippe Le Dossu d'Hébécourt. Bourlamaque later wrote to the minister of war in France that "I received positive orders from M. de Vaudreuil not to think of defending Forts Carillon and St. Frédéric, but to abandon them one after the other, as soon as the English army made its approach."[51]

and throwing Shells opened trenches at three different Places & kept working all day from landing to this day inclusive. We had one Ensign one Corporal & four Privates killed and thirty wounded. I got up two twelve-Pounders, one for each Flank of the Camp, ordered the Artillery to be got up as fast as possible, made a wharf for landing them near the left where not seen from the Fort & put them on Rafts [on the La Chute River] to bring them from the Sawmills. Some canoes passing up & down the Lake, taking the Indians off & what they can carry I suppose from the Fort. The Trenches advanced apace; I covered the working men by Pic[k]ets. I sent Lt [John] Small with the New Hampshire Regt. back to Fort George & he is to conduct that Regt with all the Expedition he can to Oswego that no hands may be wanted there for building the Fort and that Brig Gen Prideaux may have at all events on his return from Niagara a full sufficient Force to proceed to la Gallette.* Sent an order for the two Companys, one of the New Hampshire & one of the Massachusetts, to go from No. 4 & Fort Dummer to Albany to join their Regts from thence.** Made a road from the new landing Place to Lake Champlain; sent for whale boats and the large boats for guns if possible to get it down. Such a continued fire from the Fort the men were obliged to stay all night out of their Tents. Last night Part of Col Havilands Corps were alarmed & firing too quick Ensign Harrison was killed & 12 men wounded.***

25th. In the night past our working party being a little alarmed began to fire which drew on some fire from the Pic[k]ets who lay on the Lines in front of the Camp, but soon Officers stop[ped] it, with yesterdays work we shall get the Batteries on night, six 24-Pounders in the Park of Artillery. I got the English flat bottomed boat to Lake Champlain & some whale boats. Sent to the first landing Place for Provisions, had the old Sawmills inspected & ordered them to be put in order, which Capt Loring† said would be done in eight days. Sent for Col [Henry] Babcocks

*Brigadier (local rank) John Prideaux was a colonel of the 55th Regiment of Foot in 1758. He and Sir William Johnson were sent on a campaign with an army of regulars, provincials, and Indians to reoccupy the British base at Oswego and then to capture Fort Niagara. Prideaux was accidently killed by a mortar discharged from his own siege lines at Niagara. The expedition ended successfully on July 25, 1759, when Captain Pierre Pouchot surrendered his outnumbered garrison to Johnson. La Galette refers to another French outpost located near present-day Ogdensburg, New York.

**The terminology Number 4 delineates one of nine townships originally designated by the General Court of Massachusetts. Established in 1743, Fort Number 4 was commanded by Captain Phineas Stevens who with 30 soldiers in 1747 withstood an assault by a French and Indian raiding party. The town was named Charlestown in 1753 after Sir Charles Knowles who presented a sword to Stevens in commemoration of his gallant stand. The reconstructed fort, overlooking the Connecticut River in New Hampshire, is a living history museum today.

Built in 1724 for protection against the Abenakis, Fort Dummer (present-day Brattleboro) was the first permanent settlement by Europeans in Vermont.

***During the night some of the soldiers accidently fired on one another when they were convinced that the French were attacking their position. Because of these accidents, soldiers were regularly admonished not to fire at night and to use passwords at the entrenchment.

†Joshua Loring (1716-1781) was a Boston-born naval officer whose career began as a privateer during King George's War (1744-1748). With the help of Governor William Shirley of Massachusetts, Loring was commissioned a lieutenant in the Royal Navy in 1745. Traveling to England at the onset of the Seven Years' War, he was promoted and appointed to command a brig. In 1758 Loring was promoted to post captain (Royal Navy) and assigned to the construction and command of vessels on the lakes. In the 1758-1759 campaigns he was in charge of building the vessels on Lake George and Lake Champlain. During the final operations of 1760, Loring commanded the 22-gun *Onondaga* and 18-gun

[Rhode Island] Regt. to the first landing Place in the room [vicinity] of the New Hampshire. Colonel Townshend killed by a Cannon ball.* The loss of a friend is not made up by all the success that a Campaign can give to ones self personally— villain metier, celle du soldat. Ordered the Duty in the Trenches to be done by Battalion, the Royal to mount to night.

26th. The Trenches advanced apace and the Batteries to be ready this night. The Artillery will be up that we may open Batteries of

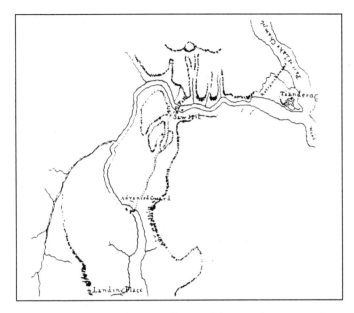

Sketch made by Jeffery Amherst of the area between Lake George and Lake Champlain 1759. From *The Journal of Jeffery Amherst* edited by J. Clarence Webster.

six 24-Pounders, and a Battery of Mortars. Everything was preparing to open the Batteries at day break. Some dispute with the Engineers and Artillery Officers who were to lay the Platforms which I cut very short by finding another to do it, at the same time telling them it was the duty of the Artillery Officers to do it but when I named Lt Col Robertson to make the Platforms, the Engineers then took it on themselves. I had ordered Major Rogers to go to night and cut the boom,** and I put up three tents and made a fire on the eastern side which had a good effect for the Enemy kept firing at it as much as if there had been a real Camp there. About ten o'clock a Deserter came in & said the Garrison was to get off and to blow up the Fort. I wrote to Major Rogers immediately to attack them, and soon we saw the Fort on fire and an Explosion but as the Deserter said a Match was laid to blow the

---

Mohawk with the Amherst offensive on the St. Lawrence River, but his performance in the operation was clouded in controversy. Three years later Loring furnished vessels on Lake Erie to quell Pontiac's rebellion. He retired to his vast Roxbury, Massachusetts, estate in 1767. Remaining loyal to the Crown, Loring fled at the outbreak of the American Revolution. Massachusetts subsequently banished him and confiscated his estate; he died in England in 1781. Loring's son Joshua, also a loyalist, was appointed the Commissory of Prisoners by General William Howe. He is best known, however, as the husband of Howe's mistress.

*Roger Townshend, brother to George Townshend who had served with Amherst in the War of Austrian Succession, was an adjutant general during the 1758 Louisbourg siege and served as Amherst's deputy adjutant general at Ticonderoga. Townshend was later buried in Albany.

**Major Robert Rogers was ordered to cut the log boom "which the enemy have laid across the point below the fort to the opposite shore."[52] According to Rogers, the boom had been "thrown across the lake opposite the fort, which prevented our boats from passing by. . .[Proceeding at night with] sixty Rangers in one English flat-bottomed boat, and two whaleboats. . .saw[ed] off their boom. . .being made with logs of timber."[53]

whole up I would not order any men into it.* However some volunteers went & brought away the Colours and I sent two other Deserters with some volunteers to try and cut the Match, who on their arrival found that there was no more danger so I sent

27th. hands and Camp Kettles to try all we could to extinguish the fire. I wrote a short Letter to Mr Pitt & sent my Brother with it that he might give an account of the whole from the 22nd to this day.** We have 16 men killed, 51 wounded and one of the light Infantry of Prideaux's missing. I destroyed the Banquet[te] I had made, struck the Tents & marched into the Lines which I ordered to be repaired & the Trenches and batteries to be levelled. Encamped at night within the Lines, ordered the Rangers, light Infantry & Grenadiers, Lymans & Wo[o]sters to fill up the Road entirely that I had made to Lake Champlain, and the Rangers to march to morrow beyond the Sawmills; [General Phineas] Lymans [1st Connecticut], [Colonel David] Wo[o]sters [3rd Connecticut], [Colonel Peter] Schuyler's [Jersey Blues], & [Colonel Eleazer] Fitch['s] [4th Connecticut Regiment], to encamp near the Fort to work at the Repairs. Sent 500 men under Col Fitch to Fort George for Provisions; ordered all French boats to be fished up & boats built for carrying 24-Pounders that I may be superior to the Enemys Sloops on the Lake.*** We took in the Fort, two 18-Pounders, one 16, seven 12, four 9, four 6, one 4, seven Swivels, two 13 Inch Mortars, one 6-1/2 one 8-Inch Howitzer with Shot Shells, 56 musquets, entrenching tools, great quantity old Iron, and 50 barrels of Powder taken out of a boat on attacking them on their retreat from the Fort.

28th. The fire was not yet totally extinguished. I pressed to get things forwarded as fast as possible that I may set out for Crown Point without loss of time.

29th. We thought we had got the fire quite out, but it appeared again a little. Br Gage set off for Oswego: Col. Fitch returned with his detachment to the Landing Place. Intelligence that the Troops which were encamped on the eastern side of the Lake were now encamped at Crown Point where the Garrison of Ticonderoga must have joined them.

---

*When a deserter reported the burning fuse at the fort, "The General offered a hundred guineas to any one of them that would go back, and sh[o]w us the match. . .but they all declared they did not know where it was laid. . .[and] there was such a quantity of powder in the Fort that they did not think us safe in our encampment."[54] The blast was "very loud and shaking" as far away as the landing at Lake George and "killed about Fifty" horses in a stable above the magazine.[55]

**Amherst sent his brother, William Amherst, an aide-de-camp, back to England with a short letter to provide a personal account of the capture of Fort Carillon to Secretary of State William Pitt. A longer account written to Pitt by Amherst on August 5 arrived in September on the same day that his brother landed in England. The August letter was soon published in The London Magazine, The Universal Magazine, and The Scots Magazine.[56]

***Sunken French bateaux were raised while the English flat-bottomed boat, three row galleys, bateaux, and whaleboats were transferred from Lake George to Lake Champlain during the last week of July.[57] Amherst ordered Captain Joshua Loring to repair the sawmill and build a brig and several other vessels capable of challenging the French fleet on Lake Champlain.

In September provincial troops raised "two Large flat Bottomed Boats yt was taken when Fort William Henry was and Sunk at ye [northern Lake George] Landing."[58] Amherst referred to the sunken vessels as scows which were to be used to carry firewood.[59] In 1761 Captain John Wrightson reported "a large French Boat at the Landing which could be Easily repaired."[60] The vessel may have been one of the sloops taken by Louis-Joseph de Montcalm's troops after the destruction of Fort William Henry in 1757.

I kept small Partys constantly looking into Crown Point. The two Sloops and a Schooner are there to cover their boats.* They depend on my not getting my boats over & being forced to build some for Cannon, but I shall be ready sooner than they imagine. Sent a Highland Regt to Landing Place to help.

30th. The Fire broke out again in the Fort; all the People at work that there was room for. I pressed to have the batteaus & whaleboats over as soon as possible.

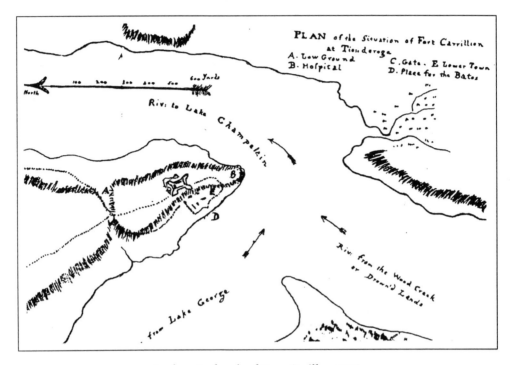

Amherst's sketch of Fort Carillon 1759.
From *The Journal of Jeffery Amherst* edited by J. Clarence Webster.

31st. I sent Col Haviland to help get the boats over [to Lake Champlain]. The fire at the Fort not quite extinguished, I ordered the Fort by the water side to be put in thorough good order. The Enemy had not quite finished it, and I will repair the Fort upon the same Plan as the Enemy had built it which will save great expense & and give no room for the Engineers to exercise their genius which will be much better employed at Crown Point. I heard some Guns from Crown Point at eleven o'clock. I am trying all I can to get forward. It is a little unlucky that three principal People in their Departments, viz., Bradstreet,** Loring and Ord are always pulling

---

*Amherst's scouts observed the schooner *La Vigilante* and two sloops (xebecs): *La Musquelongy, La Brochette,* or *L'Esturgeon.*

**John Bradstreet (1714-1774) was an American-born officer present during the successful 1745 Louisbourg siege. In 1758 he served with Abercromby as head of the "Battoe Service" and later that summer successfully led an attack on Fort Frontenac. During the French and Indian War Bradstreet held the rank of captain in the 60th Regiment of Foot and the local rank of lieutenant colonel in North America. Later in the war he was dispatched to the West Indies and Detroit (Pontiac's War). Bradstreet died in 1774, two years after being promoted to major general.

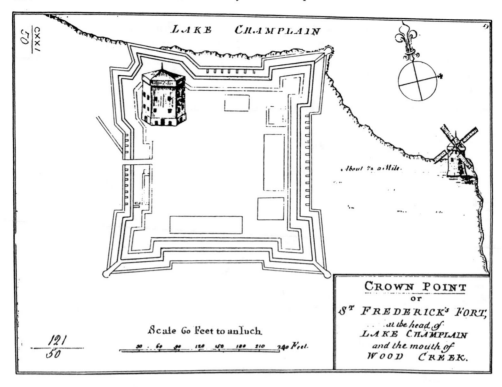

Drawing of Fort St. Frédéric 1759. (Crown Collection, New York State Library)

different ways. I try to keep them as good Friends as I can and to convince them that their duty is to forward everything for the good of the Service and to assist one another. A Deserter came in last night from Crown Point, had left it before the Garrison from hence had got there.

August 1st. I got the whale boats for the light Infantry & partly for the Grenadiers, but not batteaus enough for a Regt as the Regts are ordered to have four days bread ready baked before-hand. I can go the Instant I get the batteaus. At noon a Scouting Party came in with Intelligence that the Enemy had abandoned Crown Point, and that they have done it on the news of Quebec being taken, or supposing that I may soon have my boats to follow them and that they will find it difficult to escape me.

3rd. A Party I sent to Crown Point brought in a Deserter from [late] Forbes [Regiment] in a French boat, one that I had pardoned for Desertion at Fort George. I thought it so necessary to make an immediate example I called the commanding Officers together to judge of his Desertion and to report to me if they thought he should suffer death; on which report I ordered him to be hanged directly.

As everything was now settled for repairing the Fort [at Ticonderoga] I resolved to proceed to Crown Point tomorrow, which I could not do if the Enemy was there as I shall want many boats but I cant too soon begin securing a Post there as tis the place to cover all this country & I hope to repair Ticonderoga, make a secure Post at Crown Point & go on with the necessary preparations of a Brig and boats to go to St Johns [St. Jean, Quebec] & pursue the Enemy without any loss of time. I sent

Detail of "South East View of Crown Point" showing English gunboats,
a small radeau, and Fort St. Frédéric with its citadel demolished. Pen and ink
drawing by Thomas Davies (1759). (National Archives of Canada)

two Captains and 200 men of the Rangers through the woods to go to Crown Point
& ordered the General to beat [standard drum call for general quarters] at two in
the morning.

4th. I got the two Brigades embarked very soon except the R[oyal] Highland
Regt who had not yet got their boats, which kept me waiting some. The order of
Rowing was—Gages formed the advanced Guard, covered the Columns from right
to left, had two boats with three Pounders. The Left Column marched by the Right
consisted of the Rangers, light Infantry & Grenadiers as the first to land. The Right
Column was intended of Ruggle's & Babcocks but they could not get their boats,
& the Artillery was to have formed the 2nd Column; the Right with Schuylers &
Fitchs Regts but we could only bring a Part of the Artillery & the Regts sta[yed]
behind for want of batteaus. The third Column was of the two Brigades of Regulars,
and I had three 24-Pounders and a 12-Pounder in boats with the Columns.* The
wind blew very hard against us which made it great labour to get on. We however
reached Crown Point in the evening where I landed without opposition and I
reconnoitred the whole Ground and ordered the q[uarter] Master to mark out the
Camp; the Regts that could not get their tents lay on their Arms.

---

*According to one eyewitness, Amherst's flotilla included two newly-built radeaux with six 12-pound
cannon mounted on the sides and a 24-pounder in the bow, four row galleys with one 18-pounder
each, one flat boat, and four "bayboats with swivels."[61] In October another participant in the campaign
noted that the "two arke [radeaux] mounted 1-24 pounder each & some mort[a]rs" and mentioned
only three row galleys.[62] A contemporary newspaper account described the row galleys as mounting
"18 Pounders, each. . .placed fore and aft, and fires out at the Head, they row with 14 Oars on each
side, carry 30 men each."[63]

The Enemy has in part blown up the Fort and intended to do more.* We saved the four Barrels of Powder. I ordered the Engineers to reconnoitre the best place for erecting a Fort that I may set about it so soon as possible.** This is a great Post gained, secures entirely all the country behind it, and the situation and country about is better than anything I have seen.

5th. Part of Fitchs and Babcocks Regts arrived as likewise Ruggles's at night. I sent to Ticonderoga for spruce beer,*** ordered 100 men of the Rangers to cut a Road to Ticonderoga that cattle may be drove from thence which will be of great use, sent out a boat with a three Pounder to reconnoitre down the Lake, found a large field of peas, ordered them to be divided amongst the Army, sent Mr Rogers on the other side the Lake to see for the best Place for cutting timber to erect the Fort, gave him leave to shoot Deer; he killed three and seven Bears. I reviewed all the Ground round, ordered Posts at proper Places sent away Captain [Robert] Prescott at night to Mr [William] Pitt with news of Niagara. Sent for Spruce beer & bread from Ticonderoga, proposed to send one of Major Rogers People to try to get to Genl Wolfe† but they would not undertake it.

7th. I went out in the morning with a covering Party and reconnoitred all round, ordered the Road from the New Fort to the village to be cut out strait & to join the one making to drive cattle &c from Ticonderoga. Ordered two Redoubts [small forts]. No likelihood of the Enemys coming but I cant be too secure. Letters in the afternoon from New York that My brother sailed the 2nd. I wrote to Gen Wolfe; got Ensign [Benjamin] Hutchings of the Rangers to set out with it.

8th. As it is of consequence that I should hear from Gen Wolfe as well as he should likewise hear from me I concluded to send Capt [Quinton] Kennedy with Lt [Frederick] Hamilton, Capt Jacobs [Mohegan known as Cheekaunkun], and four Indians to go through the settlements of the Eastern Indians with a proposal from me & take their answer to Mr Wolfe whom I have directed to treat them accordingly. Last night and this morning a great storm of wind and Rain damaged some of our Batteaus. The boats with the Guns cant live in this Lake in bad weather. I ordered two Scouts to St Johns, sent 200 Rangers to cut a Road to open a communication from New England & New Hampshire [Fort Number 4] to Crown Point. Ordered

---

*Upon scrutinizing the remains of Fort St. Frédéric, James Henderson, a provincial soldier from Rutland, Massachusetts, wrote his impression of the fortification: "built of Stone and Lime the walls are about Two feet thick. . .they have destroyed all their buildings of value. The Blew up their Ci[t]adel or Magaz[i]n[e] it is a very Large heap of Stones as it now lies. . .the Building was [four] Story high all arched over The Fort is a proper square. The Citadel being an octogon."[64]

**Amherst's letter on August 5 to William Pitt disclosed that "I ordered lieutenant-colonel [William] Eyre to trace out the ground for a fort."[65] Eyre was also to supervise the rebuilding of Fort Ticonderoga, while James Montresor was in charge of the construction of Fort George.

***Spruce beer, made by boiling the cuttings from the tops of spruce trees in water and molasses, was a preventative for scurvy. Amherst provided the specific recipe in his original journal.[66]

†James Wolfe (1727-1759) followed in his father's footsteps by joining the military, serving as a young officer during the War of the Austrian Succession. Promoted to lieutenant colonel at 23 years of age in 1750, Wolfe advanced in rank to colonel early in the Seven Years' War. Given a local rank of brigadier, he distinguished himself with Amherst at Louisbourg and was elevated in 1759 to major general (local rank) and commander in chief of the expedition against Quebec. Despite debilitating illnesses, an inability to work cooperatively with his senior officers, and indecision, Wolfe won a conclusive victory over Montcalm's forces on the Plains of Abraham. Leading his troops in battle on September 13, 1759, Wolfe was mortally wounded.

a Party for cutting hay for the Cattle in the winter and a Party of 334 with a covering Party of a Comp[an]y of light Infantry & one of Grenadiers to lay in the woods to prepare timber for the Fort, sent Capt Abercromby* to Ticonderoga to see how things went on. 68 oxen arrived by the new Road from Ticonderoga for drawing the timber, &c.

9th. Enclosed the old Garden and added to it; it will be of vast help to the Troops in the winter. 400 men at work on the Ground where the Fort is to be, the first situation I think I have seen in America that is no where commanded. It will have all the advantages of the Lake and of the situation of Ground that can be wished for.

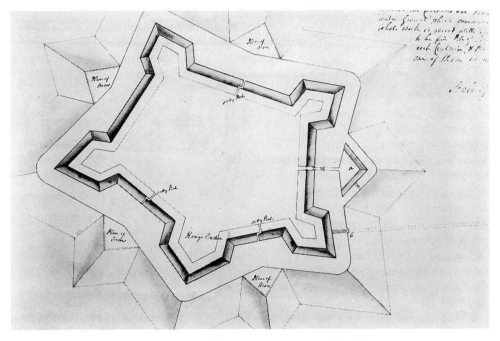

"A Draught of the Fortress building at Crown Point"
(Crown Collection, New York State Library)

10th. The work at the Fort going on pretty well, employed 800 workmen. A good deal of Rain; from all accounts more rain this summer than any People remember in this country. I ordered a Party to reconnoitre Otter River [Vermont].

11th. At day break a Party of 200 Rangers, 100 of Gages, a Company of light Infantry, and one of Grenadiers assembled under the command of Lt Col [John] Darby. They were to take two boats with three-Pounders and one [row galley] with a twelve-Pounder to explore the mouth of the Otter River, but the twelve-Pounder

*James Abercrombie (1732-1775) served during the War of the Austrian Succession and a decade later became an aide-de-camp to the following: the Earl of Loudoun (1757), James Abercromby (1758) and Jeffery Amherst (1759). Abercrombie held the rank of captain in the 42nd (Highland) Regiment. He is believed to have been the nephew of Major General Abercromby, although his family origins remain uncertain. In 1775 he was appointed an adjutant general and was mortally wounded at the Battle of Bunker Hill on June 17, 1775. Ironically, John Stark and Israel Putnam, who had served with Captain Abercrombie at Ticonderoga, were fighting with the Americans at Bunker Hill.

not rowing so well as the other boats Lt Col Darby sent it back. At one o'clock ten men of the Scouting Party of Rangers I had sent under the command of Ensign [John] Wilson to go half to the Right of the Lake & half to the Left to St. Johns, returned with a note from Capt Kennedy that Wilson thought his Party too large so sent these back & to inform me that he saw a Brigantine, a Schooner, and a topsail sloop of the Enemys and about 12 boats that they put in from the Vessels, as he supposed, on discovering his Party, that he got to the eastern side below Corliers Rock from whence he saw the Vessels at Anchor & thinks they have not seen his Party as sent no boats to the Island where he was when he supposed himself discovered. They go by water one night more and then strike into the woods. The ten Rangers said they saw the lights of the Vessels in the night; as they passed they

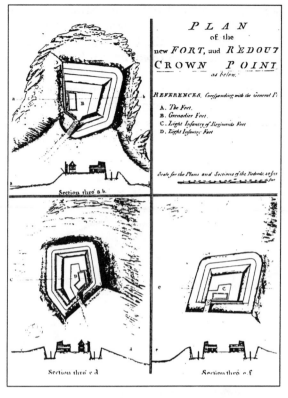

Plan of Redoubts at Crown Point 1759.
(Crown Collection, New York State Library)

met Col Darby & told him what they had discovered. I sent a [row galley with a] twelve-Pounder out to join him if he came within sight; if not to stay out and return by night to get back by the time tis dark. If the Enemy see Col Darby they will probably hasten back to St John to give the Alarm that the whole is advancing. The 12-Pounder returned at night.

16th. I had a letter from Capt Prescott of the 11th that he got to New York the 8th at night; the Packet boat arrived the 7th, and he was just going on board when he had wrote to me. A Deserter came in of the Regt of Languedoc; came from the four Vessels the Enemy has below les Isles au quatre Vents [Four Brothers Islands]. . .He says he was all winter in Garrison at Ticonderoga, that when we arrived there there were the two Batt[alion]s of Berry, one of La Reine & the Pic[k]ets of Languedoc, Bearn, LaSarre, & Roussillon, which Pic[k]ets were their winter Garrison, who were joined likewise this Spring by Canadians & some of La Marine; that when they quitted the Fort the Officer who commanded and another Officer were forced to land on the opposite side on our cannonading them, and they were three days in the woods and had seen some of our men, I suppose the Rangers I sent out; that Mons [Brigadier General François-Charles de] Bourl[a]maque is encamped at the Isle au Noix which is about six leagues on this side St Johns and the River Narrows, that he is making an Intrenchment all round & has near 100 Cannon; that the four Vessels are La Vigilante of 10 Pieces of Cannon 6 & 4-Pounders, a Schooner, a Sloop called Musquelongy. A Captain of a Man of war commands, Monsieur De le Bras has 2 brass 12-Pounders and 6 Iron six-Pounders, La Brochette of 8 Guns 6 & 4-Pounders com[m]anded by Mons. Regal, an Officer of Man of war, L'E[s]turgeon of 8 Guns of 6-& 4-Pounders. All of them have Swivels mounted. Three were built this year; one is an old one, the Pic[k]ets of Bearn & La Sarre on board, and there is another repairing.* As he told me the Officers and men went on shore to fish I sent out Capt [James] Tute [of the Rangers] and forty men to try to catch some. Sent to Capt Loring to come to me that we may prepare force enough to be superior to these Sloops. Col Bradstreet came in the Afternoon. All going well at the Landing Place I ordered him to Albany to look into the forwarding provisions up the Mohawk River for winter Garrisons at Niagara, Oswego & la Gallette.

17th. As all the timber was brought in from the opposite shore I ordered back this day the Company of Grenadiers & light Infantry. Capt. Loring came to me and said the Sawmill would go in two or three days. I told him the force the Enemy had and he said the Brig he was building was not sufficient strength without some further help, and with Mr. Ord & him we concluded the quickest and best thing to be done, as the boats we have will not carry the 24-Pounders on this Lake, is to build a sort of Radeau for carrying the six 24-Pounders which can be done in ten days. This is Ord's favourite Scheme but Capt Loring thought it likewise the best thing to be done.**

27th. The three little Forts I had ordered to be erected by the Grenadiers, light Infantry and Gages are getting on very well. I received a Letter from Col Montresor*** that the Post near Fort Edward had taken four more French Deserters who had been out sixteen-days. . .

September 1st. Sergeant [Joseph] Hopkins returned from his Scout and brought in three men of La Marine, that he took opposite to the Island [Isle-aux-Noix], whose intelligence agrees with what I have had before. All the [French] troops that went from Ticonderoga & this Place are there, besides some Canadians who were working at the Batteries & Lines on the Island. When the Garrisons got down there their

*The 10-gun schooner *La Vigilante*, under the command of Joseph Payant St. Onge, was built by Nicolas-René Levasseur at St. Jean, Quebec, in 1757. The Levasseur shipyard, with assistant shipbuilders Pierre Levasseur (son of Nicolas-René) and Louis-Pierre Poulin de Courval Cressé, constructed several 65-ton sloops in 1758-1759, including the 8-gun *La Musquelongy*, sailing under Joannis-Galand d'Olabaratz (Laubaras), the 8-gun *La Brochette*, commanded by Sieur Rigal, and the 8-gun *L'Esturgeon*. The sloops, also called "xebecs," exhibited lanteen sails, poor sailing characteristics, and were described by one French officer as "ships which do not resemble anything."[67]

**Major Thomas Ord had supervised construction of two large radeaux at Lake George in 1758 and 1759. Ord's requirements for the 84-foot radeau, which included 60-foot oak planks, taxed the capacity of the Ticonderoga sawmill.[68]

***James Montresor (1702-1776) entered the Royal Artillery in 1727 and arrived in America in 1754 as Major General Edward Braddock's chief engineer. He was promoted to lieutenant colonel and director of engineers in 1758. Serving in northern New York from 1756 to 1759, Montresor planned Fort Stanwix and supervised construction of Fort George. He returned to England in 1760 and subsequently was granted 10,000 acres adjacent to Otter Creek (Panton, Vermont). His son, John Montresor, also served as an engineer in the French and Indian War and later for the British in the American Revolution.

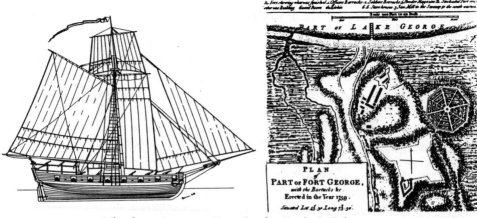

The sloop *Boscawen*. Drawing by Kevin J. Crisman
(Lake Champlain Maritime Museum)

"Plan of Part of Fort George with the Barracks &c. Erected in the Year 1759" showing
one completed bastion, a stockaded fort near the lake, and a garden. From *A Set of Plans
and Forts in America: Reduced from Actual Surveys* by Mary Ann Rocque (1765).

situation is very strong, & the deserters say they have a hundred Cannon.* That
cant be, but they have certainly got together all they could from different corners,
and I suppose some from the Ships that got up the River before Mr [Royal Navy
Rear Admiral Philip] Durell, for before that they wanted Guns. If those Ships had
not got up Canada at this instant would probably be ours, as it would have given a
General Despair.

Captain [Hugh] McKenzie returned from a Scouting Party & thought two
Rangers & a man of Gages had deserted him, as he lost them in the woods.

2nd. As the French deserters and the Sergeants account of a new Sloop agreed
that it is launched, pierced for 16 Guns, & finishing as fast as possible,** I ordered
Major Ord to prepare some fire darts to screw in, and I'll send to try & burn it. The
Enemy is trying to have a superior Force by water. I sent to Capt. Loring to come
to me that I may build a Sloop as soon as the Brig is finished and that everything
may be prepared as fast as possible.

3rd. Capt Loring came here. I settled with him to build a Sloop of 16 Guns [the
Boscawen]. Some Irons of the Sawmill broke which I ordered to be repaired. The
Guns I sent for from Fort Edward arrived at the landing Place. I sent rafts for them.

4th. It rained the whole day that no work could be done. I sent out Sergt Hopkins
with 4 Rangers, two volunteers, an officer of Ruggles & one of Whitings, and four
men who had been Sailors & the best swimmers I could find to take five darts &
hand-carcasses [canvas containers with combustible material] & try to burn the
Sloop at Isle au Noix. Had two burnt, one fire dart & one carcass to show them how
it should be done.

---

*Salah Barnard, an officer from Deerfield, Massachusetts, recorded that Sergeant Hopkins observed "a
strong breastwork with fifty (or more) Cannon. . .While he lay within a small distance of the
Island. . .he Saw one Brig & three Sloop[s] on the Side [of] the Island and one Large Brig on the Stocks
almost ready to launch."[69]

**The new sloop was the 65-ton *Waggon*, mounting six 4-pound cannon.[70]

8th. I had a Letter from Col Montresor in answer to my questions about his works, that he had raised 72,960 cubical feet, that to finish the Fort [George] will take 494,100 cubical feet and two more working Seasons to do it. I would not hesitate a moment about bringing the workmen to this Place and ordered him to shut up the Citadel Bastion by a retrenchment at the Gorge, that it will then be a small Fort of itself which with the one by the Lake side will be sufficient, as that Post is no longer a Frontier, and the Fort may be finished hereafter.*

9th. Capt Starks** returned with his Party from No 4 [Charlestown, New Hampshire]; fourteen of his men deserted, six left sick behind. He said he had made the Road & that there were no mountains or swamps to pass & as he came back it measured 77 miles. It may be much shortened. I brought in all the wood I could against winter for the Garrison; 80 Oxen from Albany, fresh Provisions now & then and a constant supply of Spruce beer kept the Army in good health & they work well which helps much towards the health of the Provincials, who if left to themselves would eat fryed Pork and lay in their tents all day long.***

10th. I rowed round the bay on the west of the Fort and to the ends of the Roads that are terminated by the bay. At my return I found a Flag of Truce was come from Mons Burlemaque by a Capt of La Reine whom Capt [Daniel?] Osborne who was out with the Guard boat had stop[p]ed 9 miles off & sent me the Letters. One from Mons Montcalm of no date, acquainting me that Capt Kennedy and Hamilton were Prisoners & talking of the Exchange of Prisoners, an Excuse to send to see what we are about and to send several Letters to their officers who are Prisoners; a Letter from Bougainville† to Capt Abercromby dated the 30th August at Quebec so that the Town was not taken then. I answered the Letters & sent Capt Abercromby to

---

*On September 8 Amherst sent a letter to Colonel James Montresor, the engineer at Fort George, with orders to "finish the Citadel Bastion, retrench [cut off] it at the Gorge. . .that it may form a small Fort of itself. . .The Hospital maybe given up. . .a small Garrison in the Fort by the Lake with barracks within it, added to the. . .Citadel Bastion will do for the present."[71] Montresor's journal noted on September 10 "a letter from General Amherst with an approbation of my proposal in finishing the Citadel, Bastion Powder Magazine &c & Barracks for 150 men."[72] In 1759 Fort George consisted of the new stone fort under construction as well as a stockaded structure closer to the lake which Reverend Henry True observed in July: "building a fort with stone and lime, where ye old breastwork was, encompassing about 2 or 3 acres of foundation is mostly laid about 40 rods from ye water; by ye water a new Redoubt built to command ye Lake."[73]

**John Stark (1728-1822), an early friend of Robert Rogers and his brothers, was briefly a captive of the St. Francis Indians in 1752. Stark served as a lieutenant and captain in Rogers' Independent Company of Rangers from 1755 to November 1759. During the American Revolution he participated in the battles at Bunker Hill, Trenton, and Princeton, and experienced his most notable success leading the Americans to victory at the Battle of Bennington in August 1777. Shortly after his promotion to major general in 1783, Stark retired from the army.

***Although provincial troops were crucial to the victory over France, British officers had little respect for them. By the same token, provincial soldiers were often not impressed by the leadership of British officers, particularly during the 1758 Ticonderoga expedition.

†Louis Antoine de Bougainville (1729-1811) was a Renaissance man with experience as a soldier, sailor, explorer, and academic, and was the author of several books, including one on calculus which resulted in his election to the Royal Society of London. Bougainville acted as an aide-de-camp (1756-1758) to General Louis-Joseph de Montcalm and served in North America until 1760. He later joined the French navy and made a voyage around the world (1766-1769). During the American Revolution Bougainville commanded the vanguard of the French fleet in the 1780 battle near Chesapeake Bay. He was later appointed a senator and grand officer of the Legion of Honour by Napoleon.

the officer with them sending at the same time a large Packet from the Prisoner officers to their Relations, &c.

11th. Twas morning before Capt Abercromby got back. Capt Disserat of the Regt de la Reine who came with the Flag of Truce said Kennedy was taken by some of the St Francois Indians who were hunting.

12th. As Capt Kennedy's Journey was now over I ordered a detachment of 220 chosen men under the command of Major Rogers to go & destroy the St Francois Indian Settlements and the French settlements on the South side of the River St Lawrence, not letting any one but Major Rogers know what about or where he was going.*

14th. Sergt Hopkins with his Party came this morning. He attempted to burn the Vessel, the 11th, at ten at night.** Had got the combustibles to the bow & one man was screwing a dart in while another was preparing another, but I suppose they made a noise for a man on board discovered them and alarmed the Guard on board & the whole Camp. They threw something overboard, fired & the Guards of the Camp fired. The men got off and were not hurt but left the combustibles at the bow and lost two Blanketts. If they had more punctually obeyed my orders and done it at two in the morning they probably had succeeded. Capt Abercromby came back. Ticonderoga will soon be finished but the Saw mill is often out of repair.*** I sent a Lieut to Fort George to bring all the masons from thence tha[t] can be spared as Lt Col Eyre† says he can now employ them. One Indian came back sick from M Roger's Party.

*On the evening of September 13, 190 hand-picked Rangers, provincials, and regulars departed in 17 whaleboats for St. Francis, a village located at the junction of the St. Francis River and the St. Lawrence, approximately 50 miles north of Montreal. Twenty-three days later, Rogers and his men burst into the Indian dwellings at St. Francis with bayonets fixed on their muskets and tomahawks flying. The village was burned to the ground. Pursued by the Indians, Rogers made a harrowing escape but 49 of his men died. The account of the St. Frances raid later became the subject of Kenneth Roberts' novel *Northwest Passage*.

**The sloop that Sergeant Joseph Hopkins had been ordered to destroy at Isle-aux-Noix was probably the 65-ton *Waggon*.[74] Hopkins also reported that "the Enemy does not intend to rig her as She is laid across the Channel wt Six Guns run out on one Side two Portholes Shut up pickets Drove in the Channel from the Island & opposite Shore to the Prow & Stern of the Vessels."[75]

***Ebenezer Dibble, an ensign in a Connecticut regiment, remarked on August 30 that " the fort [at Ticonderoga] is in a fine way for. . .Repair ye Barracks is a Mending." On October 5 he recorded barracks 98 feet long with a 60-foot width "Stone and fram[e]d 173 fe[e]t Long and 46 wide. . .one 190 fe[e]t Long and 50 wid[e] of ston[e]. . .and a mag[a]z[i]n[e] 209 fe[e]t Long and 30 wid[e] all in small Ro[o]ms and Cas[e]ments from End to End and Bom[b] pro[o]f. In the No[rth] East Corner of the fort a Larg[e] Bak[e] hous[e] and 2 ovens sa[i]d hous[e] is Bom[b] pro[o]f 32 fe[e]t Long and 26 wide arch[ed] over." Orders had also been given to "Raise a Store Hous[e]" 92 feet long, 39 wide and 34 high.[76]

†William Eyre, a captain in the 44th Regiment of Foot, served as an engineer with General William Johnson at Lake George in 1755. Eyre's management of the artillery at the Battle of Lake George was instrumental in the English victory, resulting in his promotion to major. Eyre supervised the construction of Fort William Henry, as well as Fort Edward. In command of Fort William Henry in March 1757, Eyre's garrison successfully resisted a French attack, consisting of 1,600 men under François-Pierre de Rigaud de Vaudreuil, brother of the governor general of New France. Eyre led the 44th Regiment at Abercromby's defeat in 1758, winning a promotion to lieutenant colonel nine days later. As Amherst's acting chief engineer in 1759, he was charged with the supervision of the reconstruction of the fort at Ticonderoga and the new fortress at Crown Point. Later in the year Eyre was sent by Amherst to Fort Niagara, rejoining Amherst's campaign against Montreal in 1760. On his journey home in 1765, Eyre drowned when his ship sank just before reaching the English coastline.

19th. A man of the Royal Highlanders and one of Montgomerys were brought in by seven Rangers, this makes 40 men returned of Rogers, two officers included, the two men wounded by a firelock accidentally going off. The Royal Highlander d[i]ed soon after he was brought in.

20th. The weather beginning to be cold. The fence and blockhouses forwarding apace by which all the Cattle will be kept secure, and it will be next to impossible for any small partys to creep in to pick off any men; the Barracks begun in the Fort.

22nd. I spoke to the com[m]anding officers of Regts to talk to their officers that they might keep their men at work

Drawing of radeau *Ligonier* after Thomas Davies' original. From *The Magazine of American History* 1882.

to their Business, as we must finish before winter Quarters.* The Provincials begin to grow sickly and lose some men; they are growing homesick but much less so than ever they have been any other Campaigns. They want Cloaks to keep them warm & some regulations that would not cost the Province so much as their extravagant Enlistments, and would save many men. The numbers at work every day are 3241 men, Labourers & Artificers. This should make quick dispatch but the work is great; and at the same time the works are carrying on at Fort George & the Repairs at Ticonderoga which are all most finished and the two Vessels building for which three Regiments are employed at Ticonderoga.

26th. The Lake is risen surprisingly, full three feet perpendicular; forced us to move the Magazine for provisions, the Shot, Shells &c which were on the Shore. This may be occasioned from the Pickets which the Enemy has drove in across both Channels by the Isle au Noix.**

29th. Lt [Thomas] Moncrief [1st Regiment of Foot] returned from Ticonderoga; had fixed with Capt Loring that he should carry all the provisions he conveniently could in the Brig & Sloop. Capt Loring promised to have them ready next week. In the Afternoon the Radeau was Launched & christened Ligonier. She is 84 feet long

---

*Fort Crown Point, in fact, would become the largest military fortification built by the British in North America in the eighteenth century. Designed for 4,000 troops, the main pentagon-shaped fort encompassed six acres. Three Georgian-style stone barracks, a guard house, armory, three redoubts or smaller forts (Gage's Redoubt, Light Infantry Redoubt, and Grenadier Redoubt), storehouses, a ten-acre garden, and a village were on the grounds.

**Lake Champlain flows north into the outlet of the Richelieu River. The crude barrier of pickets that the French placed at Isle-aux-Noix was not the likely cause of the rise in the water level; the heavy rains feeding tributaries into the lake were a more probable reason.

& 20 feet broad on the Platform, where the Guns run out she is 23 feet, & to carry six 24-Pounders.*

[October] 4th. Sent Lt Stevens to No 4 to take up some provisions to Wells's River, in case Major Rogers should return that way [from St. Francis]. Ordered a quantity of bread to be baked at Ticonderoga as soon as the flo[u]r arrives there that I may take a weeks bread with me, but I hear Capt Loring will not be ready as soon as he last promised. The contrary winds have hindered the floats of timber from getting here which has a little retarded the works.

5th. Two of the block houses got up for the security of the Environs. As the numbers of the Sick of the Provincials increased and several will not be fit for further Service this Campaign, I ordered them to be visited by the Director & a Surgeon of the Hospital, that the useless may be sent home. Capt [James] Dal[y]el[l] [60th Regiment of Foot] who was out in the Guard boat brought in a canoe that a Sergt of his had sp[i]ed out on the shore about eight miles down the Lake. As this may be likely [from] a small [French] Party to go to the mountains to try to see what is doing here & likewise to spy out what preparations are making at Ticonderoga I ordered a Party of 25 men to way lay them.**

9th. Sent out two Scouts. A Sergt & 6 men to go to the windmill [Windmill Point, east of Rouses Point] & so on the East side of Isle au Noix; & a Sergt and six men to point au Fer to go on the West side towards St Johns. Both the Sergts to try all they can to get me a Prisoner for Intelligence as I can have none but from thence, & the Sergts to meet me on the Lake. I likewise sent Lt Meredith of Gages with six men of that Regt to go to the Ch[az]ly River, five or six miles on this side the Point au Fer, to try to find out a carrying Place which has been made use of between that Place and Chat[e]augay of about 4 miles. The Enemy can have no suspicion of anyone being sent there; besides their Indians must be sent after Rogers. If this carrying Place is found out I may be sure when I make a sh[o]w of attacking the Isle au Noix that I can send a Party to destroy Casnawago,*** and very probably may surprise Montreal. I was forced to work the fat Oxen to keep on the works; near 300 Oxen employed. . . 200 men of [Colonel Abijah] Willards [Massachusetts] Reg [iment] arrived for the Service of the boats of the Artillery. Woosters Regt must help carry on the works & I shall not take an Artificer of the Regulars away, & leave all the Provincials except 200 for the labour. Major Ord tr[i]ed the Radeau [Ligonier] against the wind; she would not do very well. I hope the Brig & Sloop will be here to morrow.

10th. The Q[uarter] Masters having brought the flannel [cloaks] &c to the landing place I sent batteaus from each Regt. to bring it up. The Duke of Cumberland Brig arrived and anchored out of sight of any partys that may be on the mountains.†

---

*The radeau Ligonier, similar in design to the Land Tortoise and Invincible, was a unique flat-bottomed, seven-sided floating battery with upper bulwarks that angled over the crew which a contemporary newspaper called "a Floating Castle. . . contriv'd so that tis impossible for the Enemy to board her."[78]

**Brigadier General François-Charles de Bourlamaque also learned from deserters of the new British vessels and the on-going construction at Crown Point.[79]

***Caughnawaga, or St. François Xavier, was a fortified Indian mission village on the south side of the St. Lawrence River opposite Lachine (near Montreal).

†Although the 155-ton brig Duke of Cumberland had been launched on August 30, Captain Joshua Loring required more than a month to finish and rig the vessel. The brig, manned by 70 seamen and

I kept the men working all day at the Fort but had everything ready to set out so soon as the Sloop comes. Capt Loring seems to think he will not be strong enough with the Brig & Sloop, but he shall try to cut the Enemy off from Isle au Noix which is the only sure way of taking them, & if I send Guns in boats with him he will wait to get them up & the Enemys Vessels will escape.

11th. The Sloop arrived* & the Q Masters and Detachment I had sent to bring the things from the Landing place. I ordered all the Stores that were wanted on board the Sloop & the Troops to embark that I may get away the first instant I can, called the commanding officers of the Provincials to recommend the running of the works under Lt Col Eyre with all the help they could give him,** and I left the command of the Troops to Br Gen Ruggles. . .Capt Schomberg arrived. He heard I wanted an officer to fight the Sloops, but Loring very wisely did not ch[oo]se to give up the command & I would not order him to as Schomberg has come without orders & has left his Ship which is to convey all the Masts, which may be of great consequence.*** The Duke of Cumberland Brigg & Boscawen Sloop I think must have force enough to beat the Enemys Sloops. I gave all necessary orders toward it† & got ammunition on board the Sloop & ordered the Troops to strike their Tents, load their Batteaus that I might proceed directly. We sailed in four Columns with Gages for the Advanced [Guard]. The lst Column Grenadiers & light Infantry; 2nd Column the Brigade of the Royal; 3rd Column all the Artillery Stores; 4th Column the Brigade of Forbes; the Rangers & Indians forming the Rear Guard in a line to cover the Rear of the Column as Gages did the Front.

The Artillery was divided, Ligonier Radeau Center in the Front of the Center Columns; 1 Howitzer in the Front of the 2nd and another in Front of the 3rd Columns; a 12-Pounder in Front of the Ist & another in front of the 4th Column; a third 12-Pounder brought up the rear of the whole.‡

The boats for the Heads of Columns got out at two o'clock and the Columns formed. The Sloop & Brigg got out about 4 o'clock & sailed with a fair wind. I kept rowing gently all night having a light at the Radeau for the Columns to dress by it, but in the night some of the R[oyal] Highlanders mistook & followed a light that they saw either on the Brig or Sloop and at daybreak

60 marines, mounted 20 cannon, consisting of six 6-pounders and twelve 4-pounders and 20 swivelguns. Amherst had to borrow the cannon from other posts and vessels, including two 6-pounders from the sloop *Halifax* on Lake George.[80]

*The 80-foot, 115-ton *Boscawen*, commanded by Lieutenant Alexander Grant, carried four 6-pound cannon and twelve 4-pounders with 22 swivels and a crew of 60 seamen and 50 marines.[81]

**Although the Rangers and some provincial seamen were taken on the expedition, Amherst ordered the provincial regiments to work on the new fort at Crown Point. One Rhode Island provincial noted: "We Poor Provincials Must Stay to finish it while General Amherst with the Regulars is Gone to make masters themselves of the Lake and S[t.] Johns and with [Major General James] Wolf[e] and [Brigadier Thomas] Gage to Share the Glory of the conquest of Canada."[82]

***Alexander Schomberg, a captain in the Royal Navy, left the H.M.S. *Diana* without orders at Quebec to take command of Amherst's Champlain fleet, but Joshua Loring refused to step aside.

†"To obtain the free and uninterrupted Navigation of Lake Champlain," Amherst ordered Captain Joshua Loring "to take or Destroy the Enemies Vessels. . . get passed the Enemies Sloops if possible unperceived, if not, you will at Events do Your utmost to come up with and Attack them. . .cut off the Enemies communication between the Post at the Isle aux Noi[x] and their vessels."[83]

‡The flotilla included the radeau *Ligonier*, two smaller radeaux, three row galleys, bateaux, whaleboats, and several other boats.[84]

Detail of "A South View of the New Fortress at Crown Point" showing
the sloop *Boscawen* and the brig *Duke of Cumberland* at anchor.
Watercolor by Thomas Davies (1759). (Winterthur Museum)

12th. I heard some Guns; concluded our Vessels were engaged with the Enemy
& Major [Henry] Gladwin sent to me to let me know [where] they were. I made all
the sail with the Radeau [*Ligonier*] I could, and some time after a boat of the R
Highlanders came back who informed me of the mistake that had happened & that
the firing was on them as they went to the Sloops, taking them to, be our own, &
Lt Mackay a sergt & 10 men were taken, & the Enemy after taking the men out set
the batteau adrift, & Major [John] Reid said our Brig & Sloop were certainly got a
great way beyond the Enemys.* Soon after we saw the Enemys Sloops, I ordered
the Batteaus into one Column on the Western Shore & the Artillery boats all a
Breast, & Major Gladwin to keep a watch upon them. Towards night it grew bad
weather and the men being fatigued with rowing all night I took Col Schuylers
advice & got into a bay to be covered from the wind & it blew very hard.** Ordered
the men on shore to boil their pots & rest themselves by walking about. In the night
a man in a dream cr[i]ed out murder & another in his sleep fired his piece & burnt
a Sergt of Grenadiers very much.

13th. It blew a quite contrary wind & storm continued all day; tho' I was in a
bay I was forced to move several of the boats.

14th. At noon I had a letter from Capt Loring that on the 12th at day break at
which time he imagined he might be 45 miles down the Lake the Schooner [*La
Vigilante*] with two topsails appeared coming toward him and he immediately gave

*Following the light in the stern of the brig *Duke of Cumberland* instead of the radeau *Ligonier*, troops
in bateaux from the Highlander regiment found themselves among the French sloops at Four Brothers
Islands. Ensign MacKay (also spelled McKoy) and 11-20 men were taken prisoner by the French.[85]

**The army landed at Ligonier Bay, according to Commissary Wilson's orderly book.[86] A report in
the December 1759 issue of *The London Magazine* noted that Amherst had "ordered the rangers on an
island."[87]

chase. She hauled her wind & stood in between two Islands & unfortunately run aground just as he was within gunshot & soon after the Sloop [*Boscawen*] had the same fate. The Sloop was got off without taking anything out, but they were forced to take out 8 Guns & all the Troops out of the Brig [*Duke of Cumberland*] when she was got off likewise without any damage.* He then stood off to proceed down the Lake but the wind came to the Nor[th]ward and he at that instant discovered the three sloops between him & the Army, so gave chase to bring them to action before night & drove them into a bay & anchored at the mouth in order to prevent their getting out. At night I received another Letter from Capt Loring that the Enemy had sunk two of their Vessels in the bay & run the third on Shore & that he had ordered Capt [Alexander] Grant to try to save all the Guns, rigging stores &c.**

It continued to blow such a storm that the men who brought me the Letter said 'twas impossible for them to get back against it. The Water run as high as some seas in a Gale of wind. I could not send a boat to the Rangers or to Gages light Infantry. I sent out two Partys of 20 men to reconnoitre round about; the Pickets lay out advanced & the men made some Hutts pitched some Tents & made great fires.

15th. It has blown a storm with rain all night and the continuance of it renders the Lake much agitated so that it is impracticable to pass at present, but I hope it will change soon.

16th. It froze in the night and this morning the wind blows as hard as ever and has continued all day. This would be nothing if it was a month earlier, but every day is a great loss of time at present when I cant stir from hence. In the evening Capt Arnot of Gages brought back a Party of 20 men & an officer that I had sent by Land to the Regt to see if it was practicable for them to send for their Provisions by Land. Ensign Campbell found it more than 20 miles & Major Gladwin sent me word if the wind continued so contrary that no boats could go to him he would bring the Regiment here.

17th. The same contrary wind continued and it froze though it does not blow so hard. In the afternoon the two whale boats I dispatched to Capt Loring on the 13th returned, said they had tr[i]ed since that day all they could to get down but could not & were glad to get back without being drowned. Gages Regt came in. I sent out a Party every day round the Camp at some distance tho' it is impossible the Enemy can attempt anything here.

18th. Before day break I had a boat from Crown Point with Letters from Br Gen Gage from Oswego with Intelligence of three Prisoners taken near la Gallette, that Quebec was taken on the 13th of Sept, & an Hour after I had a Letter from the

---

*Captain Joshua Loring had pursued *La Vigilante*, commanded by Joseph Payant St. Onge, into the shallow water between the Sister Islands (west side of South Hero Island) where both the *Duke of Cumberland* and *Boscawen* were grounded.[88]

**Captain Loring trapped Joannis-Galand d'Olabaratz (Laubaras), commander of the French sloops *La Musquelongy*, *La Brochette* and *L'Esturgeon*, against the western shore near present-day Cliff Haven, adjacent to Crab Island. Brigadier General François-Charles de Bourlamaque at Isle-aux-Noix later reported to the Department of War that the "Commander of the Xebecs, considering it impossible for him to escape the English fleet, determined to sink the vessels at nightfall and escape with the crews through the woods. The prisoners he had taken assure us that the English army. . .was ten thousand strong."[89] In a letter dated October 18 Amherst reported that the lieutenant who had been captured by the French near Four Brothers Islands played a role in d'Olabaratz's decision to scuttle his fleet by overstating Loring's naval force: "[by] greatly magnifying our naval strength, they had come to a Resolution. . .to Sink or Drive their Vessels on Shore and then to Abandon them."[90]

Lt Governor [James De Lancey] of New York confirming the news & acquainting him of the loss of General Wolfe. This will of course bring Mons [Governor Pierre de Rigaud] Vaudreuil & the whole Army to Montreal so that I shall decline my intended operations & get back to Crown Point where I hear works go on but slowly.* One of the Enemys Sloops was so far repaired of all the damage done to her that she sailed this day down the Lake with the Brig & Sloop**. . . I sent Capt Dalyel[l] with 100 of Gages and as many Rangers to Capt Loring to assist in looking into any of the bays for him, that the Schooner may not escape and the wind being come to Southward I proceeded down the Lake to the Place where the French Sloops were sunk which I suppose may be 45 miles from Crown Point, landed the Troops on an Island at night made Fires & boiled the pot.***

19th. The wind being northerly, and an appearance of winter set in, and that it would take me perhaps ten days more to get to the Isle au Noix, which will now answer no End to make a sh[o]w of attacking, as my intention of sending a Detachment to destroy [Caugh]nawaga, La Prairie and surprise Montreal can no longer be executed. I ordered the Troops back to Crown Point to finish the works there as much as possible before we go into Winter Quarters, and we sailed & rowed back to Ligonier bay where we lay all night.

20th. I left the Radeau [*Ligonier*] with the Rangers & proceeded with the Troops for Crown Point; ordered the light Infantry & Grenadiers who were in the whale boats to row on that they might reach it by night & I stop[p]ed with the two brigades & artillery Stores about 12 miles from Crown Point & lay on the Eastern Shore.

21st. I set out again in the morning & arrived at Crown Point about two in the afternoon. The Grenadiers & light Infantry were at work at their Forts[redoubts], and the Fortress was going on pretty well.

Notes

1. J. Clarence Webster, ed., *The Journal of Jeffery Amherst* (Toronto: The Ryerson Press, 1931), 151.
2. Daniel John Beattie, "General Jeffery Amherst and the Conquest of Canada, 1758-1760," (Ph.D. diss. Duke University, 1975), 7-8.
3. Webster, 2; J.C. Long, *Lord Jeffery Amherst: A Soldier of the King* (New York: The Macmillan Company, 1933), 16; *Dictionary of Canadian Biography*, Volume 4 (Toronto: University of Toronto Press, 1979), 20; Lawrence Shaw Mayo, *Jeffery Amherst: A Biography* (New York: Longmans, Green and Co., 1916), 8.

*While the lateness of the season induced Amherst to return to Crown Point, the possibility that Bourlamaque's troops at Isle-aux-Noix could be reinforced by new troops from Montreal also influenced the decision.

**The *Musquelongy* was repaired, arriving at Crown Point on October 26. Lieutenant Alexander Grant was dispatched the next day with the sloop *Boscawen*, *La Musquelongy* (renamed the *Amherst* by Loring), and "two small Redows [radeaux]" to raise *La Brochette* and *L'Esturgeon*.[91] Grant succeeded in weighing the two sloops, but two brass cannon were missing from their carriages.[92] Two brass 12-pounders were among the British armament that had been captured by Montcalm's forces at Fort William Henry in 1757 and later mounted on the French sloops. The cannon remained on the bottom of Lake Champlain until 1968 when a swivel deck gun and two elegantly engraved brass 12-pounders were raised. After a lengthy legal controversy over ownership, the cannon were acquired by New York State and placed on display at the Crown Point Visitor Center and the Clinton Community College in Plattsburgh.

***The army camped at Schuyler Island, according to Commissary Wilson's orderly book.[93]

4. J. S. McLennan, *Louisbourg From Its Foundation to Its Fall 1713-1758* (1918; reprint ed., Halifax: The Book Room Limited, 1979), 292; See also Mayo, 89.

5. Webster, 86; See also Beattie, 91-92; Long, 77.

6. Webster, 92.

7. Caleb Rea, "The Journal of Dr. Caleb Rea, Written During the Expedition Against Ticonderoga in 1758," *Essex Institute Historical Collections* 18(1881): 199; See also John Cleaveland, "Journal of Rev. John Cleaveland Kept While Chaplain in the French and Indian War 1758-1759," *The Bulletin of the Fort Ticonderoga Museum* 10 (no. 3, 1959): 229.

8. Public Record Office, London, 285/1, War Office Records 34/64, fol. 198; See also fol. 196.

9. For an excellent graphic depiction of these forts and posts see Gary S. Zaboly, ed., "A Royal Artillery Officer with Amherst: The Journal of Captain-Lieutenant Henry Skinner 1 May - 28 July 1759," *The Bulletin of the Fort Ticonderoga Museum* 15 (1993): 362; See also Webster, 116, 119, 123, 125; PRO, CO 5/56, University Publications of America microfilm reel 4, frame 497.

10. Webster, 125; See also James Montresor, "Journals of Col. James Montresor," *Collections of the New-York Historical Society* 14 (1881): 78-79; Gertrude Selwyn Kimball, ed., *Correspondence of William Pitt* (New York: The Macmillan Company, 1906), Volume 1, 421.

11. Joshua Loring Account, Abercromby Papers, AB 802, Huntington Library, San Marino, California.

12. *Boston Gazette and Country Journal*, 28 August 1758; Salah Barnard, "Journal of Major Salah Barnard," MS Fort Ticonderoga Thompson-Pell Research Center.

13. Cleaveland, 229; See also Henry Champion, "Accounts & Journal of Captain Henry Champion of Colchester, Campaign of 1758," Connecticut State Library, Hartford, Connecticut; Rea, 199; Christopher Comstock, "Diary of Christopher Comstock 1758-59," Connecticut State Library.

14. Zaboly, 379; For the original account see Henry Skinner, "Proceedings of the Army Under the Command of General Amherst, for the Year 1759," *The Universal Magazine* (December 1759): 285; See also Lemuel Wood, "Diaries Kept by Lemuel Wood, of Boxford," *Essex Institute Historical Collections* 19 (1882): 143; Russell P. Bellico, *Chronicles of Lake George : Journeys in War and Peace* (Fleischmanns, N.Y.: Purple Mountain Press,1995), 132.

15. Commissary Wilson, *Commissary Wilson's Orderly Book, 1759* (Albany: J. Munsell, 1857), 89; John Hawks, *Orderly Book and Journal of Major John Hawks 1759-1760* (Society of Colonial Wars, 1911), 43; "Line of Vessels on Lake George under General Amherst, 1759," Public Record Office, London, Colonial Office Records 5/56, fol. 70.

16. Zaboly, 374-75, 378; Wood, 19: 149.

17. Captain John Knox, *An Historical Journal of the Campaigns in North America*, Volume 1 (1769; edited by Arthur G. Doughty, 1914-1916; reprint ed., Freeport, N.Y.: Books for Libraries Press, 1970), 485.

18. Zaboly, 381.

19. "Diary of a Soldier at Crown Point, etc., 1759," French and Indian War Collection, Octavo 2, American Antiquarian Society, Worcester, Ma.; See also Barnard, p.n.a.

20. Webster, 137; Zaboly, 378.

21. Zaboly, 381.

22. Hawks, 41-44; Wilson 87-90; Josiah Goodrich, "The Josiah Goodrich Orderbook," *The Bulletin of the Fort Ticonderoga Museum* 14 (Summer 1981): 56-57; Thomas Mante, *The History of the Late War in North-America* (1772; reprint ed., New York: Research Reprints, Inc., n.d.) 210-11; PRO, CO 5/56, UP microfilm reel 4, frames 505-6.

23. Wood, 19: 144-45; See also Henry True, *Journal and Letters of Rev. Henry True* (Marion, OH: Star Press, 1900), 10; Constantine Hardy, "Extracts from the Journal of Constantine Hardy," *New-England Historical and Genealogical Register* 60(1906): 237; Samuel Merriman, "Journal of Samuel Merriman," in *A History of Deerfield*, by George Sheldon (1895-96; reprint ed., Somersworth, N.H.: New Hampshire Publishing Company, 1972), 664; Eli Forbush's account, which implies that Amherst's fleet had anchored at Sabbath Day Point, has often been misinterpreted. Eli Forbush, "Eli Forbush to the Reverend Mr. Steven Williams, August 4, 1759," in *Fort Ticonderoga: A Short History* by S. H. P. Pell (Ticonderoga: Fort Ticonderoga Museum, 1978), 48; See also Eli Forbush, "A Letter from Carillion, August 4th, 1759," *The Bulletin of the Fort Ticonderoga Museum* 1 (July 1929): 19-23.

24. Wood, 19: 147.

25. William Amherst, *Journal of William Amherst in America*, ed., John Clarence Webster (London: Butler & Tannes Ltd., 1927), 47.

26. Ibid., 51.

27. Ibid., 52.

28. "Major General Amherst to Mr. Secretary Pitt, dated Crown- Point, August 5, 1759," *The London Magazine* (September 1759): 499; See also *The Universal Magazine* (September 1759): 147; PRO, CO 5/56, UP microfilm reel 4, frame 516; Perhaps Amherst was counting the ovens in the French village. J. Duncan Campbell, "Investigations at the French Village Fort Ticonderoga, N.Y.," *The Bulletin of the Fort Ticonderoga Museum* 10 (1958): 145.

29. Wood, 19: 185-86; John Hurbut, "The Journal of a Colonial Soldier," *The Magazine of American History* 39(1893), 396.

30. Forbush, 51.

31. Wood, 19: 148-49.

32. James Henderson, "James Henderson's Journal," in *The First Century of the Colonial Wars in the Commonwealth of Massachusetts* (Boston: Society of Colonial Wars, Mass., 1944), 206.

33. PRO 285/1, WO 34/64, fol. 157.

34. *Boston Gazette and Country Journal*, 8 October 1759.

35. Montresor, 99-100; PRO 285/1, WO 34/64, fols. 215, 164-65, 218.

36. PRO 285/1, WO 34/64, fol. 212.

37. Merriman, 666; Amherst's journal implies that 12-pound cannon were mounted on the row galleys. Webster, 179; See also PRO 293/3, WO 34/81, fol. 66.

38. "Account of the Expedition on Lake Champlain," *The London Magazine* (December 1759): 662; Thomas Mante wrote that the army stopped at "a commodious bay on the western shore, where all except the Rangers landed... the Rangers were disembarked on a neighboring island." Mante 219.

39. Wilson, 186-87; Webster, 183.

40. Kimball, 2: 237.

41. Knox, 2: 418.

42. Webster, 330; See also True, 22.

43. Mayo, 218.

44. *Dictionary of Canadian Biography*, 4: 24-25; Mayo, 235; Long 186-87; The transfer of the infected blankets to the Indians occurred before Amherst's July 7, 1763, letter. Donald H. Kent, "Communications," *The Mississippi Valley Historical Review* 41 (March 1955): 762-63; Bernard Knollenberg "General Amherst and Germ Warfare," *The Mississippi Valley Historical Review* 41 (December 1954): 489-94.

45. Long, 189.

46. Lemuel Aiken Welles, ed., "Letters of Col. Nathan Whiting," in *Papers of the New Haven Colony Historical Society* (New Haven: New Haven Historical Society, 1900), 142.

47. Webster, 141-83; See also Knox, 3: 39-67.

48. Montresor, 99-100.

49. Forbush, 48; Wood, 19: 145.

50. Merriman, 664; True 10; Hardy, 237; See also E.C. Dawes, ed., *Journal of Gen. Rufus Putnam 1757-1760* (Albany: Joel Munsell's Sons, 1886), 88.

51. E. B. O'Callaghan, ed., *Documents Relative to the Colonial History of the State of New York* (Albany: Weed, Parsons and Company, 1858), Volume 10, 1055.

52. William Amherst, 49; See also Henderson, 205.

53. Robert Rogers, *Journals of Robert Rogers* (1765; reprint ed., Ann Arbor, MI.: University Microfilms, Inc., 1966), 141.

54. William Amherst, 50.

55. Wood, 19: 149; Hurlbut, 396.

56. *The London Magazine* (September 1759): 498-99; *The Universal Magazine* (September 1759): 146-47; *The Scots Magazine* (August 1759): 439-46; See also Amherst's first letter to Pitt, PRO, CO 5/56, UP microfilm reel 4, frame 420.

57. Wood, 19: 148-49.

58. Ibid., 20: 156.

59. PRO 293/3, WO 34/81, fol. 37.

60. PRO 283/1, WO 30/50, fol. 58.

61. Forbush, 51.
62. Merriman, 666.
63. *Boston Gazette and Country Journal*, 8 October 1759; See also Samuel Niles, "A Summary Historical Narrative of the Wars in New-England with the French and Indians, in Several Parts of the Country," *Collections: Massachusetts Historical Society* (Boston: Massachusetts Historical Society, 1861), Volume, 4, Fourth Series, 524.
64. Henderson, 206.
65. *The London Magazine* (September 1759): 499.
66. Webster, 152; See also Virginia M. Westbrook, "Spruce Beer," *The Bulletin of the Fort Ticonderoga Museum* 15 (1997): 509-15.
67. André Charbonneau, *The Fortifications of Ile Aux Noix* (Ottawa: Minister of Supply and Services Canada, 1994), 331; See also "Endorsed List of the Vessels on the Several Lakes in North America, Dec. 1762," PRO, CO 5/62, UP microfilm reel 7, frame 446.
68. PRO 285/1, WO 34/64, fol. 208; See also fol. 152, 155, 207.
69. Barnard, p.n.a.
70. Haldimand Papers, "Misc. Papers Relating to the Provincial Navy 1775-1780," National Archives of Canada, Microfilm H-1649, Volume 1, B144, fol. 99; See also "Endorsed List of the Vessels," PRO, CO 5/62, UP microfilm reel 7, frame 446.
71. PRO 293/2, WO 34/80, fol. 114.
72. Montresor, 96; By the beginning of August, Second Lieutenant William Henshaw in Timothy Ruggles' Massachusetts Regiment "view'd the New Fort that is Building the Walls about 14 Feet thick Built of Stone & Lime." William Henshaw, "William Henshaw's Journal," *Proceedings of the Worcester Society of Antiquity* 25 (1912): 56; See also PRO, CO 5/56, UP microfilm reel 4, frame 504.
73. True, 18; Two weeks earlier Montresor noted plans for "the Post of Logs for 100 men at the Point." Montresor, 79; See also Webster, 130.
74. Haldimand Papers, fol. 99; "Endorsed List," frame 446; PRO 293/3, WO 34/81, fol. 2.
75. PRO 285/1, WO 34/64, fol. 212; See also *New-York Mercury*, 8 October 1759, 24 September 1759.
76. Ebenezer Dibble, "Diary of Ebenezer Dibble," *Society of Colonial Wars in the State of Connecticut Proceedings* 1 (1903): 316, 318.
77. Gregory Furness and Timothy Titus, *Master Plan for Crown Point State Historic Site* (Waterford, N.Y.: Office of Parks, Recreation and Historic Preservation, 1985), 9, 29-32.
78. *Boston Gazette and Country Journal*, 8 October 1759.
79. H. R. Casgrain, ed., *Lettres De M. De Bourlamaque au Chevalier De Lévis* (Quebec : Imprimerie De L. J. Demers & Frere, 1891), 38-39; See also Knox, 2: 192-93.
80. "Account of the Expedition of Lake Champlain," *The London Magazine* (December 1759): 662; PRO 285/1, WO 34/64, fol. 215; See also fol. 157, 164, 218; Haldimand Papers, fol. 99.
81. *The London Magazine* (December 1759): 662.
82. William Gavit, " The Gavit Letters, 1759," *The Bulletin of the Fort Ticonderoga Museum* 14 (Fall 1983): 219.
83. PRO 285/1, WO 34/64, fol. 225.
84. Merriman, 666; See also Wilson, 184.
85. PRO 272/1, WO 34/30, fol. 87.
86. Wilson, 185.
87. *The London Magazine* (December 1759): 662.
88. O'Callaghan, 1056; John C. Huden, "The Admiral of Lake Champlain," *Vermont History* 30 (January 1962): 68; Dennis M. Lewis, "The Naval Campaign of 1759 on Lake Champlain," *The Bulletin of the Fort Ticonderoga Museum* 14 (Fall 1983): 211-12.
89. O'Callaghan, 1056.
90. PRO 272/1, WO 34/30, fol. 88.
91. Webster, 185; Christopher Comstock, "Journal of Christopher Comstock 1758-1759," Connecticut Historical Society, Hartford, Connecticut, p.n.a.
92. Webster, 191; Knox, 3: 74; For a list of the guns and material found on the three French sloops see PRO, CO 5/57, UP microfilm reel 4, frames 901-2.
93. Wilson, 187.

Robert Rogers from a print in *Geschichte der Krieg* (1777) based on an original mezzotint published by Thomas Hart in 1776. There is no authentic portrait of Rogers, and this illustration probably bears little resemblance to him. (Library of Congress)

5. Robert Rogers 1760

ROBERT ROGERS was one of the most fascinating characters of the French and Indian War; his feats of bravery, bold leadership, and exceptional physical endurance during wilderness expeditions remain legendary. Rogers' exploits, particularly in the Lake George-Lake Champlain valleys, were not only described by subsequent historians, but were widely reported in colonial newspapers at the time of the French and Indian War. He was also an enterprising self-promoter, penning the *Journals of Major Robert Rogers* in 1765, which covered his experiences during the Seven Years' War in America. Nineteenth-century historian Francis Parkman characterized Rogers as "ambitious and violent. . .and so skilled in woodcraft, so energetic and resolute, that his services were invaluable."[1] Rogers' fame in the twentieth century probably reached its peak after the publication of Kenneth L. Roberts' celebrated historical novel *Northwest Passage* in 1937.

Born in Methuen, Massachusetts, on November 18, 1731, to James and Mary McFatridge Rogers, young Robert Rogers moved to the New Hampshire frontier (present-day Dunbarton) with his family in 1739. Because of recurrent Indian raids during King George's War (1744-1748), the family left their farm and was assigned to a fortified house in nearby Rumford for the last several years of the war. Although Rogers had spent some of his early childhood in a log schoolhouse, his real interests lay in the wilderness, exploring Indian trails and the headwaters of streams. After five local militiamen were killed in an ambush on August 10, 1746, Rogers, although only 14 years old, volunteered for the replacement call. He also enlisted the following year, spending six weeks scouting.* The militia experience gave Rogers a taste of adventure. At age 21 Rogers briefly worked his own farm before joining an

*According to the New Hampshire adjutant general's report, Rogers served in 1746 under Captain Daniel Ladd and with Captain Ebenezer Eastman in subsequent years.[2]

expedition in 1753 led by Captain John Goffe to survey a road to the Connecticut River and again served with the militia the following year. Apparently, Rogers' heart was never in farming; instead he relished the experience of the forest and scouting. Although his exploits endure in history, there are few descriptions of Rogers. No authentic portrait is known to be in existence. However, by oral tradition, John Stark, a New Hampshire friend and fellow Ranger, was said to describe Rogers as "six feet in stature, well proportioned, and one of the most athletic men of his time — well known in all the trials of strength or activity. . . He was endued with great presence of mind, intrepidity, perseverance."[3]

Before any of Rogers' escapades began, however, he would have a serious brush with the law. Rogers and 15 others were hauled into court in Rumford on February 7, 1755, charged with passing counterfeit money. He was released, pending trial in the Superior Court at Portsmouth, but with considerable evidence against him for an offense that could have meant the death penalty, the outlook appeared bleak. At the same time, after learning of the call for volunteers to drive the French from the northern frontier, Rogers quickly began raising recruits for the campaign. He soon ingratiated himself with the governor of New Hampshire, Benning Wentworth, who offered him a commission in the New Hampshire provincial regiment. By April in a final court appearance, Rogers was able to avoid conviction largely through his new-found political connections. By then Rogers had recruited approximately 50 men who became "Company One" of the New Hampshire regiment with himself as captain and John Stark as lieutenant.

As a contingent in the 1755 Crown Point expedition, Rogers' company escorted supply wagons from Albany to Fort Lyman (Edward). Colonel Joseph Blanchard, who headed the New Hampshire regiment, sent an introductory note with Rogers to Major General William Johnson which extolled the young provincial "as a person well acquainted with the haunts and passes of the enemy, and the Indian method of fighting."[4] Rogers was quickly sent out as a scout to determine potential routes for a French advance on Johnson's new camp at Lake George. He was scouting along the Hudson River on September 8, 1755, when Baron Jean-Armand Dieskau attacked Johnson at Lake George. Despite Rogers' failure to detect Dieskau's advance, Johnson sent him on new scouting assignments to Fort St. Frédéric and Fort Carillon, the latter then under construction. Soon provincial troops would note Rogers' scouts in their journals, including Lieutenant Colonel Seth Pomeroy of Northampton, Massachusetts, who called one of Rogers' forays "a bold adventure."[5] Johnson himself praised the 23-year-old Ranger captain: "Capt. Rodgers whose Bravery & Veracity stands very clear in my Opinion & of all who know him, tho his Regt. is gone he remains here a Volunteer, & is the most active Man in our Army."[6] On October 30 Rogers was sent northward with his men in armed bateaux to intercept French canoe patrols on Lake George and to take prisoners. Rogers and his men were successful in the Battle of the Isle of Mutton (Prisoners Island), the first naval engagement on Lake George. With only 32 men, Rogers defeated a French force of 150 in "an Engagement which I Judge was near 2 Hours."[7]

During the winter of 1756 Rogers and his men remained at Fort William Henry, which had only recently been completed. Three adventurous raids into French territory were widely reported in newspapers in the English colonies. The forays, lasting as long as 15 days in below freezing weather, resulted in the burning of the

Right: "Rangers Overlooking Lake George" as the morning mist rises. Watercolor by G. A. Embleton.
(Fort Ticonderoga Museum)

Below: "Geometrical Plan of Fort Edward" (1756) showing bridge to Rogers Island.
(Huntington Library)

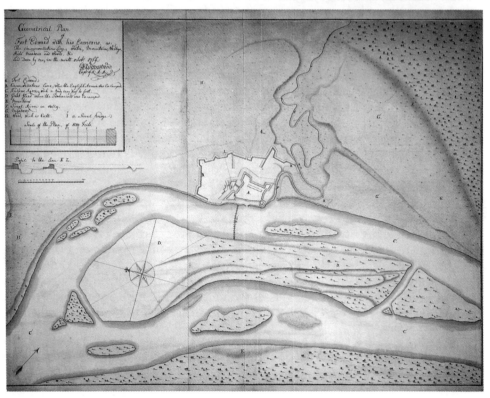

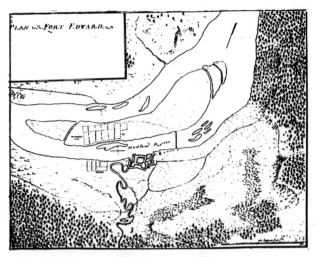

"Plan of Fort Edward" (1758) showing the hospital
on Rogers Island.
(Crown Collection, New York State Library)

village and outlying structures around Fort St. Frédéric. The excursions, some with men on ice skates, led to the refinement of winter tactics for future Ranger operations.

Early in 1756 the New York Assembly voted Rogers a gratuity for his courage, conduct, and diligence. Shortly thereafter, Rogers was summoned to Boston by Massachusetts Governor William Shirley, the commander in chief of British forces in North America. By then Shirley had recognized the necessity of a Ranger unit in forest warfare. Rogers was given orders to raise a 60-man independent company, separate from both the provincial and regular units. This was what Rogers had wanted all along. He was commissioned a captain and ordered to Lake George "to distress the French and their allies, by sacking, burning, and destroying their houses, barns, barracks, canoes, battoes. . .to way-lay, attack, and destroy their convoys of provisions by land and water."[8] Rogers' instructions also delineated pay scales which provided twice the rate for a Ranger private compared to that of provincial troops and roughly the same pay for officers as was received in the British army. The early Rangers wore a variety of homemade clothing, including a leather hunting shirt or short coat and Indian leggings. Each Ranger carried a hatchet or tomahawk, musket, powder horn, leather pouch for musket balls, and a scalping knife. By 1758, in an effort to provide for more uniformity, Rogers outfitted the Rangers in green hunting shirts and jackets. Most of the Rangers were housed on a 70-acre island* in the Hudson River, adjacent to Fort Edward where "small, peak-roofed huts" were built as living quarters; later large barracks for British soldiers, a blockhouse, and a smallpox hospital were constructed on the island.[10]

In January 1757 Rogers and his men were involved in their first major battle when a failed assault on French sleighs on Lake Champlain left his 74-man detachment in a precarious situation, deep in enemy territory between two French forts and with their position exposed. One hundred seventy-nine French regulars, Canadians, and Indians were able to intercept Rogers' men at a ravine to the west of Ticonderoga. The bloody battle, later known as the first Battle on Snowshoes, resulted in the deaths of 14 Rangers, 9 wounded (including Rogers), and 7 taken prisoner.[11] The French lost 19 killed on the field of battle and 27 wounded, of whom

---

*During the French and Indian War the headquarters of the Rangers was often called "the island." While the *New Hampshire Gazette* on October 6, 1758, used the name "Rogers' Island, near Fort Edward," the name Rogers Island may have also been associated with the family of General Thomas Rogers who owned the land during the late eighteenth and early nineteenth centuries.[9]

23 died.[12] This engagement proved the gallantry and resilience of the unit as a fighting force under the most adverse conditions.

Rogers' wound from the battle grew worse, forcing him to seek treatment in Albany. On March 5 he fell ill with smallpox which kept him bedridden until April 15, 1757. During this period, the French made a surprise attack on Fort William Henry where Ranger Captain John Stark played a crucial role in its successful defense. In the summer of 1757 most of the Rangers were assigned to the Louisbourg expedition. On June 20 Rogers sailed with these Rangers, while his brother, Captain Richard Rogers, remained at Fort William Henry where he died of smallpox on June 22, 1757.

By mid-September Robert Rogers and his Rangers had returned to New York from the failed Louisbourg expedition. While in Albany Rogers instructed 55 British volunteers in what was essentially the first Ranger school. John Campbell, the Earl of Loudoun and British commander in chief in America, asked Rogers for a written set of rules involving scouting and forest warfare. In response Rogers produced the first manual of war tactics in North America, one that would have a lasting impact on small-unit strategy to the present day. The 28 rules, dated October 25, 1757, at Fort Edward, included strategies for small patrols, handling prisoners, changing routes during forays, crossing rivers, gaining the highest ground, protecting flanks, and circling behind a pursuing enemy force.[13] Rogers, with little education, was able to formalize carefully in writing many of the tactics acquired through his experience in the wilderness.* Unfortunately for his British superiors, he did not delineate the details of survival in hostile winter conditions which had been learned through year-round scouting. Nevertheless, the rules survived the test of time and place. During World War II the Ranging Rules were again resurrected; and two decades later the American Special Forces were given Rogers' original "Rules for Ranging" as a part of their training for Vietnam.

The experience of the Rangers made an immediate impression on many officers. Lieutenant Colonel Thomas Gage, who had been at the front of Braddock's expeditionary force during its ambush in 1755, recommended regular Ranger units as a permanent part of the British army. Lord Loudoun approved the idea of a lightly-armed unit which later became the 80th Regiment. This was the inception of the light infantry. Other British officers, such as George Augustus Viscount Howe, were similarly interested in adopting the tactics of forest warfare for regular troops; Lord Howe accompanied Rogers on a scout "to learn our method of marching, ambushing, and retreating, & c."[15]

After recovering from a bout of scurvy, Rogers and 150 men departed from Fort Edward on December 17, 1757, "to Distress the Enemy at Caril[l]on & if possible to take a prisoner."[16] Rogers succeeded in seizing several prisoners, one of whom revealed "that he had heard the English intended to attack Ticonderoga, as soon as the lake was froze."[17] Plans for a winter expedition were considered by British officers and Rogers. Meeting with Lord Loudoun in New York City on January 9, 1758, Rogers presented a bold plan to capture Fort St. Frédéric with 400 men by ambushing French sleighs "and making their Drivers prisoners, after which he

---

*Some tactics of irregular warfare were familiar to New Englanders from previous clashes with Native Americans. Captain Benjamin Church's record of his experiences in King Philip's War (1675-1676), first published in Boston in 1716, suggested that he "perfectly understood the manner of Indians in fighting" and adopted guerrilla tactics learned from Native Americans.[14]

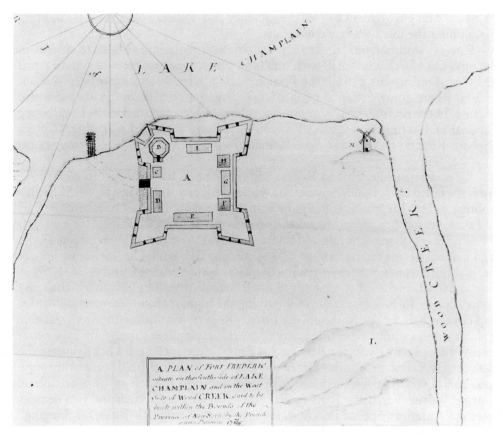

Detail of a "Plan of Fort [St.] Frédéric."
(Crown Collection, New York State Library)

would put the french Cloathing on his own Men & proceed with their Slays. . .
before they Could Discover the Deceit he could have sufficient of men in the fort
to keep the Gates open & take it by surprise."[18] Rogers' proposal was not seriously
considered, but Loudoun instead approved plans to capture Forts Carillon and St.
Frédéric with an army led by Major General James Abercromby and Brigadier
General George Viscount Augustus Howe. The idea, however, was abandoned,
largely because of the impossibility of lugging artillery through the snow. The
blame, in part however, was also placed on Rogers for not making arrangements for
building enough snowshoes for the expedition. Although Loudoun had not looked
favorably on Rogers' proposal for his winter expedition, the British commander in
chief endorsed five additional Ranger companies and Rogers succeeded in maintaining premium pay scales for his men.

Soon after plans for a winter campaign against the French forts were abandoned,
Lieutenant Colonel William Haviland, the commander at Fort Edward, sent Rogers
with 180 men on an expedition to Carillon. On March 13, 1758, Rogers' men
ambushed a party of 96 Native Americans traveling along present-day Trout Brook,
only to be surprised by another 205 of the enemy close behind. Outnumbered by

the French and Indians, Rogers and his Rangers survived four bloody attacks in an engagement known today as the second Battle on Snowshoes. Later Major General Louis-Joseph de Montcalm related that the Indians had returned to Carillon with "one hundred and forty-six scalps," but English sources reported that 104 men were killed on the field of battle, four succumbed to their wounds at Fort Edward, and 16 were taken prisoner.[19]

In July 1758 Rogers and his Rangers participated in the failed campaign against Fort Carillon which involved 15,000 British regular and provincial troops (see chapter 3). In early August, Rogers, along with Major Israel Putnam and Captain James Dalyell, was leading a detachment of Rangers, provincials, and regulars when they were attacked near Wood Creek by 500 Canadians and Indians under Joseph Marin de La Malgue. Thirty-three of the English contingent died in the battle and Putnam was nearly burned at the stake by Indian captors. Putnam, who escaped death on many occasions, was later exchanged.

During the next year Rogers continued his scouting missions, including a large-scale expedition in March 1759 that involved several skirmishes with Canadians and Indians from Fort Carillon. The expedition was an incredible feat of physical endurance which involved a 50-mile, 24-hour continuous march in freezing temperatures. By the time his detachment returned to Fort Edward, two-thirds of the men, including Rogers, had frostbitten feet.

In the summer of 1759, Rogers and his Ranger units accompanied Amherst on his successful expedition against Carillon and St. Frédéric. Amherst, in an effort to

"Rescue of Major Israel Putnam" from Indian torture by Joseph Marin de La Malgue.
Oil painting by J. L. G. Ferris.
(Continental Insurance Company Collection)

obtain news of the expedition against Quebec, sent two regular officers, Captain Quinton Kennedy and Lieutenant Frederick Hamilton, under a flag of truce to the St. Lawrence River via the Abenaki St. Francis Indian Village (St. Francois-de-Sales or Odanak). The Indians apparently saw through the ruse of the flag of truce and took the English party prisoners. In mid-September, Amherst ordered Rogers on an expedition to destroy the St. Francis village. The expedition to St. Francis, one that Rogers had advocated for several years, was to be the largest Ranger foray of 1759 and one of the most famous. On the evening of September 13, 190 hand-picked Rangers, provincials, and regulars departed in 17 whaleboats from Crown Point for St. Francis, a village located at the junction of the St. Francis and the St. Lawrence Rivers about 50 miles north of Montreal.

Ten days after setting out, Rogers and his men hid their whaleboats and provisions at Missisquoi Bay (near present-day Philipsburg, Canada) and began their trek inland. Rogers left two Stockbridge Indians to watch the vessels. Within two days the Indian sentinels caught up to Rogers with the bad news that the vessels had been discovered and burned by the French. Brigadier General François-Charles de Bourlamaque, the French commander at Isle-aux-Noix, had dispatched 300 men to overtake Rogers and posted more than 300 men at the site of the charred vessels to attack the Rangers should they return. At the same time, Rogers realized that he could not return by the Champlain route and decided upon an earlier plan of return by Lake Memphremagog and the Connecticut River. Rogers sent Lieutenant Andrew McMullen and six men back to Crown Point with a request to send Lieutenant Samuel Stevens with provisions to the junction of the Connecticut and Wells Rivers.

Review of Rangers by Major Robert Rogers and Major General Jeffery Amherst at the partially-completed British fort at Crown Point. Painting by Gary S. Zaboly.
(Timothy J. Todish Collection)

The Rangers' march through the Missisquoi swamps made it impossible for the French force to track them. The expedition reached the proximity of St. Francis on October 5, 1759. That night Rogers and two officers reconnoitered the village, observing "a high frolic or dance" among the Abenakis.[20] Amherst's orders advised Rogers to "Remember the barbarities that have been committed by the enemy's Indian scoundrels...Take your revenge...it is my orders that no women or children are killed or hurt."[21] Just before sunrise, Rogers' men burst into the settlement with bayonets fixed on their muskets and tomahawks swinging. According to Rogers, the Rangers made short order of the village: "about seven o'clock in the morning the affair was completely over, in which time we had kill[e]d at least two hundred Indians."[22] However, Captain Pierre Pouchot maintained that Rogers "found this Abenaki village entirely denuded of its warriors. He killed around thirty women & old people and brought back a number of young men prisoner."[23]

Realizing that they had no time to spare because Indian parties were sure to be close on their heels, the Rangers divided the Indian corn for their arduous trip home and departed immediately. Some Rangers, however, wasted valuable space in their knapsacks by packing Wampum necklaces, scalps, and the chalices from the church at the village. The Rangers marched southeast, following the St. Francis River, then south toward Lake Memphremagog. After a council of war, the Rangers decided to break into small parties and rendezvous at the junction of the Connecticut and Wells Rivers. However, they fell prey to piecemeal attacks by their Native American pursurers. One party of approximately 20 men led by Lieutenants James W. Dunbar and George Turner endured a brutal assault, which left only eight survivors. French accounts state that "the Indians massacred some forty and carried off 10 prisoners to their village, where some of them fell...victim to the fury of the Indian women, notwithstanding the efforts the Canadians could make to save them."[24]

The remnants of the Ranger parties were now faced with starvation. One party, led by Lieutenant George Campbell, after four days without food, had eaten their leather cartridge boxes and had "discovered some human bodies not only scalped but horribly mangled, which they supposed to be those of some of their own party.. they fell like Cannibals, and devoured part of them raw."[25] Sergeant John Evans later told of eating broiled powder horns and musket ball pouches as well as seeing "three human heads" in one of his comrade's knapsack "that he cut a piece from one of them and eat it."[26]

Amherst had earlier received Rogers' message from McMullen and had sent Lieutenant Samuel Stevens with provisions to the junction of the Connecticut and Wells Rivers. Stevens, however, made camp three miles downstream and went overland each day to the Wells River site where he periodically fired a signal with his musket. After hearing musket shots which he mistook for enemy fire, Stevens decided to depart the area shortly before Rogers arrived. Stevens was later court-martialed and dismissed from the service. Despite the disheartening situation, Rogers built a raft of pine logs, fashioning small trees into paddles. Leaving most of his party at the rendezvous point of the Wells River, he paddled south on the Connecticut River with three others as far as White River Falls (Junction). A new raft, which was made below the falls, eventually carried them to Fort No. 4 (Charleston, New Hampshire). Rogers immediately sent provisions upstream to the survivors at Wells River. After departing from the village at St. Francis, Rogers lost three officers and

46 men: 17 died at the hands of the Indians and 32 from starvation.[27] The fame of Robert Rogers was probably at its peak after the St. Francis raid, when the story appeared in large type in provincial newspapers throughout the colonies. Many Rangers were discharged at Fort No. 4; Rogers and 21 men finally returned to Crown Point on December 1, 1759.

"A North East View of Crown Point Upon Lake Champlain" by Thomas Davies 1760.
(National Archives of Canada)
"A North View of Crown Point" and the radeau *Ligonier* by Thomas Davies 1760.
(Library of Congress)

Amherst's plans for the 1760 campaign involved a complete encirclement of French forces at Montreal by three armies of British regular and provincial troops. A coordinated movement of English troops from Quebec under Brigadier James Murray would move west as Amherst's main force proceeded east on the St. Lawrence River from Lake Ontario, while a third force under Lieutenant Colonel William Haviland (brigadier in America) pushed north on Lake Champlain to capture Isle-aux-Noix prior to an advance on Montreal.

In late May of 1760, Amherst met with Rogers in Albany and ordered him on the first major expedition on Lake Champlain that year. Amherst sent Rogers to St. Johns (St. Jean) to surprise the fort's garrison and destroy vessels, boats, and provisions that were to support the French garrison at Isle-aux-Noix. In addition, Amherst instructed Rogers to send a detachment to destroy Wigwam Martinique, an Indian village on the Yamaska River, lying to the west of the St. Francis River.

On June 1, Rogers departed with 250 men from Crown Point with whaleboats and bateaux carried on the decks of the brig *Duke of Cumberland*, in addition to three sloops (probably the *Boscawen* and two of the three French sloops recovered in 1759: the *Musquelongy*, *Brochette*, or *Esturgeon*). The fleet, under Lieutenant Alexander Grant, the naval commander in 1760, sailed deep into Missisquoi Bay where Lieutenant Robert Holmes and 50 men were set ashore on June 3 with directions and instructions to annihilate Wigwam Martinique. Grant's vessels next headed for Isle La Motte. On the evening of June 4, Rogers and 213 men set forth in whaleboats and bateaux, landing on the shore of Kings Bay, located on the western side of the lake just above Isle La Motte. Two of the sloops followed the smaller boats, but Rogers sent the vessels further north near Windmill Point to distract the French. The following day Rogers and his men were mired down by heavy spring rains. On the afternoon of June 5, Rogers observed several French boats on the lake, and he feared that they might carry boarding parties to the English sloops at night. After dark he rowed out to the sloops and ordered them back to Grant's position at Isle La Motte.

The next morning Rogers learned from his scouts that a French force of 350 men from Isle-aux-Noix had landed on the west shore and was marching to intercept his detachment. With an advance warning, Rogers was able to deploy his men to their best advantage. At 11:30 in the morning, the French attacked Rogers on the Point au Fer peninsula. Using a bog for protection on the right, Rogers sent Lieutenant Jacob Farrington with 70 Rangers to the rear of the French position. As soon as Farrington began his attack, Rogers noted: "I pushed them in front, which broke them immediately I pursued them with the greatest part of my people about a mile, where they retired to a thick cedar swamp, and divided into small parties. By this time it rained again very hard."[28] Rogers reported 16 Rangers killed, and eight of his men and two light infantry wounded. Rogers collected 50 French muskets from the battle site and estimated that the Rangers had killed 40 of the enemy.[29] The three-hour clash, in which the Rangers consumed most of their 60 rounds of musket balls, was the last and most successful of the large-scale Ranger battles in the lake valleys. Most of the Ranger dead were buried on Cloak Island; the wounded and the body of Ensign John Wood were dispatched to Crown Point on a sloop.

Although the element of surprise was lost, Rogers made a second landing on the evening of June 9 on the west side of Lake Champlain with 220 men (including some reinforcements of Stockbridge Indians and light infantry). Late on the night of June 15, finding the fort at St. Jean well defended, Rogers turned his detachment toward St. Therese, about nine miles farther north on the Richelieu River. The next morning, when the gates were opened for hay carts, the Rangers rushed the stockaded fort at St.Therese. Without the loss of any men, the fort and its soldiers and civilians were captured. Rogers released the women and children, and left with 26 prisoners after burning the fort, village, provisions, wagons, canoes, and bateaux (except for eight that Rogers used for his retreat). Although a large party of French troops from Isle-aux-Noix pursued the Rangers, the latter made a successful escape.

The main French force, about a mile behind their advance units, never reached the Ranger position in time. On June 20 Rogers reembarked on Grant's ships at Windmill Point. Right after the Rangers boarded the vessels "the enemy soon after appeared on the shore where we embarked."[30] The prisoners were sent on one of the vessels back to Crown Point, while Rogers waited for Lieutenant Robert Holmes and his party to return. On the night of June 21, Holmes and his detachment rejoined Rogers after failing to locate the Indian Village at Wigwam Martinique. Two days later the Rangers were back at Crown Point where they remained until the beginning of the invasion of Canada in August 1760.

During the summer of 1760, provincial and regular units slowly gathered at Crown Point for the offensive against the French fort at Isle-aux-Noix. On June 12, 1760, Major General Jeffery Amherst had notified Lieutenant Colonel Haviland that he would have "the Command of the troops that are to Assemble at Crown Point, to advance on and Attack the Enemy" at Isle-aux-Noix as part of the "Advance on them by...three Avenues."[31] Amherst, at the same time, did not neglect his building plans, instructing Haviland to "make all the Use you can of the Intermediate Space, in finishing the Works at Crown Point; Rebuilding the Barracks at Ticonderoga; and Completing the Works at Fort George."[32] When provincial troops began arriving in June, they were invariably impressed by the new five-bastion fort at Crown Point. Captain Samuel Jenks of Chelsea, Massachusetts, remarked that Crown Point, when finished, would be "the strongest place the English ha[ve] on the continent."[33] Jenks supervised 100 men at Crown Point, working "in the King's Garden, which is the finest garden I ever saw in my life, having at least 10 acres [e]nclosed."[34] During the tedious two-month period before the embarkation of the army, Jenks noted that his fellow provincials labored on various projects during the day, but at night: "We [were] all practiseing drinking to [our] wives & sweethearts."[35]

On August 11, 1760, Haviland's 3,400-man army finally departed, initiating one part of the coordinated attack on French Canada. Robert Rogers, with 600 Rangers in whaleboats, led the columns of vessels northward on the last military campaign on Lake Champlain during the French and Indian War. As the fleet sailed, Sergeant David Holden of Groton, Massachusetts, noted that the "s[i]gnal was made on board the L[i]g[o]n[ie]r R[a]deau upon which the Army S[e]t Sail But with a Cont[r]ary wind. The Number of Vess[e]ls and Boats the fleet Consisted of is as follows viz One Brig[a]nt[i]n[e] [*Duke of Cumberland*], 4 Sloops [*Boscawen* and three captured French sloops: *La Musquelongy, La Brochette, L'Esturgeon*], 3 R[a]deau[x] [*Ligonier* and two smaller radeaux], 3 Prows [row galleys], 2 Large Boats [long boats], 263 Bateau[x] Large & Small, 41 Whale Boats, [and] 12 Canoes."[36] Battling adverse winds, the fleet made slow progress northward, stopping along the western shore the first night. Still facing contrary winds, the army barely managed to reach Button Bay by the next day. On August 13, still handicapped by the wind, the crews of six bateaux were forced to tow the *Ligonier* until ten o'clock at night, joining the rest of the fleet in the area near Ligonier Bay. Subsequent nights were spent at Schuyler Island and Isle La Motte, before the men landed on the eastern shore of the Richelieu River just south of Isle-aux-Noix on August 16. As the troops disembarked from their bateaux, the radeau *Ligonier* and row galleys "kept a fire on the enemys fort & vessels to favour our landing."[37] The following day "two of our R[a]deaux advanced close under their lines & gave them a salute, which they returned & obliged our R[a]deaux to retire. In the retreat, 8 legs were shot off from 6 men in one of the R[a]deaux."[38] The wounded men were taken to an island south of Isle-aux-Noix, known today as Hospital Island.

Over the next several days Haviland's men hurriedly constructed a long breast-work and batteries on the eastern shoreline adjacent to Isle-aux-Noix as the French troops under Colonel Louis Antoine de Bougainville frantically fired their artillery at the besiegers. Manned by only 1,650 French troops (including sailors), the garrison at Isle-aux-Noix placed its faith in a small squadron of vessels: two tartans or row galleys, the *Grand Diable* and the *Petit Diable*, the schooner *La Vigilante*, the sloop *Waggon*, several small gunboats or jacaubites, and a crude floating battery.[39] The channels on both sides of the island were protected by a defensive boom, blocking navigation to the north of the island. According to Captain Jacob Bayley from New Hampshire, the French army had "fastened 5 logs abreast with iron staples & [chain] links 1 1/2 inches in diameter, the whole anchored every 10 ft. to ye ground [in the river]. The length of the boom is about 80 yds."[40]

On the afternoon of August 23 the British and provincial troops fired their first batteries. As the general bombardment continued the next day, Lieutenant John Frost, Jr., of Maine noted in his journal: "This is the Lord's Day, and a most Ter[ri]bl[e] Day it is. Instead of going to Church, nothing but the Roaring of Cannons and mort[a]rs; the alarms of war and a Cr[y] for human Blood."[41] On August 25 Colonel John Darby, with two light infantry companies and Rogers with four Ranger companies, endeavored to end the siege by capturing the French fleet. After hauling a six-pound cannon and two howitzers along the densely-wooded east bank of the river, Darby and Rogers erected a battery to the north of the French fortress, separating the garrison at the fort from its fleet. The opening cannon shot apparently cut the cable holding the *Grand Diable*, allowing the vessel to drift in the

Right: "A Massachusetts Provincial soldier of 1760. . .on the eastern shore of Lake Champlain." Painting by Gary S. Zaboly.

Above: Detail of the same painting showing the British fort at Crown Point.

wind to the eastern shore and into the hands of English invaders. Another cannon firing, noted Lieutenant John Bradbury from Maine, resulted in "shooting the captain's head off, the others were glad to surrender on any terms."[42] Observing the grounding of the French vessels at the northern end of the channel as their crews desperately attempted to escape, Darby sent Rogers and his Rangers to seize the stranded fleet. With a covering fire from shore, Rangers swam with tomahawks in their teeth to the grounded schooner *La Vigilante*. When the melee ended, three vessels had been captured: the "Grand Diable, a Topsail Schooner [*La Vigilante*] & Sloop [*Waggon*]" according to Reverend Samuel MacClintock from New Hampshire.[43] The French garrison was now deprived of its large vessels for use in an evacuation.

On August 27, as the bombardment continued, Sergeant David Holden recorded "a thick foggy morning & the more so By the Smoke of the Cannon & b[o]mbs. . .the Cannon Crack[ed] as tho[ugh] the Heavens & Earth was Coming together for [the] Chief of the Day."[44] During the barrage a French shell landed in the British magazine, causing an explosion which injured and killed a number of provincial soldiers. By midnight on August 28, Colonel Bougainville and his troops abandoned Isle-aux-Noix, leaving about 40 troops to continue shelling the British position. The French evacuees crossed to the western shore of the Richelieu River and marched the 12 miles to St. Jean, but were delayed after becoming lost in the dark.

The following day Haviland dispatched Rogers and the Rangers after the retreating French army, but Bougainville's soldiers had already departed from St. Jean, after setting it ablaze, before the Rangers reached the village. Rogers with 400 Rangers later overtook the French army, engaging the rear guard and returning to St. Jean with "17 Prisoners amongest which was one Major & 1 Capt. of ye French army."[45] Rogers joined Colonel John Darby for a bloodless siege of Fort Chambly and thereafter was dispatched by Haviland to Montreal. After 17,000 troops of Amherst, Haviland, and Murray surrounded the 2,200-man French army at Montreal, Pierre de Rigaud de Vaudreuil, the governor-general of New France, signed the 55 articles of capitulation.

On September 12, 1760, Amherst ordered Rogers to the west, where he presided over the surrender of all French posts, including Detroit on December 1.[46] The following year Rogers accepted a commission of captain from Amherst, and led an independent company of regulars in South Carolina's Cherokee country. In 1763 he distinguished himself at the Battle of Bloody Run while attempting to break Pontiac's hold on Detroit.

Rogers' personal life and fortunes, however, took a turn for the worse after the French and Indian War. Financial difficulties, controversy, and imprisonment dogged him for much of the rest of his life. After a large portion of his war-time accounts were denied by the Crown, Rogers began years of petitions to extricate himself from debt. During the war years Rogers had borrowed funds to lend to his men against their pay as well as for his own sustenance, and owed money for various army-related activities. In 1763, after a second petition, he received a partial payment from the New Hampshire legislature for the 1755-1756 campaign at Lake George. Additional debts resulted from Rogers' failed trading partnerships (Rogers & Co. and Askin and Rogers) that sought to profit from the opening of western territories after the French and Indian War.[47] In January 1764 Rogers was jailed in New York for debt, but a group of soldiers, returning from Detroit, liberated him at gunpoint. To help cover his debts, he petitioned with others for, but failed to receive, a grant of approximately 25,000 acres on the southern and western shores of Lake George; he also failed to secure lands on Lake Champlain. In 1764, however, the governor of New Hampshire conveyed a 3,000-acre plot in present-day southern Vermont to Rogers, but the land was immediately mortgaged to repay his debts.

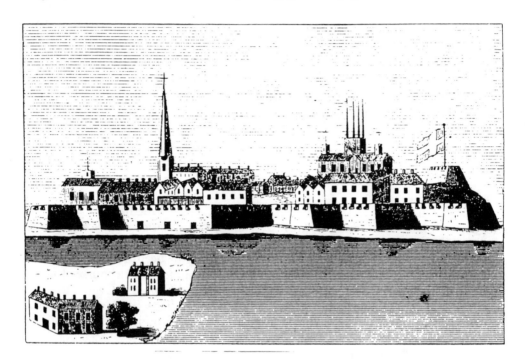

"View of Montreal and its Walls in 1760." From the *Pictorial Field-Book of the Revolution* by Benson J. Lossing.

Rogers' marriage to 20-year-old Elizabeth Browne on June 30, 1761, was also problematic. Six days after the wedding, Rogers departed for service in South Carolina; infrequent visits home plagued the union. Obtaining a loan from his father-in-law, Reverend Arthur Browne, Rogers was forced to relinquish 500 acres in Rumford, New Hampshire, as a condition for the advance. Subsequently, Rogers was served with a sheriff's writ for debt by his father-in-law.

In March 1765 Rogers secretly sailed for England in order to seek a promotion, straighten out his tangled financial affairs, and find a publisher for his story of his American exploits during the French and Indian War. Two volumes, *Journals of Major Robert Rogers* and *A Concise Account of North America*, were published in October 1765 by John Millan, bookseller.[48] The first book dealt with the scouts, skirmishes, and major battles of the war, while the second was a historical geography of the continent based on Rogers' own broad travels. The books were critically acclaimed by English reviewers. The *Monthly Review* (January 1766) called Rogers'

Journals "as authentic as they are important and necessary, to those who would acquire a thorough understanding of the nature and progress of the late military operations in North-America. The Author writes like an honest, a sensible, and a modest man. . .a brave and a skil[l]ful officer."[49] *The Gentleman's Magazine* (December 1765) remarked that Rogers' second volume was "concise and yet full; and the knowledge it contains is acquired with pleasure."[50] Although Rogers had spent most of his military career fighting Native Americans, the *Monthly Review* noted that he recognized the "virtues possessed by the Indians. . .[and] extols their surprizing patience and equanimity of mind."[51] Rogers also anonymously wrote a play entitled *Ponteach or the Savages of America: A Tragedy* published by John Millan in February 1766.[52] London critics, however, condemned the work. Given Rogers' lack of formal education, he undoubtedly received considerable assistance from his secretary, Nathaniel Potter, a graduate of the College of New Jersey (Princeton), whom he had met in New Hampshire prior to sailing for England.[53]

While in England, Rogers petitioned King George III on August 12, 1765, for funds and 200 men to search for the Northwest Passage to Puget Sound, an expedition that would take an estimated three years. The plan was turned down by the Privy Council, but Rogers was rewarded in 1765 with an appointment to command Fort Michilimackinac (near present-day Mackinaw City, Michigan), the westernmost of British strongholds. Major General Thomas Gage, the British commander in chief in North America, disclosed that the king had also appointed Rogers to "a kind of Superintendence" over the western Native Americans "but to make him if thought proper, Subordinate to Sir William Johnson."[54] Rogers and his wife arrived at Michilimackinac in August 1766. From the beginning of his administration of affairs at Michilimackinac, Rogers sought an independent course of action that would eventually lead to a confrontation with Johnson and Gage. He disregarded Johnson's instructions that trade with the Indians be confined to the immediate vicinity of the fort. Recognizing the need for fur traders to follow Native Americans on their winter hunt, Rogers approved their commercial activities outside the fort. Without authorization and at a considerable expense, he dispatched two parties in 1766 to search for a Northwest Passage. The first party was headed by Jonathan Carver, a former provincial soldier who had served at Lake George during the French and Indian War; the second was led by James Tute, who had served as a Ranger with Rogers. After joining forces in May 1767, the two explorers continued their search without success, returning to Michilimackinac at the end of August 1767.

In 1767 Rogers drafted a proposal that he later sent directly to the Board of Trade in London which recommended the establishment of a civil governor, lieutenant governor, and an elected council of Chippewas, Potawatomis, Menominees, Sauks, Winnebagos, Nippewas, Crees, Dakotas, Nipissings, Ottawas, and Sioux. Customary gifts, purchased by Rogers from merchants, were given to Native Americans, but when presented with the bills, Johnson regarded the expense as unjustified. Major General Thomas Gage subsequently notified the British Secretary of War, Lord Barrington, that "the Bills he has drawn contrary to his Instructions, and therefore payment refused, sh[o]w the Sums he has wantonly lavished in Indian Presents, done with no good intent."[55]

After an altercation with Rogers at Michilimackinac, Nathaniel Potter (Rogers' secretary) signed an affidavit against him in Montreal, charging that if Rogers' proposal for a civil government in the west were rejected, Rogers would "quit his Post and retire to the French towards Mississippi and enter into the Service of the French. . .[and] wou'd not go empty handed, but would in that case get into his hands all the goods he cou'd both from Traders and others by right or wrong he cared not how."[56] Potter subsequently departed for England but died aboard the ship and was buried at sea. On December 6, 1767, Rogers was arrested at Fort Michilimackinac for high treason. Held first under house arrest, Rogers was later placed in solitary confinement and finally clapped in irons. According to Major General Gage, Rogers' allies among the Native Americans sought his release: "a disorderly Tribe of the Chippewas went there with their arms; and threw their English Belts into the Lake, and invited other Nations to join them to release the Major from his confinement."[57] Because of the threat, the Michilimackinac garrison was placed on alert and two armed boats were employed to escort Rogers to Detroit for the journey to Montreal. With little credible evidence against him, Rogers was acquitted of all charges at the court-martial in Montreal in October 1768. Rogers, however, was incarcerated until 1769 and never reinstated at the western post.

After a brief visit to his wife and new-born son in New Hampshire in the summer of 1769, Rogers sailed for England to seek a new appointment and payment for debts incurred during his time at Michilimackinac. Gage continued to refuse funding of Rogers' expenses incurred at the post. Although Rogers was awarded his commandant's pay for service at Michilimackinac through December 1769 and received partial payment for some of his expenses, most of his debts were not covered; his petition for land on Lake Champlain fell on deaf ears, and his application for funding a new Northwest Passage expedition never materialized. Rogers eventually spent nearly two years in an English debtor's prison. He filed suit in England against Lieutenant General Thomas Gage (promoted 1770) for false imprisonment in America and for failure to pay his legitimate expenses. After his release from Fleet Prison, he withdrew his lawsuit against Gage, probably as a quid pro quo for the grant of half-pay as a retired major. Rogers, then 43 years old, sailed for American in the spring of 1775.

Back in America, Rogers was still preoccupied with financial problems, but did manage to visit his wife and six-year-old son in Portsmouth, New Hampshire. While he was traveling in a quest to resolve his fiscal difficulties, the Pennsylvania Committee of Safety, suspicious of a British officer on half-pay, detained Rogers on September 22, 1775, but he was released the next day on the assurance of not taking arms against the Americans. Rogers traveled extensively in the eastern colonies for the ensuing nine months, causing Americans to raise questions over his dealings with the British. Washington instructed Major General Philip Schuyler in Albany to maintain surveillance of the retired officer: "being much suspected of unfriendly views to this country, his conduct should be attended to with some degree of vigilance and circumspection."[58] Suppositions over Rogers' activities finally led to his arrest on orders from Washington on June 27, 1776. After interviewing Rogers, Washington recorded that "the business which he informs me he has with Congress, is a secret offer of his services, to the end that, in case it should be rejected, he might have his way left open to an employment in the East-Indies" for Great Britain.[59] Washington and his officers recommended that the Continental Congress reject

Rogers' offer. Although Rogers finally made an overture to the American side, he had never seriously entertained their cause and had sought an appointment with the British first.

On the night of July 8, Rogers escaped from the Americans and ten days later offered his services to the British. He led the Queen's American Rangers which was the unit later involved in the capture of Nathan Hale on Long Island. In 1777, after an inspector general's report, Rogers was retired on half pay and assigned to recruitment duty. In the spring of 1779, following a short visit to England, Rogers was delegated by Sir Henry Clinton to raise two battalions of Rangers, known later as the King's Rangers. On a recruiting foray to Canada, Rogers was thrown in prison in Halifax, Nova Scotia, again for his debts. After his release, he was captured on January 10, 1781, aboard a British schooner bound for New York City, by the crew of a Pennsylvania privateer.[60]

Discharged in 1782, Rogers returned alone to England the following year (his wife had divorced him in 1778). His final years were beset by debt, illness, and excessive drinking. On May 18, 1795, at the age of 63, the once-famous Ranger, who had eluded the scalping knives, tomahawks, and musket balls of the French and Indians during his service in the Champlain Valley, died in a shabby boarding house. The *Morning Post* of London observed that Rogers "performed prodigious feats of valour. He was a man of uncommon strength, but adversity, and a long confinement. . .had reduced him to the most miserable state of wretchedness."[61]

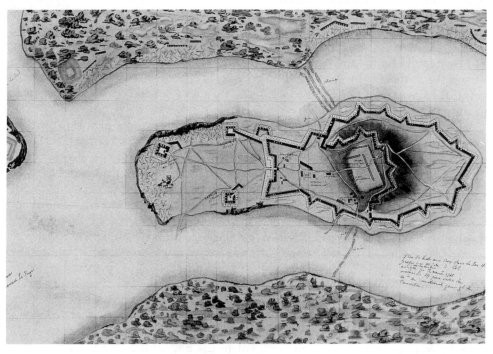

Plan of Isle-aux-Noix by Louis Antoine de Bougainville 1760.
(National Archives of Canada)

Journal of Major Robert Rogers[62]

I remained at Crown Point with my people, without effecting any thing considerable, more than in small parties reconnoit[e]ring the country about the fort, while every thing was got in readiness for embarking the army the [11th] of August [1760]; which was done accordingly, having one brig, three sloops, and four rideaus,* which latter were occupied by the royal train of artillery, commanded by Lieut. Colonel [Thomas] Ord. Our order of march was as follows, viz.

Six hundred Rangers and seventy Indians in whale-boats in the front, commanded by Major Rogers, as an advance-guard for the whole army, all in a line a-breast, about half a mile a-head of the main body, followed by the light infantry and grenadiers in two columns, two boats a-breast in each column, commanded by Col. Darby.** The right wing was composed of Provincials, commanded by Brigadier Ruggles, who was second in command of the whole army.*** The left was made up of New Hampshire and Boston troops, commanded by Col. Thomas.† The seventeenth and twenty-seventh regiments, with some few of the Royals, that formed the center column, were commanded by Major Campbell of the 17th regiment.‡ Col. Haviland was in the front of these divisions, between that and the

---

*Lieutenant Thomas Moody listed "1 Brig, Sloops 4, Ruddoes [radeaux] 3, Prows [row galleys] 3, Long Boats 2, Bate[a]u[x] 263, Whale Boats 41, Can[o]es 12."[63] The fleet included the 20-gun brig *Duke of Cumberland*; 16-gun sloop *Boscawen*; the three captured French sloops, each mounting 8 cannon: *La Musquelongy*, *La Brochette*, *L'Esturgeon*; the six-gun radeau *Ligonier*; two smaller radeaux mounting one cannon; and three row galleys (prows) also mounting one cannon each. Many of the vessels also carried a large number of swivel guns.

**John Darby held a commission of major in the 17th Regiment while serving in Amherst's siege of Louisbourg in 1758. Promoted to lieutenant colonel the following year, Darby participated in Amherst's 1759 campaign at Lake George and Lake Champlain and led a battalion of grenadiers and light infantry in the siege of Isle-aux-Noix in 1760. Elevated to colonel in 1772, he was ordered to America in 1775 but resigned from the service later the same year.

***Timothy Ruggles (1711-1795) graduated from Harvard in 1732 and was subsequently known as a capable lawyer in Massachusetts. In 1755 he served as a colonel of a Massachusetts regiment during the Battle of Lake George and led his regiment during each of the next three campaigns during the French and Indian War. In 1760 he commanded the provincial troops in the Isle-aux-Noix expedition as a brigadier general. In the postwar years Ruggles rose to chief justice of common pleas and speaker of the provincial assembly. As a loyalist in the American Revolution, he organized a battalion of loyal militia on Long Island after being exiled from Massachusetts. He later settled in Nova Scotia where he died in 1795.

†John Thomas (1724-1776) served in King George's War as a surgeon's mate. During the French and Indian War he rose to the rank of colonel in command of a regiment in the 1760 Isle-aux-Noix campaign. After the war Thomas practiced medicine in Massachusetts and joined the Sons of Liberty, raising a volunteer regiment when the Revolutionary War broke out. As a major general, he traveled north on Lake Champlain in the spring of 1776 to become senior commander of the American army in Canada. After contracting smallpox during the retreat from Canada, Thomas died at Chambly on June 2, 1776.

‡John Campbell of Strachur, Scotland, entered the army in 1745, serving during the War of Austrian Succession. He sailed to America with the 42nd Highland Regiment and sustained wounds at the 1758 battle at Ticonderoga. Promoted to major of the 17th Regiment of Foot in 1759, Campbell served during the 1759 and 1760 campaigns on Lake Champlain. Campbell returned to America with his regiment in 1776, becoming a major general in 1779. He was promoted to lieutenant general in 1787 and general in 1797. Campbell died in 1806.

light infantry, and grenadiers.* The royal artillery followed the columns, and was commanded by Colonel Ord, who had, for his escort, one Rhode Island regiment of Provincials. The sutlers, & c. followed the artillery. In this manner we rowed down the lake forty miles the first day, putting ashore where there was good landing on the west-side, and there encamped.**

The day following we lay by. The [13th], the wind blowing fresh at south, orders were given for embarking, and the same day reached a place on the west shore, within ten miles of the Isle a Mot[te], where the army encamped. It having blown a fresh gale most part of the day, some of my boats split open by the violence of the waves, and ten of my Rangers were thereby drowned.***

The [15th] we set sail again early in the morning, and that night encamped on the north-end of the Isle a Mot[te].

The [16th], before day, the army was under way, with intention to land; having but twenty miles to go, and having the advantage of a fair wind, we soon came in sight of the French fort,† and about ten in the morning Col. [John] Darby, with the Grenadiers and Light Infantry, and myself with the Rangers, landed on the east-shore, and marched and took possession of the ground opposite the fort on that side, without the least opposition. Having done this, an officer was sent to acquaint Col. [William] Haviland (who, with the remainder of the army, was at the place where we landed) that there was not the least danger to apprehend from the enemy.‡ The

---

*William Haviland (1718-1784) was a veteran British officer, serving in earlier campaigns at Lake George and Lake Champlain (see chapter 4). In 1760 Lieutenant Colonel Haviland, with a local rank of brigadier, led the expedition to Isle-aux-Noix. Haviland and Rogers had several disagreements, including the handling of discipline of Rangers in 1757 when Haviland served as commander of Fort Edward, and Haviland's attempt in 1760 to have regular officers outrank Rogers and eliminate his independent command. In both instances, the British commanders in chief (Loudoun in 1757 and Amherst in 1760) backed Rogers.

**After five years, Rogers' memory apparently slipped here. Noting contrary winds, Sergeant David Holden recorded that the fleet only "proceeded about Six miles & Landed on the west Shore"; likewise Lieutenant Thomas Moody observed that the army "mov'd but about 6 Miles."[64]

***Facing adverse winds on August 12, the fleet moved only a short distance to Button Bay. The next day the army reached the vicinity of Ligonier Bay, west of Four Brothers Islands. On August 14, struggling against strong winds and rain, the expedition proceeded as far as Schuyler Island.[65] Reverend Samuel MacClintock reported "a very heavy squall of wind & rain arose. . .8 of the Rangers, 3 of whom had been draughted from our regiment, being in a birch Canoe were unfortunately drowned by the Canoe splitting in two."[66] Lieutenant Moody also mentioned that "they say that there are 7 Battoes Missing Supposed to be gon[e] to the Bottom."[67]

†The French fort at Isle-aux-Noix was described by Sergeant David Holden as "a very Strong Fortress. . .very Strongly Piqueted [picketed] in all Round. . . The Island. . .[is] very Low & Swampy Greate[r] Part of it & Chiefly Clear[e]d."[68]

‡On the morning of August 16, Captain Samuel Jenks wrote a detailed narrative of the landing of British and provincial troops, noting that the fleet covered "4 miles & made a beautiful appearance. . . After entering the Narrows. . .the enemy's schooner [*La Vigilante*] & reddow [row galley *Grand Diable*] came out to meet us but was dr[awn] back. We formed for landing in about a mile & 1/2 from the enemy's fort, with our battoes a bre[a]st, to land on the east shore. . .without any molestation at all. The Ligonier redows [radeau] & prows [row galleys] kept a fire on the enemys fort & vessels."[69] Samuel MacClintock similarly recorded that the English force "were met by several of the French Row Gallies, with which we exchanged several shots which obliged them to retreat."[70]

next day we began to raise batteries,* and soon after to throw some shells into the garrison.** About the 24th proposal was made for taking the enemy's vessels, three of which were at anchor a little below the fort, and some of their rideaus [radeaux] likewise. It was introduced by Col. Darby, who was ordered to take the command of the party appointed for this service, which consisted of two companies of Regulars, and four companies of my Rangers, with the Indians. We carried with us two light howitzers and one six-pounder, and silently conveying them along thro' the trees, brought them opposite the vessels, and began a brisk fire upon them, before they were in the least apprised of our design, and, by good fortune, the first shot from the six-pounder cut the cable of the great rideau, and the wind being at west, blew her to the east shore, where we were, and the other vessels weighed anchor and made for St. John's, but got all aground, in turning a point about two miles below the fort.*** I was, by Col. Darby, ordered down the east shore with my Rangers, and crossed a river of about thirty yards wide, which falls into Lake Champlain from the east [Rivière du Sud]. I soon got opposite the

"Major Robert Rogers and an Indian Chief." Engraving (ca. 1770), artist unknown. The figures in this engraving were partially copied from Benjamin West's heroic painting "Death of General Wolfe at Quebec." (William L. Clements Library).

*On that day, August 17, many provincial diaries recounted one devastating incident: "A Small Artillery R[a]deau, Bore away Towards the fort whose orders was to go on till fir'd upon, accordingly he [Captain Clagg] Did & By a Six Pounder had Both his Legs Shot off after which ye Capt. soon Died, 5 more wounded, one of which had Both his Legs Shot off, the other 4 one Leg apiece Soon after one or Two Dy'd."[71]

**From August 17 to August 23 the provincial and British troops labored on breastworks and batteries on the eastern shore of the Richelieu River, opposite Isle-aux-Noix. During this period the French garrison bombarded their enemy, sometimes only "Cut[ting] of[f] the tops of ye trees" but "Daily many [men]. . .are Kill'd & Wounded."[72] The British and provincial artillery opened fire on the afternoon of August 23 when at "3 [o'clock], all ye music in camp play[e]d 10 minutes and open[e]d ye Batteries. . . which soon made the houses [on Isle-aux-Noix] fly to p[i]e[c]es."[73]

***Intendant François Bigot's letter to the French minister of war reported that "the Captain cut his cable to get at a distance, and reach the North shore; but having been killed with a part of the crew, the remainder escaped by swimming, some to the enemy, others to the island. The English thereupon rushed on board and seized that Tartane [row galley], with which they went and took the remainder of our little navy, consisting of a similar tartane, a schooner, a gabarre armed with 4 guns, and 4 boats carrying an 8-pounder."[74] Lieutenant Thomas Moody, on the other hand, wrote an account similar to Rogers' version: "our Cannon cut off the Cable of the Grand Diabl[e] and caused her to come to our shore."[75]

vessels, and by firing from the shore, gave an opportunity to some of my party to swim on board with their tomahawks, and took one of the vessels; in the mean time Col. Darby had got on board the rideau, and had her manned, and took the other two;* of which success he immediately acquainted Col. Haviland, who sent down a sufficient number of men to take charge of and man the vessels;** and ordered the

Wreck of a vessel raised after 1900 at Crown Point. This vessel may have been the row galley *Grand Diable* which had been captured at Isle-aux-Noix in 1760 and sank at Crown Point on October 22, 1761. (Postcard, James W. Spring Collection)

*Provincial soldiers reported only three vessels captured on August 25. Captain Samuel Jenks mentioned "the French great redow [radeau], th[e]ir brig, & sloop had struck to us"; while Private Lemuel Wood disclosed the capture of one Rogal[l]ey . . .a sloop and Topsail Sc[h]ooner."[76] The *Grand Diable* was actually a large row galley rather than a radeau. British and Canadian records list the names of the major vessels captured at Isle-aux-Noix in 1760: "Schooner Vigilant[e], Sloop Waggon, Row Gall[e]y Grand Diable, Row Gall[e]y Petite Diable."[77] In October 1760 General Jeffery Amherst traveled from Crown Point to Ticonderoga aboard the *Grand Diable*: "I s[e]t out in the French Grand Diable to try what sort of a boat it is & I think it not near so good as our Row Galleys."[78]

The exact design of the French row galleys and gunboats remains somewhat elusive. On August 17, 1758, Major General James Abercromby reported that the French had "contrived a kind of fourteen Oar Row Galley, called by the French *des Soups* [*les Loups*] carrying one twelve Pounder & 6 Swivels of which they had already four on the Lake."[79] These vessels may have been small gunboats or Jacaubites.[80] Another report, published in the September 8, 1760, issue of the *New-York Mercury* described a captured vessel at Isle-aux-Noix as a "Row Galley. . .mounting two 18 Pounders at the Head, another at the Stern, and full of Swivels, she rows with 24 oars."[81] This account may be referring to the row galley *Petit Diable*.

**The British fleet and captured French vessels were later docked at the King's Shipyard at Fort Ticonderoga and years later listed as "In Service till Decay'd" or "Lay'd up and Decay'd," including the brig *Duke of Cumberland*, sloop *Boscawen*, schooner *Vigilante*, sloops *Brochette*, *Esturgeon*, and *Musquelongy*, and row galley *Petit Diable*.[82] The radeau *Ligonier* apparently ended her career at Crown Point as did the row galley *Grand Diable* which sank during a storm at Crown Point in 1761 after her "row Ports fill'd."[83] Before the Tercentenary celebration of Lake Champlain in 1909, a large vessel was raised at Crown Point and displayed on the edge of the parade ground. The vessel may have been the *Grand Diable*, but a grass fire in the 1940s destroyed the vessel, thus making identification difficult. The *Duke of Cumberland* was raised at Ticonderoga in 1909 and erroneously displayed for many years as the Revolutionary War schooner *"Revenge."* Today only scant remains of the vessel survive. In 1983 the Champlain Maritime Society and Fort Ticonderoga sponsored an underwater archaeological study of the sloop *Boscawen* under the direction of Arthur B. Cohn and Kevin Crisman.[84]

remainder of the Rangers, Light Infantry and Grenadiers, to join the army that night, which was accordingly done; and about midnight the night following the French troops left the island, and landed safe on the main; so that next morning nothing of them was to be seen but a few sick, and Col. Haviland took possession of the fort.*

The second day after the departure of Monsieur Bo[ugain]ville** and his troops from the island, Mr. Haviland sent me with my Rangers to pursue him as far as St. John's Fort [St. Jean], which was about twenty [12] miles further down the lake;*** and at that place I was to wait the coming of the army, but by no means to follow further towards Montreal. I went in boats, and about daylight got to St. John's, and found it just set on fire.† I pursued, and took two prisoners, who reported, "That Monsieur [Louis Antoine de] Bo[ugai]nville was to encamp that night about half-way on the road to Montreal; and that he went from St. John's about nine o'clock the night before; but that many of their men were sick, and that they thought some of the troops would not reach the place appointed till the middle of the afternoon." It being now about seven in the morning, I set all hands to work, except proper guards, to fortify the log houses that stood near the lake side, in order that part of my people might cover the battoes, while I, with the remainder, followed Monsieur Bo[ugai]nville, and about eight o'clock I got so well fortified, that I ventured our boats and baggage under care of 200 Rangers, and took with me 400, together with the two companies of Indians, and followed after the French army, which consisted of about 1500 men, and about 100 Indians they had to guard them. I was resolved to make his dance a little the merrier, and pursued with such haste, that I overtook his rear guard about two miles before they got to their encamping ground. I immediately attacked them, who not being above 200, suddenly broke, and then stood for the main body, which I very eagerly pursued, but in good order, expecting Monsieur Bo[ugai]nville would have made a stand, which however he did not ch[oo]se, but pushed forward to get to the river [L'Acadie River], where they were to encamp, and having crossed it, pulled up the bridge, which put a stop to my march, not judging it prudent to cross at a disadvantage, inasmuch as the enemy had

---

*Lieutenant Thomas Moody noted that the regulars took possession of the fort and "found one Capt. and 30 Privates together with a great many that were sick & Wounded."[85] Some of the provincials were irritated that they had been barred from the island by British troops. Captain Samuel Jenks of Massachusetts wrote that several provincial officers "were prevented by the regulars" from crossing to the island on August 28 "when we have done [the] most part of the fatigue during the siege & our men have been more exposed than they, must now be den[ie]d the liberty to go & se[e] what they have fought for."[86]

**Louis Antoine de Bougainville (1729-1811) was the commander at Isle-aux-Noix in 1760. He had first arrived in North America in 1756 as an aide-de-camp to General Louis-Joseph de Montcalm. Bougainville, who had formulated the terms of capitulation at Fort William Henry in 1757, ironically, carried the French articles of surrender to General Jeffery Amherst at Montreal in September 1760. He later joined the French navy, serving in North America in 1780. Bougainville's career included experience as a soldier, sailor, explorer, and scholar.

***Colonel Bougainville's progress to St. Jean and Montreal had been delayed as a result of having become lost in the darkness following the evacuation of Isle-aux-Noix.[87]

†Two days later Lieutenant John Bradbury of York, Maine, "took a walk into the fort when it was all burning to ashes—10 or 12 chimneys standing -- 2 of ye houses 4 stories high: one vessel on ye stocks and one burned. The fort not very strongly fortified. The land round it clear and level, about 10 acres, but no improvement except one small garden which was destroyed."[88]

a good breast-work on the other side, of which they took possession; in this pursuit, however, we considerably lessened their number, and returned in safety.*

Notes

1. Francis Parkman, *Montcalm and Wolfe* (1884; reprint ed., New York: Atheneum, 1984), 252-53.
2. Joseph B. Walker, "Robert Rogers, the Ranger," in *A Collection of Addresses and Papers*, by Joseph B. Walker (Concord, N.H.: Joseph B. Walker, n.d.), 2; See also Allan Nevins, ed., *Ponteach or the Savages of America*, by Robert Rogers (1914; reprint ed., New York: Burt Franklin, 1971), 30, 35, 39; John R. Cuneo, *Robert Rogers of the Rangers* (1959; reprint ed., Ticonderoga: Fort Ticonderoga Museum, 1988), 8, 11.
3. Caleb Stark, *Memoir and Official Correspondence of Gen. John Stark* (1860; reprint ed., Boston: Gregg Press, 1972), 387.
4. Robert Rogers, *Journals of Major Robert Rogers* (London: J. Millan, 1765), viii.
5. Seth Pomeroy, *The Journals and Papers of Seth Pomeroy*, ed. Louis Effingham DeForest (New York: The Society of Colonial Wars in the State of New York, 1926), 121.
6. James Sullivan, ed., *The Papers of Sir William Johnson* (Albany: The University of the State of New York, 1922), Volume 2, 190.
7. E. B. O'Callaghan, *The Documentary History of the State of New-York* (Albany: Charles Van Benthuysen, Public Printer, 1851), Volume 4, 273; See also Scott Padeni, "Skirmish at the Isle of Mutton," *The Lake George Nautical Newsletter* 3 (no. 3, 1994): 1,8.
8. Rogers, 15.
9. *New Hampshire Gazette*, 6 October 1758; William H. Hill, *Old Fort Edward Before 1800* (Fort Edward: William H. Hill, 1929), 266-68.
10. Richard A. Mason, ed., *Exploring Rogers Island* (Fort Edward: The Rogers Island Historical Association, 1969), 17; David R. Starbuck, *Rogers Island Archeological Site* (Fort Edward: Rogers Island Yacht Club, 1992), 1; Hill, 220-21.
11. Rogers, 43-45; Burt G. Loescher, *The History of Rogers Rangers* (San Francisco: Burt G. Loescher, 1946), Volume 1, 137, 330, 348; See also Loudoun Papers, LO2704, Huntington Library, San Marino, California; Russell P. Bellico, *Chronicles of Lake George: Journeys in War and Peace* (Fleischmanns, N.Y.: Purple Mountain Press, 1995), 41-58.
12. Loescher, 1: 348.
13. Loudoun Papers, LO4701, Huntington Library; Rogers, 60-70; John Campbell, the Earl of Loudoun, was familiar with many tactics of irregular warfare from his experience a decade earlier in Europe. See Peter E. Russell, "Redcoats in the Wilderness: British Officers and Irregular Warfare in Europe and America, 1740 to 1760," *The William and Mary Quarterly* 35 (October 1978): 638, 645.
14. Thomas Church, *The History of King Philip's War* (Boston: Howe & Norton, Printers, 1825), 261; See also Patrick M. Malone, *The Skulking Way of War* (1991; reprint ed., Baltimore: The John Hopkins University Press, 1993), 109, 114,119.
15. Rogers, 56.
16. Loudoun Papers, LO5314, Huntington Library.
17. Rogers, 74.
18. Loudoun Papers, LO5398, Huntington Library.
19. Louis Antoine de Bougainville, *Adventures in the Wilderness: The American Journals of Louis Antoine de Bougainville 1756-1760*, trans. and ed. Edward P. Hamilton (Norman, OK: University of Oklahoma Press, 1964), 198; E. B. O'Callaghan, ed., *Documents Relative to the Colonial History of the State of New-York* (Albany: Weed, Parsons and Company, Printers, 1858), Volume 10, 703, 838; Rogers, 89-90; Loescher, 370; For the story of the second Battle on Snowshoes see Mary Cochrane Rogers, *A Battle Fought on Snow Shoes* (Derry, N.H.: Mary Cochrane Rogers, 1917), 1-30; Gary Zaboly, "The Battle on Snowshoes," *American History Illustrated*, December

---

*Sergeant David Holden reported that Rogers "lost 2 men & one or two more wounded one of which was Lt. [Nathan] Stone who was Shot Though the foot [.] The Rear of our army Landed [at Fort St. Jean] about 2 o'Clock & EnCampd [on August 30]. 31 Sunday Major Rogers Took & Brought in 17 Prisoners amongst which was one Major & 1 Capt. of ye French army."[89]

1979, 12-24; Cuneo, 74-79; Loescher, 1: 239-60, 364-88; Bellico, 77-89; Bob Bearor, *The Battle on Snowshoes* (Bowie, Md.: Heritage Books, Inc., 1997).

20. Rogers, 146.

21. Ibid., 145.

22. Ibid., 147; See also E. Hoyt, *Antiquarian Researches: Comprising a History of the Indian Wars* (Greenfield, MA: Ansel Phelps, 1824), 304.

23. Pierre Pouchot, *Memoir Upon the Late War in North America Between the French and English, 1755-60*, trans. Michael Cardy and ed. Brian Leigh Dunnigan (Youngstown, N.Y.: Old Fort Niagara Association, Inc., 1994), 249.

24. O'Callaghan, 10: 1042.

25. Thomas Mante, *The History of the Late War in North America* (1772; reprint ed., New York: Research Reprints, Inc., n.d.), 223.

26. Robert Rogers and John Stark, *Reminisences of the French War; Containing Rogers' Expeditions---- The Life and Military Services of Maj. Gen. John Stark* (Concord, N.H.: Luther Roby, 1831), 161.

27. Rogers, 159; Cuneo, 114; Burt Garfield Loescher, *Genesis Rogers Rangers: The First Green Berets* (San Mateo, CA: Burt G. Loescher, 1969), Volume 2, 61, 223.

28. Rogers, 180.

29. Ibid.

30. Ibid., 185-86.

31. Public Record Office, London, Colonial Office, 5/58, UP microfilm reel 5, frames 659-60.

32. Ibid., frame 662.

33. Samuel Jenks, "Samuel Jenks, his Journal of the Campaign in 1760," *Proceedings of the Massachusetts Historical Society* 5 (2nd Series) (1889-90): 355; See also Samuel MacClintock, *Rev. Samuel MacClintock's Journal 1760* (Crown Point, N.Y.: Crown Point Road Association, Inc., 1972), 11.

34. Jenks, 356.

35. Ibid., 364, 361, 357.

36. David Holden, "Journal of Sergeant Holden," *Proceedings of the Massachusetts Historical Society* 4 (2nd Series) (1887-1889): 396; See also P. M. Woodwell, ed., *Diary of Thomas Moody* (South Berwick, ME: The Chronicle Print Shop, 1976), 24; *New-York Mercury*, 25 August 1760.

37. Jenks, 368.

38. MacClintock, 14; See also Holden, 397; Jenks, 368; Woodwell, 26; John Bradbury, "Diary of Dea. John Bradbury," in *Bradbury Memorial*, comp. by William Berry Lapham (Portland, ME: Brown Thurston & Company, 1890), 276-77; John Frost, Jr., "Expedition Against Canada," *Old Eliot* 8 (1908): 114; Lemuel Wood, "Diaries Kept by Lemuel Wood, of Boxford," *The Essex Institute Historical Collection* 20 (1883): 291.

39. O'Callaghan, 10: 1103; André Charbonneau, *The Fortifications of Ile aux Noix* (Ottawa: Minister of Supply and Services Canada, 1994), 58, 331-36; Haldimand Papers, "Misc. Papers Relating to the Provincial Navy 1775-1780," National Archives of Canada, Microfilm H-1649, Volume 1, B144, fol. 99; "Endorsed List of Vessels," PRO CO 5/62, UP microfilm reel 7, frame 446.

40. Jacob Bayley, "Capt. Jacob Bayley's Journal," in *History of Newbury, Vermont*, by Frederic P. Wells (St. Johnsbury, VT: The Caledonian Company, 1902), 379; See also Charbonneau, 56; *New-York Mercury*, 8 September 1760.

41. Frost, 115.

42. Bradbury, 279; See also Woodwell, 30.

43. MacClintock, 16; See also Jenks, 371; Holden, 398; Woodwell, 30; Frost, 115; Wood, 293; Bartholomew Heath mentioned four captured vessels: "a brigg, one sloop and one small ruddo and one schooner." "Letter of Bartholomew Heath of N.H., Aug. 28, 1760," in *Journal and Letters of Rev. Henry True* by Henry True (Marion, OH: Star Press, 1900), 30.

44. Holden, 399.

45. Ibid., 400; See also Josephine Mayer, ed., "The Reminiscences of James Gordon," *New York History* 17 (October 1936): 428-29.

46. For Rogers' journal on the French surrender see Rogers, 201-36; See also Victor Hugo Paltsits ed., "Journal of Robert Rogers the Ranger on his Expedition for Receiving the Capitulation of Western French Posts," *Bulletin of the New York Public Library* 37 (April 1933): 265-76.

47. Josephine Janes Mayer, "Major Robert Rogers Trader," *New York History* 15 (October 1934): 390-94; See also Mayer, "Reminiscences," 429-30.

48. Robert Rogers, *Journals of Major Robert Rogers* (London: J. Millan, 1765); Robert Rogers, *A Con-*

cise Account of North America (London, J. Millan, 1765); In 1769 *Journals* was republished in Dublin, Ireland by R. Acheson; *A Concise Historical Account of All the British Colonies in North-America* was republished in London in 1775 by J. Bew.

49. Mary Cochrane Rogers, 66.
50. Ibid., 44.
51. Ibid., 56.
52. Nevins, 178-257.
53. Ibid., 102; *Dictionary of Canadian Biography* (Toronto: University of Toronto Press, 1979), Volume 4, 680-81.
54. Thomas Gage, *The Correspondence of General Thomas Gage*, comp. and ed. Clarence Edwin Carter (1933; reprint ed. Archon Books, 1969), Volume 1, 79.
55. Ibid., 2: 454; See also Alexander C. Flick, ed., *The Papers of Sir William Johnson* (Albany: The University of the State of New York, 1928), Volume 6, 146, 353.
56. E. B. O'Callaghan, ed., *Documents Relative to the Colonial History of the State of New-York* (Albany: Weed, Parsons and Company, 1856), Volume 7, 991; See also Gage, 1: 161.
57. Gage, 2: 184; Flick, 6: 319; Albert B. Corey, ed., *The Papers of Sir William Johnson* (Albany: The University of the State of New York, 1957), Volume 12, 450, 491.
58. Peter Force, ed., *American Archives*, Fourth Series, Volume 4 (Washington, D.C.: M. St. Clair Clarke and Peter Force, 1843), 696.
59. Cuneo, 263-64; Peter Force, ed., *American Archives*, Fourth Series, Volume 6 (Washington, D.C.: M. St. Clair Clarke and Peter Force, 1846), 1109.
60. For more information on Rogers' experience during the American Revolution see Cuneo, 257-78; Loescher, 2: 167-184; Nevins, 156-71.
61. *The Morning Post and Fashionable World* (London), 25 May 1795 (No. 7274).
62. Rogers, 188-93.
63. Woodwell, 24; This list was also consistent with Sergeant David Holden's description. Holden, 396.
64. Holden, 396; Woodwell, 24; See also Frost 114.
65. Woodwell, 24-25; Bradbury, 275-76; Holden, 396-97; Jenks, 367.
66. MacClintock, 13; See also Frost, 114; Bayley, 379.
67. Woodwell, 25.
68. Holden, 399.
69. Jenks, 368.
70. MacClintock, 14; See also Holden, 397; Bayley, 379.
71. Holden, 397; See also Bradbury, 276; MacClintock 14; Frost, 114; Jenks, 368; Woodwell, 26; Wood, 291.
72. Wood, 20: 292; Woodwell, 29.
73. Bradbury, 279; See also Holden, 398; Woodwell, 29; Wood, 20: 292; Jenks, 370.
74. O'Callaghan, 10: 1104.
75. Woodwell, 30.
76. Jenks, 371; Wood, 20: 293.
77. Haldimand Papers, fol. 99; "Endorsed List," frame 446.
78. J. Clarence Webster, *The Journal of Jeffery Amherst* (Toronto: The Ryerson Press, 1931), 261-62.
79. PRO, CO 5/50, UP microfilm reel 3, frame 42.
80. Charbonneau, 335-36.
81. *New-York Mercury*, 8 September 1760; See also Charbonneau, 333.
82. Haldimand Papers, fol. 99; "Endorsed List," frame 446.
83. PRO 283, WO 34/50, fols. 83, 86.
84. *The Bulletin of the Fort Ticonderoga Museum* 14 (Fall 1985) covers the excavation in detail.
85. Woodwell, 31.
86. Jenks, 373; See also Wood, 20: 293.
87. Lawrence Henry Gipson, *The Great War for the Empire: The Victorious Years 1758-1760* (New York: Alfred A. Knopf, 1949), Volume 7, 456.
88. Bradbury, 281-82.
89. Holden, 400.

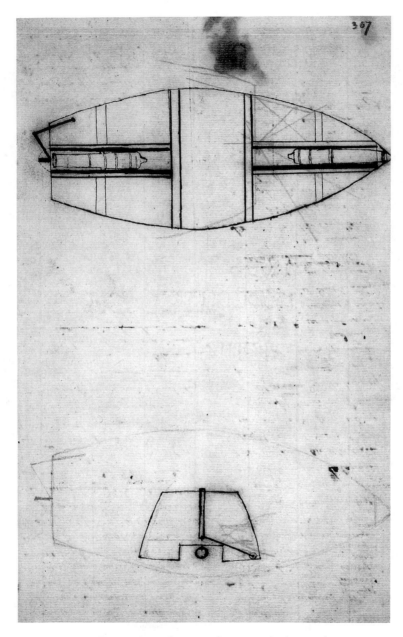

Small French gunboat at Isle-aux-Noix (ca.1759).
(National Archives of Canada)

William Gilliland. Painting by Ralph Earl (1789).
Both the artist and Gilliland were imprisoned for debt in New York City at the time.
(New-York Historical Society)

Part III: Settlement

---

6. William Gilliland 1765

T HE INTRODUCTION OF SETTLERS to the region following the French and Indian War significantly altered the landscape around Lake Champlain. On October 7, 1763, a royal proclamation empowered colonial governors to dispense land adjacent to the lake with preference to the former officers and soldiers who had served in the campaigns for the conquest of New France. William Gilliland launched his colony with a land grant and the purchase of a considerable amount of acreage from a number of former soldiers. Although Gilliland was not the first colonizer at the lake, his narration of events in the settlement of his community provides one of the best early records of the period. Gilliland's colony flourished for more than a decade on the west side of Lake Champlain along the Boquet River, but events of the American Revolution would temporarily suspend occupation of the region.

During the period following the French and Indian War, the forts remained important as transportation depots and way stations for travelers and settlers like William Gilliland. The garrisons at the forts also provided a justice system for settlers, including a place of incarceration for offenders. A number of visitors to North America, including Ralph Izard, Francis Grant, and Adam Gordon, traveled through Lake Champlain in the 1760s, chronicling their observations. In 1765 Lord Adam Gordon, a member of the British Parliament, found the "Works" at Isle-aux-Noix, the site of the 1760 siege of the French fortress, "mouldering away."[1] At Crown Point he noted that the fort "has five Bastions, Mounts 105 Guns, and has casemates for 4000 Men. . .[but] the wood Work is beginning to give. . .Scarce any Guns are Mounted, the Ditch is all cut or blown in a Lime Stone Rock, but is not finished, nor is the Glacis [sloping bank], nor is any out Work of any Sort, except three fortified redoubts with Cannons. . .Within the Fort are good Stone Barracks for Men and Officers" which were also unfinished.[2] Ralph Izard, another British traveler in 1765, recorded that "the fort at Crown Point [is] surprisingly decayed since last year. . .[but] extremely beautiful to the eye."[3] Francis Grant, a visitor from Scotland, described the fort at Crown Point in 1767 as "going fast to decay" and mentioned "several houses, inhabited chiefly by Sutlers [merchants], and some small traders."[4]

Although Lord Gordon found the fort at Ticonderoga in poor condition, Francis Grant noted "a strong redoubt [Lotbinière Battery] for the shipping, which are laid up here, consisting of a large Brigantine which mounted 20 guns, two Schooners, two Sloops, and some small craft; also a Sloop constantly employed in the summer season between this place and St. John's [Jean]."[5] The brigatine was the *Duke of Cumberland*; one of the schooners was *La Vigilante*, and one of the two sloops was the *Boscawen*; and the other *La Brochette*, *L'Esturgeon* or perhaps the *Waggon*.[6] Still in service in the 1760s, the sloop *La Musquelongy* was used to carry William Gilliland's goods from Ticonderoga to Crown Point in June 1766.[7] In 1768 Major General Thomas Gage, the British commander in chief in America, recommended that "the Sloop on Lake Champlain with the rest of the old Craft might be likewise sold if any of the Settlers would purchase them."[8] For the next several years a private contract authorized by the Crown transferred operation of the sloop to John Blackburn.[9]

After viewing the vessels at Ticonderoga, Francis Grant visited the site of Montcalm's breastwork from 1758: "These lines still remain entire, and are very strong. They extend all the way from the [La Chute] River to the Lake, about 2 miles in length, flanked at every place, they are built of large round logs of wood, and are about 8 feet thick at bottom, narrowing to the breadth of one log at top. These logs are very large, and at the angles are morticed into one another; the lines are about man height."[10] Although Gordon, Izard, and Grant failed to mention troop strength at Crown Point and Ticonderoga, both forts were typically manned by two companies of British regular troops during the 1760s.[11]

While the forts remained important outposts in the interwar period, the new settlers would shape the future of the region. The first major colonizer of Lake Champlain began his efforts to obtain a land grant before the end of the war. As early as November 10, 1759, Philip Skene, a brigade major and captain in the 27th Regiment of Foot (Inniskilling), sent a memorial (petition) to Major General Jeffery Amherst, requesting his support for a land patent for a "Settlement of a Tract of said Land agre[e]able to the Boundary Herewith presented, on the Waters of South Bay."[12] Arriving in North America in 1756, Skene subsequently served in the campaigns at Lake George and Lake Champlain and was reactivated for the 1762 expeditions to Martinique and Havana. Before his 1762 service and prior to receiving a land grant, Skene had "settled a number of poor families, and some servants, gave them houses, provisions, cattle and grain" at the southern end of Lake Champlain.[13] Upon returning to New York in 1763, Skene's frustration mounted over the failure to receive a land grant while at the same time others had been awarded parcels of land in the vicinity of Skene's original proposed boundaries specified in his petition. In 1764 Lieutenant Governor Cadwallader Colden of New York granted Skene 25,000 acres of land and King George III awarded him 20,000. The Council of the Province of New York reduced the 25,000 acres to 20,000 to coincide with the King's grant, but Skene's subsequent appeal to the Council restored the 5,000 acres in 1765 after he insisted that the 20,000 acres were intended as a separate patent.[14] Skene and his family were awarded additional acreage in subsequent years, including 3,000 acres in 1771 on the western shore of Lake Champlain in present-day Westport and Port Henry.[15] In 1773 Skene petitioned the Earl of Dartmouth (William Legge), the secretary of state for the colonies, for an appointment as the "Lieutenant Governor of Crown Point, Ticonderoga and It's dependencies."[16] Skene, however, would not receive the appointment for two years.

The second major settlement on Lake Champlain was begun in 1765 by William Gilliland, a native of Ireland who had been a soldier in the 35th Regiment of Foot during the French and Indian War. After his discharge from the army in April 1758 at Philadelphia, Gilliland moved to New York City where the following year he married Elizabeth Phagan, the daughter of a New York merchant. With funds earned from a partnership in New York City with Elizabeth's father, and a substantial dowry from the marriage, Gilliland purchased a large amount of acreage on the western shore of Lake Champlain. In 1764 he purchased 2,000 acres from John Field and more than 10,000 acres from other former officers and soldiers.[17] Subsequently, he acquired additional lands, including acreage at the mouth of the Great Chazy River, a parcel on Cumberland Head, and land opposite Valcour Island.

In February 1765 Gilliland advertised "for sober, honest, and industrious Farmers, Carpenters, Mill-Wrights, Wheel-Wrights, Black-Smiths, Coopers, and Boat-Builders who are inclinable to remove with their Families, against the fifth of May next, to the New Settlement near Crown Point."[18] On May 10, 1765, Gilliland departed from New York City for Lake Champlain with his band of tenant settlers. After a brief stop at Fort Edward, Gilliland's party arrived at Fort George on May 29.* Two days later, the party embarked from Fort George aboard four bateaux; their cattle were transported on the provision boat *Snow Shoe*, a vessel that had originally been built for Amherst's army in 1759. After spending the night of May 31 at Samuel Adams' tavern at Sabbath Day Point, Gilliland arrived in Ticonderoga the next day where he made arrangements at the old sawmill for boards which were subsequently rafted to the new settlement. On June 8 the settlers arrived at the mouth of the Boquet River; the following day a mill site was selected approximately two miles upstream at the falls on the river. Returning to the mouth of the Boquet, Gilliland and his party spread a fishing net, and "ha[u]l'd in 60 Large Fish, being mostly Masquenunge [muskellunge], Bass & Picker[e]l."[23] Within days the settlers began building a 44-foot-long house and a mill; over the years, 28 dwellings would be constructed at the community. William Gilliland had named his settlement Willsboro, based on his own name, and referred to the area surrounding the mill as Milltown.[24] While his tenants toiled at the settlement during the summer, Gilliland embarked on a 40-day trip to Canada. A second excursion in October, lasting one week, brought Gilliland to Cumberland Head to examine his property. The journal

---

*In 1765 Lord Adam Gordon described Fort George as a stockaded fort near the lake as well as a stone bastion: "You find a Small Stockade Fort, tumbling down and not tenible, built in a hurry. . . A little above this (and now called Fort George) we have a Compleat Bastion built of Stone, the Casemates of Wood; It mounts ten Guns."[19] Two years later Francis Grant remarked that "Fort George is situated at the South end of the Lake, nearly fronting the middle of it. There is no fortification except a redoubt. . .mounting 12 guns, about 200 yards from the shore, and some barracks."[20] By 1767 the garrison at Fort George had been reduced to half a company of soldiers.[21] Fort Edward on the other hand, had been abandoned by 1766.[22]

of his October trip follows this text. Gilliland returned to his family in New York City on November 20, leaving his settlers to face a harsh winter in the wilderness.

With 22 wagon loads of goods and his immediate family as well as his mother, brother, sister, and others, Gilliland set out for Willsboro from New York City on April 28, 1766. Tragedy struck, however, on May 10 when a bateau carrying his 6-year-old daughter Jane sank in the Hudson River and the child drowned. Gilliland wrote poignantly of the loss of Jane who was the "Wonder of her Age for Beauty, Stature, Politeness, discretion, Education, propriety of Language, Sweetness of temper Gracefullness of address, Strength of genius & memory, & above all of Charity, and every other Virtue. . .ever generous & Benevolent. . .many who never had seen her, who only knew her Character Bewailed her Death with Tears in their Eyes."[25] Detained by illness and grief, Gilliland did not reach Fort George until June 2; there his stores were placed aboard "Mr. Stoughtons Schooner"* for the voyage to Ticonderoga.[27] Gilliland's goods were then transferred to the sloop *La Musquelongy* at the Fort Ticonderoga dock on Lake Champlain.

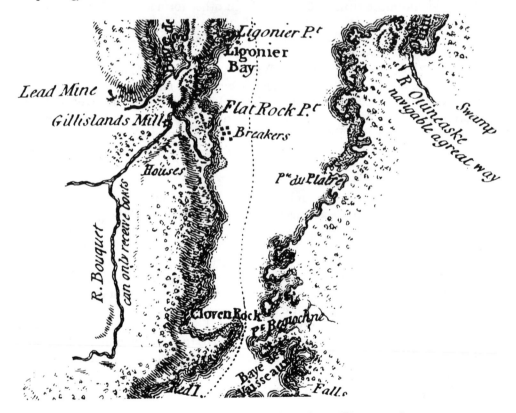

Detail of "A Survey of Lake Champlain" by William Brassier
showing William Gilliland's settlement.
(William Faden Collection, Library of Congress)

*John Stoughton, a French and Indian War veteran from East Windsor, Connecticut, had settled in Ticonderoga in 1765 with his two brothers Joseph and Nathaniel. He drowned on November 25, 1767, when his schooner, laden with three wagon loads of goods, six cows, five sheep, and one horse, sank "above the narrows" during a fierce squall.[26]

On September 2, 1766, Gilliland met at Fort George with Sir Henry Moore, the Governor of New York, Brigadier General Guy Carleton, the Lieutenant Governor of Quebec, Philip Schuyler of Albany, Charles de Fredenburgh and others who were preparing to set the official border between Quebec and the colony of New York. A year earlier, Ralph Izard had encountered several members of the same group who were attempting to find "the forty-fifth degree of north latitude, which is the settled boundary line between the provinces of New York and Canada."[28] After the group reached Crown Point on September 6, 1766, Gilliland "forewarned Cha[s] Fredenburg[h] Esq[r]. against trespassing on my Lands opposite Isle Valcour."[29] Charles de Fredenburgh, of German descent and a former captain in the British army, had settled in present-day Plattsburgh, petitioning for a large tract of land in the vicinity of Gilliland's claims. Fredenburg would build a substantial dwelling near the mouth of the Saranac River, and a sawmill three miles upstream at the falls. In 1769, several years after his original petition, he was granted 30,000 acres of land.[30]

As the survey team sailed north, Gilliland hurriedly gathered the men at his settlement and departed for his land opposite Valcour Island in order to construct a house to forestall any encroachment by Fredenburgh. While his crews were busy erecting a dwelling on the land claim, Gilliland proceeded to Wind Mill Point to rejoin the boundary committee aboard the sloop *La Musquelongy*. Gilliland returned to his pregnant wife at Willsboro on September 14; seven days later Elizabeth gave birth to another daughter, christened Jane. A day before Jane's birth, Governor Moore, Philip Schuyler, Colonel Reid, surveyor Robert Harper, and Lieutenant

"A View of the Falls of Otter Creek, Lake Champlain, North America." Watercolor by Thomas Davies (1766). At the time of William Gilliland's settlement numerous petitions had been filed for land grants on the eastern side of Lake Champlain and early settlers occupied many areas. (Royal Ontario Museum)

Adolphus Benzel, an engineer at Crown Point, stopped at Gilliland's settlement with the news that the boundary line had been fixed "about 3 Miles to the N. Ward of WindMill Point."[31]

During the winter of 1766-1767 Gilliland remained at Willsboro, surveying his land holdings along Lake Champlain. By the late 1760s and early 1770s new land grants would be made and additional settlers would change the landscape along Lake Champlain. In this period, settlers occupied portions of Chazy, Peru, Missisquoi Falls, Shelburne, Ticonderoga, Crown Point, Ferrisburgh, Panton, Addison, Chimney Point, Orwell, Shoreham, Colchester, and other areas.[32] Several land patents would also be awarded to a number of well-known officers from the French and Indian War, including Thomas Ord, who had supervised the building of the radeaux on Lake George and Lake Champlain. Ord received a 5,000-acre tract in present-day Newcomb, Essex County.[33] John Montresor, an engineer and son of chief engineer James Montresor, and two other former soldiers were granted Ligonier Point and Four Brothers Islands.[34] Before long, large tracts of contiguous shoreline along Lake Champlain would be subject to land patents. In 1772, Adolphus Benzel, who had been appointed by the British government as the "Inspector of unappropriated Land in Canada & Lake Champlain," noted that "between South Bay, and Ticonderoga, all the lands are patented on both sides of Lake Champlain."[35] As additional patents were issued, more controversy arose over boundaries. Benzel disclosed a disagreement between Skene and Gilliland over their respective land near present-day Westport: "This tract is surrounded with high mountains which abounds in rich iron ore, the limits whereof are disputed between Major Skene & William Gilliland."[36] Another problem involved the validation of French land titles. Although the British government temporarily suspended new land patents north of Crown Point in 1768 in order to examine the issue of French land holdings, the Crown resolved that consideration of French land titles would be forthcoming only when settlement and improvement of the land had occurred.[37] However, French land claims were never honored by New York.

William Gilliland's settlement along the Boquet River prospered during the early 1770s. Gilliland, however, suffered a personal loss in 1772 when his wife Elizabeth died at the age of 32. On the eve of the American Revolution, Willsboro encompassed "28 dwelling houses, and above 40 other houses, two grist and two [saw] mills" and had 98 inhabitants, according to Gilliland.[38] On March 17, 1775, the community adopted democratic principles of governance at its first formal town meeting. The American Revolution, however, would swiftly alter the tranquility of the colony. During the first two years of the Revolution, Gilliland played a prominent role in the events that were unfolding in the region. He established "the only company of minute men formed on either side of Lake Champlain" and maintained that he had "reason to think that he was the first person who laid a plan for & determined upon seizing Ticonderoga, C[rown] Point and the Kings armed vessel."[39] Gilliland was present at several council of war meetings at Crown Point in 1775 and penned a letter to the Continental Congress supporting Ethan Allen's request for authorization of the Green Mountain Boys as a paid regiment in the northern theater. Gilliland's reputation caused Major General Guy Carleton, the governor of Quebec, to offer "a reward of five hundred dollars to any person that would take [Gilliland] & carry him prisoner to Canada."[40] Ironically, nine years earlier Gilliland and Carleton had amicably participated in the determination of the boundary line between New York and Quebec.

During the summer of 1775 Gilliland's sawmills provided 5,000 board feet of lumber for Major General Philip Schuyler's emerging navy, including boards and planks for the gondolas *Hancock* and *Schuyler* and some bateaux.[41] Gilliland provided vessels for Schuyler's army under field commander Brigadier General Richard Montgomery and maintained that he had personally guided the American expedition to St. Jean, Quebec, in 1775 "from his better knowledge of the navigation."[42] After the American retreat from Canada in 1776, several thousand soldiers camped at Willsboro, where Gilliland furnished food to the defeated army at his own expense. Subsequently, Gilliland drove 100 head of cattle to Crown Point and soon removed his family and belongings to Ticonderoga. Equipment from the mills was later buried in the woods near Willsboro for safekeeping during the expected struggle for control of Lake Champlain.

Despite Gilliland's overt support of the American cause during the summer of 1776, he was suspected of disloyalty as a result of the defection to the British of several of his Willsboro tenants. On July 24, 1776, Colonel Thomas Hartley, the commander at Crown Point, wrote to Major General Horatio Gates, field commander of the Northern Army, "that the supposition that Gilliland and some others had sent down one Edward Watson and another to St. John's [St Jean, Quebec] had some foundation. They doubtless carry any intelligence they have to the enemy."[43] The accusation against Gilliland was largely ignored by Gates who authorized a court of inquiry a week later to examine Gilliland's claims for payment of goods procured for the army.[44] But Gilliland's troubles intensified after he sent a letter to Brigadier General Benedict Arnold on September 1, 1776, requesting an inquiry into the damage done at his settlement by "the troops and sailors accompanying you on your cruise. . .[that] have wantonly and wickedly committed great destruction on several of my plantations in the settlement. . .in the most insolent and licentious manner."[45] A month later Arnold wrote to Gates with the allegation that Gilliland had sent tenants to the British with information, suggesting that "I am fully of [the] opinion that Gilliland, John Watson, and [William] Mc[Au]ley have, from time to time, sent expresses to the enemy, and given them all the intelligence in their power. . .I have therefore ordered to take them prisoners to Ticonderoga."[46] Arnold enclosed Gilliland's letter, submitting that "not one syllable of which is true," and also included a deposition from Sergeant Thomas Day, a former tenant at Willsboro.[47] On October 2, 1776, Gates had Gilliland, Watson, and McAuley brought to Ticonderoga as prisoners. Gates' confinement of the party was apparently quite informal since Colonel Jeduthan Baldwin, the chief engineer at Ticonderoga, noted on October 3 that "Genl. Gates, Revd. Dr. [William] Gordon of Roxbury, Esqr. Gilliland & Mr. Mc[Au]ley Breakfasted with me."[48] Two days later Gilliland and McAuley were again with Baldwin and dined with him on October 8.

Testifying before Justice Robert Lewis, Thomas Day mused that Gilliland "contrived the plan" of the tenants that had defected to the British.[49] When criticism of Willsboro tenants for defrauding the American army occurred after one tenant had purchased military equipment from individual soldiers for "a mere trifle of rum," according to Day, Gilliland allegedly commented that "no matter how much they got out of the country: the more the better."[50] However, with no real evidence against Gilliland, the case against him proceeded no further.

The next year Gilliland futilely petitioned the Continental Congress for payment for crops sold to the quartermaster general of the army and "for the loss of personal property. . .sustained by means of Gen. Arnold."[51] At a time when Benedict Arnold was still regarded as a highly effective general by most, Gilliland denounced him for "comit[ting] the acts of tyranny and outrage. . .intoxicated with power."[52] Trouble dogged Gilliland after the altercation with Arnold. Following the American victory at Saratoga, Gilliland was confined for a few months in Albany for supposedly making disloyal statements and "for only purchasing a free article introduced to me as part of the spoils of [Lieutenant General John] Burgoyne's army, picked up after the battle of the 7th Oct. [1777]."[53]

Gilliland's land holdings at Lake Champlain were greatly reduced by actions of the state of New York during and after the American Revolution. In the course of the war, the state voided all royal grants that had not been validated by actual patents. Although Gilliland had purchased the land rights from former officers and soldiers, he had not received patents for all his holdings, including those in Clinton County, and thus lost most of his investment. He filed a caveat in 1784 "against granting to any other person lands. . .on the west side of Lake Champlain containing together 8,850 acres."[54] The following year Gilliland filed affidavits, certificates, petitions, and other documents with the state of New York supporting his earlier land claims and also proposed leasing Point au Fer and Fort Ticonderoga.[55] With dreams of a manorial estate on hold, Gilliland began selling lots in Willsboro early in 1784. During that spring more than a dozen families established farms at the old settlement.

Problems plagued Gilliland for the rest of his life. He never recovered financially from the losses incurred as a result of the Revolutionary War and during the 1780s lost money in a lumber trading venture with an unscrupulous agent. Because of a large judgment against him on behalf of his former slaves, which he refused to pay, Gilliland was jailed in New York from 1786 to 1791. Suffering from physical and emotional problems, Gilliland returned to the shores of Lake Champlain in present-day Essex where he lived with his daughter Elizabeth and son-in-law, Daniel Ross. Although Gilliland was not mentally fit in his last years, he was apparently competent enough to participate in land deals with others at Lake Champlain.[56] Following a meeting on land holdings with Platt Rogers on February 2, 1796, Gilliland, then 62 years old, strayed from the trail on his way home and froze to death. His body was located several days later. His second gravesite, at the Lakeview Cemetery in Willsboro, overlooks the land he once owned.

The following excerpt from Gilliland's 1765 journal encompasses an eight-day passage to Cumberland Bay. During the journey Gilliland explored the western side of Lake Champlain, including both mouths of the Ausable River, Ausable Chasm, Dead Creek, Little Ausable River, Salmon River, Saranac River, and Cumberland Head. He was undoubtedly the first European immigrant to describe Ausable Chasm.

Journal of William Gilliland[57]

Monday 6 October 1765 Went in a Batteau to visit my Tract of Land at Cumberland Bay, in Company with John Chick, Eliakim [or Eliakum] Ayres, John Wattson & James Sto[c]ker*—on our Passage, went on Shore on the 2 most Western of the 4 Islands found the most Eastward of those 2 being ye Largest of the 4 to Contain 4 or 5 Acres of Choice Land. & the Westward one is Rich but all Covered with Brush, it may be about 3 Acres** then pass'd Close by Sch[u]ylers Island, or Isle Chapon which looks at a distance but dry stoney light Ground, little worth***—

Aerial view of Schuyler Island and the adjacent New York shoreline.
(Photo by the author)

*John Chick was listed by Gilliland as a millwright; Eliakim (Eliakum) Ayres a wagon maker; James Stocker a weaver. John Watson (Wattson) was Gilliland's half-brother and steward at the colony in the latter's absence during the winter of 1765-66.[58]

**Four Brothers Islands, comprising a total of 14 acres, was known as Les Isles des Quatres Vents (Islands of the Four Winds) by the French. In 1764 John Montressor, Francis Mee, and Robert Wallace petitioned for a land grant of the islands as well as for Ligonier Point and Schuyler Island.[59] Montressor was an engineer during the French and Indian War and son of chief engineer James Montresor who had directed construction of Fort George. Today the undeveloped islands are a refuge for several species of birds, including cormorants, herons, egrets, and gulls. With the rise of the population of cormorants on the islands in recent years, questions have arisen regarding their impact on the destruction of trees, vegetation, and fisheries.[60]

***Schuyler Island, known by the French as Isle aux Chapons, covers 123 acres and is located approximately two miles south of Port Kent (western shore). In 1690 Captain John Schuyler, grandfather of Major General Philip Schuyler of Revolutionary War prominence, traveled through this area with militia and Mohawk warriors on his way to raid La Prairie near Montreal. The next year Major Peter Schuyler, mayor of Albany and brother of John Schuyler, also attacked La Prairie after following the same route that his brother had taken a year earlier.[61] Commissary Wilson's orderly book from Amherst's 1759 campaign (Colonel Peter Schuyler of New Jersey was an officer during the expedition) noted "Camp at Schuylers Island, 18th Oct 1759."[62] The next year Captain Samuel Jenks wrote that the bateaux fleet "ma[d]e a harbour on ye north side of an island called Schuylers Island."[63] The island would also play a role following Benedict Arnold's evacuation from Valcour Bay after the 1776 battle. During the early part of the twentieth century Schuyler Island was farmed; today it is a public island under the jurisdiction of New York State's Department of Environmental Conservation.

About six in the Evening, arrived at the high Sandy Clif[f]s, and Encamped there [Port Kent]. Between those is a Grass Swamp Containing I think about 150 Acres without any Trees but is Deep Covered with watter [Wickham Marsh]—

Seventh this Morning moved from our Encampment to the above mentioned River [Lower Mouth of Ausable River] which I Call the Callen Watter [after the Irish river Callan] & there found it alive with Ducks and Geese* it is about a Mile to Northward of the South side of the most Northerly Sandy Clif[f] & on the South side of it is a Grass Swamp of about 70 Acres [Ausable Marsh]—Put on our Potts** at the Mouth of this River which is about 60 Yards Wide and proceeded up it in order to discover it's falls and their distance from the Lake—

First Station from the Lake up the River is South 88 Degrees. West about 15 Chains.*** South 70 Degrees West 8 Chains North 50 Degrees West 16 Chains to a Grass Swamp of 50 Acres and a Dead Creek being North 65 Degrees West—Then North 60 Degrees West 6 Chains North 20 Degrees West 10 Chains North 50 Degrees East 15 Chains to a Branch that runs East to the Lake South 55 Degrees West 10 Chains to the Junction of 3 Branches then up the Mid[d]le Branch [Ausable River] North 80 West 9 Chains—when we found the left hand Branch to be Occasioned by a small Island then Soth 60 West 3 Chains to rapids that are passable for Batteaus then To one same Co[u]rse 28 Chains Smooth Good Watter the River Twice as large as Boquet [River] and more—then an Island main Channell on Right Hand going up, then from the near point of the Island.—West about 4 Chains to Rapids.† Then South 10 Chains—then South 60 Degrees West 35 Chains—then South 10 Degrees East 20 Ch. Then from South East to South West about 120 Chains to the falls which we Judge to be about 12 feet—in this place the River form'd into amost Curious Canal [Ausable Chasm] this is a prodigious Rock—It is amost admirable Sight appearing on Each Side like aregular Built Wall somewhat Ruinated and one would think that this prodigious Clif[f] was occasioned by an Earth Quake, their h[e]ight on Each Side is from 40 to 100 feet in the Different places we Seen about half a Mile of it and by it's appearance where we Stop[p]ed it may Continue very many Miles farther.

Returned to the Mouth of this River thru the North Branch [Upper Mouth of the Ausable River] to our Encamping place where we stay'd this Night, and found the Island that it is Enclosed between those Two Branches to be mostly an unprofitable Drowned Swamp‡

Eighth[.] Set out this morning from River Ausable Northerly & about a Mile

---

*During adverse weather on October 16, 1749, Peter Kalm "found a haven" at the Lower Mouth of the Ausable River, noting "the entire shore was sandy; some of the sand had the same characteristics as desert sand, namely that it was swirled about by the wind."[64]

**Potts may refer to a bag net used in fishing.[65]

***A chain is a unit of length used in surveying and is equivalent to 66 feet.

†On November 11, 1772, Adolphus Benzel, "Inspector of Unappropriated Lands in Canada and Lake Champlain," reported that a survey party that he directed "proceeded to the river au Sable upon which river we went eight or nine miles in a boat, the current being at last too rapid (but not impracticable) prevented our going further by water. I therefore directed the same party to traverse by land who returned that there was considerable quantitys of large pine timber near the banks and environs."[66]

‡Remarkably, Gilliland's campsite was probably near the present-day Ausable Point State Park Campground operated by New York's Department of Environmental Conservation. On October 15, 1749, Peter Kalm had also camped "for the night just north of Rivière au Sable."[67]

to the Northward thereof, being on the North Side of along point [Ausable Point] discovered a Considerable Creek which from the Many Thousands of Ducks we seen there we Call Duck Creek [Dead Creek]—We penetrated it and found that it is made by an overflow of the Lake into a Large Grass Swamp which was well Covered with good wild Grass fit for Hay—The ninth[.] about 300 Acres I travell[e]d up the Creek until Loss'd it which was about a Mile, here I walked on dry Land round it's most Westerly End and Came to the Lake on the North side of it, having gone from the Lake up the south side.

Proceeded thro[ugh] the Woods from Duck Creek about a Mile till I came to a Considerable Creek of Still Water, which from the Number of Trees we seen Cut by Beavers, we Call Beaver River [Little Ausable River], went up this Creek about half a Mile no appearance of Falls, but hope to discover them before the End of 2 Miles the Land adjoining being Rou[g]hly Cover'd with the best of white and Black Oak, and white and y[e]llow pine, the Land very Good from this Creek to the beginning of the Sergeants Land* which is about 1/4 of a Mile and it is valuable to a Chain or Two South of Duck Creek on Account of the great Meadow—Proceeded from Beaver River [Little Ausable River] thro[ugh] the woods to the Sergeants Land which begins at a Large White Oak Tree that stands a few yards from the strand & is Marked A on the East Side.

From hence proceeded to within about a Mile of Cragan River [Salmon River]. Doe Run which is a Small Stream that empty's it self into the Lake in a Small Bay West of the South End of Isle Valc[o]ur and found the Land to be very Good this far, and from it's appearance may [be] Good for half-a Mile farther but begins to be more Ordinary with a Mixture of Quaking Ash Some Hemlock and Spruce, not much Oak alittle or no Pine to a Rapid Stream that has Watter enough for a Grist Mill, this we Call Indian Brook [Silver Stream] and so from thence to Cragan River [Salmon River] which I take to be about the North End of Stewarts tract** went up this River about 100 yards to a 10 f[oo]t Falls by Carrying the Watter 45 yards—this is a Noble Situation for a Saw Mill as a Dam Can be made by a few Hands in a Day here is Watter for Two Mills in the Dryest Season and Dead Watter to the foot of the falls***—The Pine Ridge begins about a Mile to the North West of those falls—which is the next Pine to them and it Continues to Savaniac River [Saranac River]† and the Land is Ordinary between those but Worst next [to] the last named River—But by it's appearance is good after you are about a Mile West from the Lake—very pr[e]tty Pines in this Ridge, but not large, yet handy Saw Logs those nearest the last named River being the best and there the Ridge inclines nearest the Lake, being on the very Bank—

---

*"Sergeants Land" refers to the patents of former non-commissioned officers from the French and Indian War.

**Peter Stewart, former Masters Mate on the H.M.S. *Shannon* and H.M.S. *Shrewsbury*, had petitioned for 2,000 acres on the western side of Lake Champlain opposite Valcour Island. He later received title to the property and deeded it to Gilliland but the papers were never legally executed. [68]

***The next year Gilliand directed four men from Willsboro to build a house at Salmon River in order to establish his land claim.[69] He later named his holdings at the mouth of the river Janesboro after his daughter. The land was later owned by his grandsons William and Henry P. Gilliland.[70]

†While the name Saranac River may have originated with Native Americans, it could also be a corruption of the French name for the river, St. Amant, which Gilliland and others spelled St. Aranack.[71]

Proceeded about Two Miles up this River which found to be much larger than Boquet and Rapid from it's Mouth up—at about 400 yards from the Lake there is a Rift where the Water may be Conveniently lifted and by Carrying it about 200 yards will produce a Fall of about 10 feet which with Two feet that may be raised by a Small Stoney dam will be enough for a Mill.*

The land appears extremely well on the North Side of this Creek and abounds with Choice Oak & Pine Timber, mix'd, but is notwithstanding but light with a Sandy Bottom but still may produce a Good hearty Crop to the Distance of about half a Mile North of the River when the Land grows Worse But the Pinery [pine forest] much Better for half a Mile more then the Pinery Ends and the Land Improves.

For another half Mile to Five Chaines to the North Eastward of the South West End of along Sandy Be[a]ch at the Bottom of Cumberland Bay—in the whole of this tract at about a Mile distance from the Lake The Land appears to be very Good from thence from 6 to 12 Miles Back to the Mountains being mostly Covered with Oak, Ash, Maple, Beech Hickory Bass Elm &c. without any mixture of ever Greens from the end of the said five Chaines to Cumberland Creek [Dead Creek] the Land and Timber very Bad, op[p]osite to it having a fine Sandy Be[a]ch a Mile and Half long Cumberland River is a Black Dead Creek—no appearance of Rapid or Falls, But a Fall Could be forced [made]; On the South Side of this Creek is a Pitch pine mark'd A. at which Lieutenant Lowe['s] tract** of Cumberland Head begins, and takes in the whole of that Peninsula which I walk'd over, and found the Land to be Deep and Rich no way Hilly or Broken the Timber Chiefly Oak and there of the best kind without Ever Greens and very little Poplar or Quaking Ash except a trifle on ye Shore, and the Situation is most Beautiful and heartsome projecting near Four Miles into the Lake*** tho[ugh] only from one and a Quarter to one and a Half Miles in width—from the Bottom of Cumberland Bay we proceeded homeward on Friday the Eleventh October and Arrived that Night, on our passage V[i]ewing the Islands S[ai]nt Michael† valcour‡ & Chapon or Schuyler Island all of which we found ordinary—light Rocky, Stony Land, and Ill Timb[e]red—

Returned home the 13.th Oct.

---

*Charles de Fredenburgh, a former captain in the British army, would shortly thereafter build a house near the mouth of the Saranac River and a sawmill at the falls. Fredenburgh subsequently petitioned New York for 30,000 acres which he received in 1769.[72] However, in late 1772 Adolphus Benzel reported that "I proceeded to the River Saranac in the Bay of Cumberland where I found an empty house and a saw mill deserted in the environs. Has formerly been a considerable quantity of fine white pine destroyed by the saw mill and exportation of masts by Messrs. Fredenburg[h], [Francis] M[a]cKay, [Moses ?] Hazen & c."[73]

**Former Lieutenant Abram Lowe (also spelled Abraham Low) of the Royal American Regiment (60th Regiment) had petitioned for 2,000 acres in 1765. Lowe assigned the land to Gilliland but New York never gave a title to Lowe, so Gilliland's claim was declared invalid.[74]

***Cape Scononton was the earlier French name for Cumberland Head.[75]

†Isle St. Michel, a 35-acre island lying about two and a half miles southeast of present-day Plattsburgh, was later renamed Crab Island. American and British sailors and marines were buried on the island following the 1814 Battle of Plattsburgh Bay. The island is now owned by New York State.

‡Valcour Island, a 1,000-acre public island lying four and a half miles southeast of Plattsburgh, retained its original French name and became famous as the site of a crucial naval battle in 1776.

Aerial view of Valcour Island from the north.
(Photo by Richard K. Dean)

NOTES

1. Newton D. Mereness, *Travels in the American Colonies* (1916; reprint ed., New York: Antiquarian Press, Ltd., 1961), 443.
2. Ibid., 444.
3. [Ralph Izard], *An Account of a Journey to Niagara, Montreal and Quebec in 1765* (New York: William Osborn, 1846), 28.
4. Frances Grant, "Journal from New York to Canada, 1767," *Proceedings of the New York State Historical Association* 30 (1932): 319.
5. Grant, 319-20.
6. Haldimand Papers, "Misc. Papers Relating to the Provincial Navy 1775-1780," National Archives of Canada, Microfilm H-1649, Volume 1, B144, fol. 99; Endorsed List of Vessels, Public Record Office, London, Colonial Office Records 5/62, University Publications of America microfilm reel 7, frame 446.
7. Winslow C. Watson, *Pioneer History of the Champlain Valley* (Albany: J. Munsell, 1863), 128.
8. Clarence Edwin Carter, comp. and ed., *The Correspondence of General Thomas Gage* (1933; reprint ed., Archon Books, 1969), Volume 1, 179.
9. Carter, 2: 466, 554.
10. Grant, 320.
11. Carter, 1: 61; Carter, 2: 282, 410.
12. Public Record Office, London, CO 5/57, UP microfilm reel 4, frame 899; See also Philip Skene, "Copy of a Memorial of Major of Brigade Philip Skene to his Excellency Jeffery Amherst Esqr," *Collections of the New-York Historical Society* 5 (1921):303-5.
13. John Pell, "Philip Skene of Skenesborough," *Proceedings of the New York State Historical Association* 26 (1928): 29.
14. [E. B. O'Callaghan], comp., *Calendar of N.Y. Colonial Manuscripts: Indorsed Land Papers 1643-1863* (1864; reprint ed., Harrison, N.Y.: Harbor Hill Books, 1987), 339, 354, 356, 358-59; Doris Begor Morton, *Philip Skene of Skenesborough* (Granville, N.Y.: The Grastorf Press, 24-25; *History of Washington County, New York* (1878; reprint ed., Interlaken, N.Y.: Heart of the Lakes Publishing, 1991), 34.
15. Morton, 26; [E. B. O'Callaghan], *Indorsed Land Papers* 473, 535, 538.
16. Carter, 2: 158; See also PRO, CO 5/90, UP microfilm reel 1, frame 272.
17. Some sources use the name James or Joseph Field, but land papers recorded John Field. [E. B.

O'Callaghan], *Indorsed Land Papers*, 336-37; Winslow C. Watson, *The Military and Civil History of the County of Essex, New York* (Albany: J. Munsell, 1869), 123; See also Watson, *Pioneer History*, 26; John Pell, "The Saga of Will Gilliland," *New York History* 13 (October 1932): 392; Gilliland's original land petition in 1763 had requested 60,000 acres. [E. B. O'Callaghan], *Indorsed Land Papers*, 324, see also 336-37, 685, 692.

18. *Weyman's New York Gazetteer*, 11 February 1765.
19. Mereness, 445.
20. Grant, 321.
21. Carter, 2: 382, 410.
22. Ibid., 323; See also Carter, 1: 90; Izard, 29; Grant, 221.
23. William Gilliland, Willisborough Town-Book Commencing the 8th Day of June 1765, Plattsburgh Public Library, Plattsburgh, New York, 3.
24. Ibid., 4.
25. Ibid., 31-32.
26. Jane M. Lape, ed., *Ticonderoga-Patches and Patterns from Its Past* (Ticonderoga, N.Y.: The Ticonderoga Historical Society, 1969), 25.
27. Gilliland, 33.
28. Izard, 28.
29. Gilliland, 37.
30. [E. B. O'Callaghan], *Indorsed Land Papers*, 474; [Peter S. Palmer], *Historical Sketch of Plattsburgh, New York* (Plattsburgh, N.Y.: Plattsburgh *Republican*, 1893), 3; Allan S. Everest, *Briefly Told, Plattsburgh, New York, 1784-1984* (Plattsburgh, N.Y.: Clinton County Historical Association, 1984), 1; Marjorie Lansing Porter, *Old Plattsburgh* (Plattsburgh, N.Y.: Clinton Press, Inc., 1944), 3; Watson, *Pioneer History*, 40-41.
31. Gilliland, 39.
32. Walter Hill Crockett, *A History of Lake Champlain* (Burlington: McAuliffe Paper Co., 1909), 87-98; Watson, *Military and Civil History*, 299-314; [Palmer] *Historical Sketch*, 4; Duane Hamilton Hurd, *History of Clinton and Franklin Counties, New York* (1880; reprint ed., Plattsburgh, N.Y.: Clinton County American Revolution Bicentennial Commission, 1978), 117; Porter, 3; [O'Callaghan], *Indorsed Land Papers*, 308-9, 324, 326-40, 342, 344-45, 351, 354-59, 366-76, 378, 380-85, 397, 399-404, 406-7, 412, 427, 433, 438, 444-45, 449, 454-55, 466, 469, 472-74, 477, 484, 497-98, 500-501, 510-11, 521-23, 526-31, 533-42, 544, 546, 549-51, 553-54, 558-60, 563-64, 566-68, 572, 592, 596, 599, 603-5, 607, 615, 632; See also David E. E. Mix, *Catalogue Maps and Surveys, in the Office of the Secretary of State, State Engineer and Surveyor* (Albany: Charles Van Benthuysen, 1859), 153-54, 159-63, 166-67, 169, 172-73, 180-83, 185-93, 195-96, 198-99, 201-12.
33. Watson, *Military and Civil History*, 310; E. B. O'Callaghan, *Documents Relative to the Colonial History of the State of New-York* (Albany: Weed, Parsons and Company, Printers, 1857), Volume 8, 529; [O'Callaghan], *Indorsed Land Papers*, 378.
34. Watson, *Military and Civil History*, 309; [O'Callaghan], *Indorsed Land Papers*, 335, 366.
35. Adolphus Benzel, "Adolphus Benzel's 1772 Notes on Lake Champlain," *The Bulletin of the Fort Ticonderoga Museum* 12 (December 1969): 360; For additional material on the background of Benzel see G. G. Benedict, "Manuscript Map of Crown Point, Over 135 Years Ago," *The Vermont Antiquarian* 1 (December 1902): 37-38.
36. Benzel, 361.
37. Nell Jane Barnett Sullivan and David Kendall Martin, *A History of the Town of Chazy* (Burlington, VT.: George Little Press, Inc., 1970), 16-18.
38. Watson, *Pioneer History*, 179, 175.
39. Ibid., 177, 48, 175.
40. Ibid., 175; See also Pell, *Gilliland*, 400-401.
41. Don R. Gerlach, *Proud Patriot-Philip Schuyler and the War of Independence, 1775-1783* (Syracuse, N.Y.: Syracuse University Press, 1987), 37; Russell P. Bellico, *Sails and Steam in the Mountains: A Maritime and Military History of Lake George and Lake Champlain* (Fleischmanns, N.Y.: Purple Mountain Press, 1992), 121.
42. Watson, *Pioneer History*, 176; Although there is scant corroboration for Gilliland's pilot story, Rudolphus Ritzema, a lieutenant colonel in the 1st New York Regiment, noted that "Mr. Gillilan[d] paid us a Visit" at Isle La Motte during the expedition to St. Jean. Rudolphus Ritzema, "Journal of Col. Rudolphus Ritzema," *The Magazine of American History* 1 (1877): 98.

43. Peter Force, ed., *American Archives*, Fifth Series, Volume 1 (Washington, D.C.: M. St. Clair Clarke and Peter Force, 1848), 564.
44. Ibid., 801.
45. Peter Force, ed., *American Archives*, Fifth Series, Volume 2 (Washington, D.C.: M. St. Clair Clarke and Peter Force, 1851), 112.
46. Ibid., 592.
47. Ibid; While sailing north with the American fleet in late August 1776, Bayze Wells, however, noted that Arnold informed the captains of the vessels "that th[e]re was Compla[i]nt Made by the Inhabitants that th[ei]r houses w[e]re Rob[b]ᵈ of Furn[i]ture th[ei]r fields and Gardens of the fru[i]t th[e]reof in th[ei]r absence" and ordered that the inhabitants be reimbrused and "no Boat Should be al[l]owᵈ to go on Shore Without an Officer." Bayze Wells, "Journal of Bayze Wells of Farmington," *Collections of the Connecticut Historical Society* 7 (1899): 273.
48. Jeduthan Baldwin, *The Revolutionary Journal of Col. Jeduthan Baldwin 1775-1778*, ed. Thomas Williams Baldwin (Bangor, ME.: DeBurians, 1906), 78; See also Malcolm Freiberg, ed., "The Reverend William Gordon's Autumn 1776 Tour of the Northeast," *The New England Quarterly* 65 (September 1992): 475.
49. Force, 2: 592.
50. Ibid., 592-93.
51. Watson, *Pioneer History*, 181.
52. Ibid., 180.
53. Ibid., 183.
54. [O'Callaghan], *Indorsed Land Papers*, 652.
55. Ibid., 660, 669, 685-92.
56. Ibid., 980-81, 989-90, 998; See also Watson, *Pioneer History*, 84-85.
57. Gilliland, 20-23; For the most complete transcription of Gilliland's entire journal and details of his life see *The Journal of William Gilliland*, edited by David Kendall Martin, transcribed and annotated by Fuller Allen with an introduction by Betty J. Baldwin (Plattsburgh: Clinton County Historical Association, 1997).
58. Gilliland, 1-2; Watson *Pioneer History*, 122.
59. [O'Callaghan], *Indorsed Land Papers*, 335, 366.
60. Richard MacDonald, "The Cormorant Question," *Adirondack Life*, May/June 1997, 32-34, 36-37.
61. E. B. O'Callaghan, ed., *The Documentary History of the State of New-York* (Albany: Weed, Parsons & Co., 1849), Volume 2, 286; E. B. O'Callaghan, ed., *Documents Relative to the Colonial History of the State of New-York* (Albany: Weed, Parsons and Company Printers, 1853), 800-5; Peter S. Palmer, *History of Lake Champlain*, 4th ed.(1886; reprint ed., Fleischmanns, N.Y.: Purple Mountain Press, 1992), 41-42; Guy Omeron Coolidge, *The French Occupation of the Champlain Valley from 1609 to 1759*, 2nd ed. (1938; reprint ed., Mamaroneck, N.Y.: Harbor Hill Books, 1989), 61-63.
62. Commissary Wilson, *Commissary Wilson's Orderly Book 1759* (Albany: J. Munsell, 1857), 187.
63. Samuel Jenks, "Samuel Jenks, his Journal of the Campaign in 1760," *Proceedings of the Massachusetts Historical Society* 5 (2nd Series) (1889-90): 367.
64. Adolph B. Benson, ed., *Peter Kalm's Travels in North America* (New York: Wilson-Erickson, Inc., 1937), Volume 1, 570.
65. Richard M. Lederer, Jr., *Colonial American English* (Essex, Ct.: Verbatim, 1985), 89.
66. Benzel, 361-62.
67. Benson, 568.
68. [O'Callaghan], *Indorsed Land Papers*, 361; Mix, 160; Martin, *Journal of William Gilliland*, 13.
69. Watson, *Pioneer History*, 133.
70. Ibid., 116.
71. Ibid., 117; "Carte du Lac Champlain" in E. B. O'Callaghan, ed., *The Documentary History of the State of New-York* (Albany: Weed, Parsons & Co., Public Printers, 1849), Volume 1; "Karte Von Dem Flube Richelieu und dem See Champlain, 1744," New York State Library.
72. [O'Callaghan], *Indorsed Land Papers*, 474, see also 449, 454; [Palmer] *Historical Sketch*, 3-5; Porter, 3.
73. Benzel, 362.
74. Martin, *Journal of William Gilliland*, xxix, 15; Watson, *Pioneer History*, 193-94.
75. "Carte du Lac Champlain," O'Callaghan, *Documentary History*, Volume 1.

"Ethan Allen at Fort Ticonderoga May 10th 1775" by Frederick Coffay Yohn.
Poster commissioned by the Dixon Ticonderoga Pencil Company (1927).
(Vermont Historical Society)

Part IV: The American Revolution

---

7. Jocelyn Feltham 1775

LIEUTENANT JOCELYN FELTHAM of the British 26th Regiment of Foot was no stranger to Lake Champlain, having been first assigned to Fort Ticonderoga on June 9, 1772.[1] Three years later, Feltham would draft the most detailed report of the capture of Fort Ticonderoga by forces led by Ethan Allen and Benedict Arnold. Writing six days before the seizure of the fort, Reverend Thomas Allen, a patriot minister from Pittsfield, Massachusetts, and personal friend of Ethan Allen, "pray[ed] for success to this important expedition, as the taking. . .[of Fort Ticonderoga and Crown Point] would afford us a Key to all Canada."[2] The Ticonderoga expedition of 1775, the first offensive campaign of the American Revolution, resulted in American control of the strategic Lake George-Lake Champlain waterway and provided an important source of cannon subsequently employed to force the British from Boston.

For officers such as Lieutenant Jocelyn Feltham, duty at Fort Ticonderoga and Crown Point was usually uneventful and often allowed time for farming. The peacetime camaraderie at the forts was shattered in 1773 when a fire, which substantially destroyed Crown Point, led to a turbulent court of inquiry in Montreal. Feltham brought serious charges of misconduct against the commander at Crown Point, Captain William Anstruther of the 26th Regiment of Foot. Feltham and Anstruther had arrived at the Lake Champlain forts on June 9, 1772, and both had been first commissioned in the 26th Regiment on January 1, 1766. Both officers were recalled to Canada where Feltham accused Anstruther of "not having a Guard on his Majesty's Fort, nor a Sentry at the Magazine at the time the Barracks took fire. . .for laying the Accident of the Fire to the Negligence of the Barracks Master knowing it to be occasioned by two of his Soldiers Wives boiling Soap. . .for not giving any Assistance to either the Barrack Master [and others]. . .for allowing sundry

187

kinds of stores of Steel and Iron. . .to be taken away & plundered by the Country People. . .for not obeying General Gage's Order to dig for every thing that could be got out of the Ruins and sent to Ticonderoga, but employing his Men in Work of his own, such as Mowing, Hoeing."[3] The results of the court of inquiry, held in November 1773, were inconclusive with "palpable Contradictions in the Evidences on both Sides."[4] Major General Frederick Haldimand, acting commander in chief in Lieutenant General Thomas Gage's absence, passed on the report of the hearing to the secretary for the American colonies, William Legge, the Second Earl of Dartmouth. Although Haldimand felt that the fire was from "an accidental cause," he suggested that "the discipline of the Garrison [had been] relaxed to a great degree" and recommended a general court-martial to shed light on the contradictory evidence.[5] Eventually a court martial was authorized, but the beginning of the American Revolution eclipsed further consideration of the case. Anstruther was replaced by Captain William Delaplace, also of the 26th Regiment of Foot, who made his headquarters at Fort Ticonderoga.

On October 6, 1773, Major General Haldimand reported to Lord Darmouth that Crown Point had been abandoned and the garrison at Fort Ticonderoga would be reinforced but warned that the latter fort was "in a most ruinous condition, and will soon require some considerable repairs."[6] In the spring of 1774 Haldimand sent Captain-Lieutenant John Montresor, an engineer with the extensive experience during the French and Indian War, to evaluate and make recommendations on the Lake Champlain fortifications. In his May 13 report Montresor found Fort Ticonderoga in such "ruinous" condition "that it would require more to repair it than the construction of a new Fort."[7] Montresor recommended rebuilding Crown Point since Ticonderoga did not meet "the purpose. . .intended of protecting Navigation, Vessels, Storehouses, Wharves, Landing, &c. both with respect to its Distance and situation. . .together with the unhealthiness of the place"; Montresor found Crown Point "an amazing useless Mass of Earth" as a result of the fire and suggested an enlargement of the Grenadier Redoubt (present-day site of the Champlain monument) as the main fort, which Haldimand supported.[9] Three and a half months later General Gage endorsed Haldimand's proposal in a letter to Lord Dartmouth but added that "Establishing a Post also at Ticonderoga, might be consider'd at the same time."[10] On November 2, 1774, Lord Dartmouth approved the reestablishment of the posts at Ticonderoga and Crown Point but by then it was too late in the season to begin any construction.

By 1775 dissension in the American colonies had irreversibly escalated.* In February the Boston Committee of Correspondence voted to open communication with Canada and thereafter dispatched attorney John Brown of Pittsfield to Montreal and Quebec. Writing from Montreal on March 29, 1775, Brown advised the Boston Committee that the Canadians would remain neutral and British troops "in

---

*A long collision course between Great Britain and the American colonies began soon after the Treaty of Paris in 1763, ending the Seven Years' War (French and Indian War in North America). After the end of the war, Great Britain attempted to raise revenue in the colonies by imposing new taxes in order to help repay the swelling national debt incurred largely from the war and to pay the expenses of a standing army in North America. New taxes in the colonies, although substantially lower than the tax burden on citizens of Great Britain, came at a time when Americans no longer needed the protection of the British army against French invaders. Prior to the end of the French and Indian War, the movement to western lands was encouraged by a liberal British land policy, but a Royal Proclamation of 1763 forbade colonial governors from issuing land grants beyond the sources of rivers that emptied

this Province are ordered to hold themselves in readiness for Boston, on the shortest notice."[11] To prevent the movement of British troops to the colonies, Brown proposed "the Fort at Ticonderoga must be seized as soon as possible, should hostilities be committed by the King's Troops. The people on New Hampshire Grants [Green Mountain Boys] have [been] engaged to do this business, and in my opinion they are the most proper persons for this job."[12]. In the spring of 1775 Major General Guy Carleton, the governor of Quebec, sent reinforcements to Fort Ticonderoga at Captain William Delaplace's request, perhaps with the knowledge of John Brown's mission in Canada. It was at this time that Lieutenant Jocelyn Feltham returned to Fort Ticonderoga. Earlier, Feltham had bemoaned the fact that his recall from the outpost had resulted in a financial loss, including "some of my cattle [that] were drowned by carelessness during the winter."[13]

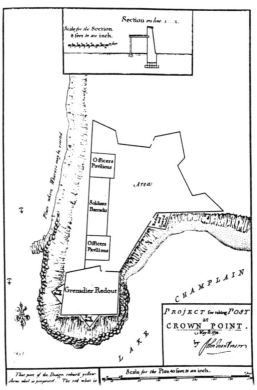

Plans for an enlargement of the Grenadier Redoubt at Crown Point by Captain-Lieutenant John Montresor (1774).
(Crown Collection, New York State Library)

After months of heightened military and political maneuvering in the Boston vicinity, the first shots of the American Revolution were fired at Lexington and Concord on April 19, 1775. Barely a week later preparations to capture Fort Ticonderoga and Crown Point were set in motion. At the head of the New Haven militia, Captain Benedict Arnold, a combative, no-nonsense, sea captain-merchant, departed for Cambridge, Massachusetts, on April 22 with a plan to take Fort Ticonderoga. Outside of Hartford, Connecticut, Arnold met Colonel Samuel Parsons, a lawyer and prominent Connecticut assemblyman, returning from Boston. Parsons had earlier expressed his concern "for the want of heavy cannon" at Boston and later wrote "I fell in with Capt. Arnold, who gave me an account of the state of Ticonderoga, and that a great number of brass cannon were there."[14]

into the Atlantic Ocean. British policy, aimed at exploiting the fur trade in the west and avoiding problems with Native Americans, created dissension among colonists seeking new land. The Quebec Act of 1774, enacted by Britain, assigned much of the western land to Native Americans and to the Province of Quebec. A combination of new taxes, changes in land policy, enforcement of British law in admiralty courts, and restrictions on currency, trade, and manufacturing gradually coalesced the opposition to arbitrary British policy. Opposition to British policy, however, had little impact on the settlers in the Lake Champlain region during most of the interwar period as immigration to the rich valley accelerated.

Arnold's idea of seizing Ticonderoga evidently had a lingering impact on Parsons who met in Hartford on April 27 with Silas Deane, a Yale-educated lawyer and member of the Continental Congress. At this meeting with Deane, several members of the Connecticut Committee of Correspondence "first undertook and projected taking that fort."[15]

When Arnold reached Cambridge, his plan for the capture of Fort Ticonderoga won favor with Dr. Joseph Warren, chairman of the Massachusetts Committee of Safety. The scheme was quickly approved by the Provincial Congress of Massachusetts; Arnold was elevated to the rank of colonel in the Massachusetts militia and issued "one hundred Pounds, in cash. . .two hundred pounds of Gunpowder, two hundred weight of Lead Balls, and one thousand Flints and also ten horses. . .to proceed with all expedition to the Western parts where you are directed to enlist. . .[400] men, and with them forthwith to march to the Fort at Ticonderoga. . .to reduce. . .[and] bring back with you such of the cannon, mortars, stores, &c., as you shall judge may be serviceable to the Army here."[16] Arnold promptly departed with Captain Eleazer Oswald, his subordinate from the New Haven militia, and approximately 20 of his Connecticut men. Arnold later rode ahead with a servant, leaving his officers to recruit volunteers along the way. After learning that another expedition was already underway, he journeyed hastily to Castleton, Vermont, the rendezvous point for the second expedition, arriving on the evening of May 8.

Meanwhile, the expedition from Hartford, Connecticut, was well underway. Shortly after the approval of the Ticonderoga expedition by the Connecticut Committee on April 27, Captains Noah Phelps and Bernard Romans and a small group of men departed from Hartford with 300 pounds borrowed from the Connecticut treasury. On April 29 Captains Edward Mott and Epaphras Bull and five others also left Hartford, recruiting 16 volunteers along the roads of western Connecticut before reaching Pittsfield, Massachusetts. Heman Allen, Ethan Allen's brother from Salisbury, Connecticut, was sent ahead to assist his brother Ethan in mobilizing the Green Mountain Boys on the New Hampshire Grants (present-day Vermont). Another brother, Levi Allen, joined the expedition on the road between Stockbridge and Pittsfield, Massachusetts. At Pittsfield the group met with Colonel James Easton and attorney John Brown, who joined the entourage and subsequently enlisted 39 more men from Massachusetts. As the small army approached Bennington, it was greeted with news that a man who had recently stopped at Ticonderoga reported "a Reinforcement from Canada & that they were fixing up the Sloop in the Lake with men & Arms, the Acct. of which Seem'd to Damp[en] our Spirits much," recorded Captain Epaphras Bull.[17] After arriving at Bennington and meeting with Colonel Ethan Allen of the Green Mountain Boys, the participants agreed to dispatch Captains Noah Phelps and Ezra Heacock (also spelled Hickok) to gather intelligence at Fort Ticonderoga.* Captain Elisha Phelps, Noah's brother, noted

---

*On May 9 Reverend Thomas Allen of Pittsfield had written to Brigadier General Seth Pomeroy in Boston with information gathered from a traveler who reported that British troops at Ticonderoga were "alarmed with an Expedition. . .[and] judged near 200 [troops] at Ticonderoga."[18] The story was proven erroneous on May 10. Benjamin Church, Jr., who signed Benedict Arnold's orders for the Fort Ticonderoga expedition, authorized by the Massachusetts Committee of Safety on May 3, 1775, was a spy for the British, but the information on the operation never reached Captain William Delaplace at Ticonderoga.

that the reconnoitering party later rejoined the expedition at Castleton and "informed us that the Regulars was not any ways appri[s]ed of our coming."[19]

On May 7 the Connecticut contingent with James Easton, John Brown, and the new recruits arrived at Castleton, meeting with Ethan Allen and the Green Mountain Boys from the New Hampshire Grants. The Grants men lived in present-day Vermont on land claimed by both New Hampshire and New York. Their leader, Ethan Allen, had migrated from Salisbury, Connecticut, in 1769 after a series of financial setbacks and legal problems. Allen was a natural leader—vigorous, enterprising, spirited and often brash in demeanor, decisive in action, with an imposing physical presence. Although noted for feats of physical strength, Allen was a multi-dimensional individual who once prepared for Yale College and later wrote cogent documents espousing democratic principles of government.[20] When the authorities of New York tried to expel settlers on the New Hampshire Grants, Allen and his Green Mountain Boys effectively blocked the legal action through overt and covert threats of violence. Even surveyors from New York were coerced into a hasty retreat from the New Hampshire Grants. During the 1770s Allen's defiant, energetic presence throughout the Grants region virtually brought New York's attempts to claim land there to a standstill. Although Allen may have ostensibly been protecting his own investment in Grants land (Onion River Company), his actions would have a long-term impact on the eventual political make-up of Vermont.

A council of war held at Castleton elected Captain Edward Mott as chairman of the committee to capture Fort Ticonderoga and Crown Point, Colonel Ethan Allen as the commander of the army, Colonel James Easton as second in command, and Colonel Seth Warner as third; the commands reflected the number of troops raised by the three individuals. A detachment of 30 men, under the command of Captain Samuel Herrick, was assigned to the capture of Skenesborough (present-day Whitehall). With matters apparently settled, Benedict Arnold galloped into Castleton and, after showing his orders from Massachusetts, demanded command of the entire expedition. According to Captain Edward Mott, Arnold contended that "we had no proper orders."[21] Technically Arnold was correct; six days after the capture of the fort, the Connecticut Committee of Correspondence suggested that the Ticonderoga expedition had been undertaken by "some individuals of this Colony, in a secret manner."[22] On May 30 Colonel Samuel Parsons noted that the Ticonderoga campaign had begun "without the knowledge and approbation of the [Connecticut] Assembly."[23] The forces at Castleton that were preparing for the seizure of Ticonderoga "were shockingly surprised" by Arnold's insistence of command of the expedition "which bred such a mutiny among the soldiers which had nearly frustrated our whole design, as our men were for. . .marching home."[24] Arnold, followed by an entourage of disgruntled Green Mountain Boys, rushed forward to overtake Allen on his way to Lake Champlain. The problem was quickly resolved when Allen assured his men that he would continue to command them. Captain Epaphras Bull noted that Arnold was temporarily placated when it was "agreed that he take the Left hand of Col. Allen."[25] With his recruits nowhere in sight, Arnold had little choice but to join Allen's campaign or be totally eclipsed from the capture of the fort.

During the evening of May 9, the intrepid raiders massed at Hands Cove in Shoreham, about two miles north of the fort on the east side of the lake. Without enough boats, only 83 men crossed the lake in the early morning hours of May 10. After another argument over who would proceed into the fort first, Allen and Arnold "entered the fortress. . .side by side" through a gate with a wicket in the south curtain wall.[26] As the invaders passed into the fort, a sentry "instantly snapped his fusee [fusil or light musket]" at Allen and ran away.[27] Passing into the parade ground, the invaders shouted "three huzzas," whereupon a second sentry charged and slightly wounded one of Allen's officers with a bayonet after which Allen immediately struck a blow with his sword "on the side of the head; upon which he dropped his gun, and asked quarter."[28] With directions to the commandant's room on the second story of the west barracks, Allen and Arnold had started up the steps when they were met by a partially-dressed Lieutenant Feltham. Mistaking Feltham for the post commander, Allen demanded the surrender of the fort. What exact words were uttered by Allen is still subject to some debate. In time Captain William Delaplace appeared fully dressed and surrendered the fort. Incredibly, the garrison at Fort Ticonderoga, comprised of 45 men and 24 women and children, was apparently unaware of the beginning of hostilities in Boston. Ethan Allen later described the hours immediately after the seizure of the fort: "the sun seemed to rise that morning with a superior lustre; and Ticonderoga and its dependencies smiled on its conquerors, who tossed about the flowing bowl [of liquor], and wished success to Congress, and the liberty and freedom of America."[29]

The capture of several nearby posts was easily accomplished. Captain Samuel Herrick and a detachment that had been dispatched earlier to Skenesborough apprehended the family of loyalist Philip Skene, including his son Andrew Skene, and his 41-foot trading schooner *Katherine*. (Skene himself was taken into custody in Philadelphia upon returning from England the following month.) After more men were ferried across the lake from Shoreham, Colonel Seth Warner was sent to Crown Point, where he and his men seized the dilapidated fort occupied by nine men and ten women and children.

After the capture of Ticonderoga, the victors reassigned troops to occupy Fort George on the southern end of Lake George. No longer garrisoned, except for two men, Fort George was nominally under the supervision of Captain John Nordberg, a 65-year-old retired British officer on half-pay living in a cottage nearby. Bernard Romans from Wethersfield, Connecticut, is generally given credit for the capture of the fort since Nordberg's subsequent petition to the Provincial Congress of New York stated that "the 12th of May last Mr. Romans came & took possession of Fort George, Mr. Romans behaved very genteel and civil to me."[30] However, Captain Epaphras Bull noted that his party "arriv'd at 9 o'clock PM [on May 11] where we met Capt. [John] Stephens with 15 Men Come on from Fort Edward to take Possession of Fort George tho' it Happen'd to be given up to 3 or 4 of our men who we sent forward before they Arr[ive]d. Soon after our Arrival Capt. Roman[s] our Engineer Came up."[31]

On the day of the seizure of Ticonderoga, Captain Edward Mott reported that "Col. Arnold challenged the command again, and insisted that he had a right to have it."[32] Once more the forces under Allen threatened to return home, inducing committee chairman Mott to promptly write orders appointing Allen commander of the garrison. Arnold immediately penned a letter to the Massachusetts Committee of Safety, complaining that Allen's men were acting "in the greatest confusion and anarchy, destroying and plundering private property, committing every enormity, and paying no attention to publick service."[33] Writing in his regimental memorandum book, Arnold recorded bitterly that Allen "assumed the [e]ntire command, & I was not Consulted or Advised With, for 4 Days which Time I spent in the Garrison As a private Person, often Insulted by him & his Officers Threat[e]ned with my Life & twice Shot at by his Men with their Fusees."[34]

Arnold's isolation finally ended on the afternoon of May 14 when Captains Jonathan Brown and Eleazer Oswald and 50 volunteers, enlisted under Arnold's original Massachusetts orders, arrived at the fort in Philip Skene's captured schooner. Wasting no time, Arnold refitted the schooner, renamed the *Liberty*, with "4 Carriage & 6 Swiv[e]l guns."[35]

On May 16 Arnold and his volunteers departed from Crown Point for St. Jean, Quebec, on a mission to capture a British sloop berthed there. Hampered by a lack of wind, the raiding party reached St. Jean on May 18, capturing the 70-ton sloop and several bateaux. Captain Eleazer Oswald noted that Arnold's troops immediately "hoisted sail and returned in triumph," meeting Ethan Allen six miles southward of St. Jean "with four boats and ninety men" on their way to occupy the British post which "Col. [Benedict] Arnold thought impracticable."[36] Since Allen's men were in "a starving condition," Arnold supplied the poorly-prepared detachment with provisions.[37] Arnold was unsuccessful in dissuading Allen from the expedition, but the next morning the leader of the Green Mountain Boys was convinced otherwise by 200 British regulars who attacked his camp on the east bank of the Richelieu River across from St. Jean.

Upon his return from St. Jean, Arnold sent a letter to the Massachusetts Committee of Safety, describing the capture of the British sloop and enclosing a detailed list of the condition of 86 cannon taken at Ticonderoga and 111 at Crown Point.[38] A day earlier, on May 18, the Continental Congress had decided to abandon Fort Ticonderoga and Crown Point; all of the artillery would be temporarily moved to Fort George. Upon hearing the news Arnold protested the decision: "Ticonderoga is the Key of this extensive Country, & if abandon'd leaves a very extensive Frontier Open to the Ravages of the Enemy."[39] Ethan Allen also warned the Continental Congress of the dire consequences of abandoning Ticonderoga and Crown Point, which would allow reoccupation of Lake Champlain by British forces. Recognizing the danger of relinquishing control of Lake Champlain, the colony of Connecticut took direct action by sending four companies of soldiers with 500 pounds of gunpowder to hold Ticonderoga. Because of vehement protests from many sectors of the colonies, the Continental Congress on May 31 rescinded its decision and officially requested the governor of Connecticut to reinforce the Lake Champlain forts. However, the two ambitious rivals, Arnold and Allen, would both see an end of their command at Lake Champlain within a month's time; Allen was replaced as commander of the Green Mountain Boys by Seth Warner in an election, and Arnold resigned his Massachusetts commission over a dispute involving a change in command at Ticonderoga.

Instead of abandoning Lake Champlain, the Continental Congress became convinced of the importance of the waterway as a staging area for an invasion of Canada. Ethan Allen's letter of May 29 to the Continental Congress suggested that "push[ing] the war against the Kings Troops in Canada, the more friends we shall

Left: Major General Philip Schuyler by Alonzo Chappel.
(New York State Library)
Right: Brigadier General Richard Montgomery. Engraving by G. R. Hall.
(New York State Library)

find in that Country. . .we should have but little to fear from the Canadians or Indians and would easily make a Conquest of that Place and set up the Standard of American Liberty."[40] Two weeks later Benedict Arnold made a detailed proposal to the Continental Congress for the invasion of Canada by taking possession of Montreal and Quebec with 2,000 men, 1,000 of whom would "proceed directly to Montreal," while 700 would "cut off Communication between St Johns [St. Jean], Chambl[y], & Montreal."[41] Once Montreal fell with the help of "friends" who would open the gates to the city, Chambly, St. Jean, and Quebec would soon surrender.[42] The conquest of Canada, according to Arnold, would "discourage the Enemies of American Liberty. . .deprive Great-Britain, of the lucrative Branch [of] the Fur Trade, and. . .an inexhaustible Granary."[43]

Arnold's offer to undertake the command of a Canadian operation was not approved by the Continental Congress since two of his antagonists from the Ticonderoga expedition, Colonel James Easton and John Brown, had disparaged Arnold's reputation in Philadelphia. Arnold, however, did have his defenders, including Barnabas Deane who wrote to his brother Silas on June 1 that Arnold maintained some semblance of order at Ticonderoga but was "greatly abused and misrepresented by designing persons."[44] The Continental Congress decided to appoint 41-year-old Philip Schuyler, who had an established name, to the position as a major general to lead the newly-formed Northern Department. Schuyler, a patrician of one of the most famous families in New York history, was a well-connected political figure and a committed supporter of the patriot cause. Thirty-seven-year-old Richard Montgomery, a former British officer who had served at Lake Champlain during Amherst's 1759 and Haviland's 1760 campaigns, was commissioned a brigadier general in the Continental Army and second in command to Schuyler.*

The subsequent invasion of Canada involved two separate armies: one that followed the traditional route via Lake Champlain and the Richelieu River and the other embarked on an arduous trail through the back rivers of present-day Maine. Schuyler, whose organizational skills were honed serving as a commissary during the French and Indian War, quickly transformed the deteriorated posts of Fort George, Fort Ticonderoga, and Crown Point into viable staging areas for a Canadian invasion. Bateaux were hurriedly constructed at Lake George while two 60-foot gondolas, the *Hancock* and *Schuyler*, each "mounting one 12 Pounder in her Bow and twelve Swivels in her Sides," were completed at Lake Champlain.[46] The new vessels supplemented the existing American fleet, consisting of the schooner *Liberty* and the captured British sloop which had earlier been renamed the *Enterprise* and armed with "2 Brass 6 Pounders and four Iron 3 [pounders] with 11 Swivels."[47]

As the army mobilized for the Canadian invasion, Major John Brown of Pittsfield, Massachusetts, aboard the sloop *Enterprise* on duty north of Isle La Motte, penned an urgent letter on August 23 to Brigadier General Montgomery with news that the British were nearing completion of two large vessels at St. Jean, beseeching the general to send part of the army immediately. Five days later Montgomery departed from Ticonderoga with 1,200 troops, reaching Isle La Motte on September 2. Two days later an ailing Major General Schuyler reached Isle La Motte and issued orders to set sail for Isle-aux-Noix, the abandoned French stronghold used during the French and Indian War. Schuyler, suffering from fever and rheumatic gout a good deal of the time at Isle-aux-Noix, was finally transported back to Ticonderoga on September 16. Plagued by illness among the troops, insufficient artillery, and an inexperienced army, the siege of Fort St. Jean lasted nearly two months.

While the American army constructed breastworks and completed batteries for the siege of St. Jean, Colonel Ethan Allen with a small group of American and Canadian volunteers rashly decided to capture Montreal. A separate party under the leadership of Major John Brown was to join Allen's assault on Montreal, but Brown withdrew after discovering that the St. Lawrence River was too turbulent to cross. Surrounded by British regulars, Canadians, and Indians, Allen was forced to surrender on September 25 after many of his men had fled, leaving "but forty-five men with me."[48]

In October fresh American reinforcements intensified the siege at St. Jean but heavy rains and strong winds hampered operations. Montgomery's forces succeeded in sinking the British schooner *Royal Savage* at her dock and a detachment under Majors John Brown and Henry Livingston subsequently captured Fort Chambly. At Longueil on October 30 Colonel Seth Warner's Green Mountain Boys thwarted a much larger British force that had been dispatched to break the siege of Fort St. Jean. With no hope of immediate relief, the isolated garrison at Fort St. Jean, under

---

*Brigadier General Richard Montgomery was described by a fellow officer "as well limbed, tall and handsome, though his face was much pockmarked. His air and manner designated the real soldier."[45]

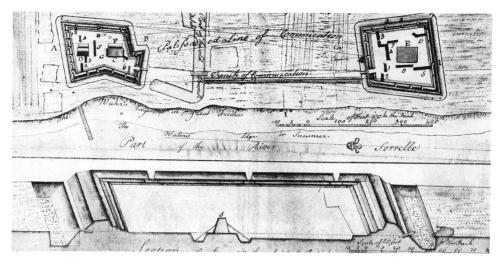

"Plan of the Two Redoubts erected at St. Johns [St. Jean]. . .in the Summer of 1775."
(National Archives of Canada)

Schooner *Royal Savage* captured at St. Jean by the Americans in 1775. From an original sketch in the Schuyler Papers of the New York Public Library. (Special Collections, Benjamin F. Feinberg Library at SUNY Plattsburgh)

the command of Major Charles Preston, capitulated on November 2. The success at St. Jean represented the first large-scale military victory of the fledging American army. The triumph also provided the Americans with two more vessels for their Lake Champlain navy: the "Royal Savage, of about 70 T[o]ns full rig[g]ed pierced for 14 Guns, 6 and four Pounders [and] one Rowagall[e]y" pierced for three guns.[49] The unfinished row galley was taken to Fort Ticonderoga in late November and later converted to the schooner *Revenge.** Troops returning to Crown Point and Ticonderoga on November 26 experienced a harrowing journey through a blinding snowstorm. Freezing temperatures resulted in the deaths of some soldiers on the open decks.****

*The captured row galley with troops from Colonel David Waterbury's regiment departed for Ticonderoga on November 21, 1775, arriving at Crown Point on November 24. The row galley was taken to Ticonderoga three days later with the sloop *Enterprise* and schooner *Royal Savage*.[50] When Charles Carroll stopped at Ticonderoga on April 22, 1776, on his way to Canada he "saw four vessels, viz: three schooners, two were taken from the enemy on the surrender of St. John's [St. Jean]."[51] The four vessels included the schooners *Liberty*, *Royal Savage*, and *Revenge*, and the sloop *Enterprise*. The gondolas *Hancock* and *Schuyler* were taken into the St. Lawrence River by the Americans.

**Reverend Benjamin Trumbull from Connecticut recorded the torturous journey on Lake Champlain aboard the sloop *Enterprise*: "Sunday Morning Nov[r]. 26th soon after Midnight there came on a

As Montgomery's army besieged Fort St. Jean, a second army, commissioned by George Washington with the support of Philip Schuyler and led by Colonel Benedict Arnold, struggled through the rugged hinterland of Maine along virgin rivers and streams. On November 9, after an arduous trek of 45 days, 600 emaciated survivors of the expedition reached the St. Lawrence River, opposite fortress Quebec. Following the surrender of St. Jean, Montgomery's troops pushed forward to Montreal and later captured eleven British vessels fleeing to Quebec City. Major General Guy Carleton, however, slipped through the American lines to take command of Quebec's defenses. On December 1, Montgomery reached Arnold's forces besieging Quebec. In a dramatic coordinated attack on both the Upper Town and Lower Town of Quebec during a fierce snowstorm on New Year's Eve, Montgomery was killed and Arnold wounded. The assault failed, leaving the American siege of Quebec stalemated. At the same time Colonel Henry Knox's Herculean effort to transport 59 cannon and mortars from Fort Ticonderoga to Boston was well underway.

Despite the failure at Quebec, the Americans had achieved considerable success in the northern theater of the war during 1775: first with the capture of Fort Ticonderoga and Crown Point, followed by naval control of Lake Champlain, triumph at Fort St. Jean, and the taking of Montreal.

The following condensed report of Lieutenant Jocelyn Feltham describes the capture of Fort Ticonderoga on May 10. Written only a month after the capture of the fort, Feltham's account is the most detailed and perhaps the least biased narration of the events on May 10. Nearly all of the British captives, including Feltham, were sent to Hartford, Connecticut. On May 31, 1775, Lieutenant Feltham and another officer were permitted to travel to New York and New Jersey where Feltham wrote this report at Captain Delaplace's behest to Lieutenant General Thomas Gage, the British commander in chief in North America. Delaplace, however, remained a prisoner in Wethersfield, Connecticut, for more than a year.* Feltham was promoted to captain-lieutenant in 1777 and captain in 1778, but his name disappeared from the list of British officers in 1780. Feltham's military legacy, nevertheless, endures in his chronicle of the capture of Fort Ticonderoga.

Snow Storm at North East, the wind was so strong that we were in continual Fear that our Sloop would part her Cable, and that we should go on shore. When the Morning Light came on, we found ourselves in such a Situation that it was Judged more safe to hoist a small Sail and run before the Wind than to lie at Anchor where we were. We hoisted a small matter of sail and were driven by the Wind near 80 Miles before Night. It snowed so fast, and the Air was so thick, that for a considerable Part of the Day, we had not a man on board who knew where we were. We once run in between two Islands where we had not more than one foot, or a foot and half of Water to spare and knew not which Way to steer with safety. But God, in his great Goodness, who had unusually appeared for us through the whole Campaign, preserved us from general and immediate Destruction. The Day was very cold as well as Stormy. Some who were obliged to be on Deck were frozen. The Army was never in greater apparent Danger than at this Time. The storm abated towards Night, and we came to an Anchor, soon after Sunset, off against Crown Point. The next Day we arrived at Ticonderoga, and carried in the Prizes which We had taken at St. John's."[52]

*Captain William Delaplace wrote to John Hancock, president of the Continental Congress on May 2, 1776, of his "many particular and severe hardships, to wit: his private stock at Ticonderoga, consisting of forty-five sheep, eleven horned cattle, household and kitchen furniture," as well as three muskets and a sword which Ethan Allen and Benedict Arnold assured him that he would not lose.[53] Delaplace was still a prisoner at the end of 1776 and upon his release sold his commission.

Lieutenant Feltham's Report to Lieutenant General Gage[54]

New York June 11th 1775.

Sir

Capt [William] Delaplace of the 26th reg^t has given me directions to lay before you in as plain a narrative as I can the manner of the surprizal of the fort of Ticonderoga on the 10th May with all the circumstances after it that I thought might be of any service in giving your Ex^y any light into the affair.

Capt Delaplace having in the course of the winter applied to Gen: Carleton* for a reinforcement, as he had reason to suspect some attack from some circumstances that happen'd in his neighbourhood, Gen Carleton was pleased to order a detachment of a subaltern and 20 men to be sent in two or three sep[a]rate parties the first party of which was sent as a crew along with Major [William] Dunbar who left Canada about the 12th April, I being the first subaltern on command was ordered down with 10 men in a few days more, to give up to Capt Delaplace with whom L^t [Arthur] Wadman was to remain, having receiv'd orders from the reg^t some time before to join there. As he was not arrived when I came I had orders to wait until he did I was 12 days there before he came which was about an hour after the fort was surprized. I had not lain in the fort on my arrival having left the only tolerable rooms there. . .for Mr Wadman if he arrived with his family, but being unwell, had lain in the fort for two or three nights preceding the 10th May, on which morning about half an hour after three in my sleep I was awaken'd by numbers of shrieks, & the words no quarter, no quarter from a number of arm'd rabble I jump'd up about which time I heard the noise continue in the area of the fort** I ran undress'd to knock at Capt Delaplaces door & to receive his orders or wake him, the door was fast the room I lay in being close to Capt Delaplaces I step[ped] back, put on my coat & waist coat & return'd to his room, there being no possibility of getting to the men as there were numbers of the rioters on the bastions of the wing of the fort on which the door of my room and back door of Capt Delaplaces room led, with great difficulty, I got into his room being pursued from which there was a door down by the stairs in the area of the fort, I ask'd Capt Delaplace who was now just

---

*Guy Carleton (1724-1808) was commissioned an ensign in the 25th Regiment of Foot in 1742. In 1758 he was appointed a lieutenant colonel in the 72nd Regiment of Foot and led the Royal Americans at Quebec, receiving a head wound during the battle on the Plains of Abraham on September 13, 1759. Carleton was seriously wounded in France in 1761 and again during the siege of Havana the following year. In 1766 he became lieutenant governor of Quebec and was elevated to the rank of brigadier general in North America; two years later Carleton became governor. An adept administrator, Carleton had a hand in formulating the Quebec Act of 1774 and worked effectively with the French minority in Canada. Carleton held fortress Quebec during the American siege of 1775-1776. In the fall of 1776 General Carleton led the British invasion of the United States via Lake Champlain, defeating Benedict Arnold at Valcour Island. However, Carleton's forces withdrew to Canada in November. After his command at Quebec ended in 1778, he returned to England only to come back to America in 1782 as commander in chief of British forces. Carleton returned to Canada as governor of Quebec in 1786, retiring from the post after ten years of service. He died suddenly at his country home in England in 1808 at the age of 85.

**The commotion that Lieutenant Feltham heard may have been "the Indian war-whoop" from the Americans as they entered the fort.[55] Ethan Allen and James Easton both recalled that the invaders shouted "three huzzas" of cheer as they reached the parade ground of the fort.[56]

Aerial view of Fort Ticonderoga.
(Photo by the author)

up what I should do, & offer'd to force my way if possible to our men, on opening this door the bottom of the stairs was fill[e]d with the rioters & many were forcing their way up, knowing the Comm^g Officer lived there, as they had broke open the lower rooms where the officers live in [the] winter, and could not find them there, from the top of the stairs I endeavour'd to make them hear me, but it was impossible, on making a signal not to come up the stairs, they stop'd, & proclaim'd silence among themselves, I then address'd them, but in a st[y]le not agreeable to them I ask'd them a number of questions, expecting to amuse them till our people fired which I must certainly. . .thought would have been the case, after asking them the most material questions I could think viz by what authority they entered his majesties fort* who were the leaders what their intent &c &c I was inform'd by one Ethan Allen and one Benedict Arnold that they had a joint command, Arnold informing me he came from instructions rec^d from the congress at Cambridge which he afterwards sh[o]wed me. Mr Allen told me his orders were from the province of Connecticut & that he must have immediate possession of the fort and all the effects of George the third (those were his words) Mr Allen insisting on this with a drawn

---

*Four years after the capture of the fort, Ethan Allen wrote that he answered "In the name of the great Jehovah, and the Continental Congress."[57] According to Benson J. Lossing (*The Pictorial Field-Book of the Revolution*), an eyewitness suggested that Allen exclaimed two more words: "In the name of the Great Jehovah and the Continental Congress, by God."[58] By oral history, Noah Callender, another eyewitness, corroborated Allen's 1779 account.[59] The recollections of eyewitnesses, however, may have been influenced by Allen's 1779 book, *A Narrative of Colonel Ethan Allen's Captivity*, which sold eight editions in only two years. In the late nineteenth century, one writer disputed Allen's words, suggesting that "Prof. James D. Butler of Madison, Wisconsin, has informed me that his grandfather Israel Harris was present, and had often told him that Ethan Allen's real language was, 'Come out of here, you d___d old rat.' "[60]

sword over my head & numbers of his followers firelocks presented at me alledging I was commanding officer & to give up the fort,* and if it was not comply'd with, or that there was a single gun fired in the fort neither man woman or child should be left alive in the fort Mr Arnold begg'd it in a genteel manner but without success, it was owing to him they were prevented getting into Capt Delaplaces room, after they found I did not command. Capt Delaplace being now dress'd came out, when after talking to him some time, they put me back into the room they placed two sentry's on me and took Capt Delaplace down stairs they also placed sentrys at the back door, from the beginning of the noise till half an hour after this I never saw a Soldier, tho' I heard a great noise in their rooms and can not account otherwise than that they must have been seiz'd in their beds before I got on the stairs, or at the first coming in, which must be the case as Allen wounded one of the guard[s] on his struggling with him in the guard room immediately after his entrance into the fort.**

When I did see our men they were drawn up without arms, which were all put into one room over which they placed sentrys and allotted one to each soldier their strength at first coming that is the number they had ferry'd over in the night amounted to about 90 but from their entrance & shouting they were constantly landing men till about 10 OClock when I suppose there were about 300,*** & by the next morning at least another 100 who I suppose were waiting the event & came now to join in the plunder which was most rigidly perform'd as to liquors, provisions, &c whether belonging to his majesty or private property,† about noon on the 10th May, our men were sent to the landing at L[ake] George, & sent over next day, then march'd by Albany to Hartford in Connecticut where they arrived on the 22^d they would not allow an Officer to go with them tho' I requested it. they

---

*Ethan Allen (*Narrative*) stated that he "ordered the commander (Capt. Delaplace) to come forth instantly, or I would sacrifice the whole garrison; at which the capt. came immediately to the door with his breeches in his hand."[61] However, it is clear from this report that a partially-dressed Lieutenant Feltham first materialized at the door. Early books on the subject repeated Allen's version of Captain Delaplace's appearance half-dressed at the door.[62]

**Captain Epaphras Bull reported that a guard at the fort's gate resisted capture "which Col[on]el Allen Seeing went with his Cutlass & Struck him on the Side of his Neck tho' no Great Wound."[63] Allen wrote that he had struck a sentry on the side of his head with his sword, causing a "slight cut."[64] Noah Callender, also present at the seizure of the fort, later maintained that the force of Allen's blow had been "obstructed by a comb which the soldier's hair was done up."[65]

***Feltham's estimate is fairly close to the numbers mentioned in American accounts. John Brown reported that 85 men had crossed the lake during the night; Ethan Allen suggested 83, and James Easton noted 80.[66] The total number of men who had assembled on the eastern shore of Lake Champlain that night was reported as 150 just after the event, according to John Brown, Ethan Allen, and Benedict Arnold.[67] However, James Easton used the figure of 240 at the lake, and a letter to the Massachusetts Congress on May 10, 1775, by James Easton, Epaphras Bull, Edward Mott, and Noah Phelps stated that a total of 210 men were present.[68]

†The day following the American takeover of Ticonderoga, Benedict Arnold wrote to the Massachusetts Committee of Safety, disclosing that 100 men at the fort were acting "in the greatest confusion and anarchy, destroying and plundering private property, committing every enormity."[69] After the victory Allen's men consumed most of the rum at the fort in celebration. The November 18, 1775, "Account of Moneys Expended by Connecticut, for Taking Possession of Ticonderoga, & c." included an item "to Capt. Delaplace for liquors supplied the Garrison—18 [pounds] 11 [shilling] 9 [pence]."[70]

‡The rest of Feltham's report covered his petition for release, the capture of the British sloop at St. Jean, and the prisoners taken at the British posts. Lieutenant Feltham listed the names of 43 men at

sent Capt Delaplace his Lady family & Lt Wadman & myself by Skenesborough to Hartford where we arrived the 21st [of May].‡

Notes

1. Clarence Edwin Carter, *The Correspondence of General Thomas Gage 1763-1775* (1933; reprint ed., Archon Books, 1969), Volume 2, 638.
2. Allen to Pomeroy, 4 May 1775, *The Historical Magazine* 1 (1857): 109.
3. Public Record Office, London, Colonial Office Records 5, Volume 91, University Publications of America microfilm reel 1, frames 311, 314, 324, 355, 378.
4. Ibid., frame 505.
5. Ibid., frames 307, 306.
6. Ibid., frame 254.
7. Ibid., frame 563.
8. Ibid., frame 564.
9. Ibid., frame 565.
10. Carter, 1: 368.
11. Peter Force, ed., *American Archives*, Fourth Series, Volume 2 (Washington, D.C.: M. St. Clair Clarke and Peter Force, 1839), 243.
12. Ibid., 244.
13. Allen French, *The Taking of Ticonderoga in 1775: the British Story* (Cambridge, MA.: Havard University Press, 1928), 36.
14. "Papers Relating to the Expedition to Ticonderoga," *Collections of the Connecticut Historical Society* 1 (1860): 182.
15. Ibid.; See also J. H. Trumbull, *The Origin of the Expedition Against Ticonderoga in 1775* (Hartford: J. H. Trumbull, 1869), 12-13.
16. Force, Fourth Series, 2: 750-51; See also "Who Took Ticonderoga," *The Bulletin of the Fort Ticonderoga Museum* 4 (January 1937): 57-58.
17. Epaphras Bull, "Journal of Epaphras Bull," *The Bulletin of the Fort Ticonderoga Museum* 8 (July 1948): 38.
18. Allen to Pomeroy, 9 May 1775, *The Historical Magazine* 1 (1857): 109; Force, Fourth Series, 2: 546; Lucius E. Chittenden, *The Capture of Ticonderoga* (Rutland, VT.: Tuttle & Company, Printers, 1872), 116.
19. "Papers Relating," 175; See also Royal R. Hinman, comp., *A Historical Collection of the Part Sustained by Connecticut* (Hartford: E. Gleanson, 1842), 29-30; Josiah F. Goodhue, *History of the Town of Shoreham, Vermont* (1861; reprint ed., Rutland, VT.: Academy Books, 1988), 12-13; Chittenden, 37, 107-8, 111.
20. Michael A. Bellesiles, *Revolutionary Outlaws: Ethan Allen and the Struggle for Independence on the Early American Frontier* (Charlottesville, VA.: University Press of Virginia, 1993), 88,96,99.
21. "Papers Relating," 171.

Ticonderoga, two at Lake Champlain, nine at Crown Point, and five at the Lake George landing. His table "Total number of prisoners sent into New England from the two garrisons of those taken on both lakes" specified 57 men and 34 women and children.[71] Feltham also attached a 700-word statement to his report to Lieutenant General Thomas Gage with descriptions of the "conspirators" and others involved in the capture of Ticonderoga, Crown Point, and Fort George.[72]

He ended the report to Gage with news that Philip Skene had been taken prisoner in Philadelphia. Enroute to America from London, Skene's ship *Sally* was diverted to Philadelphia by her captain upon learning of the seizure of the Lake Champlain forts and the probability that Skene would be wanted for questioning. Arriving in Philadelphia on June 7, Skene, with an appointment of lieutenant governor of Ticonderoga and Crown Point, was taken into custody because he "had declared [that] he had authority to raise a Regiment in America; from all this, apprehending that the said Skene is a dangerous parti[s]an of Administration, and that his papers may contain intelligence of Ministerial designs against America."[73] John Hancock, as president of the Continental Congress, boarded the *Sally* and demanded Skene's papers. On June 27 Skene was sent as a prisoner to Hartford, Connecticut, where he remained until his exchange on September 28, 1776. The next year Skene joined Lieutenant General John Burgoyne's invasion of the rebellious colonies via the Lake Champlain corridor.

22. Force, Fourth Series, 2: 618.
23. "Papers Relating," 185.
24. Force, Fourth Series, 2: 558.
25. Bull, 40.
26. Force, Fourth Series, 2: 606; See also John Pell, *Ethan Allen* (1929; reprint ed., Lake George, N.Y.: Adirondack Resorts Press, Inc., n.d.), 84; Ethan Allen, *A Narrative of Colonel Ethan Allen's Captivity Containing His Voyages & Travels* (1779; reprint ed., Rutland, VT.: Vermont Statehood Bicentennial Commission, 1988), 6-7; Force, Fourth Series, 2: 623; For the story on the boats used in crossing Lake Champlain see Goodhue, 13, 16; Chittenden, 41-42; John Pell, 82.
27. E. Allen, *Narrative*, 7; See also Force, Fourth Series, 2: 624; Chittenden, 114.
28. E. Allen, *Narrative*, 8; Epaphras Bull has a slightly different sequence for Allen's blow with his sword. Bull, 41.
29. E. Allen, *Narrative*, 9.
30. B. F. DeCosta, *Notes on the History of Fort George* (New York: J. Sabin & Sons, 1871), 11-12; See also Nordberg to Provincial Congress in New York, December 1775, *Proceedings of the New York State Historical Association* 9 (1910): 387-88.
31. Bull, 41.
32. "Papers Relating," 172.
33. Force, Fourth Series, 2: 557; William Bell Clark, ed., *Naval Documents of the American Revolution* (Washington, D.C.: Naval History Division, Department of the Navy, 1964), Volume 1, 313.
34. Benedict Arnold, "Benedict Arnold's Regimental Memorandum Book," *The Bulletin of the Fort Ticonderoga Museum* 14 (Winter 1982): 71; A condensed version of the memorandum book was published in 1884. Benedict Arnold, "Benedict Arnold's Regimental Memorandum Book," *The Pennsylvania Magazine of History and Biography* 8 (1884): 366.
35. Arnold, BFTM, 71.
36. Clark, 1: 358.
37. Ibid., 1: 366.
38. Ibid., 1: 366-67.
39. Ibid., 1: 562.
40. Ibid., 1: 564.
41. Ibid., 1: 672.
42. Ibid.; See also Robert McConnell Hatch, *Thrust For Canada: The American Attempt on Quebec in 1775-1776* (Boston: Houghton Mifflin Company, 1979), 29-31; George F. G. Stanley, *Canada Invaded 1775-1776* (1973; reprint ed., Toronto: Samuel Stevens Hakkert & Company, 1977), 27-28.
43. Clark, 1: 672.
44. "Papers Relating," 247; Hatch 30-31.
45. John Joseph Henry, *Account of Arnold's Campaign Against Quebec* (1877; reprint ed., New York: The New York Times & Arno Press, 1968), 94; For more information on Montgomery see Hal T. Shelton, *General Richard Montgomery and the American Revolution: From Redcoat to Rebel* (New York: New York University Press, 1994).
46. Benjamin Trumbull, "A Concise Journal or Minutes of the Principal Movements Towards St. John's," *Collections of the Connecticut Historical Society* 7 (1899): 146; See also Stephen H. P.Pell, ed., "Diary of the Reverend Benjamin Trumbull," *The Bulletin of the Fort Ticonderoga Museum* 15 (Spring 1989): 94-134. Trumbull's original manuscript is in the collections of the Fort Ticonderoga Museum (FTA #M-2174).
47. B. Trumbull, "Concise Journal," 146; See also Clark, 1: 1217.
48. E. Allen, *Narrative*, 19; See also James Jeffry, "Journal Kept in Quebec in 1775 by James Jeffry," *Historical Collections of the Essex Institute* 50 (April 1914): 140; Charles A. Jellison, *Ethan Allen: Frontier Rebel* (Syracuse University Press, 1969), 151-59; Bellesiles, 126-28.
49. B. Trumbull, "Concise Journal," 156; See also Henry Livingston, "Journal of Major Henry Livingston, 1775," ed. by Gaillard Hunt, *The Pennsylvania Magazine of History and Biography* 12 (1898): 17.
50. Livingston, 32.
51. Brantz Mayer, ed., *Journal of Charles Carroll of Carrollton, During His Visit to Canada in 1776* (Baltimore: Maryland Historical Society, 1876), 75; See also Allan S. Everest, ed., *The Journal of*

Charles Carroll of Carrollton (Fort Ticonderoga, N.Y.: The Champlain - Upper Hudson Bicentennial Committee, 1976), 37-38.

52. Benjamin Trumbull, "The Montgomery Expedition, 1775," *The Bulletin of the Fort Ticonderoga Museum* 1 (July 1928): 34.

53. Peter Force, ed., *American Archives*, Fourth Series, Volume 5 (Washington, D.C.: M. St. Clair Clarke and Peter Force, 1844), 1175.

54. French, 42-49; Original documents in Gage Papers and Dartmouth Papers.

55. Force, Fourth Series, 2: 623.

56. E. Allen, *Narrative*, 7; Force, Fourth Series, 2: 624.

57. E. Allen, *Narrative*, 8.

58. Benson J. Lossing, *The Pictorial Field-Book of The Revolution* (1851; reprint ed., Freeport, N.Y.: Books for Libraries Press, 1969), Volume 1, 125.

59. Goodhue, 14; See also Chittenden, 46.

60. William Cleaves Todd, "Lord Timothy Dexter," *The Historical and Genealogical Register* 40 (October 1886): 380; See also James Austin Holden, ed., "What Ethan Allen Really Said at Ticonderoga," *Proceedings of the New York State Historical Association* 9 (1910): 355.

61. E. Allen, *Narrative*, 8.

62. Ira Allen, *The Natural and Political History of the State of Vermont* (1798; reprint ed., Rutland, VT.: Charles E. Tuttle Company, Inc., 1969), 43; Lossing, 125; Goodhue, 14; Chittenden, 43.

63. Bull, 41.

64. E. Allen, *Narrative*, 8.

65. Goodhue, 14.

66. Force, Fourth Series, 2: 623-24, 1086; E. Allen, *Narrative*, 6.

67. Force, Fourth Series, 2: 556-57, 623.

68. Ibid., 556.

69. Force, Fourth Series, 2: 557.

70. "Paper Relating," 187.

71. French, 54-55.

72. French, 50-52.

73. Clark, 1: 633.

"Withstanding the Attack of Arnold's Men" at Quebec.
Engraving by F. H. Wellington from a drawing by Sydney Adamson.
(National Archives of Canada)

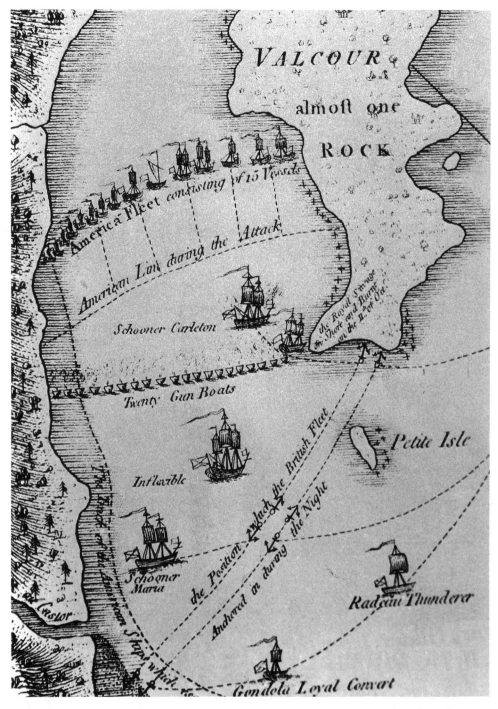

Detail of "The Attack and Defeat of the American Fleet. . .Upon Lake Champlain, the 11th of October, 1776." Engraving by William Faden, London, 1776, "From a Sketch taken by an Officer on the Spot."

(Special Collections, Bailey/Howe Memorial Library, University of Vermont)

8. Bayze Wells 1776

T HIRTY-YEAR-OLD BAYZE WELLS of Farmington, Connecticut, quickly heeded the call for volunteers at the beginning of the American Revolution, enlisting on May 10,1775, as a sergeant in Captain John Sedgwick's "Eighth Company in the Fo[u]rth Reg[i]ment Ra[i]sed by the United Colonys for the Defence of the same against the T[y]r[an]ny of Great Brit[ai]n."[1] Serving until 1778, Wells witnessed the campaigns of the northern theater, drafting the most comprehensive journal of the day-to-day events leading to the Battle of Valcour Island on October 11, 1776. Although the American fleet was defeated in the battle, its presence on the lake in 1776 effectively prevented a successful British invasion of the United States, which could have ended the Revolution by separating New England from the rest of the states. Writing in his orderly book on October 14, the day after the last engagement of 1776 between the American and British fleets on Lake Champlain, Captain Ichabod Norton, also of Farmington, Connecticut, noted that Major General Horatio Gates, the field commander of the Northern Department, extended "his h[e]arty thanks to General [Benedict] Arnold, officers, se[a]m[e]n and marines of the fleet for the Gal[l]ant Defence they made against the Super[i]ority of the Enemy."[2]

Born on August 5, 1744, Bayze Wells spent his early years uneventfully in Farmington, Connecticut. On February 1, 1769, at the age of 24, Wells married Ruth Gaylord of East Hartford, Connecticut, who was five years his junior. Living on the east side of Avon Mountain in Farmington, Wells and his young wife had three children before Bayze entered the service in 1775. Departing for Crown Point in early June, Wells traveled by foot for 12 days before reaching Fort George at the southern end of Lake George. On July 24 while on duty at Crown Point, Wells was sent on a scouting mission to Canada with Major John Brown of Pittsfield,

Massachusetts, and several others. Alternating between rowing and sailing a bateau, the reconnoitering party reached the Richelieu River in two days where they hid their boat and donned heavy packs for a trek through the forest to St. Jean and Chambly. Wells narrowly avoided capture on the harrowing journey and became separated from Brown for four days. Later, Wells was present at the American siege of Fort St. Jean on the Richelieu River, but illness forced him to return home.

On January 23, 1776, Wells was commissioned an ensign in Captain John Stevens' company of Colonel Charles Burrall's Connecticut regiment. The regiment, raised on a Continental Army basis for the Northern Department, reinforced American troops besieging Quebec City. With the arrival of a fresh British army in early May 1776, Wells became swept up in the desperate retreat of the American army from Canada. Led by Stevens, a large number of Wells' company were taken prisoner in Canada. Like hundreds of his fellow soldiers, Wells contracted smallpox and was sent to Isle-aux-Noix where "about 1500 Sick men w[e]re ordered to this Place—oh the Groans of the Sick what they undergo I Cant Expres[s]."[3] The island was evacuated between June 24 and 27th as the army made its final withdrawal from Canada. Eventually, 2,000 of the sick, including Wells, were transferred to a hospital at Fort George. Wells survived his bout with smallpox and returned to duty at Crown Point* on July 15.

Eight days later he was "ordered to our New [e]ncampment Across the Lake against S^d Ti[condero]ga no name for it as yet this [e]ncampment was A howling Wilderness."[6] A month earlier Major General Philip Schuyler had written to George Washington, suggesting "if a Fortress was Erected on the East Side of Lake Champlain nearly opposite to Tyonderoga It would equally command both Communications" and allow reinforcement by land from New England.[7] On July 8 Lieutenant Colonel Jeduthan Baldwin from Brookfield, Massachusetts, had scrutinized the terrain on the east side of the lake and shortly thereafter began work on the new fort. His supervision of the construction, however, was almost short-circuited when his clothes, uniforms, surveyor's compass, and money were stolen, prompting Baldwin to write to Brigadier General John Sullivan of New Hampshire, requesting that an earlier petition of discharge be presented to the Continental Congress, "as I am heartily tired of this Retreating, Rag[g]ed, Starved, lousey, thevish, Pockey [smallpox] Army in this unhealthy Country."[8] Baldwin, however, remained at Lake Champlain throughout 1776, directing the construction of barracks, redoubts, and a horseshoe battery on the eastern shore as well as a boom and narrow footbridge across the lake.

---

*Invariably, soldiers were still impressed by Crown Point despite the devastating fire of 1773. In May 1776 Lieutenant Colonel Joseph Vose "viewed the old fort, that was Burnt Down. I think it was the Grandest fort that was ever built in America."[4] At the same time, another officer described Crown Point as "the most famous Fort I have yet seen, the Walls are from the Bottom of the Trench about 30 or 40 Feet High the Fort is called [estimated] a Mile Round the Wall, the Trench dug out of a Rock 3 Grand Stone Barracks of 18 or 20 Rod long within the Fort, and 60 or 70 cannon. . .[re]doubts built on the Point. . .Likewise the Ruins of an old French [fort]. . .which is now so Ruined the form can hardly be Discovered."[5] On July 7 Generals Philip Schuyler, Horatio Gates, John Sullivan, Benedict Arnold and Baron Frederick William Woedtke agreed to abandon Crown Point and move the army to Ticonderoga. Despite opposition from 21 officers, the plan was carried out, leaving a small force at Crown Point under Colonel Thomas Hartley.

When news of the Declaration of Independence reached Lake Champlain,* Colonel Arthur St. Clair read aloud the eloquent text of the document and ended with "God save the free independent States of America!" whereby, according to an eyewitness, "the Army manifested their joy with three cheers. It was remarkably pleasing to see the spirits of the soldiers so raised, after all the calamities; the language of every man's countenance was, Now we are a people; we have a name among the States of this world."[10] Thereafter the fortification was known as Mount Independence.**

While many soldiers convalesced at Fort George, reinforcements arrived in July and August at the Lake Champlain forts. Many soldiers observed the ghastly sights of the bones of troops from the French and Indian War. One officer, marching along the road to Fort George, noted that "many Hundred were killed & thrown into a pond [in 1755] which gave it the name Blood[y] pond, many Bones are now to be seen in the Pond & about it."[12] At Ticonderoga, Reverend Ammi Robbins "viewed the place of Abercromb[y]s defeat in 1758. Saw many holes where the dead were flung in, and numbers of human bones,—thigh, arms, etc.,—above ground. Oh, the horrors of war."[13] Colonel Anthony Wayne, writing to a fellow officer, likened Ticonderoga to "the ancient Golgotha or place of Skulls—they are so plenty here that our people for want of Other Vessels drink out of them, whilst the soldiers make tent pins of the shin and thigh bones of Abercrumbies [Abercromby's] men."[14]

Anticipating the likely British invasion through Lake Champlain, the Americans had begun an urgent shipbuilding campaign in June at Skenesborough (present-day Whitehall, N.Y.) to supplement their existing fleet, which included the schooners *Royal Savage*, *Revenge*, and *Liberty* and the sloop *Enterprise*. On June 24 Brigadier General John Sullivan urged George Washington to build "Row gallies to Command the lakes"; the next day Brigadier General Benedict Arnold, who had designed and directed the construction of gondolas (gunboats) in Canada earlier in 1776, also wrote to Washington, recommending that "a large Number of (at least Twenty or thirty) G[o]nd[o]l[a]s, Row Gallies, & floating Batteries" be built on Lake Champlain.[15] Weeks earlier, however, Major General Philip Schuyler had already made preparations to build gondolas at Skenesborough. As the first gondola neared completion on June 22 (finished two days later), Schuyler directed his assistant deputy commissary general to have lumber "enough cut for five G[o]ndolas

---

*Although the unsigned letter describing Colonel Arthur St. Clair's reading of the document was dated July 28, the news of the Declaration of Independence had apparently reached the Champlain Valley earlier. Colonel Elisha Porter of Hadley Massachusetts, noted at Crown Point on July 16, 1776, that "This morning we rec'd the agreeable news of Independancy being declared by the Congress. About noon 2 or 3 kettles of Brandy Grog evidenced our joy at the news which we expressed in proper toasts."[9]

**The northern section of Mount Independence was acquired by Sarah and Stephen Pell in 1911 and subsequently transferred to the Fort Ticonderoga Association; in 1961 the southern section of the Mount was purchased by the state of Vermont. In 1996 the state of Vermont opened a visitor center at Mount Independence to interpret the site for the public. Foundations and artifacts from a large hospital, huts, officers' quarters, and the Southern Battery had previously been discovered in the multi-year archaeological project under the direction of Dr. David R. Starbuck. An underwater survey in 1992 by the Lake Champlain Maritime Museum under the direction of Arthur Cohn and Dr. Kevin Crisman revealed structural details of 22 crib-caissons from the Great Bridge which connected Fort Ticonderoga to Mount Independence (built in 1777). The project also yielded many artifacts, including a 12-pound cannon, bar shot, musket balls, mortar bombs, cannon balls, grapeshot, wine bottles, and tools.[11]

more."[16] At the same time Major General Guy Carleton (rank of general in North America), the governor of Quebec, wrote to Captain Charles Douglas of the Royal Navy, requesting "all the materials which can be collected for the building of armed Vessels for the Lakes."[17] The fledgling American fleet received a significant boost on July 3 when the Continental Congress empowered the Marine Committee "to contract with shipwrights to go to Lake Champlain" on very favorable terms.[18] By the third week of July, little progress had been made on the new gondolas, prompting Benedict Arnold to sail to Skenesborough in an effort to hasten construction. On July 24, after examining the gondolas on the stocks and plans for larger row galleys, Arnold suggested to Gates that "in two or three weeks, I think we shall have a very formidable fleet."[19] Five days later Gates informed John Hancock, the president of the Continental Congress, that Arnold had returned to Ticonderoga from Skenesborough where he had given "life and spirit to our dock-yard" and had agreed to undertake the command of the fleet.[20] However, the present commander, Captain Jacobus Wynkoop, had not been notified by Gates of his replacement by Arnold.

"View of a Saw Mill & Block House upon Fort Anne Creek"owned by Philip Skene and used by the Americans during the building of their fleet in 1776 at Skenesborough. From *Travels through the Interior Parts of America* by Thomas Anburey (1789). (National Archives of Canada)

In a short period of time the new gondolas were rowed to Fort Ticonderoga and Mount Independence for arming and rigging. Arnold energetically directed the outfitting of the vessels, organizing the effort to find material, cannon, and experienced seamen. On July 27, 1776, Bayze Wells recorded that he had been ordered "to work on Board Gunelow [gondola] Provid[e]nce under the command [of] a C[a]pt[ain] Simmons [Simonds]."[21] The *Providence*, one of the eight identical gondolas that would be built at Skenesborough in the summer of 1776, was a double-ended, flat-bottomed vessel with a length of 54 feet and width of 15 1/2 feet. The *Providence* was sloop-rigged with a square sail and topsail but had poor sailing qualities, except in a direct, favorable wind, which therefore required rowing by her crew much of the time. She was fitted with a 12-pound cannon in the bow mounted on a wooden slide carriage and two 9-pound cannon on the midship gun deck, with about eight 3/4 pound swivel guns mounted on brackets on the gunwales.[22] After being rigged and armed, the *Providence* set sail for Crown Point on a light wind at sunset on August 4. Arriving at Chimney Point the next day, Captain Simonds ordered the firing of the cannon on board the vessel, but a tragic accident ended the drill. Wells recorded that after the bow cannon had been swabbed with a sponge following the first firing, "Solomon Dyer who Serv[e]d the Sp[o]ng[e] went to Ram Down the Cartri[dge] there Being fire in the Gun it went of[f] While he Was Standing before the Mouth of the Cannon which Blew Both his hands & one [k]nee almost of[f]. . .Blew him overboard we Could not find him until [August] 7th he Rose and flo[a]ted we took him up and Buried him Decently."[23]

While Benedict Arnold labored at Ticonderoga to finish outfitting the fleet, Captain Jacobus Wynkoop, aboard the schooner *Royal Savage* at Crown Point, persisted in his command of the fleet, despite Arnold's appointment by Gates to the position. An incident recorded by Bayze Wells, however, must have diminished his standing with the crews of the fleet. On August 10 Wells mentioned that "a Large flock of White Gulls app[ea]r[e]d in Sight which Loom[e]d up to that Degree that the Comm[o]dore [Wynkoop] By the Assistance of his [looking] Glass thought them to be [the sails of] our Enemys."[24] Wynkoop promptly instructed the boatswain to hail with his trumpet "all the Vess[e]ls in the Harbour all the officers w[ere] ordered on Board of the Roy[a]l Savage to hold a Council."[25] The council of war ended when Captain Isaac Seaman of the schooner *Revenge* identified the seagulls with his looking glass from the top mast.

Two days later Wells was sent north in a bateau as far as Diamond Island (near the mouth of Otter Creek) to observe any British scouting parties. Upon his return to the fleet at Crown Point, he remarked in his journal that "Com[mo]dore Wynkoop was a[r]rested By General Arnold for Detaining [the schooner] Liberty."[26] A final confrontation over the command of the fleet had occurred on August 17 after Wynkoop had fired a swivel cannon from the *Royal Savage* to check the departure of the schooners *Revenge* and *Liberty* whose captains had been given orders by Arnold to sail north on a reconnaissance mission and to protect 100 American soldiers returning to Crown Point. Arnold quickly boarded the *Royal Savage*, but Wynkoop refused to recognize Arnold's authority, insisting that his earlier appointment by Major General Schuyler gave him command of the Lake Champlain vessels. The impasse resulted in an order by Gates for Wynkoop's arrest, but Arnold's request for leniency for Wynkoop resulted in the officer being sent to Schuyler's headquarters without arrest.

By August 18 the gondolas *New Haven*, *Providence*, *Boston*, *Spitfire*, and *Philadelphia* had been completed while the *Connecticut* and an unnamed gondola (later called the *New Jersey*) were "not entirely Rigg[e]d."[27] Likewise, the 43-foot *Lee*,

Benedict Arnold from *An Impartial
History of the War in America*
by James Murray (London, 1780).
(Library of Congress)

Major General Horatio Gates. Mezzotint
attributed to C. Corbutt, published by
John Morris in London (1778).
(Library of Congress)

sometimes referred to as a cutter, row galley, or gondola, was also undergoing
rigging. The vessel had been constructed from frames taken by Arnold's men in June
during the evacuation of St. Jean; at the same time three row galleys were in "great
forwardness" at Skenesborough, according to an eyewitness, "from sixty to seventy
feet in keel [overall length of 72-80 feet] and eighteen feet beam, which will mount
each six cannon and twenty swivels, and are to go with thirty-six oars, besides sails."[28]

At Crown Point on August 24, 1776, Wells received a commission as second
lieutenant effective July 24. At sunset he departed with the fleet on a cruise to the
north with the vessels arranged in the following order: the schooner *Royal Savage*
and sloop *Enterprise* in the lead, followed by the gondolas side by side (the *New
Haven* and *Boston*, the *Providence* and *Spitfire*, and *Philadelphia* and *Connecticut*),
with the rear covered by the schooners *Revenge* and *Liberty*. Benedict Arnold's
sailing orders, given by General Gates on August 7 and forwarded to George
Washington, specified an anchorage at a narrow pass of the lake but were somewhat
ambiguous, leaving Arnold with considerable discretion:

> Preventing the enemy's invasion of our country is the ultimate end of the
> important command. . .it is a defensive war we are carrying on, therefore no
> wanton risk or unnecessary display of power of the fleet is at anytime to
> influence your conduct. Should the enemy come up the Lake, and attempt to
> force their way through the pass. . .you will act with such cool, determined

valour, as will give them reason to repent their temerity. But if, contrary to my hope and expectation, their fleet should have so increased as to force an entrance into the upper part of the Lake, then, after you shall have discovered the insufficiency of every effort to retard their progress, you will, in the best manner you can, retire with your squadron to Ticonderoga.[29]

While the fleet was anchored off Willsboro two days after the departure from Crown Point, a fierce storm from the northeast forced Arnold to seek shelter for the flotilla in a bay on the eastern shore. As the fleet prepared to leave, Wells observed "the [gondola] Spitfire Being Near the Shore the Swell hove her in & She was not able to get of[f] Shore."[30] Due to the ferocity of the gale, little could be done for the stranded gunboat. After suffering minor damage to several vessels, the fleet came to anchor in Button Bay (west of present-day Vergennes, VT.) at five o'clock in the afternoon. Arnold subsequently informed Gates of the "amazing sea, and when I expected to hear the gondola [*Spitfire*] was foundered or drove on shore, she joined us, having received no damage."[31] On the evening of August 29 at Button Bay, Wells blithely recounted that "we had a most Genteel Feast of a Ro[a]st Pig Good wine Some Punch and Good old [c]ider We Drank [to] the Congress health General Arno[l]ds and Named the Point by the Name of Arnolds Point."[32]

Three days later the American fleet resumed its voyage to the north. On September 4, after several anchorages, Arnold deployed his vessels across the one-mile-wide channel at Windmill Point. The gondola *New Jersey* and cutter *Lee* reached the anchorage at Windmill Point, but the first row galley would not join the fleet until the end of the month. On September 6 Arnold ordered his gondolas ashore to "cut Fascines [branches]" to line the sides of the vessels for protection from boarding and musket balls.[33] The gondola *Boston* landed on shore without waiting for the other vessels, resulting in an ambush by Native Americans accompanied by a British officer that, according to Bayze Wells, "kill[e]d two men Right out wounded five more one of whom Died Soon after he Come on Board the Enterprise one more mortally wounded."[34]

Fearing that the British were building batteries on the shoreline at Windmill Point, Arnold moved his fleet on September 8 to the western channel of Isle La Motte. Several entries in Wells' journal during the anchorage at Isle La Motte mention illnesses. Twice in one week Wells commented that Captain Simonds of the gondola *Providence* had a "fit of the fever & Ag[ue]" which debilitated victims with a sharp fever and chills.[35] On September 16 Wells revealed that "I bath[e]d for the Itch [impetigo] with Brimstone Tallow [sulfur soap] and tar [distillate of pine or fir sap] mix[ed] together and Lay in our Cloths."[36] Diseases, including dysentery, impetigo, typhoid, smallpox, yellow fever, and malaria, were nearly inevitable at one time or another for soldiers in the American Revolution. While there was a two percent risk of being killed in battle, the odds of dying from disease or infection were 25 percent.[37]

After obtaining information on the composition of the British fleet from prisoners captured by Lieutenant Benjamin Whitcomb on September 18, Arnold wrote to Gates that he would move the fleet to Valcour Island "where is a good harbour and where we shall have the advantage. . .and if they are too many for us, we can retire."[38] Arnold's decision to relocate to another anchorage was based on the most definitive intelligence to date of the size of the British fleet which included "a Ship on the Stocks at St. John's [St. Jean] designed to mount Twenty Guns, Nine, and Twelve Pounders, several Schooners, and small Craft."[39] Although Arnold suggested to Gates "that the enemy will soon have a considerable naval force," he still did not have a comprehensive picture of the size of the emerging British fleet.[40]

"A View of St. John's. . .Taken in the Year 1776."
Drawing from *Travels through the Interior Parts of America* by Thomas Anburey (1789).
(Library of Congress)

"A View of His Majesty's Armed Vessels on Lake Champlain,
11 October 1776." Watercolor by Charles Randle (1776).
From left to right: the schooner *Carleton*, the ship-rigged *Inflexible*, a cutter-rigged gunboat, the schooner *Maria*, the gunboat *Loyal Convert*, and the radeau *Thunderer*.
(National Archives of Canada)

After completion, the British fleet included the 80-foot, three-masted *Inflexible*, mounting eighteen 12-pound cannon, which had been partially built at Quebec, and disassembled and carried to Chambly in bateaux and longboats. At Chambly the frames were transferred to wagons for the final journey to the St. Jean shipyard for reassembly. Remarkably, the *Inflexible* was "launched in twenty-eight days from laying her keel."[41] The 14-gun, 66-foot *Maria*, recaptured from the Americans on the St. Lawrence River on May 6, 1776, was taken apart and reassembled at St. Jean. Similarly, the 59-foot schooner *Carleton*, mounting twelve 6-pound cannon, was also dismantled and reconstructed at the St. Jean shipyard. The 62-foot gondola *Loyal*

Convert, an American vessel captured on the St. Lawrence River, was dragged across the rapids at Chambly. Built at St. Jean, the two-masted, 91-foot radeau *Thunderer* was reported to Arnold by a Frenchman "Antoine Geroure [Girard]. . .[but] I have every Reason to think him placed as a Spy on us."[43] Twelve 37-foot gunboats were constructed at St. Jean from frames transported from England, and a number of Canadian-built gunboats were either dragged across the Chambly rapids or built at St. Jean. British records listed 20-24 gunboats, 4 armed long boats, and 24 long boats (for provisions) used in the campaign.[44]

On September 19, on the first leg of the voyage to Valcour Island, Arnold moved his fleet of 13 vessels (the gondola *New York* had joined the flotilla on September 11) to Bay St. Armand on the western shore, about nine miles south of Isle La Motte. The schooner *Liberty*, ordered to cruise along the

Sir Guy Carleton, governor of Quebec and general in the British army. Painting, artist unknown. (National Archives of Canada)

western shore at the rear of the fleet, was nearly captured by Native Americans allied with the British. On September 28, a few days after arriving at Valcour Island, Arnold informed Gates of his anchorage on the west side of the island and restated his tactical plan "that [only a] few vessels can attack us at the same time, and those will be exposed to the fire of the whole fleet."[45] While at this anchorage, Wells noted the arrival of the row galley *Trumbull* on September 30 and six days later, the row galleys *Washington* and *Congress*. Arnold now had 16 vessels.

On October 4 General Guy Carleton, aboard the *Maria*, and Captain Thomas Pringle, the fleet commander, led the British fleet southward on the Richelieu River.* The largest ship, the *Inflexible*, which had been launched on September 29, departed later, taking several days to join the rest of the fleet. Not all of the troops with the British army accompanied the fleet into Lake Champlain; the German regiments remained on Isle-aux-Noix until October 15 and other troops remained at a camp at Lacolle River. As scouting parties searched for the American vessels, the British fleet anchored at Point au Fer where a blockhouse was ordered built and four companies were assigned to garrison the outpost. According to Major General Friedrich Riedesel, on October 10 "it was reported to General Carleton that the American fleet had been seen near Grand island. He, therefore, sailed the same afternoon as far as the two islands, and in the evening, cast anchor between Long [North Hero] and Grand islands."[47] However, Lieutenant James Murray Hadden,

*The sailing dates of the British fleet are given as October 4 and October 5 in some of the original journals.[46]

aboard one of the British gunboats, noted that the fleet "proceeded to the Southern end of Isle au Mot[t]e."[48] Whether Carleton and Pringle knew of the location of the American fleet at Valcour Island remains uncertain. Ensign John Enys, aboard the radeau *Thunderer*, remarked that "on the 10th in the evening we got intel[l]igence where they were" and three officers later charged that Captain Thomas Pringle "had information on their being there the night before" and neglected to formulate any plan of attack.[49] However, Dr. Robert Knox, aboard the *Maria* with General Carleton, recorded in his journal that orders were given to Carleton's nephew, Captain Christopher Carleton, to proceed to the "other side of Cumberland Bay" with his contingent of Native Americans and Canadian volunteers.[50] As the crew prepared the *Maria* for battle early the next morning, they "came in sight of the bay [Cumberland Bay], but to our great mortification we cou'd discover no ships."[51]

With snow on the distant Adirondack peaks, the American crews aboard the 15-vessel makeshift navy (the *Liberty* had gone to Ticonderoga for provisions) sensed the impending winter. At eight o'clock in the morning on October 11, 1776, the British fleet "appeared of[f], of Cumberland Head," Benedict Arnold reported in a letter the next day to Major General Gates.[52] With the sighting of the British fleet, Brigadier General David Waterbury (second in command), "Went on Bo[a]rd [Arnold's vessel] and told him I gave it as My [o]pinion that our fleet ought to Com[e] to Sail and Not L[ie] Where We Sho[u]ld Be Surrounded," but Arnold adamantly refused and "Said he Wo[u]ld fight them in the Bay of Valcour."[53] At "half past nine," Colonel Edward Wigglesworth, the third in command, was ordered by Arnold "into the yawl to go to the windward and observe their motions."[54] Arnold transferred his flag from the *Royal Savage* to the galley *Congress* and deployed his vessels in a line across Valcour Bay. Upon Wigglesworth's return, Arnold "ordered the 2 sc[h]ooners and 3 Gallies under way Im[m]ediately," young Pascal Charles Joseph De Angelis* wrote in his journal.[57] As the British fleet rounded the southern end of Valcour Island, the American crews caught their first glimpse of the enemy's

---

*Pascal Charles Joseph De Angelis, not quite 13 years old, was the stepson of Captain Seth A. Warner(not to be confused with Seth Warner of the Green Mountain Boys)of the galley *Trumbull*. The son of an Italian father and French mother, De Angelis was born in Oranjestad on the island of St. Eustatius in the West Indies on October 14, 1763. When he was ten years old, his family sailed aboard a ship commanded by Captain Seth A. Warner of Old Saybrook, Connecticut. His critically-ill father died during the voyage to Connecticut and his mother settled in Old Saybrook, later marrying Warner. With an above-average height and muscular build, De Angelis appeared older than his 12 years and enlisted at Old Saybrook, earning a bounty of five pounds. He enlisted again in 1780 and 1781. Serving aboard the brig *Lady Green* in the Caribbean in 1781, De Angelis was wounded and taken to Jamaica as a prisoner. Escaping the following year, De Angelis sailed aboard a merchant vessel bound for London but was impressed into the Royal Navy. He once again escaped, returning home on October 13, 1783, the day before his twentieth birthday.

De Angelis settled in East Haddam, Connecticut, where he married Elizabeth Webb in 1791 and eventually had 11 children. During his residence in East Haddam, he commanded several merchant vessels involved in the West Indies trade. With earnings from his sailing ventures, De Angelis purchased a quarter share of a large parcel of land in Oneida County, New York, known as the Holland Patent. He later built sawmills, gristmills, and other businesses, becoming the village squire in later years. De Angelis was described as "six feet in height, straight as an arrow, had black eyes, prominent nose, a high forehead, and elegant figure, and commanding presence."[55] On September 8, 1839, at the age of 75, De Angelis died; his wife lived until 1851. His diary of the Battle of Valcour Island is held at the Penfield Library, State University of New York at Oswego. An abridged version of the De Angelis diary was published in 1974.[56]

Top: Detail of "A View of New England Armed Vessels on Valcure Bay on Lake Champlain, 11 October 1776," showing the schooner *Royal Savage* in the foreground. Watercolor by Charles Randle (1776). (National Archives of Canada)

Above: "The *Royal Savage* Ashore" on Valcour Island by Carlton T. Chapman from *Scribner's Magazine*, February 1898.

vessels. The American squadron was no match for the British fleet which carried approximately twice the weight in cannon and was manned by experienced seamen and Royal Navy officers.

"About ten A Clock the fir[ing] began and the [Royal] sav[a]g[e] Schooner Run a ground," wrote Jahiel Stewart, a Massachusetts militiaman aboard the sloop *Enterprise*.[58] At the beginning of the battle the cannon from the *Inflexible* struck the *Royal Savage* "with the first three Shot, in the Bowsprit, Foremast and Quarter [deck]—the Gunner of which [later captured by the British] Exclaimed the moment she hove in sight from behind the Island of Valcour 'L[or]d G[o]d have Mercy upon us—there's a three masted Ship.'"[59] Aground on the southern tip of Valcour Island, the stranded *Royal Savage* was bombarded by the British gunboats and then boarded by Lieutenant Edward Longcroft and his crew from the gondola *Loyal Convert*, who

"General Arnold at Valcour on Lake Champlain Engages the British Fleet."
Painting by Leslie A. Wilcox.
(Naval Historical Foundation)

succeeded in capturing 20 Americans. Longcroft turned the guns of the *Royal Savage* on the American fleet, but when half of his men were killed by return fire and no assistance was forthcoming from the other British vessels, the young lieutenant abandoned the schooner.

The British gunboats, anchored in a line from the southern tip of Valcour Island to the western shoreline of the lake, played a crucial role during the engagement since the larger vessels had trouble tacking against the wind to enter the bay, just as Arnold had anticipated. Although many shots from the American vessels flew over the top of the low British gunboats, one gunboat sustained a direct hit and exploded, sending a chest aboard the vessel high in the air and the crew into the lake. "I recognized the men by the cords around their hats," wrote Captain Georg Pausch, chief of the Hesse-Hann artillery, who rescued some of the survivors.[60] Lieutenant James Manning, on one of the British gunboats, suggested "that the [gun] Boat's advantage was not to come nearer than about 700 yards, as whenever they approached nearer, they were greatly annoyed by Grape Shot [small iron balls shot from cannon]."[61] As the cannon roared from the vessels, Native Americans under the direction of Captain Christopher Carleton and Captain Alexander Fraser menaced the American crews from the New York shoreline and Valcour Island.*

---

*According to oral history, the Native Americans on the New York shoreline spared two local residents who were hiding in the bushes near their home on the lakeshore. Winslow C. Watson, a nineteenth-century historian, learned the story firsthand from the daughter who was then quite elderly (Mrs. Elmore): "While the battle raged, Mrs. Hay carrying her infant, went to a spring in a ravine near the lake, which was at that time mantled by a dense thicket. To her unutterable amazement and terror, she found herself in the midst of a large body of Indians, hideous by their war paints and savage costume,

Hour after hour the green crews of the American fleet battled the experienced artillerymen aboard the British gunboats. Arnold, who aimed the cannon himself on the exposed deck of the galley *Congress*, noted that "some of the Enemies Ships & all their Gondolas, beat & rowed up within mus[k]et Shot of us. they, Continued a Very hot fire with Round & Grape Shot until five OClock."[63] Jahiel Stewart observed that "the Cannon balls & grape Shot flew verey thick & I believe we had a great many [k]ill[e]d and I was abo[a]rd of the hospit[a]l Sloop [*Enterprise*]. . .the Doct[o]rs Cut of[f] great many legs and arm[s] and See Seven men threw overbo[a]rd that died."[64]

The schooner *Carleton*, commanded by 27-year-old Lieutenant James Richard Dacres, was the only large British vessel to sail into the thick of the battle inside Valcour Bay. Facing the brunt of the American line, the British schooner became disabled when much of her rigging was shot away. Dacres was severely wounded during the onslaught and nearly thrown overboard for dead; Robert Brown, the second in command, lost his right arm. With two feet of water in the hold, 19-year-old Midshipman Edward Pellew took control of the *Carleton*. Amidst the deadly flying metal spouting from the mouths of the American artillery, Pellew climbed forward on the bowsprit and deployed the jib sail. He then risked death a second time on the bowsprit when he reattached a rope from a long boat that was used to tow the stricken vessel to safety.

Late in the action, the *Inflexible* sailed into firing range and pounded the American fleet with repeated cannon barrages. Pascal De Angelis, aboard the galley *Trumbull*, noted that "the most Desp[e]rate can[no]nading without intermis[si]on continued till about half after 5 oclock we being about a Mile Distance from the Enemy and Sometimes 1/2 Mile. . .about 6 oclock the firing Ceas[ed]. When Directly a boat Came a Long side and took our Wounded and Carr[i]ed them on board of the Hosp[i]tal Sloop Enterprize."[65] With three-quarters of its ammunition spent, the shattered American fleet faced dire prospects. Arnold's galley *Congress* "was hulled a doz[en] times" and her main mast and yard damaged; the galley *Washington* also needed a new main mast; "the Philad[ephi]a was hulled in so many Places that She Sank, About one hour after the engagement."[66] De Angelis recorded that the *Trumbull* "received in Time of Action one Shell in our Mainmast Which Busted about half way up the mast and s[l]ivered it almost to peases [pieces] and one Twelve pound Shot under our Counter [overhanging stern section] between Wind and water and about 20 or 30 more in Different Places."[67] Soon after the end of the hostilities, a British detachment set the *Royal Savage* ablaze, causing an explosion of the gunpowder left on board the vessel. Lieutenant James Hadden, aboard a British gunboat, mused that the destruction of the *Royal Savage* "was an unnecessary measure as she might at a more leisure moment have been got off" the island.[68] The British fleet did not leave the battle unscathed: Captain Georg Pausch reflected that "the cannon of the Rebels were well served; for, as I saw afterwards, our ships were pretty well mended and patched up with boards and stoppers."[69]

and armed with guns and tomahawks. The mother, agitated and alarmed at the helpless condition, and frantically clasping her child to her breast, wept convulsively. An aged chief, she judged from his demeanour, approached, and unable to communicate consolation or an assurance of safety by language, manifested his protective feeling by gently and soothingly, wiping away her tears with the skirt of his hunting shirt; neither the mother or the child was molested."[62]

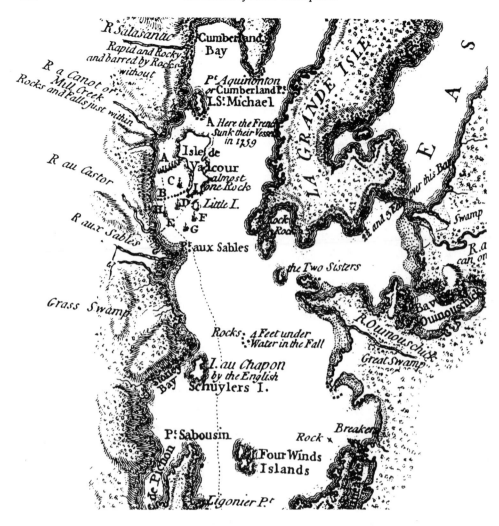

Detail of "A Survey of Lake Champlain" by William Brassier,
showing the American retreat from Valcour Island.
(William Faden Collection, Library of Congress)

Following a hasty council of war aboard the *Congress*, the Americans decided
to risk making an escape by passing by the anchored British fleet. Aided by darkness,
thick fog, and the distraction of the burning *Royal Savage*, "at about half after 7
oclock," according to De Angelis, "We Received orders from General Arnol[d] to
Get Ready and Proceed up through the Enemies Fleet and Lead the van With
Co[lo]n[e]l Wigglesworth on Board [the *Trumbull*] and to Carry a Lantern at our
St[e]rn and accordingly at half after Eight oclock we w[eigh]ed our a[n]chor and
Pro[c]eeded through the Fleet as we were ordered to make the Best of our way to
Crown point and General Arn[o]l[d] and General Waterbury in the other Gallies
to bring up the Rear. General Arn[o]l[d] on the Right and General Waterbury on
the Left so we got. . . Through and made the Best of our way all Night our

Amm[u]n[i]tion almost Expended Especially for 12 and 18 Pounders."[70] The Americans passed entirely undetected along the western shore; subsequently the commanding officers of the three British vessels: John Schank (*Inflexible*), John Starke (*Maria*), and Edward Longcroft (*Loyal Convert*) accused Thomas Pringle, the fleet commander, of mismanagement of the British vessels, including allowing the American fleet to escape since "the rear of the British line was at least one mile from the western shore."[71]

The battered American fleet became widely separated during the retreat. Most of the vessels anchored at Schuyler Island on October 12, but the schooner *Revenge*, sloop *Enterprise*, gondola *New York* and galley *Trumbull* "at light were Clos[e] to the four Brothers [Islands]," anchoring shortly thereafter at Ligonier Point, but two gunboats could not be saved: Arnold reported "two Gondolas sunk at Schuylers Island" in a letter to Major General Philip Schuyler.[73] De Angelis observed that "2 [of] the G[o]nd[o]l[a]s came along and we hail[e]d them and they told us that one of our G[o]nd[o]l[a]s was taking [water] and the other sunk whereupon we got under way."[74] One scuttled gondola, the *New Jersey*, was found by the British on October 12;[75] the other sank in deep water.*

Stern section of Benedict Arnold's last unaccounted-for gunboat, discovered intact in June 1997 in deep water near Schuyler Island. A ling rests on the stern post.
(Photo courtesy of the Lake Champlain Maritime Museum with special thanks to Benthos Inc.)

Early on the morning of October 12, the British stared into Valcour Bay in disbelief. Soon, however, "at day light" 19-year-old Ensign John Enys disclosed, "some of their fleet were Seen at a distance. Our fleet attempted to pursue them but the wind was so hard against us we were obliged [to] put back again."[77] Late on

---

*Using side-scan sonar, researchers from the Lake Champlain Maritime Museum discovered Benedict Arnold's last unaccounted-for gondola in June 1997 in the deep waters near Schuyler Island. Arthur Cohn, director of the museum, with the help of lake historian Peter Barranco, supervised the search which resulted in the find. Philip Lundeberg, curator emeritus of naval history at the Smithsonian Institution, suggested that the discovery "could prove to be the most significant maritime discovery in American history in the last half-century."[76] Arnold's last undiscovered gunboat had been the subject of several search efforts spanning 45 years, including those of Lorenzo F. Hagglund's team, the Smithsonian Institution, the National Geographic Society, the Woods Hole Oceanographic Institution and others.

October 12 the fatigued American crews struggled against powerful headwinds from the south. Captain Thomas Pringle and General Guy Carleton aboard the schooner *Maria*, along with the ship *Inflexible* and schooner *Carleton*, resumed the pursuit of the American fleet on the evening of the 12th. Pascal De Angelis on the galley *Trumbull* chronicled "this Morning at day Light [October 13] we spied Several Sail"; in response to the sighting, the crew of the sloop *Enterprise* "manned all our oars with three men to an oar."[78] Bayze Wells and Benedict Arnold both recorded the location of the American fleet near the Boquet River when the first sighting of the British fleet was made on the morning of October 13th.

"Action on Lake Champlain," October 13, 1776, depicting the pursuit of the American fleet by the *Maria*, *Carleton*, and *Inflexible*. Painting, artist unknown.
(National Archives of Canada)

Looking through his glass, Thomas Pringle with the British squadron observed "eleven sail of their fleet" on the morning of the 13th.[79] The number reflected the loss of the *Royal Savage*, the *Philadelphia*, and the two scuttled gondolas near Schuyler Island. At the time the surviving American vessels were "scattered a Bout Seven mil[e]s," according to Brigadier General David Waterbury, who was two miles behind Arnold's galley *Congress*.[80] At nine o'clock in the morning Colonel Edward Wigglesworth, several miles ahead of Arnold's vessel with the *Trumbull*, *Revenge*, *Enterprise*, and *New York*, received orders from Arnold via crew members in the yawl from the galley *Congress* "to lie by for the fleet."[81] De Angelis later remarked that "we received orders from General Arnold to heave to and engage the British."[82] Arnold sent a different message to the crew of the hospital sloop *Enterprise*, ordering "us to make all the Speed we could to ty [Ticonderoga] & all the other Ships to stop which they did."[83] Waterbury sent sailors in his stern boat to Arnold with a request to run the galley *Washington* ashore and blow it up; Arnold turned down the appeal, suggesting that "he Wo[u]ld Stop the fleet at Split Rock and th[e]re Make a Stand."[84] Waterbury briefly halted the *Washington* while his crew desperately tried to deploy two spare gondola sails as topsails, but the effort failed and the vessel made little headway since "she Was Much damaged and a Great deal of Water in [her]."[85] Alone at the rear of the fleet, Waterbury managed to "G[e]t five Mil[e]s Belo[w] Split Rock" before surrendering without firing a cannon since "she was so Shat[te]red She Was Not able to Bare firing."[86] When the *Washington* struck her colors, Wigglesworth "thought it my duty to make sail and endeavor to save the Trumbull galley if possible."[87] De Angelis, also aboard the *Trumbull*, recorded that "we were Closely

"General Arnold Destroys Remainder of His Fleet" at Arnold's Bay, Vermont.
Painting by Leslie A. Wilcox.
(Naval Historical Foundation)

p[u]rsued but by ro[w]ing and heaving out our balla[st] and making all the Sail we could we ar[r]ived at Crown Point about half after one oclock."[88]

The sloop *Enterprise*, schooner *Revenge*, and gondola *New York* also escaped. The schooner *Liberty*, returning to the fleet with provisions, quickly turned about and joined the frenzied retreat southward, reaching Ticonderoga late in the afternoon. At some point during the chase on October 13 the crew of the cutter *Lee* abandoned their vessel. Ensign John Enys later remarked in his journal that "a party of Canadians found a Gondola Named the Jersey on the opposite Side of the lake [New York shore] and Soon after a Small Sloop Named the Lee was found."[89]

On the open deck of the *Congress*, Arnold directed an ineffectual return fire against the ravaging broadsides of the British warships. Following the eastern shore of Lake Champlain with four gunboats, Arnold frantically struggled to save the crews of his remaining ships. With no options left, Arnold maneuvered the *Congress* and four gondolas into Ferris Bay (present-day Arnold's Bay), beaching and burning the vessels on the northeastern shore. According to J. F. Wasmus, a company surgeon attached to a German unit, Arnold "did not abandon his ship any sooner than when she was everywhere ablaze. Thus, he wished to prevent any of the English coming aboard and lowering the American flag, that remained hoisted until the ship was consumed by the flames."[90] Although Dr. Robert Knox, the chief medical officer of the British army, noted that Arnold had burned "the wounded and sick in them [vessels]," only one wounded man* was left (by accident) on the burning vessels.[92]

With Native Americans and British soldiers close behind, Benedict Arnold and his men, including Bayze Wells, scrambled about ten miles through the woods along the eastern shoreline. After the survivors stopped on the eastern bank south of Crown Point, boats were sent to ferry them across the lake. Peter Ferris and his family also accompanied Arnold's men; the British destroyed his farm and killed all the animals. Arnold and Colonel Thomas Hartley jointly decided to abandon Crown Point and set fire to the remaining structures of the fort. At four o'clock on the morning of October 14, Arnold finally reached the safety of Ticonderoga, "exceedingly fatigued and unwell, having been without sleep or refreshment for three days."[93]

The British fleet anchored near Crown Point on October 13, taking possession of the ruined fortress the next morning. At ten o'clock on the morning of October 14, General Guy Carleton sent Brigadier General David Waterbury and 106 prisoners under a flag of truce to the advanced post at Ticonderoga. Colonel John Trumbull, son of the Connecticut governor and deputy adjutant general to Major General Horatio Gates, met the boats and examined the prisoners who were "all warm in their acknowledgment of the kindness with which they had been treated."[94] Trumbull considered the prisoners "very dangerous" for the morale of the troops at Ticonderoga and convinced Gates to send them home "without being permitted to land."[95]

On October 14, before probing the defenses of Ticonderoga and Mount Independence, General Carleton informed Lord George Germain, the British secretary of state for the American colonies, of the victory over the American fleet and suggested that "the season is so far advanced that I cannot yet pretend to inform your Lordship whether any thing further can be done this year."[96] By late September, however, Carleton may already have had doubts concerning the British army's ability to capture Ticonderoga and its dependencies. On September 25, 1776, Ensign Thomas McCoy, who had been sent by Arnold to St. Jean to gather intelligence about the British fleet, surrendered at a British outpost after being without food for several days. (The American fleet had departed before McCoy returned.) The ensign informed the British "that there were 20,000 men at Crown Point and Ticonderoga well supplied with cannon, provisions &c."[97] The Americans, however, fully expected an attack. On October 14 the secretary to Major General Gates disclosed in a letter recalling a doctor to Ticonderoga that "the Advantage the Enemy has obtained by the very great Super[i]ority of their Fleet, gives Reason to believe we are going immediately to be attacked."[98] By October the number of troops at

---

*Lieutenant Goldsmith, who had been severely injured by grapeshot, was ordered removed from the vessel by Arnold, but the gunner set the *Congress* on fire, disregarding the entreaties of the wounded officer. "His body was seen when blown into the air," 14-year-old Squire Ferris, an eyewitness, recounted, "To the credit of Arnold, he showed the greatest feeling upon the subject and threatened to run the gunner through on the spot."[91]

Ticonderoga and Mount Independence "exceeded thirteen thousand," Colonel John Trumbull observed.

British troops boarded their bateaux at Point au Fer on October 13 for the long journey to Crown Point, but German units advanced only as far as Point au Fer from their camp at Isle-aux-Noix. Other British troops at several Canadian posts lacked sufficient bateaux to join the campaign. Just as the British troops began to arrive at Crown Point,* Carleton notified General William Howe (local rank in America) in lower New York that quartering troops at the post would not be possible, forcing their return to Canada for winter quarters since "the severe season [is] approaching very fast."[100] After a short stay at Crown Point, Lieutenant General John Burgoyne (local rank in America), second in command to Carleton, sailed back to Point au Fer in the captured row galley *Washington* and informed the German officers of Carleton's decision to end the campaign. At Point au Fer, J. F. Wasmus summarized the rationale for the decision: "the big fortification there [Ticonderoga] and the difficulties of getting near them, the steadfastness and uncertain number of the enemy, the long distance from Canada from where such necessities as ammunition, supplies and other war needs had to be transported across Lake Champlain as well as the fast approaching Canadian winter and other considerations were [the reasons] that brought this plan to naught for this year."[101]

The British, however, did not leave without testing the American garrisons at Fort Ticonderoga and Mount Independence. On Monday, October 28, Bayze Wells noted that "our Enemies Ap[p]ear[d] at the three Mile Point three [gun] Boats with A Carr[i]age Gun in Each bow one of which Came Within Cannon Shot of our North East Battery and of our Ro[w] galley [*Trumbull*] which Gave them Several Shots and we are of the Opinion Kill[d] Some men but that I Cannot tell at this time.** Fifteen other boats of A Small Size ap[p]e[a]r[d] also but at Sun Set they all Disap[p]ear[d]."[104]

At the beginning of November the British troops abandoned Crown Point and

---

*Joshua Pell, Jr., an officer in the British army, arrived at Crown Point on October 17. Pell's diary provides a detailed description of the fortification and redoubts during this period: "Crown point is a peninsula having three points or Capes, the western most point points directly down the Lake, and was fortified with a large redoubt, having four Curtains one on each Angle, the walls are Earth, rais'd to a great height, which entirely covers the buildings within; time has almost desroy'd the works, and I believe was never repair'd since taken from the French. A Barrack was building when it fell into the hands of the Rebels, which they defac'd as much as their hurry would permit, when they evacuated it. "The second point is almost three hundred yards to the east of the former, and was fortified with a small redoubt which time has render'd useless: the third point which is about the same distance from the second as the second is from the first, was fortified by the Rebels in a circular manner having various Curtains and Angles with a Battery of five Guns in the middle rais'd so high as to command the whole plain before it; they had Huts built within the works for their officers, but they destroy'd both them and works when they left it."[99]

**Persifer Frazer of the Fourth Pennsylvania Regiment suggested that one of the British vessels appeared to be reconnoitering the works: "We let them gratify their curiosity near half an hour and when they were going off we thought they would reckon us unpolite if we should take no notice of them. We saluted them with five cannon. One had the desired effect and went through their boat, killed their engineer & injured another man."[102] Michah Hildreth of Dracut, Massachusetts, recorded, "We Was alarmed and Every man to his arms and marched to his alarm post for the Enemy appeared in Sight upon the Lake and a Number of Boats Began to Land about 3 miles of[f] [at Three Mile Point] and then 1 Boat bor[e] down towards us and Come within 3 Quarters of a mile of our Bat[te]ries and We Fired 2 Cannon from ye Sandy Redou[b]t at the Boat and we understand that the Last Shot struck the Boat and kil[le]d 3 men."[103]

returned to Canada for winter quarters. The mere existence of the American fleet on Lake Champlain had caused an irretrievable delay of the British invasion. The postponement allowed the Americans time to muster substantial forces at the lake and erect significant defensive works at Ticonderoga and Mount Independence. After the British withdrawal, most of the regular troops joined George Washington's shrinking army in New Jersey and the militia was dismissed. Bayze Wells, on the other hand, remained at Ticonderoga and Mount Independence, serving in Colonel Charles Burrall's Connecticut regiment. On Thursday, December 5, Wells remarked that "this Day the State of Connecticut Kept as a Day of thanksgiven and Prayer in Immetation [imitation] of which our Battalion furnish[d] themselves with Good Victuals. . .[the officers] Made A Very Genteel feast."[105] Over the next few days Wells noted "Warm and Plea[s]ant" weather, but by mid-December stormy winter weather prevailed and the lake was frozen solid.[106] During the next month the harsh reality of winter set in—several men were found frozen to death. Wells also disclosed the disciplining of two men, noting that "one [received] 39 lashes the other 15 Lashes for Stealing," but the next day revealed that one of the soldiers "was not Sentenced by the Court Martial but Rece[i]v[d] his Punishment through [a] Mistake."[107] According to Wells, on January 30, Colonel Anthony Wayne, the commandant at the Lake Champlain posts during the winter, "came over and desired our Regiment to tarry two weeks but they Refused."[108] Against general orders, many of the men departed for home on the following evening; Wells, however, remained at his post.

Wells returned to his family in Connecticut in late February and soon re-entered the service as a first lieutenant (promoted on January 7, 1777) in Captain Jesse Kimball's company.[109] He resigned his commission on March 21, 1778, returning home to his wife and family in Farmington, Connecticut. Two of his children, Baizy and Calvin, had died in September 1777 and a daughter, Ruth, was born in November. During the seven years after his service in the Revolution, three more children were born; one died as an infant, however, and his daughter Ruth died before her second birthday. In 1785 Wells applied to the Connecticut General Assembly for reimbursement of medical expenses connected to his wartime duty, but the petition was dismissed despite testimony from Captain John Sedgwick and two depositions from physicians.[110] Wells farmed some of his 83 acres of land in Farmington and also worked as a surveyor of lands and highways in the town during the 1790s. With his property conveniently located on the Talcott Road between West Hartford and Farmington, Wells also operated a tavern for travelers. In 1795, just before he turned 51 years old, Wells eleventh and last child was born.

On October 24, 1814, the old soldier, who had survived the battles on Lake Champlain with Benedict Arnold, passed away at the age of 71. His wife Ruth received a widow's Revolutionary War pension and lived for another 21 years. Bayze Wells is buried in the North Cemetery (Old Center Cemetery) in West Hartford, Connecticut.

The following section of Bayze Wells' Revolutionary War journal begins on September 19, just as Benedict Arnold initiated the voyage of the American fleet to Valcour Island from Isle La Motte, and ends on October 14 when Wells and his exhausted comrades returned to Ticonderoga after burning their vessels in present-day Arnold's Bay in Panton, Vermont.

Journal of Bayze Wells 1776[111]

Th[u]rsday 19th Sep^tr this Day the wind Northerly and Clear about ten A M the fleet hove up and Stood up the Lake as far as Bay [St. Armand] on the North Side of Cumberl[a]n[d] head A[r]riv^d th[e]re about five P. M. and Came too in about Seven fathom and an half of Water Good Bottom Schooner Liberty being on A Cru[i]se up and Down the Lake was Decoy^d by A man in french Dress in A Small Cove on the West Shore Opefet [opposite] the North End of Isle [La] mott[e] the above man making bel[i]eve he Was in Distress and wanted to Come on board Capt Pr[e]m[i]er ordered his boat to back St[e]rn Near the Shore and then order the man to Swim on board he waded in to his middle and told them he Could not Swim and he must go Back he went back and give three Cahoops and immediately there arose about Six hundred ma[i]nly Dres[sed] in indian Dress and fired upon our boat and upon the Schooner and Wounded five of our men two we are afraid mortally Capt Pr[e]m[i]er fired upon them about an hour and there Was Several Seen Carried of[f] from the Shore.*

Fr[i]day 20th Sep^tr this Day the wind Southerly but Small Serj^t m^clowra being on Guard the Lieu^t of the Gondola N^w york was ordered to Rel[i]eve him he Came within Swivel Shot and fired upon m^clowra without any Prov[o]cation but Did no Damage at twelve Oclock Ansel Fox was Ca[tte]d [flogged] twelve Strokes on his Naked Butt[o]cks for sleeping on his watch the wind incre[as]ed at South and held very Strong all night the Painter [bow rope] of the Battoe Parted and. . .went A Drift. A more Wind[y] night I Sc[a]rce Ever Knew.

Sat[u]rday 21 Sep^tr this day the wind Southerly and Cloud[y] the wind much Abated. the General ordered five Battoes and two Schooners to go on Shore after five Battoes that Went A Drift they took our Guard Boats Crew of[f] the Shore that w[e]re Drove on Shore by the wind Last night this Day I Recv^d three Letters from home.

Sabbath 22^d Sep^tr this Day the wind Southerly but Small and Var[i]able this

---

*Two days later Benedict Arnold reported the incident in a letter to Major General Horatio Gates: "The Liberty was ordered to cruise off the Isle-la-Motte until two o'clock, and then join the fleet. On her return, opposite to the Isle-la-Motte, a Frenchman came down and desired to be taken on board; the Captain suspected him and went near the shore with his boat, stern in, swivels pointed, and match tiled [match of hemp rope and a primer consisting of a paper tube holding powder]; the Frenchman waded near a rod from the shore, but when he found he could decoy the boat no farther, he made a signal to the enemy, when three or four hundred Indians, Canadians, and Regulars, rose up and fired on the boat; they wounded three men. The boat returned the fire with their swivels and small-arms, and the schooner fired several broadsides of grape before they dispersed, though several were seen to fall."[112] J. F. Wasmus, a surgeon with the German troops, disclosed that Lieutenant Thomas Scott of the 24th Regiment had been sent with 24 Indians and two Canadians to reconnoiter the American position. Scott and his detachment were about to leave "when the 2 Canadians went to the bank and called to the Rebels to take them along: they were deserters. Thereupon the Rebels immediately lowered a boat with 10 men and rowed toward the bank. The Savages sneaked through the bushes close to the bank to receive the Rebels at their landing. The Rebels, however, might have noticed something as they turned their boat around and went in the other direction. At that moment, the Savages shot at them, and 8 Rebels fell from their thwarts [seats] backwards into the water. The other 2 applied all their strength to get back to the ships. Now the Rebels poured whole volleys into the woods and fired for more then an hour but could not harm anything but trees, for Lieut. Scott was already safe."[113]

morning at Eight. A. M. Ananius Tubbs was Ca[tt]ᵈ twelve Strokes on his Naked Butt[o]cks for Sleeping on his watch the wind increased at South west until night Lieuᵗ Fox & Serjᵗ [Josiah] Whitney made us A Vis[i]t

Monday 23ᵈ Sepᵗʳ this Day the wind Southerly and fresh and Some Cloud[y] I went on Guard at twelve OClock & Was Rel[i]evᵈ at Six in the morning at 3 P. M. the Capᵗ [Reed] of Gondolo Nʷ York Came on board to V[i]ew the hands on board Agre[e]able to General Arnoldˢ Orders Last Evening

Tuesday 24ᵗʰ Sepᵗʳ this Day wind at West Nor[th]west the General Gave A Sailing Signal about Seven A. M. the whole fleet hove up I[m]mediately and Stood up the Lake as far as Sᵗ Antonies [St. Armand] Bay about ten miles from Cumberland head on the west Side Isle Belcore [Valcour] and Came too in about Six fathom of water Good bottom.

Wednesday 25ᵗʰ Sepᵗʳ this Day Westerly wind and Clear about ten A. M. the General [Arnold] invited all Capᵗˢ & Lieuᵗˢ to Dine with him on the Isle of Bellchore accordingly we went and had A most agre[e]able Entertainment. about twelve Oclock we heard the Report of Several Can[n]on toward Sᵗ Johns [St. Jean]

Th[u]rsday 26ᵗʰ Sepᵗʳ this Day the Wind South and Clear at twelve Oclock Orders for the Whole fleet to fire at mark accordingly we Did at one P. M. one Round Each fired about one mile at an Empty Ca[s]k anchor[e]d the Wind incre[a]seᵈ until at So[u]th it Sno[w]ᵈ this night*

Fryday 27ᵗʰ Sepᵗʳ this Day the wind Southerly and Cloud[y] at one P. M. orders that all the fleet Should fire one Round with all th[eir] Guns at mark. the wind hast [come] up at Nor[th]west So fresh the General adjorn[e]d it. about Seven P. M. our Boatswain a[r]rivᵈ on board With A New Rudder he informᵈ me that he Left C[rown] Point in order to join the fleet on monday 23ᵈ he met with Schooner Liberty Capᵗ Pr[e]m[i]er informed him that the fleet Lay at Sch[uy]ler Island and ordered him not to go any further he Did accordingly a[r]rivᵈ th[e]re and finding no fleet th[e]re Put about and Return[e]d to C. Point and Got A boat to Come with him they not [k]no[w]ing wh[e]re the fleet Lay Run by as far as P. A fair [Point au Fer] then Disparing of Ever Seeing the fleet again tackᵗ about and Stood for Crown Point a[r]rivᵈ to Cumberl[a]n[d] head and met with the Schooner Revenge which brought them too and Piloted them to the fleet.

Sat[u]rday 28ᵗʰ Sepᵗʳ this Day the wind Northerly and Clear I went on Guard at twelve oclock and Came of[f] at Six at three P. M. the whole fleet fired at mark one Round in Each Gun the [gondola] Providence made the best Shots in the fleet. this Day Lieuᵗ Fox Dinᵈ With us we had A mess of Greens which was Equ[a]l to any in the month of may.

Sabbath 29ᵗʰ Sepᵗʳ this Day the wind Southerly and Cloud[y] and Rain which increa[s]ed until midnight then Abated Serjᵗ Paul Wells went on Guard in my Room I being not Very well.

Monday 30ᵗʰ Sepᵗʳ this Day the Wind Continued at South and flying Clouds about two P. M. Ro[w] galle[y] Trumb[u]ll Capᵗ [Seth] Warner a[r]rivᵈ Saluted the fleet with Seven Guns the [schooner Royal] Savage Saluted her with three Guns the above Galley Carries Eight Great Guns & Sixteen Swivels.

---

*The living conditions for the 45-man crew aboard the 54-foot gunboats during a month and a half period of deteriorating weather must have been miserable, given the limited space on the vessels, which required the men to sleep in shifts on the open decks.

Tuesday 1ˢᵗ Octʳ this the wind Northerly and Clear at Eight A M. Mʳ Stiles Returnᵈ from A Scout Down the Lake had b[e]en Gone Eight Days he brought News yᵗ the Enemy had fortifyᵈ Strong on I[s]le a[ux] No[i]x and at River La[colle] and that he lay Conceal[e]d and A boat Past by him in which the General Burgo[y]ne was which he knew.* Disco[u]rse Past between the General and two other Officers was that they intended to Send th[eir] Schooner up in Sight of the Yanke[e] fleet and then Retreat and lead our fleet Down against th[eir] battery and then Sink them all this Day we Could See Sno[w] on the mountains.

Wednesday 2ᵈ Octʳ this Day the wind Northerly and Clear. I went on Guard at midnight and Came of[f] at five OClock in the morning the wind Shifted Round in the South and Blow[e]d A Gale from about Six P. M. to the morning following the [schooner Royal] Savage Drifted against us

Th[u]rsday 3ᵈ Octʳ this Day the wind Continued Southerly and Very Strong we w[e]re Oblig[d] to Pay out the whole Length of our Cables to Keep out of the way of the Royal Savage the Wind Continued Strong at South until night then Abated it Set in and Rain[e]d all night.

Friday 4ᵗʰ Octʳ this Day the Wind Northerly and Cloud[y] we Sent our boat on board Galley Trumb[u]ll and Got two barrels of Pork & two Ditto of Bread the wind Continued Northerly until Nex[t] Morning.

Sat[u]rday 5ᵗʰ Octʳ this Day the wind Northerly and Clear. I went on Guard at twelve Oclock and Came of[f] at Six in the morning Lieuᵗ Jacob Fox made us A Vis[i]t.

Sabbath 6ᵗʰ Octoʳ this Day the wind Southerly and Cloud[y] this morning I am not well about twelve oclock Ro[w] galley Washington Capᵗ [John] thacher a[r]rivᵈ this Ves[s]el Carries Nine Carr[i]age Guns Sixteen Swivels. about one P. M. Ro[w] galley Congress Capᵗ [James] Arnold Ar[r]ivᵈ this galley Carries ten Carr[i]age Guns and Sixteen Swivels these Ves[s]els Saluted the fleet with firing a Round the Com[mo]dore Saluted Each of them with five Guns. General Waterbury** A[r]rivᵈ Came in [the galley] Washington and join[e]d our fleet they brought A Barrel of Rum for Each Gondola

Monday 7ᵗʰ Octʳ this Day the wind Northerly and Cloud[y]. this morning I feel Some bet[t]er Sc[h]ooner Liberty a[r]rivᵈ and join[e]d the fleet had been Gone up to ticonderoga about A Week to be repa[i]r[e]d they brought us Some Stores of fresh beef and Sug[a]r.

Tuesday 8ᵗʰ Octʳ this Day the [wind] Southerly and Cloud[y]. about Sun Set we

*According to Benedict Arnold, Eli Stiles reported "Two Thousand men on the Island, In Tents, That he saw a Schooner Mounting Twelve Guns Two Gondolas Compleated with thre[e] Guns in Each & a Square Sail, One Gondola Launched & Not Compleated. & Two on the Stocks one of them Just set up, that a Number of People were encamped at Rive[r] a Cote [Lacolle] where they have Erected a Battery of heavy Cannon—He also Saw Many Tents on Hospital Island & on the West Shore between that & Isle Aux Noix—that he passed Windmill Point in the night & he believes there was Four hundred Indians there."[114]

**David Waterbury (1722-1801) began his military career as an ensign in the Connecticut militia in 1747 at the time of King George's War (1744-1748). He was an officer during the French and Indian War, including duty in Abercromby's disastrous 1758 expedition to Ticonderoga. Colonel Waterbury marched his Connecticut regiment to Fort Ticonderoga in July 1775 and served during the siege of Fort St. Jean in the fall. Appointed Brigadier General and second in command to Benedict Arnold, 54-year-old Waterbury also participated in the supervision of the vessels under construction at Skenesborough in 1776.

"The Engagement of October 11th—The American Guns Converging on the [schooner] *Carleton*" by Carleton T. Chapman from *Scribner's Magazine*, February 1898.

"The Running Fight. . .The American flotilla. . .retreating"
by Carleton T. Chapman from *Scribner's Magazine*, February 1898.

brought Eight Gallons of West india Rum and two Gallons of [c]ider brand[y] and three bushels of Potatos.

Wednesday 9th Oct[r] this Day the wind Southerly and Cloud[y].

Th[u]rsday 10, Oct[r] this Day the wind Southerly and Cloud[y].

Friday 11 Oct[r] this Day the wind at North and Clear th[e]re was Sno[w] to be Seen on the mountains on the West Shore about Eight A. M. the Guard boat Came in and fired an Alarm and brought News of the Near Ap[p]ro[a]ch of our Enemy about ten A. M. A twenty two Gun Ship [18-gun *Inflexible*] hove in Sight and two Sixteen Gun Schooners [14-gun *Maria* and 12-gun *Carleton*] and two Sloops [gondola *Loyal Convert* and a sloop-rigged long boat] and one flo[a]ting Battery [*Thunderer*] which mounted twenty Six Guns [actually 14 cannon and two howitzers which included] Six twenty four Pounders and A Large number of boats [bateaux]. they Soon Gave us Battle We Return[e]d the Same to them they Soon Disabled one of our Sc[h]ooners [*Royal Savage*] and Oblig[d] our men to Le[a]ve her and Get on Shore the Battle Lasted Eight hours Very hot they Landed men on Shore on both Sides of us Which took Some Lives* about four P. M. one of th[eir] Schooners [*Carleton*] was Disabled so that they w[e]re oblig[d] to Come and tow her off With boats** at Sun Set they Blow[d] up our Schooner [*Royal Savage*] and Set her on fire*** and Seast [ceased] firing and Retreated as Near as I Can Gues[s] we Lost about fifty Kill[d] and wounded.† After Dark orders was Given for our fleet to Retreat to Crownpoint accordingly we Did and Come by them undiscovered‡ and Ar[r]iv[d] to Sch[uy]lers Isleland and Came too the wind being hard against us.

Sat[u]rday 12, Oct[r] this Day the wind at South. in the morning our Enemies

---

*Pascal De Angelis mentioned that during the "time of action the Regulars and Indians [led by Captains Christopher Carleton and Alexander Fraser] Fired with Small arms From the Shore at the Galley Washington who soon put them in Sil[e]nce by a few Cann[i]ster Shot."[115] Cannister shot was an "anti-personnel scatter projectile" consisting of shot tightly packed in a tinned iron cylinder or can which was discharged from cannon.[116]

**Jahiel Stewart, aboard the *Enterprise*, observed that the *Carleton* "came up verrey bold and the battel was verrey hot we Cut her Rigen [rigging] most all away & bored her threw and threw & She was forst [forced] to tos[s] of[f] us."[117] The vessel was saved by the heroic efforts of 19-year-old Edward Pellew (see main text).

***Both the schooner *Royal Savage* and the gondola *Philadelphia* were lost at Valcour Island. After discussing his plans with Stephen H. P. Pell, director of the Fort Ticonderoga Museum, Lorenzo F. Hagglund, a New York salvage engineer, wrote a letter on September 9, 1929, to Dr. Charles Adams, director of the New York State Museum, outlining "a small expedition to recover some revolutionary relics in the vicinity of Lake Champlain."[118] In 1934 Hagglund and his crew raised the remains of the *Royal Savage* and a year later recovered the intact *Philadelphia*. Today the original *Philadelphia* is on display at the Smithsonian's National Museum of American History and a full-size replica is exhibited at the Lake Champlain Maritime Museum at Basin Harbor.

†Benedict Arnold reported that "the whole killed and wounded amounted to about sixty" and Colonel Edward Wigglesworth, third in command, noted "about fifty killed and wounded."[119]

‡Ensign John Enys, aboard the *Thunderer*, suggested that the deployment of the British fleet "in a Semicircle round the Mouth of it [Valcour Bay], in Such Manner that it might well be thought they could not have escaped, which however they did in the course of the Night by passing between us and the shore unper[c]eived by any one."[120] Charles Terrot, an assistant engineer with the British forces, wrote that "Nobody could tell how the rebels escaped."[121] British officers later criticized the British naval commander, Thomas Pringle, for mooring the fleet "at least one mile from the western shore" which allowed the Americans to retreat unnoticed.[122]

"Arnold Leaving the *Congress*" from *Harper's New Monthly Magazine*, November 1861.

appear^d in Sight the General ordered that the whole fleet to Get under way* the Enemy Came hard against us So that we w[e]re Oblig^d to Le[a]ve three Gondolas and make the best of our way with boats two of which we D[e]stroy^d and one of them the Enemies made A Pri[z]e of.** The Rest made th[eir] Escape this Day by Rowing all night

Sabbath 13 Octr this Day the wind at North we being against the mouth of Gillilands Crick [Boquet River]*** the Enemy hove in Sight and P[u]rsued us with all Speed they Soon overtook the two Rear Ro[w] galleys and Oblig^d o[ne] of them to Strike her Colors and Come too† the Galley Congress Retreated and fought they Soon Came up With four Gondolas and the Congress who w[e]re Oblig^d to Run a Shore and blow them up‡ and take to the land with the Loss of but few we march^d by land as far as against Crown point and Lo[d]g^d in the woods.

monday 14 Octr we trav[e]l^d by Land as far as against Putn[a]m Point and th[e]re met boats which took us on board we Ar[r]iv^d to Ticonderoga about Sun Set†‡

---

*Benedict Arnold noted that "at 2 oclock P. M. [at Schuyler Island] the 12th weighed Anchor with a fresh Breeze to the Southward. The Enemy's Fleet at the same time got under Way, our Gondolas made very little way a Head."[123] Some of the vessels, especially the shattered galley *Washington*, made little progress. The *Revenge, Enterprise, New York*, and *Trumbull* had anchored for repairs at Ligonier Point, opposite Four Brothers Islands on October 12, and "lay there till half after one at Night," according to Pascal De Angelis, "When 2 [of] the G[o]nd[o]l[a]s came along and we hail[e]d them and they told us that one of our G[o]nd[o]l[a]s was taking [water] the other sunk whereupon we got under way and Beat down the Rest of the Night."[124]

**Bayze Wells' statement on October 12, which noted leaving three gunboats, has puzzled historians for generations. Benedict Arnold mentioned "two Gondolas sunk at Schuyler Island," one of which included the *New Jersey* that was found by the British and taken into the Royal Navy.[125] Wells may have included the *Philadelphia* in the three gondolas since his October 11 entry failed to report the sinking of the vessel. On the other hand, Wells possibly may have counted the cutter *Lee* which had been abandoned by her American crew during the retreat. The other gondola that sank was perhaps the *Spitfire* or *Connecticut*.[126]

***"At six o'clock the next morning," Benedict Arnold recorded, "we were about off Willsborough."[127] Pascal De Angelis noted in his journal: "this Morning [October 13] at day Light we Saw the Enemies Ship [*Inflexible*] and 2 schooners [*Carleton* and *Maria*] But a Little a st[e]rn of our fleet."[128]

†Although Benedict Arnold had given orders to "Stop the fleet at Split Rock and Make a Stand," the fleet was scattered over seven miles and could not regroup for battle.[129] The British vessels "at about 9 oclock came up with our fleet," Pascal De Angelis observed, "and fired at the Washington Galley and Congress Galley and after Four or five Shot the Washington Galley Strik[e] without firing one Gun."[130] In an effort "to save the Trumbull galley if possible," Colonel Edward Wigglesworth ordered that the oars be "double manned. . .and made all the sail we could, and by throwing over our ballast got off clear."[131]

‡Benedict Arnold directed the return fire from the exposed decks of the galley *Congress* during a running battle, which lasted several hours, as the remnants of the crippled American fleet fled southward along the eastern shore of Lake Champlain. With no chance to escape, Arnold ordered the *Congress* and four gondolas into Ferris Bay, named for Peter Ferris, whose farmhouse bordered the small inlet (present-day Arnold's Bay in Panton, Vermont). According to Joseph Cushing, a marine sergeant on the galley *Congress*, Arnold "set them [vessels] on fire, but ordered the colours not to be struck; and as they grounded, the marines were directed to jump overboard, with their arms and accoutrements, to ascend a bank about twenty-five feet elevation, and form a line for the defence of their vessels and flags against the enemy, Arnold being the last man who debarked."[132]

†‡Wells probably crossed the lake about five miles south of Crown Point, landing at the mouth of Putnam Creek.

Left:
Raising of the gondola *Philadelphia* at Valcour Island in 1935. (Smithsonian Institution)
Right:
Colonel Lorenzo F. Hagglund (with helmet) and crew on recovery barge at
Valcour Island, 1935. (Vermont Historical Society)
Below:
Exact replica of the gunboat *Philadelphia* at the Lake Champlain Maritime Museum.
The original vessel is on display at the Smithsonian Institution. (Photo by the author)

Notes

1. Bayze Wells, "Journal of Bayze Wells of Farmington," *Collections of the Connecticut Historical Society* 7 (1899): 241.
2. Ichabod Norton, *Orderly Book of Capt. Ichabod Norton* (Fort Edward, N.Y.: Press of Keating & Barnard, 1898), 37.
3. Wells, 267; See also Lewis Beebe, "Journal of a Physcian on the Expedition Against Canada, 1776," *The Pennsylvania Magazine of History and Biography* 59 (October 1935): 336; William Chamberlin, "Letter of General William Chamberlin," *Proceedings of the Massachusetts Historical Society* 10 (2nd Series) (1896): 498.
4. Joseph Vose, "Journal of Lieutenant-Colonel Joseph Vose," *The Colonial Society of Massachusetts* 7 (Transactions 1900-1902): 251.
5. *From Cambridge to Champlain* (Middleboro, MA.: Lawrence B. Romaine, 1957), 29.
6. Wells, 267.
7. William Bell Clark, ed., *Naval Documents of the American Revolution* (Washington, D.C.: Naval History Division, Department of the Navy, 1966), Volume 2, 589.
8. Jeduthan Baldwin, *The Revolutionary Journal of Col. Jeduthan Baldwin 1775-1778*, ed. Thomas Williams Baldwin (Bangor, ME.: De Burians, 1906), 60.
9. Elisha Porter, "The Diary of Mr. Elisha Porter of Hadley 1776," *Magazine of American History* 29 (January - June 1893): 201.
10. Peter Force, ed., *American Archives*, Fifth Series, Volume 1 (Washington, D.C.: M. St. Clair Clarke and Peter Force, 1848), 630.
11. Arthur Cohn, *The 1992 Fort Ticonderoga - Mount Independence Submerged Cultural Resource Survey* (Lake Champlain Basin Program, 1995), Report 4A; Kevin Crisman, *The 1992 Mount Independence Phase One Underwater Archaeological Survey* (Lake Champlain Basin Program, 1995), Report 4B; Dennis E. Howe, *This Ragged, Starved Lousy, Pocky Army* (Concord, N.H.: The Printed Word, 1996); David R. Starbuck, "Building Independence on Lake Champlain," *Archaeology*, September - October 1993, 60-62.
12. *From Cambridge to Champlain*, 28.
13. Ammi R. Robbins, "Journal of Rev. Ammi R. Robbins," in *History of Norfolk*, comp. by Theron Wilmot Crissey (Everett, MA.: Massachusetts Publishing Company, 1900), 101.
14. Charles J. Stille, *Major-General Anthony Wayne and the Pennsylvania Line in the Continental Army* (Philadelphia: J. B. Lippincott Company, 1893), 37; See also Vose, 251.
15. Clark, 2: 701-2, 731.
16. Ibid., 680, see also 306, 317, 436, 494-95, 710.
17. Ibid., 657.
18. William James Morgan, ed., *Naval Documents of the American Revolution* (Washington, D.C.: Naval History Division, Department of the Navy, 1970), Volume 5, 897.
19. Force, Fifth Series, 1: 563.
20. Ibid., 649.
21. Wells, 267.
22. Philip K. Lundeberg, *The Gunboat Philadelphia and the Defense of Lake Champlain in 1776* (Basin Harbor, VT.: Lake Champlain Maritime Museum, 1995), 57-60.
23. Wells, 268.
24. Ibid.
25. Ibid.
26. Ibid., 269.
27. William James Morgan, ed., *Naval Documents of the American Revolution* (Washington, D.C.: Naval History Division, Department of the Navy, 1972), Volume 6, 224.
28. Force, Fifth Series, 1: 988.
29. Ibid., 826.
30. Wells, 271.
31. Force, Fifth Series, 1: 1267.
32. Wells, 272.
33. Morgan, 6: 734.
34. Wells, 275; The officer was Lieutenant Scott of the 24th Regiment. See "A Journal of Carleton's

and Burgoyne's Campaigns," *The Bulletin of the Fort Ticonderoga Museum* 11 (December 1964): 252.

35. Wells, 267-77.

36. Ibid., 278.

37. Harold L. Peterson, *The Book of the Continental Soldier* (Harrisburg, Pa.: The Stackpole Company, 1968), 172; By the end of July 1776, 1,497 soldiers had been admitted to the Fort George hospital. Force, Fifth Series, 1: 857; See also Howe, 6-7.

38. Peter Force, ed., *American Archives*, Fifth Series, Volume 2 (Washington, D.C.: M. St. Clair Clarke and Peter Force, 1851), 481; See also Morgan, 6: 884.

39. Morgan, 6: 884; See also an intelligence report from a German prisoner. Force, Fifth Series, 2: 421.

40. Force, Fifth Series, 2: 481, for additional intelligence reports see 421, 482, 835, 982; See also Morgan, 6: 1081, 1084; James Wilkinson, *Memoirs of My Own Times* (1816; reprint ed., New York: AMS Press, Inc., 1973), 87.

41. Edward Osler, *The Life of Admiral Viscount Exmouth* (London: Smith Elder & Co., 1835), 11.

42. Howard I. Chapelle, *The History of the American Sailing Navy* (New York: W. W. Norton & Company, 1949), 105; "An Account of the Expedition of the British Fleet on Lake Champlain," New York State Archives, #1008 Revolutionary War Manuscripts; Eleanor M. Murray, "The Burgoyne Campaign," *The Bulletin of the Fort Ticonderoga Museum* 8 (January 1948): 6; The artillery on the *Thunderer* varies with sources as does the length—one original source has the length of the *Thunderer* at 100 feet. "A Journal of Carleton's and Burgoyne's Campaigns," 256.

43. Morgan, 6: 857-58; See also Wilkinson, 87; A letter to Benedict Arnold dated September 23,1776, from Colonel Thomas Hartley seems to imply that the British had a radeau: "the Grand Diable (which I understand is the largest vessel of the Enemy)." The letter was among Arnold's papers taken by the British before the *Royal Savage* was destroyed. "Documents sur la Révolution Américaine,"*La Revue De L'Université Laval, Québec* 2 (June 1948): 928.

44. "An Account of the Expedition of the British Fleet on Lake Champlain"; Morgan, 6: 883, 1344; Robert Beatson, *Naval and Military Memoirs of Great Britain from 1727 to 1783* (1804; reprint ed., Boston: Gregg Press, 1972), 46; Osler, 11; Elizabeth Cometti, ed., *The American Journals of Lt. John Enys* (Syracuse: Syracuse University Press 1976), 18; Horatio Rogers, ed., *Hadden's Journal and Orderly Books: A Journal Kept in Canada and Upon Burgoyne's Campaigns in 1776 and 1777, by Lieut. James M. Hadden, Roy. Art.* (Albany: Joel Munsell's Sons, 1884), 16. The original journal and orderly books of Lieutenant Hadden are presently in the Fort Ticonderoga Museum Collection.

45. Force, Fifth Series, 2: 591.

46. Rogers, 16; Helga Doblin, trans. and Mary C. Lynn, ed., *An Eyewitness Account of the American Revolution and New England Life: The Journal of J. F. Wasmus, German Company Surgeon, 1776-1783* (Westport, CT.: Greenwood Press, 1990), 31; Joshua Pell, Jr., "Diary of Joshua Pell, Junior," *Magazine of American History* 2 (1878): 46; James Phinney Baxter, ed., *The British Invasion from the North, The Campaigns of Generals Carleton and Burgoyne from Canada, 1776-1777, With the Journal of Lieut. William Digby* (Albany: Joel Munsell's Sons, 1887), 159.

47. William L. Stone, trans., *Memoirs, Letters, and Journals of Major General Riedsel* (1868; reprint ed., New York: The New York Times & Arno Press, 1969), Volume 1, 70.

48. Rogers, 17; See also J. Robert Maguire, "Dr. Robert Knox's Account of the Battle of Valcour, October 11-13, 1776," *Vermont History* 46 (Summer 1978): 148.

49. Cometti, 18; John Schank, John Starke, and Edward Longcroft, "An Open Letter to Captain Pringle," *The Bulletin of the Fort Ticonderoga Museum* 1 (July 1928): 18.

50. Maguire, 148.

51. Ibid.

52. Morgan, 6: 1235; See also Donald Wickman, ed., "A Most Unsettled Time on Lake Champlain: the October 1776 Journal of Jahiel Stewart," *Vermont History* 64 (Spring 1996): 92; The Hay household was said to have signaled Arnold's fleet on the approach of the British vessels. Winslow C. Watson, *Pioneer History of the Champlain Valley* (Albany: J. Munsell, 1863), 70.

53. William James Morgan, ed., *Naval Documents of the American Revolution* (Washington, D.C.: Naval History Division, Department of the Navy, 1976), Volume 7, 1295.

54. E. Vale Smith, *History of Newburyport* (Newburyport, MA.: n.p., 1854), 357.

55. *History of Oneida County, New York* (Philadelphia: Everts & Fariss, 1878), 569.
56. For a shortened version of the De Angelis diary see Charles M. Snyder, "With Benedict Arnold at Valcour Island: The Diary of Pascal De Angelis," *Vermont History* 42 (Summer 1974): 195-200. About one half of De Angelis' October 11 entry, describing the battle, the Indian attack from shore, damage to the fleet, and the retreat, was omitted from this version.
57. Pascal Charles Joseph De Angelis, "The Lake Champlain Fight," diary 1776, Marshall Family Papers, MS 9, Penfield Library, State University of New York at Oswego; See also Snyder, 198; Morgan, 6: 1235; E. Smith, 357.
58. Wickman, 91; See also E. Smith, 357; Cometti, 19; Morgan 6: 1235; Morgan, 7: 123; Georg Pausch, *Journal of Captain Pausch*, trans. and ed. William L. Stone (Albany: Joel Munsell's Sons, 1886), 82.
59. Charles Douglas, letter 29 October 1776, National Archives of Canada reprinted in *North Country Notes*, April 1963, 2; See also Schank, Starke, and Longcroft, 18.
60. Pausch, 83.
61. Rogers, 23.
62. Watson, 70.
63. Morgan, 6: 1235.
64. Wickman, 92.
65. De Angelis, Marshall Family Papers.
66. Morgan, 6: 1235.
67. De Angelis, Marshall Family Papers.
68. Rogers, 24; British boarding parties did save Benedict Arnold's papers before the *Royal Savage* was burned. They are now held by Laval University in Quebec. The papers include letters from other officers which date from September 21, 1775, and end on October 5, 1776. Although some of the letters have been published in Peter Force's *American Archives* (Fifth Series, Volume 2) and William James Morgan's *Naval Documents of the American Revolution* (Volume 6), others apparently have not been published in the United States. In addition to the military correspondence, some letters, written by his sister Hannah Arnold, deal with news about his young sons. "Documents, sur la Révolution Américaine," *La Revue De L'Université Laval*, Québec 2 (December 1947): 344-49; 2 (March 1948): 642-48; 2 (April 1948): 742-48; 2 (May 1948): 838-46; 2 (June 1948): 926-34.
69. Pausch, 83.
70. De Angelis, Marshall Family Papers.
71. Schank, Starke, and Longcroft, 19.
72. De Angelis, Marshall Family Papers; See also Snyder, 198; E. Smith, 358.
73. Morgan, 6: 1276.
74. De Angelis, Marshall Family Papers; Snyder, 198.
75. Force, Fifth Series, 2: 1180; Morgan, 6: 1245; Baxter, 162; "A Journal of Carleton's and Burgoyne's Campaigns," 257.
76. *Post-Star* (Glens Falls), 1 July 1997.
77. Cometti, 20.
78. De Angelis, Marshall Family Papers; Snyder, 199; Wickman, 94.
79. Force, Fifth Series, 2: 1069.
80. Morgan, 7: 1295.
81. E. Smith, 358.
82. *History of Oneida County*, 569.
83. Wickman, 94.
84. Morgan, 7: 1295.
85. Ibid.
86. Ibid.
87. E. Smith, 358.
88. De Angelis, Marshall Family Papers; Snyder, 199.
89. Cometti, 21-22.
90. Wasmus, 33; This story was also corroborated by James Wilkinson. Wilkinson, 91.
91. Samuel Swift, *History of the Town of Middlebury* (Middlebury, VT.: A. H. Copeland, 1859), 89; See also Art Cohn, "An Incident Not Known to History: Squire Ferris and Benedict Arnold at Ferris Bay, October 13, 1776," *Vermont History* 55 (Spring 1987): 97-112.

92. Maguire, 148.
93. Force, Fifth Series, 2: 1080.
94. John Trumbull, *Autobiography, Reminiscences and Letters of John Trumbull from 1756 to 1841* (New Haven, CT.: B. L. Hamlen, 1841), 35.
95. Ibid., 36.
96. Force, Fifth Series, 2: 1040; Morgan, 6: 1258.
97. Baxter, 147.
98. Horatio Gates Papers, Microfilming Corporation of America, reel 3, frame 1206.
99. Pell, 46-47.
100. Morgan, 6: 1336.
101. Wasmus, 34.
102. Persifer Frazer, "Letters from Ticonderoga, 1776," *The Bulletin of the Fort Ticonderoga Museum* 10 (January 1962): 455; See also Persifer Frazer, "An Account of a Skirmish on or Near Lake Champlain," 28 Oct. 1776, New York State Archives, #14007.
103. Micah Hildreth, "Micah Hildreth of Dracutt His Book," in *History of Dracut*, by Silas R. Coburn (Lowell, MA.: Press of the Courier-Citizen Co., 1922), 149-50; See also Jonathan Burton, *Diary and Orderly Book of Sergeant Jonathan Burton*, comp. and ed. by Isaac W. Hammond (Concord, N.H.: Republican Press Association, 1885), 35; Phineas Ingalls, "Revolutionary War Journal, Kept By Phineas Ingalls of Andover, Mass., April 19, 1775—December 8, 1776," *The Essex Institute Historical Collections* 53 (1917): 91; Simon Mudge, "A Journal of the March to Continental Army," in *Memorials: Mudge*, by Alfred Mudge (Boston: Alfred Mudge & Son, 1868), 205; Rufus Wheeler, "Journal of Lieut. Rufus Wheeler of Rowley," *The Essex Institute Historical Collections* 68 (October 1932): 376; Nathaniel Brown Dodge, "A Letter and Diary of 1776," *Vermont Quarterly* 21 (1953): 34-35; Norton, 48; Baldwin, 83-84.
104. Wells, 286.
105. Ibid., 289-90.
106. Ibid., 290.
107. Ibid., 292.
108. Ibid., 293.
109. Charles J. Hoadly, *The Public Records of the State of Connecticut* (Hartford: Press of the Case, Lockwood & Brainard Company, 1894), 314; Henry P. Johnston, ed., *The Record of Connecticut Men in the Military and Naval Service During the War of the Revolution 1775-1783* (Hartford: The Case, Lockwood & Brainard Company, 1889): 230.
110. Nelson R. Burr, *From Colonial Parish to Modern Suburb: A Brief Appreciation of West Hartford* (n.p., 1982), 28.
111. Wells, 279-85.
112. Force, Fifth Series, 2: 440.
113. Wasmus, 30.
114. Morgan, 6: 1084; Force, Fifth Series, 2: 835.
115. De Angelis, Marshall Family Papers.
116. Peterson, 136.
117. Wickman, 92.
118. L. F. Hagglund to Charles C. Adams, 9 September 1929, New York State Museum.
119. Force, Fifth Series, 2: 1038; E. Smith, 358.
120. Cometti, 20.
121. Charles Terrot, "Naval Action on Lake Champlain, 1776," *American Neptune* 8: 3 (1948): 256; See also Charles Terrot to John Frott, 17 October 1776, Fort Ticonderoga Thompson-Pell Research Center. This correspondence is believed to be the basis for William Faden's famous map of the battle. Faden's original map engraving entitled "The Attack and Defeat of the American Fleet under Benedict Arnold, by the King's Fleet Commanded by Captn. Thos.Pringle, upon Lake Champlain. The 11th of October 1776" is in the collection of the Fort Ticonderoga Museum.
122. Schank, Starke, and Longcroft, 19.
123. Morgan, 6: 1276.
124. De Angelis, Marshall Family Papers; See also Snyder, 198; E. Smith, 358.
125. Morgan, 6: 1276; Force, Fifth Series, 2: 1079, 1179; Haldimand Papers, National Archives of Canada, Microfilm C-3242, Volume 722A, fol. 21.

126. Arthur B. Cohn, "New Discoveries in the Archaeology of the Lakes" (paper presented at the annual meeting of the North American Society for Oceanic History, Bolton Landing, N.Y., May 8, 1999).

127. Force, Fifth Series, 2: 1079.

128. De Angelis, Marshall Family Papers; See also Snyder, 199.

129. Morgan, 7: 1295.

130. De Angelis, Marshall Family Papers; See also Snyder, 199.

131. E. Smith, 358-59.

132. Charles R. Smith, *Marines in the Revolution: A History of the Continental Marines in the American Revolution 1775-1783* (Washington, D.C.: History and Museums Division, Headquarters, U.S. Marine Corps, 1975), 32; See also Wilkinson, 91; For information on the shipwrecks of Arnold's Bay see Russell P. Bellico, *Sails and Steam in the Mountains: A Maritime and Military History of Lake George and Lake Champlain* (Fleischmanns, N.Y.: Purple Mountain Press, 1992), 198-201; For an account of the archaeological site excavation of the Peter Ferris homestead see David R. Starbuck, *The Ferris Site on Arnold's Bay* (Basin Harbor, VT.: Lake Champlain Maritime Museum, 1989).

An 1899 photograph of the remains of the row galley *Congress* retrieved from Arnold's Bay. Two surviving frames are presently on display at the Lake Champlain Maritime Museum. (Vermont Historical Society)

Detail of "The Surrender of General Burgoyne at Saratoga." Painting by John Trumbull.
Enos Hitchcock is the fifth figure from the left. Colonel Daniel Morgan
is the figure in the foreground wearing white. (National Archives)

9. Enos Hitchcock 1777

FOLLOWING THE ABORTED BRITISH INVASION of the American colonies through Lake Champlain in 1776, a similar plan was formulated and advocated in London during the winter of 1777 by John Burgoyne, who had been second in command during the 1776 operation. Appointed to head the 1777 expedition, Major General Burgoyne (local rank of lieutenant general in North America) reached Quebec with his army in early May. The British strategy involved a plan to sever the American colonies along the Hudson River by the convergence at Albany of Burgoyne's forces and General William Howe's army stationed in southern New York. (Howe, the British commander in chief, was the younger brother of George Augustus Howe who had been killed during the campaign against Fort Carillon in 1758.) Lieutenant Colonel Barry St. Leger (local rank of brigadier general) would lead the third prong of the planned invasion with a diversionary force of approximately 2,000 Native Americans, Tories, and regulars through the Mohawk Valley to Albany. By the end of June the American forces at Ticonderoga and Mount Independence would face Burgoyne's formidable professional army of more than 7,000 British regulars, German mercenaries, and auxiliary personnel.

Enos Hitchcock, a chaplain with the American army, was attached to troops deployed at Ticonderoga. Hitchcock, a descendant of a family whose roots in America dated to the early seventeenth century, was born in Springfield, Massachusetts, on March 7, 1744, to Peletiah and Sarah Parsons Hitchcock.[1] His grandfather, Luke Hitchcock, a prominent citizen of Springfield, had been a tavern keeper, captain of the militia, and sheriff of Hampshire County. Enos Hitchcock's family resettled in Brookfield (central Massachusetts) around 1760. Following graduation from Harvard College in 1767, Hitchcock was subsequently certified to preach by a council of ministers from Cape Cod. On January 13, 1771, he married Mrs. Achsah

(Upham) Jordon, a widow from Truro, Massachusetts, and four months later was ordained a colleague of the pastor at the Second Church in Beverly, Massachusetts.

Like many clergymen, Hitchcock volunteered during the American Revolution, serving as chaplain of Colonel Ebenezer Learned's 3rd Continental Infantry and later with several other units at Ticonderoga in 1776. Unfortunately, his diary for this period has never been found. With continued support from his parishioners, Hitchcock left his home in Beverly on April 8, 1777, for the long journey to Ticonderoga to assume his duties as chaplain of Colonel Thomas Marshall's 10th Massachusetts Regiment. After three days of travel, he arrived in Brookfield, where his mother still resided. While in Brookfield, Hitchcock was inoculated for small-pox, a scourge of eighteenth-century armies. The process involved spreading the secretion from an infected patient into a cut or scratch on the person being inoculated. Although the primitive vaccination had been a controversial medical practice during the first two years of the war, George Washington had authorized the procedure for the Continental Army in 1777. Hitchcock also swallowed a "mecurial pill" every day for a week in addition to various powders and purgatives.[2] Ten days after the smallpox inoculation, mild symptoms of the disease appeared and lasted for 13 days while Hitchcock remained in the Brookfield hospital. He finally left for Ticonderoga on May 15, lodging along the way in the small towns of Massachusetts, Vermont, and New York. Reaching Ticonderoga on May 23, Hitch-cock would soon enjoy dinners of venison, veal, and fish, but six weeks later would find himself in the thick of a hasty evacuation and dodging "flying ball" at Skenesborough.[3]

Plans for the defense of the Lake Champlain posts had been formulated six months earlier. Writing to the committee of the Continental Congress responsible for the army in the north, Philip Schuyler, the commander of the Northern Department, recommended on November 6, 1776, that "a fort [be] built on Mount Independence to cover batteries near the lake side and the redoubt on the Ticon-deroga side. . .the navigation should be effect[ive]ly stopped by sinking cassoons at small distances, and joined together by string pieces. . .to serve [as] a bridge between the fortifications."[4] At the end of the month the committee endorsed Schuyler's plans, including his idea for the construction of "very large and strong vessels" on Lake Champlain and blocking access through Lake George: "two large Floating-Bat-teries be built on Lake Champlain to cover the Boom and the Bridge. . .and the passage of. . .[Lake George] be also obstructed in like manner by caissons from island to island in the Narrows."[5] In addition, the committee suggested that "the Hospital at Fort George be continued for. . .contagious diseases, and that there be a General Hospital erected on Mount Independence."[6]

On December 28 the Continental Congress approved the plans for the Northern Department. A month and a half later Schuyler met in Albany with Chief Engineer Jeduthan Baldwin (who had constructed a narrow footbridge across Lake Champlain in 1776), ordering him to proceed immediately to Lake George to assess the practicality of building an obstruction across the lake (Baldwin later determined that it was not feasible) and then to continue to Ticonderoga for work on the bridge. On February 26 Colonel Baldwin directed his men to cut timber for the 1,700-foot span; three days later he noted that they "began to build the Great Bridge, from Ticon-der[o]ga to Independ[e]nt point."[7] Twenty-two caissons or heavy log cribs were partially constructed on the ice and later placed on the lake floor.* The piers were connected by "separate floats, each about fifty feet long and twelve wide," according to James Thacher, a hospital surgeon's mate with the Americans.[11] On the north side of the bridge, Thacher also noted, that the Americans had built "a boom composed of large pieces of timber. . .and by the side of this is placed a double iron chain."[12] Later, Lieutenant August Wilhelm Du Roi, an officer with a German regiment, praised the bridge "which does honor to human mind and power. . .It may be compared to the work of Colossus in the fables of heathen."[13]

Aerial view of Fort Ticonderoga and Mount Independence.
(Photo by the author)

On April 2, with work progressing on the bridge, Colonel Baldwin sent plans for the new fort at Mount Independence to Major General Schuyler. The engineering of the new fortifications was directed by Baldwin with the help of several assistants, including Colonel Thaddeus Kosciuszko, a Polish military engineer who arrived at Ticonderoga on May 12. Kosciuszko was moderately critical of some of Baldwin's "unnecessary works," especially the blockhouses.[14] Two months later, however, British and German observers found the engineering impressive. Colonel Johann Friedrich Specht (local rank of brigadier general), the commander of the first brigade of the left wing of Burgoyne's army, noted that "the fortifications. . .had been laid out very competently on [Mount] Independence and. . .were admired by [our] experts of military engineering."[15] Likewise, Lieutenant Du Roi suggested that Mount Independence "was well done and showed no lack of clever engineers among

---

*The piers or log cribs, probably built one course at a time, were carefully lowered into holes cut or chopped in the ice and guided to the bottom of the lake by the use of long poles. The log cribs were held down by rocks lying on platforms, consisting of intermediate log crossmembers.[8] Expanding an earlier survey of the piers by the Champlain Maritime Society in 1983, an archaeological team from the Lake Champlain Maritime Museum located 21 of the original caissons in 1992.[9] The researchers also discovered 900 artifacts, including a 12-pound cannon (9 feet, 4 inches long), mortar bombs, barshot, spades, tools, bottles, iron grapeshot, a musket, and other relics.[10]

the rebels."[16] Julius Friedrich Wasmus, a company surgeon with the German troops, wrote a detailed description of the finished works on Mount Independence: "at the foot of this mountain lies a retrenchment of 29 cannon on gun emplacements. Above this line on a beautiful height stand 5 cannon in an entrenchment above the bank. One hundred and fifty paces further up lies an octagonal, star-shaped, palisaded fort where there are cannon and about 8 barracks en queue [in a line]."[17] In addition, cabins or huts, artificer's shops, lookout posts, and a 250-foot hospital were built on the site.[18]

Despite the completion of extensive defensive preparations at Mount Independence and additional redoubts and blockhouses at Ticonderoga, the Americans were ultimately ill-prepared for the onslaught of British forces in 1777. A letter sent to George Washington in January 1777 by Major General Schuyler recommended 10,000 troops to defend Ticonderoga. Washington, however, ignored the plea for reinforcements for the north, anticipating that the main British advance under General William Howe would be against Philadelphia. He also assumed that if Howe's forces were not sufficiently reinforced from England, "they will bring round all the Troops from Canada to reinforce 'em here."[19] "If we shou'd draw a large force together at Ticonderoga," and the British failed to attack, Washington noted to Schuyler, "they wou'd be an useless Body of Troops there," compromising the defense in the south.[20] Although Washington had ordered regiments from New Hampshire and Massachusetts to Ticonderoga, as late as June 14 Schuyler was still dispatching urgent messages to officials in the two states for immediate reinforcements. In addition, the American navy on Lake Champlain was not strengthened, although "two strong schooners of sixty feet keel" and row galleys were ordered constructed at Lake George.[21] On Lake Champlain the Americans had only six vessels, all from 1776: the galley *Trumbull*, gondola *New York*, schooners *Liberty* and *Revenge*, sloop *Enterprise*, and galley *Gates*, the last vessel completed immediately after the Valcour battle.

In contrast, the British expedition had a substantial squadron of warships, including several captured from the Americans in 1776. The fleet,* under the command of Captain Skeffington Lutwidge, included the ship *Inflexible*, schooners *Maria* and *Carleton*, gondolas *Loyal Convert* and *Jersey*, cutter *Lee*, radeau *Thunderer*, and a new three-masted ship, the 26-gun, 96-foot *Royal George*. On June 15 Lieutenant General John Burgoyne departed from St. Jean** aboard the schooner *Maria*, receiving a cannon salute from the schooner *Carleton*. During the forthcom-

---

*Joshua Pell, Jr., an officer with the British expedition, also noted a seven-gun vessel called the *Land Crab*, carrying 30 men.[22] Pell, however, may have called the flat-bottomed gondola *Loyal Convert* the *Land Crab* since he omitted the former vessel from his list. In February 1777 Lieutenant Thomas Anburey remarked that "we have raised up the Lakes, in addition to the force of last summer, a curious vessel, called a Radeaux, which formerly belonged to the French, and was sunk by the Americans near this place [St. Jean]: it is a castle of itself, of a monstrous constructure, and will hold a great number of men; she is intended to convey the heavy artillery across the Lakes."[23] Anburey, who was not present during the 1776 campaign, was actually referring to the 91-foot radeau *Thunderer* which had been constructed in 1776 and rebuilt for the 1777 campaign. Surgeon Julius Friedrich Wasmus noted that "the radeau or Floating Battery, which I described last year [armed on two decks in 1776] is still here and has even grown taller by one story."[24]

**In 1777 Fort St. Jean was described as "2 small forts, or rather. . .Redoubts, thrown up of earth. Each one has a dry ditch (moat) and palisades connected by a communication line, which [e]ncloses the barracks for the garrison."[25]

Right: Lieutenant General John Burgoyne sailed from St. Jean aboard the schooner *Maria*. Detail from an engraving printed in London for Robert Sayer and Jno. Bennett. (Special Collections, Bailey/Howe Memorial Library, University of Vermont)

Below: "A South West View of St. John's [St. Jean] sh[o]wing the Fort and the Detach'd Redoubt with the Blockhouse opposite" and the British fleet, including the three-masted ships *Inflexible* and *Royal George*. Watercolor by James Hunter. (National Archives of Canada)

ing expedition Burgoyne would have the unequivocal allegiance of his troops because of the uncommon fairness and consideration with which he treated the men under his command. He often mingled with the soldiers in their camp, admonished officers not to strike or swear at their troops, and encouraged officers to follow his own example and speak informally with the men. With drums beating and music playing, the fleet of bateaux and gunboats carrying German and English troops made uneven progress southward along the Richelieu River on June 16. Making stops at Lacolle River, Point au Fer, and Isle La Motte, the flotilla reached Cumberland Head on June 18, the rendezvous point for the army.

After two days at Cumberland Head, "General Burgoyne with great pomp, went on board the Lady Mar[ia]; and immediately the booming of cannon from the ship announced that the army w[as] about to start."[26] As the bateaux fleet sailed majestically southward, Julius Friedrich Wasmus recorded: "the beauty of this sight is beyond description."[27] Landing on the shore of a bay on the western side of the lake, the army pitched its tents.* In the evening Burgoyne sailed with several vessels for the camp of Brigadier General Simon Fraser at the Boquet River. At three o'clock in the morning of June 23, troops under Major General Friedrich Adolphus Riedesel, the commander of the German forces, made preparations to leave the bay but a violent storm led to a postponement of the departure. Early the next morning the bateaux armada reembarked, but a severe thunderstorm, accompanied by a pelting

*Surgeon Wasmus noted: "disembarked at Ligonier Bay. . .we pitched our tents on the top of the mountain."[28] The bay may have been present-day Willsboro Bay since after departing from the inlet on June 24 the troops rowed for several hours before reaching "4 islands, called Four Brothers."[29] Major General Friedrich Adolphus Riedesel, commanding the German troops, wrote on June 23 that the bateaux fleet had failed to pass Ligonier Point due to severe weather and on the following day five vessels were forced to land "on the Isle aux Quatres Vents [Four Brothers Islands]."[30]

hail and followed by a dense fog, hampered the voyage of the intrepid invaders. By late morning the army finally passed Four Brothers Islands.

At two o'clock in the afternoon the troops reached Burgoyne at Fraser's camp along the Boquet River, where the remnants of William Gilliland's mill and settlement were observed. At the Boquet camp Burgoyne met with his Native American allies, the Iroquois, Algonquins, Abenakis, and Ottawas, "in all about four hundred."[31] Speaking through an interpreter, Burgoyne urged the warriors to "strike at the common enemies of Great-Britain" but "positively forbid bloodshed, when you are not opposed in arms. Aged men, women, children, and prisoners, must be held sacred from the knife or hatchet. . .you shall be allowed to take the scalps of the dead. . .but, on no account. . .are they to be taken from the wounded."[32] Shortly thereafter, Burgoyne issued a proclamation (dated June 20) encouraging Americans to join his "glorious task. . .[in] re-establishing the blessings of Legal Government."[33]

On June 25 the army set out for Crown Point, stopping for the night at Button Bay before reaching the old fortress on the 26th. At Crown Point the British and German regiments made final preparations for the attack on Mount Independence and Fort Ticonderoga; during this time all of the vessels joined the fleet, including the galley *Washington* which arrived on June 27, carrying 20 cannon slated for the siege. At ten o'clock on the night of June 28, Lieutenant Thomas Blake, a carpenter from New Hampshire turned citizen soldier, observed "some of their gunboats up the lake as far as the Three Mile point and fired upon our gunboats."[34] By then the

"Gen[l.] Burgoyne Addressing the Indians" at the Boquet River by H. Warren.
(National Archives of Canada)

undermanned garrisons at Fort Ticonderoga and Mount Independence were cognizant of their predicament. On June 24 Major General Arthur St. Clair, the commander of the forts since June 12, reported sightings of the British fleet to Major General Philip Schuyler. St. Clair wrote again the following day, suggesting that the existing garrison would not have "the least prospect of our being able to defend the post, unless the militia come in" and feared they would have to abandon both posts but did not "see that a retreat will, in any shape, be practicable."[35] On July 3, just before the British siege began, 900 American militia arrived at Mount Independence, bringing total troop strength at both forts to approximately 3,400 men, about half the British invasion force. On the 30th of June, Brigadier General Fraser's troops landed at Three Mile Point while the British warships formed a line across the lake; Captain Enos Stone of Lenox, Massachusetts, recorded "two ships, four schooners, twenty Boats."[36] Preparing for the worst-case scenario of evacuation, Enos Hitchcock sent his baggage to Mount Independence. The next day the main body of German and British troops advanced toward Ticonderoga from Crown Point accompanied by several armed vessels and "Music and Drums of the different Regiments. . .continually playing. . .[which made] the Scene and passage extremely pleasant."[37] As Burgoyne looked on from the decks of the *Royal George*, the troops disembarked on both sides of the lake approximately four miles from the American position. On July 2 the rebel batteries fired on Brigadier General Fraser's troops while the Americans consolidated their forces by withdrawing from Mount Hope and the La Chute River. In a short period of time the British advanced to Mount Hope, effectively ending American access to Lake George. The Native Americans with Fraser's corps attacked the American "Piquet [picket] Guard at [the] French Lines," leaving casualties on both sides from the skirmish.[38]

Despite being outnumbered, the American defenders steadfastly clung to the hope that they could hold the line. At Mount Independence on July 3 the rebels "hoisted a white flag with 13 stars and 13 red stripes," German surgeon Wasmus recorded in his journal.[39] After Captain James Henry Craig and the light infantry took possession of present-day Mount Defiance, and Lieutenant William Twiss, an engineer, confirmed the commanding position of the mountain top, Major General William Phillips assigned 400 troops on July 4 to begin construction of "a Road to the top of a high Mountain called Sugar Loaf Hill [Mount Defiance]."[40] Lieutenant Colonel Christian Prätorius, with the German corps, recorded a road "16 feet wide and 3 leagues long" which was used in bringing the cannon (some taken from the radeau *Thunderer*) to the summit.[41] In all, six cannon were hoisted secretly along the west slope to the top of the mountain.*

Ironically, a year earlier, Colonel John Trumbull, the deputy adjutant general to Major General Horatio Gates in 1776, had proposed fortifying the summit with cannon, demonstrating the viability of the plan by proving that a cannon fired from Mount Independence or Fort Ticonderoga could reach Mount Defiance, and he subsequently climbed the mountain with Benedict Arnold and Anthony Wayne. In May 1777 Colonel Thaddeus Kosciuszko reported to Major General Gates that "the sides of the hill though steep, may, by the labor of strong fatigue [work] parties, be

---

*Although Lieutenant August Wilhelm Du Roi with a German regiment noted, "as no horses had been supplied, the men had to pull up the cannon with great difficulties," Lieutenant William Digby recorded that the cannon were "drawn up by most of the cattle belonging to the Army."[42]

so shaped as to permit the ascent of the heaviest cannon."[43] Gates later endorsed the idea in a letter to Major General St. Clair, but the plan failed to gain his support.

The Americans were startled on July 5 when work on the British battery on Mount Defiance became apparent. After assessing the situation, St. Clair turned to an aide and proposed evacuation since the American position had become a "desperate one."[44] In the early evening St. Clair hastily called a council of war with Brigadier Generals Matthias Alexis Roche de Fermoy, Enoch Poor, John Paterson, and Colonel Pierce Long, who unanimously decided that "a retreat ought to be undertaken as soon as possible" before the evacuation route could be blocked.[45] A few hours later officers were informed piecemeal that a retreat would begin after midnight. "About one o'clock in the morning," Lieutenant Blake chronicled, the men were ordered to strike their tents and cross the bridge to Mount Independence where they discovered boats being loaded in near chaos.[46] Enos Hitchcock placed his baggage on the gondola *New York* and on one of the schooners, departing for Skenesborough at three o'clock in the morning. Captain Moses Greenleaf from Massachusetts recorded that during the tumultuous preparations to leave "Gen Fermoy's House was set on fire which gave the Enemy notice of our retreat."[47] Although the fire was observed by the British and German troops, they were still surprised the next morning to find that the Americans had abandoned their posts. On the afternoon of July 5 several German officers had observed "unusually heavy smoke on Mount Independence and we assumed. . .the brushwood or some wooden fortifications had caught fire."[48]

The American fleet, including a large number of bateaux filled with provisions, departed in the moonlight for Skenesborough, not arriving until "three o'clock in the afternoon" of July 6.[49] Although the Americans had labored arduously to build the Great Bridge, "the boom and one of the intermediate floats were cut with great dexterity and dispatch," soon after they had departed, according to Lieutenant General Burgoyne.[50] The British gunboats passed immediately through the opening;

"A View of Ticonderoga from the Middle of the Channel in Lake Champlain, 1777."
Watercolor by James Hunter (1777), depicting two British gunboats, long boats,
Native American canoes, and American shore batteries on the west side of the lake.
(National Archives of Canada)

after another half-hour of labor, Captain Lutwidge's larger vessels also began their pursuit of the beleaguered Americans. At Skenesborough the British found the evacuees "posted in a stockaded fort [built in June], and their armed gallies in the falls below."[51] "Captain [John] Carter, with part of his brigade of gun-boats," Burgoyne wrote, "immediately attacked, and with so much spirit, that two of the vessels very soon struck [galley *Trumbull* and schooner *Liberty*]; the other three [galley *Gates*, schooner *Revenge*, and Sloop *Enterprise*] were blown up;* and the enemy. . .set fire to the fort, mills, storehouses, bateaux, &c."[53] Enos Hitchcock found himself in the middle of the deadly fire at Skenesborough as he loaded baggage into a bateau for a frantic escape along Wood Creek.

On the morning of July 6 the last of the Americans left Mount Independence at "about sunrise," according to Lieutenant Thomas Blake.[54] Major General Arthur St. Clair headed the largest contingent of rebel forces, approximately 2,500, on a circuitous journey to Castleton, Vermont, with plans to rejoin the rest of the army at Skenesborough. The rear guard of St. Clair's troops comprised of about 1,000 men, led by Colonel Ebenezer Francis of the 11th Massachusetts Regiment, Colonel Nathan Hale of the 2nd New Hampshire Regiment, and Colonel Seth Warner of a Continental regiment of Green Mountain Boys, encamped about six miles from Castleton in Hubbardton (present-day East Hubbardton). Unbeknown to the Americans, Brigadier General Simon Fraser and his troops and Major General Friedrich Adolphus Riedesel with German soldiers, including some of Lieutenant Colonel Heinrich Breymann's corps, began a pursuit of them on the morning of July 6. After trudging along the wilderness road through Vermont all day, the pursuing army rested overnight. Fraser resumed his march at three o'clock on the morning of July 7 and in a short while his Indian scouts reported the location of the American camp after rebel sentinels had fired on them. Fraser immediately pushed forward and launched an attack while troops from Hale's regiment were occupied "cooking their provisions."[55] Fraser's corps quickly proceeded with an attack on Warner's and Francis' troops as Riedesel rushed forward to join the fray. Colonel Francis "fought bravely to the Last. . .he first rec'd a Ball through his right Arm still. . .Continued at the head of our Troops till he rec'd the fatal wound thro' his Body Entering his right breast, he drop'd on his face," Moses Greenleaf recounted.[56]

After nearly two hours of battle, the Americans scattered into the forest. The casualties were high on both sides and the British had taken a large number of prisoners, including "one colonel, seven captains, ten subatlerns, and 210 men."[57] Sixteen-year-old Ebenezer Fletcher, a fifer in Colonel Nathan Hale's New Hampshire regiment, was found lying on the ground in his own blood from a musket ball wound in his back. A British soldier briskly pulled off his shoes, "supposing me to be dead," Fletcher later recounted.[58] A British officer, however, forced the soldier to return the shoes and helped Fletcher into the British field hospital where a doctor removed the ball from his back. A succession of men soon stripped Fletcher of all his valuables. The first man took his silver shoe buckles, leaving an old brass pair in

---

*During the enlargement of the Champlain Canal (1907-1912) "two more large cannons, making a total of four" were dredged from the harbor at Whitehall.[52] The cannon were believed to be from the galley *Gates* and two are on display on the lawn of the state armory in Whitehall. Although most of the quoted accounts of the Skenesborough engagement fail to mention the gondola *New York*, a stem piece identical to those of other known gondolas was recovered at Whitehall and is presently on exhibit at the Lake Champlain Maritime Museum at Basin Harbor.

exchange, another took his handkerchief, and a third his fife. The Indians, with nothing left to take, insulted Fletcher and his fellow prisoners verbally, calling them "Yankees and rebels."[59]

At three o'clock on the morning of July 9, following heavy rains, the American prisoners began their march back to Fort Ticonderoga; the injured, however, remained behind. Just before the wounded were taken to Ticonderoga, "the wolves came down in numbers from the mountains to devour the dead," attracted by the "great stench."[60] Young Fletcher never made the move back to Ticonderoga. He remained in the field hospital for two weeks before escaping into Vermont's forests, eventually finding his way home to New Ipswich, New Hampshire, after a harrowing journey. In a short while, Fletcher was arrested, apparently for desertion, and sent to the American army in Pennsylvania.

Meanwhile, as the Hubbardton battle raged, the Americans who had fled Skenesborough were in Fort Anne, a picketed fort 11 miles to the south. Lieutenant Colonel John Hill and men from the 9th Regiment of Foot pushed forward to a position near the fort. After the Americans learned from a spy that Hill's force numbered less than 200 men, they attacked his troops, "sustaining 3 hours of continuous fire."[61] With ammunition running low and after hearing an Indian war whoop (actually imitated by a British officer), the rebels withdrew to Fort Anne. Realizing that British reinforcements were on their way, the Americans burned the fort and evacuated to Fort Edward.

Rather than pursue the fleeing American army, Burgoyne ordered his exhausted troops back to Skenesborough to wait for "a fresh supply of provisions."[62] This provided Major General Schuyler with valuable time to obstruct the passage of Wood Creek and accumulate reinforcements. On July 9 Schuyler ordered Brigadier General John Fellows of the Massachusetts militia to Wood Creek to fell trees and begin clogging the passage to the Hudson River. Three days later Enos Hitchcock recorded the arrival at Fort Edward of Brigadier General John Nixon with Continental troops and "the Gen^ls from Ti[conderoga]."[63] St. Clair's weary forces, who then remained just south at Fort Miller, had taken a difficult seven-day-long roundabout trek to join the American army, gathering at the Hudson River. Nixon's brigade, which annexed Fellow's militia, was sent north to burn any remaining sawmills and drop trees into the creek. "Th[e]re was no pains Spared by the Americans in obstructing his [Burgoyne's] passage," Captain Rufus Lincoln observed, which required 40 bridges to be constructed later by the British.[64] Colonel James Wilkinson subsequently credited Thaddeus Kosciuszko's engineering direction with rendering "Wood Creek unnavigable."[65]

Burgoyne's decision to proceed the 23 miles from Skenesborough to Fort Edward via Wood Creek, rather than transferring his troops and supplies using the traditional route through Lake George where only 13 miles of a solid road separated the lake from the Hudson River, remains the subject of debate. After returning to England, Burgoyne defended his choice in *A State of the Expedition from Canada*, published in London in 1780. He suggested that a movement of his army back to Ticonderoga in order to enter Lake George would have created "the general impression [of]. . .a retrograde motion."[66] "The natural conduct of the enemy in that case," Burgoyne submitted, "would be to remain at Fort George," thus requiring a lengthy siege "and in the mean time they would have destroyed the road

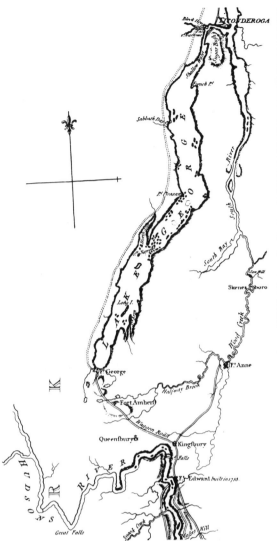

John Burgoyne. Painting by Sir Joshua
Reynolds (1767).
(Library of Congress)

Detail of "A Topographical Map of Hud-
sons River. . ." by Claude Joseph Sauthier
(1776) showing Lake George and the southern section of Lake Champlain. From *The
North American Atlas* by William Faden
(1777).
(Library of Congress)

from Fort George to Fort Edward."[67] In addition, Burgoyne maintained that "the
great number of boats. . .for the transport of the troops over Lake George, were by
this course [Wood Creek route] spared for the transport of the provision[s], artillery,
and ammunition" from Canada.[68] However, others in Burgoyne's ranks disagreed:
"Many here were of [the] opinion the general had not the least business in bringing
the army to Skenesborough," Lieutenant William Digby mused in his journal, "they
were also of [the] opinion [that] we should have pushed directly to Fort George"
where wagons and horses could probably be captured, instead of "waiting for horses
from Canada."[69] Digby also complained of the excess baggage and the large number
of "loyalists, women and every other hanger on" that slowed the invading army.[70]
Lieutenant August Wilhelm Du Roi charged that "Governor [Philip] Skene had
much to do with pushing forward over South Bay. . .his entire fortune having been

Brigadier General John Stark at
Bennington. (New York State Library)

used for the establishment [of Skenesbor-
ough]. . .his desire would be fulfilled to have
Wood Creek cleared of trunks and logs, so
it could be used for boats, while on the side
of the creek a road would be made."[71]

Although Lake George would not be
used as the invasion route to the Hudson
River for the main army, it was employed
for the transportation of artillery and provisions. On July 8 the gunboats returned to
Ticonderoga from Skenesborough for portage to Lake George. "Carriages resembling a
Waggon without the body" were utilized to
haul the gunboats and bateaux from the La
Chute River to the northern landing on
Lake George.[72] On July 27 more than two
dozen gunboats and bateaux embarked for
Fort George located at the southern end of
the lake. The fort had already been abandoned and burned along with several newly-
constructed vessels on July 16. The
Americans withdrew with 20 cannon and
nearly 13 tons of powder. Militarily vulner-
able and dilapidated, Fort Edward was abandoned on July 23 (except for a few hundred

"Battle of Bennington" (artist unknown). Engraving from
Kingsford Illustrations: Battles, Ships, Forts. (National Archives of Canada)

soldiers). The troops from Fort Edward bivouaked at Moses Creek (present-day Moses Kill), about five miles south of the fort, while others encamped on nearby Paterson's Island (present-day Griffin or Thompson Island).

On July 30 Philip Schuyler's army retreated again; Chaplain Hitchcock left "Paterson's Island," lodging at Schuyler's summer home in "old Saratoga" (present-day Schuylerville) on the 31st. By then the repeated withdrawals had taken a toll on the already-tarnished reputation of Major General Schuyler. The Continental Congress had approved a resolution to investigate the circumstances leading to the abandonment of Ticonderoga and Mount Independence. Malicious rumors dogged Generals Schuyler and St. Clair following the evacuation from Lake Champlain. Surgeon James Thacher disclosed the outrageous stories in his journal, which accused the generals of "act[ing] the part of traitors. . .paid for their treason by the enemy in silver balls, shot from Burgoyne's guns into our camp, and. . .collected by order of General St. Clair, and divided between him and General Schuyler."[73] Congress recommended to George Washington that he replace Schuyler, but the commander in chief would not subscribe to political intrigue. On August 4 Congress voted overwhelmingly to replace Schuyler with Major General Horatio Gates. Schuyler, however, would not be informed of his replacement by Gates for another ten days. The next year Schuyler and St. Clair were court-martialed but were found not guilty.

In August Burgoyne's planned thrust into the center of the northern states would begin to unravel. On August 3, couriers arrived in Burgoyne's camp with a message (in a hollow silver bullet) written on July 17 from General William Howe, informing him that "my intention is for Pennsylvania, where I expect to meet Washington; but, if he goes to the northward, contrary to my expectations, and you keep him at bay, be assured I shall soon be after him to relieve you."[74] The long planned junction with Howe's army in Albany would now be impossible. Two days later Burgoyne was less than candid with his men: Brigadier Specht reported that "Gen. Burgoyne also told us today that he has gotten reliable news from General Howe in a hollow lead ball according to which we could be absolutely certain that not only was his army progressing in accordance with our wishes but that we would see a respectable corps of theirs join our army in a short time."[75]

While Burgoyne awaited provisions from Canada, he dispatched Lieutenant Colonel Friedrich Baum, commander of the Dragoon Regiment, on a mission to raid Bennington, Vermont, for "supplies of cattle, horses, and carriages," as well as "the great deposit of corn, flour."[76] Burgoyne later blamed Major General Reidesel for the idea of the ill-fated expedition: "It was at this time Major-general Reidesel conceived the purpose of mounting his regiment of drago[o]ns."[77] Although Reidesel had suggested a raid for horses earlier, he later maintained that Bennington was a dangerous undertaking "being at too great a distance" but Burgoyne "was not a man to be dissuaded."[78] On August 10 Baum's army of approximately 800 Germans, Canadians, Indians, Tories (including Philip Skene), and British regulars departed from Fort Miller (evacuated earlier by the Americans). Instead of finding welcoming loyalists and fleeing American soldiers at Bennington, Baum's forces encountered determined volunteers led by Brigadier General John Stark of the New Hampshire militia and Seth Warner with his Green Mountain Regiment of the Continental Army. Stark, a former Ranger captain who had served with Robert Rogers during the French and Indian War, had refused to relinquish command of his New

Hampshire troops to Major General Benjamin Lincoln, a Continental officer appointed by Congress to assume command over the militias converging in Vermont. After Baum sent a message to Burgoyne describing the size of the American force at Bennington, Lieutenant Colonel Heinrich Breymann was dispatched with 600 men to reinforce Baum. On August 16, just before Breymann's troops reached their comrades, Stark initiated an attack on the invaders. Surgeon Wasmus soberly remarked that "in a short time, our tallest and best dragoons were sent into eternity."[79] Breymann's corps hurried forward when they heard the sounds of musket fire, but they were too late to make a difference in the battle, firing ineffectively from a distance. The two-hour battle was a decisive victory for the Americans; Enos Hitchcock recorded 664 captured (more than half Germans) and 280 killed or wounded.[80]

A second British failure during the invasion of New York occurred shortly after the Bennington debacle. Lieutenant Colonel Barry St. Leger was sent from Canada "to make a diversion on the Mohawk River."[81] Leading an army of nearly 2,000 men, consisting of British regulars, Hessians, Tories, and Indians (representing approximately one-half of the force), St. Leger reached Fort Stanwix on August 3 and set in motion a siege of the American garrison. Fort Stanwix, a stockaded fort originally built in 1758, lay at the portage (present-day Rome, N.Y.) between the Mohawk River and Wood Creek to the west, which linked the Great Lakes to the Hudson River. Rebuilt in 1776 and renamed Fort Schuyler, the outpost was garrisoned by 550 New York Continental troops under Colonel Peter Gansevoort. Brigadier General Nicholas Herkimer subsequently led a relief column of approximately 800 militia to break the siege at the fort but was ambushed on August 6 by St. Leger's Native American allies led by Thayendanagea (Joseph Brant). The bloody six-hour engagement, known as the Battle of Oriskany, resulted in high casualties on both sides, including the 56-year-old Herkimer. With the report of the failure of Herkimer's army, Philip Schuyler proposed sending a new detachment to stop St. Leger, but his officers feared that a reduction in forces at the Hudson River would weaken defenses there. Major General Benedict Arnold, however, volunteered to lead the reinforcements, and on August 13 Chaplain Hitchcock noted "Gen. Arnold set out for Fort Schuyler [Stanwix]."[82] Before the new American division arrived at the fort, a Tory was coerced into entering St. Leger's camp to spread an exaggerated account of the size of Arnold's approaching column. The ruse, combined with the waning support of St. Leger's Indians, resulted in their defection and St. Leger's withdrawal. The second element of the British offensive was now over, leaving Burgoyne isolated with overextended supply lines.

Major General Horatio Gates, the new commander of the Northern Army, finally reached his troops camped near the Hudson River on August 19. In early September Gates and his officers selected an elevated plateau, known as Bemis Heights, on the west side of the river in Saratoga as the site of defensive breastworks and redoubts. Chaplain Hitchcock arrived at Bemis Heights on the 13th, noting "entrenchments throwing up, from ye Hill to ye River."[83] In one week Colonel Thaddeus Kosciuszko and 1,000 men had substantially completed the work; at the same time Burgoyne occupied Schuyler's summer house a few miles to the north in present-day Schuylerville. By mid-September the American force outnumbered Burgoyne's army.

On September 19, Enos Hitchcock wrote that "about ten °clock accounts receiv[d] that the Enemy are Advancing."[84] As Burgoyne approached with about 4,000 troops divided into three columns, Benedict Arnold persuaded Gates to dispatch Colonel Daniel Morgan's riflemen (Morgan was a veteran of Arnold's 1775 attack on Quebec City) to ambush the invasion force. "At half after one," Hitchcock observed, the battle began and renewed at three-forty and "lasted three Hours very hot. . .the action ceased, as night approached."[85] Both Arnold and Burgoyne exposed themselves to the deadly flying shot while directing their troops from the front lines. The engagement, known as the Battle of Freeman's Farm or the First Battle of Saratoga, occurred about a mile north of Bemis Heights. The following day Captain Benjamin Warren of the 7th Massachusetts Regiment remarked that "the loss of the enemy is very great; the field was covered with dead almost for several acres."[86] Although Burgoyne referred to the battle as a "victory," others in his ranks, including Lieutenant Thomas Anburey, feared that the Americans now had the "real advantages resulting from this hard-fought battle. . .our army being so much weakened by this engagement."[87]

Two days after the battle, Enos Hitchcock reported "news of Col° Brown taking the French lines &c—thirteen Cannon discharged on the Occasion & three Cheers given."[88] In order to create a diversion and tie-up some of Burgoyne's troops in rearward positions, Major General Benjamin Lincoln, then stationed at Pawlet, Vermont, sent three 500-man detachments to Skenesborough, Mount Independence, and Ticonderoga. Lieutenant Colonel John Brown's mission "to release the prisoners [from the Hubbardton battle] & destroy the stores" was accomplished, but his call for the surrender of Fort Ticonderoga and Mount Independence by the British garrisons was ignored.[89] After destroying a number of British vessels at the northern Lake George landing, Brown and his men departed with a "Small Sloop mounting 8 Guns & 2 British Gun Boats" and 17 bateaux with plans for a surprise attack on the British supply depot at Diamond Island on Lake George.[90] However, a Tory sutler (merchant) escaped from Brown's party and warned the British garrison on the island. On September 24, after an hour-long

Major General Horatio Gates. From a painting by Alonzo Chappel. (New York State Library)

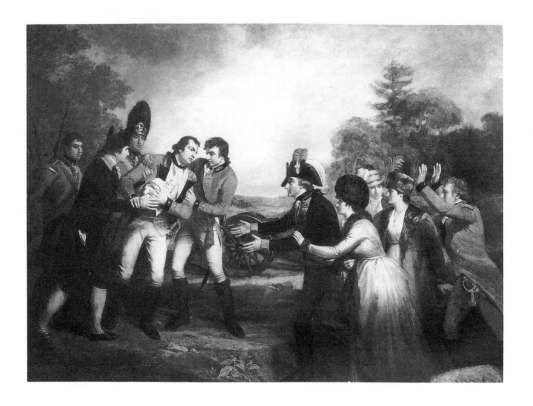

cannonade with Captain Thomas Aubrey's shore batteries, Brown "r[a]n my Boats up a Bay a considerable distance and burnt them."[91] One gunboat was abandoned during the action and another was retrieved later from the bay (probably Dunhams Bay) by the British.

Burgoyne's main army in Saratoga was now in a precarious situation with supply lines to Lake Champlain effectively cut by the Americans and the chances of a junction with British forces in New York City under Lieutenant General Henry Clinton only a remote possibility. Clinton's only assistance would be a diversion on the Hudson River. After discussing several strategies with his officers on October 7, Burgoyne advanced toward Bemis Heights with three divisions, comprised of 1,700 British regulars and German soldiers and a mixed detachment of 600 Tories, Canadians, and Native Americans. It became painfully obvious in a short period of time that this large-scale reconnaissance was a risky maneuver for Burgoyne's outnumbered detachments. The American riflemen and light infantry opened a devastating fire on the British columns and were soon joined by several other regiments. "At half after four it [the firing] came on very heavy & lasted till Dark," Enos Hitchcock observed, "our troops drove them 3/4 of a Mile, pursued to their Encampment."[92]

Confined to his quarters because of a dispute with Major General Gates, 36-year-old Benedict Arnold finally could not contain himself any longer and leaped onto his horse, galloping to the field of battle. Taking command of several regiments, Arnold led the attack against the tenacious German units. Eventually, all of Burgoyne's divisions fell back to their redoubts. Facing point-blank grape and

Above: "View of the West Bank of the Hudson's River 3 Miles above Still Water," depicting the British camp after the October 7, 1777, battle. The funeral procession for Brigadier General Simon Fraser is shown on the hillside to the right. Engraving from a drawing in *Travels through the Interior Parts of America* by Thomas Anburey (1789). (Library of Congress)

Facing page, top: "Arnold at Saratoga" from *A Brief History of the United States* by J.D. Steele and E.B. Steele (1871).

Bottom: "Death of [Brigadier General] Simon Fraser [at] Saratoga, 1777." Oil on canvas by Samuel Woodforde (1800). Baroness Frederika von Riedesel attended the British general throughout the night, but Fraser died the next morning. (National Archives of Canada)

musket fire, Arnold led the charge against the enemy redoubts until wounded in the leg. Burgoyne later credited Arnold's actions with the British failure to capture the American works, suggesting that Arnold "gave, instead of receiving battle."[93]

Having lost four times as many men as the Americans, Burgoyne began an evacuation to Fort Edward the next evening, leaving 340 wounded men behind. American riflemen pursued the British, who managed to retreat only about four miles in a heavy rain; on October 10 more American brigades were ordered forward to stop the British retreat. Hitchcock departed at one in the afternoon, finding "a great number of Horses dead, Carts & Waggons broke. . .articles Strew[n]ed by the way" and Schuyler's home burning.[94] "A number of Cannon Shot exchanged," Hitchcock wrote, "[Brigadier] Gen.[l] Fellows prevented them passing the River [Batten Kill]. . .took their Boats."[95] On October 11 Chaplain Hitchcock noted "a moderate cannonade & Scattering Musketry all Day," followed by "Some Cannonading" on the next day.[96] With no chance to escape, Burgoyne and his officers sent a draft of surrender terms to Major General Gates on October 13. However, reports that a British force under Major General John Vaughan was sailing north on the Hudson River caused Burgoyne to delay the final agreement for several days. Although Vaughan's small force sailed to within 50 miles of Albany, no help ever reached Burgoyne's army.

Given the uncertainty of British reinforcements from the south, Gates agreed to accept the more lenient terms of a convention over his original demand for capitulation. On October 17 the surrender terms were formally signed and the British and German troops paraded onto an open field and stacked their weapons (in present-day Schuylerville). Observing the proceedings, Hitchcock wrote that Burgoyne arrived at noon and the army "began to pass [cross] the River [Fish Creek] about two & continued till near sunset. . .the number of the Enemy who marched out, besides women [about 300] and children, five thousand two hundred—the whole conducted with great Order & decency & ou[ght] to inspire every Soul with Sincere Gratitude."[97] Colonel Jeduthan Baldwin, who had constructed bridges during the last days of the campaign, remarked in his journal that the spectacle of the British laying down their arms was "the most agreeable sight that ever my eyes beheld."[98] Well-respected by the officers in the American army, Hitchcock was one of the figures (the eighth person from the left) featured in Colonel John Trumbull's famous painting, "The Surrender of General Burgoyne at Saratoga."

The Lake George and Lake Champlain Valleys remained occupied by the British until November 8 (the decision to destroy all the fortifications and evacuate was not made until the end of October). Lieutenant Du Roi noted that Fort George, as well as the breastworks on Diamond Island, was burned and other structures demolished, including those at the northern Lake George landing, the bridge and sawmill at the La Chute River, and the old French lines. Before daybreak on the day of departure, November 8, the wooden buildings on Mount Independence and Ticonderoga were burned: "the log houses, the store houses, the hospital, all the huts and cottages, everything which could be ruined by fire, in flames. . .the floating bridge was also cut down and burned. We embarked and departed. Immediately after, the explosion at Fort Ticonderoga took place; it had been filled with powder to which fire was set [at] the last moment."[99] The British, however, were not finished with the Champlain Valley, initiating destructive raids in 1778, 1779, and 1780. The 1780 incursion, the

"Surrender of Burgoyne." Painting by Frederick Coffay Yohn.
(Continental Insurance Company Collection)

largest military expedition since 1777, also wreaked havoc as far south as Stillwater, Ballston, Queensbury, Fort Edward, Fort Anne, and Fort George.

With a three-month leave of absence granted by Major General Gates, Chaplain Hitchcock left Albany on October 29, 1777, overtaking Lieutenant General Burgoyne and the British and German prisoners in Palmer, Massachusetts, on their way to Boston. After staying with his mother (his father had died in 1776) in Brookfield, Hitchcock rode to Worcester in the company of Burgoyne. On November 6 he finally reached home during "a N[ew] E[ngland] Storm."[100] Hitchcock served as a chaplain to the end of the war. During his military tenure he dined with many notable officers, including Benedict Arnold. In 1780 he witnessed the hanging of John André who had conspired with Arnold. Held in high esteem by George Washington, Hitchcock was often invited to the commander's headquarters to dine and preach. In a sermon entitled "A Devout Soldier," given at West Point in 1782, Hitchcock suggested that "social & mil[i]tary virtues ought to derive stability & lustre from religion. To the distinguished character of a patriot & soldier it should be your highest glory to add the more distinguished character of a virtuous, good, man—then you can quit this stage in the full blaze of honor."[101]

While on furlough from the army in 1780, Hitchcock preached a few sermons at the First Congregational Society in Providence, Rhode Island, and was subsequently installed as pastor on October 1, 1783 (he had resigned from the parish in Beverly, Massachusetts, on April 6, 1780). As a pastor in Rhode Island, Hitchcock had a circle of friends which included the presidents of Harvard College, Brown University, and Yale College, as well as John Hancock, governor of Massachusetts. However, times were not always happy for Hitchcock—his 11-year-old daughter Achsah died in April 1784.

In the 1780s Enos Hitchcock passionately embraced the cause of education, becoming a strong advocate of free public schools (*Discourse on Education*, 1785). In 1791 he joined a committee of college presidents, politicians, and prominent citizens to promote education. Hitchcock's most ambitious educational effort, a two-volume book entitled *Memoirs of the Bloomsgrove Family*, was published in 1790 and dedicated to Martha Washington. Written as a series of fictitious letters and anecdotes, the book encompassed principles of childrearing, education, health care (including brushing one's teeth), and individual integrity. To Hitchcock, education could be compared to "an inexhaustible fountain, [which] may be drawn upon perpetually, without being drained"; but education can be focused too narrowly: "the object of it has been to teach what to think, rather than, how to think."[102] "Virtuous principles are of incomparably more worth," according to Hitchcock, "than mere science."[103] "These virtues. . .are few, simple, and to be taught in the early years of infancy" by parents.[104] To Hitchcock, the first seven years of life were critical: If "the minds of children [are] left uncultivated, with examples of vice continually before them" children will become "pest[s]" on society.[105] Hitchcock's childrearing principles also included a warning on spoiling children: "indolence, incapacity for vigorous exertion, and dul[l]ness of apprehension, are the effects of furnishing children with every thing they want."[106] His second book, *The Farmer's Friend, or the History of Mr. Charles Worthy*, published in 1793, had similar themes. Shorter works included *Discourse on Dignity and Excellence of the Human Character, Illustrated in the Life of General George Washington* (1800) and a simplified catechism, *Catechetical Instructions and Forms of Devotion for Children and Youth* (1798).

Enos Hitchcock passed away on February 26, 1803; his wife Achsah died shortly thereafter, but the exact date is uncertain. His unmarried adopted daughter, believed to be a stepdaughter, Martha Hitchcock Jordon, died three months after Hitchcock himself.

The following section of Enos Hitchcock's diary begins on May 23, 1777, when he arrived at Fort Ticonderoga and ends when the Americans evacuated Fort Anne on July 8.

Diary of Enos Hitchcock[106]

May

23. Lodged at Averys [? Elisha Avery Deputy Commissary], breakfasted at Capt. [Nathan] Wa[t]kins [12th Massachusetts Regiment]—Set off from Skene [sborough] 10 o'clock, wind Contra, arrived at Ticonderoga* 6 P. M. fair Day.

24. Dined upon flowr puding** & Venison Steak.

25. Sunday. Heard Mr. [Chaplain Samuel] Cotton A. M. Mr. [Chaplain William] Plumb dined with us upon roast & stewed Venison, 6 °Clock began Service interrupted by the floating away of y^e Bridge,*** very warm.

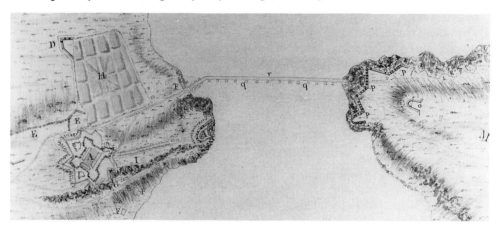

Detail of a "Plan of Ticonderoga and Mount Independence" by Lieutenant Charles Wintersmith (1777) showing the "Great Bridge" linking the two fortifications.

(Special Collections, Bailey/Howe Memorial Library, University of Vermont)

26. Generals Poor & Patterson, Col^{os} Baldwin, Scamel, Wilkinson & Hays dined here.† Pudding, Veal &c.

27. Rained in morning. Prayers omited—fair Day

---

*In 1777 Lieutenant August Wilhelm Du Roi described Fort Ticonderoga as "layed out in a regular square with 4 bastions and 2 Ravelins [freestanding bastions] on the north side, thrown up of earth, revetted [faced] however, as far as the dry ditch with quarry-stone. . .There are barracks for 600-800 men in the fort, built of quarry-stone. . .[and] huts between the old Fort of Ticonderoga and the French Lines."[107]

**Hitchcock probably dined on Yorkshire pudding made from a batter of flour, salt, eggs, and milk baked under venison or other meats.

***On May 25 Colonel Jeduthan Baldwin, the chief engineer, mentioned that "the boom & Bridge in a heavy gale of wind gave way & with some difficulty they were brought back to place."[108] The 1,700-foot Great Bridge was initially completed on May 10, but additional work was done on the boom on May 29 and the floating bridge was moved to the opposite side of the piers on June 14.

†Enoch Poor, brigadier general Continental Army; John Paterson, brigadier general Continental Army; Jeduthan Baldwin, colonel and chief engineer; Alexander Scammell, colonel Third New Hampshire Regiment; James Wilkinson, lieutenant colonel Continental Army and deputy adjutant general of the Northern Department; Udney Hay, lieutenant colonel and assistant deputy quartermaster general of the Northern Department.

28. Wrote Home by a Marblehead man, very warm—receiv^d Letter from Home 19 May—the Enemies fleet discovered a little below Split Rock*—General Patterson supped with us upon fish

29. Very warm, some Cannon heard down ye Lake—nothing further appears

30. Went up to ye Landing to see Mr. [Captain James] Leach [Massachusetts Militia]—not well—very hot

31. Wrote Home by Parsons No. 2 & to Revd Willard** with a thirty Dollar Bill Capt Whitcombe*** brings up an account y^t. ye Enemy are gone down ye Lake—very warm

June

1. Sunday. No Service A. M. dined at the Generals [brigade headquarters]—Letters from General Gates inform of Col^o [Return Jonathan] Meigs^s [Sherburne's Continental Regiment] capturing 70 men on Long Island & destroying some Stores also y^t the Troops in Canada are going to the South[w]ard—Divine Service at Six ^oClock I Chron [Chronicles Chapter] 19, [verse] 17, very warm.

2. Rained a little last Night, cleared of[f] this morning pleasant, a cool Southerly wind—Went to the Landing P. M. Mr. Leach better—wrote Home No. 3, by a person going to Lynn [Massachusetts]—fair, pleasant Day

3. Wrote Home by the Post No. 4, the Field officers sent a memorial of their grieviences to the general Court—Col.^o [Samuel] Brewer [12th Massachusetts] & I wrote to the Rev.^d Mr. Foster—Show[e]ry—drank Tea at Col.^o [Thomas] Marshals [10th Massachusetts]

4. Receiv.^d of Paymaster twenty pounds—paid Col.^o Francis† six pounds, my

---

*On May 28 Colonel Jeduthan Baldwin remarked that "a scout Return[e]d from Split rock (Lt. Liford) & says that the Enemy was there with two Vessels 7 Gunboats & about 40 Battoes."[109] Thomas Liford was a first lieutenant in Benjamin Whitcomb's New Hampshire Rangers. The next day, scouts reported "that the Enemy fired yesterday about 80 Cannon, besides a Number of Volleys of Small arms at & near Split rock."[110]

**Hitchcock wrote his second letter home, perhaps carried by Second Lieutenant Josiah Parsons (11th Massachusetts Regiment) or Ensign Nathan Parsons (10th Massachusetts). The other letter was written to his friend Reverend Joseph W. Willard, who became president of Harvard College in 1781.

***Benjamin Whitcomb served as a second lieutenant in Timothy Bedel's regiment of New Hampshire Rangers in 1776, winning a promotion to first lieutenant in May. He was probably the most daring scout employed by the Americans during the war. Seeking information on the size of the British fleet, Benedict Arnold sent Whitcomb into Canada in July 1776 to bring back a prisoner. A few miles from the St. Jean shipyard, Whitcomb wounded Brigadier General Patrick Gordon, who managed to escape but died a week later. Ensign John Enys, serving in the British army, reported that Whitcomb "was im[m]ediately pursued by part[ie]s of Soldiers and Indians [but] found means to escape them all."[111] After learning Whitcomb's name, Major General Guy Carleton offered a reward of 50 guineas for the Ranger, dead or alive. Despite the danger, Whitcomb returned to Canada and captured Alexander Saunders, a quartermaster, and a non-commissioned officer and delivered both to Arnold. Whitcomb was promoted to captain in October and to major in November 1777; he retired in 1781 and lived until 1828.

†Ebenezer Francis (1743-1777) was born in Medford, Massachusetts, later moving to Beverly where he married in 1766. Francis was friendly with Reverend Hitchcock whose parish was in the same community. Commissioned a lieutenant during the Lexington Alarm of April 1775, Francis became a captain in Colonel John Mansfield's Massachusetts regiment a month later. Appointed a colonel of the 11th Massachusetts Regiment in November 1776, Francis led the unit to Ticonderoga early the next year. The 33-year-old patriot was killed at the Battle of Hubbardton on July 7, 1777 (see main text). Lieutenant Thomas Anburey, an officer in Burgoyne's campaign, later noted that the American

proportion of the Stores together with 2.^{lb} 8.^{s} 6^d paid before; paid [Lieutenant] Col^o [Noah Moulton] Litt[l]efield [11th Massachusetts] 2:^{lb} 18:^{s} 5^d Expenses on the Road paid Capt [Billy] Porter [11th Massachusetts] 30 Dollars which I borrowed to send Home—cool westerly wind—fair Day—a Picker[e]l sent [to] us two feet & 3/4 long

5. Bought q^r Venison at 9^S—Col.^{o} Hale* dined with us upon fish & a Venison St[e]ak—officers of the Brigade turn^d out to exercise agre[e]able to orders—drank Tea with Major [William] Hull [8th Massachusetts]—Heada[ch]e—no Prayers—fair & pleasant.

6. The morning opens very fine but we happened to lay in Bed till almost Eight ^{o}Clock—slept very sound after a fine Supper of Venison St[e]aks, this may seem strange, but it cured my Heada[ch]e—fair & pleasant, dined upon roast Venison Stuf[hash]

7. A soldier in Col.^{o} Marshals Reg.^{t} set on ye Gallows 1/2 an Hour & receiv.^{d} 100 Stripes for enlisting twice & deserting. Col.^{o} Hays dined with us upon Venison So[u]p &c fair & pleasant—Report of ye Capture of ye Milford.

8. Sunday. Divine Service at 1/2 past ten A. M. Mr. Plumb pr[eache]d Exod[us]: 15, present Col.^{s} Marshals—Brewers & Francis's Reg^{ts}; at 1/2 Six P. M. pr[eache]d myself Ps[alms]: 119: 115, fair and pleasant, but something warm and dry

9. Went fishing up east Crick [east of Mount Independence]—News from Canada—by two Frenchmen, y.^{t} [Lieutenant General John] Burgo[y]ne arrived 10th of May without Troops—y.^{t} many of the Soldiers had died—the Hessians uneasy—500 French imprisoned for refusing to enlist—300 at Isle la Noix, 200 St Johns, a Reinfor[ce]ment of 4000 expected—cloudy A. M. cleared of[f] P. M.

troops had been "rallied by that brave officer, Colonel Francis, whose death, though an enemy, will ever be regretted by those who feel for the loss of a gallant and brave man."[112] Ironically, ten months later, Anburey, then a prisoner in Massachusetts, would meet the fallen colonel's mother and write a poignant passage about the chance encounter. While purchasing vegetables, a group of British officers were approached by an elderly, grief-stricken woman, inquiring of her son who had been killed at Hubbardton. After learning that the officers had indeed been at Hubbardton and had known Francis, she further questioned them on the whereabouts of his papers, pocketbook, or watch—any remembrance; whereupon, Captain William Ferguson pulled the watch, which had been purchased from a drummer boy, from his pocket and handed it to the woman with the words "God bless you."[113] "On seeing it, it is impossible to describe the joy and grief that was depicted in her countenance," Anburey remarked, "I never in all my life, beheld such a strength of passion; she kissed it, looked unutterable gratitude at Captain Ferguson, then kissed it again. . .our feelings were lifted up to an inexpressible height; we promised to search after the papers, and I believe, at that moment, could have hazarded life itself to procure them."[114]

*Nathan Hale (1743-1780), not to be confused with the Nathan Hale hanged as a spy in 1776, was born in Hampstead, New Hampshire. First serving as a captain in the New Hampshire Minutemen in 1775, Hale rose to the rank of colonel in the 2nd New Hampshire Regiment in 1777. At the Battle of Hubbardton Colonel Hale was duped into surrendering approximately 70 men from his regiment after a squad of British soldiers pretended to have surrounded his detachment with a much larger force. On July 20, 1777, Hale was freed at Ticonderoga and proceeded home to Ringe, New Hampshire, on a limited parole, which prohibited his serving with the Americans until exchanged. A month later Major General Horatio Gates issued orders to have Hale "immediately apprehended, and brought prisoner to Albany, to answer an accusation of high treason."[115] On September 13, 1777, Enos Hitchcock noted that "Col.^{o} Hale is under confinement at Albany."[116] Apparently Hale was never formally tried on the charges and returned home. Since no prisoner exchange ever occurred, Hale surrendered himself to the British on June 14, 1779. He died on September 23, 1780, while imprisoned on Long Island.

10. Wrote Home p.ʳ Post No. 5, & to Rev.ᵈ Fisk—dined on Fish, fair & pleasant, purchased two tickets No.ˢ 57111669 & 70 jointly with Cap.ᵗ Greenleaf.*

11. Radishes with breakfast—fine roast Beef for diner glorious news of Genˡ Washington's gaining a compleat Victory over the Enemy at Bound Brook—no particulars**—fair pleasant Day—something dry

12. Wrote home No. 6, by Mr. Plumb, to Mr. Foster & Mr. Hall—General Sinclair & Formay arrived in Camp about 9 o'Clock,*** rained in the Morning—purchased two [lottery] Tickets No. 57,674 & 58,449 jointly with Col.ˢ Francis & Littlefield & Major [William] Lithgow [11ᵗʰ Massachusetts]—sent my Journal Home to this date.

13. Mr. Plumb set off for Boston at 4 ᵒClock P. M. Show[e]ry—two persons br[ough]t in supposed to be Spies, who give an account that the Enemy are coming up 10,000 strong.

---

*Chaplain Hitchcock split the purchase of two lottery tickets with Captain Moses Greenleaf. (Lottery proceeds comprised less than one percent of the revenue raised for the war effort.) Moses Greenleaf (1755-1812) was commissioned a second lieutenant in the Massachusetts militia in 1775 and promoted to first lieutenant the following year. On November 6, 1776, he was appointed captain in the 11th Massachusetts Regiment under Colonel Ebenezer Francis. Greenleaf survived the Battle of Hubbardton on July 7, 1777, spent the winter at Valley Forge with Washington's army, and participated in the Battle of Monmouth in 1778. He left the army in 1780, later spending two years as the Deputy Collector of Excise and Customs in Newburyport, Massachusetts. Greenleaf then earned a living as a farmer in Maine and died in 1812 at age 57. His original diary of the 1777 campaign is presently held by the Massachusetts Historical Society and was published in *The Bulletin of the Fort Ticonderoga Museum* in 1997.

**George Washington moved the American army to Middle Brook, New Jersey (near Bound Brook), between May 28 and May 31, 1777. Although the British army under General William Howe was not far away, no battle occurred in this region.

***Arthur St. Clair (1737-1818) served as an ensign in the 60th Regiment of Foot at the siege of Louisbourg in 1758 and as a lieutenant during the 1759 capture of Quebec. After his wife received a substantial inheritance, St. Clair moved from Boston to Pennsylvania where he became a large landholder. From the rank of colonel in the Pennsylvania Militia in 1775, St. Clair rose to the rank of major general in the Continental Army by February 1777, having served in the campaigns at Three Rivers (Canada), Trenton, and Princeton. Upon the withdrawal from Ticonderoga in 1777, St. Clair faced immediate criticism. Soon after the evacuation a letter by St. Clair was published in several newspapers. In a letter St. Clair defended his decision by suggesting that the garrisons at the Lake Champlain posts were undermanned: "two thousand and eighty-nine only, were fit for duty, many of those mere boys" and maintained that the retreat saved the army.[117] The next year St. Clair was exonerated at a court-martial, but rumors questioning his loyalty dogged him for the rest of the war. He held staff positions until his retirement on November 3, 1783. Following the war St. Clair served two years in Congress (1785-1787), and was president of the body in the last year. He became the first governor of the Northwest Territory (1789-1802) and in 1791 was appointed commander in chief of the army with a rank of major general. Leading an expedition into the Ohio Territory late in 1791, St. Clair had his army nearly wiped out by a combined force of Miamis, Shawnees, Delawares, and six other Indian nations, suffering one of the worst defeats in the history of the U.S. Army with over 600 men killed and more than 250 wounded. The next year a Congressional committee cleared St. Clair of responsibility for the disaster. He lived his last few years in relative poverty and died in 1818 after being thrown from a pony-drawn wagon.

Matthias Alexis Roche de Fermoy, a French citizen born in Martinique, was commissioned a brigadier general in the Continental Army in 1776 after purporting to be a French colonel of engineers. He served in the Trenton campaign in December 1776 and inexplicably left his post as commander of a delaying force at Princeton. Transferred to the Northern Department in 1777, he subsequently burned his quarters on Mount Independence, against orders, on the night of the evacuation. After failing to receive a promotion from Congress, Fermoy resigned early the next year and returned to the French West Indies.

14. The Regiment past muster—visited the Hospital at Mount Independence, the new Hospital about one third covered—250 long & 24 wide*—warm and pleasant

15. Sunday. Divine Service at Six °Clock, P. M. Matt[hew] 16, 26.—pleasant

16. Capt. [Samuel] Page [11th Massachusetts] &c arrived—receiv.d Letters by Him from Master Herrick to the 30th of May, fair & pleasant.

17. Wrote Home No. 7, & to Mr. Plumb by Post—visited Hospital A. M.—the Camp alarmed about noon by some firing without the Lines—two men were taken & some killed near McIntoshes by some Indians, who were pursued by Scouts, who on their return met with Lieut Taylor who went out yesterday with a party of twelve men which was suddenly encompassed by them, exchanged several Shots wounded the Lieut: who escaped with two men, the others killed or taken—one dead Body found bro[ugh]t in belonging to Col.° Hale's Reg.t**

18. This morning 8 of Lieut Taylors men came in, one swam over the Lake—another Col.° Hale's men found in McIntoshes field—[Major] General [Philip] Sch[u]yler came into Camp to-day—Major Lithgow went to Fort George on Court Martial—Rev.d [Thomas] Allen of Pittsfield came into Camp.

19. One Harris of Col.° Hales Reg.t killed by an accidental discharge of his own Gun—this morning Cap.t Whitcomb came in who went out yesterday, bro[ught] an Indian S[c]alp killed by Taylors party—dined on roast Beef—fair Day—spent the evening in writing Letters by Cap.t Raymond

20. Wrote Home No. 8 & to Rev. Forbes Mr. Herrick & Brother David [Hitchcock]—Major [William] Hull [8th Massachusetts] dined with us upon Roast Beef &c—Cap.t Raymond set off for N. England; fair Day

·21. Appointed Chaplain to gen.l Pattersons Brigade—fair Day

22. Sunday. Major Lithgow returned from Fort George, bro[ugh]t dispatches from Gen.l Washington to Schuyler, giving an account of the Enemies getting to Morrisania***—confirming the late reports from Canada &c. fair Day but no Service, the men on fatigue [work detail] & moving into Tents—

General Schuyler left Camp—

23. Dined at Gen.l Poors—receiv.d a letter from Rev.d Ward p.r Post—Major Hull, Cap.t [Isaac] Gray [Massachusetts Militia] & others dined with us

24. Col.° [James] Mead [Vermont Militia] came into Camp about 12 °Clock last Night, informs that the Enemy were very near Crown-point at Sundown—The morning opens fair & very warm—warm all Day

25. Col.° Marshal dined with us

---

*The remains of the General Hospital were excavated in 1990 by volunteers working under the direction of archaeologist Dr. David R. Starbuck.[118]

**According to Lieutenant Thomas Blake of the First New Hampshire Regiment, the first attack by the Indians occurred "on the road that leads from Ticonderoga to [the] Lake George landing."[119] Captain John Calfe of the New Hampshire Militia noted that "on their Return Back to Crown Point they [the Indians] met 13 of our Rangers who were out on a Scout and kill'd two of them and wounded two more," including Lieutenant Nathan Taylor of the New Hampshire Rangers.[120] The first incident probably occurred near the land (215 acres purchased from Samuel Deall) owned by James MacIntosh, who operated a tavern situated between the Lower Falls of the La Chute River and the garrison grounds. Alexander McIntosh's land was located just north of Ticonderoga (near present-day Streetroad).[121]

***Although there were skirmishes in Morrisania, New York (present-day Bronx), in the latter years of the American Revolution, there was no significant action there in 1777. Perhaps Hitchcock had confused the name with the British position near Millstone or Middlebush, New Jersey, in June 1777.

26. Some men fired upon by Indians one killed & S[c]alped, one S[c]alped & came in wounded in several parts, a Shower P. M.

27. Rained last Night attended with much lightning—A Report of a number of Indians going to Skene[sborough]—very warm work upon our House—Shower at noon

28. An account of two large Vessels sailing down the Lake—turned out at Gunfiring attended Prayers on the Brigade parade before Sunrise—warm Day—about Sunset one of their Vessels was discovered this side [of] five mile point by a boat of ours & three a little below, upon seeing our Boat (80 Rods distant) they hoisted two, chased & fired upon it, several fires were exchanged which soon communicated to ye guard Boat who gave the Signal & an Alarm was fired—about half after 9 °Clock,* I had just got into Bed, but immediately turned out & went parade, found the Brigade generally turned out & very Spirited—dismissed at half after eleven to lay on arms—Lieu.^t Huax deserted to the Enemy

29. Sunday. Rise at gunfiring (1/2 past 2 °Clock) nothing happened Attended prayers, dismissed at Sunrise, men all on Duty

30. Alarmed at [blotted out on original] °Clock last Night by firing from the Picket guard—it proved false—about 7 °Clock the guard Boats coming in—8 a number of Enemies Boats heave in sight, alarm Guns—Several Cannon discharged at the French lines at a party of Indians & others—Some Musketry with.^t the Picket drove in**—at noon men dismissed to get Refreshment—sent our Bag[g]age to Mount Independ.^c—towards Night two Ships, several Sloops a lar[g]e number of Gun Boats & others stretch across the lake within one & 1/2 mile of the Jersey Battery***—Mr. Shaw came in with other Posts a little before Night, receiv.^d Letter from Home No. 3, Revd Foster & Fish & Brother David—extreme Hot

July

1. No disturbance last Night. Attended prayers before Sunrise—the Enemy in Statu quo—good news from Genl Washington of the defeat of How[e]s Army, that gen.^l Sullivan was in possession of Brunswick, Genl Green in possession of an advantage post between that & Amboy—& that the Enemy were fleeing precipitately†—some firing at the [saw] mills

*Lieutenant Henry Sewall of the 12th Massachusetts Regiment suggested that "some spy boats from the enemy" were discovered about ten in the evening of June 28.[122] Lieutenant Thomas Blake noted that "some of their gunboats" had sailed as far as Three Mile Point and fired on the American vessels.[123]

**Lieutenant Thomas Blake mentioned that "a party (chiefly Indians) came to our lines, fired upon the pi[ck]ets (that were posted about 100 yards from the works) a few times and then returned."[124]

***On June 30 Captain Moses Greenleaf observed that "the Enemy Advances within Two Miles with Two Twenty Gun Frigates & about fifty Boats, Land a Number of Troops about two Miles from us."[125] Colonel Jeduthan Baldwin recorded that "early in the morning the Enemy appeared at 3 mile point with 18 Gunboats. . .this afternoon two large Ships appeared one 20 guns & the other a 16 gun Ship 22 tenders they warped up in a line with the Boats across the lake."[126] Lieutenant William Digby with the British army disclosed that the ships *Royal George* and *Inflexible* were anchored near the line of gunboats "with a large boom ahead to prevent fire ships coming down from the fort."[127]

†The news was misleading. Although there were a few skirmishes and much maneuvering of armies in New Jersey, George Washington did not actually engage the British army in a major battle, and General William Howe withdrew for a campaign against Philadelphia. Major General John Sullivan, Major General William Alexander, and Brigadier General Nathaniel Greene and others were involved in the 1777 New Jersey campaign with Washington. The "Good news," nevertheless, was celebrated at Ticonderoga, according to Captain Enos Stone, with the firing of "13 cannon as a S[a]lute to the 13 United States" at noontime on July 1.[128]

2. The Mills & Block Houses [at the La Chute River] evacuated as not tenable & burnt—about 2 °Clock—

four Boats came towards the J[e]rsey Battery—one Cannon discharged at them, three Signal Guns from the Enemies Ships—the Lines were soon man[n]ed about three °Clock a firing between the Picket & a party of Indians & Regulars it lasted more than half an Hour the Picket retreated with the los[s] of about five killed & Six wounded most of them bro[ugh]t in—the Enemy followed up till Col.° Francis Reg.ᵗ fired over the Parapet some twice, some three Times—some Cannon was discharged at them they soon retreated*—the men dismissed about Six °Clock—one Regular Soldier was taken—two Hessians deserted came to Mount Independᵉ—they say the Enemy are 5600 strong.

3. A peac[e]able Night, things in Statu quo—about 700 M[i]l[i]tia came into Camp P. Mr. [Chaplain Augustine] Hibb[a]rt [of the New Hampshire Militia] with them—the Enemy get possession of Mount Hope—Some Cannon fired at them opposite the Jersey Battery very warm

4. The Enemy at work on the rising ground fronting French Lines several Cannon fired at them—extreme hot

5. Wrote Home by Mr. Shaw No. 9, the [enemy] discovered on the Mount S. W. of Ti** some firing towards night—wind came in Cool & Crisp at 5 P. M. at N. W.—about 6 °Clock [orders] came for every man to furnish himself with 24 rounds Extra & five Days provision, the Bumb [radeau *Thunderer*] drew in Shore & boats approach the Jersey Battery—at seven orders came for every man to be under Arms & march to their respective Alarm Posts—about nine orders for all to be ready with all their Effects to obey further orders—with great Reluctance I left our new dwelling at past nine came over to Mount Independence, got the Baggage down to the wharf & put it on board the Schooner & Gundeloe***

6. Sunday. at three °Clock hoisted Sail under a very small breeze with all our Vessels & set off for Skene[sborough]†—the land Army march at the same time for Castleton, Col.°[Ebenezer Francis] commands the rear Guard 500 men—arrived at Skeene two Clock P. M. in about an Hour the Enemies Gun boats came up & fired at one of our Row gallies, a brisk & mutual Can[n]onade followed for near half an

---

*This skirmish occurred at the site of Montcalm's original breastwork which had been repaired by the Americans.

**A British battery established on the top of present-day Mount Defiance precipitated the evacuation of Fort Ticonderoga and Mount Independence (see main text for more details).

***Orders for the evacuation reached the officers at different times. Major Ebenezer Stevens first heard the news from Major General St. Clair at "about seven o'clock in the evening," while Captain Moses Greenleaf received word "at Nine o Clock," but Captain Enos Stone did not learn of it until "11 Night" and Lieutenant Thomas Blake "about one o'clock in the morning."[129] The sudden night retreat caused "the Umost Confusion," according to Captain John Calfe.[130]

†Under the command of Colonel Pierce Long of the New Hampshire Militia, the American vessels employed in the retreat to Skenesborough included the galleys *Gates* and *Trumbull*, gondola *New York*, schooners *Liberty* and *Revenge*, sloop *Enterprise*, and a large number of bateaux. James Thacher later recalled that the boats were "deeply laden with cannon, tents, provisions, invalids and women. . .the night was moon-light. . .the sun burst forth in the morning with uncommon lustre. . .the water's surface serene and unruffled. . .a scene so enchantingly sublime. . .the drum and fife afforded us a favorite music; among the hospital stores we found many dozen bottles of choice wine, and, breaking off their necks, we cheered our hearts with the nectareous contents. . .but in less than two hours we were struck with surprise and consternation by a discharge of cannon from the enemy's fleet."[131]

Hour during which time I was imployed amidst flying ball in getting some of my baggage on board a boat above the falls, which with difficulty I effected & put off up Wood Crick the shoalness of the Water & many logs in it render it extrem[e]ly difficult passing in boats; set off between three & four °Clock & with much difficulty & hard labor, working all night in the water we reached Fort Ann[e]* about

7. At ten °Clock, some boats in our rear cut off by Savages, the men mostly got in, but scattering partys continue to come in—about noon a Skirmish happened between a small Scouting party & a few Indians & some regulars we lost three, killed & four wounded,—some Stores came in from Fort Edward—fair Day

8. Rested comfortably last Night, the Garrison was alarmed once but I did not turn out—about 9 °Clock a scouting party of a 100 men was sent out to go down the Crick to recover some lost Bagage, but soon met with a party of regular Troops about 300 a brisk firing came, 60 more went to reinfore them & then 30 & 20 more—the engagement last an Hour & half very warm—our loss was 10 killed and wounded—the Enemies supposed to be 40 or 50 killed and wounded, our men drove them from a little Breast[work] they had built up a hill—four of the Enemy were bro.ᵗ in, viz Dʳ. Ciely of Lord Leigoniers Reg.ᵗ well—Cap.ᵗ Mongumery wounded in the Knee & two privates dangerously wounded**—a Council of war was called at which I was present, it was agreed upon to evacuate. . .the G[a]rrison considering the weak State it was in as to ammunition, & the large Reinforcement we had authentic assurance was on their way to the Enemy—left Fort Ann[e] in flames*** between three & four °Clock P. M. travelled without Stop[p]ing to Fort Edward 14 miles in a heavy rain reached it at dark

*Departing late from Mount Independence Captain John Calfe wrote that the British "came upon us Just as we Landed [at Skenesborough] and fired on us very Smartly with Shipping [British gunboats commanded by Captain John Carter], which occasioned a great Confusion, and many came of[f] and Left all their Effects behind and Traveled on for Fort Ann[e], where just arrived about Midnight."[132]

When the British arrived at Skenesborough, James Thacher observed that "The officers of our guard now attempted to rally the men and form them in battle array, but this was found impossible; every effort proved unavailing, and in the utmost panic they were seen to fly in every direction for personal safety. In this desperate condition, I perceived our officers scampering for their baggage; I ran to the batteau, seized my chest, carried it a short distance, took from it a few articles, and instantly followed in the train of our retreating party. We took the route to Fort Anne, through a narrow defile in the woods, and were so closely pressed by the pursuing enemy, that we frequently heard calls from the rear to 'march on, the Indians are at our heels.' Having marched all night we reached Fort Anne at five o'clock in the morning, where we found provisions for our refreshment. A small rivulet called Wood Creek is navigable for boats from Skeensboro' to Fort Anne, by which means some of our invalids and baggage made their escape; but all our cannon, provisions, and the bulk of our baggage, with several invalids, fell into the enemy's hands."[133]

**Lieutenant Colonel John Hill, with an advance unit of the 9th Regiment of Foot, had pursued the Americans close to Fort Anne. With information on the limited size of the British detachment, the Americans began a counterattack, "which continued for several hours," according to James Thacher: "the enemy, being almost surrounded, were on the point of surrendering, when our ammunition being expended, a party of Indians arriving and setting up the war-whoop. . .the Americans were induced to give way and retreat [the war-whoop came from a British officer]. One surgeon [Dr. Ciely] with a wounded captain [William Stone Montgomery] and twelve or fifteen privates were taken and brought to our fort [Fort Anne]."[134] Montgomery later succumbed to his wounds.

***A short time later Brigadier Johann Friedrich Specht described Fort Anne as "nothing but a square of palisades in which embrasures [openings for cannon] have been fitted. Before leaving, the enemy had set fire to it whereby a wooden barrack and a similar magazine, which had stood in this square, had been reduced to ashes. Actually no more than half of the palisades had burned; for a sudden, heavy rain must have extinguished the flames."[135]

Fort Ticonderoga.
(Photo by the author)

NOTES

1. William B. Weeden, ed., "Diary of Enos Hitchcock, D. D., A Chaplain in the Revolutionary Army with a Memoir," *Publications of the Rhode Island Historical Society* 7 (1899): 87; *Dictionary of American Biography*, Volume 5 (New York: Charles Scribner's Sons, 1961), 72; One source stated that Hitchcock was born in Brookfield, Massachusetts, but also noted that his epitaph read "Rev. Enos Hitchcock, D. D., born Springfield, Mass." Mrs. Edward Hitchcock, *The Geneology of the Hitchcock Family* (Amherst, MA.: Press of Carpenter & Morehouse, 1894), 424.
2. Weeden, 107.
3. Ibid., 118.
4. Peter Force, ed., *American Archives*, Fifth Series, Volume 3 (Washington, D. C.: M. St. Clair Clarke and Peter Force, 1853), 1585-86.
5. Ibid., 1586, 1592.
6. Ibid., 1592.
7. Jeduthan Baldwin, *The Revolutionary Journal of Col. Jeduthan Baldwin 1775-1778*, ed. Thomas Williams Baldwin (Bangor, ME.: DeBurians, 1906), 94.
8. Arthur Cohn, *The Great Bridge "From Ticonderoga to Independent Point"* (Lake Champlain Basin Program, 1995), Report 4C, 20-21; Kevin Crisman, *The 1992 Mount Independence Phase One Underwater Archaelogical Survey* (Lake Champlain Basin Program, 1995), Report 4B, 48-49.
9. Arthur Cohn, *The 1992 Fort Ticonderoga - Mount Independence Submerged Cultural Resource Survey* (Lake Champlain Basin Program, 1995), Report 4A, 12.
10. Ibid., 11; Crisman, 15, 17-19, 22-24; Dennis E. Howe, *This Ragged, Starved Lousy, Pocky Army* (Concord, N.H.: The Printed Word, 1996), 75-79.
11. James Thacher, M.D., *Military Journal of the American Revolution* (Hartford, CT.: Hurlbut, Williams & Company, 1862), 80; Thacher may have taken the measurements from Burgoyne's work published in 1780. John Burgoyne, *A State of the Expedition from Canada* (1780; reprint ed., New York: The New York Times & Arno Press, 1969), Appendix VII, xxx.
12. Thacher, 80.
13. Charlotte S. J. Epping, trans., *Journal of Du Roi the Elder* (Philadelphia: University of Pennsylvania, 1911), 97.
14. Miecislaus Haiman, *Kosciuszko in the American Revolution* (New York: The Kosciuszko Foundation and The Polish Institute of Arts and Sciences, 1975), 15.
15. Helga Doblin, trans. and Mary C. Lynn, ed., *The Specht Journal: a Military Journal of the Burgoyne Campaign* (Westport, CT.: Greenwood Press, 1995), 53.
16. Epping, 97.
17. Helga Doblin, trans. and Mary C. Lynn, ed., *An Eyewitness Account of the American Revolution and New England Life: The Journal of J. F. Wasmus, German Company Surgeon, 1776-1783* (Westport, CT.: Greenwood Press, 1990), 59; See also Thomas B. Furcron, "Mount Independence, 1776-1777," *The Bulletin of the Fort Ticonderoga Museum* 9 (Winter 1954): 240-41.
18. David R. Starbuck, *Mount Independence and the American Revolution 1776-1777* (Montpelier, VT.: Vermont Division for Historic Preservation, 1991), 14; David R. Starbuck, "Military Hospitals on the Frontier of Colonial America," *Expedition* 39 (No. 1, 1997): 35-38; Howe, 20; See also Donald H. Wickman, "Built with Spirit, Deserted in Darkness: the American Occupation of Mount Independence 1776-1777," (master's thesis, University of Vermont, 1993).
19. John C. Fitzpatrick, ed., *The Writings of George Washington* (Washington, D. C.: Government Printing Office, 1932), Volume 7, 273.
20. Ibid., 274.
21. William James Morgan, ed., *Naval Documents of the American Revolution* (Washington, D. C.: Naval History Division, Department of the Navy, 1980), Volume 8, 187-88; See also William James Morgan, ed., *Naval Documents of the American Revolution* (Washington, D. C.: Naval History Division, Department of the Navy, 1976), Volume 7, 1255-56, 627.
22. Joshua Pell, Jr., "Diary of Joshua Pell, Junior," *The Magazine of American History* 2 (1878): 107.
23. Thomas Anburey, *Travels through the Interior Parts of America* (1789; reprint ed., New York: The New York Times & Arno Press, 1969), Volume 1, 169.
24. Doblin, *Journal of Wasmus*, 51; See also Epping, 87.
25. Epping, 86.

26. William L. Stone, trans., *Memoirs, Letters, and Journals of Major General Riedesel* (1868; reprint ed., New York: The New York Times & Arno Press, 1969), Volume 1, 106.

27. Doblin, *Journal of Wasmus*, 53.

28. Ibid.

29. Ibid., 55.

30. W. Stone, *Memoirs of Riedesel*, 108-9; See also Doblin, *Specht Journal*, 219.

31. Burgoyne, 10.

32. Ibid., Appendix VI, xxii-xxiv; See also Anburey, 283, 286-87.

33. F. J. Hudleston, *Gentleman Johnny Burgoyne* (Garden City, N. Y.: Garden City Publishing Co., 1927), 146.

34. Thomas Blake, "Lieutenant Thomas Blake's Journal," in *History of the First New Hampshire Regiment*, by Frederic Kidder (Albany: Joel Munsell, 1868), 26; See also Henry Sewall, "Diary of Captain Henry Sewall, of the Army of the Revolution, 1776-1783," *Historical Magazine* 10 (August 1871): 137.

35. William Henry Smith, *The Life and Public Services of Arthur St. Clair* (Cincinnati: Robert Clarke & Co., 1882), 409.

36. Enos Stone, "Capt. Enos Stone's Journal," *The New England Historical & Genealogical Register* 15 (October 1861): 300; See also Donald H. Wickman, " 'Breakfast on Chocolate': The Diary of Moses Greenleaf, 1777," *The Bulletin of the Fort Ticonderoga Museum* 15 (1997): 496; John Calfe, "Capt. John Calfe's Book," in *A Memorial of the Town of Hampstead, New Hampshire*, comp. by Harriette Eliza Noyes (Boston: George B. Reed, 1899), 289; Baldwin, 108; Sewall, 137; Oddly, when St. Clair informed Schuyler (July 1, 1777) of the "two ships, eighteen gun boats, and three sloops, lying off the Three Mile Point," he concluded "This does not look like their being strong." "The Trial of Major General St. Clair, August, 1778," *Collections of the New-York Historical Society* 13 (1880): 69.

37. Horatio Rogers, ed., *Hadden's Journal and Orderly Books: A Journal Kept in Canada and Upon Burgoyne's Campaign in 1776 and 1777, by Lieut. James M. Hadden, Roy. Art.* (1884; reprint ed., Boston: Gregg Press, 1972), 82.

38. Wickman, "Diary of Greenleaf," 496.

39. Doblin, *Journal of Wasmus*, 58.

40. Rogers, 84; See also Burgoyne, Appendix VII, xxviii, xxix; Anburey, 319-20; Simon Fraser, "Gen. Fraser's Account of Burgoyne's Campaign on Lake Champlain and the Battle of Hubbardton," *Proceedings of the Vermont Historical Society* (October 18 and November 2, 1898): 143-44.

41. Helga Doblin, tran. and ed., "Journal of Lt. Colonel Christian Julius Prätorius 2 June 1777 - 17 July 1777," *The Bulletin of the Fort Ticonderoga Museum* 15 (Winter 1991): 64.

42. Epping, 93; James Phinney Baxter, ed., *The British Invasion from the North, The Campaigns of Generals Carleton and Burgoyne from Canada with the Journal of Lieut. William Digby* (Albany: Joel Munsell's Sons, 1887), 205.

43. Haiman, 18.

44. James Wilkinson, *Memoirs of My Own Times* (1816; reprint ed., New York: AMS Press, Inc., 1973), 184.

45. Ibid., 185.

46. Blake, 28; See also E. Stone, "Capt. Enos Stone's Journal," 301; Calfe, 290.

47. Wickman, "Diary of Greenleaf," 497.

48. Doblin, *Specht Journal*, 52; Doblin, *Journal of Prätorius*, 64.

49. Thacher, 83.

50. Burgoyne, Appendix VII, xxx.

51. Ibid., xxxi.

52. *Ticonderoga Sentinel*, 16 November 1911; See also *Lake George Mirror*, 2 September 1910.

53. Burgoyne, Appendix VII, xxxi; See also Pell, 108; Anburey, 1: 347; Rogers, 91; James Minor Lincoln, *The Papers of Captain Rufus Lincoln of Wareham, Mass.* (1904; reprint ed., Arno Press, Inc., 1971), 14; On July 7, 1777, the day after the battle, Julius Friedrich Wasmus reached Skenesborough where he observed the *Trumbull* and *Liberty*. On July 8 he described much of the devastation: "the enemy had burned a 2-masted ship here [at the waterfall]; it had sunk but the masts could still be seen. A burned battery. . .Most of the more than 200 bateaux had been burned, a great deal of ammunition, provisions and other items had been thrown into the water." All the

houses had been burned down "except one stone house." Wasmus surmised that the destruction of the village "was done out of hatred for Colonel [Philip] Skene, who owned this region and who was with our army." Doblin, *Journal of Wasmus*, 60.

54. Blake, 28.
55. Anburey, 1: 326.
56. Wickman, "Diary of Greenleaf," 497.
57. Burgoyne, Appendix VII, xxxiii; See also Doblin, *Journal of Prätorius*, 66.
58. Charles I. Bushnell, ed., *The Narrative of Ebenezer Fletcher* (1827; reprint ed., Freeport N. Y.: Books for Libraries Press, 1970), 14.
59. Ibid.
60. Baxter, 246.
61. Doblin, *Journal of Prätorius*, 66.
62. Burgoyne, 17.
63. Weeden, 119-20.
64. Lincoln, 15; See also Rogers, 94-95.
65. Haiman, 21.
66. Burgoyne, 17.
67. Ibid.
68. Ibid., 18.
69. Baxter, 227-28.
70. Ibid., 226.
71. Epping, 114.
72. Rogers, 96.
73. Thacher, 86; See also Wilkinson, 198.
74. Burgoyne, Appendix X, xlix.
75. Doblin, *Specht Journal*, 62-63.
76. Burgoyne, Appendix XII, lxiii, 19.
77. Ibid., 18.
78. W. Stone, *Memoirs of Riedesel*, 127.
79. Doblin, *Journal of Wasmus*, 71.
80. Weeden, 128; See also Luther Roby, *Reminiscences of the French War; Rogers' Expeditions and Maj. Gen. John Stark* (Concord, N. H.: Luther Roby, 1831), 192.
81. Burgoyne, Appendix IV, xiii.
82. Weeden, 127.
83. Ibid., 134.
84. Ibid., 148.
85. Ibid., 148-49.
86. David E. Alexander, ed., "Diary of Captain Benjamin Warren on Battlefield of Saratoga," *The Journal of American History* 3 (1909): 212.
87. Burgoyne, Appendix XIV, lxxxviii; Anburey, 1: 417.
88. Weeden, 149-50; At noon the British "heard them huzzaing in their camp, after which they fired 13 heavy guns, which we imagined might be signals for an attack." Baxter, 276.
89. "Brown's Attack of September 1777," *The Bulletin of the Fort Ticonderoga Museum* 11 (July 1964): 212; See also Helga Doblin, trans. and Mary C. Lynn, ed., *The American Revolution, Garrison Life in French Canada and New York: Journal of an Officer in the Prinz Friedrich Regiment, 1776-1783* (Westport, Ct.: Greenwood Press, 1993), 78-81, 90-94.
90. William James Morgan, ed., *Naval Documents of the American Revolution* (Washington, D. C.: Naval History Division, Department of the Navy, 1986), Volume 9, 969.
91. J. Brown to B. Lincoln, 26 September 1777, *The New-England Historical & Genealogical Register* 26 (January 1872): 151.
92. Weeden, 153.
93. Burgoyne, 26.
94. Weeden, 155.
95. Ibid., 155-56.
96. Ibid., 156.
97. Ibid., 159.
98. Baldwin, 125.

99. Epping, 110; See also Doblin, *American Revolution, Garrison Life*, 86.

100. Weeden, 163.

101. Ibid., 106.

102. Enos Hitchock, *Memoirs of the Bloomsgrove Family* (1790; reprint ed., Upper Saddle River, N. J.: Literature House, 1970), Volume 1, 14-15.

103. Ibid., 47.

104. Ibid., 51.

105. Ibid., 138, see also 141.

106. Weeden, 109-19.

107. Epping, 94, 181.

108. Baldwin, 103.

109. Ibid.

110. Ibid., 104.

111. Elizabeth Cometti, ed., *The American Journal of Lt. John Enys* (Syracuse, N. Y.: Syracuse University Press, 1976), 18.

112. Anburey, 1: 336-37.

113. Ibid., 2: 209.

114. Ibid., 2: 209-10.

115. Rogers, Appendix 15, 488.

116. Weeden, 134.

117. *Boston Gazette and Country Journal*, 26 July 1777; See also Smith, 425-26.

118. Starbuck, "Military Hospitals," 36-38, 41, 43; Howe, 20-22.

119. Blake, 26.

120. Calfe, 289; See also Wickman, "Diary of Greenfield," 494.

121. Jane M. Lape, ed., *Ticonderoga: Patches and Patterns from Its Past* (1969; reprint ed., Ticonderoga, N. Y.: The Ticonderoga Historical Society, 1997), 265, 20; [E. B. O'Callaghan], comp., *Calendar of N. Y. Colonial Manuscripts: Indorsed Land Papers 1643-1863* (1864; reprint ed., Harrison, N. Y.: Harbor Hill Books, 1987), 345; Loyalist James MacIntosh served as a spy for the British during the 1777 campaign. See Simon Fraser, "Inquisition of a Spy," 18 June 1777, Fort Ticonderoga Thompson-Pell Research Center and *The Bulletin of the Fort Ticonderoga Museum* 10 (1959): 240-45.

122. Sewall, 137.

123. Blake, 26.

124. Ibid., 27.

125. Wickman, "Diary of Greenleaf," 496.

126. Baldwin, 108; See also Sewall, 137.

127. Baxter, 201.

128. E. Stone, "Capt. Enos Stone's Journal," 300.

129. "Trial of St. Clair," 93; Wickman, "Diary of Greenleaf," 497; E. Stone, "Capt. Enos Stone's Journal," 301; Blake, 28.

130. Calfe, 290.

131. Thacher, 83.

132. Calfe, 290.

133. Thacher, 83-84.

134. Ibid., 84; See also Calfe, 290; Doblin, *Specht Journal*, endnote 74, 119; R. Lamb, *Journal of Occurrences During the Late War* (1809; reprint ed., New York: Arno Press, Inc., 1968), 142.

135. Doblin, *Specht Journal*, 59.

Detail of a "View on the Hudson River." Sketch by Isaac Weld
from his *Travels Through the States of North America.*

Part V: Temporary Peace

---

10. Isaac Weld 1796

Although there were a few published accounts of earlier journeys by foreigners in America, Isaac Weld's *Travels Through the States of North America, and the Province of Upper and Lower Canada* was the first comprehensive guide in a long line of British volumes on life in the United States and Canada. Traveling by foot, horseback, boat, and carriage, Weld visited Pennsylvania, Virginia, Maryland, New Jersey, New York, Michigan, and Canada. The 21-year-old traveler came to America "for the purpose of examining with his own eyes into the truth of the various accounts which had been given of the flourishing and happy condition of the United States of America," but his dim view of Americans caused Weld to leave "without entertaining the slightest wish to revisit it."[1] Weld's narrative encompassed descriptions of cities, farms, crops, waterways, wildlife, history, weather patterns, the intricacies of the economy, politics, and the natural wonders of North America. Sailing on a rented bark on Lake Champlain in the summer of 1796, Weld remarked that "the scenery along various parts of the lake is extremely grand and picturesque" and noted that the water "in the broad part [of the lake]. . .is as pure and transparent as possible."[2]

Isaac Weld, born on March 15, 1774, in Dublin, Ireland, was the eldest son of Isaac and Elizabeth Kerr Weld. His grandfather, Isaac Weld, was the first of three family members named after the eminent scientist Sir Isaac Newton (1642-1727), who had been a friend of young Weld's great-grandfather, Dr. Nathaniel Weld. Weld's grandfather and great-grandfather were both members of the ministry. Weld's father, on the other hand, held a lucrative government position in the Irish customs office. During young Isaac Weld's lifetime, ample family wealth permitted private schooling and funds for extensive travel in North America. As a boy he attended the school of Samuel Whyte in Dublin and later studied at Palgrave in

Norfolk County, England, under Rochemont Barbauld. His final tutelage, ending in 1793, occurred under the direction of Dr. William Enfield in Norwich, England.

In 1795 Isaac Weld decided to sail to North America to verify the optimistic stories that he had heard about the United States since "war was spreading desolation over the fairest parts of Europe. . .soon any one of its inhabitants might be forced to seek refuge in a foreign land."[3] After a difficult voyage of two months, Weld and his dedicated servant (whom he scarcely mentions in his *Travels*) arrived in Philadelphia in November 1795. His subsequent travels in America brought him into contact with a broad cross-section of people. He wrote detailed descriptions of many major cities, including that of the new capital, Washington, D.C., and visited Monticello and Mount Vernon.

Traveling at a time when facilities for tourists were rudimentary at best, Weld often lodged in primitive taverns and farmhouses, and on occasion camped out. He repeatedly complained about the lack of privacy and of the crowded conditions in local taverns where a dozen travelers were forced to sleep in a single room, containing "five or six beds, and in which they laid down in pairs."[4] While at taverns, Weld could not help but notice that Americans were constantly debating political issues: "it is scarcely possible for a dozen Americans to sit together without quarrelling about politics."[5] Even when the travelers retired to their communal bedroom, "the conversation was again revived, and pursued with as much noise as below, till at last sleep closed their eyes, and happily their mouths at the same time" and he mused that if Americans could argue in their sleep "they would have prated on until morning."[6] Weld, however, was impressed by the egalitarian atmosphere in taverns where several eminent lawyers from Virginia and a Supreme Court justice were indistinguishable from other guests, "for these kind of gentlemen in America are so very plain, both in their appearance and manners, that a stranger would not suspect that they were persons of. . .consequence."[7]

After traveling through several states, Weld came to the conclusion that "there is no country on the face of the globe" where partisan politics and political issues "are more frequently the topic of conversation amongst all classes, and where such subjects are more frequently the cause of rancorous disputations and lasting differences amongst the people."[8] Generally, the young traveler determined that Americans were loath to acquiesce to authority and that a "spirit of dissatisfaction. . .forms a leading trait in the character of the Americans as a people."[9]

Like other British travelers who would later write about Americans, including Francis Trollope, Basil Hall, and Thomas Hamilton, Weld found fault with American manners and behavior. In his preface to *Travels*, Weld acknowledged the acrimonious nature of many of his comments on American manners but insisted that his attitude was impartial and not a "hasty prejudice."[10] In fact, Weld maintained that he had "crossed the Atlantic strongly prepossessed in favour of the people and the country. . .[but] returned with sentiments of a different tendency. . .result[ing] solely from a cool and dispassionate observation."[11] In response to questions by a traveler with "the appearance of a gentleman," Weld complained, "the lower classes of people will return rude and impertinent answers. . .to show how much they consider themselves upon an equality with him. . .[since] there is no other way of convincing a stranger that he is really in a land of liberty, but by being surly and ill mannered in his presence."[12] As Weld stopped in various communities during his journey he would invariably be accosted by local inhabitants with questions, but he considered the inquiries "idle and impertinent curiosity. . .[from] ignorant, boorish fellows" who often turned the conversation into a political debate, causing Weld "to turn from them with disgust."[13] Referring to travelers on their way to Kentucky, Weld acidly noted: "Of all the uncouth human beings I met with in America, these people from the western country were the most so; their curiosity boundless."[14] On the other hand, Weld found warm "hospitality and friendly civilities" from the residents of New York City which induced him to "rank [it] as the most agreeable place I have visited in the United States."[15] While in Vermont he also noted that American farm families were hospitable, for they "will cheerfully lie three in a bed, rather than suffer a stranger to go away who comes to seek. . .lodging."[16]

Weld reserved most of his negative observations for the lower and middle classes in America, finding the upper classes similar to those of England. While he found the "common people" of Virginia "more inclined to hospitality, and to live more contently on what they possessed" than in other parts of America, he described them as "rather of an indolent habit, and inclined to dissipation. Intoxication is very prevalent, and it is scarcely possible to meet with a man who does not begin the day with taking one, two, or more drams, as soon as he rises. . .there is hardly a house to be found with two rooms in it, but where the inhabitants have a still."[17] Although Weld noted that the women of the region did not have the drunken habits of the men, "their morals are in like manner relaxed."[18]

While in Philadelphia, Weld made sweeping generalizations about the appearance of American women: "the women, in general, whilst young, are very pretty; but by the time they become mothers of a little family they lose all their beauty, their complexions fade away, their teeth begin to decay, and they hardly appear like the same creatures."[19] He noticed the nearly universal decay of teeth with age for both men and women, but observed that the teeth of Black Americans and Indians remained bright and healthy.

Weld's *Travels* describes a variety of fascinating details about American society in 1796. He remarked that the people in the communities along the James River in Virginia, "are extremely fond of an entertainment which they call a barbacue. It consists in a large party meeting together, either under some trees, or in a house, to partake of sturgeon or pig roasted in the open air. . .an entertainment chiefly confined to the lower ranks, and like most others of the same nature, it generally ends in intoxication."[20] In Richmond he complained of widespread gambling, cockfighting, and billiard rooms "always full of a set of idle low-lived fellows."[21] Weld often found himself traveling beyond his original destinations in Maryland and Virginia "in order to avoid scenes of rioting and quarrelling that I have met with at the taverns."[22] "Whenever these people come to blows," Weld wrote, "they fight just like wild beasts, biting, kicking, and endeavouring to tear each other's eyes out with their nails. . .called gouging. . .but what is worse than all, these wretches in their combat endeavour to their utmost to tear out each other's testicles. Four or five instances came within my own observation."[23]

Weld also mentioned the resourcefulness of individuals and American society in general. In Pennsylvania he noted the first turnpike in the state which collected tolls on an improved road between Philadelphia and Lancaster. In Lancaster, Weld described in great detail the "rifled barrel guns. . .esteemed by the hunters, and are sent to every part of the country."[24] He was "surprised at finding so many men with military titles" in America but provided an explanation: "every freeman from the age of sixteen to fifty years, whose occupation does not absolutely forbid it, must enrol[l] himself in the militia. . .[which] is not assembled oftener than once in two or three mo[n]ths, and as it rests with every individual to provide himself with arms and accoutrements, and no stress being laid upon coming in uniform, the appearance of the men is not very military."[25]

Weld paid considerable attention to the working of the economy and understood the interrelationship of agriculture, trade, manufacturing, and finance in explaining economic growth. Americans were the most mobile people on earth, according to Weld, but they did "not change from place to place in this manner merely to gratify a wandering disposition; in every change he hopes to make money."[26] Weld concluded that "Americans of every class and description are actuated in all their movements; self-interest is always uppermost in their thoughts; it is the idol which they worship."[27] Americans, Weld noted, were always on the prowl for cheap land. Land speculation was rampant in the United States, often leading to "the most nefarious practices" of artificially raising land prices to swindle buyers.[28] Weld favored Britain's colony to the north where excessive land speculation was held in check by the government. Weld also disclosed the wide income disparity in America, particularly in Virginia, where "immense estates are held by a few individuals, who derive large incomes from them, whilst the generality of the people are but in a state of mediocrity."[29]

Although Weld observed fairly adequate slave quarters on plantations, he reflected the irony of owners "talking of the blessings of liberty" while their workers lived "in a state of bondage. . .there is ample cause for humanity to weep at the sight."[30] In contrast to the plantations of eastern Virginia, Weld found more equality among German settlers in the western part of the state where "poverty also is as much unknown in this country as great wealth. Each man owns the house he lives in and the land he cultivates, and every one appears to be in a happy state of mediocrity."[31]

In the summer of 1796 Weld left Philadelphia for New York City on the first leg of a trip to Canada. Just prior to his departure, he met two English travelers who were preparing to set off on the same journey. The small entourage passed through New Jersey and reembarked on a 55-foot Hudson River trading sloop in New York City, reaching Albany at four o'clock in the morning on July 4. "A drum and trumpet, towards the middle of the day," Weld wrote, "gave notice of the commencement of the rejoicing, and on walking to a hill about a quarter of a mile from the town," he observed 60 uniformed men fire a few volleys from their small arms and discharge a three-pound cannon before a group of 300 spectators.[32] Weld was surprised at the unremarkable celebration but mused that the "phlegmatic [self-possessed] people in this neighbourhood intent upon making money, and enjoying the solid advantages of the revolution, are but little disposed to waste their time in what they consider idle demonstrations of joy."[33] Weld viewed about 1,100 houses in Albany and noted that "in the old part of the town the streets are very narrow, and the houses frightful; they are all built in the old Dutch taste, with the gable end towards the street, and ornamented on the top with large iron weather-cocks; but in that part which has been lately erected, the streets are commodious, and many of the houses are handsome. . .the streets well paved and lighted."[34]

After a few days, Weld's party left Albany, stopping along the way to view Cohoes Falls which Weld sketched and later had engraved professionally in England. At Saratoga Weld found "the works thrown up. . .by the British and American armies during the war, there are now scarcely any remains."[35] Passing through Fort Edward, Weld discerned little of the old fort* but heard the detailed story of Jane McCrea's death (see chapter 9). Leaving Fort Edward, Weld traveled by carriage to Fort Ann on a long causeway, consisting "of large trees laid side by side transversely"; spaces between the logs caused the wheels to become stuck frequently.[38] Because of the rough ride over the logs, the English excursionists alighted from the carriage with their hunting weapons and walked parallel to the road through the woods, observing a forest "much more majestic. . .than any that we had before met with on our way from Philadelphia."[39] Between Fort Ann and Whitehall (formerly Skenesborough), where the road improved, the Englishmen returned to their carriage, but the exhausted horses stopped, requiring the driver to ride one of the animals bareback while an English servant coaxed the other horses along. After five hours the party finally reached Lake Champlain at Whitehall.

Isaac Weld was only one of several travelers to Lake Champlain in the 1790s. Most excursionists used the traditional Lake George route to reach Lake Champlain at Ticonderoga, but Weld sailed the entire length of the lake, beginning his voyage at Whitehall. Following a passage on Lake George, James Madison and Thomas Jefferson visited Ticonderoga and Crown Point in 1791. By then, Lake Champlain had become a thriving commercial waterway linking Canada to the United States. While staying at a tavern at Chimney Point, Vermont, Madison noted that the main exports via Lake Champlain were wheat, flour, pot and pearl ash with "trade of the lake. . .divided between Canada & N. York. . .The future & permanent course of trade will depend much on the improvements that may be made in the communication with the Hudson. Some preliminary steps have been taken by the Legislature of N. York, for connecting the navigation of this river [the lake south of Crown Point was often referred to as a river] with Wood Creek. . .Dry goods can be imported rather cheaper through Canada than through N. York with the present duties on them. Tobacco, French brandy, tropical fruits are smuggled from the U. S. through Lake Champlain into Canada."[40] Lumber was also a major item of commerce on the lake; two years before Madison and Jefferson's journey to the northern lakes, Reverend Nathan Perkins from Hartford, Connecticut, had scrutinized "a raft of Lumber. . .which covered an acre of water & had two huts on it."[41]

With plans for canals making headway in other parts of the United States, the New York legislature in 1792 authorized the incorporation of two private canal companies, the Western Inland Lock Navigation Company and the Northern Inland Lock Navigation Company, with Philip Schuyler, a senator and former major

---

*Peter Sailly (1754-1826), a notable Champlain Valley settler, described the remnants of Fort Edward in his 1784 diary: "the ruins of the rampart and ditch only remain. The rampart is built of wood and is quite high. The inclosure of the fort is not extensive. I saw beyond the fort a graveyard where were buried the officers and soldiers who died of wounds received in the attack upon Ticonderoga, on Lake Champlain, in 1758."[36] Sailly also visited Fort George which he found "yet in good repair" and at the site of Fort William Henry observed "the remains of old ramparts of earth. They were covered with wild cherry trees."[37]

general in the Continental Army, as president of the two companies. The Northern Company spent $100,000 surveying a route from the Hudson River to Lake Champlain along Wood Creek and clearing timber from the creek, but the project was found to be too expensive for the company to complete. Despite the failure, a vibrant trading relationship developed from the Richelieu River in Canada to the American communities along Lake Champlain.

"Timber Raft on Lake Champlain."
(Print, author's collection)

Aware of the plans for a canal through Wood Creek, Isaac Weld mused that Whitehall ("Skenesborough") would "doubtless, soon become a trading town of considerable importance" serving the downstate markets of Albany and New York City.[42] After finishing the Lake Champlain section of his journey, Weld entered the Richelieu River, disembarking at St. Jean, Quebec, where he hired a light wagon for the trip to La Prairie and Montreal. On the first of August he departed from Montreal on a sailing bateau for Quebec City. His description of Quebec included an account of the 1759 battle between the forces of Major General James Wolfe and Lieutenant General Louis-Joseph de Montcalm. This integration of history with his travels, also used in other parts of his book, would be a forerunner of popular nineteenth-century guidebooks of North America. Weld's work, however, also delved into the details of the economy, trade, climate, and agriculture.

Weld and his party planned a visit to Niagara Falls and returned to Montreal by carriage to make preparations for the next excursion. At Montreal he procured "a large travelling tent, and camp equipage, buffalo skins [for bedding], a store of dried provisions, kegs of brandy and wine" for a voyage west in a large bateau on the St. Lawrence River and Lake Ontario.[43] On September 7 Weld left Kingston, Ontario, arriving at Fort Niagara three days later. He was not disappointed with Niagara Falls "which may justly be ranked amongst the greatest natural curiosities in the known world."[44] Weld then followed the Niagara River to Lake Erie and sailed west, eventually reaching Detroit in October 1796. Sailing for Presque Isle (present-day

Whitehall Harbor.
(Gayer Collection, New York State Library)

Erie, Pennsylvania) on Lake Erie on the return trip, Weld had a memorable voyage aboard an overcrowded schooner. During a fierce storm the vessel nearly sank as shrieking, seasick passengers frantically "began to write their wills on scraps of paper."[45] Because of the damaged condition of the schooner, plans to land at Presque Isle were abandoned and Weld disembarked at Fort Erie. At nearby Buffalo Creek, Weld hired Indians to guide him through the forests of western New York. Forced to walk along rivers too shallow for boats, Weld and his party finally found part of the Tyoga River deep enough for canoes and subsequently navigated the Susquehannah River to Wilkes-Barre, Pennsylvania, reaching Philadelphia in December. The following month Weld departed from New York City for home.

Despite Weld's harsh descriptions of the Americans whom he met on his journey, he mentioned some positive characterizations of the fledging nation, including an equitable justice system: "there is no country, perhaps, in the world, where justice is more impartially administered, or more easily obtained by those who have been injured."[46] He was also an admirer of the spectacular natural wonders of America. Although Weld maintained that "when abroad he had not the most distant intention of publishing his travels," his book, *Travels through the States of North America and the Provinces of Upper and Lower Canada, During the Years 1795, 1796, and 1797*, was published in one quarto volume in 1799, illustrated with drawings by Weld which were engraved in London. The work was reprinted in two volumes in 1800 and 1807 and translated into French in 1800 and Italian in 1819; two German versions and a Dutch version were also published. Weld's criticisms of America in the book did not go unanswered. Timothy Dwight, president of Yale College, later wrote that he had been induced to write *Travels in New-England and New-York* because "misrepresentations, which foreigners, either through error or design had published of my native country. . .The United States have been regarded by this class of men as fair game, to be hunted down at pleasure."[47]

The success of Isaac Weld's book brought him instant recognition. He was elected a member of the Historical and Literary Society of Quebec and the Royal Dublin Society. In 1801 the lord lieutenant of Ireland enlisted Weld to write a position paper on emigration to North America in an effort to redirect settlers from America to Canada. (As a result of his work, he was promised accession to his father's lucrative Irish customs post, but when his father died in 1824, the position no longer provided an adequate income.) In 1802 Weld married Alexandria Home in Edinburgh; no children resulted from the marriage. Weld enhanced his stature as a topographer in 1807 with the publication of *Illustrations of the Scenery of Killarney and the Surrounding Country*, which included 18 engravings of his scenic drawings. During his journeys on the lakes of southwest Ireland to depict the scenes for the book, Weld used a boat that he had constructed from compressed brown paper. Eight years later, in the spring of 1815, Weld and his wife made a perilous 758-mile voyage aboard the 14-horsepower steamboat *Thames* from Dublin, Ireland, to Limehouse (East London).

In 1838, as the senior honorary secretary of the Royal Dublin Society, Weld compiled the *Statistical Survey of the County of Roscommon* which recommended industrial exhibitions, including the triennial exhibitions which were later adopted by the Society. In 1849 Weld became vice president of the Royal Dublin Society.

In his later years Weld traveled widely in Italy. His half-brother, Charles Richard Weld (1813-1869), also traveled extensively, writing a series of tour books, including *A Vacation Tour in the United States and Canada* published in London in 1855 which he dedicated to Isaac Weld.* On August 4, 1856, Isaac Weld died at the age of 81 near Bray in the county of Dublin.

The following edited version of Isaac Weld's *Travels* covers his trip from Whitehall, New York, to the rapids at Chambly, Quebec, during the summer of 1796.

---

*Charles Weld had toured both Lake George and Lake Champlain, but his excursion was marred by smoke from forest fires in the Adirondack Mountains.[48]

Travels Through the States of North America[49]

We at last reached the little town of Skenesborough,* much to the amusement of every one who beheld our equipage, and much to our own satisfaction; for, owing to the various accidents we had met with, such as traces [straps connecting the harness] breaking, bridles slipping off the heads of horses, and the noble horses themselves sometimes slipping down, &c. &c. we had been no less than five hours in travelling the last twelve miles [from Fort Ann].

Skenesborough stands just above the junction of Wood Creek with South River, as it is called in the best maps, but which, by the people in the neighbourhood, is considered as a part of Lake Champlain. At present there are only about twelve houses in the place; but if the navigation of Wood Creek is ever opened, so as to connect Lake Champlain with the North River [Hudson River], a scheme which has already been seriously thought of, it will, doubtless, soon become a trading town of considerable importance, as all the various productions of the shores of the lake will then be collected there for the New York and Albany markets.** Notwithstanding all the disadvantages of a land carriage of forty miles to the North River, a small portion of flour and pot-ash, the staple commodities of the state of New York, is already sent to Skenesborough from different parts of the lake, to be forwarded to Albany. A considerable trade also is carried on through this place, and over Lake Champlain, between New York and Canada. Furs and horses principally are sent from Canada, and in return they get East Indian goods and various manufactures. Lake Champlain opens a very ready communication between New York and the country bordering on the St. Lawrence; it is emphatically called by the Indians, Caniad—Eri Guarunte, the mouth or the door of the country.***

Skenesborough is most dreadfully infested with m[o]squitoes; so many of them attacked us the first night of our sleeping there, that when we arose in the morning our faces and hands were covered all over with large pustules, precisely like those of a person in the small pox. This happened too, notwithstanding that the people of the house, before we went to bed, had taken all the pains possible to clear the

---

*In 1786 the town of Skenesborough was reorganized under the name of Whitehall.

**The Northern Inland Lock Navigation Company, incorporated in 1792, stimulated considerable discussion in the region.[50] Little progress was made on the proposed canal, which would have connected the Hudson River to Lake Champlain at Whitehall through Wood Creek, before the project was abandoned. In 1793 Benjamin Lincoln, a former major general in the Continental Army who had been appointed by George Washington as an Indian commissioner, also commented on the canal. Lincoln suggested that the "waters of an eastern Wood Creek, which empty into Lake Champlain, may with great ease be united with the waters of the Hudson, near Fort Edward. . .[with] some canals and locks made in different places, which business is now commenced, and will, I presume, be completed without difficulty, a water communication will be opened to a great part of the state of Vermont. . .it will open communication by water with Quebec, so that the waters of the Hudson and the St. Lawrence will be united."[51] The Champlain Canal, uniting the Hudson River and the lake at Whitehall, did not open until 1823, while the Chambly Canal, which provided a continuous waterway between the St. Lawrence River and Lake Champlain, was not opened until 1843.

***In early 1756 Major General William Johnson sent a letter to England with the papers and maps of Jean-Armand Dieskau. In the packet, Johnson provided a detailed sketch of the region with explanations of various names, noting that the Indians called Lake Champlain "Caniadere-guaront which. . .signiff[i]es the Lac [lake] that is ye Gate or Door."[52]

room of them, by fumigating it with the smoke of green wood, and afterwards securing the windows with gauze blinds; and even on the second night, although we destroyed many dozens of them on the walls, after a similar fumigation had been made, yet we suffered nearly as much. These insects were of a much larger size than I ever saw elsewhere, and their bite was uncommonly venomous. General Washington told me, that he never was so much annoyed by m[o]squitoes in any part of America as in Skenesborough, for that they used to bite through the thickest boot.* The situation of the place is indeed peculiarly favourable for them, being just on the margin of a piece of water, almost stagnant, and shaded with thick woods.

Shortly after our arrival in Skenesborough, we hired a small boat of about ten tons for the purpose of crossing Lake Champlain. It was our wish to proceed on the voyage immediately; but the owner of the boat asserting that it was impossible to go out with the wind then blowing, we were for three days detained in Skenesborough, a delicious feast for the hungry m[o]squitoes. The wind shifted again and again, still it was not fair in the opinion of our boatman. At last, being most heartily tired of our quarters, and suspecting that he did not understand his business as well as he ought to have done, we resolved not to abide by his opinion any longer, but to make an attempt at beating out; and we had great reason to be pleased with having done so, as we arrived in Canada three days before any of the other boats, that did not venture to move till the wind was quite aft.

We set off about one o'clock; but from the channel being very narrow, it was impossible to make much way by tacking. We got no farther than six miles before sun-set. We then stopped, and having landed, walked up to some farm houses, which appeared at a distance, on the Vermont shore [probably in present-day West Haven], to procure provisions; for the boatman had told us it was quite unnecessary to take any at Skenesborough, as there were excellent houses close to the shore the whole way, where we could get whatever we wished. At the first we went to, which was a comfortable log-house, neither bread, nor meat, nor milk, nor eggs, were to be had; the house was crowded with children of all ages, and the people, I suppose, thought they had but little enough for themselves. At a second house, we found a venerable old man at the door, reading a news-paper, who civilly offered it to us for our perusal, and began to talk upon the politics of the day; we thanked him for his offer, and gave him to understand, at the same time, that a loaf would be much more acceptable. Bread there was none; we got a new Vermont cheese, however. A third house now remained in sight, and we made a third attempt at procuring something to eat. This one was nearly half a mile off, but, alas! it afforded still less than the last; the people had nothing to dispose of but a little milk. With the milk and the cheese, therefore, we returned to our boat, and adding thereto some biscuits and wine, which we had luckily on board, the whole afforded us a frugal repast.

The people at the American farm houses will cheerfully lie three in a bed, rather than suffer a stranger to go away who comes to seek for a lodging. As all these houses, however, which we had visited, were crowded with inhabitants, we felt no great inclination to ask for accommodation at any of them, but determined to sleep on board our little vessel. We accordingly moored her at a convenient part of the shore,

*Isaac Weld had met George Washington and provided a lengthy eyewitness description of the first president in his book.[53] During July 1783 Washington had made an inspection tour of the military posts in the region, stopping at a tavern in the town of Fort Edward and visiting Fort George, Fort Ticonderoga, and Crown Point.[54]

and each of us having wrapped himself up in a blanket, which we had been warned to provide on leaving New York, we laid ourselves down to sleep. The boat was decked two-thirds of her length forward, and had a commodious hold; we gave the preference, however, because more airy, to the cabin or after part, fitted up with benches, and covered with a wooden awning, under which a man could just sit upright, provided he was not very tall. The benches, which went lengthwise, accommodated two of us; and the third was obliged to put up with the cabin floor; but a blanket and a bare board, out of the way of m[o]squitoes, were luxuries after our accommodations at Skenesborough; our ears were not assailed by the noise even of a single one the whole night, and we enjoyed sounder repose than we had done for many nights preceding.

The wind remained nearly in the same point the next morning, but the lake being wider, we were enabled to proceed faster. We stopped at one house to breakfast, and at another to dine. At neither of these, although they bore the name of taverns, were we able to procure much more than at the houses where we had stopped the preceding evening. At the first we got a little milk, and about two pounds of bread, absolutely the whole of what was in the house; and at the second, a few eggs and some cold salted fat pork; but not a morsel of bread was to be had. The wretched appearance also of this last habitation was very striking; it consisted of a wooden frame, merely with a few boards nailed against it, the crevices between which were the only apertures for the admission of light, except the door; and the roof was so leaky, that we were sprinkled with the rain even as we sat at the fireside. That people can live in such a manner, who have the necessaries and conveniences of life within their reach, as much as any others in the world, is really most astonishing! It is, however, to be accounted for, by that desire of making money, which is the predominant feature in the character of the Americans in general, and leads the petty farmer in particular to suffer numberless inconveniences, when he

Romanticized view of Ticonderoga showing the boat landing and Larabee's Point on the right. Detail of a drawing by Harry Fenn from *Picturesque America* edited by William Cullen Bryant. (Author's collection)

can gain by so doing. If he can sell the produce of his land to advantage, he keeps a small part of it as possible for himself, and lives the whole year round upon salt provisions, bad bread, and the fish he can catch in the rivers or lakes in the neighbourhood; if he has built a comfortable house for himself, he readily quits it, as soon as finished, for money, and goes to live in a mere hovel in the woods till he gets time to build another. Money is his idol, and to procure it he gladly foregoes every self-gratification.*

From this miserable habitation, just mentioned, we departed as soon as the rain was over, and the wind coming round in our favour, we got as far as Ticonderoga that night. The only dwelling here is the tavern, which is a large house built of stone. On entering it we were shown into a spacious apartment, crowded with boatmen and people that had just arrived from St. John's [St. Jean], in Canada. Seeing such a number of guests in the house, we expected nothing less than to be kept an hour or two till sufficient supper was prepared for the whole company, so that all might sit down at once together, which, as I have before said, is the custom in the country parts of the United States. Our surprise therefore was great at perceiving a neat table and a comfortable little supper speedily laid out for us, and no attempts made at serving the rest of the company till we had quite finished. This was departing from the system of equality in a manner which we had never witnessed before, and we were at a loss for some time to account for it; but we presently heard that the woman of the house had kept a tavern for the greater part of her life at Quebec, which resolved the knotty point. The wife is generally the active person in managing a country tavern, and the husband attends to his farm, or has some independent occupation. The man of this house was a judge, a sullen demure old gentleman, who sat by the fire,** with tattered clothes and dishevelled locks, reading a book, totally regardless of every person in the room.***

The old fort and barracks of Ticonderoga are on the top of a rising ground, just

---

*This is one of Weld's favorite criticisms, sprinkled throughout his book of *Travels*. Visiting America in 1827, Frances Trollope (1780-1863) subsequently wrote *Domestic Manners of the Americans* (published 1832), in which she compared Americans to bees in a hive "actively employed in search of that honey of Hybla, vulgarly called money; neither art, science, learning, nor pleasure can seduce them from its pursuit."[55]

**Weld's own footnote: "Though this was the 14th day of July, the weather was so cold that we found a fire extremely agreeable."[56]

***The tavern was located in the "Old King's Store" which in later years was described as being "near the present steamboat landing from [Lake] Champlain at Ticonderoga."[57] Charles Hay had been a prosperous merchant in Montreal when the American Revolution began. Rejecting a British commission to enter the war against the Americans, Hay was imprisoned for several years during the war. He was released after suing for false imprisonment and later moved to Poughkeepsee, New York. After spending two years in business in the Fort George area, Hay moved to Ticonderoga where he became a judge. His brother, Udney Hay, had been the deputy quartermaster general at Fort Ticonderoga in 1777.

In May 1791 James Madison and Thomas Jefferson stayed at the inn during their Lake George-Lake Champlain tour. Jefferson rated the accommodations as "midling."[58] In July 1800, 24-year-old Abigail May of Boston also stayed at the tavern, then operated by the widow of Judge Hay: "she gave us a fine dinner, of Chickens, Ham, green Peas, Cucumbers, Custards &cc—after which we amused ourselves with reading, and viewing the Lake—the Piazza stands over it, and Commands a view charming indeed."[59] In August 1805 Elkanah Watson described the tavern as an "old one story long stone house kept by Mother Hays, a squat old Englishwoman."[60]

"Ticonderoga" from the *Cyclopedia of Useful Knowledge.*
(Author's collection)

behind the tavern; they are quite in ruins,* and it is not likely that they will ever be rebuilt, for the situation is very insecure, being commanded by a lofty hill called Mount Defiance. The British got possession of the place [during] the last war by dragging cannon and mortars up the hill, and firing down upon the fort.**

Early the next morning we left Ticonderoga, and pursued our voyage to Crown Point, where we landed to look at the old fort. Nothing is to be seen there, however,

---

*In 1784 Peter Sailly (accompanied by William Gilliland) visited Fort Ticonderoga, noting that the fort consisted of "double ramparts of very high and strong walls of stone. . .We saw the retrenchments of the French and English armies in the vicinity. . .The Americans in the late war built a bridge across the lake which separates Mount Independence from Ticonderoga. We saw its remains. We also saw the ruins of several batteries, which the French erected to guard the entrance of the lake [Lotbinière Battery]."[61] Probably one of the best descriptions from this period was written in 1800 by young Abigail May, who found "the ruins, much more magnificent then I supposed existed in our new country, built of stone, and the stone alone remaining—wood, glass, all devour'd by the insatiable monster [carted away by settlers]—but the chimnies are intire, the walls of the houses, and peaks of the roof—the windows and door frames—the ramparts, fortifications (or whatever name they bear) yet remain—but over grown with nettles and weeds, such a scene of desolation I never beheld—we alighted, I paced over the stones awe struck—this, said our guide was the house of the commanding officer—I paus'd—w[h]ere now is thy distinction, thought I, as I passed what once was the threshold, a cold chill ran through my veins, Ah! thought I, how often has a proud step and gay heart passed thee, that now beats no more—we were sh[o]wn the sally ports [gates]—the Guard room—the bakers room—and descended into some subterraneous cells supposed to be places of confinement—A powder room &cc—our guide though he knew a great deal—but I wish'd he knew more, I wanted to know. . .every particular, of a spot that interested my feelings so much—but could obtain very imperfect information—that a vast sight of blood has been spilt on [this] spot, all agree—for several miles round, every object confirms it—the heaps of stones on which the soldiers used to cook—the ditches, now grass grown, and forsaken graves !! all, every thing makes this spot teem with melancholy reflections—I knew not how to leave it, and ascended the waggon with regret—I should like to pass a day there alone."[62] Five years later Elkanah Watson suggested that the ruins of Ticonderoga exhibited "the appearance of an ancient castle of Europe, enveloped in the mist of ages."[63]

**In July 1777 British troops of Lieutenant General John Burgoyne's invasion force succeeded in hauling cannon to the summit of Mount Defiance, forcing the American army under Major General Arthur St. Clair to evacuate Fort Ticonderoga and Mount Independence.

"Fort Ticonderoga." Oil on canvas by Samuel W. Griggs.
(Adirondack Museum)

but a heap of ruins; for shortly before it was given up by the British, the powder magazine blew up, by which accident a great part of the works was destroyed;* since the evacuation of it also, the people in the neighbourhood have been continually digging in the different parts, in hopes of procuring lead and iron shot; a considerable quantity was in one instance got out of the stores that had been buried by the explosion. The vaults, which were bomb-proof, have been demolished for the sake of the bricks for building chimneys. At the south side alone the ditches remain perfect; they are wide and deep, and cut through immense rocks of limestone; and from being overgrown towards the top with different kinds of shrubs, have a grand and picturesque appearance. The view from this spot of the fort, and the old buildings in it overgrown with ivy, of the lake, and of the distant mountains beyond it, is indeed altogether very fine. The fort and seven hundred acres of good cleared land adjoining to it, are the property of the state of New York, and are leased out at the rate of one hundred and fifty dollars, equal to 33£.10s. sterling per annum, which is appropriated for the use of a college.** The farmer who rented it told us,

---

*In 1773 the British fort at Crown Point was substantially damaged by a fire accidently started by two wives of soldiers who were boiling soap. The cause of the fire resulted in a contentious court of inquiry (see chapter 7).

**Acting on an agreement made in 1796, the New York State legislature in 1801 formally conveyed the land at the Crown Point forts to Columbia and Union Colleges. The grounds thereafter passed through a series of private owners, but in 1910, 26 acres, including the garrison grounds of Fort St.

he principally made use of the land for grazing cattle; these, in the winter season, when the lake is frozen, he drove over the ice to Albany, and there disposed of.

Crown Point is the most advantageous spot on the shores of Lake Champlain for a military post, not being commanded by any rising grounds in the neighbourhood, as Ticonderoga is; and as the lake is so narrow here, owing to another point running out on the opposite side, that it would be absolutely impossible for a vessel to pass, without being exposed to the fire of the fort. The Indians call this place Tek-ya-dough-nigarigee, that is, the two points immediately opposite to each other*: the one opposite to Crown Point is called Chimney Point: upon it are a few houses, one of which is a tavern.** While we staid there we were very agreeably surprised, for the first time, with the sight of a large birch canoe upon the lake, navigated by two or three Indians in the dresses of their nation. They made for the shore and soon landed; and shortly after another party, amounting to six or seven, arrived, that had come by land.***

Lake Champlain is about one hundred and twenty miles in length, and is of various breadths: for the first thirty miles, that is, from South River [southern section of Lake Champlain] to Crown Point, it is in no place more than two miles wide; beyond this, for the distance of twelve miles, it is five or six miles across, but then again it narrows, and again at the end of a few miles expands. That part called the Broad Lake, because broader than any other, commences about twenty-five miles north of Crown Point, and is eighteen miles [actually 12 miles] across in the widest part. Here the lake is interspersed with a great number of islands, the largest of which, formerly called Grande Isle, now South Hero, is fifteen [12] miles in length, and, on average, about four in breadth. The soil of this island is fertile, and it is said that five hundred people are settled upon it. The Broad Lake is nearly fifty miles in length, and gradually narrows till it terminates in a large river called Chambly, Rich[e]lieu, or Sorelle, which runs into the St. Lawrence.

The soundings of Lake Champlain, except at the narrow parts at either end, are in general very deep; in many places sixty and seventy, and in some even one hundred

Frédéric and Crown Point, were deeded back to the state of New York by the Witherbee, Sherman and Co., of Port Henry. Today the site is operated by New York State's Office of Parks, Recreation and Historic Preservation.

*Major General William Johnson's dispatches to England in January 1756 mentioned that "the Entrance between Fort St. Frederic & Crown PT. into the Lake ye Indians call Tek'-ya-doughniyariga signifying two Points of high Land opposite to each other."[64]

**Chimney Point has had a long history of occupation, first by Native Americans and then by Europeans. In 1690 Captain Jacobus de Warm was sent by the governor of New York to construct an advance post near Crown Point; two months later Chimney Point became the site of a "little stone fort."[65] French soldiers and workmen built a small stockaded fort on the point in 1731 before the construction of Fort St. Frédéric. When the French army departed from the region, only the chimneys of the homes of French settlers remained standing on the east side of the lake, hence the name (based on tradition). In the late eighteenth century a tavern at Chimney Point served travelers on the lake, including James Madison and Thomas Jefferson. After the turn of the twentieth century, the inn was known as Hotel St. Frederic; the building is now the Chimney Point State Historic Site and may encompass some of the ruins of the original forts of 1690 and 1731.

***Isaac Weld provides a long account (omitted here) of "Captain Thomas, a chief of the Cachenonaga nation," who "had along with him at Chimney Point thirty horses, and a quantity of furs in the canoe, which he was taking for sale to Albany."[66]

fathoms.* In proportion to its breadth and depth, the water is more or less clear; in the broad part it is as pure and transparent as possible.** On the west side, as far as Cumberland Bay, the lake is bounded for the most part by steep mountains close to the edge of the water; at Cumberland Bay the ridge of mountains runs off to the north-west, and the shore farther on is low and swampy. The East or Vermont shore is not much elevated, except in a few particular places; at the distance of twelve miles, however, from the lake, is a considerable mountain. The shores on both sides are very rocky; where there are mountains these rocks jut out very boldly; but at the east side, where the land is low, they appear but a little above the water. The islands also, for the most part, are surrounded with rocks, in some parts, shelving down into the lake, so that it is dangerous to approach within one or two miles of them at particular sides. From some parts of the eastern shore the rocks also run out in the same manner for a considerable distance. Sailing along the shore when a breeze is blowing, a hollow murmuring noise is always heard from the waters splashing into the crannies of these rocks. There are many streams which fall into the lake: the mouths of all those on the western side are obstructed by falls, so that none of them are navigable.*** Of those on the eastern or Vermont side, a few only are navigable for small boats, and that for a short distance.†

The scenery along various parts of the lake is extremely grand and picturesque, particularly beyond Crown Point; the shores are there beautifully ornamented with hanging woods and rocks, and the mountains on the western side rise up in ranges one behind the other in the most magnificent manner.‡ It was on one of the finest evenings possible that we passed along this part of the lake, and the sun setting in all his glory behind the mountains, spread the richest tints over every part of the prospect; the moon also appearing nearly in the full, shortly after the day had closed,

---

*The deepest part of the lake (400 feet) lies north of Split Rock and west of McNeil Cove (Charlotte, Vermont).

**Other contemporary travelers also mentioned the water quality of Lake Champlain. In 1791 Thomas Jefferson suggested that the lake was "narrow and turbid from Ticonderoga to beyond the Split rock about 30 miles, where it is said to widen and grow more clear."[67] Jefferson, however, had traveled only as far as Crown Point. In 1802 Timothy Dwight characterized the water at Ticonderoga as "turbid with clay, and disgusting to the eye."[68]

***The Upper Mouth and Lower Mouth of the Ausable River may have been among the tributaries on the western shore that Weld noticed. In 1805 Elkanah Watson explored the river and observed the Grand Flume of Ausable Chasm: "Adgates Falls, and the passage of the river among cloven rocks. . .About one mile below the falls, we crossed the High Bridge, formed by timbers which span a chasm of forty-five feet in width, and one hundred and thirty feet, at this point, in depth. Travellers who have descended to the base of this abyss, pronounce it one of the most extraordinary and imposing natural curiosities in America, not exceeded in the interest and solemnity with which it impresses the mind—although of a totally different character—by the cataract of Niagara. Yet these amazing scenes are rarely visited, and are scarcely known to exist."[69]

†Weld was apparently unaware of Otter Creek, navigable for more than seven miles to Vergennes. In 1789 Reverend Nathan Perkins of Hartford, Connecticut, "viewed ye falls of ye Otter Creek & ye works there [sawmills, a gristmill, iron forge, and brewery]. The falls 40 feet, a great curiosity."[70] Arnold's Bay, on the east side of the lake south of Otter Creek, was another point of interest visited by a few contemporary travelers. In 1805 Elkanah Watson observed the remains of Benedict Arnold's fleet of 1776, "lying in charred and blackened fragments in a deep bay."[71]

‡Viewing the shoreline in 1784, Peter Sailly remarked that "in general I have never in my life seen anything which approaches the beauty [of] the borders of Lake Champlain, although they are uninhabited."[72]

afforded us an opportunity of beholding the surrounding scenery in fresh though less brilliant colors. Our little bark was now gliding smoothly along, whilst every one of us remained wrapt up in silent contemplation of the solemn scene, when suddenly she struck upon one of the shelving rocks: nothing but hurry and confusion was now visible on board, every one lending his assistance; however, at last, with some difficulty, we got her off; but in a minute she struck a second time, and after we had again extricated her, even a third and a fourth time; at last she stuck so fast, that for a short time we despaired of being able to move her. At the end of a quarter of an hour, however, we again fortunately got her into deep water. We had before suspected that our boatman did not know a great deal about navigation of the lake, and on questioning him now, it came out, that he had been a cob[b]ler all his life, till within the last nine months, when he thought proper to change business, and turn sailor. All the knowledge he had of the shores of the lake, was what he had picked up during that time, as he sailed straight backward and forward between St. John's and Skenesborough. On the present occasion he had mistaken one bay for another, and had the waves been as high as they sometimes are, the boat would inevitably have been dashed to pieces.

The humble roof of another judge, a plain Scotch labourer, afforded us shelter for this night. It was near eleven o'clock, however, when we got there, and the family having retired to rest, we had to remain rapping and calling at the door for half an hour at least, before we could get admittance. The people at last being roused, opened their doors, cheerfully got us some supper, and prepared their best beds for us. In the morning, having paid our reckoning to the judge, he returned to his plough, and we to our boat to prosecute our voyage.

We set off this day with a remarkable fine breeze, and being desirous of terminating our voyage as soon as possible, of which we began now to be somewhat tired, we stopped but once in the course of the day, and determined to sail all night. A short time after sunset we passed the boundary between the British dominions and the United States. Here we were brought to by an armed brig of twenty guns, under English colours, stationed for the purpose of examining all boats passing up and down the lake; the answers which we gave to the several questions asked being satisfactory, we were accordingly suffered to proceed. Since the surrender of the posts, pursuant to the late treaty with the United States, this brig has been removed, and laid up at St. John's.* When night came on, we wrapped ourselves up in our blankets, as we had done on the first night of our voyage, and laid down upon the cabin floor, where we might possibly have slept until we got to St. John's, had we not been awakened at midnight by the loud hollas of the sentinel at the British fort on Isle aux Noix.** On examining into the matter, it appeared that the boat had

---

*Sailing south on the Richelieu River in 1793, Benjamin Lincoln was forced to "report ourselves again to a British garrison, thence to a British armed vessel which was anchored near the fort" at Point au Fer.[73] The armed vessel was the schooner *Maria*, used by the British at the Battle of Valcour Island. In 1794 the *Maria* was replaced by the 16-gun schooner *Royal Edward* (built in 1779).[74] Point au Fer was legally ceded to New York by Jay's Treaty, ratified by the Senate on June 24, 1795, and slated to be implemented on June 1, 1796. However, during Weld's journey in July 1796, the *Royal Edward* was apparently still at Point au Fer.

**At Isle-aux-Noix in 1784 Peter Sailly found "four forts on the island. . .Three of the forts are not garrisoned."[75] William Twiss, the engineer who accompanied Lieutenant General John Burgoyne's army to Ticonderoga in 1777 (chapter 9), had supervised construction of several redoubts on the island in 1782.[76] During the War of 1812, the island became an important military base and shipbuilding

been driven on shore, while our sleepy pilot enjoyed his nap at the helm; and the sentinel, unable to imagine what we were about, seeing the boat run up close under the fort, and suspicious of some attack, I suppose, had turned out the whole guard; by whom, after being examined and re-examined, we were finally dismissed. We now took the command of the boat upon ourselves, for the boatman, although he was more anxious to get to St. John's than any one of us, and though he had himself in some measure induced us to go on, was so sleepy that he could not keep his eyes open. Relieving each other at the helm, we reached St. John's by day-break; one hundred and fifty miles distant from Skenesborough.

Immediately on our landing we were conducted to the guard house, where we had to deliver to the serjeant on duty, to be by him forwarded to the commanding officer, an account of our names, occupation, and place of abode, the strictest orders having been issued by the governor not to suffer any Frenchmen or other foreigners, or any people who could not give an exact account of their business in Canada, to enter into the country.

Fort Chambly. Engraving by J.& C. Walker from an aquatint by J. Bouchette.
(Author's collection)

St. John's is a garrison town; it contains about fifty miserable wooden dwellings, and barracks, in which a whole regiment is generally quartered. The fortifications are entirely out of order, so much so that it would be cheaper to erect fresh works than to attempt to repair them. There is a king's dock yard here, well stored with timber, at least when we saw it; but in the course of the summer, after the armed brig which I mentioned was laid up, all the timber was sold off. The old hulks of

center. Fort Lennox, the largest fortification ever built on the island, was constructed between 1819 and 1829. Today the fort is a National Historic Park open to the public.

several vessels of force were lying opposite the yard.* In proportion to the increase of trade between New York and Lower Canada, this town must improve, as it is the British port of entry on Lake Champlain.

The country about St. John's is flat, and very bare of trees, a dreadful fire in the year 1788 having done great mischief, and destroyed all the wood for several miles: in some parts of the neighborhood the people suffer extremely during winter from the want of fuel.

At St. John's we hired a light waggon, similar to those made use of in the United States, and set off about noon for La Prairie, on the banks of the river St. Lawrence. By the direct road this is only eighteen miles distant; but the most agreeable way of going thither is by Chambly, which is a few miles farther, on account of seeing the old castle built there by the French. The castle stands close to the rapids in Chambly or Sorell River, and at a little distance has a grand appearance; the adjacent country also being very beautiful; the whole together forms a most interesting scene. The castle is in tolerably good repair, and a garrison is constantly kept in it.**

Notes:

1. Isaac Weld, *Travels Through the States of North America* (1799; reprint ed., New York: Johnson Reprint Corporation, 1968), Volume 1, preface iii, Volume 2, 376; See also *The Dictionary of National Biography*, Volume 20 (London: Oxford University Press, 1921-1922), 1070.
2. Weld, 1: 300-301.
3. Ibid., preface iii.
4. Ibid., 103.
5. Ibid., 102.
6. Ibid., 103.
7. Ibid., 102.
8. Ibid., 413.
9. Ibid., 108-9.
10. Ibid., preface iv.
11. Ibid.
12. Ibid., 30.
13. Ibid., 134-35.

*The names of the ships that Isaac Weld observed are unknown. However, a large number of vessels used during the Revolutionary War are believed to have ended their careers at St. Jean, including vessels taken from the Americans—the cutter *Lee*, galleys *Trumbull* and *Washington*, gondolas *Jersey* and *Loyal Convert*, and schooner *Liberty*. The British vessels eventually laid up at St. Jean probably included the ships *Inflexible* and *Royal George*, schooners *Carleton* and *Maria*, and five supply vessels (ranging from 42 to 65 feet in length): the *Camel*, *Commissary*, *Delivery*, *Ration*, *Receipt*, and six 30-foot, sloop-rigged tenders: *Dilligence*, *Dispatch*, *Lookout*, *Nautilus*, *Spitfire*, and *Spy*.[77] The radeau *Thunderer* had sunk near Windmill Point after colliding with a rock in late 1777, and two vessels were acquired by Gideon King of Burlington in 1790 for commercial purposes. Some of the other vessels were probably sold as well. Many of the remaining vessels were destroyed during the construction of the Chambly Canal (1831-1843).

**Three years earlier Benjamin Lincoln had described Fort Chambly as "a handsome well-built fort."[79] Originally built as a wood structure in 1665 by Captain Jacques de Chambly, the fort guarded the gateway to the Richelieu River and safeguarded French colonists from marauding Iroquois. Rebuilt as a stone fortification between 1709 and 1711, Fort Chambly was captured by British forces under Major Robert Rogers and Colonel John Darby in 1760. The fort was seized by the Americans under Brigadier General Richard Montgomery in 1775 but evacuated the following year during the American retreat from Canada. Garrisoned by British troops until 1870, the fort thereafter fell into disrepair. In 1983 Parks Canada began a restoration and reconstruction of the fort and today it is open to the public.

14. Ibid., 234.
15. Ibid., 2: 375.
16. Ibid., 1: 290.
17. Ibid., 206.
18. Ibid.
19. Ibid., 22.
20. Ibid., 187.
21. Ibid., 191.
22. Ibid., 192.
23. Ibid.
24. Ibid., 117.
25. Ibid., 237-38.
26. Ibid., 126-27.
27. Ibid.; During the Lake Champlain trip, Weld again mentioned that for Americans "money is their idol." Ibid., 292.
28. Ibid., 403-5.
29. Ibid., 146.
30. Ibid., 149.
31. Ibid., 233.
32. Ibid., 272-73.
33. Ibid., 273.
34. Ibid., 271.
35. Ibid., 277.
36. Peter Sailly, "Diary of Peter Sailly on a Journey in America in the Year 1784," *New York State Library History Bulletin* 12 (February 1919): 63; In 1780 Francois-Jean, Marquis de Chastellux (1734-1788) described Fort Edward: "Formerly it consisted of a square, fortified by two bastions on the east side, and by two demi-bastions on the river side; but this old fortification has been abandoned, because it was too easily commanded from the heights, and a large redoubt, with a simple parapet and a wretched palisade, has been built on a more elevated spot: within are small barracks which can accommodate two hundred soldiers." Marquis de Chastellux, *Travels in North America in the Years 1780, 1781 and 1782*, trans. and ed. Howard C. Rice, Jr. (Williamsburg, Va.: Institute of Early American History and Culture, 1963), Volume 1, 215.
37. Sailly, 64.
38. Weld, 1: 280-81.
39. Ibid., 280.
40. J. Robert Maguire, ed., *The Tour to the Northern Lakes of James Madison & Thomas Jefferson May-June 1791* (Ticonderoga, N.Y.: Fort Ticonderoga, 1995), 16, 18; See also Robert A. Rutland et al., ed. *The Papers of James Madison* (Charlottesville: University of Virginia Press, 1983), Volume 14, 26-27.
41. Nathan Perkins, *A Narrative of a Tour through the State of Vermont* (Woodstock, VT.: The Elm Tree Press, 1920), 27; See also H. N. Muller, "Floating a Lumber Raft to Quebec City, 1805: The Journal of Guy Catlin of Burlington," *Vermont History* 39 (Spring 1971): 116-24.
42. Weld, 1: 284.
43. Weld, 2: 21.
44. Ibid., 108.
45. Ibid., 303.
46. Weld, 1: 130.
47. Timothy Dwight, *Travels in New-England and New-York* (London: William Baynes and Son, 1823), Volume 1, iv, xvi.
48. Charles Richard Weld, *A Vacation Tour in the United States and Canada* (London: Longman, Brown, Green, and Longmans, 1855), 84-85.
49. Weld, 1: 283-305; This passage is identical to earlier editions (including page numbers). See Isaac Weld, Jr., *Travels through the States of North America and the Provinces of Upper and Lower Canada, during the Years 1795, 1796, and 1797*, 3rd ed.(London: John Stockdale, 1800), Volume 1, 283-305.
50. Chilton Williamson, "New York's Struggle for Champlain Valley Trade 1760-1820," *Proceedings of the New York State Historical Association* 39 (October 1941): 431-32; See also Gertrude E.

Cone, "Studies in the Development of Transportation in the Champlain Valley to 1876," (M. A. thesis, The University of Vermont, 1945), 73.

51. Benjamin Lincoln, "Journal of a Treaty Held in 1793, with the Indian Tribes North-West of the Ohio, by Commissioners of the United States," *Collections of the Massachusetts Historical Society* 5 (3rd Series) (1836): 112.

52. Public Record Office, London, Colonial Office 5/46, University Publications of America microfilm reel 1, frame 639.

53. Weld, 1: 104-7.

54. John H. G. Pell, "General George Washington's Visit to Fort Ticonderoga in July 1783," *The Bulletin of the Fort Ticonderoga Museum* 14 (Fall 1983): 260-62; See also George Washington, "Expense Account of Washington," *New York History* 13 (1932): 180-81; John C. Fitzpatrick, ed., *The Writings of George Washington* (Washington, D.C.: U.S. Government Printing Office, 1938), Volume 27, 65-67.

55. Frances Trollope, *Domestic Manners of the Americans*, ed. John Lauritz Larson (St. James, N.Y.: Brandywine Press, 1993), 26; See also Roger Haydon, ed., *Upstate Travels: British Views of Nineteenth-Century New York* (Syracuse: Syracuse University Press, 1982), 6.

56. Weld, 1: 293.

57. Flavius J. Cook, *Home Sketches of Essex County: Ticonderoga* (Keeseville, N.Y.: W. Lansing & Son, 1858), 29.

58. Maguire, 33.

59. Abigail May, "The Journal of Abigail May," printed copy, New York State Historical Association, No. 1, 77 (see original in the Schlesinger Library of Radcliffe College of Havard University); See May's Lake George journal in Russell P. Bellico, *Chronicles of Lake George: Journeys in War and Peace* (Fleischmanns, N.Y.: Purple Mountain Press, 1995), 191-203.

60. Maguire, 10.

61. Sailly, 64-65.

62. May, 76; See also Bellico, 200.

63. Winslow C. Watson, ed., *Men and Times of the Revolution; or, Memoirs of Elkanah Watson* (New York: Dana and Company, Publishers, 1856), 353.

64. PRO, CO 5/46, University Publications of America microfilm 1, frame 639.

65. Guy Omeron Coolidge, *The French Occupation of the Champlain Valley from 1609 to 1759* (1938; reprint ed., Mamaroneck, N.Y.: Harbor Hill Books, 1989), 59.

66. Weld, 1: 296-98.

67. Maguire, 29.

68. Timothy Dwight, *Travels; in New-England and New-York* (New Haven, CT.: S. Converse, 1822), Volume 3, 342; See also Bellico, 212.

69. Watson, 356.

70. Perkins, 27; See also James E. Peterson, *Otter Creek: The Indian Road* (Salisbury, VT.: Dunmore House, 1990), 88.

71. Watson, 353.

72. Sailly, 66.

73. Lincoln, 175.

74. Allan S. Everest, *Point au Fer on Lake Champlain* (Plattsburgh, N.Y.: Clinton County Historical Association, 1992), 38.

75. Sailly, 66.

76. André Charbonneau, *The Fortifications of Ile aux Noix* (Ottawa: Minister of Supply and Services Canada, 1994), 100.

77. Haldimand Papers, National Archives of Canada, microfilm C-3242, Volume 722A, fol. 30-31, microfilm H-1649, Volume 1, B144, fol. 142.

78. Lincoln, 175.

Thomas Macdonough at Plattsburgh Bay. Engraving by J. B. Forrest
from a painting by John Wesley Jarvis.
(Author's collection)

Part VI: War of 1812

11. Thomas Macdonough 1814

OF ALL THE MEN AND WOMEN who ventured to Lake Champlain in the nineteenth century, only Thomas Macdonough achieved the status of a true national hero as a result of his tenure at the lake. On the day of the defeat of the British fleet at Plattsburgh Bay on September 11, 1814, a ferocious battle that Winston S. Churchill would later call "the most decisive engagement of the war," the 30-year-old master commandant wrote a simple message to William Jones, the secretary of the navy, "The Almighty has been pleased to Grant us a Signal Victory on Lake Champlain in the capture of one Frigate, one Brig, and two Sloops of War of the Enemy."[1] Theodore Roosevelt, writing in his book *Naval War of 1812*, praised Macdonough's skill and seamanship, suggesting that "Down to the time of the Civil War he is the greatest figure in our naval history. A thoroughly religious man, he was as generous and humane as he was skil[l]ful and brave; one of the greatest of our sea-captains, he has left a stainless name behind him."[2]

Thomas Macdonough was born on December 31, 1783, to Thomas McDonough and Mary Vance McDonough. The sixth of ten children, young Macdonough (who later changed the spelling of his name) spent his first year in a small log cabin six miles from present-day Middletown, Delaware, in New Castle County. In 1784 the family relocated to a large brick residence in the same area on lands owned by James McDonough, grandfather of young Thomas. Emigrating from Ireland, James McDonough had settled in rural Delaware in 1725 and subsequently became a physician. His eldest son, Thomas (father of our hero), also became a physician. In 1776, six years after his marriage to Mary Vance, Dr. Thomas McDonough was appointed a major in a battalion raised on a Continental basis in Delaware and participated in the campaigns of Long Island and White Plains where he was wounded. He later served on the Delaware Privy Council, as a colonel in the Delaware Militia (1781-1782), and as a judge in New Castle County.

When he was eight, Thomas Macdonough's mother and grandfather both died; three years later in 1795 his father also died. After attending a country school, Macdonough, then in his teens, worked as a clerk in nearby Middletown, Delaware. At the time, his older brother James appeared to have a more interesting life as a midshipman in the U. S. Navy, including duty on the frigate *Constellation*.* Using family connections, 16-year-old Thomas Macdonough "on the 5th February, 1800, . . .received a warrant as midshipman in the Navy. . .from John Adams, then President, through the influence of Mr. [Henry] Latimer, a Senator from the state of Delaware."[3]

Macdonough's first assignment involved action against French ships in the West Indies. With war flaring between Great Britain and France in the 1790s, the British navy began seizing neutral ships, including American vessels which were believed to be carrying contraband goods. The issue was settled in 1796 in Jay's Treaty, by which the Americans accepted the British stance on contraband goods in exchange for British withdrawal from military posts along the northern U. S. border. Perceiving the new American position as favoring the British, French naval ships began seizing American merchant vessels bound for British ports. When attacks on American shipping persisted, President John Adams ordered a naval offensive against French vessels (Quasi-War 1798-1800). On May 15, 1800, Macdonough was assigned to the 116-foot, 24-gun *Ganges* which later succeeded in capturing three French vessels. While on board the *Ganges*, Macdonough was felled by Yellow Fever and sent to "a dirty Spanish hospital" in Havana where he nearly died.[4]

After France finally acknowledged America's neutral rights in a peace treaty signed in 1801, many U. S. naval vessels were sold, including the *Ganges*, and a large number of crews and officers were discharged. Again connections aided Macdonough, who was retained in the service. In 1802 Macdonough sailed for the Mediterranean aboard the 164-foot, 36-gun frigate *Constellation*, assigned to end the menace of the Barbary corsairs of Algiers, Morocco, Tripoli, and Tunis. Encouraged by other maritime powers, the Barbary pirates were able to interfere with the merchant vessels of emerging maritime competitors such as the United States. American ships and crews were systematically seized and held for ransom by the North African pirates.

When diplomacy failed in the 1790s, construction of a number of powerful frigates was authorized by Congress. In 1803 Macdonough returned to the Mediterranean aboard the 157-foot, 36-gun frigate *Philadelphia*. The *Philadelphia*, unfortunately, was captured by the Tripolitans after running aground, while Macdonough was temporarily serving as the second officer aboard a captured Moorish vessel, the 30-gun *Meshboha*. Macdonough was reassigned to the 84-foot, 12-gun schooner *Enterprise*, commanded by Lieutenant Stephen Decatur, which had been dispatched along with the frigate *Constitution* under Captain Edward Preble to rescue the *Philadelphia*. After plans to recover the vessel were found to be impractical, Decatur, Macdonough, and a small cadre of volunteers sailed to the *Philadelphia* in the captured 60-foot ketch *Intrepid*. In a daring exploit on February 16, 1804, the men

---

*In 1799 James McDonough's navy career ended when his leg was amputated following a severe injury sustained during the capture of the 40-gun French frigate *L'Insurgent* during the Quasi-War.

boarded the fully-manned *Philadelphia*, moored in the inner harbor of Tripoli, and burned it.

Macdonough remained in the Mediterranean during 1804, serving as Stephen Decatur's first officer of a gunboat division which captured two Tripolitan gunboats in a rigorous hand-to-hand engagement. Decatur soon promoted young Macdonough to acting lieutenant. While the *Enterprise* was undergoing repairs in Venice, Macdonough proceeded to Ancona, Italy (south of Venice on the Adriatic Sea), where he outfitted four small vessels as gunboats to be used against Tripoli. After a land attack led by marines (first stanza of the Marines' hymn) and a simultaneous bombardment by three navy brigs on Derna (present-day northwest Libya), the Pasha of Tripoli requested peace, which was concluded on June 3, 1805. Thomas Macdonough was subsequently transferred to the 94-foot, 16-gun *Syren* as acting first lieutenant.

Following his Mediterranean duty, Macdonough was ordered to Middletown, Connecticut, in October 1806 to aid Captain Isaac Hull in supervising the construction of four 55-foot gunboats. (During Thomas Jefferson's presidency, 173 gunboats were built for the American navy.[5]) After three months, Macdonough left Middletown (where he had met his future wife, Lucy Ann Shaler) for a new assignment as an officer aboard the recently-completed, 105-foot, 18-gun sloop *Wasp* at the Washington Navy Yard. In January 1807 he received notification of his permanent commission as lieutenant. The *Wasp* sailed for Europe in 1807 and during the following year patrolled the coast of the United States, enforcing the Embargo Act of December 1807. With a resumption of war between Great Britain and France in 1803, both nations eventually forbade the trade of neutral vessels with their enemy. Because American merchant vessels could not be protected under these circumstances, President Jefferson persuaded Congress to authorize an embargo that essentially prohibited nearly all trade with foreign nations.

Following a short period on the 139-foot, 28-gun frigate *John Adams*, Macdonough served as the first lieutenant on the 141-foot, 32-gun frigate *Essex* during 1809. When he left the *Essex* for a gunboat command in Connecticut, 38 members of the crew of the frigate signed a letter, offering their "heartfelt sorrow" upon his departure and "most sincere thanks and acknowledgments for your officer-like Conduct and Philanthropy during the time we have had the happiness of being under your Command as Second officer."[6] Although he enjoyed the opportunity of courting Lucy Ann Shaler in Middletown, Macdonough found that the command of gunboats offered little advancement in the navy. With meager funds for a marriage, Macdonough applied for and received permission for a furlough in June 1810 to take command of the commercial brig *Gulliver* and subsequently completed a lucrative year-long voyage to India. After arriving back in Boston, he returned to Middletown, Connecticut, and promptly sent a letter to the secretary of the navy, requesting a second furlough for another commercial voyage to India which was denied. Although Macdonough nearly resigned from the navy over the issue of the furlough, in the end he was granted additional time. Leaving New York City on March 14, 1812, as the captain of the merchant ship *Jeannette Snow*, Macdonough encountered a severe storm which caused his vessel to leak, forcing a return to port.[7]

Macdonough's abortive voyage coincided with new tensions over trade restrictions by the American government. With the plummeting of U. S. exports following the Embargo Act of 1807, Congress passed the Nonintercourse Act of 1809 which reopened world trade, with the exception of France and Great Britain. The following year the Macon Bill authorized the president to allow trade with Great Britain and France but suggested that trade prohibitions would be reimposed against the country that did not end its interference with American shipping. France disingenuously responded by repealing her trade sanctions, leading President James Madison to threaten Great Britain with a renewal of the trade embargo. Britain reacted to the warning by increasing her interference with American shipping, including outright confiscation of merchant vessels, and escalated the impressment of American seamen into the Royal Navy.

A 90-day embargo enacted by Congress on April 4, 1812, prevented the *Jeannette Snow* from returning to sea, so Macdonough traveled to Middletown, Connecticut. Facing increased political pressure, President Madison asked Congress for a declaration of war against Great Britain on June 1, 1812. On June 26 Macdonough sent a letter to Paul Hamilton, the secretary of the navy, requesting an assignment. A few weeks later Macdonough received orders to proceed to the frigate *Constellation* in the Washington Navy Yard to serve as her first lieutenant. Finding the *Constellation* months away from sailing due to uncompleted repairs, Macdonough received permission to command a squadron of gunboats in Portland, Maine. On September 7, 1812, Macdonough took charge of a fleet of eight gunboats headquartered in Portland.

Three weeks after his arrival in Portland, the secretary of navy ordered Macdonough to "immediately proceed to Lake Champlain, & make every arrangement necessary—Six vessels, have been purchased, by the War Departm[en]t & there are two gunboats built by the Navy Department, on the Lake; the whole of which, is to be under Your direction & command."[8] After a fatiguing four-day journey by carriage and horseback through the mountains of New Hampshire and Vermont, Macdonough arrived in Burlington in early October. The navy at Lake Champlain consisted of two gunboats at Basin Harbor, Vermont, under the command of Lieutenant Sidney Smith. The two 40-ton gunboats (numbers 169 and 170) had been built in Whitehall by John Winans in 1809, under the supervision of navy Lieutenant Melancthon T. Woolsey, son of the New York Customs Collector.[9] Several commercial sloops had been purchased by the War Department in the summer of 1812, including the 65-foot *President*, 64-foot *Bull Dog*, 61-foot *Hunter*, and three of the following: the *Champlain*, *Fox*, *Juno*, and *Jupiter*.[10]

Macdonough had arrived in a region that opposed the government's efforts to enforce the embargo. Earlier, Thomas Jefferson had proclaimed the Lake Champlain Valley "to be the seat of a conspiracy to defeat the execution of the law."[11] On March 12, 1808, Congress had passed an embargo which extended trade prohibitions to inland routes connecting Canada and the United States. Defiance of the law, however, was prevalent in the Champlain Valley; in the winter of 1809 at meetings held in towns on both sides of the lake, citizens came to the conclusion that the enforcement of the embargo "in its nature [is] odious and oppressive."[12] Smuggling was rampant and attempts to end the activity sometimes had disastrous results. For example, in August 1808 during an attempt to apprehend the infamous *Black Snake*, a 40-foot vessel used in smuggling potash, two government officials and a private citizen had been killed.

Despite the potential risks, commerce between Canada and the United States actually increased during the embargo years. Goods imported from Canada were blatantly advertised in Vermont newspapers and prominent businessmen, including Gideon King of Burlington and John Jacob Astor of New York City, engaged in smuggling operations. Legal trickery also allowed merchants to take possession of their contraband goods after posting a bond which would later be returned, less a ten percent fee. More disheartening for Macdonough was the shipment of war supplies to the British army and navy in Canada.

Soon after his arrival at Lake Champlain, Macdonough sailed two of the sloops, the *Hunter* and *Bull Dog*, and gunboats 169 and 170 to Whitehall for strengthening and refitting. Three of the smallest sloops were deemed too old to carry guns and the sloop *President* was temporarily retained by the army. In early November Macdonough sailed his fleet to Burlington to supplement transport sloops conveying troops to Plattsburgh in preparation for an American advance into Canada. The botched invasion, however, forced the disorganized army's return to Plattsburgh. Shortly thereafter, Macdonough brought his fleet into Shelburne Bay for winter quarters and additional modifications. Late in December he informed the navy secretary of the status of his fleet, including the "Sloop President Mounting six cullumbiards [Columbiads combined features of a cannon and howtizer] and two long twelves—Sloop Growler [renamed from *Hunter*] with two twelves and four sixes and one long eighteen on a circle [pivot mount]—Sloop Eagle [renamed from *Bull Dog*], with six sixes and one eighteen on a circle—And two Gun Boats carrying a long Twelve each."[13]

Earlier in December Macdonough traveled to Middletown, Connecticut, to marry Lucy Ann Shaler, whom he had first met six years earlier, when she was only 16 years old and Macdonough 22. The couple had experienced long separations while Macdonough was away at sea, but whenever he returned to America, a visit to Middletown was on his itinerary. His furloughs (1810-1812), involving the command of commercial ships, were believed to be related to his need to supplement his navy income prior to marriage. In the late spring of 1812, while waiting for orders from the navy secretary, Macdonough had joined the Episcopal Church in Middletown. It was at this church on December 12, 1812, that Macdonough, attired in his full dress uniform, married 22-year-old Lucy Ann, daughter of Nathaniel and Lucretia Ann Shaler. After a trek of nearly a week in a two-wheeled carriage, the Macdonoughs arrived in Burlington. The young bride would endure two years of relative idleness in which "sewing, reading, and knitting d[id] not fill the vacuum."[14]

By the spring of 1813, after mounting additional cannon, Macdonough's fleet of five vessels with 36 cannon clearly outmatched the British fleet, consisting of three small gunboats and several armed bateaux stationed at Isle-aux-Noix in the Richelieu River. Macdonough's superiority, however, would not last long. An unexpected wind burst near Cumberland Head capsized one of the gunboats, causing Macdonough to take both gunboats out of service. Then the sloop *President*, Macdonough's flagship, ran aground on a rocky ledge near Plattsburgh and had to be hauled out for repairs. Finally, the *Growler* and *Eagle* were captured in early June by the British in the Richelieu River when Lieutenant Sidney Smith crossed the border, contrary to Macdonough's orders, and was forced to surrender after being engaged by British gunboats and shore parties for "three hours and a half."[15]

Fortunately, the new secretary of the navy, William Jones, a knowledgeable chief of naval operations with prior experience in the Continental Navy and merchant shipping, immediately empowered Macdonough with "unlimited authority" to rebuild the Lake Champlain navy by purchasing two sloops and building four or five gunboats.[16] During the summer of 1813 Macdonough was occupied at Burlington outfitting two additional vessels: the *Preble* (formerly the merchant sloop *Rising Sun*) and the sloop *Montgomery*. At the same time the British were busy planning a destructive raid against the northern communities along the lake "to create a diversion" and to destroy public buildings "and likewise all Vessels...found along the shore which can aid the Enemy," but private property was to be respected.[17]

On the morning of July 29 a British expeditionary force, consisting of two sloops, the 64-foot *Broke* and 60-foot *Shannon* (renamed from the American sloops *Eagle* and *Growler*), three gunboats, and 47 bateaux departed from Isle-aux-Noix. Later known as "Murray's Raid," the invasion force of 1,000 men was led by Lieutenant Colonel John Murray, while the naval vessels were commanded by Captain Thomas Everard, on temporary assignment from the H.M.S. *Wasp*, and Captain Daniel Pring, serving as second in command. On July 31 British troops burned "the Enemy's Blockhouse, arsenal, Barracks, and public Store houses at Plattsburgh" and, contrary to orders, also plundered private homes.[18] There was no resistance from the Americans since Major General Benjamin Mooers had moved his inadequate force of New York militia three miles out of town after local citizens pleaded with him to avoid a battle in order to "save our village & property from ruin."[19]

The British left Plattsburgh on August 1, taking the 13-ton merchant sloop *Burlington Packet* back to Canada. The British force then divided, with one division of two gunboats and the bateaux contingent under Murray sailing north where his soldiers destroyed a hospital and barracks at Swanton, Vermont. Before reaching Swanton, Murray's forces also created havoc at Point au Roche, and prior to returning to Isle-aux-Noix, a detachment from his division burned barracks, blockhouses, and a warehouse in the town of Champlain. The second division under Everard and Pring proceeded to Burlington with the sloops *Broke* and *Shannon* and one gunboat. Reaching Burlington on August 2, the raiders found the harbor "under the protection of the Guns mounted on a bank of 100 feet high without a breast work, two scows [probably the gunboats 169 and 170] mounting one Gun each...and several field pieces on the shore."[20] After a short exchange of cannon fire, the British vessels withdrew. Although Everard could not destroy Macdonough's fleet, he was able to fulfill one part of his instructions—to gain information on the composition of the American squadron. British sailors later captured several small vessels in Shelburne Harbor, and the 50-ton commercial sloop *Essex*, becalmed further south. The *Essex* was burned after towing the vessel proved futile.

For the rest of the summer Macdonough's men worked feverishly to complete modifications on the sloops *Preble* and *Montgomery* and to arm two small rented sloops, the *Frances* and *Wasp*. While at Burlington on August 14, 1813, Macdonough received formal notification (dated July 24) of his promotion to master commandant (a rank later renamed commander). While Macdonough was often referred to as commodore, the title was an honorary rank only. Although the new American vessels were ready for duty before the end of August, Macdonough was forced to wait for men drawn from the army to complete the crews. The fleet, consisting of the sloops *President*, *Preble*, *Montgomery*, *Frances*, *Wasp*, and two gunboats, set sail for Plattsburgh during the first week of September. The arrival of Macdonough's squadron at Plattsburgh forced Captain Daniel Pring and the British fleet, then anchored off the northeast shore of Cumberland Head, into a hasty retreat across the border.

During September Macdonough's fleet was used to escort transport vessels loaded with troops from Burlington to Plattsburgh and later from Plattsburgh to the Great Chazy River. The troops were destined for a Canadian invasion, under the command of Major General Wade Hampton. The 4,000-man army, however, was later turned back by a smaller Canadian force and returned to Plattsburgh in November. In the meantime, on October 18, Macdonough notified the secretary of the navy that he had "launched two Boats and Mounted on each a long 18 at Plattsburgh."[21] The new 50-foot gunboats came in handy in early December when Captain Daniel Pring's gunboats ventured as far as Cumberland Head where his crews set fire to an empty warehouse. Macdonough dispatched his four gunboats (later named by Macdonough the *Ludlow*, *Wilmer*, *Alwyn*, and *Ballard* after navy lieutenants who had been killed in action) under Lieutenant Stephen Cassin on a three-hour pursuit of the British flotilla. In response to Macdonough's request to enlarge the Lake Champlain fleet, Secretary Jones recommended in December "building fifteen Galleys. . .the first class, 75 feet long and 15 wide to carry a long 24 and 42 pound carronade, row [with] 40 oars. . .Second Class, 50 feet long and 12 wide to carry long 18 and 32 carronade and row [with] 26 oars."[22] In expectation of a major shipbuilding program, Macdonough brought his fleet seven miles up Otter Creek to Vergennes for winter quarters. His choice of Vergennes as a shipyard was based on the variety of resources available in the community, including abundant water power, eight forges, sawmills, a blast furnace, a rolling mill, an air furnace, and large stands of timber in the vicinity.[23]

Late in January William Jones finalized the authorization for construction of the vessels but allowed Macdonough the choice of 15 gunboats or a ship and three or four gunboats. Shortly thereafter, Macdonough learned that the British were building a large vessel at Isle-aux-Noix and therefore decided on a ship. He later received authorization for four galleys. The navy gave the contract to Adam and Noah Brown of New York City, builders of a number of successful warships, including those of Oliver Hazard Perry's fleet on Lake Erie. On February 22 Secretary Jones promised Macdonough that the Browns would "launch a Ship of 24 Guns; on Lake Champlain, in 60 days" and authorized the purchase of "a New Boat 120 feet long, near Vergennes, intended for a Steam Boat" that Lieutenant Stephen Cassin, second in command, had mentioned to Jones during his trip to Washington, D.C.[24] The navy subsequently purchased the hull for $1,200 from the Lake Champlain Steam-boat company and Macdonough had the vessel completed as a schooner (*Ticonderoga*).

On April 11, only 40 days after construction had begun, Noah Brown launched the 26-gun, 143-foot ship. Macdonough named the ship *Saratoga*, after he learned that his first choice, *Jones*, had already been taken for a new brig on Lake Ontario. Nineteen days later Macdonough reported on the state of the fleet at Vergennes to

Secretary Jones: "The *Saratoga* rigged, her Sails are made. . .The new gallies are also finished."[25] The 75-foot galleys, named the *Allen, Borer, Burrows, Centipede, Nettle,* and *Viper,* each mounted one 24-pound cannon and one 18-pounder and carried two masts with triangular sails and had 40 oars each.[26] Macdonough also advised Secretary Jones that he had "to abandon the idea of fitting" the unfinished hull at Vergennes as a steamboat but to rig her as a 20-gun schooner due to "the machinery not being complete. . .the extreme liability of the machinery. . .I have scarcely known the Steam Boat,* now running here, to pass the Lake without something happening to her."[27] He also suggested that the new naval fleet on the lake would have a "deficiency to man all the vessels, of 245."[28] At the time, two of his lieutenants, two midshipmen, and a sailing master were attempting to recruit sailors in New York City, Boston, and Salem. The problem with the recruiting drive, Macdonough acknowledged, related to "the Sailors having an objection to the Gun Boats or Gallies, and entering any service in preference to this," forcing him to recruit from the army.[28]

While Macdonough was struggling to complete his Lake Champlain fleet, Lucy Ann Macdonough was making the best of life in Vergennes. After becoming pregnant while the Macdonoughs were living in Burlington, Lucy Ann had returned to her parents' home in Middletown, Connecticut, during the summer of 1813. However, Lucy Ann lost the baby, an unnamed son. In January 1814 Thomas Macdonough journeyed to his in-laws' home in Middletown and returned to Vermont with his young wife. Lucy Ann subsequently wrote to her mother from Vergennes on March 16 that "the good woman with whom I live takes every pains to make me comfortable. I worked up [sewed] a cap for her sister and she sent me a pie. The people here are very clever but it is not a season when they can be very sociable, as you are liable to drown in mud [due to a mild winter]."[30] On March 24 Lucy Ann again wrote to her mother, but her attitude toward her landlady had changed: "The lady who charitably took us to board, has concluded she can keep us no longer; accordingly we depart bag and baggage on Tuesday."[31] The Macdonoughs moved to the home of "Col. Fisher; the females of the family are pleasant, but how long they will be content to keep us is uncertain. There is an universal dread of officers among the enlightened inhabitants of V[ergennes]. They are so domestic that they have not as yet invited us to drink tea with them, but say they intend to. However, the mud is so much worse than ever it was in Hartford [Connecticut] that it is almost an impossibility to get out of the house."[32] Lucy Ann, however, did reconnect with a friend from Middletown who was then living in Middlebury.[33]

On April 6, 1814, customs collector Peter Sailly sent an urgent message to Macdonough warning him that the British might sail to "Otter Creek and block you in" by sinking vessels filled with stones at the mouth of the creek and suggested placing "strong batteries" at the entrance of the waterway.[34] Five days later, Major

---

*Built by John and James Winans in 1809, the 125-foot, 167-ton steamboat *Vermont* was nearly captured by the British in May 1814. On October 15, 1815, a connecting rod punctured a hole in the hull, sinking the vessel near Bloody Island in the Richelieu River. In 1953 the Lake Champlain Associates, Inc., (one of the principals included Lorenzo Hagglund, salvager of the *Royal Savage* and *Philadelphia*) raised the hull of the *Vermont* and placed the remains on a site along the Port Kent Road across from Ausable Chasm for display in a yet-to-be built maritime museum. The museum never materialized and much of the vessel was destroyed in 1973 to clear the land for a campsite.

General James Wilkinson, whose army had just been repulsed in Canada, reiterated Sailly's concerns for the safety of the fleet and also recommended "plant[ing] a heavy battery at the mouth of the creek."[35] Wilkinson and Macdonough thereafter selected a site for the battery that would later be named for Macdonough's second in command, Stephen Cassin. The battery consisted of seven 12-pounders on naval carriages and was subsequently manned by 50 men under Captain Arthur Thornton from Burlington, and Lieutenant Stephen Cassin.

On May 12 the 120-foot schooner *Ticonderoga* was launched. At the same time the British fleet under Captain Daniel Pring was on its way "for the purpose of attacking the enemy's force laying in. . .Otter Creek near Vergennes, if found practicable or oth-

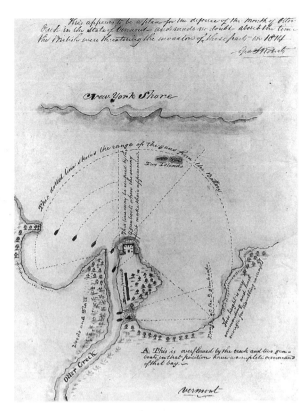

Plan of defense of the mouth of Otter Creek showing Fort Cassin battery (1814).
(New York State Library)

erwise to block up the Channel near the entrance."[36] Pring's fleet included the new 82-foot, 16-gun brig *Linnet*, built at the shipyard at Isle-aux-Noix under the direction of shipwright William Simons, the 11-gun sloop *Finch* (renamed from *Broke*), seven gunboats, the 44-foot sloop *Canada* (sloop *Mars* captured from the Americans), a tender with provisions and two merchant vessels (one was probably the captured *Burlington Packet* renamed the *Icicle*).[37] The latter two vessels would have been used to block the Otter Creek channel. Delayed by "Southerly winds," Pring did not reach Otter Creek until May 14, whereupon "the Gun boats commenced cannonading at day break with great effect, and at five AM the Linnet was swept within range for the purpose of covering. . .[a] landing" of gunboat crews to storm the American battery.[38] Not having enough troops to capture the battery, Pring deemed it prudent to withdraw after less than two hours of shelling. In the afternoon, however, three British gunboats entered the Boquet River to take government flour stored at a gristmill in Willsboro, but American militia were on the alert as a result of an incursion by a British gunboat a day earlier. The militia's fire disabled one of the vessels, requiring her to be towed away.[39] The main benefit of Pring's raid was intelligence gained on the size and composition of the American fleet which had been extracted from two men captured in a small boat on the open lake. Pring

"On the Stocks, and Nearly Finished, the Fine
Frigate *Confiance*." From *The Boys of 1812*
by James Russell Soley (1887).

submitted a detailed chart describing each ship, including armament and officers in command.[40] Responding to the information, British officials signed an agreement with shipbuilder William Simons to build a 147-foot, 37-gun vessel at Isle-aux-Noix, the largest warship ever built for service on Lake Champlain and comparable to an ocean-going navy frigate.

On May 26 Macdonough's flotilla, including the *Saratoga*, *Ticonderoga*, *Preble*, *President*, *Montgomery*, and six new galleys, emerged from Otter Creek and sailed for Plattsburgh. (The four 50-foot gunboats were temporarily disarmed, awaiting crews and cannon.) On June 11 Macdonough confirmed the news of additional British shipbuilding at Isle-aux-Noix to Secretary Jones, informing him "that the Keel of a Ship to carry 32 Guns was laid," and suggested that "Schooners or Brigs carrying [eighteen] 18 pds." may be needed.[41] Macdonough moved his fleet to Point au Fer, blocking the British fleet in the Richelieu River and again wrote to Jones, suggesting that the British fleet would "be much larger than us—I should, therefore, propose building. . .a Brig or Schooner."[42] Concerned over budget problems, Jones ignored Macdonough's plea. Unwilling to risk the loss of Lake Champlain, President James Madison in late June overrode Jones for the only time during the war. On July 5 Jones authorized Adam Brown to proceed immediately to Vergennes and build Macdonough's 18-gun brig. Isolated at the Point au Fer anchorage, Macdonough did not become aware of the decision until Adam Brown boarded the *Saratoga* on July 18 to review plans for the new brig. In the meantime, Lucy Ann had returned to Middletown in June, five months into her second pregnancy.

While Macdonough and his men prepared for the impending confrontation with the British fleet, the smuggling of goods to Canada by Americans continued to jeopardize the military effort. In June, Macdonough had learned "that two spars intended for the Masts of the Ship building at Isle aux Noix were on their way to Canada. . .from the United States. I sent Sailing Master [Elie] [La] Vallette to destroy them which he did."[43] In early July Macdonough asked for volunteers to slip across the border to destroy masts that had been smuggled from the United States.

Twenty-one-year-old Midshipman Joel Abbot and several sailors stepped forward for the mission. After discovering the masts hidden along the shore, Abbot and his men towed them into the open lake at night and "cut them up and returned to the ship after three days absence, so weak & exhausted [they had]. . .to be hoisted on board. The masts were destroyed the very night before they were to be taken to the frigate [*Confiance*]."⁴⁴ Smuggling of other goods persisted as well; Governor-General George Prevost of Canada admitted that "two thirds of the [British] army are supplied with beef. . .[from] Vermont and New York."⁴⁵

While American crews manned their vessels off Point au Fer, a 19-year-old graduate of Yale College recorded a personal glimpse of Macdonough and his men. After receiving some introductory letters, Joseph Heatly Dulles and a classmate from Yale, James Potter, traveled to the mouth of the Great Chazy River (opposite Point au Fer) where they boarded the *Saratoga* on Sunday, August 14. When Macdonough boarded the flagship, Dulles noted, "the greatest silence" occurred; "the Com. behaved very politely, but spoke very little, he has a fine countenance and what is much more is a most amiable man, no less loved than esteemed by his officers and crew. . .the officers put the most unbounded confidence in his bravery and prudence. He never uses any profane language. . .his manner is all mildness."⁴⁶ Dulles described the *Saratoga* as "very low [in the water] for her size and her appearance is deceptive; she is much broader than she appears [beam of 36 feet], having fine quarters."⁴⁷ Dulles and Potter had wine and dinner on the *Saratoga*, consisting of "a fine roast pig, Roast fowls, Hushed fowls, fried fish and some other dishes. . .des[s]ert and blackberries."⁴⁸ According to Dulles, Macdonough "gave the signal for attention before grace was asked; this motion of his hand with his countenance was the most beautiful and expressive gesture I ever saw; there was something pecular in his look and the wavering of his hand I cannot hit, tho. the motion is still before me."⁴⁹

Dulles also met whiskered "Dragoon officers. . .all Southerners. . .nearly all had servants."⁵⁰ In mid August when Dulles and Potter visited the army, Major General George Izard had command of 5,100 American soldiers, including 4,500 camped at Chazy and Champlain and 600 assigned to the construction of forts at Plattsburgh.* The troops in New York also included the regiments of Brigadier General Alexander Macomb who had been assigned to Burlington earlier during the spring. In July Izard had petitioned for a transfer to the west because he then believed the fighting would take place along the Niagara frontier. However, when reports of mounting British reinforcements reached Izard, he promptly wrote back to the secretary of war to withdraw his request, but his orders were never altered.

At the end of August the American fleet was finally complete. On August 11, only 19 days after its keel was laid, the new 120-foot brig was launched in Vergennes. Nine days earlier Macdonough had written to Secretary Jones requesting a name for the brig, "or may I call her the Eagle?"⁵² But when newly-promoted Master Commandant Robert Henley (Jones' choice to command the brig) arrived in

---

*While waiting in Plattsburgh for a fresh breeze to sail back to Vermont, Dulles visited the three forts (Fort Brown, Fort Moreau, and Fort Scott) under construction south of the Saranac River. The three forts, Dulles observed, made "a complete cross fire on an attack made in any direction, they all have deep wide ditches around them. . .The forts are built of wood and are so positioned that the strongest can command the other two if they should be taken possession by the enemy."⁵¹ Although Dulles seemed to appreciate the three forts, he had a dim view of wartime Plattsburgh, describing the town as "overrun with grog shops and taverns. . .all looks vulgar. . .The streets are very dirty; on the whole its a pretty dirty place as far as I can judge."⁵²

The American brig *Eagle* was launched from the Vergennes shipyard only 19 days after construction began. Drawing by Kevin J. Crisman. (Lake Champlain Maritime Museum)

"The [American] Fleet as viewed from Chazy, New York" showing the brig *Eagle* in the background and galleys in the foreground. (Shelburne Museum)

Vergennes, he quickly wrote directly to Jones with his name for the vessel—the *Surprise*.[53] The 20-gun brig *Surprise* reached Macdonough's squadron on August 27. However, Macdonough's list of vessels forwarded to the navy secretary on the same day listed the brig without a name.[54] With no explanation, the brig's entry log on September 6 noted that "the name of the Brig was this day changed to the Eagle."[55] The aborted gesture to name the brig would not be the last breach of command protocol by Henley.

By early September events began propelling the American and British forces toward a final confrontation. Meeting in Ghent, Belgium, the peace commissioners from Great Britain and the United States had become deadlocked over demands for each other's territory. To support their land claims, the British would have to occupy some of the regions that they were demanding. In early June, Lord Bathurst, the British colonial secretary of state, had instructed Governor-General Prevost to secure a toehold in the Champlain Valley: "any advanced position on that part of your frontier which extends towards Lake Champlain, the occupation of which would materially tend to the security of the Province," but avoid "being cut off" by overextension.[56] Governor-General Prevost would later suggest that his actions were "to establish the Army at Plattsburg and to detach from thence a Brigade for the destruction of Vergennes & its Naval establishment."[57]

Without a change of orders from the secretary of war, on August 27 Major General George Izard reluctantly began his withdrawal of 4,000 troops from Plattsburgh for the journey to the western frontier. The movement of Izard's army left 32-year-old Brigadier General Alexander Macomb at Plattsburgh with fewer than 2,000 regular soldiers fit for service and 900 ill with dysentery and typhus. Macomb's management of the remaining troops, however, would prove crucial in preventing British troops from overrunning the forts at Plattsburgh. On August 31, only two days after the last of Izard's troops had departed, the British invasion force began pouring across the border. Macomb immediately called on Governor Martin Chittenden of Vermont for militia support, and requested Major General Benjamin Mooers to activate the militia of the northern New York counties. Because British troops were on the New York shore, Macdonough withdrew his fleet from the Point au Fer post on August 31 and headed for Plattsburgh. But light headwinds the next day required the laborious towing of the *Saratoga*, *Ticonderoga*, and *Eagle* most of the distance to Plattsburgh Bay.

On September 6 Prevost's army arrived in the vicinity of Plattsburgh, forcing the Americans to withdraw their forces to the three forts on the south side of the Saranac River. At the time Macomb had about 3,400 troops; 1,400, however, were sick (one-half on Crab Island) and 250 were serving on Macdonough's vessels. By September 11, General Samuel Strong had reached Plattsburgh with 2,500 volunteers from Vermont, wearing "green sprigs in their hats."[58] With fewer than one-third the men, Macomb had to contend with the best European troops, many of which had defeated Napoleon's army. By the eve of the battle approximately 8,200 British soldiers had overrun Plattsburgh and another 2,100 would occupy posts between there and the border.[59] Nevertheless, Macomb was not discouraged, parading his troops to magnify his numbers and planting false information to mislead the British invaders.

As the British army advanced on Plattsburgh, Macdonough moved his fleet to a prearranged position about 100 yards off Cumberland Head where an elaborate anchoring pattern was put into place. Two anchors placed off the bow and stern permitted each vessel to be turned 180 degrees, or end to end, within the mooring lines, allowing fresh guns from the opposite side of a ship to bear on the enemy. Macdonough's anchoring strategy would make it possible for the Americans to use their firepower to best advantage. The American vessels had superiority in short-range carronades, the British in long-range cannon. Macdonough's final battle fleet was comprised of the *Saratoga*, *Ticonderoga*, *Eagle*, *Preble*, six galleys (*Allen*, *Borer*, *Burrows*, *Centipede*, *Nettle*, and *Viper*) and four gunboats (*Alwyn*, *Ballard*, *Ludlow*, and *Wilmer*). The *President* and *Montgomery* were assigned to transport duties, and 16 of the latter's crew were transferred to the *Eagle*. To fill the complement of the undermanned *Eagle*, 40 army prisoners (freed from ball and chain), five hospital patients, and six musicians (one with his wife) were taken aboard the brig. Between September 7 and September 11, the two opposing armies and the American fleet at Plattsburgh Bay waited for the arrival of the British warships.

On September 1, as carpenters worked feverishly to complete the 147-foot, 36-gun *Confiance* at Isle-aux-Noix, Captain George Downie of the sloop of war *Montreal* reached the island shipyard to replace Captain Peter Fisher, who had commanded the British fleet for little more than two months. Downie assumed command on September 3 and dispatched Captain Daniel Pring with the sloops and gunboats "to protect the left Flank of our army advancing towards Plattsburgh" and to establish a base at Isle La Motte.[60] Pressured by Governor-General Prevost,

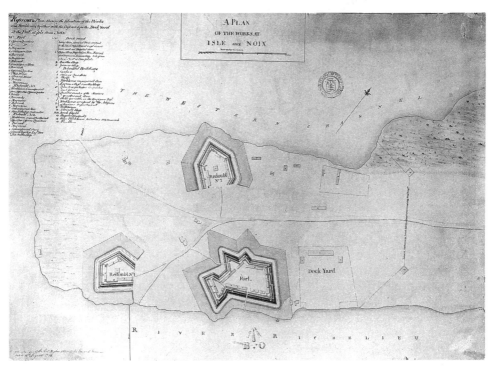

Plan of the east side of Isle-aux-Noix during the War of 1812 showing the shipyard.
(National Archives of Canada)

Downie moved the unfinished *Confiance* southward on the Richelieu River on September 7. Meeting at Ash Island, the *Confiance* and *Linnet* then proceeded to a temporary anchorage at Point au Fer where Downie answered Prevost's urgent request to sail to Plattsburgh. Downie angrily reiterated that the *Confiance* "is not ready now, and, until she is ready, it is my duty not to hazard the Squadron."[61] Later on the same day, the entire British fleet, including the ship *Confiance*, brig *Linnet*, sloops *Chub* and *Finch*, and 12 gunboats, rendezvoused off Little Chazy River. On September 10 Downie attempted to set sail for Plattsburgh but adverse winds forced cancellation of the orders and the carpenters on the *Confiance* resumed their work. Confident of victory, Downie hosted an elaborate banquet on shore at Chazy Landing during the evening with numerous toasts of wine and rum.[62]

Early the next morning with a fresh wind from the north, the British fleet headed for a showdown with the Americans at Plattsburgh. Downie had faith in the superiority of his squadron, particularly after Prevost had informed him that the crew of the new American brig was comprised of "Prisoners of all descriptions."[63] At 5:15 A.M., following a prearranged signal to Prevost's land forces, the *Confiance* scaled her guns by firing blank charges to clean the bores of the cannon. As Downie's vessels moved southward along Cumberland Head, the crews observed the tops of the masts of Macdonough's fleet anchored on the other side of the peninsula. Shortly thereafter, Downie reconnoitered the American position from a small boat and discharged the last of the artificers working on the *Confiance*. Convinced of a British victory, shipbuilder William Simons remained on board the flagship. Downie's

Cumberland Head. Before the battle the crews aboard the British fleet observed the tops of the masts of Macdonough's vessels anchored on the other side of the peninsula.
(Photo by Richard K. Dean)

plans called for sending the *Linnet*, supported by the *Chubb*, against the *Eagle*, anchored at the northernmost position; the *Confiance* would fire her starboard guns at the *Eagle* and her port ones at the *Saratoga*; the gunboats were to attack and board the *Ticonderoga* and also engage the *Preble*.

Before eight o'clock Downie began tacking into Plattsburgh Bay, fighting northerly winds as Macdonough had envisioned. As the British fleet maneuvered toward the American line, Macdonough knelt on the quarterdeck and led his men in a short prayer. When the *Confiance* moved into view of the *Eagle* on the way to her station, Master Commandant Robert Henley impulsively fired a salvo at too great a distance to reach the British flagship. On the way to engage the *Eagle*, the *Linnet* shelled the *Saratoga*, but the cannonballs fell short, except for one, which demolished a hen-coop on the flagship, releasing a prize gamecock kept by the American sailors which "flew upon a gun-slide, and, clapping his wings, crowed lustily and defiantly. The sailors cheered" the incident as a good omen, according to Macdonough's clerk, James Sloan of Oswego.[64] Shortly thereafter, Macdonough fired one shot at the *Confiance* from a 24-pound cannon as a signal to his crews to commence action. The *Confiance* was soon hit repeatedly, including barrages from "the Enemy's Gun Boats" and lost "two Anchors* shot away from her Larboard [port] bow."[65] Holding his fire, Downie continued to tack toward his predetermined position, but uneven wind and damage to the *Confiance* forced him to anchor further away from the *Saratoga* than anticipated. After mooring the *Confiance*, Downie ordered a double-shotted broadside from his 24-pound guns which instantly smashed through the open decks of the *Saratoga*, killing or wounding 40 sailors and shaking the vessel so intensely that half the crew was flattened on the deck. About 15 minutes after the commencement of the general action, "a shot from the enemy struck one of the Confiance's 24-pounders, and threw it completely off the carriage, against Captain Downie, who was standing close in the rear of it."[67] Although Downie's skin was unbroken, he died almost instantly, his watch in his waistcoat pocket flattened and frozen at the time of the fatal injury. A short time later, Macdonough, somehow escaped injury when a falling spar knocked him senseless. Shortly thereafter, he was thrown again to the deck after being hit by the severed head of his gun captain; Acting Lieutenant Elie La Vallette was also knocked to the deck of the *Saratoga* by a decapitated head.[68]

After reaching his assigned position, Captain Daniel Pring of the *Linnet* discharged a volley upon the bow of the *Eagle*. The lightly constructed *Chubb* also opened fire on the *Eagle* but was hit early in the engagement by two devastating broadsides from the American brig, which destroyed her rigging and killed five men and wounded 16, according to Midshipman John Bodell.[69] After having "two of his Finger Ends cut off and wounded in the Thigh by a Splinter," Lieutenant James McGhie, the sloop's commander, went below deck as did most of the remaining

---

*In August 1996 divers William Vanstockum and his son Ken found a ten-foot anchor half-buried in the sediment of Plattsburgh Bay. The huge anchor was temporarily removed from the lake with a crane operated by Captain Frank Pabst. The anchor was identified by its British broad-arrow emblems, Quebec painted on one of the flukes, and H.M.S. and 1813 carved into the metal. It is believed to be one of the anchors that Macdonough shot away from the bow of the *Confiance*. The anchor was returned to the lake and raised again in September 1998 for preservation treatment at the Lake Champlain Maritime Museum.[65]

crew.[70] The stricken vessel floated untended into the American lines, where McGhie ordered the colors struck.

When the naval engagement commenced, Governor-General Prevost opened an artillery bombardment and a volley of Congreve rockets upon the American forts in Plattsburgh. Although 14 miles away, Stephen Keese Smith, only eight years old at the time, observed "the dense smoke of the battle" and joined with his young friends in putting "our ears on the ground and felt it shake from the firing of the cannon."[71] Viewing the battle from Cumberland Head, Julius Hubbell of Chazy also felt the ground shake with firing so rapid it sounded like "one continuous roar, intermingled with spiteful flashing from the mouths of the guns and dense clouds of smoke soon hung over the two fleets."[72]

At the southern end of the American line the *Ticonderoga* and *Preble* came under close attack from the *Finch* and several British gunboats—the *Marshall Beresford*, *Murray*, *Popham*, and *Blucher*, while the *Drummond* fired from a distance. When the *Preble* faced a heightened onslaught an hour into the battle, her commander, Lieutenant Charles Budd, left his station, "retir[ing] in shore with her colours struck, where however she afterwards rehoisted them."[73] Writing fitness reports a year later, Macdonough concluded that Budd "did not behave well on the 11th Septr. [1814]."[74] With the departure of the *Preble*, Acting Lieutenant William Hicks renewed the attack on the *Ticonderoga*, but the light sloop was no match for the American schooner—her "fore stay cut away—main boom nearly cut through. . .and nearly all my running rigging cut away" and three and a half feet of water filled the sloop's hold from five shots below the waterline.[75] The *Finch* ran aground on Crab Island where the vessel came under immediate attack from two field pieces manned by invalids from the hospital.

Witnessing the carnage from a distance, the crews of the other British gunboats, largely composed of French-speaking Canadian militia, could not be persuaded to

"Macdonough's Victory on Lake Champlain," Engraving (1856).
(New York State Library)

"Battle of Lake Champlain." Line Engraving by Julian O. Davidson of a bird's-eye view of the battle. (*Century Magazine*, December 1890). (National Archives of Canada)

Detail of "MacDonough's Victory on Lake Champlain" showing Macdonough's flagship *Saratoga*, the brig *Linnet*, and the American row galleys. Engraving by Benjamin Tanner from a painting by Hugh Reinagle (1816). (New York State Library)

"Macdonough's Victory on Lake Champlain." Pen and Ink by Thomas Birch (1815).
(Collection of the New-York Historical Society)

row closer to the battle. Early in the engagement Lieutenant Mark Raynham, commander of the gunboats, fled with the gunboat *Yeo* to the security of the hospital sloop *Icicle*. While the crew of the *Ticonderoga* was fighting valiantly to repulse the onslaught of the four active British gunboats, the acting first lieutenant of the American schooner, John Stansbury, disappeared. Two days later his body came to the surface of the lake, cut in two by a cannonball.[76] Coming to the aid of the *Ticonderoga*, the American galley *Borer*, under Midshipman Thomas Conover, was stopped by a fusillade that killed three crew members and wounded a fourth. Lieutenant Stephen Cassin, commander of the *Ticonderoga*, returned the fire. A short time later the British gunboat *Murray* retreated after the commander of the vessel had his leg sheered off by one of the *Ticonderoga*'s cannonballs.

Meanwhile, at the northern end of the action, Master Commandant Robert Henley of the *Eagle* left his station because the starboard anchor spring on his brig had been shot away, resulting in the vessel's turning in a direction which rendered her remaining guns ineffective. Henley reanchored the *Eagle* between the *Saratoga* and the *Ticonderoga*, a move which soon subjected the *Saratoga* to the *Linnet*'s guns after the latter vessel had driven off the American galleys. As the battle continued, Macdonough's remaining starboard cannon were disabled by blasts from the *Confiance*. (Guns of both fleets also fell silent due to the unintentional overloading with shot or reversing of the order of charges during the chaos of the frenetic action.) Setting in motion his prearranged maneuver, Macdonough ordered the *Saratoga* completely turned around, using springs attached to cables and kedge anchors. While springs had been employed before, the combination with lines to kedge anchors was innovative. Using the undamaged guns on the port side, Macdonough hammered the *Confiance*. Already torn to pieces, the British flagship had filled with so much water, despite 16 shot plugs in the hull, that the wounded below deck had to be continually moved to prevent drownings. Lieutenant James Robertson, the commander of the *Confiance* after Downie's death, also tried to turn his ship, but the tactic failed and his crew refused to return to their stations. Robertson and his fellow officers surrendered the shattered *Confiance* to avoid "a Wanton and useless waste of human blood."[77] Captain Daniel Pring of the *Linnet*, however, fought valiantly for another 15 minutes while the fresh guns of the *Saratoga* pounded his stricken brig. With the rest of the fleet out of action and a foot of water above the lower deck, Pring finally surrendered. A short time later, the sloop *Finch*, stranded near Crab Island, ran up her colors. The British gunboats and the sloop *Icicle* promptly fled, firing a cannon at a "public" house on Cumberland Head in response to local residents who derisively blew horns and beat tin pans in celebration of the British defeat.[78]

Without the British fleet, Governor-General Prevost found it "impracticable" to remain in Plattsburgh.[79] During the British occupation of Plattsburgh, 32-year-old Brigadier General Alexander Macomb had remained steadfast in the face of a superior enemy force. If he had abandoned the three American forts, as some of his officers had recommended, Macdonough's position in the bay might have been compromised. Despite a valiant effort, militia units from New York and Vermont could not stop the invaders from fording the Saranac River. British troops, carrying a large number of scaling ladders, were poised on the south bank of the river for an assault on the American forts when Prevost ordered a retreat. The crews of the British batteries, however, did not end their bombardment until late in the afternoon. In the darkness of the early morning hours of September 12, the British army began its trek back to Canada. Mary Sheldon, a resident of Plattsburgh who was

Detail of "MacDonough's Victory on Lake Champlain," depicting the retreat of the British gunboats/galleys and the sloop *Finch* aground on Crab Island. Engraving by Benjamin Tanner from a painting by Hugh Reinagle (1816). (New York State Library)

"Battle of Plattsburg, 1814" showing the engagement at the Saranac River. Wood engraving from an original by Alonzo Chappel. (National Archives of Canada)

only seven years old at the time of the battle, later recalled that during the British retreat her father had overheard an "officer cursing and swearing about the damned Yankees, because the British had been beaten."[80] During the retreat others heard "the rolling of the British cannon and ammunition wagons [which] made a noise like distant thunder."[81]

When the naval engagement ended, many of the vessels were on the verge of sinking, and their masts, spars, and rigging destroyed. Midshipman William Lee of the *Confiance* likened the shattered masts and torn sails on his ship to "many bunches of matches and the other like a bundle of rags."[82] British casualties were estimated at 54 to 57 killed and 116 wounded (including 40 killed and 83 wounded on the *Confiance*), while American losses were also high with 52 killed and 58 wounded.[83] William Simons, the civilian builder of the *Confiance* who decided to witness the

"Battle of Plattsburg" Woodcut. (National Archives of Canada)

battle aboard the flagship, was among those killed. Following the surrender of their fleet, the British officers boarded the *Saratoga* to present their swords formally, but Macdonough, according to an eyewitness, bowed and responded, "Gentlemen, return your swords into your scabbards and wear them. You are worthy of them."[84]

The next day the grim task of burying the dead began. Simeon Doty, a 17-year-old militiaman from Alburg, Vermont, sailed to Crab Island for burial duty: "They were broken up and smashed up a great deal."[85] When Doty boarded the *Confiance* for bodies, he noticed Captain Downie's corpse covered with a flag, and "the decks were not cleared off but were bloody. My brother [Harry Doty] fainted when he saw the blood and the dead."[86] The American and British sailors were buried side by side in trenches on Crab Island. Three days after the battle, a formal burial of 15 officers, including Captain George Downie, took place at the Riverside Cemetery in Plattsburgh. Writing to his superiors on September 12, Captain Daniel Pring of the *Linnet* acknowledged "the humane treatment the wounded have received from Commodore M[a]cDonough."[87] Representing the surviving officers of the *Confiance*, Lieutenant James Robertson on September 15 expressed "gratitude and esteem" to Macdonough for his "unbounded liberality and humane attention not only extended to themselves but to the unfortunate wounded seamen and marines."[88]

Upon learning of the victory at Lake Champlain, Americans marked the triumph with great bonfires and fireworks in many parts of the country. New York State later presented 2,000 acres of land to Macdonough, and Vermont purchased 200 acres on Cumberland Head as a gift to the victorious naval commander. Macdonough was promoted to captain, and Congress struck a gold medal in his honor. A dinner of celebration, presided over by Peter Sailly, was held at the United States Hotel in Plattsburgh on September 23. Three days later Burlington repeated the celebration with 21 toasts, outdoing the 17 toasts offered at the Plattsburgh dinner.

On October 30, 1814, as the fleet was being prepared for winter quarters at Whitehall,* Macdonough received orders to leave Lake Champlain. (On September 13 Macdonough had written to the secretary of the navy, requesting a transfer to New York City for "health" reasons.[92]) On November 11, the day after relinquishing command of the Lake Champlain fleet, Macdonough received a letter from 26 fellow officers, expressing their "most poignant regret. . .[in] losing our commander, our preceptor, our example, or our friend,. . .[you will] leave a void which we doubt never can be filled."[93] At the end of November the secretary of the navy issued orders for Macdonough to proceed to New York City to take command of the 156-foot *Fulton First* (originally called *Demologos*), a steam-powered floating battery designed

---

*The largest vessels from the battle were placed in "ordinary" (mothballed) in March 1815 and never left Whitehall again. However, the sloops *Preble*, *Montgomery*, *President*, *Chubb*, *Finch*, and the gunboats and galleys (except the *Allen*) were later sold to the public. The remaining vessels were moved into East Bay (Poultney River) during 1820. Visiting Whitehall in 1820, William Dunlap observed that "the Ships of War appear going to wreck"; a year later Professor Benjamin Silliman of Yale College noted that the vessels were "mere wrecks, sunken, neglected and in ruins."[89] Nevertheless, in 1850 the vessels were still seen by Benson J. Lossing.[90] In 1949 a large section of the brig *Linnet* was pulled out of East Bay, and in 1958 the remains of the schooner *Ticonderoga* were raised and are presently on display under a shed at the Skenesborough Museum. The Champlain Maritime Society (1981-1983) and the Lake Champlain Maritime Museum (1995) completed extensive archaeological studies of the brigs *Eagle* and *Linnet*, and the galley *Allen* under the direction of Arthur Cohn and Kevin Crisman.[91]

by Robert Fulton and built by the Brown brothers. Although Macdonough did not relish the assignment, he had the distinction of being the first commander of a steam-powered war vessel. On his way home before proceeding to New York City, Macdonough was honored in Troy with a formal dinner and in Albany was presented with a deeded lot, given another formal dinner, a naval ball, and a fireworks display in celebration of his victory at Lake Champlain.

On December 10 Macdonough finally reached Middletown, Connecticut, where Lucy Ann and his six-week-old son, Thomas Nathaniel, were waiting. After more celebrations in Middletown and later in New York City, Macdonough was briefly recalled to Whitehall by the new navy secretary, Benjamin Homans, to prepare the American fleet for a possible attack by the British. Although intelligence had revealed British preparations to build another fleet at Isle-aux-Noix, Macdonough found no evidence of an imminent winter raid. On February 17, 1815, the United States Senate ratified the Treaty of Ghent (signed on Christmas Eve 1814); the victory at Plattsburgh had played a crucial role in persuading the British to abandon their demands for territorial concessions along the northern border of the United States.

Despite the unremitting public accolades, Macdonough remained the same unpretentious officer that he had been before the battle. In responding to a resolution in his honor by the Vermont legislature, Macdonough wrote to Governor Martin Chittenden that he considered his "humble services on this frontier. . .greatly overrated."[94] After the battle a friend from Delaware characterized Macdonough as "extremely modest and reserved. . .I never heard him speak a word of his exploits" or talk of the battle on Lake Champlain.[95] Similarly, another old family friend, Caesar Augustus Rodney, suggested that Macdonough was "perfectly free from vanity and pride. His glorious affair on Champlain has not produced the slightest change in his character."[96]

Because of health problems,* Macdonough sought an assignment in a more moderate climate. In 1815 he journeyed to Washington, D.C., to request a command with the Mediterranean fleet, but was instead sent to Portsmouth, New Hampshire, to superintend construction of the 74-gun ship *Washington*. Meanwhile, his son Thomas Nathaniel died. Writing to his sister Lydia on June 27, 1815, Macdonough lamented that the "poor dear boy. . .was but 12 hours sick with an inflammation in the lungs and cutting teeth at the same time. Two sweet boys have I now lost in less than two years."[98] Thomas and Lucy Ann Macdonough would lose three more of their ten children: a six-month-old daughter, Mary Ann Louisa, died in 1817; a son, William Joseph, died in 1821 at the age of two years and eight months; and one-year-old Frances Augusta died in 1824.

Finally receiving an assignment in a temperate climate, in the summer of 1818 Macdonough took command of the 44-gun frigate *Guerriere* for a cruise to the Mediterranean. Several officers on the *Guerriere*, including Joseph Smith, Elie A. F. La Vallette, Thomas A. Conover, Joel Abbot, and Charles T. Platt, had served under Macdonough on Lake Champlain. All would have long careers as officers in the U. S. Navy; Smith and La Vallette would later become rear admirals. While in the

---

*The first biography of Thomas Macdonough, published in *The Analectic Magazine and Naval Chronicle* in March 1816, revealed that "his health was somewhat affected by his long stay on the lake, which, at some seasons, is very unhealthy to strangers."[97] Macdonough's illness, also contracted by Lucy Ann, was tuberculosis, often called "consumption" during the nineteenth century.

Mediterranean in July 1819, Macdonough and several officers were relieved of duty by Commodore Charles Stewart as a result of a dispute stemming from a technicality during a court-martial at which Macdonough presided. After receiving legal advice upon returning home, Macdonough admitted to the secretary of the navy that his court had erred. The Navy Department accepted his apology and ordered his reinstatement with the Mediterranean squadron, but Macdonough requested a new assignment.

On March 11, 1820, Macdonough was given command of the 197-foot, 74-gun *Ohio*, then under construction at the New York City Navy Yard. Although the ship was launched on May 31, the vessel would not be completed for some time and thereafter remained in ordinary for several years, allowing Macdonough time at home in Middletown. He also visited Vermont in the summer of 1820 and two years later traveled to Niagara Falls, Quebec, and Plattsburgh. (He had returned to Plattsburgh in 1816 to help choose a site for fortifications.) In 1823 Macdonough wrote a brief 12-page autobiography, providing one of the few original sources on his naval career.[99] At that time he had four surviving children: James Edward Fisher (born 1816), Charles Shaler (born 1818), Augustus Rodney (born 1820), and Thomas (born 1822).

After repeated requests for sea duty, Macdonough assumed command of the frigate *Constitution* ("*Old Ironsides*") in the spring of 1824, sailing for the Mediterranean at the end of October. Elie A. F. La Vallette, who had served with Macdonough on the *Saratoga* a decade earlier, was again at his side as the first lieutenant of the frigate. Macdonough also had his four-year-old son, Augustus Rodney, on the voyage. On August 9, 1825, while Thomas Macdonough was in command of the *Constitution*, 35-year-old Lucy Ann Macdonough died in Middletown, a month and a half after the birth of a daughter, Frances Augusta. Lucy Ann may have died of tuberculosis (or from complications from childbirth), but the exact cause is unknown. In a letter to a friend a year earlier, Lucy Ann had suggested that she sought the wherewithal "for lengthening a life which I have for many months known could not continue long."[100] The news of his wife's death caused further deterioration of Macdonough's fragile health. On October 24, 1825, Macdonough, his son, and William Turk (the *Constitution*'s surgeon) sailed for home aboard the merchant brig *Edwin*. On November 10, six hundred miles off the capes of Delaware, the hero of Lake Champlain died at the age of 41 from "pulmonary consumption [tuberculosis]."[101] Dr. William Turk noted that "Commodore Macdonough failed so fast a few days before his death as to be conscious himself that his end was approaching. . .I never witnessed a death before so perfectly free from pain and distress. He fixed his eyes upon me with fortitude and composure and appeared to have fallen gently to sleep."[102]

Macdonough's coffin reached New York City on November 27 and was placed on the *Fulton First*, the vessel which he had commanded ten years earlier. Four days later at a formal funeral with the marine and navy bands, many army and navy officers, public officials, and family paid tribute to the fallen hero. He was subsequently buried in the Riverside Cemetery in Middletown, Connecticut, beside his wife. Their five children were placed with guardians; one son, Charles Shaler Macdonough, later made a career in the navy and briefly served as an officer on the *Constitution*, his father's last command.

The following report on the Battle of Platts-burgh Bay was written by Thomas Macdonough two days after the engagement and sent to the secretary of the navy.

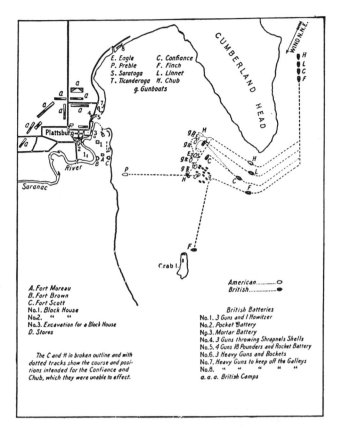

E. Eagle   C. Confiance
P. Preble   F. Finch
S. Saratoga   L. Linnet
T. Ticonderoga   H. Chub
          g. Gunboats

CUMBERLAND HEAD

WIND N.N.E.

Plattsburg

River

Saranac

Crab I.

American..........O
British............●

A. Fort Moreau
B. Fort Brown
C. Fort Scott
No.1. Block House
No.2.   "   "
No.3. Excavation for a Block House
D. Stores

The C and H in broken outline and with dotted tracks show the course and positions intended for the Confiance and Chub, which they were unable to effect.

British Batteries
No.1. 3 Guns and 1 Howitzer
No.2. Pocket Battery
No.3. Mortar Battery
No.4. 3 Guns throwing Shrapnels Shells
No.5. 4 Guns 18 Pounders and Rocket Battery
No.6. 3 Heavy Guns and Rockets
No.7. Heavy Guns to keep off the Galleys
No.8.   "   "   "   "   "
a. a. a. British Camps

Map of the "Battle of Lake Champlain" from *Sea Power in its Relations to the War of 1812* by A. T. Mahan.

"Battle of Lake Champlain----McDonough's Victory." Engraving from a painting by Alonzo Chappel. (New York State Historical Association)

Report of Thomas Macdonough[102]

U.S. Ship Saratoga,
Plattsburgh Bay, Sept. 13, 1814.

Sir: I have the honor to give you the particulars of the action which took place on the 11th Inst[ant] on this Lake.

For several days the Enemy were on their way to Plattsburgh, by Land and Water; and it being understood that an attack would be made at the same time by their land and naval forces, I determined to await at anchor the approach of the latter.

At 8 A. M. the lookout boat announced the approach of the Enemy. At 9 he anchored in a line ahead, at about 300 yards distance from my line;* His Ship [*Confiance*] opposed to the Saratoga, his Brig [*Linnet*] to the Eagle, Cap. Rob.ᵗ Henley,** his Gallies, thirteen in number,*** to the Schooner [*Ticonderoga*], Sloop [*Preble*], and a division of our Gallies—One of his Sloops [*Chubb*] assisting their Ship and Brig, the other [*Finch*] assisting their Gallies. Our remaining Gallies with the Saratoga and Eagle.

In this situation, the whole force, on both sides, became engaged: the Saratoga suffering much from the heavy fire of the Confiance. I could perceive at the same

---

*Some differences regarding the time of the battle appear in the original sources. Captain Daniel Pring of the brig *Linnet* noted that "at ten minutes after eight, the Confiance having two anchors shot away. . .was obliged to anchor."[103] Lieutenant William Hicks of the sloop *Finch* suggested that at "8.30 A M The Confiance and Linnet commenced action."[104] Hicks, however, may have been referring to a single barrage from the *Linnet* before the British brig and *Confiance* had actually anchored. Daniel Records, acting sailing master on the brig *Eagle*, noted that "At half past 9 A. M. we opened fire upon the Enemys Ships."[105]

**Robert Henley (1783-1828), born in Williamsburg, Virginia, on January 5, 1783, and educated at William and Mary College, had entered the navy as a midshipman on April 8, 1799. Serving under Commodore Thomas Truxtun on the frigate *Constellation*, Henley distinguished himself during an engagement with the French ship *La Vengeance* on February 1, 1800 (Quasi-War). After a furlough of several years, Henley resumed his naval career, earning a promotion to lieutenant on January 29, 1807. In 1813 Henley led a squadron of gunboats against British ships at Hampton Roads, Virginia, and a year later pressured the secretary of the navy through several friends (including Commodore Oliver Hazard Perry) for a new assignment. Receiving a master commandant promotion on August 12, 1814, Henley was ordered to Lake Champlain to command the new brig under construction at Vergennes. After arriving at Vergennes, Henley, ignoring Macdonough's command, imprudently wrote directly to the secretary of the navy with his own name for the brig. His name for the brig, *Surprise*, was later changed to the *Eagle*, Macdonough's original suggestion. The animosity between Henley and Mac-donough continued after the battle at Plattsburgh. In a subsequent fitness report to the Board of the Navy Commissioners, Macdonough noted that Henley's "disposition I take to be Malicious."[106] Henley received a gold medal from Congress for his part in the Plattsburgh battle but wrote a number of letters complaining of Macdonough's failure to recognize his proper role in the battle. He proceeded to Washington, D. C., in the fall of 1814 and was later given command of a fleet of gunboats in Wilmington, North Carolina. Henley was promoted to captain in 1825 and died in Charleston, South Carolina, on October 7, 1828, at the age of 45.

***Although Macdonough mentioned 13 British galleys (gunboats), most evidence points to 11 or 12 gunboats at the battle. The Americans may have mistaken the 32-foot hospital sloop *Icicle* for a gunboat. The gunboats, ranging from 44 to 64 feet in length and mounting one or two cannon, were named *Sir James Yeo*, *Sir George Prevost*, *Sir Sidney Beckwith*, *Brock*, *Murray*, *Wellington*, *Tecumseh*, *Drummond*, *Simcoe*, *Marshal Beresford*, *Popham*, and *Blucher*.[107]

time, however, that our fire was very destructive to her. The Ticonderoga, Lt. Commandant Cassin,* gallantly sustained her full share of the Action. At 1/2 past 10 o'clock the Eagle, not being able to bring her Guns to bear, cut her Cable, and anchored in a more eligible position between my Ship and the Ticonderoga, where she very much annoyed the Enemy, but unfortunately leaving me exposed to a galling fire from the Enemy's Brig.**

Our Guns on the Starboard side, being nearly all dismounted, or not manageable, a Stern anchor was let go, the bower cable cut, and the Ship winded [turned] with a fresh broadside on the Enemy's Ship [*Confiance*], which soon after surrendered. Our broadside was then sprung to bear on the Brig [*Linnet*] which surrendered in about 15 minutes after.

The Sloop [*Chubb*] that was opposed to the Eagle had struck some time before, and drifted down the line----the Sloop [*Finch*] which was with their Gallies having struck also.----Three of their Gallies are said to

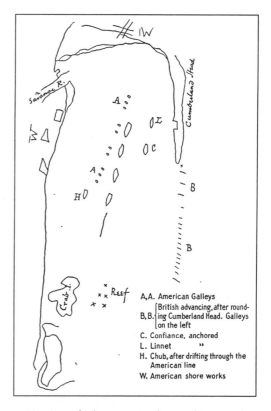

A,A. American Galleys
B,B. { British advancing, after rounding Cumberland Head. Galleys on the left
C. Confiance, anchored
L. Linnet   "
H. Chub, after drifting through the American line
W. American shore works

Tracing of Thomas Macdonough's pencil sketch of the battle from *Sea Power in its Relations to the War of 1812* by A. T. Mahan.

---

*Stephen Cassin (1783-1857) was born in Philadelphia on February 16, 1783. Entering the navy as a midshipman on February 21, 1800, he served with distinction aboard the frigate *Philadelphia* with Stephen Decatur during the war with Tripoli. Cassin was promoted to lieutenant on February 12, 1807, and became Macdonough's second in command at Lake Champlain in 1813. His father, John Cassin, at the same time was a navy post-captain in command of the naval forces in Delaware. Stephen Cassin was promoted to master commandant, retroactive to September 11, 1814, and granted a gold medal by Congress in recognition of his gallant behavior during the Plattsburgh battle. Macdonough later commented to the Board of the Navy Commissioners that Cassin was "a Man of firmness when put to the test. . .whose Judgement is good. . .and who behaved very well on the 11th Sept. 1814."[108] Cassin later battled pirates in the West Indies and was promoted to captain on March 3, 1825. He was placed on the reserve list in 1855 and died on August 27, 1857, in Georgetown, District of Columbia.

**Perhaps to deflect any criticism, Robert Henley's report to Macdonough was exceedingly praiseworthy of his own officers during the action. Henley disclosed 27 wounded in the report, a figure which Macdonough felt was an exaggeration and thus reduced the number, based on the surgeon's examination of the *Eagle*'s crew. Inexplicably, Henley's account was missing in the dispatches sent by Macdonough to William Jones, the secretary of the navy. Feeling that he had not been accorded proper credit, Henley sent his own report directly to the navy secretary in which he suggested that his decision to move the *Eagle* resulted in the surrender of the *Confiance* and *Linnet*. He also enclosed his original count of the wounded and his original report, "which he [Macdonough] had since informed me had been lost."[109] Macdonough responded on October 9 that Henley's "statement is unquestionably very erroneous and will I fear, ultimately be injurious to himself."[110] In a fitness report the following spring, Macdonough termed Henley "very deficient in Seamanship. . .[but] he behaved like a brave man on the 11th Sept. last, though his vessel was badly Managed."[111]

be sunk,* the others pulled off. Our Gallies were about obeying with alacrity [promptness], the Signal to follow them, when all the Vessels were reported to me to be in a sinking state—it then became necessary to annul the Signal to the Gallies, and order their men to the Pumps.

I could only look at the enemy's Gallies going off in a shattered condition, for there was not a Mast in either squadron that could stand to make sail on; the lower rigging, being nearly all shot away, hung down as though it had been just placed over the Mast heads.

The Saratoga had Fifty five rounds shot in her Hull—the Confiance one hundred and five.** The Enemy's shot passed principally just over our heads,*** as there were not 20 whole hammocks in the nettings at the close of the action which lasted, without intermission, two hours & twenty minutes.

The absence and sickness of Lt. Raymond Perry† left me without the services of that excellent officer—much ought fairly to be attributed to him for his great care and attention in disciplining the Ship's crew, as her first Lieutenant. His place was filled by a gallant young Officer, Lt. Peter Gamble,‡ who I regret to inform you, was killed early in the action.

Acting Lt. Vallette†† worked the 1st & 2nd divisions of Guns with able effect. Sailing Master Brum's‡‡ attention to the Springs, and in the execution of the order

---

*Reports of the sinking of three British galleys/gunboats during the engagement were erroneous; all of them had escaped.

**A later survey of the *Confiance* indicated that 250 to 300 shot holes were present in the hull.[112] Just after the battle, Benajah Phelps of South Hero Island remarked that the outside planks of the *Confiance* were "stuck solid full of [cannon]balls that looked just like some of the new fashioned houses, plastered on the outside."[113]

***In the chaos of the battle, a number of inexperienced gun crews on the *Confiance* failed to readjust the quoins (gun-wedge controlling the cannon's elevation) which loosened after each shot. With repeated firings, the trajectory of the cannonballs was raised higher and higher, causing them to fly into the rigging.

†Raymond H. Perry, brother of Oliver Hazard Perry, was a member of a Rhode Island family with a long tradition of naval service—his father and all four brothers had careers as officers in the U. S. Navy. Raymond H. Perry became a midshipman on July 24, 1807, and was promoted to lieutenant on March 5, 1813. Perry arrived at Lake Champlain on August 24 to take the place of John Stansbury who had been moved to the schooner *Ticonderoga* as acting lieutenant. Stansbury was killed, as was Perry's replacement on the *Saratoga*, Peter Gamble. Both of the officers were buried in the Riverside Cemetery in Plattsburgh; marble monuments were erected in 1843 to identify the grave sites.[114]

‡Peter Gamble, son of an officer who served in the American Revolution and whose two brothers served as officers in the marine corps and navy, had been appointed a midshipman on January 16, 1809, and promoted to lieutenant on March 17, 1814. Gamble was kneeling down to sight a bow cannon on the *Saratoga*, "when a shot entered the port, split the quoin, drove a part of it against his breast, and laid him dead without breaking the skin."[115]

††Elie A. F. La Vallette was appointed a sailing master on June 25, 1812. In a fitness report written in 1815, Macdonough characterized La Vallette as "an excellent young Man, a good Seaman, sober, steady, studious & brave."[116] La Vallette was promoted to lieutenant on December 9, 1814, and later served with Macdonough on the *Guerriere* and as first lieutenant on the *Constitution* (Macdonough's last command). La Vallette was promoted to master commandant (commander) on March 3, 1831, captain on February 23, 1840, and rear admiral (retired list) on July 16, 1862. He died four months after his last promotion.

‡‡Philip Brum, appointed sailing master on February 15, 1813, was commended by Macdonough for his role in the battle in a letter to the secretary of the navy on September 20, 1814: "Sailing Master

to Wind the Ship, and occasionally at the Guns, meets with my entire approbation,—also Capt. Young's* commanding the acting Marines, who took his men to the Guns.

Mr. Beale,** Purser was of great service at the Guns and in carrying my orders throughout the Ship, with Midshipman Montgomery.***

Master's Mate, Joshua Justin,† had the command of the 3rd division—his conduct during the action was that of a brave and correct Officer. Midshipmen [Walter L.] Monteath,[John H.] Graham, Williamson, [Charles T.] Platt, [Samuel?] Thwing, and Act[in]g Mids[hipman] [James M.] Baldwin, all behaved well, and gave evidence of their making valuable Officers.‡

The Saratoga was twice set on fire by hot shot from the Enemy's Ship.‡†

I close, sir, this communication with feelings of gratitude for the able support I received from every Officer and Man attached to the Squadron which I have the honor to command.

I have the honor to be, With great respect, sir, Yr. most obedient servant,
T. Macdonough

Hon[orable] Wm. Jones   Secretary of the Navy   Washington

Brum of this Ship gave the clearest evidence of a brave and good officer."[117] In a fitness report written the next year, Macdonough praised him again as "a Man who I would have been much pleased to see promoted for his good Conduct on the 11th Sept. as Master of the Saratoga. he is a Seaman a Man of steady and Manly habits. . .I think him a valuable officer."[118] Brum never received a promotion and was dismissed from the navy on April 29, 1817.

*Captain White Youngs of the 15th Infantry played a vital role in the battle as commander of the acting marines aboard Macdonough's fleet. Two days after the engagement, Macdonough sent a letter to Brigadier General Alexander Macomb commending Youngs: "I beg leave to recommend Capt. Youngs to your particular notice. During the action his conduct was such as to meet with my warmest approbation. I feel much indebted to him for his personal valor and example of coolness and intrepidity to his own men as well as to the sailors. He volunteered in a sinking boat to carry my order to the galleys for close action in the hottest part of it and supplied the guns with his men as fast as the sailors were disabled."[119] On September 15 Youngs escorted the British prisoners on the steamer *Vermont* for the first leg of their journey to Greenbush, New York. He was honored with a brevet major promotion for his gallant conduct on September 11, 1814. Youngs resigned from the army in 1819 and died three years later.

**Appointed a navy purser on July 24, 1813, George Beale handled accounts and dispersed funds for Macdonough, who reported that "his principles and Judgement are good. I consider him an excellent purser."[120]

***N. L. Montgomery entered the service as a midshipman on December 10, 1810, and was promoted to lieutenant on December 9, 1814, in recognition of his courageous service during the battle. In 1815 Macdonough referred to Montgomery as "a promising young Man of good habits he was with Comm[odore] [John] Rogers with [the frigate] President & lost an Arm, his merits as to knowledge of his profession hand[i]ly entitle him to a Lts. Commission he behaved well on the 11th Sept."[121] Montgomery died at sea on July 30, 1824.

†Nine days after the battle, Macdonough wrote to the secretary of the navy, recommending Justin for promotion: "Permit me Sir to intercede for Master Mate Joshua H. Justin who commanded the 3rd division on board this Ship. He merits in my opinion a Warrant as Master or Midshipman."[122] Justin was promoted to midshipman on November 30, 1814.

‡Macdonough commended a few of these officers in his fitness reports and several of them had long careers in the U.S. Navy, including Charles Platt, a native of Plattsburgh.[123]

‡†The source of the hot shot remains a mystery. While hot shot was observed hitting the *Saratoga*, British officers categorically denied that their vessels were responsible. Robert Anderson Brydon, a sailing master on the ship *Confiance*, suggested that the shot "must have come from the Enemy's

Notes

1. Winston S. Churchill, *Churchill's History of the English- Speaking Peoples*, ed. Henry Steele Commager (New York: Dodd, Mead & Company, 1965), 319; Naval Records Collection, National Archives, Washington, D. C., Record Group 45, Microcopy 125, Roll 39, fol. 38.

2. Theodore Roosevelt, *The Naval War of 1812* (New York: G. P. Putnam's Sons, 1882), 399.

3. Rodney Macdonough, *The Macdonough-Hackstaff Ancestry* (Boston: Press of Samuel Usher, 1901), 10-11; See also Dumas Malone, ed., *Dictionary of American Biography* (New York: Charles Scribner's Sons, 1933), 19.

4. Rodney Macdonough, *Life of Commodore Thomas Macdonough* (Boston: The Fort Hill Press, 1909), 21.

5. Spencer C. Tucker, *The Jeffersonian Gunboat Navy* (Columbia: University of South Carolina Press, 1993), 181-200.

6. Macdonough, *Life of Commodore Thomas Macdonough*, 91-92.

7. W. M. P. Dunne, "The Battle of Lake Champlain 11 September 1814," (manuscript, 1994), 6.

8. William S. Dudley, ed., *The Naval War of 1812: A Documentary History* (Washington, D. C.: Naval Historical Center, Department of the Navy, 1985), Volume 1, 319.

9. H. N. Muller III, "The Commercial History of the Lake Champlain - Richelieu River, 1760-1815" (Ph.D. diss., University of Rochester, N. Y., 1968), 210; H. N. Muller, "Smuggling into Canada: How the Champlain Valley Defied Jefferson's Embargo," *Vermont History* 38 (Winter 1970): 7; Tucker, 200.

10. Allan S. Everest, *The War of 1812 in the Champlain Valley* (Syracuse: Syracuse University Press, 1981), 64; *The Battle of Plattsburgh: What Historians Say About It* (Albany: New York State Commission Plattsburgh Centenary, 1914), 60; Dennis M. Lewis, *British Naval Activity on Lake Champlain during the War of 1812* (Plattsburgh: Clinton County Historical Association, 1994), 2; Dudley, 1: 325; H. N. Muller III, "Commercial History," 159, 264.

11. Gertrude E. Cone, "Development of Commerce on Lake Champlain," *North Country Life*, Winter 1960, 42; See also Gertrude E. Cone, "Studies in the Development of Transportation in the Champlain Valley to 1876," (M. A. thesis, The University of Vermont, 1945).

12. H. N. Muller, "Smuggling into Canada," 20.

13. Dudley, 1: 371.

14. Charles G. Muller, "Commodore and Mrs. Thomas Macdonough: Some Lights on Their Family Life," *Delaware History* 9 (October 1961): 347; See also Virginia M. Burdick, *Captain Thomas Macdonough: Delaware Born Hero of the Battle of Lake Champlain* (Wilmington, DE.: Delaware Heritage Press, 1991), 84.

15. National Archives of Canada, Ottawa, Record Group 8, Microfilm C-3502, Volume 1170, fol. 226.

16. William S. Dudley, ed., *The Naval War of 1812, A Documentary History* (Washington, D. C.: Naval Historical Center, Department of the Navy, 1992), Volume 2, 513; Macdonough, *Life of Commodore Thomas Macdonough*, 120-21.

17. NAC, Record Group 8, Microfilm C-3172, Volume 679, fol. 291.

18. Ibid., fol. 340.

19. Everest, *War of 1812*, 116.

20. NAC, Record Group 8, Microfilm C-3172, Volume 679, fol. 341; For more information on Burlington's role during the war see Karen Stites Campbell, "Propaganda, Pestilence, and Prosperity: Burlington's Camptown Days During the War of 1812," *Vermont History* 64 (Summer 1996).

21. NRCNA, Record Group 45, Microcopy 147, Roll 5 (part 2), fol. 144b.

22. Ibid., Microcopy 149, Roll 11, fol. 163.

23. Walter Hill Crockett, *A History of Lake Champlain: The Record of Three Centuries 1609-1909* (Burlington, VT.: Hobart J. Shanley & Co., 1909), 257.

24. NRCNA, Record Group 45, Microcopy 149, Roll 11, fol. 223; See also Kevin James Crisman,

(FN. CONTINUED) Batteries, as none of our Squadron had means of preparing red hot Shot."[124] James Fenimore Cooper, in his *History of the Navy of the United States* (1839), maintained that "the Americans found a furnace on board the Confiance, with eight or ten heated shot in it."[125]

The History and Construction of the United States Schooner Ticonderoga (Alexandria, VA.: Eyrie Publications, 1983), 3-5.

25. NRCNA, Record Group 45, Microcopy 147, Roll 5 (part 2), fol. 115a.

26. A. Bowen, *The Naval Monument* (Boston: George Clark, 1830), 152; *Niles' Weekly Register*, 1 October 1814; Byron N. Clark, *A List of Pensioners of the War of 1812* (Burlington, VT.: Research Publications Company, 1904), 60; Howard I. Chapelle, *The History of the American Sailing Navy* (New York: W. W. Norton & Company, Inc., 1935), 298, 532-34, 541, 556.

27. NRCNA, Record Group 45, Microcopy 147, Roll 5 (part 2), fol. 115f.

28. Ibid., fol. 115e.

29. Ibid., fol. 121b.

30. C. G. Muller, "Commodore and Mrs. Thomas Macdonough," 347.

31. Ibid., 348; See also Charles G. Muller, *The Proudest Day: Macdonough on Lake Champlain* (New York: The John Day Company, 1960), 346.

32. C. G. Muller, "Commodore and Mrs. Thomas Macdonough," 348.

33. Samuel Swift, *History of the Town of Middlebury* (Middlebury, VT.: A. H. Copeland, 1859), 443.

34. Macdonough, *Life of Commodore Thomas Macdonough*, 139.

35. Ibid., 140.

36. NAC, Record Group 8, Microfilm C-3174, Volume 683, fol. 160.

37. Ibid.; See also NAC, Record Group 8, Microfilm C-3526, Volume 1219, fol. 89; Joyce Gold, *The Naval Chronicle for 1812* (London: Joyce Gold, 1814), Volume 32, 157; Lewis, 18, 46-47.

38. NAC, Record Group 8, Microfilm C-3174, Volume 683, fol. 161; See also NRCNA, Record Group 45, Microcopy 147, Roll 5 (part 2), fol. 128 a, b, c.

39. Morris F. Glenn, *The Story of Three Towns* (Ann Arbor, MI: Braun-Brumfield, 1977), 245.

40. NAC, Record Group 8, Microfilm C-3174, Volume 683, fol. 163.

41. NRCNA, Record Group 45, Microcopy 147, Roll 5 (part 2), fol. 145 a, b, c.

42. Ibid., fol. 146c.

43. Ibid., fol. 153.

44. Joel Abbot Papers, Microfilm 25, Special Collections, Nimitz Library, U. S. Naval Academy, Annapolis, MD., fol. 173.

45. A. T. Mahan, *Sea Power in Its Relations to the War of 1812* (Boston: Little, Brown, and Company, 1905), Volume 2, 363.

46. Joseph Heatly Dulles, "Extracts from the Diary of Joseph Heatly Dulles," *The Pennsylvania Magazine of History and Biography* 35 (1911): 279; A fictionalized account of Dulles' comments were published in Macdonough, *Life of Commodore Thomas Macdonough*, 153-56.

47. Dulles, 280.

48. Ibid., 281.

49. Ibid.

50. Ibid., 277.

51. Ibid., 284; See also Allan S. Everest, *The Military Career of Alexander Macomb* (Plattsburgh: Clinton County Historical Association, 1989), 51, 54-55; Everest, *War of 1812*, 165.

52. NRCNA, Record Group 45, Microcopy 147, Roll 5 (part 3), fol. 12b.

53. Kevin J. Crisman, *The Eagle* (Shelburne, VT.: The New England Press, 1987), 48.

54. NRCNA, Record Group 45, Microcopy 147, Roll 5 (part 3), fol. 25b.

55. Crisman, *Eagle*, 61.

56. Everest, *War of 1812*, 166.

57. NAC, Record Group 8, Microfilm C-3527, Volume 1222, fols. 194-95.

58. Swift, 441.

59. Byron N. Clark, "Accounts of the Battle of Plattsburgh, 11 September, 1814," *The Vermont Antiquarian* 1 (March 1903): 79; William Wood, ed., *Select British Documents of the Canadian War of 1812* (Toronto: The Champlain Society, 1920), Volume 1, 117; Clark, *Pensioners*, 49, 53; Everest, *War of 1812*, 167.

60. William Wood, ed., *Select British Documents of the Canadian War of 1812* (Toronto: The Champlain Society, 1926), Volume 3, Part 1, 368.

61. Ibid., 380.

62. Nell Jane Barnett Sullivan and David Kendall Martin, *A History of the Town of Chazy* (Burlington, VT.: George Little Press, Inc., 1970), 102.

63. Wood, 3: 381.

64. *The Battle of Plattsburgh: What Historians Say About It*, 38; See also *Niles' Weekly Register*, 1 October 1814; "Biographical Sketch of Captain Thomas Macdonough," *Analectic Magazine and Naval Chronicle* 7 (March 1816): 224; Benson J. Lossing, *Pictorial Field-Book of the War of 1812* (New York: Harper & Brothers, Publishers, 1869), 867; Bowen, 159.

65. *Press-Republican* (Plattsburgh), 8 August 1996; *The Post-Star* (Glens Falls), 12 September 1998.

66. Wood, 3: 369.

67. William James, *Naval Occurrences* (London: T. Egerton, 1817), 410; See also Wood, 3: 374.

68. J. Fenimore Cooper, *The History of the Navy of the United States of America* (Philadelphia: Lea & Blanchard, 1839), 444-45; James Russell Soley, *The Boys of 1812 and other Naval Heroes* (Boston: Estes and Lauriat, 1887), 288; C. H. J. Snider, *In the Wake of the Eighteen-Twelvers* (1913; reprint ed., London: Cornmarket Press Limited, 1969), 218-19; Macdonough, *Life of Commodore Thomas Macdonough*, 182; Clark, *Pensioners*, 48; *The Battle of Plattsburgh: What Historians Say About It*, 15; Macdonough, *Macdonough-Hackstaff Ancestry*, 21.

69. Wood, 3: 422-23.

70. Ibid., 423.

71. Allan S. Everest, *Recollections of Clinton County and the Battle of Plattsburgh 1800-1840* (Plattsburgh: Clinton County Historical Association, 1964), 57.

72. Everest, *War of 1812*, 185.

73. Wood, 3: 473.

74. NRCNA, Record Group 45, Old Subject File NI, Report of Thomas Macdonough, May 6, 1815, fol. 3.

75. Wood, 3: 496.

76. Cooper, 444; Lossing, 872.

77. Wood, 3: 375.

78. Bess H. Langworthy, *History of Cumberland Head* (Plattsburgh, N. Y.: n. p., 1961), 23; Everest, *Recollections*, 26, 49.

79. NAC, Record Group 8, Microfilm C-3526, Volume 1219, fol. 280.

80. Everest, *Recollections*, 18.

81. Ibid., 25.

82. Lossing, 870.

83. Bowen 152; Wood, 3: 479; Everest, *War of 1812*, 185; The number of British casualties varied in some accounts. James, cixii; Robert Wilden Neeser, *Statistical and Chronological History of the United States Navy 1775-1907*, Volume 2 (1909; reprint ed., New York: Burt Franklin, 1970), 57; NRCNA, Record Group 45, Microcopy 125, Roll 39, fol. 52e.

84. Macdonough, *Life of Commodore Thomas Macdonough*, 185.

85. Everest, *Recollections*, 49.

86. Ibid.; Fourteen-year-old Benjamin Phelps from South Hero Island boarded the *Confiance* after the battle and observed "Blood, blood was everywhere! The decks was covered with arms and legs and heads, and pieces of hands and bodies all torn to pieces!" *Dedication of the Thomas Macdonough Memorial* (Plattsburgh: Plattsburgh Centenary Commission, 1926), 67.

87. Joyce Gold, *The Naval Chronicle, for 1815* (London: Joyce Gold, 1815), Volume 33, 257.

88. Macdonough, *Life of Commodore Thomas Macdonough*, 190.

89. William Dunlap, *Diary of William Dunlap* (New York: New-York Historical Society, 1930), Volume 2, 544; Benjamin Silliman, *Remarks Made on a Short Tour Between Hartford and Quebec in the Autumn of 1819*, 2nd ed. (New Haven, CT.: S. Converse, 1824), 192.

90. Lossing, 873.

91. Crisman, *Eagle*, 113-243; Arthur B. Cohn, ed., *A Report on the Nautical Archeology of Lake Champlain: Results of the 1982 Field Season of the Champlain Maritime Society* (Burlington, VT.: The Champlain Maritime Society, 1984), 47-77; R. Montgomery Fischer, ed., *A Report of the Nautical Archeology of Lake Champlain: Results of the 1983 Field Season of the Champlain Maritime Society* (Burlington, VT.: The Champlain Maritime Society, 1985), 13-19; Erika L. Washburn, "The Story of the H.M.S. *Linnet*, a Brig from the War of 1812," *Underwater Archaeology* (1996): 117-21; Eric B. Emery, " 'Gallies are Unquestionably the Best Description of Vessels for the Northern Parts of this Lake': The Excavation and Study of the U.S.N. Row Galley *Allen* on Lake Champlain," *Underwater Archaeology* (1996): 134-39.

92. NRCNA, Record Group 45, Microcopy 125, Roll 39, fol. 52c & d.

93. Macdonough, *Life of Commodore Thomas Macdonough*, 207.

94. Ibid., 210.

95. Burdick, 81.

96. Ibid.

97. "Biographical Sketch," 215.

98. C. G. Muller, "Commodore and Mrs. Thomas Macdonough," 349.

99. Macdonough, *Life of Commodore Thomas Macdonough*, 20-32; See also Macdonough, *The Macdonough-Hackstaff Ancestry*, 12-14, 17-18.

100. C. G. Muller, "Commodore and Mrs. Thomas Macdonough," 352.

101. Inscription on monument to Thomas Macdonough at Riverside Cemetery, Middletown, Connecticut.

102. NRCNA, Record Group 45, Microcopy 125, Roll 39, fol.51a-d.

103. Gold, *The Naval Chronicle, for 1815*, 255.

104. Wood, 3: 495.

105. Crisman, *Eagle*, 226.

106. NRCNA, Record Group 45, Old Subject File NI, Report of Thomas Macdonough, May 6, 1815, fol. 1.

107. NAC, Record Group 8, Microfilm C-3840, Volume 1709, fol. 116, Microfilm C-3526, Volume 1219, fol. 279; Bowen, 153; Clark, *Pensioners*, 61; James, 409; Wood, 3: 402, 406, 429-30, 433, 450, 459, 476; Two 35-foot gunboats were also in use during this period. See Lewis, 47.

108. NRCNA, Record Group 45, Old Subject File NI, Report of Thomas Macdonough, May 6, 1815, fol. 1-2.

109. Crisman, *Eagle*, 86-87.

110. Ibid., 87.

111. NRCNA, Record Group 45, Old Subject File NI, Report of Thomas Macdonough, May 6, 1815, fol. 1.

112. Crisman, *Eagle*, 79.

113. James A. Holden, ed., *The Centenary of the Battle of Plattsburgh* (Albany: The University of the State of New York, 1914), 30.

114. *An Account of the Celebration of the Anniversary of the Battle of Plattsburgh* (Plattsburgh: R. G. Stone, Plattsburgh Republican, 1843), 5.

115. Lossing, 867.

116. NRCNA, Record Group 45, Old Subject File NI, Report of Thomas Macdonough, May 6, 1815, fol. 3.

117. Ibid., Microcopy 125, Roll 39, fol. 74b.

118. Ibid., Old Subject File NI, Report of Thomas Macdonough, May 6, 1815, fol. 7.

119. Macdonough, *Life of Commodore Thomas Macdonough*, 284.

120. NRCNA, Record Group 45, Old Subject File NI, Report of Thomas Macdonough, May 6, 1815, fol. 6.

121. Ibid., 4.

122. Ibid., Microcopy 125, Roll 39, fol. 74a.

123. For information on the midshipmen that Macdonough mentioned see NRCNA, Record Group 45, Old Subject File NI, Report of Thomas Macdonough, May 6, 1815, fol. 3, 9; See also NRCNA, Record Group 45, Microcopy 125, Roll 39, fol.74a & b; Edward W. Callahan, ed., *List of Officers of the Navy of the United States and of the Marine Corps from 1775 to 1900* (1901; reprint ed., New York: Haskell House Publisher, Ltd., 1969), 37, 226, 387, 438, 545; Lossing, 867; *An Account of the Celebration*, 2, 3, 5. Wounded in the battle, James M. Baldwin was eventually buried alongside his comrades in the Riverside Cemetery in Plattsburgh.

124. Wood, 3: 413, see also 408; James, 415.

125. Cooper, 441; See also Macdonough, *Life of Commodore Thomas Macdonough*, 168.

Lake-Champlain Steam-Boat

CONGRESS,

RICHARD W. SHERMAN, Master.

—◦✦◦—

FOR the better accommodation of Parties of Pleasure, and others, who may wish to view the remains of those ancient fortresses, Ticonderoga and Crown Point, and other more recently memorable places on the Lake, such as the Battle Ground of Macdonough's Naval Engagement—Plattsburgh, &c.—the Congress will leave Whitehall, as usual, every Thursday morning, at 5 o'clock, and if desired, will stop one hour at Ticonderoga—one hour at Crown Point, and arrive at Vergennes, at 6 P. M.—will leave Vergennes at 5 o'clock the next morning, and stop at Burlington and Plattsburgh, to give passengers an opportunity of seeing those places ; and will meet the Phoenix, about half past 2 o'clock, at Cumberland Head, on her way from St. Johns ; so that those who do not wish to visit Canada, may return in the Phoenix, and arrive at Whitehall again, at 6 o'clock next morning—having, in two days only, performed this delightful excursion, and viewed the principal interesting scenery of the Lake.

Lake-Champlain, July 24, 1821.

Part VII: The Northern Tour

---

12. Tyrone Power 1835

T HE NINETEENTH CENTURY ushered in a new wave of travelers to Lake Champlain as the "Northern Tour" became increasingly popular. Visiting America between 1833 and 1835, Tyrone Power traveled to nearly every region of the country and later wrote the two-volume *Impressions of America*, published both in London and Philadelphia in 1836. Unlike Isaac Weld and many other British writers, Power's view of the United States was strikingly positive—"a mighty country, in the enjoyment of youth and health."[1] After his passage on the steamboat *Phoenix II* during the summer of 1835, he remarked on the beauty of Lake Champlain: "I have looked on many lakes, and by none have been more delightfully beguiled than by a contemplation of this during some nine hours of sunshine, sunset, and twilight, the last alone too brief."[2] The Irish actor would return three more times to America. One hundred years after his death, his great-grandson of the same name would become as famous an actor as his great-grandfather had been.

Many changes had occurred in the Champlain Valley between 1814 and 1835 as military tensions abated and trade with Canada flourished. However, remnants of the earlier confrontation with Great Britain still dotted the landscape. Passing through Whitehall in November 1818, Scottish traveler John M. Duncan noted that "the unfortunate [George] Downie's fleet, and that of his antagonist [Thomas Macdonough], now dismantled and roofed over, are moored by the edge of the stream a few miles from Whitehall."[3] A year later Professor Benjamin Silliman of Yale College observed that "a few seamen showed their heads through the grim

---

Facing page: Broadside (poster) of the Lake Champlain Steam-boat
company advertising excursions to the historic sites on the lake.
(Special Collections, Bailey/Howe Memorial Library, University of Vermont)

American and British vessels from the War of 1812 in storage at Whitehall.
(Shelburne Museum)

port-holes. . .Sparless, black and frowning, these dismantled ships look like the coffins of the brave. . .sad monuments of the bloody conflict."[4] In 1821 Silliman found the ships "lying a little way down the lake, mere wrecks."[5]

At the other end of the lake the Americans began construction of a fort at Rouses Point in 1817 to guard the border with Canada. President James Monroe inspected the site during his 1817 summer tour of the Northeast; a year later, however, the brick octagonal fort began settling and the masonry cracked because it lacked a solid foundation. Shortly thereafter, surveyors assigned under the Treaty of Ghent, which had settled the War of 1812, determined that the fort was nearly a mile into Canadian territory. The fort was abandoned and subsequently nicknamed "Fort Blunder."[6] Travelers on the lake sometimes mentioned the fortress. In 1818 John M. Duncan, for example, referred to the structure as a "very fine semicircular stone fort," and in 1831 Theodore Dwight's *Northern Traveller and Northern Tour* guidebook suggested that it resembled "a kind of large castle, built of hewn stone, with perpendicular walls, and three tiers of embrasures [openings for cannon]."[7] The Webster-Ashburton Treaty of 1842 ceded the land to the United States, and in 1844 construction began on a new fort, named for Brigadier General Richard Montgomery of the American Revolution.

With the end of the War of 1812, commerce resumed along Lake Champlain, and major port cities experienced substantial economic growth. Just prior to Tyrone Power's tour, Whitehall was described as "200 dwellings and stores and 1,500 inhabitants."[8] Plattsburgh at this time contained "about 350 dwellings, besides the court house and prison for the county. The number of inhabitants is about 2,500," while Burlington encompassed "about 300 houses and stores, two banks, a court-house, jail, and 3 churches," and "330 feet above the level of the lake, stands the University of Vermont [founded in 1791]."[9] A decade earlier Benjamin Silliman observed "one hundred and sixty dwelling-houses, and forty-three stores, offices, and mechanics' shops" in Burlington and noted that the faculty at the university "consists of a President, five professors, and two tutors."[10]

During the two decades prior to Tyrone Power's visit in 1835, eleven steamboats served the growing transportation needs of the inland sea, including the *Vermont*

"View of Burlington" from an original wood engraving. (Author's collection)

(1809-1815), *Phoenix* (1815-1819), *Champlain* (1816-1817), *Congress* (1818-1835), *Phoenix II* (1820-1837), *General Greene* (1825-1833, converted to a sloop), *Franklin* (1827-1838), *MacDonough* (1828-1841), *Washington* (1827-1843), *Water Witch* (1832-1836, converted to a schooner), and *Winooski* (1832-1850). Theodore Dwight, however, noted in his guidebook that commercial goods were most often carried by "great numbers of small schooners. . .and within a few years numerous canal boats, some of them fitted with masts for schooners for sailing."[11]

Because the Northern Inland Lock Navigation Company (chartered in 1792) had failed to complete a canal between the Hudson River and Lake Champlain, in 1817 the New York legislature authorized the construction of a new canal linking the two waterways. In November 1819 the first successful trial of the canal between Fort Edward and Whitehall was celebrated in the latter town by "the discharge of cannon and other demonstrations of joy. . .The locks. . .nine in number, were in the finest order," according to a contemporary newspaper account.[12] On October 8, 1823, the entire Champlain Canal was officially opened from Whitehall to

"Northern View of Whitehall" from a wood engraving (1841). (Author's collection)

Waterford. Arriving in September before the last lock was completed at Waterford, the 60-foot sailing canal boat *Gleaner*, built in St. Albans, Vermont, was the first boat through the new waterway.[13] The celebration of the opening of the canal at Waterford included "every demonstration of joy and rejoicing from the shores, loud huzzas, the ringing of bells and the firing of cannon, music, processions, and [a] military parade."[14] The Champlain Canal was an immediate success with thousands of boats passing through the canal by the end of the first year of operation.[15] By the middle of 1836, revenue earned from tolls on the Champlain and Erie Canals had completely paid off the remaining original debt incurred in their construction.[16] The opening of a continuous water route from New York City to Canada expanded the bustling commercial ports along all of Lake Champlain.

By the time of Tyrone Power's voyage on Lake Champlain, the Northern Tour had become well-known through the publication of a number of popular American guidebooks. Professor Benjamin Silliman's *Remarks, Made on a Short Tour, Between Hartford and Quebec in the Autumn of 1819* (published in 1820 with a second edition in 1824) combined observations of the countryside with a historical narrative. This format was used earlier by Timothy Dwight, president of Yale College and Silliman's mentor, in his *Travels in New-England and New-York* (published in 1821, four years after his death). Gideon Miner Davison's guidebook *The Fashionable Tour; or, a Trip to the Springs, Niagara, Quebec, and Boston, in the Summer of 1821* (published in 1822, it appeared in ten editions by 1840) followed a similar format. In 1825 Henry Dilworth Gilpin's *A Northern Tour: Being A Guide to Saratoga, Lake George, Niagara, Canada, Boston* covered a good deal of the same material and quoted heavily from Silliman's earlier book. Theodore Dwight, nephew of the late Timothy Dwight, had the first of seven editions of *The Northern Traveller* published in 1825. An avid traveler, Theodore Dwight, like others, combined historical material with a detailed description of scenery.

Tyrone Power's travels in North America were preceded by his earlier adventures as a young man. William Grattan Tyrone Power was born on November 2, 1797, in Kilmacthomas, Ireland (southeast Ireland). When Tyrone was only a year old, his father, a member of an affluent Waterford family, died while seeking a new home for his wife and son in America. His mother, Marie Maxwell Power, thereafter decided to move with her infant son to England. After being robbed on a road in Ireland and surviving a harrowing voyage from Dublin, in which their ship wrecked on the Welsh coast, Marie and young Tyrone settled in Cardiff, Wales (on the Bristol Channel, about 130 miles west of London). Power's mother had a distant relative in the printing business in Cardiff, and young Tyrone is believed to have had an apprenticeship with the firm.[17] The company handled the printing for the theater in Cardiff, and Tyrone Power became acquainted with a troupe of traveling stage players. At the age of 14, to the intense dismay of his mother, Power ran away from home and followed the troupe of actors on its circuit, later playing minor roles. In 1815, after several years on the road with different theatrical companies, Power began a two-year stint on the stage in Newport (Isle of Wight, south of London). In Newport he met his future wife (Miss Gilbert), whom he married in January 1817 when he was 19 years old and she was 18. Power continued performing and also began writing during this period. His appearance on the Dublin stage in late 1817 in the role of Romeo (*Romeo and Juliet*) received mixed reviews. While he was acting in Newcastle-upon-Tyne (northern England), Power's first son, William Tyrone Power, was born in June 1819.

In 1820, with the security of his wife's recent inheritance, Power left the theater and embarked on an expedition to South Africa to settle a new territory at Algoa Bay. Arranging for the care of his wife and son with friends, Power sailed for the Cape of Good Hope in June 1820. After a year of many exploits while surveying the interior of the Cape colony, Power became convinced that the prospects of the area (including the desirability as a home for his family) were dim, so he returned home.[18] In the summer of 1821 Power returned to the stage in London, but real success eluded the young actor and he seriously considered a military appointment in Sierra Leone (West Africa). He continued, however, with his acting career and three years later succeeded in the role of a drunken Irishman, Larry Hoolagan, "keeping the audience in a perpetual roar."[19] Late in October 1826 Power's break came when Charles Connor, the leading Irish comedian on the London theater circuit, died of apoplexy (stroke). Power was given Connor's role in several productions and became an immediate success.

Tyrone Power

Power thereafter concentrated his roles on Irish characters; contemporary theater critics often lauded his performances as superior to those of the late Charles Connor.[20] After three or four hours on stage, Power would stand before the audience, "fresh, smiling, and untired."[21] His entertaining nature was not limited to the stage, and he was described "as merry and entertaining in private. . .full of humorous anecdote, and conversible on many topics."[22] He appeared in the best London theaters, earning very high wages for long engagements. Power was described by a close friend as "about five feet eight inches in height, with a light complexion, blue eyes, and brown hair. His form compact, light, and agile; his face intelligent, animated and expansive. Although the richest humour sparkled in his eyes, and fell from his lips without effort, he could embody either pathos or strong passion with adequate intensity when required."[23]

As Power's acting career soared, his interest in writing also flourished. Initially writing for magazines and monthly periodicals, Power also wrote several well-received novels, including *The Prediction* (1829), *The Lost Heir* (1830), *The Gypsy of Abruzzo* (1831), and *The King's Secret* (1831), as well as a number of plays. At this time he envisioned the day when writing would replace his career on the stage. Combining his two talents, Power decided on a stage tour of America which would also allow him to record his observations of the young nation.

On July 16, 1833, Power embarked on a three-year journey of North America which included stage appearances in the larger towns and cities. Power suggested that he "set out with the intention of keeping such a close record of my feelings [in a journal]. . .with the premeditated design also of giving them to. . .[the] public."[24]

Inset: Tyrone Power from *Appleton's Cyclopaedia of American Biography* (1888).

After arriving in New York City on August 20, 1833, Power journeyed to Philadelphia, Boston, and Baltimore, returning to New York City at the end of December. During the next year he crisscrossed the Middle Atlantic States, New England, and the South. On March 22, 1835, after a long stay in Louisiana, Power departed on the schooner *Shakspeare* [sic] for New York City. On May 30 he began his trek to Canada via the Hudson River and Lake Champlain, visiting Montreal and Quebec before returning to New York by the same route in preparation for his trip back to England. Power boarded the packet ship *Algonquin* at New Castle, Delaware, on June 20, 1835, for "a most delightful passage" home.[25]

"View of Plattsburg" from an original wood carving (1842). (New York State Library)

Power's two-volume *Impressions of America* enjoyed wide popularity although it differed greatly from the books of other contemporary British travelers to America. British travelers were typically well-to-do and regarded the common citizens of America as crude. They were often critical of the lack of class distinction in America and disapproved of grass roots democracy. For example, Captain Basil Hall's three volume *Travels in North America in the Years 1827 and 1828* gained a wide readership in Great Britain and the United States. Hall complained about virtually everything, infuriating Americans more than any earlier British writer.[26] Hall's trip on a crowded steamboat on Lake Champlain in 1827 elicited a typical description:* "The machinery was unusually noisy, the boat weak and tremulous. . .I went upon deck once or twice [at night], when worried almost to death by the incessant bustle, but the scenery was not very interesting."[28] On the appearance of a town on the horizon, Hall "asked an American gentleman what place it was. 'Oh! don't you know? That is Plattsburgh—and there is the very spot where our Commodore Macdonough defeated the English squadron.'—I went to bed again,"

---

*Even before steamboats appeared on Lake Champlain, some British travelers expressed acrimonious sentiments about their journey on the lake. Sailing aboard the *Dolphin* in November 1807, John Lambert described the sloop as "a wretched vessel" and noted that "the sails were in rags, the pumps choked up and broken; and we were obliged to bale out the water from under the cabin every two hours with a tin kettle. To increase our difficulties we had two ignorant men to pilot us."[27]

wrote the disgruntled retired British naval officer.[29] Captain Hall's wife, Margaret Hunter Hall, wrote detailed descriptions of America in the form of letters to her sister which were not published until 1931. She had negative views of the United States similar to those of her husband, disapproving of democratic equality and the personal habits of Americans. However, she did find "romantic scenery" along Lake Champlain.[30]

The 1832 publication of Mrs. Frances Trollope's hypercritical *Domestic Manners of the Americans* became a resounding commercial triumph in England, but the controversial tome was considered the "most prejudiced" of all British books on America.[31] Trollope was continually distressed by "republican equality" in America and she was particularly upset by her interaction with those whom she considered below her social class: "the eternal shaking hands with these ladies and gentlemen was really an annoyance, and the more so, as the near approach of the gentlemen was always redolent of whiskey and tobacco."[32] A year after the publication of *Domestic Manners of the Americans*, a traveler found that Trollope's book was for sale on every corner in American cities and superseded all political and economic controversies of the day: "at every table d'hote, on board. . .every steamboat, and in all societies, the first question was, 'Have you read Mrs. Trollope.' And one-half the people would be seen with a red or blue half-bound volume in their hand."[33]

Although a few British writers had offered some positive comments on America, including Francis Hall (*Travels in Canada and the United States, in 1816 and 1817*) and James Stuart (*Three Years in North America*), the negative authors were more widely read. Stuart's positive views of America were directly challenged by Richard Weston's *A Visit to the United States and Canada in 1833*. Tyrone Power's work was one of the first popular books that defied convention and contradicted earlier British writers. Several other contemporary books would ultimately help change British opinion about the United States, particularly Alexis de Tocqueville's *Democracy in America* (1835) and Harriet Martineau's *Retrospect of Western Travel* (1838).

"I blame none of my predecessors for their general views," Tyrone Power remarked in the preface to *Impressions of America*, "but claim the right of differing from them wherever I think fit."[34] Power found Americans "clear-headed, energetic, frank, and hospitable."[35] He specifically answered some of the complaints made by earlier English writers by "enter[ing] my protest against the sweeping ridicule it has pleased some writers to cast upon these doings here [Washington, D.C.]; since I saw none of those outrageously unpresentable women, or coarsely habited and ungainly men, so amusingly arrayed by some of my more observant predecessors."[36] Although admitting that American women "have seen little of what is called the world," Power, nevertheless, praised their knowledge, intelligence, and spirit, and said that their "manners, refined, feminine, and naturally graceful, might with infinite advantage be studied by some of the ungentle censors."[37] Even though Americans were "not conventionally polished," Power asserted, "you will rarely find [them] either rude or discourteous."[38] During his travels "through the roughest part of these States in every sort of conveyance, and. . .thrown amongst all classes of the community," Power "never received one rude word," but "observed more ill-breeding, and selfish rudeness at a fashionable rout [formal social gathering] in England."[39]

Power, however, did encounter problems during his tour of America. On the

Albany. From *Random Recollections of Albany (II)* by Gorham A. Worth.
(New York State Library)

evening of his stage performance in Albany in June 1834, fewer than ten people attended because of bad weather. On Power's request, the management and the audience agreed to a postponement until the following night. But the citizenry in neighborhood bars were in an uproar over the perceived affront by the actor, and "inflammatory handbills and a scurrilous print" the next day exacerbated the situation.[40] On the evening of his performance, the theater was filled with angry men who booed and hooted down Power's first attempt at his repertoire. He provided the audience with an explanation for the postponement, but the second attempt met with the same fate; however, Power continued through the entire set. Recognizing the unfairness of the situation, a number of citizens came to his defense, allowing the performances scheduled for the next three nights to go forward in perfect order. The turn of events left Power with a positive feeling about the people of Albany: "I have never been able to regret a momentary vexation which obtained for me many friends, and made known to me the sterling good feeling existing in Albany."[41]

Power also encountered difficulties with various modes of transportation in America, including being on a train when one of the passenger cars overturned. (He assisted the victims.) On another part of his trip, Power spent several uncomfortable summer days on an Erie Canal packet boat between Niagara and Schenectady. He had expected "a couple of days' quiet travel," but by the time his boat reached Lockport the temperature had risen to 110 degrees and Power noticed "several horses dead upon the banks of the canal."[42] Stagecoaches had to be canceled because 40 horses had died from the heat. "During the day," Power recounted that "many of our men frequently threw themselves overboard, clothes and all [into the canal]."[43] Although the information provided little comfort, "the oldest inhabitants on the line of the canal assured us they never remembered any heat of three days' continuance which could compare to this."[44] On another journey through New Jersey, his horse's leg plunged through the boards of a bridge; luckily the leg was not broken and Power rode on, but he covered 18 miles in the wrong direction. Power later called the incident "a blundering adventure, but served me with a hearty laugh. . .my left temple continued swollen for two or three days; and my horse was laid up for a month."[45]

Erie Canal packet boat similar to the vessel that Tyrone Power traveled on.
(Postcard, author's collection)

Power made many observations during his three years in America. Although directions were difficult to obtain from Dutch youths in Pennsylvania, Power found that the young people in an Irish village were "ready and willing to show you any place or road they know any thing or nothing, about."[46] He also liked Westerners: "their off-hand manner makes you at once at your ease with them: they abound in anecdote[s] growing out of the state in which they live, full of wild frolic and hardy adventure."[47] He disagreed with the stereotypical view of "the Yankee as a naturally cold-blooded, selfish being. . .they are proverbial as the kindest husbands and most indulgent fathers."[48] Power was also intrigued by various American contraptions, including a large horseboat on the Niagara River "propelled by paddle-wheels similar to those of a steamboat, only wrought by horse-power,—an animal tread-mill in fact. . .[the horses] were scampish-looking steeds, their physiognomical expression was low and dogged."[49]

Power devoted considerable space in his book to a description of Washington, D.C., including vignettes of major political figures—Henry Clay, Daniel Webster, Martin Van Buren, Andrew Jackson, and others. He took particular note of the egalitarian nature of White House receptions: "I learn that in [the] true spirit of democracy, the doors on these occasions are open to every citizen without distinction of rank or costume; consequently the assemblage at such times may be oddly compounded."[50] Power's book was not devoid of complaints: "There was nothing that puzzled me more. . .than the utter indifference with which the Americans look upon the exceedingly unworthy condition of their capital, when considered in relation with the magnitude, the greatness, and prosperous condition of their common country. During months of every session, the roads leading through the district of Columbia are all but impassable" because of mud or dense clouds of dust.[51] Power obtained a simple explanation from several Congressmen: "they cannot satisfactorily account to their constituents for voting sums of money to adorn or render convenient a city these may never see, and for whose very existence they have no care."[52]

Power concluded his book with several pages of praise for the United States, including the comment that "I shall ever love America for the happy home it has proved to the provident amongst the exiles of Ireland," but he acknowledged their "constant struggles for equal rights."[53] He also found that immigrants were charitable to relatives left in Europe: "There is not a part of the country to which I have wandered, where I did not find that a like gentle recollection of the destitute left at home prevailed. . .The donors [who had sent money home] are themselves the poorest of the poor."[54]

After returning from America during the summer of 1835, Power spent time with his family at their home near Tunbridge, England, where his two eldest sons attended college. In August he resumed his lucrative stage career in England but had time to complete *Impressions of America* by early January 1836 and in April produced a romantic musical in London. In July 1836 he again departed from Liverpool for a year-long stage tour in America. After his return to England in 1837, Power renewed his acting career on the London stage during the summer. By then his remuneration was so substantial that any thoughts of leaving the theater were dismissed. In July 1838 Power embarked on a third theater tour of the United States, subsequently appearing in New York City, Philadelphia, and Baltimore, before returning to England in December. While at the height of his career in Great Britain, the popular actor decided on yet another trip to America, primarily to look after his problematic investments, including a title dispute over land that he had purchased in Texas and to recover 3,000 pound sterling invested in the Second Bank of the United States. (In the midst of a deflationary period in America, many banks suspended payment.)

Power left England in late August 1840 and reembarked for home on the steamship *President* on March 11, 1841. The largest ocean-going steamer at the time, the *President* had earlier attracted thousands of curious onlookers in England to view her "imposing mass; her sides black and towering as an impenetrable fortress."[55] A close friend of Power later recalled that in 1840 the actor had concluded that the *President* was "an ugly-looking brute, and I won't go on her."[56] However, Power did book his return passage on the steamer. Three days into the voyage, while battling a severe tempest between the shoals of Nantucket and George's Bank, the *President* disappeared. Not a single survivor or piece of wreckage was ever found.

Forty-four-year-old Tyrone Power left behind a wife, four sons, and three daughters. His second son Maurice decided upon a stage career but died in 1849. His grandson Frederick Tyrone Power also became an actor but died while filming a Hollywood movie in 1931. Tyrone Power's most famous descendant, Tyrone Edmund Power (Frederick's son) also followed in his great-grandfather's footsteps as an actor. After a number of successful Hollywood film roles, the movie idol joined the U.S. Marines during World War II, resuming his flourishing career after the war. In 1958, 44-year-old Tyrone Edmund Power, like his father, died of a heart attack while filming a movie.

The following narrative, written by Tyrone Power, describes a journey through the Champlain Valley in 1835. Although Power did not depict all areas of the lake, he captured the aura of Lake Champlain.

Detail of "Burlington Bay." Drawing by Harry Fenn in *Picturesque America* edited by William Cullen Bryant. (Author's collection)

Journal of Lake Champlain[57]

Saturday, May 30th [1835]. Went on board the De Witt Clinton steam-boat* about six P.M. and in the brightest possible night sailed up the most beautiful of rivers. We were not crowded; my excellent friend C----e was in company, on his way to take unto him a wife, and consequently the trip was to me unusually agreeable. We kept pacing the deck until we had passed through the deep shadows of the highlands, and floated over the silvery expanse of Newburg[h] Bay.

Sunday, 31st. Before six A.M. we were set ashore at Albany. Breakfasted at the Eagle, and at nine A.M. left for Saratoga by the rail-road; thence by stage to Whitehall. The day was fine, the roads rough enough to be sure. To the north lay the mountain state of Vermont, and to the south a ridge of bold well-wooded heights. At Glenfalls we passed the Hudson [River] by a wooden bridge thrown over the very foot of the cataract; luckily, whilst in the act of crossing, a trace [strap to the harness] came unhitched, and we pulled up to order matters, just at the centre of the misty abyss. Thus were we afforded ample leisure to look on the wild fall, which, when in the wilderness, must have been a glorious scene; for, disfigured as it now is by a mill or two of the ordinary kind, it is still magnificent.**

Our ride from this place to Whitehall reminded me much of some part of North Wales: the enclosures are small, irregularly shaped, and surrounded by walls of stone; many rills [rivulets or brooks] of clear water are crossed, making their way to the Hudson through rough courses bestrewn with fragments of rock: close on the left the river is itself visible every now and then, whilst in the distance rise a confused heap of wild mountains.

Numerous comely looking pigs, together with groups of round-faced fat children, barefooted and bareheaded, complete the resemblance.

For the last seven miles the road was of the roughest kind; but our coachman rattled along merrily, getting us to Whitehall by ten P.M.

Monday, June 1st. At about one we quitted the comfortable inn here, and the busy little town of Whitehall; and in the fine steamer Phoenix*** thridded

---

*The 373-ton sidewheeler *De Witt Clinton* had been built at Albany in 1828 and was converted to a barge in 1843.

**In the 1830s Theodore Dwight described the Hudson River at Glens Falls in his guidebook, *The Northern Traveller*: "The river here makes a sudden descent of 37 feet, over a rock of dark blue limestone. . .The projection of two large masses of rock divides the water into three sheets. . .A dam is thrown across just above the falls, which supplies a Cotton Manufactory of Stone with water, as well as several mills. . .the mouths of two caverns are found facing the north, in different places among the rocks. . .This place is made the scene of some of the most interesting chapters of Mr. [James Fenimore] Cooper's novel of *The Last of the Mohicans*."[58] In August 1824, prior to writing his famous novel, Cooper viewed Glens Falls in the company of four English travelers. One of the English tourists, Edward Stanley (later prime minister of England), recorded that "Mr. Cooper, the American Novelist, who was of our party on this occasion, was much struck with the scenery which he had not before seen; and exclaimed 'I must place one of my old Indians here.' "[59]

***More than a decade earlier Professor Benjamin Silliman wrote that "Whitehall is situated at the bottom of a narrow defile in the mountains, and has the bustle and crowded aspect of a port, without the quiet and cleanliness of a village. Some of the houses are situated on elevations and declivities, and some in the bottom of the vale—some are of wood, and others of brick, but I was gratified to see many of them handsomely constructed of stone."[60] In 1833 English traveler Richard Weston mentioned that [threaded] our way out of the swampy harbour formed by the head-waters of the lake.

The hills about us rose boldly, and were covered with a variety of trees now clothed in their freshest leaves, therefore beautiful to look on. For many miles the channel continues narrow, at times confined by a steep wall of marble surmounted by rich flowering shrubs; then, for a short distance, laving [flowing along] the edge of some rich meadow slope.* At last, the lake expanded gloriously, reminding me, at a first glimpse, of the Trossachs [valley in central Scotland], save that here was less grandeur and deep shadow, the outlines of the mountains were softer and the valleys more fertile.

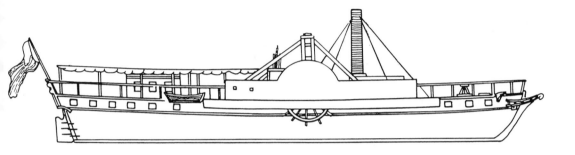

The Steamboat *Phoenix II.*
Drawing by Kevin J. Crisman from the poster "The Steamboats of Lake Champlain."
(Lake Champlain Maritime Museum)

The green mountains of the State of Vermont now bounded the lake upon the north, and on the south rose the Giant-mountains of the State of New York. These were for ever changing in form, as we crossed and re-crossed the lake in order to land or receive passengers from stated points. This circumstance also brought us acquainted with several very lovely locations. Beneath the old fort of Ticonderoga

"the houses in this place, as every where else, are built of wood, though stone and lime abound in the neighbourhood. I am convinced the Americans build houses only for themselves, not for their descendants."[61]

The 150-foot *Phoenix II* was completed in 1820 at Vergennes as a replacement for the 146-foot *Phoenix* which had burned and sunk near Colchester Shoal (north of Burlington) the previous year. Six lives were lost in the catastrophe. Today the wreck of the original *Phoenix*, lying at depths of 60 to 110 feet, has been designated an Underwater Historic Preserve by the state of Vermont. The *Phoenix II* and the 108-foot steamboat *Congress* were the first vessels to be advertised as providing a "delightful excursion" with views of forts, the site of Macdonough's 1814 naval battle, etc.[62] During his 1825 tour of America, the Marquis de Lafayette traveled from Burlington to Whitehall aboard the *Phoenix II*, adorned for the occasion with American and French flags and other decorations.

*In 1825 Henry Dilworth Gilpin described the southern section of Lake Champlain as "nothing more than a narrow sluggish river, without apparent motion, among the high rocky and mountainous ridges, between whose feet and the lake, there is generally a considerable extent of low, wet, marshy ground."[63] This part of the lake remains very primitive and perhaps the beauty and wildlife may be more appreciated by tourists today than in 1825.

we halted for a few minutes;* and at Crown-point our stay was long enough to allow. . .a rough sketch being taken of the roofless barracks and the ruined works.**

In the course of our progress we ran into two or three of the sweetest bays imaginable, where the calm lake was shadowed by steep mountains, down whose sides leaped little tributary streams that rushed sparkling and foaming into its turbid bosom.

It is most certain that, had these beauties been given to England or to Scotland, they would each and all have been berhymed [in verse] and bepainted until every point of real or imaginable loveliness had been exhausted: for myself, I have looked on many lakes, and by none have been more delightfully beguiled than by a

Facing page: Fort Ticonderoga in the nineteenth century.

Top left: Detail of "Fort Ticonderoga, from Eastern Shore." Drawing by Harry Fenn in *Picturesque America* edited by William Cullen Bryant. (Author's collection)

Top right: Detail of "Fort Ticonderoga." Drawing by Harry Fenn in *Picturesque America* edited by William Cullen Bryant. (Author's collection)

Center: "Ruins of Fort Ticonderoga—Lake Champlain" by W. R. Miller, engraved by S. V. Hunt. (Author's collection)

Bottom: "Ruines du Fort Ticonderoga" by Jacques Gerrard Milbert. (New York State Library)

*Theodore Dwight's 1831 edition of *The Northern Traveller* noted that the "walls still remain of all [the barracks at Fort Ticonderoga] except those on the eastern side. . .two stories high; and these, with chimneys, several of which are standing are the principal objects seen from a distance. . .At each corner was a bastion or a demi-bastion; and under that in the north-eastern one is a subterranean apartment, the access to which is through a small entrance near the corner of the court yard. It communicates with two magazines at the further end."[64] Dwight also described the Grenadiers' Battery (Lotbinière Battery) "situated on a rocky point towards the east from the main fortress. . .[once] connected by a covered way, the traces of which are distinctly visible. It is surrounded by a wall faced with stone, with five sides, one of which measures about 180 feet; but [collapsing]. . .The remaining parts are nearly entire, and about 10 feet high."[65] Despite trees that blocked the view, he traced the remnants of the old French lines originally built by Montcalm in 1758 and rebuilt by subsequent armies.

Nathaniel Hawthorne sat alone in one of the roofless barracks (probably in 1832) which "appear[ed] to have occupied three sides of a large area, now overgrown with grass, nettles, and thistles. The one in which I sat was long and narrow, as all the rest had been, with peaked gables. The exterior walls were nearly entire, constructed of gray, flat, unpicked stones. . .There were a few particles of plastering near the chimney. . .I closed my eyes on Ticonderoga in ruins, and cast a dream-like glance over pictures of the past, and scenes of which this spot had been the theater."[66]

James Stuart, a British traveler who also visited Ticonderoga in this period, made note of the new owner of the fort's grounds: "Mr. [William Ferris] Pell of New York, who prevents any farther dilapidation of the works, and has put the whole in good order,—especially the garden, formerly called the King's garden, to which he has been at pains to bring varieties of trees, shrubs, and fruits."[67]

**Theodore Dwight observed three sets of ruins at Crown Point in the 1830s: the Grenadiers' Battery (on the site of the present-day Champlain monument), Fort St. Frédéric (which then enclosed a garden), and the fortress built by Major General Jeffery Amherst. The latter ruin "appear[ed] much like Ticonderoga from a distance, showing the walls and chimneys of the old barracks, and walls of earth surrounding them. . .The fortress is surrounded by a ditch walled with stone, except where it has been blasted into the solid rock of blue limestone. . .The walls are about 20 or 25 feet high, and there is a convenient path running entirely round up the top, interrupted only by the gates at the north and south sides. . .Opposite the north gate is a small ledge of rocks; and close by, the remains of a covered or subterraneous way to the lake shore. On entering the fortress, the stranger finds himself in a level, spacious area, bounded on the left, and in front, by long ruinous buildings of stone, two stories high, and the first 220 feet long, while the ruins of similar ones are seen on two sides on the right. . .a portion of the shingled roof [officers barracks] which remains serves to cover a little hay mow and the nests of robins."[68]

contemplation of this during some nine hours of sunshine, sunset, and twilight, the last alone too brief. Atmosphere, I am aware, does much; and this was one of those lovely days whose influence expands the heart and takes the reason prisoner.

After quitting Burlington,* where we encountered the returning steam-boat [*Franklin*], and received a large accession of force, I retired to my berth, and enjoyed the soundest possible sleep.

Tuesday, 2d. On deck at six A.M.: found the lake had assumed a river-like appearance [Richelieu River]; the channel narrow, the banks low and swampy. The day, too, was as much changed as the scene from yesterday, for a drizzling rain was falling, and clouds looked heavy and threatening.

As we neared St. John's** we had a slight [brief] custom-house visitation; and soon after landing, were served with an excellent breakfast; after which came the bustle of departure. A string of carriages, of the same build used throughout the States, occupied half the little street, all loading heavily with baggage and bipeds [people], till by nine we got in motion, forming quite a caravan.

The road lay for a time along the bank of the new canal*** destined to unite the head-waters of the lake with the St. Lawrence, and was a pleasant succession of ditch and bog-hole. It got better after a few miles' jolting, but was nowhere tolerable, or creditable to his Majesty's dominions.

Return Trip

Friday 12th [June 1835]. Left St. John's with a couple of gentlemen in a canoe, for Isle aux Noi[x], there to abide the coming of the steamboat. The heat was intense, but our canoe men were a pair of lusty old lads, Canadians, and they pulled us up stream merrily at the rate of six miles an hour, keeping close beneath the trees growing out of the lake, here a narrow channel merely.

We found Fort Lennox garrisoned by a party of the 32d regiment, under the

---

*Visiting Burlington in 1832, Nathaniel Hawthorne later wrote a detailed description of the busy port, noting "a sandy beach, sweeping beneath a woody bank, around the semi-circular bay of Burlington. The painted light-house, on a small green island [Juniper Island], the wharves and warehouses, with sloops and schooners moored alongside, or at anchor, or spreading their canvas to the wind, and boats rowing from point to point, reminded me of some fishing town on the sea-coast. . . On closer inspection, the vessels at the wharves looked hardly sea-worthy—there being a great lack of tar about the seams and rigging, and perhaps other deficiencies, quite as much to the purpose. . .Our next movement brought us into a handsome and busy square, the sides of which were filled up with white houses, brick stores, a church, a court-house, and a bank. Some of these edifices had roofs of tin, in the fashion of Montreal. . .There was a pleasant mixture of people in the square of Burlington, such as cannot be seen elsewhere, at one view: merchants from Montreal, British officers from the frontier garrisons, French Canadians, wandering Irish, Scotchmen of a better class, gentlemen of the south on a pleasure-tour, country squires on business; and a great throng of Green Mountain boys, with their horse-wagons and ox-teams, true Yankees in aspect, and looking more superlatively so, by contrast with such a variety of foreigners."[69]

**St. Jean (St. Johns), Quebec, served as an important military post during the French and Indian War, the American Revolution, and the War of 1812. Benjamin Silliman observed the ruins of the fort at St. Jean in 1821: "A few troops are stationed here, but the ancient fort, which was very extensive, and still looks very venerable, with its high earthen walls and falling barracks, is an interesting ruin. . .In wandering about the ruins of the fort, I observed the cemetery of the garrison; their monuments and boards painted black, and the inscription is in white painted letters."[70]

***Although work began on the 12-mile Chambly Canal in October 1831, financial and political problems delayed the completion of the canal until November 1843.[71]

command of Major Swinburne, who was resident here with his family. The fort is regularly and well built, and the defences are in excellent order, save that the facing of the ditch, being of wood, is tumbling in at most points, to the great danger of the foundation. As this place is considered worthy a garrison, it would be as well that this ditch should be faced with stone, in a way becoming the other defences, all of which appear to be built in the best manner, and are in good preservation.*

At three o'clock P.M. the steamer was announced in sight, and we hastened to the little wharf where the captain always lands to show his clearance; a matter of form which is strictly observed.

The inhabitants; at least the civilians, were all assembled on the wharf, for this arrival was the event of the day. The little group was composed of two or three officers' ladies, with their families. Amongst these I noticed one pretty black-eyed English girl, who I fancied looked after the boat as it left the shore, and was whirled along side the steamer, with a mournful glance, wherein I read the word home written as plainly as I ever read it in a book.

"I wish you were returning to your home, my sweet girl," replied I, in the same language; "and that I might be your escort, you should be well and honestly guarded, at all events."

In a moment I was for ever sundered from this object of my commiseration yet had my eyes only been as expressive as hers, all I have set down here might have been read therein.

Away we sped along the winding lake, turning from shore to shore, now visiting one pretty landing, now another; a mode of proceeding that is amidst such scenery, perfectly delightful.

Saturday, 13th. Breakfasted at Whitehall, and took the middle line to Albany, traversing a wild sterile country, over bad roads and worse bridges, until we reached Sandy-hill [Hudson Falls], where the noble Hudson bursts upon the view.

From this point to Albany the river is never lost sight of; and a grateful sight the beautiful stream afforded to a sun-dried, half-smothered traveller, to turn from the dusty track and contemplate its cool waters and pleasant groves.

Notes

1. Tyrone Power, *Impressions of America; During the Years 1833, 1834, and 1835* (Philadelphia: Carey, Lea & Blanchard, 1836), Volume 1, vi.
2. Ibid., Volume 2, 183.
3. John M. Duncan, *Travels Through Part of the United States and Canada in 1818 and 1819* (Glasgow: Hurst, Robinson, & Company, 1823), Volume 2, 233.

*Isle-aux-Noix was a significant military post in three wars. After the end of the War of 1812, naval construction was suspended at the shipyard on the island. In 1820 William Dunlap noticed "various Vessels of War half finished left as the peace [of] 1814 found them."[72] In 1831 British traveler Godfrey Vigne "observed several schooners on the stocks, remaining, like the ships at Kingston [Ontario], as they were at the close of the war, and several old gun boats."[73] In the summer of 1819 new construction for a defensive fortification was begun at Isle-aux-Noix and continued for the next ten years. Fort Lennox would be named for Charles Lennox, the Duke of Richmond and governor general of Canada who had died in 1819. Theodore Dwight's 1831 guidebook noted "a long wall and battery on the south side, with angles; beyond which are seen a large stone building, and the roofs of others on the left and right of it, forming the storehouses, &c. of the post. The channel is on the east side, and very narrow, faced for a considerable distance by another battery."[74]

4. Benjamin Silliman, *Remarks Made on a Short Tour Between Hartford and Quebec in the Autumn of 1819*, 2nd ed. (New Haven: S. Converse, 1824), 192-93.
5. Ibid., 192.
6. Warder H. Cadbury, "The Men Who Built Fort Blunder," *The Antiquarian* 6 (Fall 1989): 7-12; See also Roberta Kane, "The Fort that Almost Lived Twice," *Adirondack Bits'n Pieces*, Winter 1983-84, 21-22; Peg Barcomb, *Rouses Point* (Rouses Point: p.n.a., 1977), 5-6.
7. Duncan, 2: 229; Theodore Dwight, Jr., *The Northern Traveller and Northern Tour with Routes to Springs, Niagara & Quebec*, 4th ed. (New York: J. & J. Harper, 1831), 192; See also Silliman, 208.
8. Gideon Minor Davison, *The Traveller's Guide: Through the Middle and Northern States, and the Provinces of Canada*, 5th ed. (Saratoga Springs: G. M. Davison, 1833), 239.
9. Ibid., 323, 327.
10. Silliman, 409, 411.
11. Dwight, 185.
12. *Albany Argus*, 30 November 1819. The opening ceremonies were attended by State Senator Martin Van Buren, future president of the United States, and Charles Budd of the U.S. Navy, "who kindly permitted the use of one of the boats from the fleet [probably the row galley *Allen*]."
13. Arthur Cohn and Marshall True, "The Wreck of the *General Butler* and the Mystery of Lake Champlain's Sailing Canal Boats," *Vermont History* 60 (Winter 1992): 35; See also W. S. Cann, *History of Chittenden County* (Syracuse: D. Mason & Co., Pub., 1886), 312.
14. Horatio Gates Spafford, *A Gazetteer of the State of New-York* (Albany: B. D. Packard and Horatio Gates Spafford, 1824), 97.
15. Ulysses Prentiss Hendrick, *A History of Agriculture in the State of New York* (Albany: New York State Agricultural Society, 1933), 246; See also F. Daniel Larkin, *New York Canals: A Short History* (Fleischmanns, N.Y.: Purple Mountain Press, 1998), 48.
16. Alvin F. Harlow, *Old Towpaths* (New York: D. Appleton and Company, 1926), 146.
17. *The Dictionary of National Biography*, Volume 16 (London: Oxford University Press, d.n.a.), 260.
18. J. W. Calcraft, "Tyrone Power; a Biography—Part I," *The Dublin University Magazine* 40 (September 1852): 269-71.
19. J. W. Calcraft, "Tyrone Power; a Biography—Part II," *The Dublin University Magazine* 40 (November 1852): 564.
20. *Dictionary of National Biography*, 16: 260.
21. Calcraft, Part II, 565.
22. Ibid., 566.
23. J. W. Calcraft, "Tyrone Power: a Biography—Part III," *The Dublin University Magazine* 40 (December 1852): 732.
24. Power, 1: 14.
25. Ibid., 2: 218.
26. Allan Nevins, *American Social History: As Recorded by British Travellers* (New York: Henry Holt and Company, 1923), 140.
27. John Lambert, *Travels through Canada and the United States of North America 1806, 1807, & 1808*, 2nd ed. (London: C. Cradock and W. Joy, 1814), Volume 2, 6, 8.
28. Basil Hall, *Travels in North America* (1829; reprint ed., Akademische Druck, 1964), Volume 2, 5-6.
29. Ibid., 7.
30. Una Pope-Hennessy, ed., *The Aristocratic Journey* (New York: G. P. Putnam's Sons, 1931), 59. Mrs. Hall was also positive about Lake George: "I never saw anything more beautiful. It is really exquisite."
31. Nevins, 159.
32. Frances Trollope, *Domestic Manners of the Americans*, ed. John Lauritz Larson (St. James, N.Y.: Brandywine Press, 1993), 59.
33. Nevins, 160.
34. Power, 1: viii.
35. Ibid., 1: vii.
36. Ibid., 1: 146.
37. Ibid., 1: 254.
38. Ibid., 1: 147.
39. Ibid., 2: 171, 1: 147.

40. Ibid., 1: 212.
41. Ibid., 1: 213.
42. Ibid., 1: 247.
43. Ibid., 1: 249.
44. Ibid.
45. Ibid., 2: 27.
46. Ibid., 1: 116.
47. Ibid., 1: 179.
48. Ibid., 1: 82.
49. Ibid., 1: 234; For an excellent history of horseboats see Kevin J. Crisman and Arthur B. Cohn, *When Horses Walked on Water: Horse - Powered Ferries in Nineteenth-Century America* (Washington, D.C.: Smithsonian Institution Press, 1998).
50. Power, 1: 147.
51. Ibid., 1: 161.
52. Ibid., 1: 162.
53. Ibid., 2: 214-15.
54. Ibid., 2: 215-16.
55. Calcraft, Part III, 725.
56. Ibid., 726.
57. Power, 2: 181-83, 206-7.
58. Dwight, 163-65.
59. Edward Stanley, *Journal of a Tour in America 1824-1825* (London: R & R Clark, Ltd., 1930), 34.
60. Silliman, 182.
61. Richard Weston, *A Visit to the United States and Canada in 1833* (Edinburgh: Richard Weston and Sons, 1836), 162.
62. Ogden Ross, *The Steamboats of Lake Champlain 1809 to 1930* (1930; reprint ed., Quechee, VT.: Vermont Heritage Press, 1997), 35.
63. Henry Dilworth Gilpin, *A Northern Tour: Being a Guide to Saratoga, Lake George, Niagara, Canada, Boston* (Philadelphia: H. C. Carey & I. Lea, 1825), 224.
64. Dwight, 181-82.
65. Ibid., 182; See also Alex Bliss, "A Visit to Fort Ticonderoga in 1825," *The Bulletin of the Fort Ticonderoga Museum* 8 (Summer 1949): 160-62.
66. Nathaniel Hawthorne, "A Visit to Ticonderoga 100 Years Ago," *The Bulletin of the Fort Ticonderoga Museum* 4 (January 1936): 14-15; Alfred Weber, Beth L. Lueck, and Dennis Berthold, *Hawthorne's American Travel Sketches* (Hanover, N.H.: University Press of New England, 1989), 67-68.
67. James Stuart, *Three Years in North America*, 3rd ed. (Edinburgh: Robert Cadell, 1833), Volume 1, 170.
68. Dwight, 186-88.
69. Weber, Lueck, and Berthold, 43-45; See also Frances Wright, *Views of Society and Manners in America*, ed. Paul R. Baker (Cambridge, MA.: The Belknap Press of Harvard University Press, 1963), 157.
70. Silliman, 400.
71. P.-André Sévigny, *Trade and Navigation on the Chambly Canal: A Historical Review* (Ottawa: National Historic Parks and Sites Branch, Parks Canada, 1983), 22.
72. William Dunlap, *Diary of William Dunlap* (New York: New York Historical Society, 1930), Volume 2, 544.
73. Godfred T. Vigne, *Six Months in America* (London: Whittaker, Treacher, & Co., 1832), Volume 2, 219.
74. Dwight, 193.

"Split Rock" from *Nelson's Guide to Lake George and Lake Champlain* (1866).

13. Benjamin C. Butler 1873

Bᴇɴᴊᴀᴍɪɴ C. Bᴜᴛʟᴇʀ's 1873 guidebook *From New York to Montreal* combined the history of the momentous events at Lake George and Lake Champlain with practical tourist information. Butler had a deep commitment to the history of the region, having written *Lake George and Lake Champlain from their First Discovery to 1759*, which was published by the Weed, Parsons and Company of Albany in 1868. In the first chapter of this book, Butler mused that travelers at fashionable summer resorts may "perhaps [be] careless or ignorant of the great events that once transpired beneath their feet or within their vision. Yet the possession of these places has engaged the attention of kings, cabinets and parliaments."[1]

The era of tourism in the nineteenth century was aided by the continuing evolution of the transportation network in America. In 1868 Butler observed that by "taking the fine steamers of the Lake Champlain company, the traveler passing 'through by daylight' looks upon the scenes replete with historic lore. . .Every American, at least once in his life, should visit Lake George and Lake Champlain, and view for himself the scenes made historic by the events imperfectly described in the following pages."[2] By the 1840s the steamboats, which Basil Hall (chapter 12) had criticized earlier, had been replaced with modern vessels. Boarding an American steamboat at St. Jean, British traveler Alexander MacKay commented that the vessel "in her appearance and all her appointments [was] one of the most magnificent of the kind I had seen in America. She was a floating palace."[3] Novelist Charles Dickens also praised Lake Champlain steamboats for "their conveniences, cleanliness, and safety" and singled out the steamer *Burlington* as "a perfectly exquisite achievement of neatness, elegance, and order. The decks are drawing-rooms; the cabins are boudoirs, choicely furnished and adorned with prints, pictures, and musical instruments; every nook and corner in the vessel is a perfect curiosity of graceful comfort

Lake Champlain Steamers

Top: The steamboat *Adirondack* plied the lake from 1867 to 1875. (Delaware and Hudson Collection, New York State Library) *Middle:* The steamboat *United States*, retired in 1873. (Special Collections, Benjamin F. Feinberg Library, SUNY Plattsburgh) *Above, left:* The steamboat *Vermont II* began service in 1871. (Special Collections, Bailey/Howe Memorial Library, UVM) *Above, right:* The wrecked steamboat *Champlain* on the side of the mountain north of Westport (1875). (Special Collections, Bailey/Howe Memorial Library, UVM)

and beautiful contrivance. . .[a] floating palace."[4] The guidebooks of London-based Thomas Nelson and Sons noted that "the appearance of [Lake Champlain] steamers at night is exceedingly grand. The wood with which their fires are fed send forth clouds of the most brilliant sparks, which issue from their funnels like a magnificent pyrotechnic display. . .they have the appearance of monstrous fiery serpents as they go rushing past."[5] However, by the time of Butler's guidebook, most Champlain steamers had been converted to coal; the 251-foot *Adirondack*, completed at Shelburne Harbor in 1867, was the first of the Champlain Transportation Company steamboats to be specifically designed to use coal.

Between the time of Tyrone Power's 1835 journey through Lake Champlain and Benjamin C. Butler's guidebook of 1873, more than a dozen steamboats were built at the lake. The largest passenger steamers of this period included the *Burlington* (1837-1854), *Whitehall* (1838-1853), *Saranac* (1842-1855), *Francis Saltus* (1844-1859), *United States* (1847-1873), *Montreal* (1855-1880), *R. W. Sherman/America* (1851-1866), *Canada* (1853-1870), *Adirondack* (1867-1875), *Oakes Ames/Champlain* (1868-1875),* and *Vermont II* (1871-1903). All of these vessels were at one time or another owned by the Champlain Transportation Company, which dominated steamboat traffic on both Lake George and Lake Champlain. Under Colonel LeGrand Cannon's leadership, the CTC had completed the acquisition of the Lake George Steam Boat Company in 1868, and during the same year the company agreed to a friendly takeover by the Rensselaer and Saratoga Railroad. By the summer of 1870, railroads, including the Whitehall and Plattsburgh, Vermont Central,

Train emerging from the Willsboro Tunnel.
(Seneca Ray Stoddard Collection, NYS Museum)

Plattsburgh and Montreal, Vermont and Canada, and Rutland Railroad, connected many of the communities along or near Lake Champlain.[8] Subsequent years would witness further expansion and consolidation of the lines. In 1871 the Delaware and

*The most famous vessel of this period, the 258-foot steamboat *Oakes Ames*, was originally built to carry loaded railroad cars between Burlington and Plattsburgh. The 1871 guidebook of R. S. Styles' Steam Printing House noted that the *Oakes Ames* was "remarkable for her great strength, and a speed scarcely [ever] impeded by any stress of weather."[6] Two years later the steamer was acquired by the Champlain Transportation Company and converted into a luxurious passenger vessel. The Styles' guidebook had suggested that "steamboat navigation extending over sixty years. . .has experienced but a single disaster [*Phoenix* 1819], demonstrat[ing] the skill and prudence of the officers and the excellence of the vessels."[7] Four years later, however, Pilot John Eldredge, apparently sleepy from taking morphine, crashed the *Champlain* (formerly *Oakes Ames*) full speed into the mountainside four miles north of Westport.

Hudson Canal Company leased in perpetuity all of the assets of the Rensselaer and Saratoga Railroad, including the two steamboat operations. Under the Delaware and Hudson, the firm's train schedules were coordinated with their steamboat runs, allowing continuous service between New York City and Montreal (the D & H had also acquired the Whitehall and Plattsburgh and the Montreal and Plattsburgh Railroads). In 1875 the company opened its newly-constructed rail line from the Baldwin Landing on northern Lake George to the Montcalm Landing on Lake Champlain at Ticonderoga. Seven years later the Delaware and Hudson brought railroad lines from Glens Falls to its steamboat landing at the southern end of Lake George. Although the Lake George operation benefited from increased passenger traffic because of the convenient access by train to the depot at the southern end of the lake, the expanded network of railroads along Lake Champlain reduced the number of passengers on the Lake Champlain steamboats. As a result, the Champlain Transportation Company solicited summer tourists through advertisements which emphasized the history and scenery of the lake.[9]

Contemporary guidebooks noted that the waters of Lake Champlain were "crowded with shipping of all kinds; steamers, tugs, sloops, schooners, canal-boats, barges, and small craft. . .constantly passing to and fro, giving life and animation to the scene."[10] The vast majority of commercial vessels at the time of Benjamin C. Butler's tourist guide were related to the expansion of canal traffic. The Chambly Canal, completed in 1843, allowed canal boats to pass from the St. Lawrence River to St. Jean and then continue to Lake Champlain. As the demand for resources for an industrial economy accelerated, traffic on the Champlain Canal and Lake Champlain "doubled on the average, in every eight years," reaching 1,100,000 tons in 1863.[11] An amendment to New York's constitution was passed in 1854 authorizing enlargement of the Champlain Canal locks; by 1877 all locks on the canal conformed to the enlarged Erie Canal standards.[12] Two basic types of canal vessels dominated the bulk cargo trade on the lake: one type involved sloop- and schooner-rigged canal boats which sailed on the open lake and were towed through the canal by a horse or mule after the removal of its masts. The second type was towed both in the canal and on the open lake; in the latter instance it was tied together with 30 or 40 other boats and towed by a steamboat.

From their origin on Lake Champlain in the late eighteenth century, ferryboats continued to ply the waters of the lake during the tourist era of the nineteenth century. At one time or another, ferry crossings connected Benson Landing to Putnam Station, Chipman Point to Wright, Orwell to Montcalm Landing, Larrabee Point to Ticonderoga, Chimney Point to Crown Point and Port Henry, Adams' Landing (Arnold's Bay) to Barber's Point, Basin Harbor to Westport, Hawley's Bay (Kingsland Bay) to Grog Harbor, Charlotte to Essex, Burlington to Port Kent, Grand Isle to Cumberland Head, Alburg to Rouses Point, and several other points. Hotels and taverns located at ferry landings enjoyed a booming business during the heyday of the ferries. But as rail connections expanded along Lake Champlain during the latter half of the nineteenth century, many of the ferries declined in importance.

For a time, however, horse-powered ferries on Lake Champlain caught the attention of some travel writers such as Zadock Thompson, a noted Vermont historian and naturalist, who remarked in his 1845 guidebook that "[Charles] McN[ei]l's [and Henry R. Ross'] Ferry, between Charlotte landing and the village

Lake Champlain Ferries

Top left: Sail ferry at the Chimney Point-Crown Point-Port Henry crossing. Drawing by Harry Fenn from *Picturesque America. Top right:* Cable ferry crossing in the southern section of Lake Champlain. (Special Collections, Bailey/Howe Memorial Library, UVM) *Above left:* Ferryboat *Ethan Allen* at Larrabee's Point, Vermont. (Postcard, Mahlon and Gina Teachout Collection) *Above right:* "Ferry off Larrabee's Point, Vermont" by John George Brown. (Shelburne Museum)

of Essex. . .is one of the oldest and best ferries across the lake. The passage is by horseboat [*Eclipse*], and is performed in about 30 minutes."[13] Thompson used the same description in his 1851 guide, but his 1854 edition mentioned that "the passage is by a small steamboat called the Boquet."[14] However, in the same guide he noted that "a horse ferry plies between this place [Westport] and Basin Harbor."[15] Between 1826 and the early 1860s the horse ferries *Experiment*, *P. T. Davis*, and *Gipsey* (also written *Gypsy*) plied the route between Chimney Point and Port Henry; the *Eclipse* operated from 1828 to 1847 on the Charlotte-Essex passage; and the *Eagle* ran from 1832 into the 1840s on the Basin Harbor-Westport crossing.[16] Eventually steam-powered vessels dominated the remaining crossings on Lake Champlain.

The period from the 1840s to the 1870s witnessed a steady stream of travel guidebooks concentrating on the Northern Tour. By the 1870s travel was particularly "fashionable" and was considered a measure of social status, drawing affluent urban dwellers to elegant hotels in picturesque settings.[17] However, as more modest hotels, boarding houses, and rail transportation expanded, less affluent travelers also visited Lake Champlain.

Zadock Thompson had his first edition of a *Guide to Lake George, Lake Champlain, Montreal and Quebec* published in 1845. One of the earliest guidebooks to focus on Lake George and Lake Champlain, the popular travel guide was reissued in 1848 and revised in 1851, 1854, 1857, and republished anonymously by Chauncey Goodrich and Company in 1858 after Thompson's death.[18] Although Thompson's format, which combined history with scenic details, had been used by earlier guidebook writers, his description of sites along the lakes influenced the tone of many later guides, including that of Benjamin C. Butler. Thompson's history of the lakes presented in his guidebooks relied on his earlier book *History of Vermont* (1833). This latter work borrowed heavily from Samuel Williams' second edition of *The Natural and Civil History of Vermont* (1809) and Nathan Haskins' *History of the State of Vermont* (1831).[19] While subsequent guidebooks often paraphrased Thompson's work, including Thomas Nelson and Sons' *Lake George and Lake Champlain*, others such as John Disturnell's *A Trip through the Lakes of North America* quoted his material extensively.[20]

By the 1860s and 1870s a new crop of guidebooks was available to travelers on the Northern Tour. L. M. Fouquet's 1867 guidebook *Lake Champlain, Lake George! Lake Memphremagog, The Adirondacs! and Mount Mansfield* covered a good deal of historical material on the region, including 12 pages on the dramatic 1819 burning of the steamer *Phoenix,* in which six passengers perished.[21] The amount of space devoted to the steamboat disaster seems surprising, given the intent of the guidebook to promote tourism. Fouquet borrowed some passages directly from the Nelson guidebook (*Lake George and Lake Champlain*) and included a promotion for his own hotel in Plattsburgh, the Fouquet House. Other guidebooks in the 1860s were more broadly based but also covered Lake Champlain and its history in detail:Charles H. Sweetser's *Book of Summer Resorts* (1868) and Charles Newhall Taintor's *The Hudson River Route* (1869).[22] In 1871 the R.S. Styles' Steam Printing House published the 168-page *A Descriptive and Historical Guide to the Valley of Lake Champlain and the Adirondacks*, the longest and most detailed guide to date on the lake. Although the Styles' guidebook was published without an author's name, it has generally been attributed to historian Winslow C. Watson. A few years later Edwin R. Wallace's equally long *Descriptive Guide to the Adirondacks and Handbook of Travel* was published and reprinted in annual editions for more than 20 years.[23] Wallace's work, however, used extensive verbatim sections from the Styles' guide.

Although guidebooks provided the best detailed information for travelers, they lacked the emotion often evoked in individual tourists by the beauty of Lake Champlain. In 1851, 21-year-old George Wurts, a newspaper employee from New Jersey, wrote in his journal that "it is impossible to describe the scenery on this beautiful lake. Little fairy like islands lie sleeping everywhere upon its bosom—and as we thread our devious course through them new scenes of beauty continually expand, each lovelier than the last. . .two giant ranges seem to be giant sentinels keeping eternal watch and ward over this lovely lake. . .the Green Mountains were clothed in a most delicate purple tint. . .The lofty Adirondacks were of a most beautiful blue."[24] Several years later, S. H. Hammond and L. W. Mansfield, aboard the steamboat *America,* observed "a thousand romantic bays, that steal landward around jutting promontories, lying in the deep shadow-like entrances to immense caverns; a hundred beautiful islands; green fields stretching away to the base of the hills, tall precipices rising in ragged and beetling [overhanging] cliffs right up from the deep waters, upon the tops of which stand old primeval trees, like sentinels upon the battlements of some ancient castle."[25]

Benjamin C. Butler made a substantial contribution to the historical writings on Lake George and Lake Champlain which would influence later generations of writers. He was also noted for his successful business, military, and political careers. This may seem surprising given the characterization of his early years by an acquaintance as "a wayward boy, whose father, after the wife's death, lost control of him, lacking patience or reasonable forbearance."[26] Benjamin Clapp Butler was born in Oxford, New York, on April 20, 1821, to James Clapp and Julia Hyde Butler Clapp. Benjamin's father was a successful lawyer who had studied in Aaron Burr's law office in 1804 and settled in Oxford in 1808. His mother, "educated in the best English schools," was the eldest daughter of Dr. Benjamin Butler and had married James Clapp in 1815. In 1832 young Benjamin's mother died at the age of 38, leaving five children.[27] Noted for an acrimonious personality coupled with severe digestive problems, James Clapp had no patience with his independent son. Young Benjamin's grandfather, Dr. Benjamin Butler, who had given up medicine and was then engaged in sheep raising and land speculation, intervened and, with the consent of his son-in-law, moved the boy into his own home. Young Benjamin attended Oxford Academy from 1837 to 1840; a classmate later described him as "very bright, quite erratic, well-read, and of independent mind."[28]

Complying with a provision in his grandfather's will and legalized by an act of the state legislature, Benjamin Butler Clapp had his name changed to Benjamin Clapp Butler.[29] Benjamin and his aunts shared his grandfather's estate, following the latter's death in January 1839. After his education at the Oxford Academy, Benjamin studied law in Saratoga. His estrangement from his father, however, persisted after the death of his grandfather. In an 1844 letter, James Clapp suggested to Benjamin that he may have wasted his inheritance on a legal career: "I fear it has all, or mainly, been dissipated in the idle pursuit of a profession which, neither your early education or natural talent fitted you for. The profession of the law, as you well know, is overstocked with lawyers."[30] Clapp concluded the letter by noting that "these remarks are general and not intended to wound" and that he would be "grati-fied. . .by any honest employment that would forever save you from vice and crime. . .I shall always pray for your success and sincerely hope that you are no longer the victim of delusion."[31] Clapp himself was a lawyer, as was another son, James. Suffering from mental illness, the elder Clapp committed suicide at the age of 68 on January 8, 1854.

In June of 1854 Benjamin C. Butler married Mary Anne Skinner of Albany. By then Butler had a thriving profession as a lawyer and civil engineer at Lake Luzerne, New York, having established a law and surveying office there in 1845. On December 27, 1856, at a meeting of prominent members of the community, Butler urged the formation of the Warren County Agricultural Society. The following year Butler was elected president of the newly-created organization, serving until 1861 and again from 1865 to 1866.[32] A large annual agricultural fair was one of the activities organized by the Society, a tradition which continues to the present day. In 1860 Butler was elected to the New York State Assembly, but the outbreak of the Civil War cut short his political career. Two days after the war began, Butler volunteered, first serving as paymaster for the 22nd Regiment. In October 1861 Butler commenced his service as lieutenant colonel of the 93rd Regiment of New York Volunteers, with nearly half of its members being recruited from Warren County by Butler himself. The 1,000-man regiment subsequently fought at Fredericksburg, Chancellorsville, Antietam, the Wilderness, Cold Harbor, Spottsylvania, Petersburg, and in another half dozen bloody engagements. After the first two years of war, only 260 men of the original 1,000 remained. Butler was mustered out of the service in February 1865 and immediately returned to Lake Luzerne.[33] Soon after the war's end, Butler became instrumental in the construction of Saint Mary's Episcopal Church. In fact, "he has been said to have vowed on a Civil War battlefield that, were he spared, he would return home and build a church."[34] Noted for his eloquent public lectures, Butler donated the proceeds from his oratory to the building fund for Saint Mary's. The sword that Butler carried during the Civil War is presently held by the church.

Butler's writing career flourished after the Civil War in the form of a history book and guidebooks. (He had also been the editor of the *Saratoga Sentinel*.) His most substantive effort, the 240-page *Lake George and Lake Champlain, from their First Discovery to 1759*, was published in three editions (1868, 1869, and 1870). Butler relied on a number of authoritative secondary sources as well as first-hand military journals and orderly books, but placed considerable emphasis on the original letters and reports published in E. B. O'Callaghan's massive works, *The Documentary History of the State of New-York* (4 volumes) and *Documents Relative to the Colonial History of the State of New-York* (10 volumes), suggesting with the use of these volumes that "we arrived at a proper knowledge of events, which had either been wrongly located, or exaggerated, or obscured."[35] Butler's history text detailed Samuel de Champlain's 1609 voyage, the military raids and expeditions of King William's War (1689-1697), Queen Anne's War (1702-1713), and King George's War (1744-1748), and devoted six of the ten chapters to the French and Indian War (1755-1763). He not only presented the facts of the wars but brought a certain passion to the subject, juxtaposing the beauty of the lakes with the forlorn ruins of the region's fortifications: "Forts William Henry and Carillon, the salients of the two most powerful and most civilized nations of the globe, over whose scarp [inner side of a ditch surrounding a rampart] and counterscarp nature has thrown her protecting mantle of forest and turf—venerable in your ruins, ye[t] stand at either gateway of these classic waters, monuments of a heroic age, and of the wrestling of giants for the possession of a continent. Beneath your shadow the bones of thousands lie unrecognized though honorable dust, while every glen, bay, island and mountain, furnishes some legend which has made their names household words in American homes...Thy peaceful shore has seen the course of carnage and misery, the butchery of the tomahawk, and wasting of a siege."[36]

Butler's early history of Lake George and Lake Champlain laid the groundwork for his 11-chapter guidebook, *From New York to Montreal*, published in 1873 by the American News Company. Departing from New York City aboard a steamboat (or alternatively on the Hudson River Railroad), Butler delineated the sights and communities on the trip to Albany and Saratoga Springs, including hotel accommodations. His guidebook also covered Lake Luzerne, Schroon Lake, and other communities west of Lake George. Butler was also very much a part of the business of tourism, having built the elegant Wayside Inn* in Lake Luzerne in the early 1870s. He is often credited with bringing the tourist industry to the Luzerne area, devoting seven pages of his 1873 guidebook to the town. The detailed historical narratives in Butler's guidebook included descriptions of Fort Edward, Whitehall, Glens Falls, Lake George, Lake Champlain, Montreal, Quebec City and other areas. Because of the expansion of the rail network by the 1870s, Butler devoted his last chapter to the route "from Philadelphia to Saratoga via the Delaware & Hudson Canal Co.'s railroad. . .[aboard their] commodious drawing-room cars."[37] After the 155 pages of text, the guidebook highlighted an additional 37 pages of advertisements for hotels, steamboat lines, railroads, and medicinal springs. An updated 173-page version of Butler's guidebook, retitled *The Summer Tourist; Descriptive of the Delaware & Hudson Canal Co's Railroads, and their Summer Resorts* was published in several editions beginning in 1879 by the General Passenger Department of the D and H. The new guide included additional illustrations and some expanded sections on Lake Champlain; eight pages with four drawings were devoted to Ausable Chasm, reflecting the increase in tourist interest in the attraction.[38]

Butler resumed his political career in the 1870s, serving as a town supervisor of Luzerne in 1875 and 1876, and was elected to the New York Assembly in 1880. During this period many of his speeches and remarks before the legislature were published, including *Home-Spun to Calico* (1877), *The Hudson River Reservoirs* (1881), and *The New Capitol: A Criticism* (1881). In 1879 he also produced a large map, *The New York Wilderness: Hamilton County and Adjoining Territory*, published in Albany by Weed, Parsons, & Co., which delineated state and private lands in the Adirondacks.

On November 16, 1882, Benjamin C. Butler died at the age of 61, leaving his wife but no children. While the *Glens Falls Republican*'s obituary listed heart disease as the cause of his death, the *New York Times* and later sources suggested "disease of the liver."[39] Although Butler was "not a man of extraordinary ability," the *Glens Falls Republican* noted, "the versatility of his talents and his unusual energy made him a man of decided mark."[40] Butler's wife, Mary Anne Skinner Butler died in January 1901 at the age of 81.

The following description of Lake Champlain has been excerpted from Butler's 1873 guidebook *From New York to Montreal*. Some of his longer historical passages have been omitted because the material is covered in earlier chapters of this book. A number of typographical errors have been corrected in this text; his previous book on Lake George and Lake Champlain did not include these printing errors.

---

*The Swiss-inspired, five-story Wayside Inn exhibited high Victorian Gothic-style architecture. Overlooking Lake Luzerne on a 20-acre parcel, the 95-room inn accommodated 200 guests with additional space for another 100 tourists in 10 to 11 large cottages located on the grounds. The resort also encompassed a casino, farm, horse barn, and docks for rowboats. During the 1870s guests included Sarah Bernhardt, Ulysses S. Grant, William McKinley, J. Pierpont Morgan, Commodore Vanderbilt, and many others. The facility remained open until the 1930s, burning on April 5, 1938. Today the Hadley-Luzerne Central School is located on the site of the old hotel.[37]

Lake Champlain[41]

It is a great highway of commercial intercourse and pleasure travel. Four steamers form a day and a night line, two of which, the Adirondack and the Vermont, are models of elegance, convenience and tasteful furnishing. This line [Champlain Transportation Company] has been in existence for fifty years, and during that time has transported over a million passengers, with but one accident by fire, and without the loss of a life.*

The steamboat wharf is about a mile from Whitehall station, just below "the elbow." Near this place may be seen the hulks of the fleets which contended for the mastery at Plattsburgh in 1814.**

Just below is Put's Rock, the scene of Putnam's midnight ambuscade and battle with Marin.*** Beyond is South Bay, through which Dieskau made his disastrous expedition to the head of Lake George.† The lake through to Ti, winds among steep hills, and has the appearance of a river. Rank aquatic grasses grow upon the low lands [on] each side of it, for which reason the French named it *La grand Marias* [the Great Marsh].

*The 251-foot *Adirondack* was built in 1867 and the 262-foot *Vermont II* in 1871. The aging 240-foot *United States*, completed in 1847, was also owned by the Champlain Transportation Company at this time but was retired in 1873. The fourth steamboat that Butler makes reference to here is questionable—the 132-foot *A. Williams*, built in 1870, was not acquired by the CTC until 1874 (as was the *Oakes Ames*) and the 224-foot *Montreal* had been relegated to towing service before the publication of his guidebook. The remains of the *Adirondack*, the *United States*, and the *A. Williams* lie today at the bottom of Shelburne Harbor, along with several other dismantled steamers. The one accident by fire that Butler alludes to occurred in September 1819 when the 146-foot *Phoenix* caught fire and sank north of Burlington; six lives were lost in the tragedy. Only two years after the publication of Butler's guidebook, the 258-steamer *Champlain* (formerly *Oakes Ames*) crashed into the side of the mountain north of Westport; no lives were lost in this accident but the vessel was a total loss.

**The ship *Saratoga*, schooner *Ticonderoga*, brig *Eagle*, and galley *Allen* from Thomas Macdonough's 1814 squadron, along with the British prizes, the ship *Confiance* and brig *Linnet*, were moored in East Bay (Poultney River) in 1821. In 1824 and again in 1869 portions of the *Confiance* washed out of East Bay and several years later were blown up (300 pounds of copper, however, were salvaged). The *Saratoga* may have also swung out into the main channel and was later dismantled. The remains of the *Eagle*, *Allen*, and *Linnet* still lie in East Bay. A section of the bow of the *Linnet* was removed in 1949, and the *Ticonderoga* was taken out in 1958 and is presently displayed under a shed at the Skenesborough Museum.[42]

***Put's Rock, just south of South Bay, has been associated with Major Israel Putnam (1718-1790) who was captured on August 8, 1758, after a fierce skirmish with a large Canadian, French, and Indian raiding party. Tied to a tree, Putnam endured tomahawks thrown near his head and the butt of a musket smashed into his face after the weapon had misfired against his chest. Saved by the crossfire of renewed British and French musketry, Putnam was untied and forced to carry many of the French knapsacks as the raiding party retreated. At a camp that evening the Indians again lashed him to a tree and started a fire at his feet, but fortunately a rain shower extinguished the flames. A second attempt to burn Putnam ended when Captain Joseph Marin de La Malgue broke through the crowd of his Indian allies, kicked the brush away, and cut Putnam down. Forty-year-old Putnam was later exchanged and lived to serve as a major general in the American army during the Revolutionary War.[43]

†In 1755, traveling by water as far as South Bay, Jean-Armand Dieskau (Baron de Dieskau), the French commander in chief, led an army of regulars, Canadian militia, and Indians in an attack on the provincial army of Major General William Johnson encamped at the southern end of Lake George. The French force was defeated and Dieskau captured. Butler had covered the historical background of the battle earlier in his guidebook under the Lake George section.[44]

Left: The Phelp's House at Chipman Point, Vermont, located approximately three miles south of the Ticonderoga steamboat landing. (Postcard, Mahlon and Gina Teachout Collection) *Right:* Ruins of Fort Ticonderoga. (New York State Historical Association)

BENSON, thirteen miles from Whitehall, and ORWELL, seven miles further on, are the two first landings.

TICONDEROGA is twenty-four miles from Whitehall.

The village of Ticonderoga is situated at the lower fall about half way between the two lakes. Considerable additions are being made to the manufacturing facilities upon the water power, which is a very fine one. The bridge and sawmill, which were burnt by the French on the approach of Lord [George Augustus] Howe and the British army, were located here [in 1758].

Fort Ticonderoga or Carillon is a peninsula one hundred feet high, which contains about five hundred acres. Water lies upon three sides, and a deep swamp extends partly across the fourth.

Between the swamp and the lake, the French built in 1756 this stately fort, Carillon, a name signifying chiming water.*

This celebrated fortification has been held in the military possession of three distinct nations, and is the common theater of their glories and triumphs, and of their defeats and disasters. Most of the ramparts, the gate way, the walls of the barracks, the battery, the glacis [sloping bank], and the redoubt known as the water battery [Lotbinière or Grenadiers' Battery] remain, and will attract and reward the attention of the tourist.**

---

*The name Carillon, which translates to a chime in French, was said, according to tradition, to be derived from the cascade of water at the outlet of Lake George. While there is no definitive evidence, the name Carillon may have been associated with Philippe de Carrion, a former officer of the French Carignan Regiment who erected a log shed at Ticonderoga to facilitate the smuggling of furs between Albany and New France.[45] On January 17, 1756, Major General William Johnson sent the captured letters and papers of Baron de Dieskau to England. A map and a list of place names compiled from provincial scouting reports were also enclosed in the packet, including an explanation for the word Ticonderoga: "The French Fortifyed Post which they call Carillon call'd by the Indians Ticonderoge signifying ye Confluse of two Rivers."[46]

**In 1848 historian Benson J. Lossing carefully examined the site of Fort Ticonderoga, including Major General Louis-Joseph de Montcalm's 1758 battle lines—"the mounds and ditches of which are still very conspicuous."[47] Lossing viewed the remains of the two-story limestone barracks: "Near the southeastern angle of the range of barracks is the bakery; it is an under-ground arched room. . .the entrance steps are much broken, and the passage is so filled with rubbish that a descent into it is difficult.

Top: United States Hotel at Larrabee's Point. (Postcard, Mahlon and Gina Teachout Collection)
Above left: Ruins of Crown Point. (Photo by the author)
Above right: Crown Point Lighthouse built in 1858. (Postcard, author's collection)

LARRABEE'S POINT, [location of the United States Hotel] or Shoreham, is on the Vermont side, two miles beyond Ticonderoga.

CROWN POINT. The barracks were also built of solid stone, some of which are now standing.*

PORT HENRY. This is one of the most thriving villages on the shore of the lake and is situated in the town of Moriah. It is in the midst of a great iron district. Immense quantities of ore have been dug from the hills, which, instead of affording any evidence of appreciable diminution of the remaining supply, seem to prove the boundless magnitude of this source of wealth. As the excavations widen and deepen, the quantity and the quality of the mineral appears to increase and improve. The

It is about twelve feet wide and thirty long. On the right is a window, and at the end were a fire-place and chimney, now in ruins. On either side of the fire-place are the ovens, ten feet deep. . .This bakery and the ovens are the best-preserved portions of the fortress. . .The guide [Isaac Rice] informed me that many years ago he assisted in the labor of loading a vessel with bricks and stones taken from the fort, to build an earthern-ware factory on Missisqu[o]i Bay. . .Year after year the ruins thus dwindle."[48] (Two and a half pages of historical background on Fort Ticonderoga from Benjamin C. Butler's guidebook are omitted since the material is covered earlier in this book.)

*Benjamin C. Butler's long historical explanation of Crown Point is entirely omitted here because it duplicates earlier material in this book. Zadock Thompson's 1854 guidebook provides a more detailed description of the ruins, noting that "the ramparts are about 25 feet thick, and from 15 to 25 in height, and are riveted with solid masonry. . .the whole circuit, measuring along the top of the rampart,

ores in this district are magnetic, and yield about 60 per cent of iron. The exportation is about 300,000 tons per annum. The two principal firms are Witherbee, Sherman & Co. and the Port Henry Iron Company. The Bay State Iron Company, whose furnaces are at Port Henry, manufacture about 18,000 tons of iron per annum. The first mine opened in this town was the Cheever ore bed from which the yield is 60,000 tons per annum.* The Barton Bed and the New Bed are also important mines.

The ore is divided into three kinds, the price of which is $7, $6, and $4.50 per ton. It is sent by the cargo to all the furnaces down the Hudson River, and as far west as Pittsburgh and Cleveland, where it is mixed with other ores.

SPLIT ROCK. This is the most remarkable natural curiosity on the lake. It is an enormous mass of rock about half an acre in extent and thirty feet above the level of the water, which has been detached from the neighboring cliff, and is separated from it [by] twelve feet. It is put down on [William] Tryon's colonial map, as REGIOCHNE, but by the Iroquois it was known as Regeo Rock.** It derived this name from the fact that, long before the whites ever came to this country, a celebrated Indian

Aerial view of Split Rock. (Photo by the author)

chief by the name of Rogeo, while on an excursion, was acidentally drowned off this rock, and ever after, the Indians as they passed, were accustomed to throw a

including the bastions, is 853 yards. . .Within the fort were four large stone buildings, designed for barracks and other uses, one of which is now wholly removed [armory], and another 287 feet long, is mostly thrown down [unfinished barracks]. The walls of the other two, being one 192 and the other 216 feet long, and two stories high are nearly entire. These were used as barracks, are built of solid masonry with chimneys. . .In the northeastern bastion is a large well, said to be 90 feet deep, and from this bastion was the descent to the covered way or underground communication with the lake. The walls of the covered way have fallen in, so as to render it impassable, but it may be traced through its whole length by a depression along the surface of the ground."[49] Styles' 1871 guide mentioned the ruins of Fort St. Frédéric, which could "be easily traced. The oven, the covered way and magazine are still discernible."[50]

*Prior to the American Revolution, Philip Skene's ironworks in Skenesborough (Whitehall) utilized ore from his land patent in the Cheever area.[51] At the turn of the nineteenth century, forges in the Champlain Valley continued to rely on ore from Skene's original ore bed. After the opening of the Champlain Canal, large-scale mining operations dominated the area, lasting until the 1970s.

**William Brassier's 1762 map referred to Split Rock as "Cloven Rock," and Gaspard-Joseph Chaussegros DeLery's 1748 map called it "Rocher fendu [boulder or rock split]."[52] Benjamin C. Butler based some of his information on an 1868 article in the *Historical Magazine* which detailed the 1696 land grant of Godfrey Dellius that extended as far north as "Rock Rosian [Regio]."[53] In 1750 John Lydius, an entrepreneur who traded extensively with Native Americans, provided an affidavit before the mayor of Albany in which he maintained "that he had always heard that the purchase made by Godfrey Dellius, in the year 1696, was commonly esteemed to extend to the rock Regio. . .about twenty leagues further North than Crown Point."[54] Erected in 1939, the New York State historical sign on route 9N overlooking Whallon Bay reads "Split Rock called Roche Regio by Indians."

stone toward it for good luck. It was further noted as being the recognized boundary between the Mohawk hunting grounds and those conceded to the Northern Indians residing on the St. Lawrence. These various nations conceded their rights of sovereignty to the French and English crowns. These rights were confirmed to each other by the respective governments, by the Treaty of Utrecht in 1713, and commissioners were appointed to ascertain and fix upon such boundaries, who, however, never took action in the premises.* Time rolled on, and the French built and occupied Crown Point and Ticonderoga. Seigniories [land grants] were laid out under the name and style of Hocquart and Al[ainville], which covered the above territory, also a portion across the lake, including the valley of Otter Creek, and extensive settlements were made.** After the conquest of the country [in 1759-1760] by Lord [Major General Jeffery] Amherst, the English officers, seeing these fair lands, applied for patents from the colonial authorities, which were met by a protest from the French proprietors and late occupants. The whole matter was referred to a commission of crown lawyers, who, after hearing the testimony on both sides, decided that, REGIO ROCK was the true boundary between New York and Canada, and that Crown Point and Ticonderoga, being confessedly within the bounds occupied by the Mohawk Indians as their hunting ground, the claim of the French was without title and void.***

WESTPORT. This is ten miles from Port Henry, and lies at the head of North-West Bay. Nearly opposite is Otter Creek, which is navigable for eight miles, to Vergennes. At this last place, in 1814, [Thomas] Macdonough's fleet was constructed. A British flotilla attempted to burn the vessels while on the stocks, but were prevented by Lieutenant Cassin, who beat them off. The fort which was subsequently constructed received its name of Fort Cassin from this circumstance.†

Twelve miles beyond is the charming village of Essex. The hospitable brick

---

*The Treaty of Utrecht, signed on April 11, 1713, ended Queen Anne's War (1702-1713) in North America. The Treaty provided that Split Rock was the boundary between French and English land claims, but the limits were not adhered to.

**Sieur Gilles Hocquart's 1743 land grant extended along the eastern shore of Lake Champlain somewhere near Basin Harbor on the northern border to a point south of Chimney Point and east on Otter Creek to present-day Middlebury. Hocquart, the intendant of New France until 1748, later sold his seigniory to Michel Chartier de Lotbinière, the builder of Fort Carillon. In 1738 Seigneur d'Alainville had been granted a large parcel of land encompassing most of present-day Ticonderoga and the north end of Lake George. Lotbinière later claimed the Alainville seigniory, but was not compensated with any land in Canada by the British government after the end of the French and Indian War.[55]

***Following the Treaty of Paris in 1763, which ended the Seven Years' War (French and Indian War in North America), the British government approved grants of land on the northern frontier by colonial governors. Former officers and soldiers who had served in the northern campaigns were given special consideration for land patents. In 1768 the British government temporarily suspended land grants north of Crown Point which conflicted with previous French claims. The American Revolution postponed the final decision on French claims; after years of litigation and several court decisions, French titles to the land along Lake Champlain were denied.[56]

†On May 14, 1814, a British fleet under Captain Daniel Pring was repelled at the mouth of Otter Creek by a battery of seven 12-pound cannon behind a horseshoe-shaped earthwork manned by men under Captain Arthur Thornton and Lieutenant Stephen Cassin, Macdonough's second in command. The point of land on the northern side of the entrance to Otter Creek thereafter was named Fort Cassin/Fort Cassin Point; but no new fortifications were ever built there. At the turn of the century travelers confused the remains of the Fort Cassin House with the original fort. Today a careful observer can discern the remnants of the 1814 earthworks.

Lake Champlain Industries
Top: Commercial operations on Otter Creek in Vergennes. (Special Collections, Bailey/Howe Memorial Library, UVM) *Right:* "Falls at Vergennes, VT." by S. H. Washburn (ca. 1875). (Shelburne Museum) *Below left:* Detail of "Birds Eye View of Burlington and Winooski, VT." by E. Meibek (1877), showing the steamer *Adirondack* and lumber stacked on the Burlington docks. (Special Collections, Bailey/Howe Memorial Library, UVM) *Below right:* Burlington Manufacturing Company Marble Works. (Special Collections, Bailey/Howe Memorial Library, UVM)

Mansion of the late General Henry H. Ross is now a pleasant summer hotel [Royce's Hotel]. A few miles north of Essex, on the Boquet river, were the first English settlements made in Essex County. Here, in May, 1765, the celebrated pioneer, William Gilliland, of New York, with his colony, cattle and horses, erected dwelling-houses, and at the falls, two miles above, built mills and made clearings.

In 1777 Burgoyne occupied the ground, and held high carnival with the Indian tribes.*

Beyond this point we approach the islands representing the cardinal points of the compass, and known as the Four Brothers. Near these occurred a naval encounter between the flotilla of [Benedict] Arnold, and the British under Governor

*In late June 1777 Lieutenant General John Burgoyne and his British invasion force landed at the mouth of the Boquet River. Burgoyne admonished about 400 Iroquois, Algonquin, Abenaki, and Ottawa warriors to "strike at the common enemies of Great-Britain."[57]

[Guy] Carlton in 1776.* Opposite, upon one of the highest peaks of the Green Mountains, apparently carved on the imperishable rock, is Camel's Hump [4,083 feet in height].

ROCK DUNDER, a few miles further north, a dark naked cliff, rises in a cone thirty feet above the lake. On the left of this is Juniper Island, and the right is Shelburne Bay, a narrow sheet of water extending four miles inland. Here is the harbor and ship yard of the Champlain Transportation Company, where their gallant steamers are built and moored during the winter.

Detail of "Burlington Bay" showing Juniper Island. Drawing by Harry Fenn from *Picturesque America*. (Author's collection)

BURLINGTON. The city of Burlington has a population of fifteen thousand. Its streets are broad, and lined with beautiful shade trees. It has many elegant private residences, and the eminence in its rear is crowned by the buildings of the Vermont University, and Agricultural College. The corner stone of the central edifice was laid by General Lafayette in 1825.**

The tomb of Ethan Allen lies in the cemetery. The late [Episcopal] Bishop [John Henry] Hopkins had his elegant and picturesque residence and seminary at Sharp-Shins Point [Lone Rock Point], two miles down the shore of the lake.

The lumber mart of Burlington is hardly second to any in the world, and has very extensive planing mills connected with it.***

Col. LeGrand B. Cannon† has a delightful residence here, and his large and spacious grounds [just south of Burlington] are continually open to visitors.

*The running battle between the American and British fleets occurred south of Split Rock on October 13, 1776 (see chapter 8).

**On June 29, 1829, Marquis de Lafayette laid a corner stone for a building at the University of Vermont: "The ceremony...took place in [the] presence of the pupils of the university, their professors, the magistrates of the city, and a great concourse of citizens."[58] About midnight Lafayette boarded the steamer *Phoenix II* and departed to the "loud farewells of the crowd who lined the shores" and a 13-gun salute.[59]

***Burlington became the center for Canadian lumber imports following the opening of the Chambly Canal in 1843. With the expansion of railroads, Burlington benefited from a direct connection to eastern cities and served as a major port for American canal boats using the Champlain Canal. (Canadian canal boats were prohibited from leaving Lake Champlain by international regulations.) Stockpiles of lumber adjacent to the wharves often covered 30 or 40 acres and numerous lumber forwarding companies and manufacturing firms were located in the area. Despite the commercial activity, visitors appreciated the charm of the city: in 1870 novelist Henry James called Burlington "a supremely beautiful town...The lower portion by the lake-side is savagely raw and shabby, but as it ascends the long hill...it gradually becomes the most truly, I fancy, of New England country towns...and ascends a stately, shaded, residential avenue to no less a pinnacle of dignity than the University of Vermont."[60]

†After purchasing a stock interest in the Champlain Transportation Company, LeGrand B. Cannon served as a director of the company in 1856 and then as president from 1864 to 1895. Cannon revitalized the CTC by modernizing the company's fleet and improving the financial well-being of the firm. He

The best hotels are the American, Van Ness and Lawrence House, which are spacious and superior.

The views from Burlington are superb. Ten miles width of lake makes a capital foreground for the famous wilderness of northern New York, above whose unbroken forests rise the peaks of Whiteface, McIntyre [Algonquin Peak] and Tahawas [Mt. Marcy]; the latter being six thousand feet high. Sixty peaks are visible from the cupola of the University.

Passengers desiring to go to the celebrated Mt. Mansfield House at Stowe, can take the cars of the Vermont Central Railroad for Waterbury station, thence by stage for ten miles through the finest scenery of the glen mountains.

PORT KENT. Nearly opposite to Burlington is Port Kent. The stone mansion of the late Elkanah Watson is on the hill. Col. Watson originated the first Agricultural Society in the State of New York, and his narrative of a journey made at the

"Burlington-Lake Champlain. Taken from College Hill" from *Nelson's Guide to Lake George and Lake Champlain* (1866).

age of 19, [beginning] in the year 1777, is the best record we now have of the principal towns and villages of the Revolutionary period.* He died in 1842, and the place is occupied by his descendants.

Four miles in the interior is Keeseville, midway between the two villages is the celebrated Au Sable Chasm, sketches of which are beginning to be seen in the National Academy of Design.

About a mile and a half from Keeseville, the Au Sable River makes a leap of twenty feet into a semi-circular basin of natural beauty. A mile further on another precipice sends the water down a hundred and fifty feet amid the wildest scenery. Following the stream now rapidly narrowing and deepening and foaming we shortly come to the chasm.

The river here is encased in a channel five feet wide, whose walls are from ninety to a hundred and twenty feet high. Lower down, toward the lake, the walls are fifty feet apart, descending perpendicularly and extending in a lateral canal, with occa-

reestablished "neatness and order" on the steamboats, insisting "on the courteous behavior of officers and men" and inaugurated the wearing of uniforms by crew members.[61] In 1868, cooperating with his brother-in-law George H. Cramer, president of the Rensselaer and Saratoga Railroad, Cannon facilitated the sale of the CTC to the railroad. A few years later the Rensselaer and Saratoga Railroad leased all its assets to the Delaware and Hudson Canal Company, including the Lake George and Lake Champlain steamboat lines. Cannon was a member of the D&H board of directors at the time and remained president of the CTC.

*Elkanah Watson's journal, edited by his son, historian Winslow C. Watson, was published in 1856 under the title *Men and Times of the Revolution; or, Memoirs of Elkanah Watson, including his Journals of Travels in Europe and America, from the year 1777 to 1842.*

"Birmingham Falls, Ausable Chasm"
from *Picturesque America*.
(Author's collection)

sional widenings, for more than half a mile. The entire scenery is wild beyond description.

Lateral fissures, deep and narrow, project from the main ravine at nearly right angles. Through one of these crevices the abyss is reached by a stairway of two hundred and twelve steps.*

KEESEVILLE. This is a fine manufacturing town, with [horse] nail factories, twine and wire works and a rolling mill, an examination of which will well repay the tourist. A chalybeate [medicinal] spring gushes forth on the premises of Mr. John R. Wills. There are several pleasant drives about the town, among which is one [about 11 miles south of Keeseville] to a defile known as POKE O'MOON-SHINE [Mountain]. The Au Sable and the Adirondack House are pleasant places for the wayfarer.

PLATTSBURGH is a village of some 8,000 people, one hundred and five miles from Whitehall. The place is distinguished as the scene of the victory of [Thomas] Macdonough and [Alexander] Macomb over the British naval and land forces under Commodore [George] Downie and Sir George Provost, and familiarly known as the Battle of Plattsburgh.**

The Saranac River affords a fine water power at this place, which is chiefly occupied by lumber mills. Those owned or worked by C. F. Norton & Co. contain ten gates [saw frames], and average eighteen thousand pieces per day. The logs are floated down from the interior, for a distance of eighty or ninety miles. The village contains a number of fine public and private institutions, prominent among which is the Catholic convent or nunnery. Foquet's Hotel has for seventy years been a prominent institution of its kind. The present edifice was [completed] in 186[5], on the site of the one which was the year previous consumed by fire.***

*Benjamin C. Butler's 1880 guidebook, entitled *The Summer Tourist; Descriptive of the Delaware & Hudson Canal Co's Railroads, and their Summer Resorts*, added considerable detail to the description of Ausable Chasm, including names for geological formations.[62] Ausable Chasm had emerged as one of the great natural attractions for tourists just after publication of Butler's first guidebook. Seneca Ray Stoddard's 1874 guide, *The Adirondacks Illustrated*, noted that "until recently there had been but little done to open the chasm to the comfortable inspection of the public. . .However, in 1873, a company of Philadelphians secured nearly all the land surrounding, have commenced the erection of a hotel near by [Lake View House], and built stairways, galleries and bridges so that nearly the entire length can now be traversed with comfort, the remainder in a boat."[63]

**Butler's history of the Battle of Plattsburgh is omitted here (see chapter 11).

***L. M. Fouquet's 1867 guidebook provided a brief history of Fouquet's Hotel: "The first hotel bearing this name was built by John Louis Fouquet in 1798, and was destroyed by fire during the engagement of 1814. In 1815 it was rebuilt by John L. Fouquet and his son D.L.—the former of whom died in 1828. The hotel was kept as a summer resort until June [18]64, when it was accidently destroyed by fire. The present structure was commenced by D. L. Fouquet & Son, in August [18]64, and was

"Foquet's Hotel, Plattsburgh, N.Y." from the *Descriptive Guide to the Adirondacks and Handbook of Travel* by Edwin R. Wallace (1875).

Leaving Plattsburgh, we first pass between Cumberland Head and Grand Isle, and reach Isle La Motte, twelve miles from the first-named place. A fort was built on this, in 1666, by [Captain de] la Motte, a French officer, and it continued to be an important military and naval station through the French and Revolutionary War.* Beyond is the entrance to the beautiful Missisquoi Bay. Eight miles beyond is Rouse's Point.

This is the junction of three railroads, to wit, the Vermont and Canada,

opened to the traveling public in June [18]65."[64] Other hotels in the Plattsburgh area included the Cumberland House and Witherill Hotel.

Fouquet and other contemporary guidebooks furnished some other details about Plattsburgh. Fouquet commented that the city "contains about 5,000 inhabitants, and on the [Saranac] river there are several mills and manufactories. . .This is one of the United States [Army] military posts, where the Government ha[s] extensive barracks. . .The steamers touch here daily during the season of navigation, and there is a good break-water done for the protection of shipping in the harbor of Cumberland Bay."[65] The Taintor Brother's 1872 guide, *Summer Routes to Lake Champlain and the Adirondacks*, mentioned the remains of the 1814 forts, Fort Brown, Fort Moreau, and Fort Scott (named for Jacob Jennings Brown, Jean Victor Moreau, and Winfield Scott): "The ruins of these works still exist, in a fair state of preservation, and will be visited with deep interest by the tourist."[66] Styles' 1871 guidebook made note of the wreck of the schooner *Royal Savage* from the Battle of Valcour Island on October 11, 1776: "At the southern extremity of Valcour, just in front of a tiny grass plot, lie the remains of the Royal Savage, a large schooner of twelve guns, sunk in Arnold's battle. Many abortive attempts have been made to raise the wreck, which is visible in low water."[67] The remains of the vessel were raised by Colonel Lorenzo F. Hagglund in the summer of 1934.[68]

*Fort St. Anne, a 144-foot log structure with four bastions, was built by French troops under Captain de la Motte in 1666; the outpost was abandoned about 1671, but the island itself was used in various capacities in succeeding wars.

"Plattsburg[h]-Lake Champlain"
from *Nelson's Guide to Lake George and Lake Champlain* (1866).

Ogdensburgh and Champlain, and Montreal and Lake Champlain. The first named road has a stupendous bridge across the lake, a mile in length, which contains a draw or floating track, three hundred and fifty feet long.*

The Alburgh Springs (sulphur and lithia) are two miles east from Rouse's Point. The hotel [Alburgh Springs House] is near Missisquoi Bay. A steamer makes excursion trips among the islands and to Plattsburgh twice a week.

The Missisquoi Springs are situated on the beautiful winding river of the same name. The nearest point of railway communication is St. Albans. The springs are thirteen in number, all within the space of an acre of land, and all possessed, apparently, of different qualities, one spring being cathartic and another diuretic; one is offensive to the taste and smell, another, the principal one, is free from all odor. This spring is from four to five feet deep, and the water rises in small jets through the minute apertures of a white, marble like, hardpan. Stages run regularly from St. Albans to Sheldon, in connection with the hotels situated among the springs. [The Missisquoi Hotel, Missisquoi Springs Hotel, Bellevue and Vermont, Congress Hall, and Missisquoi Valley House].

The Welden House at St. Albans is in every way first-class, and contains about two hundred rooms.**

*Opening on September 1, 1851, a wood trestle railroad bridge, fitted with a 300-foot-long drawboat, connected Alburgh, Vermont, with Rouses Point.

**A contractor engaged in the construction of the Welden House was the only fatality in the chaotic raid on the banks of St. Albans by 22 Confederate soldiers in October 1864.

Notes

1. B. C. Butler, *Lake George and Lake Champlain, from their First Discovery to 1759* (Albany: Weed, Parsons and Co., 1868), 8.
2. Ibid., 4.
3. Alex. MacKay, *The Western World; or, Travels in the United States in 1846-47* (1849; reprint ed., New York: Negro Universities Press, 1968), Volume 2, 191.
4. Charles Dickens, *American Notes* (1892; reprint ed., New York: St. Martin's Press, 1985), 194; Traveling in America in 1844, Rev. G. Lewis found his Lake Champlain steamer "a perfect model of neatness and comfort, as fresh and fair in all her appointments as if this were her first appearance on the Lake." Rev. G. Lewis, *Impressions of America and the American Churches: From Journal of the Rev. G. Lewis* (1848; reprint ed., New York: Negro Universities Press, 1968), 368.
5. *Nelson's Guide to Lake George and Lake Champlain* (London: T. Nelson and Sons, 1866), 28. Their 1859 and 1865 guides had the same description.
6. *A Descriptive and Historical Guide to the Valley of Lake Champlain and the Adirondacks* (Burlington: R. S. Styles' Steam Printing House, 1871), 42. Winslow C. Watson is believed to have been the author of this guidebook.
7. Ibid., 44.
8. Jim Shaughnessy, *The Rutland Road*, 2nd ed. (1981; reprint ed., Syracuse: Syracuse University Press, 1997), 28.
9. Jim Shaughnessy, *Delaware & Hudson* (1967; reprint ed., Syracuse: Syracuse University Press, 1997), 259.
10. *Nelson's Guide*, 28.
11. Andrew G. Meiklejohn, "The Champlain Canal—Remarks of Hon. Andrew G. Meiklejohn," 5 April 1864, Special Collections, New York State Library, 4.
12. Thomas X. Grasso, *Champlain Canal* (Syracuse: The Canal Society of New York State, 1985), 4.
13. Z. Thompson, *Guide to Lake George, Lake Champlain, Montreal and Quebec* (Burlington: Chauncey Goodrich, 1845), 22.
14. Z. Thompson, *Northern Guide. Lake George, Lake Champlain, Montreal and Quebec, Green and White Mountains, and Willoughby Lake* (Burlington: Stacy & Jameson, 1854), 19.
15. Ibid., 17.
16. Kevin J. Crisman and Arthur B. Cohn, *When Horses Walked on Water: Horse-Powered Ferries in Nineteenth-Century America* (Washington, D. C.: Smithsonian Institution Press, 1998), 114-126.
17. Dona Brown, *Inventing New England: Regional Tourism in the Nineteenth Century* (Washington, D. C.:Smithsonian Institution Press, 1995), 75.
18. The latter guidebook had virtually the same title except for Lake Horicon which reflected James Fenimore Cooper's campaign to change the name of Lake George. *Lake Horicon, (Lake George,) Lake Champlain, Montreal and Quebec* (Burlington: C. Goodrich and Company, 1858).
19. J. Kevin Graffagnino, "The Vermont 'Story': Continuity and Change in Vermont Historiography," *Vermont History* 46 (Spring 1978): 83; J. Kevin Graffagnino, "Zadock Thompson and The State of Vermont," *Vermont History* 47 (Fall 1979): 244.
20. [John Disturnell], *A Trip through the Lakes of North America* (New York: J. Disturnell, 1857), 294-95, 303-4, 309-10.
21. L. M. Fouquet, comp., *Lake Champlain, Lake George! Lake Memphrenmagog, The Adirondacks! And Mount Mansfield* (Burlington, R. S. Styles' Steam Book and Job Printing Establishment, 1867), 48-59.
22. Charles H. Sweetser, *Book of Summer Resorts* (New York: John A. Gray & Green Printers, 1868), 190-206; [Charles Newhall Taintor], *The Hudson River Route* (New York: Taintor Brothers, 1869), 110-20.
23. E. R. Wallace, *Descriptive Guide to the Adirondacks and Handbook of Travel* (New York: The American News Company, 1875).
24. George Wurts, "Journal of a Tour to Niagara Falls, Montreal, Lake Champlain, &c.," *Proceedings of the New Jersey Historical Society* 69 (1951): 357.
25. S. H. Hammond and L. W. Mansfield, *Country Margins and Rambles of a Journalist* (New York: J. C. Derby, 1855), 288.
26. C. C. Clarke to Charles T. Titus, 24 August 1903, Benjamin C. Butler Collection, Hadley

Luzerne Historical Society, Lake Luzerne, New York; See also original document in Rare and Manuscript Collections, Carl A. Kroch Library, Cornell University, Ithaca, New York.

27. Mary Dolbeare Butler Devereux to Julia Rosa Newberry, December 1874, Benjamin C. Butler Collection, Hadley Luzerne Historical Society; See also original document in Rare and Manuscript Collections, Carl A. Kroch Library, Cornell University.

28. C. C. Clarke letter.

29. Henry J. Galpin, *Annals of Oxford, New York, with Illustrations and Biographical Sketches of Some of its Prominent Men and Early Pioneers* (Oxford, N.Y.: New York Times Books and Job Printing House, 1906), 519.

30. James Clapp to Benjamin Clapp Butler, 13 October 1844, Benjamin C. Butler Collection, Hadley Luzerne Historical Society; See also original document in Rare and Manuscript Collections, Carl A. Kroch Library, Cornell University.

31. Ibid.

32. H. P. Smith, *History of Warren County* (Syracuse: D. Mason & Co., Publishers, 1885), 274-76.

33. Ibid., 226, 247, 250; See also "Record of Butler Post," 2 February 1913, newspaper account, Benjamin C. Butler Collection, Hadley Luzerne Historical Society.

34. *The Story of Saint Mary's Episcopal Church 1865-1988* (Lake Luzerne, N. Y.: St. Mary's Episcopal Church, n. d.), 2.

35. Butler, *Lake George and Lake Champlain*, 3.

36. Ibid., 7-8.

37. B. C. Butler, *From New York to Montreal* (New York: American News Company, 1873), 131.

38. B. C. Butler, *The Summer Tourist; Descriptive of the Delaware & Hudson Canal Co's Railroads, and their Summer Resorts* (Boston: Franklin Press, Rand, Avery & Co., 1880), 147-54.

39. *Glens Falls Republican*, 21 November 1882; *New York Times*, 27 November 1882; *The Story of St. Mary's*, 20.

40. *Glens Falls Republican*, 21 November 1882.

41. Butler, *From New York to Montreal*, 98-116.

42. Kevin J. Crisman, *The Eagle* (Shelburne, VT: The New England Press, 1987), 108; Sidney Ernest Hammersley, *The Lake Champlain Naval Battles of 1776-1814* (Waterford, N. Y.: Col. Sidney E. Hammersley, 1959), 22-24; Doris B. Morton, *Whitehall in the War of 1812* (Whitehall, N. Y.: Washington County Historical Society, 1964, Mimeographed), 8.

43. Frances Parkman, *Montcalm and Wolfe* (1884; reprint ed., New York: Atheneum, 1984), 377-78; Thomas Mante, *The History of the Late War in North-America* (1772; reprint ed., New York: Research Reprints Inc., n.d.), 159; M. Pouchot, *Memoir Upon the Late War in North America Between the French and English, 1755-60*, trans. and ed. Franklin B. Hough (Roxbury, MA.: W. Elliot Woodward, 1866), 123; Robert Rogers, *Journals of Major Robert Rogers* (1765; reprint ed., Ann Arbor, MI.: University Microfilms, Inc., 1966), 117-19.

44. Butler, *From New York to Montreal*, 88-89.

45. Roger R. P. Dechame, "Why Carillon?" *The Bulletin of the Fort Ticonderoga Museum* 13 (Fall 1980): 432-46.

46. Public Record Office, London, Colonial Office Records 5, Volume 46, University Publications of America microfilm reel 1, frame 638.

47. Benson J. Lossing, "A Visit to Ticonderoga 1848," *The Bulletin of the Fort Ticonderoga Museum* 1 (January 1929): 24.

48. Ibid., 24-25.

49. Thompson, *Northern Guide*, 16-17.

50. Styles' *Descriptive and Historical Guide*, 29.

51. Morris F. Glenn, *The Story of Three Towns: Westport, Essex and Willsboro, New York* (Ann Arbor, MI.: Braun-Brumfield, 1977), 266-67; Patrick Farrell, *Through the Light Hole* (Utica, N. Y.: North Country Books, Inc., 1996), 5, 8.

52. Library of Congress Map Collection; E. B. O'Callaghan, ed., *The Documentary History of the State of New-York* (Albany: Weed, Parsons & Co., 1849), Volume 1, opposite page 557.

53. Hiland Hall, "The New York Dellius Patent," *The Historical Magazine* 3 (Second Series) (February 1868): 74.

54. Ibid., 75; E. B. O'Callaghan, ed., *Documents Relative to the Colonial History of the State of New-York* (Albany: Weed, Parsons and Company, Printers, 1855), Volume 6, 569; B. C. Butler, *Lake*

George and Lake Champlain from their First Discovery to 1759, 2nd ed. (New York: G. P. Putnam & Son, 1869), 16-17.

55. Guy Omeron Coolidge, *The French Occupation of the Champlain Valley from 1609 to 1759* (Harrison, N. Y.: Harbor Hill Books, 1979), 86, 95-99, 113-14.

56. Nell Jane Barnett Sullivan and David Kendall Martin, *A History of the Town of Chazy: Clinton County, New York* (Burlington: George Little Press, Inc., 1970), 16-22.

57. John Burgoyne, *A State of the Expedition from Canada* (1780; reprint ed., New York: The New York Times & Arno Press, 1969), 10, Appendix VI, xxii-xxiv.

58. A. Levasseur, *Lafayette in America in 1824 and 1825; or, Journal of a Voyage to the United States* (Philadelphia: Carey and Lea, 1829), Volume 2, 214.

59. Ibid., 215.

60. Henry James, *Lake George to Burlington* (Burlington: Rumble Press, 1991), p.n.a.

61. Ogden Ross, *The Steamboats of Lake Champlain 1809-1930* (1930; reprint ed., Quechee, VT.: Vermont Heritage Press, 1997), 108-9.

62. B. C. Butler, *The Summer Tourist*, 147-54.

63. S. R. Stoddard, *The Adirondacks: Illustrated* (Albany: Weed, Parsons & Co., Printers, 1874), 47; See also Duane Hamilton Hurd, *History of Clinton and Franklin Counties, New York* (1880; reprint ed., Plattsburgh: Clinton County American Revolution Bicentennial Commission, 1978), 205-6.

64. Fouquet, 11.

65. Ibid.

66. [Charles Newhall Taintor], *Summer Routes to Lake Champlain and the Adirondacks* (New York: Taintor Brothers, 1872), 8.

67. Styles' *Descriptive and Historical Guide*, 34-35.

68. Russell P. Bellico, *Sails and Steam in the Mountains: A Maritime and Military History of Lake George and Lake Champlain* (Fleischmanns, N. Y.: Purple Mountain Press, 1992), 192-93.

Benjamin C. Butler. (Hadley-Luzerne Historical Society)

"At Bluff Point, Lake Champlain, 1890," showing the Hotel Champlain.
Drawing by William Thomas Smedley from *Harper's Weekly*, August 16, 1890.

14. Augusta Brown 1895

DURING THE SUMMER OF 1895, 54-year-old Augusta Brown and three female friends from Brooklyn embarked on a month-and-a-half-long journey from New York City to Canada via the Champlain Canal and Lake Champlain aboard a freight canal boat. A newspaper account noted that the group of excursionists was "supplied with a kodak, an artist and a determination to have a right good time. . .[on the] chartered Bertha Bullis."[1] Brown, the artist on the trip, began her journal with the remark that "people who seldom see a canal boat gliding along over a quiet mirror of water, have little idea how great an undertaking it is to carry the merchandise of a country through its winding ways. To get a better idea of this, and also to pass away, in a novel fashion, a few weeks of the summer, a party of four impecunious [possessing little money] women made up an excursion to Quebec and Montreal," suggesting that trains or steamboats "would have been dusty, hot and fatiguing, and their speed prevented a full and perfect enjoyment of the scenery en route."[2] Brown produced a remarkable description of life on canal boats as well as a substantial number of drawings of scenes along the way. A veteran traveler, she was not disappointed with her Champlain Canal trip, viewing "new scenes of beauty every moment."[3]

Lake Champlain reached its zenith of national attention as a tourist destination at the end of the nineteenth century. In 1890 William H. H. Murray, famous for his Adirondack book, *Adventures in the Wilderness*, championed Lake Champlain in his new work, *Lake Champlain and Its Shores*: "It is surrounded by natural scenery of the highest order. Its shores and bays are alive with historic memories. . .Here are ruins of ancient forts. Here the lines of old-time earthworks still stand. Here nature has accumulated chasm, gorge, and mountains for the lover of the grand and picturesque to admire."[4] With heightened public interest in the lake, three popular

"Hotel Champlain from the East."
Photograph from *Historic Lake Champlain* by Seneca Ray Stoddard (1898).

regional guidebooks offered updated annual editions: Charles H. Possons' *Guide to Lake George*; *Lake Champlain and Adirondacks*, Seneca Ray Stoddard's *Lake George (Illustrated) and Lake Champlain: A Book of To-Day*, and Edwin R. Wallace's *Descriptive Guide to the Adirondacks*.

At the end of the nineteenth century the travel industry gravitated toward grand hotels as "affluent tourists were increasingly content with easier forms of conspicuous consumption."[5] Completed in 1890, the gigantic Hotel Champlain was set in a 265-acre park at Bluff Point just south of Plattsburgh. Four hundred feet in length and 75 feet wide, the four-story edifice exhibited three towers—two were six stories high and the center tower nine stories, rising to a height of 125 feet. In his 1895 guidebook Seneca Ray Stoddard noted that the "long colonades; broad piazzas. . .breezy porticos and balconies hung along its sides or perched high up on [its] tower and sharply sloping roof—give grace and lightness to the structure that rises above the tops of the trees crowning the rugged bluff."[6] With every modern convenience available, President William McKinley used the hotel as his summer White House in 1897 and again in 1899.

Other first class hotels dotted the landscape in larger communities and at tourist points along the way. The Fouquet House, Witherill Hotel, Devlin House, Cumberland Hotel, and other inns were located in Plattsburgh. The Hotel Windsor at Rouses Point offered a lakeshore setting with large rooms, fireplaces, spacious common halls, 300 feet of verandas, and facilities that included "billiards, tennis, croquet,. . .telegraph and telephone [and] steam yachts, sail and row boats, carriages and saddle horses connected with the house."[7] Near the end of the 1890s the Hotel Burlington was described as having "an electric system of call bells throughout, an electric elevator, and suit[e]s of rooms with baths and all modern conveniences."[8] Other hotels in Burlington included the Van Ness House and the American House. At Ausable Chasm visitors stayed at the Hotel Ausable (built after the Lake View House burned) and Trembleau Hall. Inns and hotels also accommodated tourists at Alburgh Springs, St. Albans, Highgate Springs, Maquam Bay, Grand Isle, South

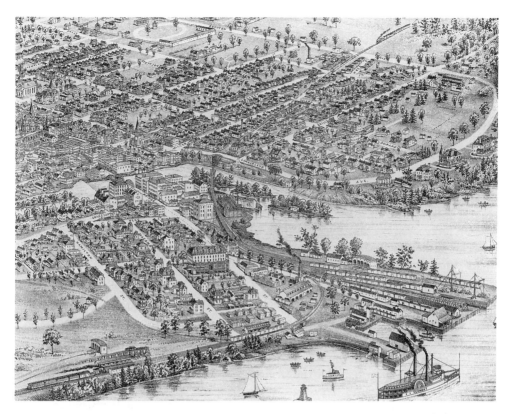

"1899 Plattsburgh, N.Y." Bird's eye view drawn by Christian Fausel.
(New York State Library)

"Port Henry, N.Y." Bird's eye view drawn by L. R. Burleigh.
(New York State Library)

Hero, Basin Harbor, Vergennes, Westport, Port Henry, Ticonderoga, Larrabee Point, Whitehall, and in other communities.

Not all tourists came to Lake Champlain to relax in the large hotels, however. In October 1884 Moses Brown (no relation to Augusta Brown) traveled in a 14-foot Adirondack guideboat fitted with a small mattress during his journey through the lake. In contrast to noisy steamboats, Moses Brown's quiet guideboat allowed him to draw close to the lake's wildlife, surprising "hundreds of wild ducks which were swimming and flying about" in the vicinity of the Canadian Border.[9] North of Port Kent he encountered "a flock of wild geese which startled me, exceedingly, as they made a great racket 'honking' and splashing, as they rose off the water."[10] Although he struggled to keep his guideboat from being swamped during a treacherous gale in which "waves broke clear over the bow and rear decking," the young sailor still enjoyed the beauty of the lake. Unexpectedly, a lull in the storm spread "a flood of golden light from the sun over the mountains and there burst on my vision a scene of celestial beauty and magnificence such as I had never before witnessed," Moses Brown recounted: "a picture which only comes to one once in a lifetime and once seen, is never forgotten, a picture worth every foot of my hard and perilous journey to see. . .a glimpse of Paradise itself."[11] Removing his dripping hat, he looked in awe at the autumn scene high above the lake, "glowing with red, yellow and green colors; while beyond, rising with their white peaks [the Adirondack Mountains] covered with snow. . .the flood of light from the sun, striking only on this plateau, brought out the coloring and had the effect of making it appear to be in the heavens, above the clouds."[12] Unfortunately, "the scene lasted but a few minutes," Moses Brown lamented, "and on came the dreadful storm again more violent than before."[13] Brown rode out the storm, covering 38 miles on the lake in one day, stopping only for a supper at a lakeside farmhouse on the New York shore.

By the 1890s the reputation of Lake Champlain as a unique water resource led to increased recreational activities. On the lakefront in Burlington, the Lake Champlain Yacht Club had built a "large and commodious clubhouse" with a "fleet of nearly forty well-built boats" and offered members spectacular views of the lake and mountains.[14] Founded in 1887, the club's membership was characterized as "cosmopolitan. . .naturally composed of gentlemen of intelligence, public spirit and standing."[15] While the annual dues were termed "too slight to be burdensome to any," the officers of the club were relatively well-heeled citizens, including William Seward Webb,* the commodore of the club.[16]

Events at the lake, such as the American Canoe Association meets held at Willsborough (Willsboro) in 1891 and 1892, drew new attention to Lake Champlain. As part of the entertainment during the 1891 meet, Florence Watters Snedeker observed, "a strange object with gaping red jaws, pointed tail and crest—the fabled Champlain sea-serpent! As the idea dawns upon the astonished people they break into wild applause—all except a poor little dog in one of the canoes, who yelps with

---

*Dr. William Seward Webb and his wife, Eliza Vanderbilt Webb, owned the 3,800-acre Shelburne Farms, encompassing a palatial mansion and an immense horse-breeding barn on grounds planned by Frederick Law Olmsted. Dr. Webb, the son-in-law of William Henry Vanderbilt, became president of the Vanderbilt-owned Wagner Palace Car Company in 1883 and later served as president of the Rutland Railroad (1902-1905). Dr. Webb's daughter-in-law, Electra Havemeyer Webb, and son, J. Watson Webb, founded the nearby Shelburne Museum in 1947. Today Shelburne Farms is a 1,400-acre nonprofit working farm and national historic site; Dr. Webb's former residence serves as an inn.

The Lake Champlain Yacht Club in Burlington. (Postcard, author's collection)

terror. The serpent gnashes its jaws. Its scales glisten. It passes, surrounded by admiring, harpoon–flinging crews. Mighty laughter springs up before it, and dies slowly in its wake."[17]

The increase in tourism at Lake Champlain was aided by accessibility to the region via an expanded rail network. The Delaware and Hudson Canal Company's* completion of the New York and Canada Line in November 1875 made it possible to travel entirely by rail from New York City to Montreal with stops at all major communities along the western side of Lake Champlain. The Rutland Railroad, the Vermont and Canada, and the Vermont Central controlled rail traffic on the eastern side of the lake at the same time. The ownership of the Champlain Transportation Company and the Lake George Steamboat Company by the Delaware and Hudson permitted an uninterrupted journey by train and steamboat from New York City to Canada. J. Arbuthnot Wilson took delight in his trip on Lake Champlain aboard "a Yankee steamer with a broad awning covering the hurricane-deck, and easy chairs of the purest Sybarite [an ancient city bathed in luxury] persuasion inviting you rather to gentle slumber than due appreciation of the beautiful scenery. Of course the steamer is about three stories high, and is fitted up as much like a Fifth Avenue hotel...She has a dining-room where attentive...waiters serve you up a seven-course

---

*The Delaware and Hudson Company pursued an aggressive policy of acquisition and expansion during the late nineteenth century, which resulted in the domination by the company of both rail and steamboat transportation at Lake George and Lake Champlain. In 1870 the D & H leased in perpetuity the Albany & Susquehanna Railroad. In the following year it leased all the assets in perpetuity of the Rensselaer & Saratoga Railroad, which included the Champlain Transportation Company and its subsidiary, the Lake George Steamboat Company. In early 1873 the Whitehall & Plattsburgh Railroad, the Montreal & Plattsburgh Railroad, and the New York and Canada Railroad were consolidated into a second New York & Canada Railroad under the financial control of the D & H. By 1875 the D & H had opened a branch line from the northern Lake George steamer landing at Baldwin to the Montcalm Landing on Lake Champlain at Ticonderoga. The southern steamboat landing on Lake Champlain was moved from Whitehall to the Montcalm Landing in 1875. In 1882 the D & H brought passenger rail lines from Glens Falls directly to the steamboat dock at Caldwell at the southern end of Lake George.[18]

dinner. . .saloons fitted out in all the glories. . .she has private state-rooms where languid New York ladies retire for their siesta."[19]

The 1870s, however, brought a reduction in passenger service available on the lake through the Champlain Transportation Company. In July 1875 the 258-foot steamboat *Champlain* was wrecked north of Westport (see chapter 13), and the 251-foot *Adirondack* was retired later in the same year as a result of the shift of passengers to railroads. Because the southernmost steamboat landing on the lake was changed from Whitehall to Ticonderoga in 1875 and the northernmost terminal relocated from Rouses Point to Plattsburgh in the following year, the mileage covered by the CTC steamboats shrank from 125 miles to 81. In 1876 the CTC passenger fleet consisted of the 262-foot *Vermont II*, built in 1871, and the 132-foot *A. Williams*, which had been acquired by the company in 1874 for use in ferry service and tourist excursions. (The 224-foot *Montreal* had been relegated to towing duties in 1868 and burned in 1880.) However, two non-CTC passenger steamboats plied the lake during the 1880s and 1890s. In 1881 the 142-foot *Maquam* was built for excursion service by the St. Johnsbury and Lake Champlain Railroad and in 1882 the 168-foot *Reindeer* was completed for the Grand Isle Steamboat Company for passenger duty between Burlington and St. Albans. Although the *Maquam* would be acquired by the Champlain Transportation Company in 1897, the *Reindeer* was never owned by the CTC—one of the few steamers to be so distinguished in the long history of steamboats on Lake Champlain. With revenue on the rise in the 1880s, the CTC decided to build a new steamer as a replacement for the aging *A. Williams*. The 205-foot *Chateaugay*, the first iron-hulled steamer to be employed by the company, began service in 1888. In addition to the large steamboats, many ferries and small passenger steamers also operated on the lake during this period. The *Water Lily*, for example, ran between Westport and Vergennes, enabling passengers to make connections to the CTC steamers at the Westport steamboat landing.

Rejecting a typical tourist excursion on one of the large passenger steamboats, Augusta Brown traversed Lake Champlain on a nondescript utilitarian canal boat.

The steamboat *Reindeer*, owned by the Central Vermont Railroad, was the largest steamboat to navigate Otter Creek to Vergennes, Vermont.

(Postcard, Mahlon and Gina Teachout Collection)

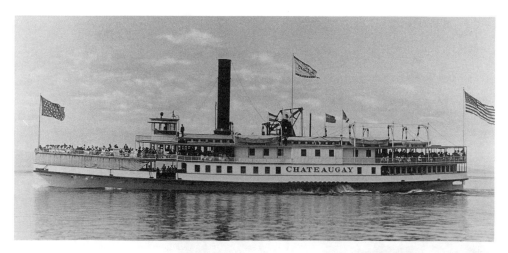

Above: The 205-foot steamboat *Chateauguay* began service on Lake Champlain in 1888. (Special Collections, Bailey/Howe Memorial Library, University of Vermont)

Right: The steamboat *Maquam* at the American Canoe Association camp in the 1880s. Photo by Seneca Ray Stoddard. (New York State Museum)

She passed through the 64-mile Champlain Canal, in operation since 1823, and the 12-mile Chambly Canal, opened in 1843. Canal boats continued to be the backbone of bulk transportation during the late nineteenth century. Two classes of canal boats plied Lake Champlain during this period: one type had to be towed both on the lake (by steamboat) and through the canal (by mules or horses); the other carried removable masts which allowed the boat to be towed through the canal but to sail on the open lake. Brown traveled on the first type of boat. The size of canal boats changed with the enlargement of the Champlain Canal. An amendment to the New York Constitution in 1854 authorized the enlargement of locks to match the larger Erie Canal locks (110 feet by 18 feet), whenever the Champlain locks needed to be rebuilt.[20] Work on the Champlain Canal, however, proceeded unevenly. Because of increased pressure from business groups during the spring of 1860, the New York legislature authorized an enlargement of the prism (width and depth) of the Champlain Canal and the rebuilding of some of the locks. The widening and deepening of the canal was completed in 1862, allowing larger vessels to be used after that date.[21] Shipyards began building larger schooner-rigged canal boats in place of sloop-rigged vessels. Other design changes included round bows on all canal boats, mandated by legislation in 1862 to lessen damage caused by collisions. By 1877 the enlargement of all Champlain Canal locks to 110 feet by 18 feet, which had been commissioned 23 years earlier, was finally completed.[22]

Canal Schooners
Clockwise from top left: "A Glimpse of Plattsburgh from the Harbor," detail, showing a canal schooner from *Historic Lake Champlain* by Seneca Ray Stoddard (1898). Canal schooner *Hiram Walker* at Burlington (1892). (Vermont Historical Society) Steering wheel of canal schooner *O.J. Walker* and tiller bar of the canal schooner *General Butler*, both in Vermont Underwater Historic Preserve sites. (Photos by the author)

By the late nineteenth century railroads offered stiff competition for canal boats, thus leading to the removal of all tolls on New York canals in 1882. Sailing canal boat operators were the first segment of the industry to begin downsizing; the Essex (N.Y.) shipyard of Hoskins and Ross, for example, completed its last sailing canal boat in 1878.[23] Traffic on the canal and lake, however, reached a peak of 1,520,757 tons in 1890, but fell to less than half that amount by 1907 "due to the disappearance of the fleet of sloops and schooner-rigged canal boats" which faced competition from the Delaware & Hudson rail lines on the west side of Lake Champlain.[24] Despite the competition from railroads, between 1,500 and 1,800 canal boats operated on Lake Champlain from 1870 to 1915.[25]

Augusta Brown's excursion aboard the towed canal boat *Bertha M. Bullis* in 1895 occurred at a time when this form of commercial transportation was still a vital part of the economy. She recognized the importance of canals and ended her journal with the comment that "the reader will see (if he has had patience to wade through these dry notes) the necessity for having more water in our water-ways; more width to the narrow channels; more and better service in transporting our boat freight; and last, but not least, stronger boats propelled by steam. When this is accomplished who could resist the temptation of a trip to Canada in a Canal-boat?"[26] Less than a decade later, the state legislature authorized rebuilding the Champlain Canal as a larger barge canal.

Canal boat under tow in the Champlain Canal. (Canal Society of New York State)

Augusta Woodruff Brown was born in December 1840 in Brooklyn, New York, to Solyman and Elizabeth Brown. The second child of seven, Augusta never married and resided with her family into adulthood. Her father, Solyman Brown (1790-1876), who had completed an undergraduate degree and master's degree at Yale College, was known as a clergyman, poet, teacher, dentist, and artist.[27] Augusta's literary and artistic talents were to some degree the result of her exposure to her father's prolific work. Solyman Brown began and ended his career as a minister, but also worked in his early years as a classics instructor in a private school and later achieved eminence as the father of modern dentistry.* His interest in the dental profession began in the 1820s as a result of his association with the prominent New York City dentist, Eleazar Parmly. While practicing dentistry in 1834, Solyman Brown married Elizabeth Butler, daughter of the owner and editor of the *Mercantile Advertiser*.

In 1844 the Brown family, which now included two daughters, Columbia and

---

*During the late 1830s and early 1840s, Solyman was instrumental in establishing the first dental society (Society of Surgeon Dentists of the City and State of New York) and the world's first dental periodical (*American Journal of Dental Science*). His 1839 article entitled "Remarks on Professional Morality" outlined the first code of ethics for dentists.[28] Solyman Brown's diffuse publications on dentistry included the 176-page *Dentologia: A Poem on the Diseases of the Teeth*, "Treatise on Mechanical Dentistry," *An Essay on the Surest Methods of Degrading the Profession of Dental Surgery*, and *The Importance of Regulating the Teeth of Children*, the latter representing the first treatise on orthodontia published in the United States. He also wrote a substantial number of poems, political treatises, and essays from 1818 to 1829 and in later years completed *Llewellen's Dog: a Ballad, The Cholera King, and Other Poems*, the *Union of Extremes: a Discourse on Liberty and Slavery*, and a novel on the American Revolution, published posthumously.[29]

Augusta, and two-year-old Edward, moved to Leraysville, Pennsylvania, where Solyman served as a minister, teacher, and dentist in a short-lived utopian community. A second son, E. Parmly Brown, was born in Pennsylvania. (He later became a prominent dentist in New York City.) Returning to New York State in 1846, Solyman preached in the Swedenborgian churches in Ithaca and Danby where he continued to practice dentistry. He brought his family back to New York City in the early 1850s, opening the Dental Depot, a dental supply house, in 1853 and later became a partner in the New York Teeth Manufacturing Company. In 1860, 69-year-old Solyman and 47-year-old Elizabeth Brown's Brooklyn household consisted of Columbia (21), Augusta (19), Edward (17), Parmly (15), Flora (13), Helen (11), Virginia (7), and Elizabeth's mother, Charlotte Butler, only two years older than Solyman.[30] In 1862 Solyman moved back to Ithaca with his family, serving as a Swedenborgian minister in nearby Danby until his retirement in 1870. Augusta, then 28 years old, and her younger sisters Helen and Virginia were still living at home with their parents in Ithaca in 1870.[31] In 1876, at the age of 86, Solyman died at the home of a married daughter in Dodge Center, Minnesota.

In subsequent years Augusta Brown lived in Brooklyn, working as a housekeeper to a succession of families. Over the years, she honed her writing talents, including poetry, as well as her artistic skills. Her position oftentimes involved traveling with her employers, and she usually wrote long descriptive letters of the trips to her sister Virginia. While in San Francisco in April 1888, Augusta visited Sausalito, Alcatraz Island, Angel Island, the Golden Gate passage, and Oakland and composed an eight-page letter to Virginia in which she observed that "the millionaires all live in the summer at San Rafael & the billionaires at Menlo Park."[32] In 1893 Augusta lived on Montague Street in Brooklyn and worked for Mrs. Henry Manning, the matriarch of a well-to-do family. Writing to Virginia in October 1893, Augusta detailed a recent trip taken with Mrs. Manning and her friends to Niagara Falls, where Augusta "went down an elevator to the Whirl Pool rapids—Mr. Shaw & I donned the rubber suits and went behind the Canada Falls. . .[and] took a steam up to the foot of the Falls on the Maid of the Mist."[33] In the letter she complained to her sister that she had a case of pleurisy because of Mrs. Manning's insistence on keeping the windows open in their train car. (Mrs. Manning also got sick.) On her return to Brooklyn, Augusta resumed more mundane duties: sorting "apples and pears. . .canning. . .sweeping & dusting."[34]

Augusta Brown's canal boat trip of 1895 was a departure from her earlier excursions with wealthy employers—this time she traveled with four women aboard a slow freight canal boat. The exact inspiration for the trip is unknown; perhaps the publicity associated with plans to improve New York's canals had something to do with the trip or, more likely, the 1886 article describing the cruise of four artists and writers from *The Century Magazine* aboard the canal boat *Seth G. Cowles* (renamed from the *Wm. Denny*) had influenced their choice of travel.[35] Like the *Century* artists, who used pen names or nicknames, Brown's group "decided upon taking the sobriquets [nicknames] of 'Snip,' 'Snap,' 'Snorum,' and 'Dauber' by way of brevity."[36] Unlike the *Century* party, which had cleaned and converted the "entire central portion of the [boat's] hold, a space of sixty or seventy feet, [into a]. . .salon" equipped with fine tapestries, antique armchairs, a writing desk, an oak chest, silk draperies, lamps, and other amenities, Brown and her friends traveled on a standard canal boat with a full load of coal.[37]

Brown and her fellow travelers departed from New York harbor on the evening of July 2 aboard the tugboat *E. R. Levy*, which gathered a caravan of canal boats before they reached their chartered boat, the 93-foot *Bertha M. Bullis*, docked on the New Jersey shore. As the captain of the tug hunted for the *Bullis* in the dark, Augusta noticed that "the moon had made a long and beautiful twilight, and the shores, lighted by myriads of electric and gas lights, seemed an endless panorama, crowned by the wondrously brillant dome of the 'World Building,'* and tipped by the illuminated spire of 'Madison Square Garden.'"[39] After the tug captain located the *Bullis*, Augusta placed her baggage aboard the vessel; Her luggage consisted of "a small telescope bag, containing a change of clothes, a warm shawl and an umbrella. . .a shade hat and an extra pair of shoes. Nor must I forget the tin horn which the Captain of the Quartette [nicknamed "Snap"] used on numerous occasions."[40]

Since the *Bertha M. Bullis* had not yet been loaded with her cargo of coal, the departure was delayed for one more day. On July 4, at one in the morning, the *Bullis* left as part of an immense tow "of seventy two boats drawn by three tugs."[41] Later in the morning Augusta observed American flags flying, despite the rainy day. About noontime, one of the women, "our jolly Captain 'Snap' hailed one of the tugboats [*Mabel*] steaming near us," and persuaded the captain to take the foursome aboard.[42] After a dinner of homemade mince pie, Boston baked beans, and cocoa, Augusta made a quick sketch of the *Mabel* for the captain: "It was a water color truly, as the rain continued almost un-intermittingly all day."[43] The long tow snaked its way northward, "form-ing many regular and ir-regular S's," while passing bends in the river.[44] On July 5 the tug *Mabel* was replaced by the *Saranac*; after breakfast the leader of the quartet, the bold "Capt. Snap, drew the boat alongside

"Tow Winding through Highland, West Point."
Drawing by Augusta Brown (1895). (New York State Museum)

by means of her trumpet, and soon we four were transferred to that vessel. Here, too, we visited the pilot-house, helped the captain and his mate eat white fish, potatoes and bread."[45] In the early evening Augusta's boat reached the lock at Troy, which allowed entry to the Champlain Canal via the Waterford Side Cut Locks. She noted a "lively scene, with fifteen or twenty men and boys" assisting at the lock.[46] "Inside this immense Lock it is awful and weird. The sides are so high and regular and the noise of the inrushing water as the gates are closed behind us, and

---

*Completed in 1890, the 16-story World Building housed Joseph Pulitzer's *New York World* newspaper on Park Row. Topped by a gold dome and flagpole, the stylish building was the tallest structure in New York City at the time.[38]

the sluices [water channel controlled by a floodgate] opened before us, seeming like a great, boiling cauldron, rising faster and higher every second, but chilly and damp instead of hot with steam."[47] Augusta recalled that "a most enchanting pull [followed]. . .all the while the moon stealing in and out among the branches, dropping sudden reflections to make clear our way, discovering deep coves or rustic docks along the shore; then disappearing only to wake up darker shadows. To break the stillness startled bullfrogs croaked remonstrance, or else splashed heavily in the water, as if they thought we infringed too closely upon their domain."[48] The *Bullis* docked for the night at Waterford and remained there all the next day because of a lack of available tow animals. Finally, on the following morning, Augusta and her fellow travelers began their journey through the Champlain Canal, "that seldom visited region, except by canal-boat, mules and small boys on [a] swimming bent; that winding stream with its well trodden tow-path; its countless bridges and mysterious locks."[49] This section of her diary, covering the Champlain Canal and Lake Champlain, is reproduced in its entirety at the end of this text.

After reaching St. Jean, Quebec, Augusta and her party boarded a train for a short stay in Montreal, making arrangements with another canal boat captain for their passage from Sorel to Quebec City since the *Bertha M. Bullis* was not going to the latter destination. Following their visit to Montreal, they reached Sorel via the river boat *Saguenay*, joining a fleet of 14 canal boats being towed to Quebec. As their lumber-laden canal boat moved slowly east, Augusta worried that one of the passengers "a restless little boy of four or five. . .incessant[ly] running about with [a] saw or pole or long pieces of plank" without any parental attention, might come to disaster.[50] "But what added more interest and some terror," Augusta wrote, "were the antics of [crewman] Frank Bouchard on the boat behind us. . .continually performing most daring feats, such as walking a tight or slack rope between boats, jumping from one to another when many feet apart."[51] After several days in Quebec, the women boarded a western-bound canal boat at three in the morning for a 24-hour trip to Three Rivers. From Three Rivers the excursionists traveled to Sorel on the steamboat *Montreal*. Once at Sorel they met Captain Bullis, who was part of a tow going east on the St. Lawrence River to Nicolet. When the canal boat tow from Three Rivers that was bound for St. Jean and Lake Champlain failed to stop for them at Sorel, the women accepted Captain Bullis' offer for another trip east on the St. Lawrence. Eventually the group returned to Sorel; but because there was no tow available at the time, Augusta returned alone by train to Troy and then by steamboat to Brooklyn; two of the other women ("Snip" and "Snorum") remained on the *Bertha M. Bullis* for a week-long journey to Whitehall. At Saratoga they met "Snap" who then accompanied them to Troy for the steamer to Brooklyn. "Snap" had left the party at Sorel, traveling by train to Saratoga, and later returning to New York harbor alone on the tugboats *Pocohontas* and *Mabel*.

In subsequent years Augusta Brown continued her employment as a live-in domestic worker in Brooklyn. In 1900, at the age of 59, she worked for John and Maria Ridsdal of Montague Street. Unlike her previous employers, John Ridsdal was not considered well-to-do, living in a rented apartment with his wife and working as a clerk at age 65.[52] Augusta's traveling adventures, however, were not over. In July 1907 she embarked on a three-month grand tour of Europe, writing a ten-page diary during the trip. Traveling with her cousin Emma Sanford, a nurse who was also single, Augusta visited Belgium, Germany, Switzerland, and France. She was still a hardy traveler at the age of 66. Her return voyage aboard the steamship *Grosser Kurfurst* was rough and stormy: "[We] were washed with heavy seas, and I was about the only woman who took a meal in the Saloon; then I spent almost all the time reading on one of the divans."[53]

Augusta often visited her sister Virginia and her husband, Harry E. Blake, in North Adams, Massachusetts. While in North Adams, she wrote a four-page story entitled "Three Berkshire Cyclists Take an Extended Trip," describing a six-day bicycling adventure to Lake George and Ticonderoga by "three academy students" from North Adams.[54] In the last years of her life she lived with her sister Virginia Blake in Elsmere, New York. Her grand niece, Sibyl Blake Selkirk, remembers Augusta as "an old lady with black dresses that swept the floor. . .and she was very helpful to everyone."[55] In 1934 Augusta sent a check to her grand niece for her one-year-old son, noting in a letter that "I used to send a check to my nieces and nephews to start a little bank account"; the letter included a typewritten poem that she wrote for the child with instructions that "perhaps you will keep [it] for him until he is old enough to read type-writing."[56]

On October 16, 1937, Augusta died in Elsmere, New York, at the age of 96.[57] She is buried in the Blake plot in the South View Cemetery in North Adams, Massachusetts. Her 1895 journal and drawings were donated to the New York State Museum in 1996; earlier, two volumes of her drawings of flowers had been given to the Brooklyn Botanic Gardens. Like many of her generation, Augusta Brown witnessed the transformation of America from a country of gas lights, horse-drawn wagons, canal boats, and steamboats into a nation of electric lights, automobiles, and airplanes.

The following excerpt from her journal begins with the entrance to the Champlain Canal in Waterford and ends in St. Jean, Quebec.

"Saddle Mule," showing canvas covering
for protection from insects.
Drawing by Augusta Brown (1895).
(New York State Museum)

Off on a Canal Boat[58]

About four o'clock next morning we were taken through three Locks [at Waterford] and there waited until nine o'clock for our team. It was composed of three mules, to say nothing of the driver; said mules being designated as "the lead," "the swing"and "the saddle."As for the driver, enough cannot be said,—besides walking behind the mules on a dusty, shadeless road, with the long tow-line flopping in and out of the water, and sometimes catching on snags or other boats; guiding them over, or around, bridges and locks for twelve hours a day, he has an immense amount of strong language to use, both to team and Captains; in the case of the mules, accompanied with considerable kicking, except when he has taken off his heavy shoes and swung them over the tow-line, to rest his feet.

On account of flies and insects many of the mules are covered with a square piece of white canvas, scalloped on the sides, and with holes for their ears to pass through. Comfortable and cool as this may be for them, it is anything but picturesque. But fortunately, the animals are so far ahead that one need not insult them by laughing.

Many amusing incidents occur on this sixty-five mile "walk" to Whitehall. Besides walking on the tow-path, picking berries and flowers, we had evening practice in physical culture, singing by moonlight, and chatting with the passing boatmen and drivers. About noon one day, we were grounded by a passing yacht which seemed to want the entire channel, by no means broad and deep just there. It took one hour and much labor to get by.

The Captain informed us there had been ample appropriation made by the State to keep the Canals in good condition, but by a misappropriation of the funds, (or some other fault), there is a poor bottom and a scarcity of water almost all summer on this route.* This causes long delays in getting out of the "tangles" and "wedges" [two boats stranded or wedged in a narrow channel], and great unnecessary exertion on the part of the boatmen who spend hours in hard poling; and in consequence the poor mules have to suffer in ineffectual attempts to start. This is trying to the tempers of all, and what wonder the mules become "kickers." If human they would "strike" instead. The drivers grow more abusive and profane, but the Captains have to bear it all uncomplainingly as they are dependent upon the towing lines and cannot afford to speak their minds. Not so the steersman, who is hired for the Canal trip only. In fact he seldom ceased speaking, nor was his language the most choice. The Steersman and the Captain "took turns" about at the tiller, as the boat needs careful guiding both day and night, through these narrow banks and winding ways.

July 9th, reached Schuylersville about nine A. M. and walked up to the station to meet Snap, who was to return from Saratoga to join us here.** Learning that we

*The administration of New York canals had been plagued by charges of mismanagement for years. Several decades earlier the Canal Board had been "accused of being in collusion with contractors. The committee of investigation found that there had been a waste of public funds in the letting of contracts, amounting to several millions of dollars, for work half done or wholly unperformed."[59] Although the project had been authorized in 1876, by 1890 only one third of the Champlain Canal had been widened to 44 feet on the bottom and dredged to a depth of six feet. Funds appropriated in 1895 were inadequate to enlarge the prism of the Champlain Canal to match the last enlargement of the Erie Canal.[60]
**"Snap," the most extroverted of the four women, had boarded a train at Mechanicville to visit a friend in Saratoga.

could not go before one A. M. in order to give the mules four hours rest, we started to view the Monument, but came across a gentleman who took us first to the old Schuyler Mansion, built more than a century ago; also to the site of the first Schuyler house burned down in 1745 by the Indians, and never rebuilt.* Some years after the land was graded for the new place and the old ruined cellar filled in. When the Canal was carried through, one bank came close to these old stone walls, and last spring, to mend the tow path, some of the bank was dug away and unearthed the ruins. Under a few feet of gravel, charred timbers and fallen stones, were found the bones of the seven inmates who were burned, and quite a number of imperishable household articles, in different stages of preservation. We poked about the spot and found old nails, pieces of the old brick, English make [china], and some of the old charred oak. Photographers had been there to get pictures of the old cellar walls and chimney, and part of a brick oven. The gravel diggers were waiting for orders from Washington as to whether they should go on with their digging or preserve the site.

So much time had been spent at this interesting spot and viewing the Mansion and its surrounding grounds, that we had little time left for the Monument. As it was we returned too late for our boat, and each with a bundle of fruit to add to our store of provisions, had also brought along a watermelon too large for us to carry, in charge of a young man. After walking down the tow-path half a mile or so, we overtook another boat; the Captain hauled up and took us on board, and here we spent a pleasant afternoon and evening, talking and eating, napping and being entertained by the family generally. This was the "Eustace," bound for Quebec, owned by a Mrs. Bouchard, whose eldest son was Captain, (she had a son [Fred] on another boat whom we met soon after) also a boy of ten, a girl of eight and a small boy of six. Quite a care for a widowed mother.

She gave us quite an interesting account of her life on a canal boat. Her husband was in poor health and had been advised to live out doors, so bought a canal boat as he was not able to do farm work. This prolonged his life many years; he died about three years ago leaving her with four or five boys and a small girl to bring up. In the winter the boat lies in a large basin at the foot of Twenty-fifth Street, Brooklyn, N. Y., and the children go to a public school from November until April, and have a pretty good education. Owing to their isolated home life, confined so much to a canal cabin, they learn very little of the mischief of street children and are more amenable to the Mother's government. But in the limited quarters of a canal-boat cabin there are but few books or amusements, and the girls learn early to help the mother with the housework, and the boys become expert sailors, see much of life in many places and invariably prefer the water to the land.

Once in a while we caught a glimpse of our "B. M. B." as some turn in the Canal permitted, only to lose sight of it in another moment. Our Captain had rigged up an awning for us which had to be taken down as we approached the Canal bridges; but we knew her by the carriage which our Captain had on the deck, taking it up

---

*Augusta and her party viewed the 155-foot-tall Saratoga Monument, built in 1883 to commemorate Lieutenant General John Burgoyne's surrender of the British army on October 17, 1777, to Major General Horatio Gates. They also inspected Major General Philip Schuyler's country home which had been rebuilt after having been burned by Burgoyne's troops during the Saratoga campaign.

In November 1745 Paul Marin de La Malgue, accompanied by his son, Joseph Marin de La Malgue, led a raiding party of 509 French regulars and Indians which succeeded in destroying Saratoga. Philip Schuyler, Major General Philip Schuyler's uncle, was killed in the raid.[61]

into Canada, and in which we had many comfortable hour[s] without fear of upsetting or being run away with. After a while the top had to be taken off and the wheels removed, and still we could enjoy what we called sleigh rides without snow and cold, quite an advantage if you have umbrellas to keep off the sun. All this time we were enjoying our fruit, and the kind hospitality of Mrs. Bouchard and her children.

Makeshift awning on deck of the canal boat *Bertha M.Bullis*. Canal Boat *Bertha M. Bullis* on the Champlain Canal. Drawings by Augusta Brown (1895). (New York State Museum)

About nine o'clock we hauled up at a Lock, and bidding our kind friends "good night," went "Home." At this Lock, at Moses' Kill, we learned that a lock-gate at Fort Edward, a few miles above, had burst off and washed down stream. So Capt. Bullis decided to put his boat into a dry-dock and have her caulked on the bottom, as she leaked badly. Next morning we found ourselves high and dry on some posts and beams inside what had been the night before a side-lock full of water. We climbed down a pair of steps and there found some men at work, and a hole having been bored in the bottom of the boat, she was slowly emptying.

The canal boat *Bertha M. Bullis* in dry dock. Drawing by Augusta Brown (1895).
(New York State Museum)

Then our good Captain hunted up a trusty nag of thirty years, put the carriage on "terra firma," and we soon started on a five mile drive to Fort Edward, where Snap and Snorum had some friends they wished to call upon. Capt. Snap took the whip and lines and by dint of much coaxing and urging, with encouraging remarks from the rest of the party, when we were not out of the carriage botanizing, as our good Snip was, at every approaching hill, while we lightened the load or helped to push the carriage, a double surrey, up some of the bridge-hills which are very steep. Our dear Snip had proved a botanist, and on every occasion decorated our cabin with flowers, and now was half the time out gathering them, catching up when our Rosinante [the old, worn horse of Don Quixote] stopped in every possible shade to rest and cool off. Fortunately, we had carried our lunch with us, which beguiled one of the slow hours away before we reached Fort Edward. After making a comprehensive tour of the town, we at last mounted a steep hill to Judge Waite's [A. Dallas Wait] place, made a long call on Dr. Waite and Madame Poté, visited the cupola occupied by a Dr. Shultz, and from which is a very fine panoramic view, then the barn where Dr. S. is building a canoe to go to Lake George in during August. Under some shady trees in the yard we tied our noble steed, and boarded the trolley car* for a ride of six miles through Sandy Hill [Hudson Falls] to Glens Falls, a beautiful town with many charming residences. Here we left Snip and Snap to spend the night with the cousin of the latter, and join us again when we reached Fort Edward. Starting home again behind our rested horse, we were not so long returning. A beautiful sunset, and a tea of sandwiches and bananas varied the monotony of the drive.

Next morning the caulking was finished, a coat of tar smeared on, and at one A. M. we saw our lock refilled, our mules attached and ourselves again on the way, going over the same region as the morning before, only under the bridges instead of over them. I must not forget that the morning had been spent in visiting the yards and sheds where boats are made and mended, thoroughly but not practically learning the caulking business as well as one of the branches of it, i. e. picking over oakum and making it into strands and bales for use.** It takes one man a month to prepare a bale, one hundred pounds, which sells for $7.00 or $7.50. We also went at eleven o'clock to an old district school kept by a Miss Powers from Fort Edward. There were about ten scholars, all chewing pitch [gum from pine trees]; their desks were all jack-knife carved; pond lilies decorated the teacher's desk in basin and fruit cans. At twelve o'clock we went down into a hollow for a drink of sulfur water at a spring, but did not much relish it, in fact preferred Hudson River water from a barrel.

Soon after leaving the dry-dock we were run into by a line-scow named "Belle Sheehan," our tow-line caught in its bow while all the men on board were engaged looking at a kicking mule our driver was trying to keep in position. Of course the

---

*The trolley belonged to the Hudson Valley Railway Company, a consolidation of the Glens Falls, Sandy Hill, and Fort Edward Street Railways and the Stillwater and Mechanicville Street Railway. The trolley lines were originally horse drawn but by 1895 were powered by electricity. The Delaware and Hudson Company later acquired the trolley line, but by the end of the 1920s many of the routes had been abandoned because of competition from automobiles. In November 1928 all operations ended and 50 wooden trolley cars were burned at the Glens Falls storage yard.[62]

**Oakum was made from old rope or hemp. Boat yards generally received the material in bales which required rolling it into string-like shapes of various diameters and then winding it into balls. Oakum was soaked in pitch before being applied to a boat's seams with a caulking iron and a mallet.[63]

sharp iron end of the scow struck in between fenders and front timbers and broke two of the planks above the water line; this wrenched them so that a leak started below, and our Captain's usual good temper had a severe test. And it was very aggravating just after his having paid thirty-one dollars for repairs. (And he could get no redress.)

The sun was bright, but a delightful breeze made the day perfect. Just after our accident we came across a load of lumber, perched upon which were our two absent

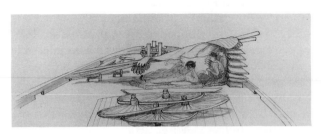

"Temporary Awning." Drawing by
Augusta Brown (1895). (New York State Museum)

members ["Snap" and "Snorum"], who had to be helped aboard while the boats passed each other. This was done successfully, and at five P. M. we reached Fort Edward and the now mended lock. . . About eight o'clock we reached the highest point of land,* where stands a barn, down the roof of which water flows when it rains, from one side joining the Hudson River and from the other Lake Champlain. We did not stop to prove it. Our loungers had rigged up a temporary screen from the sun by piling up half a dozen flat fenders, leaning the tent poles against these and laying the partially folded awning over them. Here we sewed and read and napped.

About midnight we were all wakened by our boat getting in a "wedge" with two others passing; by dint of an hours hard work and loud talking we were off again, but at five o'clock next morning the same strong language and hard poling wakened us again. Our progress now was down stream, and our mules had less work and we moved a little faster. Now all the locks were "down locks"; and the scenery was very picturesque, between the Green Mountains on our right and the mountains East of Lake George on our left; the canal, very circuitous, turns sharp, and new scenes of beauty every moment. Then came the "seven mile level" without locks or other incidents, until we reached Whitehall just before noon.

Our first walk was to the Post Office; then to a hotel where we took a room and rested. Visited a few of the stores; climbed the high cliff on the east side, and saw the narrow river through which we were to wind our way to the Lake. The tent was again raised on deck, and at night Snap and Snorum had their bed and bedding carried on deck, and under that slept for the rest of the trip, except when we spent the nights at hotels.

Next day we heard our tug was expected the following night, so we wandered about town again, and read aloud. In the afternoon Snorum took a stroll all alone,

---

*Approaching the highest point of the Champlain Canal from the south, canal boats were lifted higher in the locks, and then descended in the locks north of the summit. An abundant water supply at the summit of a canal is critical to the efficient operation of the system. The Glens Falls Feeder Canal was completed at the summit of the Champlain Canal in 1829 as a source of water, but also as a navigable waterway serving commercial enterprises located in Glens Falls. After a century of successful use, traffic on the feeder virtually ended in 1931 and the canal was officially closed for navigation in 1941.[64]

Above: Whitehall basin.
(Canal Society of New York State)

Right: Detail of "Potter Panorama" of Whitehall.
(New York State Museum)

Below: Canal boat at Whitehall
lock.
(Canal Society of New York State)

Canal boats (*Edward Clarke*, *James A. Doyle*, and *John J. Phalen*)
under construction at Whitehall. (Canal Society of New York State)

visited some churches, the Railroad Station a mile away, and again viewed us from
the cliff as we lolled about the deck in the shade of huge piles of lumber.

In the night a sudden gust of wind and rain drove Snap into the cabin for shelter,
but Snorum braved it out. Next day ten boats started by daylight in the tow, but
by the time we reached Fort "Ti" the number had reached forty.* We had no chance
to climb the hill at Fort "Ti."** nor to get off at Battery Point [Lotbinière or
Grenadier's Battery], but had a little time to look around at the long draw-bridges
beyond. Nor did we hear the "carillon," or music of the falls, as the waters of Lake
George tumbling down the steep outlet, are called [see footnote chapter 13].

Passing through the drawbridge*** just before two o'clock, we had a most
delightfully cool breeze, which kept our awning flapping and hair flying. The water
of the Lake is a delicate Nile green, clear enough to see to the bottom fifteen or
twenty feet deep, if the wind is not making white caps. We visited quite a number
of the boats, comparing cabins, as we stopped at different places to drop off or take
up boats. Though all seemed alike in a general way, some were very much nicer than
others. The "B. M. B." had a large room, a bedroom and a kitchen while some had
the bedroom only curtained off, and others had four rooms, as the "Palisade," with

---

*In a story describing a canal boat trip published in *Harper's New Monthly Magazine* in 1896, Howard
Pyle noted that upon leaving Whitehall and entering Lake Champlain, canal boats were two abreast
and stretched "sometimes to a mile in length; for the southern reaches of Lake Champlain are narrow
and tortuous...the long line of slow moving boats takes upon it the appearance of some strange gigantic
water-serpent with a smoking head, wriggling now here through the cleft of a wooded mountain height,
now winding there its jointed coil around a jutting point of bright green marsh."[65]

**Howard Pyle found the grounds adjacent to the crumbling walls of the fort to be inhabited by flocks
of sheep during the same time period as Augusta Brown's trip. "The scene is very lovely," Pyle noted,
but "one has only to scratch the soil upon which he stands to turn up bullets and grape-shot
embedded...in the peaceful bosom of mother earth—mementos of those bitter days."[66]

***Completed in 1871, an 1,830-foot-long railroad bridge, utilizing a 300-foot drawboat section to
allow for the passage of vessels on the lake, connected Willow Point, Ticonderoga, to the south side
of Beadles Cove at Larrabees Point (Vermont). Train service across the bridge continued until late
1920. On May 24, 1923, the Interstate Commerce Commission approved the permanent abandonment
of the crossing. A side-scan sonar survey of the area in 1992 by the Lake Champlain Maritime Museum
revealed the remains of two drawboats used for the portable section of the bridge. The first of the
300-foot drawboats was in service from 1871 to 1888 and the second from 1888 to 1902.[67]

Top: South Bay. (Photo by Richard K. Dean) *Above:* "Grenadier's Battery." *Below:* "Fort Ti. and Grenadier's Battery." Drawings by Augusta Brown (1895). (New York State Museum) *Right:* Ticonderoga (ca. 1903). (Postcard detail, author's collection)

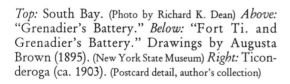

rolling doors between, so that all could open into one in the day time. Most of the boats have awnings over the cabins, with swings and hammocks underneath, the top of which reaches back so as to shelter the steersman from sun and rain.

Small children play about under them, tied to a post when left alone, as there is great danger of their falling off into the water; and in the Lakes or Rivers, there is little hope of picking them up.*

One captain swung a hammock across his cabin and slept in that altogether. Had no steersman so [he] had to be on deck night and day. At Fort St Frederick** we had to stop a few hours as some of the machinery on the Tug got out of order. Captain Antoine Murray had two young ladies on board [the 94-foot tug *H. G. Tisdale*] to whom he was showing the various towns, so we were informed by Pilot Luther Bullis, our Captain's cousin, so we had our suspicions about the danger we had been in regarding broken machinery. When the tug stopped, it was quite a curiosity to see the boats from the rear push ahead in the strong current,—almost an entire circle was formed with many zig-zags on the line before we came to a full stop, and the boats ceased bumping into each other. Two young men went ashore in a row boat, and Snap sent a note by them to the tug Captain requesting him to stop, if possible, at Port Kent long enough for us to visit Ausable Chasm. He sent back word that he would do so as he had to stop there anyway. We found out afterwards that his own relations lived there.

Passed Westport in the night, and were nearing Cleft Rock [Split Rock] when we rose at 6 in the morning. There is a tradition that during the French & Indian War an Indian acted as spy; was chased in his canoe down the lake; as he neared this point he passed through the cleft, and disappeared. It being night, his pursuers did

---

*In 1896 Howard Pyle related two melancholy stories. Sitting on their respective cabins one evening while their boats were moored side by side, two boat captains turned their conversation to the tragedies of their children lost in canal boat accidents. One "in a sort of passive monotone, began telling about how they had lost their two only children; how one of the children had fallen overboard and had been drowned, and how the other had fallen from the cabin roof, upon which it had been playing, and had died in a little while—an hour or so. He went into all the particulars of what must at the time have been a great and overwhelming tragedy, and his wife every now and then put in a word or two, adding to or confirming what was said. She rocked back and forth in her rocking-chair as they talked, and there was no sound of passion in their words—only a passive submission to what had happened, and which could not be mended. But what they said seemed to awaken an echo of the past tragedy in our own captain's life; for he began telling about how he had had a daughter (she would, he said, have been twenty-two years old if she had lived). He told how he had left her playing upon the deck one day while he went up to the collector's office for his papers. His wife was down in the cabin cooking supper. By-and-by she came up, and saw the little one's straw hat floating in the water. There was no ripple or sign to show what had happened. They never, he said, saw anything of the child again."[68]

**Charles Possons' 1891 guidebook mentioned that Fort St. Frédéric "is a popular excursion point, parties journeying many miles to visit the historic locality. The Champlain Transportation Co. makes it a regular landing for excursionists. Substantial walks lead from the dock to the ruins, and a fine pavilion has been erected for dancing or assemblies."[69] He also noted the presence of treasure hunters: "Money digging still continues in the neighborhood."[70] William H. H. Murray's *Lake Champlain and Its Shores*, published in 1890, described the remains of the English village (ca. 1760-1775) on the Bulwagga Bay side of Crown Point where "signs of ancient fences and enclosures of gardens and door-yards may still be seen. . .[and] an old street. . .ancient cellars. . .two large graveyards."[71] Both writers also observed that the barracks at Crown Point were still standing.

not see it, and passed swiftly by, giving him a chance to come out from behind and go back with his news.*

The day was somewhat misty, tinging the mountains a delicate blue, but still we could see the streaks of granite on their sides looking like snow valleys or glaciers.

Near Essex the Lake grows very broad, the water is still clear looking, but without that lovely green tinge which made it so beautiful yesterday. The Green Mountains seem to have reached their northern limit, and those we see far off are "deeply, darkly, desperately Blue." I wonder if we could see the White Mts. from the lake level on a clear day? I fear not.

Arrived about four at Port Kent where we took a carriage to the Chasm, and were well paid for the trip. This is a most remarkable natural curiosity; the Ausable River forcing its way through a hill nearly two miles

Ausable Chasm.
(Postcard detail, author's collection)

long, making a cut more than two hundred feet deep.** A walk of a mile and row of another took us to the lake level and we returned to the tow just about dark and soon started for the broadest part of the lake. The wind had been gaining in strength all day and at night helped us on, but making a rough and rocking sea, and in the morning the white caps loomed up all around us, and Captain Murray was obliged to turn the tow around inside the long break water at Rouse's Point. This was no slight work, but it would have been impossible to carry such a long line through the drawbridge.*** A few light boats for the point were taken to the dock, then the rest of us were taken four at a time, and tied between the dock and the bridge to wait until a change or abatement of wind. It took us skirt-hampered females some

*Many legends connected with landmarks at Lake Champlain were repeated over the generations. Benjamin C. Butler's nineteenth-century book *Lake George and Lake Champlain, from their First Discovery to 1759* noted that "it was a superstition of the Indians that in passing the rock [Split Rock] they should cast a stone or other article toward it for good luck."[72]

**Accessible via a steamboat landing and a train depot located at Port Kent, Ausable Chasm emerged as a major tourist attraction in the late nineteenth century, particularly after the commercial development of the site in the 1870s. Guidebooks in the 1890s devoted whole sections to the Chasm. Possons' guidebook suggested that "thousands of tourists pronounce their visit to the Chasm as being the most enjoyable and gratifying of their summer experience. . .By means of artificial stairways, galleries and bridges, erected and owned by the Ausable Chasm Co., and by boats, this stupendous work of nature can be traversed its entire length."[73] Visiting Ausable Chasm in 1884, Moses Brown commented that "it is, really, a remarkable place. The guides met us at the end of the walking part of the gorge, in a huge boat, more tub than boat, capable of holding 20 people, and embarking, we went through the flume and down some rapids. These were quite steep and it was good fun."[74]

***The mile-long wooden trestle drawbridge, connecting Rouses Point to Alburgh, Vermont, opened for railroad traffic in 1851. The Ticonderoga drawbridge, completed 20 years later, was modeled after this structure. The Rouses Point Bridge allowed for the passage of vessels on the lake by means of a removable 300-foot drawboat section, which was replaced in 1868 by a center-pivot swing bridge. The latter mechanism continued in service until the crossing was abandoned in the 1950s.[75]

time to climb over boats and reach the shore, by the aid of many helping hands, among them the ever ready ones of Mrs. Bouchard's Fred, who was on the boat "Blohm," just ahead of us, he and the Captain of his boat became our good knights on many a tramp over boats and water.

The clearance papers have all to be shown here at the Custom Office, so all the Captains have to go ashore. The wind blew furiously all day and all night and all the next day, so there we lay in a conglomerate mass, a community of boats,— a canal town, No less than one hundred and fifty souls with their homes about them; all sorts and conditions of men, women and children, from the free and independent excursionist, the aristocratic canal boat owner and captain, to the cunning baby in arms, and the coal heaver on the open flat boat.

Thanking Captain Murray of the "Tisdale" for enabling us to visit the Chasm, we resigned ourselves to being tied to the usual old post that has held canal boats from time immemorial. Putting up the awning over the carriage to keep out the wind and cold rain, we fell reading again the adventures of Don Quixote, until two of the party fell asleep, another resorted to the cabin to do her week's ironing and listen to the Captain's wife [Martha] who amused us daily with stories and anecdotes, of which she seemed to have an inexhaustible supply. Having been for four years a Captain in the Salvation Army she had seen much of life, and could always fit a joke in to the occasion.

Snorum began a lively flirtation with the Captain of a neighboring boat, and never lost an opportunity to cheer him up, as he was a lonely widower. He once told her she reminded him of his first wife. Whether he had been blessed with a second we did not know.

About seven o'clock the tug appeared and towed up six boats at a time through the drawbridge, where we were left until five next morning, beyond the power of wind and wave. Reached Lacol[l]e Bridge [a swingbridge in Quebec] about seven when the whole tow, four abreast, was turned round and "dropped" through. Then slowly turned again in the shallow, narrow river. This took just two hours to accomplish, as some boats were constantly getting aground. At this point the "pin flats"* hoisted sail and left us far behind, as the wind was just right. The empty pin flats, "lighters," hoist two sails, both the same size, sailing away before the breeze quite finely, but loaded with ten or twenty feet of lumber there is only room for one sail.

The service of the Champlain Transportation Co. is far inferior to that of the Hudson River Towing Co. The tugs are not powerful enough and they do not have enough of them for the number of boats, nor do they run frequently for the accommodation of the Captains; who, as in the mule service, feel obliged to put up with it, though it often is a loss to them of an entire trip during a short season, three or four hundred dollars.

Arrived at St. Johns about 5 P. M. and decided to leave the boat for the sake of a little longer stay in Montreal, so climbing over boats loaded high with hay or pulp-wood, finally we scrambled to the dock and made our way to the Post Office and after a restaurant-tea took the 7 o'clock train for Montreal.

---

*"Pinflats" were Canadian sailing canal boats typically used to carry lumber or pulpwood to American ports on Lake Champlain.[76]

Notes

1. "Off on a Canal Boat: A Cruise on the Bertha Bullis to Canada," (newspaper account, p.n.a.), in Augusta Brown, "Journal of Augusta Brown," New York State Museum, Albany.
2. Augusta Brown, "Journal," 1.
3. Ibid., 17.
4. W. H. H. Murray, *Lake Champlain and Its Shores* (Boston: De Wolfe, Fiske & Co., 1890), 140.
5. Dona Brown, *Inventing New England: Regional Tourism in the Nineteenth Century* (Washington, D. C.: Smithsonian Institution Press, 1995), 72.
6. S. R. Stoddard, *Lake George (Illustrated) and Lake Champlain. A Book of To-Day* (Glens Falls, N. Y.: S. R. Stoddard, 1895), 133; See also Charles H. Possons, *Possons's Guide to Lake George; Lake Champlain and Adirondacks* (Glens Falls, N. Y.: Chas. H. Possons, Publisher, 1891), 163-64.
7. Possons, 176.
8. S. R. Stoddard, *Lake George (Illustrated) and Lake Champlain. A Book of To-Day* (Glens Falls, N. Y.: S. R. Stoddard, 1898).
9. Moses Brown, "1500 Miles in a 14 ft. 'Adirondacker' on Canal, Lake and River, Fall of 1884," Adirondack Museum, Blue Mountain Lake, N. Y., 217. Moses Brown's guideboat is presently at the Adirondack Museum. See Hallie Bond, "What is 'Museum Quality'? A Curator Looks at Boat Restoration," *WoodenBoat*, September/October 1998, 86.
10. Moses Brown, 224.
11. Ibid., 221.
12. Ibid., 222.
13. Ibid.
14. Murray, 153, 158-59.
15. Ibid., 158.
16. Ibid., 160.
17. Florence Watters Snedeker, *A Family Canoe Trip* (New York: Harper & Brothers, 1892), 107-8; The fake monster was apparently confused with the real thing. See Marjorie L. Porter, *Vermont Life*, Summer 1970, 48; For a record of sightings of the Champlain monster see Joseph W. Zarzynski, *Champ: Beyond the Legend* (Wilton, N. Y.: M-Z Information, 1988), 156-205, 208-16.
18. Jim Shaughnessy, *Delaware & Hudson* (1967; reprint ed., Syracuse: Syracuse University Press, 1997), 83, 109, 129, 144, 151, 169, 255; For information on the Delaware & Hudson Company's canal operations see Larry Lowenthal, *From the Coalfields to the Hudson: A History of the Delaware & Hudson Canal* (Fleischmanns, N.Y.: Purple Mountain Press, 1997).
19. J. Arbuthnot Wilson, *Belgravia: An Illustrated London Magazine*, October 1883, 419. Although Wilson's article was published in 1883, the trip was probably taken in the early 1870s.
20. Thomas X. Grasso, *Champlain Canal* (Syracuse: The Canal Society of New York State, 1985), 4; William J. McKelvey, Jr., *Champlain to Chesapeake: A Canal Era Pictorial Cruise* (Exton, PA.: Canal Press Incorporated, 1978), v.
21. Henry Wayland Hill, *An Historical Review of Waterways and Canal Construction in New York State* (Buffalo: Buffalo Historical Society, 1908), 156; See also Arthur B. Cohn et al., *The Archaeological Reconstruction of the Lake Champlain Canal Schooner General Butler* (Ferrisburg, VT.: Lake Champlain Maritime Museum, 1996), 27.
22. Grasso, 4; McKelvey, v.
23. Cohn, *General Butler*, 27.
24. Hill, 178; See also Alvin F. Harlow, *Old Towpaths* (New York: D. Appleton and Company, 1926), 156.
25. Frank H. Godfrey, *The Godfrey Letters* (Syracuse: The Canal Society of New York State, 1973), 28.
26. Augusta Brown, "Journal," 45.
27. *Dictionary of American Biography*, Volume 2 (New York: Charles Scribner's Sons, 1929), 156; Stanley J. Kunitz and Howard Haycraft, *American Authors 1600-1900* (New York: The H. W. Wilson Company, 1938), 106; Solyman Brown was described as "a typical tall New Englander. A forceful public speaker, with marked mechanical ability and literary talent, he did much for the elevation of dentistry." *Dictionary of American Biography*, 156.

28. Leonard Elkins, "Early Articles on Dental Ethics and Practice Administration," *New York State Dental Journal* 27 (February 1961): 87.

29. Ibid., 87-88; *Dictionary of American Biography*, 155-56; Kunitz and Haycraft, 106.

30. Population Schedules of the Eighth Census of the United States 1860, National Archives Microfilm Publications, Microcopy n.d., roll 769, Kings County (Ward 10), N. Y., Volume 53, 492.

31. Population Schedules of the Ninth Census of the United States 1870, National Archives Microfilm Publications, Microcopy 593, roll 1104, Tompkins County, N. Y., Volume 100, 43.

32. Augusta Brown to Virginia Brown Blake, 21 April 1888, Sibyl Blake Selkirk Family Papers.

33. Augusta Brown to Virginia Brown Blake, 19 October 1893, Sibyl Blake Selkirk Family Papers.

34. Ibid.

35. F. Hopkinson Smith and J. B. Millet, "Snubbin' Through Jersey," *The Century Magazine*, August 1887, 483-96, 697-711.

36. Augusta Brown, "Journal," 3.

37. Smith and Millet, 485.

38. Mona Domosh, *Invented Cities: The Creation of Landscape in Nineteenth-Century New York & Boston* (New Haven: Yale University Press, 1996), 65-66, 72-73.

39. Augusta Brown, "Journal," 2.

40. Ibid., 1.

41. Ibid., 4.

42. Ibid.

43. Ibid.

44. Ibid., 5.

45. Ibid.

46. Ibid., 6.

47. Ibid.; See also McKelvey, 31.

48. Augusta Brown, "Journal," 6.

49. Ibid., 8.

50. Ibid., 25.

51. Ibid.

52. Population Schedules of the Twelfth Census of the United States 1900, National Archives Microfilm Publications, Kings County, N. Y., Volume 62, line 53.

53. Augusta Brown, "Trip to Europe in 1907 with Cousin Emma: Seeing the Mountains, Lakes and Rivers of Western Europe," Sibyl Blake Selkirk Family Papers, 9.

54. Augusta Brown, "Three Berkshire Cyclists Take an Extended Trip" (undated), Sibyl Blake Selkirk Family Papers, 1.

55. Sibyl Blake Selkirk, telephone interview by author, 9 July 1998.

56. Augusta Brown to Sibyl Blake Selkirk, 24 October 1934, Sibyl Blake Selkirk Family Papers.

57. *Times-Union* (Albany), 17 October 1937.

58. Augusta Brown, "Journal," 8-23.

59. Hill, 155.

60. Ibid., 159; See also Larkin, 81.

61. Guy Omeron Coolidge, *The French Occupation of the Champlain Valley from 1609 to 1759* (1938; reprint ed., Mamaroneck, N. Y.: Harbor Hill Books, 1989), 140; Benson J. Lossing, *The Life and Times of Philip Schuyler* (1872; reprint ed., New York: Da Capo Press, 1973), Volume 1, 54-56; See also Bayard Tuckerman, *Life of General Philip Schuyler 1733-1804* (1903; reprint ed., Freeport, N.Y.:Books for Libraries Press, 1969), 28-29; Nathaniel Bartlett Sylvester, *History of Saratoga County, New York* (1878; reprint ed., Interlaken, N. Y.: Heart of the Lakes Publishing, 1979), 39.

62. Craig Williams, "In the Footsteps of Augusta Brown," in *Proceedings: First Annual Conference of Heritage Tourism in the Adirondack Region*, ed. by David Starbuck (Glens Falls, N. Y.: Adirondack Regional Chambers of Commerce, 1996), 43; Shaughnessy, 218, 309.

63. Fred. G. Godfrey, *The Champlain Canal: Mules to Tugboats* (Monroe, N. Y.: LRA, Inc., 1994), 56; Arthur B. Cohn et al., *Underwater Preserve Feasibility Study of the Lake Champlain Canal Schooner O. J. Walker* (Ferrisburg, VT.: Lake Champlain Maritime Museum, 1996), 97.

64. Grasso, 3; McKelvey, 15; Williams, 44; Godfrey, *Champlain Canal*, 71.

65. Howard Pyle, "Through Inland Waters," *Harpers New Monthly Magazine*, June 1896, 72.

66. Ibid., 74.

67. Peter Barranco, Jr., *Ticonderoga's Floating Drawbridge; 1871-1920* (Lake Champlain Basin Program, 1995), Report 4E, 10-16, 18-40, 48.
68. Pyle, May 1896, 837.
69. Possons, 121.
70. Ibid., 127.
71. Murray, 90-91.
72. B. C. Butler, *Lake George and Lake Champlain, from their First Discovery to 1759*, 2nd ed. (New York: G. P. Putnan & Son, 1869), 17.
73. Possons, 148, 151.
74. Moses Brown, 227-28.
75. Barranco, 2-4, 18.
76. John E. O' Hara, "Erie's Junior Partner," (Ph. D. diss. Columbia University, 1951), 234-35; P. André Sévgny, *Trade and Navigation on the Chambly Canal: A Historical Review* (Ottawa: National Historic Parks and Sites Branch, Parks Canada, 1983), 36-53; E. P. P., "A St. Lawrence Trader," *Mariner's Mirror* 5 (1: 1919): 23; Irving R. Wiles, "A St. Lawrence Trader," *Mariner's Mirror* 6 (2: 1920): 53-55.

"Pin Flat." Drawing by Augusta Brown (1895).
(New York State Museum)

Seneca Ray Stoddard at Ausable Chasm (ca. 1870s). (Adirondack Museum)

15. Seneca Ray Stoddard 1915

ALTHOUGH BEST KNOWN for his photographic record of the Adirondacks, Seneca Ray Stoddard can also be cited for his remarkable work as a writer, painter, lecturer, mapmaker, inventor, and conservationist. As a native of the region, Stoddard was intimately familiar with the Adirondacks, including Lake George and Lake Champlain, having spent considerable time over several decades photograph-ing and surveying the region, as well as gathering material for his annual guidebooks. When Stoddard passed away in 1917, the *Glen Falls Times and Messenger* noted that he "toiled not for himself alone, but for this community and the Adirondack region; the great north woods, where for more than 50 years he has sought to call attention of the outside world to their glories."[1] His 1892 Adirondack slide presentation before a packed New York State Assembly in Albany, which was later shown to audiences across the state, was instrumental in coalescing support for the passage of the bill establishing the Adirondack Park.

Seneca Ray Stoddard witnessed many changes at Lake Champlain during the decades that his guidebooks were published. His books always included new information for travelers on the Champlain steamboats. Transportation on the lake underwent several evolutionary changes after the turn of the century. The remaining wooden-hulled steamboats of the Champlain Transportation Company were retired in the first decade of the new century. After 31 years of service, the steamboat *Vermont II* was retired at the end of the 1902 season and replaced by the 262-foot steel-hulled *Vermont III* the following year. Although the new steamer had the same length, the *Vermont III*'s maximum width of 62 feet was nearly 60 percent wider than her predecessor's, making her the largest vessel ever built at the lake. Decorated in white and gold with red carpeting in the stateroom hall and furnished with elegant mahogany furniture, the *Vermont III* resembled a floating palace. Passengers were

Above left: The steamer *Ticonderoga* in Burlington harbor. (Postcard, author's collection)
Top: The *Vermont III* began service in 1903. (Postcard, author's collection)
Above right: The steamboat *Chateaugay*, built in 1888 and remodeled as a car
ferry in 1925. (Special collections, Bailey/Howe Memorial Library, University of Vermont)

accommodated in 50 staterooms, which offered running water, heat, and electricity.
Assigned to the Ticonderoga-Plattsburgh route, the 1,800-horsepower *Vermont III*
cruised at 23 miles per hour.

The last wooden-hulled CTC steamboat, the 142-foot *Maquam*, was retired three
years after the *Vermont II* and replaced with the 220-foot steel-hulled *Ticonderoga*
in 1906. Although designed as a day vessel, the *Ticonderoga* had five staterooms
available for passengers during the day or overnight when the vessel was docked.
The luxurious stateroom hall was finished with cherry trim, butternut-paneled
doors, a stenciled ceiling, and a richly-patterned carpet.[2] The *Ticonderoga* was
assigned to the Port Henry-Plattsburgh run (also stopping at Westport, Essex,
Burlington, and St.Albans), while the 18-year-old steamer *Chateaugay* was transferred to the excursion trade, previously the duty of the *Maquam*.

At the turn of the century, economic and political pressures mounted to improve
the canal system of New York State which in a short period of time culminated in
the construction of the New York Barge Canal. While the Panama Canal received
more publicity, the New York Barge Canal represented as impressive an engineering
feat and was actually ten times longer with several more elaborate locks.[3] By 1898
tonnage carried on New York canals had fallen to a 41-year-low as railroads surpassed
canals, carrying ten times the freight. The political process leading to an improved
canal system proved troublesome, however. When a nine-million-dollar appropriation in 1895 was found to be inadequate to finish deepening the canals, rumors of
fraud and incompetence spread across the state. Soon after taking office in 1899,

Top left: Whitehall's commercial district facing the canal. (Postcard, author's collection)
Above left: Harbor at Whitehall. (Canal Society of New York State)
The Champlain Barge Canal at Whitehall looking south. (Photo by Richard K. Dean)

New York Governor Theodore Roosevelt appointed a seven-member committee to study the state's canal system and recommend a long-term policy. After a thorough investigation, the committee suggested that the Erie, Oswego, and Champlain Canals be enlarged. Roosevelt endorsed the findings, concluding that "we must act in the broadest and most liberal and energetic spirit if we wish to retain the state's commercial supremacy."[5] Despite opposition by railroad interests, a referendum on a bond issue for an enlarged barge canal was approved by voters in 1903. Although the original legislation would not have deepened the Champlain Canal to the 12-foot depth planned for the other two canals, politicians and businessmen (particularly mining and paper interests) from the Champlain Valley were successful in gaining approval of similar dimensions for the Champlain Barge Canal.

Although a section of the New York Barge Canal opened for navigation at Waterford on May 15, 1915, the entire length of the barge canal would not be opened for another three years. The new barge canal eliminated traditional tow paths; from then on canal boats were towed by tug boats through the canal and the canalled section of the Hudson River. From Troy to Whitehall the Champlain Barge Canal extended 63 miles with 12 locks, each 328 feet in length and 45 feet wide.[7] As a result of the enlargement of the locks, barges that were three times the size of the late nineteenth-century canal boats could pass through the canal and into Lake Champlain. By the time the new canal opened, sailing canal boats had disappeared from the lake, and the days of small family-owned (towed) canal boats were numbered. Tonnage on the New York Barge Canal did not attain the old canal's twentieth-century peak set in 1903 until the 1930s, reaching its greatest tonnage in 1951.[8] Faced with competition from a number of sources, including oil pipelines, the St.Lawrence Seaway, railroads, and trucks, the commercial use of the barge canal declined after the 1950s; today the canal has a new life as a recreational waterway.[9]

With the approach of the three-hundredth anniversary of Samuel de Champlain's 1609 exploration of Lake Champlain, an appreciable upswing of public interest in the lake's history occurred. In September 1908 Stephen H. P. Pell "visited [Fort] Ticonderoga for the first time in twenty-five years and was greatly impressed with the possibilities of the place. . .the property. . .had always remained in the family, but no member had taken the slightest interest in it."[10] In 1883, at the age of eight, Stephen H. P. Pell had his curiosity stirred when he discovered a bronze flint box in the ruins of the fort. Pell's great-grandfather, William Ferris Pell, had acquired the property in 1820 after having first leased it for several years from Columbia and Union Colleges. In 1908 Stephen H. P. Pell began repairing the family summer home, the Pavilion, built in 1826 following a fire that had destroyed William Ferris Pell's first house. For a good part of the nineteenth century the Pavilion had been used as a hotel, but for 15 or 20 years prior to 1908 it had been leased to a farmer. (One room was used as a horse stable.)[11] The restoration of the fort's West Barracks, funded by Pell's father-in-law, Colonel Robert Means Thompson, was completed for the Tercentenary celebration of 1909. The first year's excavation of the fort yielded a treasure trove of historic artifacts, according to Pell, including "buttons, buckles, knives, forks, porcelain, earthenware, hundreds of cannon balls, bullets, and grapeshot, and. . .a punch bowl, in which. . .'Success to General Amherst' " was written.[12] An examination of documents in British, French, and Canadian archives aided in the reconstruction of the fort and the outer defenses. The Pell family's commitment to preserving the history of the fort and its dependencies (Stephen H. P. Pell and Sarah G. T. Pell acquired a large portion of Mount Independence in 1911) continued in subsequent decades.

The Pavilion, originally built in 1826. (Postcard, author's collection)

The grandest celebration of Lake Champlain, the Tercentenary of Samuel de Champlain's epic voyage, occurred in July 1909. Preparations for the events began several years earlier and included plans by the Tercentenary Committee for raising the wreck of Benedict Arnold's 1776 flagship *Royal Savage* sunk at Valcour Island. However, hard-hat divers concluded that the schooner *Royal Savage** was too "deeply imbedded in the sand" to raise it.[18]

The Tercentenary celebration began in Vergennes, Vermont, on July 3, 1909, with religious services, an Algonquin dance exhibition, a display of three small U.S. Navy vessels, a parade, speeches, and a banquet.[19] Moving to Crown Point on July 5, the observance involved mock battles, Indian pageants, speeches, a parade, and fireworks. After being towed from Canada, a replica of the *Don de Dieu*, the ship that had brought Samuel de Champlain to Canada in 1608, lay at anchor off Crown Point. Performed aboard a 300- by 70-foot barge, the Indian pageants, involving 168 Iroquois, dramatized "Hiawatha," Champlain's voyage on the lake, and his 1609 battle.[20] Similar exercises were held the next day at Fort Ticonderoga with the addition of a speech by President William Howard Taft, who noted the long struggle by France, Great Britain, and the United States over Lake Champlain's strategic "passageway."[21] President Taft toured the restored portions of the fort with the Pell family and viewed the wreck of Amherst's 1759 brig *Duke of Cumberland*, raised earlier in 1909 and mistakenly identified at the time as Benedict Arnold's schooner *Revenge*. Taft later embarked on the steamboat *Ticonderoga* for a voyage to Port Henry where he boarded a train for Plattsburgh. On July 7 he gave speeches at Cliff Haven and at the Plattsburgh army barracks, as did the governors of New York and Vermont and the ambassadors from Great Britain and France. The festivities also included Indian pageants performed at the mouth of the Saranac River, a parade, a banquet, and fireworks. The following day, virtually the same activities were repeated in Burlington before an audience of 40,000 people. After a banquet there, the presidential party returned to Washington, D.C., but the Tercentenary ceremonies continued for another day at Isle La Motte. The final chapter in the observance of the Tercentenary occurred several years later. On May 3, 1912, American

---

*Although the *Royal Savage* was not raised for the Tercentenary, the divers from Burlington discovered many relics aboard a 45-foot section of the wreckage, including silver spoons, musket balls, and cannonballs.[13] In September 1929 Lorenzo F. Hagglund, manager of the Under-Water Metal Cutting Company operating with the Merritt-Chapman and Scott Corporation, wrote to Charles C. Adams, director of the New York State Museum, seeking cooperation in the recovery of "some Revolutionary relics" in Lake Champlain.[14] Hagglund had been stationed in Plattsburgh for officer training in 1917 and his interest in the lake's history was sparked during the 1929 Crown Point bridge construction when his divers recovered artifacts from the lake, including a small cannon.[15] For several years during the early 1930s Hagglund corresponded with the museum director, proposing a plan to raise the *Royal Savage* for display in the state museum. In May 1934 Hagglund wrote again to Adams, suggesting a "plan to raise and condition the remains of this hull. . .The proper place for this collection would be the New York State Museum and it is my idea to offer the material recovered to your museum as a loan exhibit and also give the museum the option to acquire the exhibit at any time upon payment of the cost of obtaining and preserving this material. . .[a sum of] less than $1,000.00."[16] Hagglund raised the vessel during the summer of 1934 but was later informed that there wasn't sufficient space to exhibit the vessel at the museum. After Hagglund raised a second vessel, the gunboat *Philadelphia*, at Valcour Island, state authorities began enforcing section 54 of the Education Law, asserting state ownership of artifacts lying on the bottom of the lake.[17] The wreck of the *Royal Savage* was stored in a small barn in Willsboro for many decades, and in 1995 it was sold to a private party in Pennsylvania for future display in a new museum.

dignitaries accepted the gift of Auguste Rodin's bronze bust of "La France" from an official French delegation. The sculpture was later placed on the Champlain Memorial Lighthouse. On July 5, 1912, the lighthouse, exhibiting a large bronze statuary grouping of Samuel de Champlain, an Indian, and a French soldier, was formally dedicated. The next day, a 12-foot bronze statue of Champlain set on a granite pedestal was dedicated in Plattsburgh.

Left: President William Howard Taft at the Tercentenary
celebration at the Plattsburgh army barracks on July 7, 1909.
From *The Champlain Tercentenary* by Henry Wayland Hill (1913).
Right: Champlain Memorial Lighthouse before the dedication ceremonies on
July 5, 1912. From *The Champlain Tercentenary: Final Report* (1913).

The 1909 Tercentenary brought national attention to the history of Lake Champlain; the July issue of *The Travel Magazine*, for example, was devoted entirely to Lake Champlain and the Tercentenary celebration. The magazine recognized the transition in modes of transportation with an article written by Raymond Beck of the Automobile Club of America, entitled "An Auto Trip to Lake Champlain," which provided convoluted directions from New York City to "the Great Lake for the Tercentenary Celebration."[22] Beck recommended an overnight stay at Caldwell (Lake George Village), noting that "we have traveled thus far over most excellent macadam roads, the scenery has been superb, and we are now about to encounter some rough touring roads" to Plattsburgh.[23] "The first thirty-four miles is mostly good dirt road with some macadam," Beck observed, but "the middle part of the route is considerably rough mountain road, with some sandy spots. There are no bad grades, but most beautiful scenery. From Ke[ese]ville to Lake Champlain (Bluff Point) we again strike macadam."[24] His specific directions included following trolley lines from Caldwell to Warrensburg where a right fork was negotiated before following telegraph wires. The route eventually brought auto travelers through the towns of Chestertown, Schroon Lake, Underwood, New Russia, Elizabethtown, and Lewis. Separate directions were also provided from Schroon River to Crown Point and Fort Ticonderoga. To reach the Tercentenary festivities in Vermont, Beck suggested that drivers board the steamboat at Plattsburgh with their automobiles for the regularly scheduled trip to Burlington.

Seneca Ray Stoddard also changed with the times, using an automobile to evaluate road conditions for his illustrated road maps, published between 1909 and 1915. Advertisements in Stoddard's guidebooks reflected the new era as hotels listed "automobile parties to Fort Ticonderoga and other points of historic interest" and garages for the cars of motoring tourists.[25] As less expensive cars, particularly the Ford Model

State road south of Plattsburgh.
(Postcard, author's collection)

T, reached the mass market, travel became more democratized, leading to an expansion of boarding houses, cottages, and camping sites in the Adirondacks.[26] By publishing annual guidebooks and photographs during the late nineteenth and early twentieth centuries, Seneca Ray Stoddard furthered the growth of tourism in the Adirondacks and at Lake George and Lake Champlain.

Born on May 13, 1843, in Wilton, New York, (south of Glens Falls) to Charles and Julia Ray Stoddard, Seneca Ray traced his family lineage as far back as Anthony Stoddard, who had emigrated from England in 1639. While the Stoddard family included several Harvard-educated ministers, Seneca Ray's father, Charles Stoddard, had little education and spent most of his life as a farmer.[27] As a youngster, Seneca Ray had to adapt to many changes, including several moves with his family, the death of his mother in 1851, and his father's remarriage soon after. In 1862, after the Stoddard family had moved to the Troy area, nineteen-year-old Seneca Ray was employed by the Gilbert Car Company located in Watervliet on Green Island, painting landscape scenes on the interior of railroad passenger cars.[28] Although decorative scene painting on railroad cars was on the wane, the experience would shape Seneca Ray Stoddard's life-long career. At the age of 21, Stoddard moved to Glens Falls, opening a sign and ornamental painting business which he later expanded with the help of a partner. By the fall of 1867 Stoddard had turned to the fledgling medium of photography. He may have learned the process of wet-plate photography at the Glens Falls gallery of George W. Conkey, who dealt in portrait photography and stereoscopic prints.[29] In 1868, with his business on a sound financial footing, Stoddard married 18-year-old Helen Augusta Potter, the daughter of a well-to-do family with whom Stoddard had lived during his first years in Glens Falls. The Stoddards later settled into a home on Elm Street where they raised two children. Seneca Ray nurtured his photography business there while maintaining an interest in landscape art.

New opportunities awaited Seneca Ray during the 1870s. Before the publication of his guidebook series, Stoddard had honed his writing skills while working part-time for Glens Falls newspapers. In 1872 he produced his first viewbook of Lake George (11 scenes) and the next year his guidebook *Lake George; (Illustrated.) A Book of To-Day* was published. The guide covered the stagecoach ride to the lake (humorously) and provided descriptions of hotels, steamboats, islands, and scenic points, as well as a history of the lake. Witty comments and a few whimsical stories were sprinkled throughout the text. The next year he published a similar-sized guide entitled *Ticonderoga: Past and Present*, covering the history of the fort and the "present state of the ruins" with etchings and maps showing the location of the walls and underground passages.[30] The volume on Ticonderoga was published only once (1873), but the Lake George guide, which included information on Saratoga, Lake Luzerne, and Schroon Lake, was republished in annual editions.

Stoddard had also become interested in the Adirondacks, undoubtedly influenced by the popularity of William H. H. Murray's 1869 book *Adventures in the Wilderness; or, Camp-Life in the Adirondacks*. In the fall of 1870 Stoddard embarked on his first long photographic and painting expedition to the Adirondacks, accompanied by his brother-in-law and assistant, Charles Oblenis. A second Adirondack expedition by the pair, lasting 22 days during September and October 1873, provided Stoddard with material for his first Adirondack guidebook. Traveling aboard the steamboat *Vermont II*, the duo first visited the towns along Lake Champlain and Ausable Chasm before journeying inland. Stoddard and Oblenis ventured to all the well-known areas of the Adirondacks, meeting the famous guides and characters of the mountains: Orson Schofield Phelps ("Old Mountain Phelps"), Alvah Dunning, Mitchell Sabattis, Mart Moody, Bill Nye, and Paul Smith. Stoddard's first edition of *The Adirondacks: Illustrated*, published the following year, was an immediate success and was republished in updated editions for the next 40 years. While Stoddard's guidebook offered practical information on routes, distances, canoe trips, hotels, walking trails, guides, and descriptive details of the region, it was also an entertaining text. In addition, his early guides were appealing for their ample illustrations, consisting of etchings and drawings often based on his photographs. (At the back of the volume, Stoddard advertised some of his photographs of Ausable Chasm, Lake Champlain, steamboats, Fort Ticonderoga, Crown Point, and scenes of the Adirondacks.)

The popularity of Stoddard's *Adirondacks: Illustrated* may be related to the amusing vignettes spread throughout his book. Perhaps inspired by Mark Twain, Stoddard apparently mastered his humorous writing style while working for Glens Falls newspapers, and successfully applied it to his first Lake George guidebook. His 1874 *Adirondacks: Illustrated*, however, made fuller use of humor. For example, his section on Lake Champlain began with a description of Samuel de Champlain as "the first white sporting man. . .who, in 1609, joined a company of native tourists on a gunning expedition. . .where he fell in with a party of Iroquois and succeeded in bagging a satisfactory number."[30] In the guidebook, Stoddard retold a story which he had learned from pilot Ell B. Rockwell, who had originally heard the story when the distinguished Civil War general Philip H. Sheridan and President Ulysses S. Grant had traveled aboard the steamer *Vermont II* in 1872. According to Stoddard, Sheridan had offered a drink to an old farmer in northern New York, who asked with whom he had the honor of drinking. When Sheridan provided his last name, the old farmer asked quizzically if he was any relation to the Civil War general, "whom he considered the greatest man living."[31] Sheridan affirmed his identity, "pompously straightening up and enjoying the effects" of the farmer's words, but "the old chap gazed at the short, thick-set form before him, and his look of blended wonder and reverence changed to disgust, as he growled out, 'Not—by—a—damn—site—little—feller—General—Sheridan's over—seven—feet—high.' Phil left, feeling that he had tried to pass himself off for a great man, and been caught in the act."[32] When the leader of a tour to Ausable Chasm, H. H. Bromley, the proprietor of the Chasm House, couldn't name a towering rock overhead, Stoddard mused "Poor Fellow! . . .already shows signs of approaching baldness, caused by frequent attempts to dig out appropriate and nice sounding names for the many objects of interests near by. 'Call it Moses,' suggested the Professor, and 'Moses' it was christened by unanimous consent. 'Who was Moses?' " was soon asked by someone.[33] Stoddard's stories invariably included droll references to his traveling companion, the professor (actually his brother-in-law), who "abstains from the absorption of that mysterious compound known as hash, on account of the uncertainty of its origin. Revolts at [the] sight of sausages, as it is unpleasantly suggestive of a dear little dog that he once loved."[34]

By the late 1870s Stoddard's professional stature in the region had been firmly established, and he earned a stable income, partially derived from his two popular guidebooks. *Lake George; (Illustrated.) A Book of To-Day* was published from 1873 to 1915 in several versions. From 1874 to 1877 the guide was retitled *Lake George, Saratoga, Luzerne, and Schroon Lake*, reflecting a broadening of coverage. The next three editions of the guidebook returned to the original Lake George title for the hard-cover copies but included Saratoga on the soft-cover editions. The 1881 through 1888 guides had dual titles: on the front cover—*Lake George: (Illustrated.) A Book of To-Day* and on the back cover of the same volume, printed upside down—*Saratoga*. The text describing Saratoga was printed upside down to separate the two sections of the guide. In 1889 Stoddard changed the title to *Lake George (Illustrated.) and Lake Champlain. A Book of To-Day*, a title he continued to use until the final year of publication in 1915. Later editions, however, placed the *Illustrated* in parentheses after Lake Champlain. Offered in both soft- and hard-cover editions, his popular guide *The Adirondacks: Illustrated* was published until 1914.[35]

Today, Stoddard is best remembered for his photographs (perhaps 10,000) taken over a period of four decades in the North Country. From the early 1870s through the 1890s, he made repeated forays into the Adirondacks, visiting even the most remote areas of the wilderness. Stoddard continued producing his images of Lake George and Lake Champlain well into the twentieth century. Many of his photographs remain the representative illustrations of the Adirondack region of this period. His style of photography has been associated both with the Hudson River school because of its emphasis on scenic landscapes and with "luminism," which

Overleaf:
Top: "High Art, Blue Mountain, Sept. 15, 1879."
Seneca Ray Stoddard with his portable darkroom. (Adirondack Museum)
Bottom: Campfire scene in the Adirondacks (1888).
Photo by Seneca Ray Stoddard. (Stoddard Collection, New York State Museum)

featured variations of light on scenery. John Fuller's critique of Stoddard's work in the *History of Photography* suggests that his "crystalline images of the smooth water have earned Stoddard a position in the luminist pantheon."[36] Photographs showing reflections of mountainsides, shorelines, and steamboats in still lake water are trademark Stoddard luminist images. Stoddard's artistic inclinations never interfered with his commercial objectives. He marketed his pictures at hotels, in bookstores, on steamboats, and through the largest retailer of photography in America, E. & H. T. Anthony & Co. of New York City.

Before gelatin dry plates were adopted in the early 1880s, collodion wet-plate glass negatives required processing in the field, most often in a tent. Even with dry plates, photography was a laborious procedure, requiring heavy, unwieldy equipment. In addition to taking photographs, Stoddard developed several innovations in photography, including a photographic plate holder, patented in 1882 and produced by an Auburn, New York, firm. A decade later he supervised the building of the largest camera in the world designed to capture the Alaskan landscape. However, the enormous camera, for use with 20- by 49-1/2-inch negatives, never worked properly. He pioneered the use of powered magnesium metal for flash photography, invented by German chemists. Using flash powder and other techniques, he was able to create remarkable pictures of Adirondack campfire scenes and of bats at Howe Caverns. (He sometimes used dark filters in creating some night scenes and also retouched his campfire images by hand.) Employing a multiple flash arrangement, he made unique illuminated images of immense objects, including the Washington Square Arch in New York City, the Statue of Liberty, buildings at the Chicago World's Fair, and later of the Eiffel Tower, the Arc de Triomphe, the Sphinx, and the Rock of Gibraltar. However, his initial attempt at photographing a large object at night, the Washington Square Arch, nearly ended in disaster when an explosion, caused by an excessive amount of powder, sent him to the hospital. Stoddard also created spectacular panoramic photographs from Adirondack peaks while heading the photographic section of the state topographical survey under Verplank Colvin. His skill in photography induced a number of corporations and groups, including the Delaware and Hudson Company, the Adirondack Railroad, the Central Vermont Railway, and the American Canoe Association, to engage him as their official photographer.

Stoddard achieved recognition of his photography through slide shows given in cities during the winter and at Adirondack hotels in the summer. Long before the advent of movies or television, his presentations of 200-225 hand-tinted lantern slides projected on a huge 30-foot square canvas were breathtaking. His most important show, on behalf of pending legislation to create an Adirondack Park, was delivered in Albany on February 25, 1892, before a standing-room-only audience of the New York State Assembly. The *Albany Evening Journal* noted that Stoddard's objective was to stir public interest for "the idea of protecting the forest and keeping it in its natural state," and the *Albany Argus* concluded that "the law-makers who saw this program were greatly impressed."[37] Stoddard crisscrossed New York during the following months, showing his slides and advocating preservation of the Adirondacks. Finally on May 20, 1892, the bill to initiate the Adirondack Park was passed by the New York legislature and signed into law.

Seneca Ray Stoddard's talents also included cartography, and he produced some of the most important maps of the region during the late nineteenth and early twentieth centuries. He developed a mastery of surveying by assisting Hiram Philo, a proficient Glens Falls surveyor, who was Stoddard's brother's father-in-law. Stoddard also gained valuable surveying skills through his association with Verplanck Colvin during the mapping of the Adirondack high peaks. In 1880, after nearly four years of preparation, Stoddard finished his highly acclaimed "Map of the Adirondack Wilderness." While he used data from many sources, his cartographic effort is considered one of the important original contributions to the mapping of the Adirondacks.[38] Travelers could judge distances by gauging the concentric circles plotted to represent ten-mile intervals which radiated from Mount Marcy. The year after the completion of his 1880 field work, Stoddard published a four-color map of Lake George (including separate inserts for individual communities along the lake), which he revised and reprinted through 1915. A similar Lake Champlain map was first published in 1890 and continued in print until 1911. One of Stoddard's most ambitious projects involved a detailed hydrographic chart of Lake George which required thousands of depth measurements between 1906 and 1908. First published in its entirety in 1909, the chart remained the basis for charts of the lake well into the second half of the twentieth century. Just after finishing the field work for the Lake George chart, Stoddard started a new endeavor—an illustrated auto road map of the Adirondacks and the Champlain Valley, which he marketed between 1909 and 1915.[39]

Seneca Ray Stoddard also exhibited a taste for adventure, completing a 2,000-mile voyage in an 18-foot sailing canoe from Glens Falls via the Hudson River and along the Atlantic coast to Nova Scotia over a period of five summers (1883-1887). In 1892 Stoddard traveled to Alaska to photograph the rugged terrain and during the winter of 1894 brought his cameras to Havana, Cuba, and Florida. During the summer of 1894 he made a complete tour of the American West, producing 700 negatives. Stoddard toured the Mediterranean, Near East, and Egypt in 1895; Great Britain, the Scandinavian countries, Russia, and the North Atlantic islands in 1897; and France and Germany in 1900. Invariably, Stoddard employed pragmatic financial arrangements to fund his trips by trading passage for advertisements in his guidebooks, selling souvenir photo albums of the voyage to passengers, or photographing passengers and crew members for cash.

Stoddard's diverse writing efforts continued throughout his career and included *The Story of Atlantis* (1890), a book-length account of his canoe trip to Nova Scotia; *In Mediterranean Lands: The Cruise of the Friesland 1895* (1896), a 348-page book of travel; *Jan the Golden* (1902), a 220-page novel; and two short stories.[40] Over the years he also produced many picture books such as *Historic Lake Champlain* (1898). From May 1906 to September 1908 Stoddard published the *Northern Monthly*, a periodical dedicated to the preservation of the "Great North Woods" and its stories and traditions.[41] But the venture was a financial failure.

Stoddard's wife of 38 years, Helen Augusta Stoddard, died on October 28, 1906, at the age of 56.[42] She and Seneca Ray had raised two children: Charles Herbert Stoddard, who graduated from West Point and served in the Spanish-American War, the Philippine-American War (1898-1902), and World War I, and became a prominent attorney; and LeRoy Ray Stoddard, who graduated from Cornell Medical School and became a plastic surgeon in New York City. For years Helen Augusta

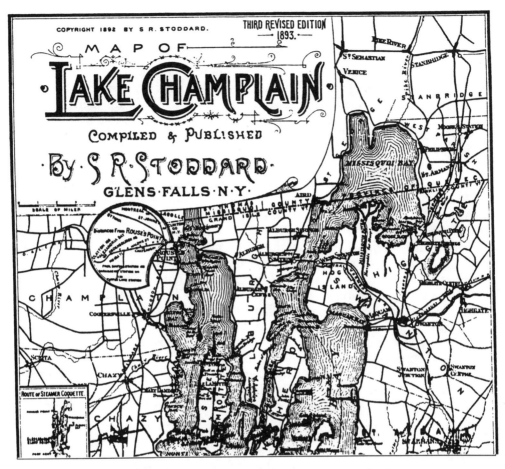

Detail of Seneca Ray Stoddard's 1893 Lake Champlain map.

Stoddard had been in charge of producing the photographic prints (with the help of several female employees) in Seneca Ray's Glens Falls studio. Two years after Helen Augusta's death, Seneca Ray married Emily Doty, who had worked for the family for several decades as a printing assistant and housekeeper.

The once vigorous Seneca Ray Stoddard spent the last two years of his life (1915-1917) coping with declining health. From late December 1916 to his death on April 26, 1917, Stoddard was confined to his bed. Although he was believed to have been suffering from arteriosclerosis, his obituary noted that his illness "appeared to be more mental than physical."[43] The newspaper account observed that "Mr. Stoddard was a sturdy friend to those he called friends. He saw only the good in people and remained always silent if this could not be expressed. Thoroughly unselfish he lived, while gentleness appeared to govern his conduct throughout life."[44] Emily Doty Stoddard, his second wife, died in 1936; both of his sons by his first marriage died in 1943.

The following narrative is a condensed version of Stoddard's last guidebook (1915) on Lake Champlain.

Lake Champlain [45]

Leaving the station at Whitehall the train runs north through the principal street of the town, and entering a tunnel emerges in sight of the narrow section of the lake, crossing a marsh-bottomed basin, toward a notch cut out of its northern rim. Just before entering this rock-cut, we see on the east a short double crook, in the narrow lake, known as "Fiddler's Elbow," where, under water [in East Bay or the Poultney River], are the hulks of some of the vessels engaged in the Battle of Plattsburgh in 1814. On the high point of rocks just over and slightly to the north of the Elbow is Fort Putnam, where General Israel Putnam lay in ambush, waiting for the French and Indians under the command of Marin.*

Montcalm Landing (formerly Ticonderoga Station), is 23 miles north of White-hall.** Ticonderoga-Orwell auto ferry crosses here. Steamer *Vermont[III]* here deposits her load of passengers from the north, bound south by train via Whitehall or via Baldwin for points on Lake George, and receives tourists from Lake George and the south for the return trip to Plattsburgh and the north. The *Vermont[III]*. . .is 262 feet long 35 foot beam (62 foot beam over all) and is provided with [50] state rooms for guests and passengers. It is lighted throughout by electricity and has an electric search light. It leaves Plattsburgh at 6:45 a.m., and, touching at intermediate landings, arrives at this point about noon. Returning, leaves on arrival of passengers from Lake George and the south. The dinners served on Lake Champlain have been noted for years for their wholesomeness, and for the plethora of good things with which the table is loaded. On the other hand, the appetite which a ride over Lake George or Lake Champlain gives a body is also a constant source of wonderment— and it costs just a dollar here to do justice to the one and satisfy the other. A trip through Lake Champlain on this boat is a delightful experience, Fort Ticonderoga (ruins) are 24 miles north of Whitehall, and can be seen on the promontory lying about one mile north of Montcalm Landing. Here were enacted the principal events in the play of the lake. Here savage tribes contended for the country on either hand, and here two great nations struggled for the prize of a continent which neither could retain, while precious blood flowed like water for this, the key of the "gate of the country," by its position elected to become historic ground.***

The Ruins of To-Day.—The old battery on the bluff, above the fort steamboat landing, is said to have been [the] original Carillon [Lotbinière or Grenadiers' Battery]. Back on higher ground are the barrack walls, trenches, and bastions. On the west, beyond the outlet of Lake George is Mount Defiance. Opposite the fort at the southeast, the lake is narrowed down by the near approach of Mt. Inde-

*By tradition this landmark ("Put's Rock" on Stoddard's map) was believed to be the location of a battle on August 8, 1758, between English and provincial forces led by Majors Robert Rogers and Israel Putnam, and French troops and Indians led by Captain Joseph Marin de la Malgue. (Putnam was an American general during the Revolutionary War.)

**Because the Champlain Transportation Company's steamboat service to Whitehall had been replaced by trains, Stoddard omitted a narrative of the southern part of the lake but did include a map showing various landings.

***Stoddard's eight-page narrative covering Samuel de Champlain's battle with the Iroquois and the history of Fort Ticonderoga is omitted here because the material has been covered in previous chapters of this book.

Left: The restored West Barracks of Fort Ticonderoga. (Postcard, author's collection)
Right: Barracks at Crown Point. (Delaware and Hudson Railroad Collection, New York State Library)

pendence, which was also fortified while [Major General Arthur] St. Clair held command [1777]. Between the two points ran the chain, or floating bridge. The lake here turns toward the north, the water washing three sides of the promontory. Across the locust-covered flat, just north of the ruins, from a point near the drawbridge, lay Ethan Allen's route in 1775.

The name is the composite of a dozen or more Indian terms with something of the same sound, as Ticonderoga, Tieuderoga, Cheonderoga, etc., the words used by the natives meaning the coming together or meeting of waters. Carillon, the French name, means "music racket, a chime" [see footnote chapter 13].

The Old Fort and Garrison grounds consisting of about 700 acres were ceded by the state toward the close of the century to Columbia and Union Colleges, and in 18[20] purchased by William [Ferris] Pell, the great-grandfather of the present owner, Stephen H. P. Pell. Efforts have been repeatedly made to interest both the state and national governments in the care of the old fort, the owners expressing a willingness to sell at a nominal price if the preservation could be guaranteed, but in vain. They have now undertaken the restoration of the old building as nearly on original lines as can be determined.

Larrabee's Point is on the Vermont shore, a mile north of the ruins. For hotel see page 198 [the 100-guest Larrabee's Lake House].

Crown Point Landing is 11 miles north of Fort Ticonderoga.

Crown Point Ruins are six miles north of Crown Point Landing. The lake is here narrowed down by the land extending from the west on which the ruins stand, its easternmost point marked by a stone lighthouse. Chimney Point approaches from the east side. Beyond the light-house, at the narrowest place in the passage, are the scarcely visible remains of Fort St. Frederic built by the French in 173[4]. Crown Point Fort standing over toward the west was commenced by [Major General Jeffery] Amherst in 1759, and completed at an expense of over ten million dollars. The extensive earth-works, and the walls of the barracks, still in a good state of preservation, indicated the strength and extent of the fortification—from which, however, no gun was ever fired at an approaching foe. Dr. Bixby designates the shores of the peninsula west of the ruins as the probable site of Champlain's battle with the Iroquois in 1609. In absence of positive proof there is much historical evidence to indicate that the battle did really occur here. No historic point on the lake is thrust forward "from the west shore" into more avoidable prominence.*

The land on which the ruins stand, 25 acres in extent, was presented to the State in 1910 by Witherbee Sherman & Co., of Port Henry, to be held forever as public property.

The Champlain Memorial is erected here at the extremity of the point. It takes the form of a monumental light house, built jointly by the states of Vermont and New York. A heroic statue of Champlain in bronze faces the east and in the base is Rodin's symbolic "La France," which was presented by France to the United States and installed with becoming ceremonies by a distinguished company of citizens of our sister Republic, who came over the ocean for that purpose. The Monument is a fitting memorial to the discover[er], who gave his name to the noble lake.

Port Henry, two miles northwest of Crown Point Ruins, is exceedingly picturesque, with a number of elegant private residences, occupied by the iron magnates of that section.

The Lee House is an excellent hotel. J. E. McNulty, proprietor. Rates $2-$3 per day. Open all the year. Free bus to trains.

The *G. R. Sherman*, steam ferry boat, runs six round trips daily (4 trips Sundays) through the summer months between Port Henry and Chimney Point on the Vermont shore, landing at Fort Frederic on signal. Boat leaves Port Henry at 7:30 a.m. and Chimney Point at 8, and at two-hour intervals thereafter. Fare for automobiles or double teams, with driver, between points, 65 cents; single horse, 40 cents; for the single passenger, 15 cents.**

Moriah is two miles west of Port Henry. Schroon River is 17 miles (Jackson's Hotel, Carson); thence west to Newcomb (36 miles) and to Long Lake, a total of 50 miles. Stage daily, Sundays excepted.

The Lake Champlain and Moriah R. R. is seven miles long, extending from Port Henry to the ore beds at Mineville 1,300 feet above. The grade at one point is 256-1/2 feet to the mile. The average is 211 feet. It contains three "Y's [in the tracks]," where the nature of the ascent renders a curve impracticable.

Westport is a pretty little village, on a deep bay, setting into the western shore of Northwest Bay, 25 miles north of Fort Ticonderoga and 40 miles south of Plattsburgh. It is a favorite gateway into Elizabethtown and Keene Valley and possesses in its broader environment attractions that recommend it to the summer visitor above most interior resorts.

The Westport Inn stands on the brow of an abrupt eminence a hundred feet above the lake and overlooks a tennis lawn shaded by fine elms, the picturesque steamboat landing, the great sweeping amphitheater of hillside leading away to right and left, the circling shore of the bay and the beautiful chain of Green Mountains across in Vermont. The house has broad piazzas and is neat and well furnished from

---

*Stoddard is referring to a monograph by Dr. George F. Bixby, entitled *First Battle of Lake Champlain*, which makes the case that Samuel de Champlain's battle occurred at Crown Point rather than at Ticonderoga.[46] However, because Champlain had noted "a rapid which I saw afterwards," he had probably been at Ticonderoga and had observed the lower falls of the La Chute River.[47]

**The 75-foot ferry *G. R. Sherman*, a double-ended propeller-driven steamer built with cabins on each side of the vessel, began service in 1890 and was retired in 1929 as a result of the opening of the bridge at Crown Point.[48]

The Westport Inn. (Postcard, author's collection)

basement to belvedere [upper viewing areas]. It has cozy parlors and dining-room, with large open fire-places. The table is superior and the service most efficient. There are bath rooms and perfect drainage. Water comes from a wonderful mountain spring 500 feet above the lake. A number of detached cottages add to the attractions, furnishing altogether accommodations for 150 guests. Golf links on rolling ground afford an excellent course with interesting hazards. Good boating and fishing facilities and bathing places with fine bottom, and convenient bath houses, are here. The golf club house has billiard and pool tables and a shower bath. There are two small steamers and a launch for rent. The Champlain steamers touch four times each day at the wharf at the foot of the grove. Excursions by these steamers, running at convenient hours, are popular. Long distance telephone and W[estern] U[nion] telegraph in the house. H. P. Smith, who has been connected with the Inn since its opening, is manager.

Westport Inn Garage and livery is at foot of hill on the way to the station. M. E. Lott, proprietor.

Glenwood Inn, at the north edge of the village, spreads an exceptionally good and wholesome table. Rates $2 per day. Special on application. John L. Sherman, proprietor. It has most of the commercial travel and is open all the year. Free carriage to station.

The Westport, a small house at the station, should not be confounded with "The Westport Inn," mentioned above.

Elizabethtown is 7 miles west of the station. By auto stage [large automobile] connecting with principal trains, $1. A small propeller runs from Westport to Vergennes daily, on arrival of steamer *Vermont[III]* from the south, returning in the morning to connect with the south-bound boat.*

Split Rock Mountain extends along the west shore, terminating in a sharp point 8 miles north of Westport. Barn Rock (a corruption probably of Barren Rock) shows the upturned edges of strata lying at a sharp angle with the surface in a bold point

*Two passenger steamers of the Daniels' Steamboat Line at Vergennes, the 63-foot *Victor* built in 1897 and the 58-foot *Alexander* completed in 1899, ended service in 1916 because of increased competition from automobiles and automobile ferries.[49]

enclosing a deep harbor. "The Palisades" a little way north are grand perpendicular cliffs. Rock Harbor, a mile further north, shows an "effort," where Gotham's [New York City] one time Boss, Tweed tried his hand at digging ore.* Grog Harbor—a charming little cove despite its name—is near the northern end of Split Rock Mountain.**

Split Rock is at the northern end of the mountain bearing the same name. In the uncertain records of old Indian treaties, it is claimed that this rock marked the boundry line between the tribes of the St. Lawrence and those of the Mohawk Valley.

Otter Creek enters the lake from the east something over five miles north of Westport. This is the longest river in Vermont and is navigable to Vergennes whose spires may be seen some distance inland. Fort Cassin stood at the mouth of Otter Creek. Bits of the ruins are still visible. Within the creek a portion of the American squadron was fitted out in 1814, which, under Commodore [Master Commandant Thomas] M[a]cDonough defeated the British Commodore [Captain George] Downie, at Plattsburgh, in September of that year.

Top: Across from Split Rock Mountain, the Lodge at Basin Harbor, Vermont, accommodated 60 tourists nightly in the 1915 season. (Postcard, Mahlon and Gina Teachout Collection)
Above: The Palisades along Split Rock Mountain. (Postcard, author's collection)

Vergennes is eight miles back from the lake as Otter Creek runs, although in an air line but little more than half that distance. It is one of the oldest cities in New England, chartered in 1788. It is also the smallest incorporated city in the country. The city limits include an area of 1-1/4 x 1-1/2 miles.

Essex, a small village on the west shore, is 10 miles north of Westport. The Boquet River empties into the lake four miles north of Essex landing. It is navigable for about a mile. It was a rendezvous of [Lieutenant General] John Burgoyne's flotilla, in the advance on Ticonderoga, in 1777, and in 181[4] was entered by [three] British gunboats to work the destruction of the little village of Willsborough, a mile inland [see chapter 11].

Willsborough Point, a low peninsula about four miles long by one wide, separates Willsborough Bay from the main lake.

---

*William Marcy Tweed (1823-1878), political boss of New York City's Tammany Hall, purportedly invested in the Split Rock Iron Mine located on the mountainside above Louis Clearing Bay. Tweed died in prison in 1878, convicted of forgery and grand larceny. The financially-troubled mining operations at Split Rock ended production about 1883.[50]

**By tradition Grog Harbor received its name from an incident in 1776 when rum, found in a British bateaux, was dumped into the bay.[51] Another story, however, relates the name to a 1756 episode which Robert Rogers mentioned in his journal.[52]

The Four Brothers are near the middle of the lake east of Willsborough Point. Here occurred the running engagement between Benedict Arnold and Captain Pringle, in 1776, in which the English were victorious.* Juniper Island is northeast of the Brothers [and is] surmounted by a lighthouse [built in 1826].

After leaving Essex Landing the boat passes the Vermont side in the approach to Burlington. Back inland are the two highest peaks of the Green Mountains—Mansfield, 4,360 [4,393] feet above the tide, and Camel's Hump [4,083 feet], the L[i]on Couchant [Couching Lion] of the French.

Shelburne Harbor is east of Pottier's Point. Here are the shipyards of the Champlain Transportation Company. It is worthy of note that but one year after Robert Fulton's steamboat was launched on the Hudson River a steamboat was launched at Burlington. It could run five miles an hour without heating the shaft!**

Rock Dunder is a prominent object, as we near Burlington. It is a sharp cone, 20 feet high above water, believed by Winslow C. Watson, the historian, to be the famous "Rock Regio" so frequently mentioned in colonial records.***

Top: View of Shelburne Point. (Photo by Richard K. Dean)
Above: The *Vermont III* at the Champlain Transportation Company's Shelburne shipyard. (Vermont Historical Society)

Burlington is a city of nearly 25,000 inhabitants, 80 miles north of Whitehall. Burlington has quite an extensive lumber market and also a varied line of manufacturing interests, including cotton and woolen textiles, refrigerators [ice boxes], chairs, screens, blinds, doors, sash and machinery. Two railroads center [converge] here, the Portland and the Central

---

*The running battle between Benedict Arnold's remaining vessels and the British fleet under Captain Thomas Pringle occurred along the eastern shore of the lake south of Split Rock (see chapter 8).

**John and James Winans, both of whom had worked on Robert Fulton's steamboat, completed the 125-foot steamboat *Vermont* in 1809. The vessel sank near Bloody Island in the Richelieu River in 1815 after its connecting rod punctured the hull. The remains of the vessel were raised in 1953 and transported to a site on the Port Kent Road across from Ausable Chasm for display in a new maritime museum. The enterprise never materialized and most of the vessel was destroyed in 1973 to clear the land for a commercial campground.

***Rock Dunder, an immense solitary rock island approximately a half-mile northeast of Shelburne Point, is important in Abenaki tradition. Noted regional historian Winslow C. Watson made the case in *The Military and Civil History of the County of Essex, New York (1869)* that Rock Dunder was in fact "Rock Reggio," the legendary boundary separating the Algonquin and Mohawk lands.[53] Watson based his argument on a few original accounts and an early French map published in *Documents Relating to the Colonial History of New-York* which showed the word "Rougio" in the vicinity of present-day Burlington.[54] Other contemporaries of Watson, including Benjamin Clapp Butler, insisted that evidence pointed to Split Rock as "Regio Rock."[55]

Vermont. Direct train service is had with noted eastern mountain and coast resorts. The distance from Burlington to Montreal, 95 miles; to Fabyans [Crawford Notch, N.H.], 120; to Portland, 211; to Lake Winnipesaukee, 140, to Concord, 174; to Boston, 230.

The Champlain Transportation Company operating the lake steamers has its general office here.

The steamer *Ticonderoga* is 220 feet long, 57 feet 9 inch beam over all, hull of steel, with three water tight bulkheads, steered and heated by steam, and lighted by electricity; is a modern, up-to-date vessel in every respect, and is in construction very similar to the *Sagamore* on Lake George.

Burlington, Vermont
Above: Municipal Beach. *Top left:* Located on the Burlington waterfront, the Central Vermont Railroad Terminal was replaced by the new Union Station in 1915. *Left:* Street scene. (Postcards, author's collection)

The steamer *Chateaugay* is in service June 15 to September 15 each year, and is employed in handling excursion traffic during the summer months, and on Mondays and Saturdays performs regular service between Burlington and St. Albans Bay.

The Lake Champlain Yacht Club has a convenient club house a little way north of the steamboat landing.

Colchester Point reaches half way out across the broad lake north of Burlington, and still further west are Colchester reefs and light-house—a blood-red light marking the outermost rock at night.

Port Kent is on the west shore of the lake 10 miles from Burlington.

Trembleau Hall, on the high land a half mile north of the station, is most attractive. Capacity 125. Farrell & Agate, proprietors. Rates $3.00 to $4 per day, $15.75 to $21 per week. Free carriages to trains and boats.

For excursions a gentle climb may be had to the top of Trembleau Mountain at the south, or a walk to the mouth of the AuSable River at the north, or a trip to AuSable Chasm three miles away, by the electric car which runs at convenient intervals—this last being one of the essentials of the day and place.

The AuSable Inn is delightfully situated on a slight rise overlooking the lake. . .two minutes' walk from the shore, just north of the station at Port Kent.

To those who like the comforts of home—and who does not—the AuSable Inn will appeal.

The proprietors, M. E. and D. A. Weatherwax, have long studied the needs of the tourists, and as they call their place, "a resting place for the traveler," they have made it truthfully fit its title.

The K[eeseville] AuS[able] C[hasm] & L[ake] C[hamplain] R[ailroad] runs from Port Kent, passing over AuSable Chasm (3 miles) near its head, affording a good view of Rainbow Falls and continuing 2 miles further reaches Keeseville, the end of the road. At AuSable Chasm Station busses are taken (25 cents round trip) for Hotel AuSable Chasm ($4 up per day). Accommodations are here in house and cottages for 200. A large share of the patronage of the house is in excursion parties. House and chasm are owned by [a] stock company. F.W. Adams, Manager.

AuSable Chasm affords a fine illustration of rock fracture and erosion. Admission is gained through the lodge, a picturesque octagonal building near its head. Entrance fee, 75 cents. The boat ride is 50 cents additional, including carriage back to hotel or station. Large parties are admitted at reduced rates. Guides are unnecessary, as guide-boards and signs call attention to notable places. The chasm is something over a mile in length from Rainbow Falls to the Basin and upwards of a hundred feet in depth, the enclosing walls at points rising vertically from the water.

Returning to the steamer, we see, three miles north of the landing at Port Kent, the sandy mouth of the AuSable River. AuSable means "of sand." Across from this point is the widest uninterrupted portion of the lake, the distance being nearly eleven miles [12 miles wide].

Hotel Champlain is situated on a lofty bluff on the west shore of Lake Champlain overlooking a mighty expanse of water on the east and north. South and west extends a far reaching plain of checkered field and forest that vanishes into blue where the Adirondacks in a great panorama of serrated mountain peaks rise beyond. With so near mountain heights to dwarf its own strong setting Bluff Point commands scenes wonderfully varied, yet restful to a degree that few places can approach.

Valcour Island lies below like a garden bordered with its varying belt of shrubbery. Beyond dotted here and there with islands, stretches the broad lake to the shores of Vermont, the Green Mountains beyond rising into the heights of Camel's Hump and Mount Mansfield. North and east are Grand Isle and Great Back Bay; at the north, Cumberland Head, the sweeping circle of Plattsburgh Bay, where occurred that splendid naval battle of 1814—the last, as the battle of Valcour, 1776, was the first, with the mother country—and nearer, the little island [Crab Island] where sleep the dead of that eventful day.

Surrounding the hotel is a wooden park of eight hundred acres traversed by winding drives and shaded walks, with rustic seats and pavilions at notable viewpoints. A number of commodious cottages subject to special assignment of guests are scattered about on the grounds. A wide sandy beach—the Beach of the "Singing

Sands" extends along the lake shore with bathing houses, boat house, etc. Tennis court (with dirt floor) is on the lawn in front of the house on the west. Along the lake shore toward the south, and extending over rolling country westward is an eighteen-hole golf course with commodious club house. This course has been recently greatly improved and extended, and is a prime favorite among discriminating players.

Hotel Champlain is furnished in Louis XVI style and in its equipment combines every modern convenience, and is absolutely fire-proof.*

This house, like the Fort William Henry Hotel at Lake George, is in the Delaware & Hudson Company chain, and is under the management of Albert Thieriot, General Manager of hotels and dining service department for the company.

Cliff Haven, site of the Champlain Summer School, is just north of Bluff Point—in summer a busy village and a center of intellectual advance.**

Isle San Michel (of old called Crab Island) is

The new Hotel Champlain, completed in 1911.
(Postcard, author's collection)

the burial place of the sailors and marines who fell in the Battle of Plattsburgh.*** North of this, and projecting well out across the lake, is Cumberland Head, from which the shore recedes toward the north and west, then comes back in a wide sweep, embracing Cumberland Bay.

The Battle of Plattsburgh took place here in 1814. Stripped of detail, the account of this decisive battle is as follows: On Sabbath morning, September 11th, 1814, the American land forces under [Brigadier] General [Alexander] Macomb, and the American fleet under Commodore [Master Commandant Thomas] Macdonough, were simultaneously attacked by the British land and water forces, under General Sir George Provost and Commodore [Captain George] Downie. The engagement

---

*The first Hotel Champlain, built in 1890, burned to the ground in May 1910. Completed in 1911, the new hotel exhibited simpler architecture, but offered up-to-date amenities, including a 50-car garage. Since 1969 the building has been the home of Clinton Community College.

**Chartered by the Regents of the State of New York in 1893, the Catholic Summer School moved to a 450-acre site at Cliff Haven in 1896. Although the main focus of the school was education, a wide variety of recreational opportunities at the facility created a resort-like atmosphere. The school/resort closed in the 1930s, and after years of idleness, the buildings were demolished to make room for homes.

***A large stone obelisk, called the "Soldiers' and Sailors' Monument in Macdonough National Park," was erected on the north end of the 35-acre island in 1907 to mark the mass grave of the dead from the 1814 Battle of Plattsburgh.[56] A 135-foot limestone obelisk, complete with an interior stairway and capped by a bronze eagle with a 22-foot wingspan, was dedicated as the Thomas Macdonough Memorial in front of the Plattsburgh City Hall in 1926.

resulted in a complete victory for the Americans, only a few small boats of the enemy effecting a successful retreat—which served them right for breaking the Sabbath.

The Barracks, occupied by several companies of soldiers forming a regular U.S. Army post, are near the lake shore, about a mile south of Plattsburgh.*

Plattsburgh, on the west shore of Cumberland Bay, is a thriving city of 8,000 inhabitants. It is of considerable commercial importance** being on the direct line between New York and Montreal, 311 miles from the former and 74 miles from the latter. "Plattsburgh is thoroughly cosmopolitan, with an opinion to offer on every question of the day, exerting no mean influence through its wide-awake daily news papers and its notable weekly, the Plattsburgh Republican" —instituted in 1811— and notwithstanding its age, one of the most reliable and ably conducted Democratic weeklies in the State. The town has numerous churches, high and grades schools, State Normal School.***

The New Cumberland is on the main street and leads as the commercial hotel. It has electric elevator, steam heat, and electric lights. Rates $2.50.

The Wither[i]ll Hotel is a fine house, with an excellent reputation. W.H. Howell, proprietor, Rates, $2.50 up. It has a grill room and caters acceptably to automobile tourists.

It is quite the correct thing for parties bound south over Lake Champlain,

---

*The history of the Plattsburgh Barracks dates from the War of 1812; the purchase of 200 acres of land a few miles south of Plattsburgh on December 30, 1814, was the genesis of a permanent military base. In 1837 stone barracks were constructed (Ulysses S. Grant was once quartered in these barracks.); from 1894 to 1897 additional brick barracks were completed at the post. Public outcry over the sinking of the *Lusitania* by a German submarine in 1915 led directly to the "Plattsburgh Movement," beginning with a two-week military training camp for 1,200 civilians in August 1915 at Plattsburgh.[57] Theodore Roosevelt, former Rough Rider and president, delivered a pro-war speech at the camp directed against Woodrow Wilson, raising a furor in Washington, D.C. In any event, the camp was successful in providing some of the impetus for the formation of the Military Training Camps Association in 1916 and the passage of the National Defense Act of 1916, which included provision for the Officers Reserve Corps and a Reserve Officers Training Corps (ROTC). The experience gained from the training camps for students in 1913 and 1914, including those at Vermont's Fort Ethan Allen, was also instrumental in shaping the legislation. Sixteen thousand men trained at Plattsburgh during the summer of 1916, with more to follow in the next two years, thus providing the backbone of the officer corps during World War I. Plattsburgh continued as an army base until early 1944, when it was turned over to the U.S. Navy for use as a naval training station (until January 1945). After the war the facility served as a college (Champlain College), and in the mid-1950s it was converted to a Strategic Air Command (SAC) base, closing with the end of the Cold War.[58]

**There were dozens of manufacturing concerns in Plattsburgh at this time. However, one famous concern, the Lozier Motor Company, faced bankruptcy in 1915. Once a maker of bicycles in Toledo, Ohio, the Lozier Company relocated to Plattsburgh in 1900, building a new plant on a ten-acre site for the manufacture of boats and marine engines. After a careful examination of the best European automobiles, the company began producing cars of exceptional quality, offering the latest technological advances. (The vehicles were also very expensive—$5,500 for a touring car in 1905.) A Lozier was named U.S. Championship Race Car for 1910-1911 and placed second in the first running of the Indianapolis 500 in 1911. A reorganization of the company by Detroit investors resulted in the replacement of top management and the opening of another plant in Detroit. The company thereafter abandoned the luxury car market for lower-priced models, but this highly-competitive field overwhelmed Lozier, and the Plattsburgh plant closed in August 1914.[59]

***In 1889 the New York State legislature approved the establishment of the State Normal School in Plattsburgh for the training of teachers. In 1938 the institution initiated a four-year teaching degree program; ten years later the college became the State University of New York at Plattsburgh. Today the campus consists of 35 buildings on 300 acres.

arriving in Plattsburgh at night, to go aboard the steamer *Vermont[III]*, where excellent accommodations are provided, and rise and breakfast at their leisure after the boat leaves her dock in the morning.

Cumberland Head, near which occurred the naval battle of 1814, is three miles from Plattsburgh. Continuing northward the west shore is low but picturesque in its irregular line of deep bays and projecting points, but of little interest historically except for the old fort that once stood on Point au Fer, built, according to the best authorities, in 1774.*

Chazy Landing is of special note as the place where Sweet's Auto Ferry [*The Twins*] ties up on the [New]York side and crosses over to Isle La Motte on call, opening up a most delightful route extending the length of the main islands to near Burlington, (Ferriage, $1.00). The roadbed is largely slate and unusually good in all seasons.

Rouses Point, according to the United States Coast Survey, is about 107 miles north of Whitehall. It is a place of considerable commercial interest, and the most important port of entry on the frontier.

Hotel Columbia is at the southern border of the village of Rouses Point, which here stretches a mile along [the] shore north and south. It is open only during the summer and caters specially to automobilists.

The Champlain House is at Champlain, N.Y., on the road to Montreal from the south. It is under new management. It is a house for traveling men and makes a special appeal to automobile parties. Of both it receives its full share, and rightly so. Rates are $2.00 per day and upward; $12.00 to $14.00 a week.

Fort Montgomery, a little way north of the long bridge, is an interesting ruin belonging to the United States.** About a mile north of this a belt of woodland marks the boundary line between the United States and Canada.

The islands of Lake Champlain lie principally in its northern and broader parts. The larger ones are North and South Hero and Isle La Motte, which, with others of less note, and with Alburgh Tongue—extending from the north centrally 11 miles south of the Dominion line—constitute Grand Isle, a county belonging to the State of Vermont.

The Rutland Railroad extending from Bellows Falls on the east and Chatham

---

*The 500-acre peninsula of Point au Fer played an important role during the military campaigns of the eighteenth century. In June 1760 Robert Rogers and his Rangers battled French forces on the Point. The British constructed a modest two-story rectangular stone fortification there in 1774. Advancing into Canada in 1775, the Americans took control of the outpost and improved the works slightly. From late 1776 and for the following 20 years, the British occupied the peninsula. During the British campaigns of 1776 and 1777, as well as the raids later in the Revolutionary War, Point au Fer served as a strategic staging area. As a result of Jay's Treaty, legally effective June 1, 1796, the peninsula became part of New York State.[60]

**Fort Montgomery was named for Brigadier General Richard Montgomery, who had been killed during the American assault on Quebec at the beginning of the Revolutionary War. Construction of Fort Montgomery, the second American attempt to build a fort on the border (see chapter 12), began in 1844, and ended in 1870 before the fortress was completely finished. Although the cannon were tested between 1865 and 1870, the huge fort itself was never garrisoned. By 1910 the guns had been removed, and sixteen years later the fort and 140 acres were sold at an auction for $45,000. Stones from the fort were removed and used in the construction of buildings at Rouses Point, but the most substantial degradation of the fort occurred during the 1930s when a large amount of stone was removed during the building of the Rouses Point Bridge, which opened in 1937. A relatively large intact section of the fort (south end) still survives under private ownership.[61]

View from parade ground of Fort Montgomery.
(Delaware and Hudson Railroad Collection, New York State Library)

and White Creek at the south, via Rutland to Burlington, and continuing to Colchester Point, strikes boldly out into Lake Champlain [on a three-mile, rip-rapped causeway], giving one the novelty of sailing over the waters on a railroad train. By this long fill of solid rock the south end of South Hero is reached.

South Hero, the largest of the islands, is 12 miles long and fills about one-third the width of the lake. Hotels and farm-houses furnish accommodations at from $7 a week upwards. The station for the southern portion is South Hero, near the little hamlet of the same name which is picturesquely situated on the south side of Keeler's Bay. Locust Grove, Island House, Squires' Spring House and others furnish entertainment. The land is rolling, with wide spreading orchards, and farms under a high state of cultivation. The roads are notably good for driving and bicycling.

Squires' Spring House is about a half mile north of South Hero station. It faces east overlooking Keeler's Bay. Accommodations are here offered for about 50 guests.

Gordon's Landing is on the west shore of the island about 4 miles from Squires' Spring House and directly east of the city of Plattsburgh to which steamboats run daily during the season. Accommodations are offered at the farm house of D. I. Center for about 20 guests. Four miles north of South Hero station is Grand Isle station.

The Island Villa is on the east side on a point extending into the Great Back Bay three miles from Grand Isle station. Frank A. Briggs, proprietor. Carriages meet all trains, fare 50 cents.

Ladd's is at the north point of South Hero. Here a swinging bridge connects with North Hero opening [Sandy Point to Knight Point] to give free passage to the steamboats that ply between Plattsburgh and other lake ports and the various landings on the Great Back Bay.

North Hero Station is 8 miles north of Grand Isle Station, near the hamlet of North Hero on City Bay, which opens east into Great Back Bay. Steamer daily, except Sundays, from this point, to Plattsburgh.

The Irving House looks east over this bay. It is cozy and inviting with a modest but specially wholesome and inviting table. Rates $2 per day, $10 to $14 per week. J. H. Dodds, proprietor.

All that has been said of the beauty of South Hero Island applies with equal force to North Hero, the character of the landscape in all its fascinating variety being much the same.

Pelots Point is on the west shore of North Hero Island and here a third crossing of the lake is effected to Alburgh Tongue.

Isle La Motte is 9 miles north of Cumberland Head. It is 5-1/2 miles long by about 1-1/2 wide. About its southern extremity are valuable black marble quarries [including Fleury's, Fisk's, Hill's, and Holcomb's quarries]. On its west shore, midway, is the site of a fort, built in 181[4], and near its north end the ruins of Fort St. Anne, built in 1[6]66.* The post-office, located centrally, is Isle La Motte, Vt. Communication with the New York shore is had by ferry to Chazy Landing and to Alburgh Tongue by bridge at the north end of the island (Isle La Motte station on the Rutland Railroad). A number of small inns and farm houses, where summer boarders may find accommodations, are scattered about North Hero, Isle La Motte, and Alburgh Tongue.

Alburgh Tongue is a broad peninsula, extending into the lake from the north.

Alburgh Springs is near the east shore of this Tongue, a mile north of Alburgh Station seven miles east of Rouse's Point.

The Great Back Bay, on the east of these central islands, is a revelation. It might remain undiscovered for years by the voyager through from north or south if not especially sought for. Glance at the map and you will note that it forms by considerable the larger body of the lake at its north end. It is entered through the narrow passage at the north. At the south it is cut across by Sand-Bar Bridge. At the north the water is dotted with numerous small islands. East, St. Albans Bay enters deep into the mainland.

Continuing northward around Hog Island (made an island by the united waters of Maquam and Charcoal Creeks) the spreading delta of the Missisquoi River is found. Extends north Missisquoi Bay, four miles wide. . .into the Dominion of Canada an equal distance. Highgate Springs is on the shore of the bay, backward southeast from the Delta. It is 14 miles north of St. Albans and about two miles south of the Canada line.

And here we must say good-bye, and—whether your course leads westward to the sparkling waters that mirror the Thousand Islands: northward to the splendors that cluster around Mount Royal and the quaint places of Quebec, or eastward, to where you lose yourself among the mighty fastnesses [secluded regions] of the White Hills of New Hampshire—wish you "Bon voyage" and many happy returns.

---

*On September 4, 1814, prior to the British advance on Plattsburgh, Captain Daniel Pring of the Royal Navy took possession of the west side of Isle La Motte and ordered "a Battery of 3 Long 18 Pounder Guns to be constructed for the support of our position abreast of little Chazy [River] where the supplies for the Army were ordered to be landed."[62]

In 1666 French regulars under Captain Pierre de Saint-Paul, Sieur de la Motte-Lussière built Fort Sainte-Anne, a four-bastioned log fortress on the northwest end of present-day Isle La Motte.[63] In 1894 St. Anne's Shrine was constructed on the site of the fort's chapel to commemorate the first Catholic Mass celebrated there in 1666. Nearby, a large granite statue of Samuel de Champlain stands, sculpted in the Vermont Pavilion at Expo 67 in Montreal and dedicated at the island in 1968.

Notes:

1. The *Glens Falls Times and Messenger*, 26 April 1917.
2. For more information on the *Ticonderoga*, see Richard M. Strum, *Ticonderoga: Lake Champlain Steamboat* (Shelburne, VT.: Shelburne Museum, Inc.,1998).
3. Michele A. McFee, *A Long Haul: The Story of the New York State Barge Canal* (Fleischmanns, N.Y.: Purple Mountain Press, 1998), 18; F. Daniel Larkin, *New York State Canals: A Short History* (Fleischmanns, N.Y.: Purple Mountain Press, 1998), 82.
4. Henry Wayland Hill, *An Historical Review of Waterways and Canal Construction in New York State* (Buffalo: Buffalo Historical Society, 1908), 247.
5. Francis P. Kimball, *New York---The Canal State* (Albany: The Argus Press, 1937), 37; See also Charles T. O'Malley, *Low Bridges and High Water on the New York State Barge Canal* (Utica, N.Y.: North Country Books, 1991), 12-13.
6. H. W. Hill, *Waterways and Canal Construction*, 301, 303.
7. McFee, 26; Frederick Stuart Greene and Thomas F. Farrell, *The New York State Canal System* (Albany: State Public Works, 1928), 19, 24; William J. McKelvey, Jr., *Champlain to Chesapeake: A Canal Era Pictorial Cruise* (Exton, Pa.: Canal Press Incorporated, 1978), v; See also Fred G. Godfrey, *The Champlain Canal: Mules to Tugboats* (Monroe, N.Y.: LRA Inc., 1994), 93-94.
8. McFee, 174,184.
9. Ibid., 182-84, 198-99, 201; Larkin, 87; Richard Garrity, *Canal Boatman: My Life on Upstate Waterways* (Syracuse: Syracuse University Press, 1977), 196.
10. Stephen H. P. Pell, "The Restoration of Fort Ticonderoga," *The Travel Magazine*, July 1909, 464.
11. Ibid; S. H. P. Pell, *Fort Ticonderoga: A Short History* (Ticonderoga: Fort Ticonderoga Museum, 1957), 99.
12. Pell, "The Restoration," 464.
13. *Plattsburgh Evening News*, 16 October 1908; *Glens Falls Daily Times*, 23 October 1908.
14. Lorenzo F. Hagglund to Charles C. Adams, 9 September 1929, New York State Museum.
15. Hagglund to Adams, 29 October 1930, New York State Museum.
16. Hagglund to Adams, 3 May 1934, New York State Museum.
17. Dorothy Smith, *Historic Vessels in Lake Champlain and Lake George* (Albany: The University of New York, 1937), 123.
18. Henry Wayland Hill, *The Champlain Tercentenary: First Report of the New York Lake Champlain Tercentenary Commission*, 2nd ed. (Albany: J. B. Lyon Company, State Printers, 1913), 86.
19. *The Tercentenary Celebration of the Discovery of Lake Champlain and Vermont* (Montpelier: Lake Champlain Tercentenary Commission of Vermont, 1910), 30-45.
20. H. W. Hill, *The Champlain Tercentenary: First Report*, 86-88.
21. Ibid., 186.
22. Raymond Beck, "An Auto Trip to Lake Champlain," *The Travel Magazine*, July 1909, 481.
23. Ibid., 482.
24. Ibid.
25. S. R. Stoddard, *Lake George and Lake Champlain (Illustrated): A Book of To-Day* (Glens Falls, N.Y.: S. R. Stoddard, 1914), 134.
26. Lynn Woods, "An Adirondack Auto Biography: Cars Were the Driving Force Behind a Landscape Changed Forever," *Adirondack Life*, May/June 1996, 34-43, 86-87.
27. Elijah W. Stoddard, *Anthony Stoddard, of Boston, Mass., and his Descendants: A Genealogy*, Revised ed. (New York: Press of J. M. Bradstreet & Son, 1865), 1-2,8,10,12,20; Maitland C. De Sormo, *Seneca Ray Stoddard: Versatile Camera-Artist* (Utica, N.Y.: North Country Books, Inc., 1972), 17-18.
28. H. P. Smith, ed., *History of Warren County* (1885; reprint ed., Interlaken, N.Y.: Heart of the Lakes Publishing, 1981), 451; Jeanne Winston Adler, *Early Days in the Adirondacks: The Photographs of Seneca Ray Stoddard* (New York: Harry N. Abrams, Inc., 1997), 38; De Sormo, *Stoddard Camera-Artist*, 19.
29. Adler, 59-60; See also Smith, 284,656.
30. S. R. Stoddard, *The Adirondacks: Illustrated* (Albany: Weed, Parsons & Co., Printers, 1874), 9.
31. Ibid., 40.
32. Ibid.

35. Ibid.,49.

34. Ibid.,37.

35. De Sormo, *Stoddard Camera-Artist*, 38; Guidebook collection at the Sherman Library, Port Henry, New York.

36. John Fuller, "Seneca Stoddard and Alfred Stieglitz: The Lake George Connection," *History of Photography* 19 (Summer 1995): 152; See also Adler, 110-15,130; John Wilmerding, *American Light: The Luminist Movement 1850-1875* (New York: Harper & Row, Publishers, 1980), 143,284-85; William Crowley, *Seneca Ray Stoddard: Adirondack Illustrator* (Blue Mountain Lake, N.Y.: Adirondack Museum, 1982), 16,18.

37. De Sormo, *Stoddard Camera-Artist*, 70; Maitland C. De Sormo, "Seneca Ray Stoddard: Pioneer Photographer in the Adirondack," *The Conservationist*, February-March 1973, 22.

38. Crowley, 10.

39. De Sormo, *Stoddard Camera-Artist*, 34; Crowley, 10.

40. Ibid., 164; Seneca Ray Stoddard, *Old Times in the Adirondacks*, ed. Maitland C. De Sormo (Saranac Lake, N.Y.: Maitland C. De Sormo, 1971), 14; Adler, 82,171.

41. Fuller, 152; De Sormo, *Stoddard Camera-Artist*, 142.

42. *Glens Falls Morning Star*, 29 October 1906.

43. *The Post-Star* (Glens Falls), 27 April 1917.

44. Ibid.; See also *The Glens Falls Times and Messenger*, 26 April 1917.

45. S. R. Stoddard, *Lake George and Lake Champlain (Illustrated) A Book of To-Day* (Glens Falls, N.Y.: S. R. Stoddard, 1915), 124-68.

46. W. Max Reid, *Lake George and Lake Champlain* (New York: G. P. Putnam's Sons, 1910), 20-29; See also Guy Omeron Coolidge, *The French Occupation of the Champlain Valley from 1609 to 1759* (Mamaroneck, N.Y.: Harbor Hill Books, 1989), 12-13.

47. H. P. Biggar, ed., *The Works of Samuel De Champlain* (Toronto: The Champlain Society, 1925), Volume 2, 93; See also Morris Bishop, *Champlain: The Life of Fortitude* (New York: Alfred A. Knopf, 1948), 354.

48. Charles B. Warner and C. Eleanor Hall, *History of Port Henry, N.Y.* (1931; reprint ed., Salem, MA: Higginson Book Company, 1998), 17-18; Morris F. Glenn, *Lake Champlain Album* (Alexandria, VA.: Morris F. Glenn, 1979), Volume 2, 27; Ruth O'Connor, "History of the Champlain Valley," (p.n.a., Bixby Library, Vergennes, VT.); Jerry P. Williams and Ralph Nading Hill, *Lake Champlain Ferryboats* (Burlington, VT.: Lake Champlain Transportation Company, 1990), 21.

49. Morris F. Glenn, *Glenn's History of Lake Champlain: Occasional Lists of Shipping on Lake Champlain* (Alexandria, VA.: Morris F. Glenn, 1980), Volume 2, 5; Beatrice M. Casey, Bixby Library files.

50. Morris F. Glenn, *The Story of Three Towns: Westport, Essex, and Willsboro, New York* (Ann Arbor, MI.: Braun-Brumfield, 1977), 63-64.

51. Ibid., 34, see also 35-37.

52. Robert Rogers, *Journals of Major Robert Rogers* (1765; reprint ed., Ann Arbor, MI.: University Microfilms, Inc., 1966), 21; B. C. Butler, *Lake George and Lake Champlain from their First Discovery to 1759*, 2nd ed. (New York: G. P. Putnam & Son, 1869), 138-39.

53. Winslow C. Watson, *The Military and Civil History of the County of Essex, New York* (Albany: J. Munsell, 1869), 37-38.

54. E. B. O'Callaghan, ed., *Documents Relative to the Colonial History of the State of New-York* (Albany: Weed, Parsons and Company, Printers, 1855), Volume 9, 1023; The original map "Carte Du Lac Champlain" is in the collection of the National Archives of Canada.

55. Butler, 16-17.

56. *A Summer Paradise* (Albany: The Passenger Department of the Delaware and Hudson Company, 1914), 228; Allan S. Everest, *Briefly Told: Plattsburgh, New York, 1784-1984* (Plattsburgh: Clinton County Historical Association, 1984), 40.

57. John Garry Clifford, *The Citizen Soldiers: The Plattsburgh Training Camp Movement, 1913-1920* (Lexington, KY.: The University Press of Kentucky, 1972), 66-71; Donald M. Kingston, *Forgotten Summers: The Story of the Citizens' Military Training Camps, 1921-1940* (San Francisco: Two Decades Publishing, 1995), 4; Donald B. Webster, " 'Teddy Roosevelt's Private Army'; The United State Military Training Camp, Plattsburgh, N.Y., 1915-1916," *Military Collector & Historian* 44 (Winter 1992): 163-65.

58. Marjorie Lansing Porter, *Plattsburgh 1785----1815----1902: Plattsburgh Barracks 1814* (Burlington: George Little Press, 1964), 95-118; Everest, *Briefly Told*, 42; Clifford, 61-69, 70-75, 84-85, 153, 259.

59. Ashley Rogers, "The Lozier Story," *Adirondack Bits 'n Pieces*, Winter 1983-84, 12-15; Helen W. Allan et al., *Clinton County: A Pictorial History* (Plattsburgh: The Bicentennial Celebrations Committee, 1988), 111; Everest, *Briefly Told*, 51.

60. Allan S. Everest, *Point Au Fer* (Plattsburgh: Clinton County Historical Association, 1992), 3-42; R. Rogers, 178-80.

61. Robert Kane, "The Fort that Almost Lived Twice," *Adirondack Bits 'n Pieces*, Winter 1983-84, 21-23; Peg Barcomb, *Rouses Point* (Rouses Point: p.n.a., 1977), 6.

62. William Wood, ed., *Select British Documents of the Canadian War of 1812* (Toronto: The Champlain Society, 1926), Volume 3, Part 1, 368.

63. Coolidge, 28-29, 200.

Seneca Ray Stoddard's map of the northern section
of Lake Champlain from his 1915 guidebook.

Index

Abbass, D. K., 105

Abbot, Joel, 305, 317

Abenakis, 57, 66, 68, 120, 150-51, 244, 363, 419

Abercrombie, James, 127

Abercromby, James, 79-82, 87, 90-92, 94, 103, 118, 127, 131-32, 148, 164

Adams, Charles, 229, 405

Adirondack House, 366

Adirondack Park, 401, 411

Adirondack (steamboat), 350-51, 358, 363, 378

Alainville, Seigneur d', 362

Albany, 52-53, 104, 152, 239, 251, 256, 276-77, 281, 317, 336, 340, 345, 411

Alburgh, VT., 395

Alburgh Springs, 368, 374

Alburgh Springs House, 367

Alburgh Tongue, 424, 426

Alexander (steamboat), 417

Algonquins, 16, 28-29, 37, 42, 244, 363

Allen, Ethan, 176, 186-87, 191-93, 195, 197-99, 200, 415

Allen (galley), 302, 308, 316, 358

Allen, Thomas, 187, 190, 263

Alwyn (gunboat), 301, 308

American Canoe Association, 376, 379, 411

American House, 365, 374

Amherst, Elizabeth Cary, 115-16

Amherst, Jane Daylson, 102, 115

Amherst, Jeffery, 100-38, 149-50, 152, 154, 156, 165, 172

Amherst, John, 101, 117

Amherst, William, 101, 107-8, 114, 117, 122

Anburey, Thomas, 242, 253, 260-61

Anglais de Bassignac, Jean d', 82

Anstruther, William, 187

Arnold, Benedict, 177-78, 187, 189-93, 194, 197-200, 205-11, 214, 217-22, 224-27, 229, 231, 245, 252-53, 255-57

Arnold, James, 227

Arnold's Bay, 221, 224, 231, 288

Ash Island, 309

Astor, John Jacob, 299

Aubrey, Thomas, 255

Augustus, William (Duke of Cumberland), 102

Ausable Chasm, 178, 180, 288, 357, 365-66, 395, 400, 408-9, 421

Ausable House, 366

Ausable Inn, 421

Ausable Marsh, 180

Ausable Point State Park Campground, 180-81

Ausable River, 66-67, 180-81, 288, 365, 395

A. Williams (steamboat), 378

Ayres, Eliakim, 179

Baldwin, Jeduthan, 17, 206, 240-41, 256, 259-60, 264

Baldwin Landing, 352

Ballard (gunboat), 301, 308

Barnard, Salah, 130

Barn Rock, 417

Barranco, Peter, 219

Barrin de la Gallissonnière, Rolland-Michel, 69

Barrows, Abner, 82, 94

Basin Harbor, 298, 353, 362, 418

Bateaux, 58, 78-79, 83, 88, 94-95, 144, 154

Battle of Bennington, 131, 250, 252

Battle of Freeman's Farm, 253

Battle of Hubbardton, 260, 262

Battle of Lake George, 74, 92, 132

Battle of Plattsburgh Bay, 309-16, 319-23, 422

Battle of the Isle of Mutton, 144

Battle of Valcour Island, 214-9, 228-29

Battle on Snowshoes (first), 146

Battle on Snowshoes (second), 149

Baum, Friedrich , 251

Bayley, Jacob, 155

Beale, George, 323

Bedout, Jean-Antoine, 64

Bemis Heights, 252-53, 255

Bennington, VT., 251-52

Benzel, Adolphus, 176, 180, 182

Bertha M. Bullis (canal boat), 381, 383-84, 388

Bigot, François, 163

Bixby, George F., 415-16

Bixby Island, 110

Blackburn, John, 172

Black Snake (sailing vessel), 298

Blake, Thomas, 246-47, 263-65

Blanchard, Joseph, 144

Bloody Island, 302, 419

Bloody Pond, 207

Blucher (gunboat), 311, 320

Bluff Point, 421-22

Bodell, John, 310

Boquet River, 171, 173, 176, 220, 231, 243-44, 303, 363, 418

Boquet (steamboat), 353

Borer (galley), 302, 308, 313

Boscawen (sloop), 110, 130, 135-38, 153, 161, 164, 172

Boston (gunboat), 209-11

Bougainville, Louis Antoine de, 81, 84-86, 91, 95, 131, 155-56, 160, 165

Bouquet, Henry, 115

Bourlamaque, François-Charles de, 80-81, 87-88, 92, 94, 107-8, 119, 128, 134, 137, 150

Bradbury, John, 156, 165

Braddock, Edward, 74, 118, 129, 147

Bradstreet, John, 80, 123, 129

Brassier, William, 361

Breymann, Heinrich, 247, 252

Brock (gunboat), 320

Broke (sloop), 300, 303

Brown, Adam, 301, 304

Brown, John, 188-92, 194-95, 200, 205, 253, 255

Brown, Moses, 376, 395

Brown, Noah, 301

Brown, Robert, 217

Brown, Solyman, 381-82

Brum, Philip, 322

Bry, Théodore de, 29

Budd, Charles, 311

Bull Dog (sloop), 298-99

Bull, Epaphras, 190-92, 200

Bullis, Luther, 394

Bulwagga Bay, 59, 394

Burgoyne, John, 201, 223, 238-39, 242-46, 248-49, 251-53, 255-57, 261, 363, 387

Burlington, VT., 299, 302-3, 305, 316, 330, 339, 344, 349, 363-65, 376, 378, 405, 419-20

Burlington Manufacturing Company Marble Works, 363

Burlington Packet (sloop), 300, 303

Burlington (steamboat), 349, 351

Burrows (galley), 302, 308

Butler, Benjamin C., 349, 355-68, 371, 395, 419

Butler, Mary Anne Skinner, 355, 357

Button Bay, 154, 162, 211, 244

Calfe, John, 263, 265-66

Callender, Noah, 199-200

Cambrian Sea, 15

Camel's Hump, 364, 419

Campbell, George, 151

Campbell, John (Earl of Loudoun), 103, 147-48, 161

Canada (sloop), 303

Canada (steamboat), 351

Canal boats, 352, 379-80, 391-92

Cannon, LeGrand B., 351, 364-65

Canoes, 52, 58

Carillon (derivation of name), 359

Carleton, Christopher, 214, 216, 229

Carleton, Guy, 175-76, 189, 197-98, 208, 213-14, 220, 222-23, 260

Carleton (schooner), 212, 217, 220, 228-29, 231, 242, 291

Carrion, Philippe de, 359

Carter, John, 247, 266

Cartier, Jacques, 22, 27, 40

Carver, Jonathan, 158

Cassin, Stephen, 301, 303, 313, 321, 362

Castleton, VT., 247

Catholic Summer School, 422

Caughnawaga, 134, 138

Centipede (galley), 302, 308

Chambly, 28, 194, 206, 212, 291

Chambly, Jacques de, 291

Chambly Canal, 344, 352, 364, 373, 379

Champlain (sloop), 298

Champlain (steamboat), 331

Champlain II (steamboat), 350, 358, 378

Champlain, Hélène Boullé, 30

Champlain, N.Y., 300, 305

Champlain, Samuel de, 21-38, 40-42, 46, 405, 408, 416

Champlain Barge Canal, 403

Champlain Canal, 247, 331-32, 352, 364, 379, 381, 383-84, 386, 388, 390, 403

Champlain House, 424

Champlain Maritime Society, 241, 316

Champlain Memorial Lighthouse, 406, 416

Champlain Sea, 16

Champlain Transportation Company, 351-52, 358, 364-65, 377-78, 394, 396, 401, 414, 419-20

Charlotte, VT., 288

Chartier de Lotbinière, Michel, 88, 362

Chaste, Aymar de, 22

Chateaugay (steamboat), 378-79, 402, 420

Chazy, N.Y., 306

Chazy Landing, 309, 424, 426

Cheever ore bed, 361

Chick, John, 179

Chimney Point, 46, 48, 209, 277, 287, 362, 415-16

Chipman Point, 359

Chittenden, Martin, 307, 317

Chub (sloop), 309-10, 316, 320-21

Church, Benjamin (King Philip's War), 147

Church, Benjamin, Jr. (American Revolution), 190

Churchill, Winston S., 295

Clapp, James, 355

Clerk, Matthew, 80

Cliff Haven, N.Y., 112, 405, 422

Clinton, Henry, 160, 255

Clinton Community College, 138, 422
Cloak Island, 153
Cohn, Arthur B., 164, 207, 219, 316
Cohoes Falls, 277
Colchester Point, 420, 425
Colchester Shoal, 341
Colden, Alexander, 90
Colden, Cadwallader, 172
Collet(Cober), Father Hippolyte, 70
Colvin, Verplanck, 412
Confiance (frigate), 304-5, 308-10, 313-16, 320-21, 323-24, 358
Congress Hall, 368
Congress (row galley), 213-14, 217-18, 220-22, 227, 230-31, 331, 341
Conkey, George W., 407
Connecticut Committee of Correspondence, 190-92
Connecticut (gunboat), 209-10, 231
Conover, Thomas, 313, 317
Constellation (frigate), 296, 298, 320
Constitution (frigate), 318, 322
Cooper, James Fenimore, 324, 340
Corlaer Bay, 112
Courcelles, Daniel de, 46
Crab Island, 182, 311, 314, 316, 421
Craig, James Henry, 245
Crisman, Kevin J., 164, 207, 316
Crown Point, 20, 37, 46, 50, 56, 59, 61, 101, 108-10, 112-14, 122-25, 128, 132-33, 136-38, 150, 152-54, 161, 171, 175-77, 187-89, 191-93, 195, 197, 201, 205-7, 209-11, 221-23, 231, 244-45, 263, 276, 282, 286-88, 342, 360, 362, 394, 405, 407, 415-16
Cumberland Bay, 112, 179, 182, 214, 288, 422-23

Cumberland Head, 173, 225-26, 243, 299, 301, 308-9, 311, 314, 316, 367, 421-22
Cumberland House/Hotel, 367, 374, 423
Cushing, Joseph, 231
Cutter, Ammi Ruhamah, 77

Dacres, James Richard, 217
Dalyell, James, 134, 138, 148
Daniel's Steamboat Line, 417
Darby, John, 127-28, 155-56, 161-63, 291
Davison, Gideon Miner, 332
Day, Thomas, 177
Dead Creek, 181-82
Deane, Barnabas, 194
Deane, Silas, 194
De Angelis, Pascal Charles Joseph, 214, 217-21, 229, 231
Decatur, Stephen, 296, 321
De Lancey, James, 138
Delaplace, William, 188-90, 192, 197-98, 200
Delaware & Hudson Company, 351-52, 357, 365, 377, 380, 411, 422
Dellius, Godfrey, 361
Desandrouins, Jean-Nicholas, 79-82, 88, 90, 95
Devlin House, 374
Diamond Island (Lake George), 209, 253, 256
Dibble, Ebenezer, 132
Dickens, Charles, 349
Dieskau, Jean-Armand (Baron de Dieskau), 74, 144, 281, 358-59
Digby, William, 245, 249, 264
Disturnell, John, 354
Dolphin (sloop), 334
Doreil, André, 84
Doty, Simeon, 316
Douglas, Charles, 208
Downie, George, 308-10, 316, 329

Drucour, Chevalier de, 103
Drummond (gunboat), 311, 320
Duke of Cumberland (brig), 110-12, 134-37, 153-54, 161, 164, 172, 405
Dulles, Joseph Heatly, 305
Dunbar, James W., 151
Duncan, John M., 329-30
Dunlap, William, 316, 345
Duprat, Sieur, 89, 91, 93
Durell, Philip, 130
Du Roi, August Wilhelm, 241, 245, 249, 256, 259
Duval, Jean, 26-27
Dwight, Theodore, 330-31, 340, 342, 345
Dwight, Timothy, 280, 288, 332
Dyer, Solomon, 209

Eagle (brig), 306-8, 310, 313, 316, 320-21, 358
Eagle (sloop), 299,
Earl of Halifax (sloop), 84, 105-6, 135
East Bay (Poultney River), 316, 358, 414
Eastman, Ebenezer, 143
Easton, James, 190-91, 194, 200
Eldredge, John, 351
Embargo Act of 1807, 297-98
Enterprise (sloop), 195-96, 207, 210, 215, 217, 219-20, 221, 229, 231, 242, 247, 265
Enys, John, 214, 219, 221, 229, 260
Essex, N.Y., 178, 363, 395, 418
Essex (sloop), 300, 380
Evans, John, 151
Everard, Thomas, 300
Eyre, William, 80, 105, 115, 126, 132, 135

Farrington, Jacob, 153
Fellows, John, 248, 256

Feltham, Jocelyn, 187-89, 192, 197-201

Ferguson, William, 261

Fermoy, Matthias Alexis Roche de, 246, 262

Ferris, Peter, 222, 231

Ferris, Squire, 222

Ferris Bay, 221

Ferryboats, 352-53

Field, John, 173

Finch (sloop), 303, 309, 311, 314, 316, 320-21

Fish Creek, 256

Fisher, Peter, 308

Fitch, Eleazer, 122

Fletcher, Ebenezer, 247-48

Fort Amherst, 104

Fort Anne, 54, 56, 248, 257-58, 266, 277

Fort Blunder, 330

Fort Brown, 305, 367

Fort Carillon, 78-79, 81, 83-84, 87, 89, 91, 93, 101, 104, 107, 117-18, 147-48

Fort Cassin, 362, 418

Fort Cassin House, 362

Fort Chambly, 65, 156, 195, 290-91

Fort Dummer, 120

Fort Duquesne, 74, 79

Fort Edward, 75, 78, 84, 104-5, 118, 129, 132, 144-49, 173, 192, 248-51, 256-57, 266, 276, 282, 331, 388-90

Fort Ethan Allen, 423

Fort Frontenac, 54, 84, 123

Fort Gage, 104

Fort George, 105, 108, 113, 118, 120, 124, 126, 129, 131-33, 154, 173-74, 179, 192-93, 195, 201, 205-7, 240, 248-49, 256-57, 263, 277, 282-84, 286-87

Fort Lennox, 290, 344-45

Fort Massachusetts, 50

Fort Michilimackinac, 158-59

Fort Miller, 52, 248, 251

Fort Montgomery, 424-25

Fort Moreau, 305, 367

Fort Niagara, 54, 56, 104, 112, 120, 129, 132, 279

Fort Nicholson, 52

Fort Number Four, 50, 120, 131, 151-52

Fort Ontario, 74

Fort Orange, 45, 46

Fort Oswego, 74, 120, 129, 137

Fort Richelieu, 46

Fort St. Anne, 366, 426

Fort St. Frédéric, 62, 65, 81, 84, 101, 104, 106, 108, 119, 124-26, 144, 146-49, 287, 342, 361, 394, 415-16

Fort St. Therese, 153

Fort Schuyler, 252

Fort Scott, 305, 367

Fort Stanwix, 252

Fort Ticonderoga, 17, 108, 111, 113, 119, 124, 126, 128, 133-34, 154, 164, 172-74, 178, 187-89, 191, 193, 195-97, 201, 208, 221-23, 229, 231, 239-42, 244-46, 248, 250-51, 253, 256, 258-59, 261, 265-66, 276, 282-87, 342-43, 359-60, 404-7, 414-15

Fort William Henry, 75-78, 87, 104, 122, 132, 138, 144, 147, 165, 276

Fouquet, L. M., 354, 366

Fouquet, Marshal Louis-Charles-Auguste, Comte de Belle-Isle, 86

Fouquet Hotel, 366-67, 374

Four Brothers Islands, 63-64, 67, 110, 128, 137, 179, 231, 243-44, 363, 419

Four Mile Post, 104

Fox (sloop), 298

Frances (sloop), 300-301

Francis, Ebenezer, 247, 260, 262, 265

Francis Saltus (steamboat), 351

Franklin, Benjamin, 52, 54

Franklin (steamboat), 331, 344

Fraser, Alexander, 216, 229

Fraser, Simon, 243, 245, 247, 255

Frazer, Persifer, 223

Fredenburgh, Charles de, 175, 182

Frost Jr., John, 155

Fuller, Archelaus, 81

Fulton, Robert, 317

Fulton First (steam vessel), 316, 318

Gage, Thomas, 81, 118, 135, 137, 147, 158-59, 172, 188, 197, 201, 209

Gamble, Peter, 322

Gansevoort, Peter, 252

Gates, Horatio, 177, 205-6, 208, 210-11, 214, 222, 225, 245-46, 251-53, 255-57, 260-61, 265, 387

Gates (row galley), 242, 247

General Butler (canal schooner), 380

General Greene (steamboat), 331

Germain, George, 222

Gideon King, 291

Gilbert Car Company, 407

Gilliland, Elizabeth Phagan, 173, 175

Gilliland, Henry P., 181

Gilliland, William, 170-82, 285, 363

Gilpin, Henry Dilworth, 332, 341

Girard, Antoine, 213

Gladwin, Major, 136-37

Glasier, Benjamin, 93

Gleaner (canal boat), 332

Glens Falls, N.Y., 340, 377, 389, 407-8, 412

Glens Falls Feeder Canal, 390

Glenwood Inn, 417

Goffe, John, 144

Goldsmith, Lieutenant, 222

Gordon, Adam, 171-73

Gordon, Patrick, 260

Gordon, William, 177

Gougou, 22-23

Graham, John H., 323

Grand Diable (row galley), 155, 162-64

Grand Isle, 110, 287, 367, 421

Grand Isle Steamboat Company, 378

Grant, Alexander, 110, 135, 137-38, 153-54

Grant, Francis, 119, 171-73

Grant, Ulysses S., 357, 408, 423

Great Back Bay, 421, 425-26

Great Bridge, 207, 240, 246, 256, 259

Great Chazy River, 173, 301, 305

Greene, Nathaniel, 264

Greenleaf, Moses, 246, 262, 264-65

Green Mountain Boys, 189-91, 193

Grenadier Redoubt (Crown Point), 189, 342

Grog Harbor, 418

Growler (sloop), 299

G. R. Sherman (steam ferry), 416

Hadden, James Murray, 213, 217

Hagglund, Lorenzo F., 219, 229, 232, 302, 367, 405

Haldimand, Frederick, 188

Hale, Nathan, 247, 261

Halfway Brook Post, 104

Hall, Basil, 274, 334, 349

Hall, Francis, 338

Hall, Margaret Hunter, 335

Hamilton, Frederick, 126, 131, 150

Hamilton, Paul, 298

Hamilton, Thomas, 274

Hammond, S. H., 354

Hampton, Wade, 301

Hancock, John, 197, 201, 208, 258

Hancock (gunboat), 195-96

Hands Cove, 191

Hardy, Constantine, 118

Harris, Israel, 199

Hartley, Thomas, 177, 206, 222

Haskins, Nathan, 354

Haviland, William, 108, 112, 118-20, 122, 148, 152, 154, 156, 162, 164-65

Hawthorne, Nathaniel, 17, 342, 344

Hay, Charles, 284

Hay, Udney, 259, 284

Heacock, Ezra, 190

Henderson, James, 108, 126

Henley, Robert, 305, 310, 313, 320-21

Herbin, Frederic-Louis, 70

Herkimer, Nicholas, 252

Herrick, Samuel, 191-92

H. G. Tisdale (tug), 394, 396

Hicks, William, 311, 320

Highgate Springs, 426

Hildreth, Michah, 223

Hill, John, 248, 266

Hiram Walker (canal schooner), 380

Hitchcock, Achsah Jordon, 240, 258

Hitchcock, Enos, 238-40, 245-48, 251-53, 255-66

Hocquart, Sieur Gilles, 362

Hog Island, 426

Holden, David, 154, 156, 162, 166

Holmes, Robert, 153-54

Homans, Benjamin, 317

Hopkins, John Henry, 364

Hopkins, Joseph, 129-30, 132

Horse-powered ferries, 337, 352-53

Hoskins and Ross, 380

Hospital Island, 155

Hotel Ausable, 374, 421

Hotel Burlington, 374

Hotel Champlain, 372, 374, 421-22

Hotel Columbia, 424

Hotel St. Frédéric, 287

Hotel Windsor, 374

Howe, George Augustus, 79, 81, 89, 95, 102, 121, 147-48, 239, 359

Howe, William, 223, 239, 242, 251, 264

Hubbardton, VT., 247-48, 261

Hubbell, Julius, 311

Hudson Falls, N.Y., 345, 389

Hudson Valley Railway Company, 389

Hunter (sloop), 298-99

Hurlbut, John, 108

Hurons, 28-29, 42, 45

Hutchings, Benjamin, 126

Icicle (sloop), 303, 313-14, 320

Inflexible (ship), 212-13, 215, 217, 220, 229, 231, 242-43, 264, 291

Invincible (radeau), 106, 109, 118, 134

Iroquois, 16, 22, 28-30, 37-38, 45-47, 50, 66, 244, 361, 363

Irving House, 426

Island Villa, 425

Isle-aux-Noix, 94, 109, 112-13, 118, 128, 121, 129-30, 132-35, 137-38, 150, 152-56, 160-65, 169, 171, 195, 206, 213, 223, 227, 261, 289, 299-301, 303-4, 308, 317, 345

Isle La Motte, 46, 64, 153-54, 162, 195, 211, 213, 225, 243, 308, 367, 405, 424, 426

Isle St. Michel, 182, 422

Izard, George, 305, 307

Izard, Ralph, 171-72, 175

Jacobs, Captain, 92, 126

James, Henry, 364

Jay's Treaty, 289, 424

Jefferson, Thomas, 277, 284, 287-88, 297

Jenks, Samuel, 154, 162, 164-65, 179

Jersey Battery, 264-65

Jewett, Benjamin, 82
Jogues, Father Isaac, 45-46
Johnson, William, 52, 56, 81, 92-93, 95, 115, 120, 132, 144, 158, 281, 287,358-59
Jones, William, 295, 300-302, 304-5, 321, 323
Jungström, Lars, 51-52
Juniper Island, 344, 364, 419
Juno (sloop), 298
Jupiter (sloop), 298
Justin, Joshua H., 323

Kalm, Peter, 44-45, 51-52, 54-70, 180
Katherine (schooner), 192
Keeseville, N.Y., 365-66, 406
Kennedy, Quinton, 126-27, 131-32, 150
King, Gideon, 299
King George's War, 45, 50, 57, 62, 143
King Hendrick, 49
King Philips's War, 147
King's Bay, 153
King's Garden, 342
King's Rangers, 160
King William's War, 46
Kisensik, 78
Knox, Henry, 197
Knox, Robert, 214, 222
Kosciuszko, Thaddeus, 241, 245, 248, 252

La Brochette (sloop), 112, 123, 129, 138, 153-54, 161, 164, 172
La Chute River, 37, 81, 87, 89, 91, 94, 107, 120, 172, 245, 250, 256, 265, 416
Lacolle River, 227
Lafayette, Marquis de, 341, 363
Lafitau, Father Joseph, 40
La Galette, 120, 129, 137
Lake Champlain Associates, Inc., 302

Lake Champlain Maritime Museum, 18, 219, 229, 232, 241, 247, 310, 316, 392
Lake Champlain monster, 36, 376-77
Lake Champlain Yacht Club, 376-77, 420
Lake George Steamboat Company, 351, 377
Lake Luzerne, 355-57
Lake Memphremagog, 150-51
Lake St. Sacrement, 56, 61-62, 87-88
Lake View House, 366, 374
Lambert, John, 334
La Musquelongy (sloop), 112, 123, 129, 137-38, 153-54, 161, 164, 172, 174-75
Land Crab (vessel), 242
Land Tortoise (radeau), 83-84, 105, 109, 134
Larrabee's Lake House, 415
Larrabee's Point, 360, 392, 415
Latimer, Henry, 296
La Vallette, Elie, 304, 310, 317-18, 322
La Vigilante (schooner), 65, 110-11, 123, 129, 136-37, 155-56, 162, 164, 172
Lawrence House, 365
Le Don de Dieu (ship), 26-27, 405
Le Dossu d' Hébécourt, Louis-Philippe, 107, 119
Lee, Charles, 82
Lee, William, 315
Lee (cutter), 209, 211, 221, 242, 291
Lee House, 416
Legge, William, 173, 188
Le Roux, Bartholomew, 95
L'Esturgeon (sloop), 112, 123, 129, 138, 153-54, 161, 164, 172
Levasseur, Nicolas-René, 129
Lévis, François de, 79, 81, 83, 87, 90-94

Liberty (schooner), 193, 195-96, 207, 209-10, 213-14, 221,225-26,242,247,265, 291
Liford, Thomas, 260
Ligonier, John, 102-3, 115
Ligonier Bay, 112, 154, 162, 243
Ligonier Point, 179, 219, 231, 243
Ligonier (radeau), 109-10, 118, 133-36, 152, 154, 161
Lincoln, Benjamin, 252-53, 289, 291
Lincoln, Rufus, 248
Linnaeus, Carl, 51
Linnet (brig), 303, 309-10, 312-14, 316, 320-21, 358
Little Chazy River, 309
Lone Rock Point, 364
Long, Pierce, 246, 265
Longcroft, Edward, 215-16, 219
Loring, Joshua, 104-5, 108-10, 120-23, 129-30, 133-37
Lossing, Benson J., 199, 316, 359
Lotbinière Battery, 172, 285, 342, 359, 392, 414
Louisbourg, 79, 84, 103, 123, 126, 147
Louis Clearing Bay, 418
Lowe, Abram, 182
Loyal Convert (gunboat), 212, 215, 229, 242, 291
Lozier Motor Company, 423
Ludlow (gunboat), 301, 308
Luminism, 409, 411
Lundeberg, Philip, 219
Lusignan, Paul-Louis Daze-mard, 56-57, 62, 70
Lutwidge, Skeffington, 242, 247
Lydius, John, 52, 361
Lyman, Phineas, 119, 122
Lyon, Lemuel, 81

MacClintock, Samuel, 156, 162

Macdonough, Lucy Ann Shaler, 297, 299, 302, 317-18
Macdonough, Thomas, 294-305, 307-14, 316-23, 329, 358, 422
MacIntosh, James, 263
MacKay, Alexander, 349
MacKay, Ensign, 112, 136
MacKay, Francis, 182
Macomb, Alexander, 305, 307, 314, 323
Macon Bill, 298
Madison, James, 277, 284, 287, 298, 304
Manning, James, 216
Mansfield, L. W., 354
Maquam (steamboat), 378-79, 402
Marais, Sieur de, 28, 30, 33
Maria (schooner), 212-14, 220, 229, 231, 242-43, 289, 291
Marin de la Malgue, Joseph, 84, 149, 358, 387, 414
Marin de la Malgue, Paul, 387
Mars (sloop), 303
Marshall Beresford (gunboat), 311, 320
Martineau, Harriet, 335
Massachusetts Committee of Safety, 193, 200
May, Abigail, 284-85
McAuley, William, 177
McCoy, Thomas, 222
McCrea, Jane, 277
McDonough, James, 296-97
McGhie, James, 310-11
McIntosh, Alexander, 263
McKenzie, Hugh, 130
McKinley, William, 357, 374
McMullen, Andrew, 151
McNeil, Charles, 352
McNeil Cove, 288
Merriman, Samuel, 110, 118
Millan, John, 157-58
Missisquoi Bay, 150, 153, 368, 426

Missisquoi Hotel, 368
Missisquoi Springs, 368
Missisquoi Springs Hotel, 368
Missisquoi Valley House, 368
Mohawks, 16-17, 28, 47, 50
Monckton, Robert, 102
Moncrief, Thomas, 133
Monroe, James, 330
Montagnais, 27-29, 38, 42
Montcalm, Louis-Joseph de, 72-74, 78-95, 122, 126, 131, 149, 165, 359
Montcalm Landing, 352, 377, 414
Monteath, Walter L., 323
Montgomery, N. L., 323
Montgomery, Richard, 177, 194, 197, 291, 330
Montgomery (sloop), 300-301, 304, 308, 316
Montgomery, William Stone, 266
Montreal (steamboat), 351, 358, 378
Montresor, James, 80, 104, 118, 126, 129, 131
Montresor, John, 129, 176, 179, 189
Monts, Pierre du Gua de, 23-26
Moody, Thomas, 161-63, 165
Mooers, Benjamin, 300
Moore, Henry, 175
Morgan, Daniel, 238, 253
Moriah, 360
Morison, Samuel Eliot, 30
Mott, Edward, 190-92, 200
Motte, Captain de la (Pierre Saint-Paul, Sieur de la Motte-Lussière), 46, 367, 426
Mount Defiance, 81, 245-46, 265, 285
Mount Hope, 245, 265
Mount Independence, 207-8, 222-24, 239-42, 244-47, 251, 253, 256, 259, 261-66, 285, 404

Mt. Mansfield House, 365
Murray, Antoine, 394
Murray, James, 112, 152, 156
Murray, William H. H., 15, 17, 373, 394-96, 408
Murray (gunboat), 311, 313, 320
Murray's Raid, 300

Nelson, Thomas, 351, 354
Nettle (galley), 302, 308
New Hampshire Grants, 189-91
New Haven (gunboat), 209-10
New Jersey (gunboat), 209, 211, 219, 231, 242, 291
New York Barge Canal, 402
New York (gunboat), 213, 219, 221, 231, 246
Nichols, Joseph, 94
Nicholson, Francis, 47, 49, 54
Nipissings, 57
Nixon, John, 248
Nonintercourse Act of 1809, 298
Northern Inland Lock Navigation Company, 277-78, 231
Northern Tour, 329, 332, 354
North Hero Island, 213, 424-26
Northwest Passage, 158-59
Norton, Ichabod, 205
Norton, John, 50

Oakes Ames/Champlain II (steamboat), 351, 358
Oblenis, Charles, 408
O'Callaghan, E. B., 356
O. J. Walker (canal schooner), 380
Olabaratz, Joannis-Galand d', 112, 129, 137
Onion River Company, 191
Ord, Thomas, 105-6, 109, 118, 122, 129, 134, 161-62, 176

Oswald, Eleazer, 190, 192
Ottawas, 57, 244
Otter Creek, 16, 127, 175, 209, 288, 301-4, 362-63, 378, 418

Pabst, Frank, 310
Paleoindians, 16
Palisades, 418
Panton, VT., 231
Parker, John, 78-79
Parkman, Francis, 143
Parsons, Samuel, 189-91
Paterson, John, 246, 259
Paterson's Island, 251
Pausch, Georg, 216-17
Pavilion, 404
Pell, Joshua, Jr., 223, 242
Pell, Sarah G. T. , 207, 404
Pell, Stephen H. P., 207, 209, 404, 415
Pell, William Ferris, 342, 404, 415
Pellew, Edward, 217, 229
Pelots Point, 426
Perkins, Nathan, 277, 288
Perry, Oliver Hazard, 301, 320, 322
Perry, Raymond H., 322
Petit Diable (row galley), 155, 164
Phelps, Benajah, 322
Phelps, Elisha, 190
Phelps, Noah, 190, 200
Phelp's House, 359
Philadelphia (gunboat), 209-10, 220, 229, 231-32, 405
Phillips, William, 245
Philo, Hiram, 412
Phips, Sir William, 47
Phoenix (steamboat), 341, 354, 358
Phoenix II (steamboat), 329, 331, 340-41, 364
Pilotois, 35
Pinflats, 396
Pitt, William, 79, 92, 95, 103, 105, 108, 112-13, 115, 122, 126

Plains of Abraham, 85, 94, 126, 198
Platt, Charles T., 317, 323
Plattsburgh, N. Y., 175, 301, 304, 307-8, 311, 314, 318, 320, 330, 334, 366, 374-75, 378, 380, 422-23
Plattsburgh Barracks, 405, 423
Plattsburgh Bay, 295, 299-300, 310, 421
Plattsburgh Movement, 423
Point au Fer, 134, 153, 178, 213, 222, 243, 289, 304-5, 309, 424
Point au Roche, 300
Pomeroy, Seth, 144
Pont-Gravé, François, 22, 24, 26-28
Poor, Enoch, 246, 259
Popham (gunboat), 311, 320
Port Henry, 360-62, 375, 416
Port Henry Iron Company, 361
Port Kent, 180, 365, 376, 395, 421
Port-Royal, 24-25
Porter, Elisha, 207
Posson, Charles H., 374, 394-95
Potter, James, 305
Potter, Nathaniel, 158-59, Pouchot, Pierre, 80-82, 95, 120, 151
Poulin de Courval Cressé, Louis-Pierre, 129
Poutrincourt, Jean de Bien-court de, 25
Power, Tyrone, 329, 332-42, 344-45
Power, Tyrone Edmund, 338-39
Pownall, Thomas, 104
Prätorius, Christian, 245
Preble (sloop), 300-301, 304, 308, 310-11, 316, 320
Premier, Captain, 225-26
Prescott, Robert, 126
President (sloop), 298-99, 301, 304, 308, 316

Prevost, George, 305, 307-8, 311, 314
Prideaux, John, 104, 120
Pring, Daniel, 300-302, 308, 310, 316, 320, 362, 426
Pringle, Thomas, 214, 219-20
Printup, William, 52
Providence (gunboat), 209-11, 226
Putnam, Israel, 79, 84, 89, 127, 149, 358, 414
Putnam, Rufus, 89, 93
Putnam Creek, 231
Put's Rock, 358, 414
Pyle, Howard, 392, 394

Quasi War, 296
Quebec Act of 1774, 113, 189, 198
Queen Anne's War, 47, 54, 362
Queen's American Rangers, 160

Radeaux, 108, 125, 154-55, 161-62
Ramezay, Jean-Baptiste-Ni-colas-Roch de, 86
Raynham, Mark, 313
Rea, Caleb, 93
Records, Daniel, 320
Reed, Captain, 226
Reid, John, 136
Reindeer (steamboat), 378
Rensselaer and Saratoga Railroad, 351-52, 365, 377
Revenge (schooner), 196, 207, 209-10, 219, 226, 231, 242, 247, 265
Riedesel, Frederika von, 255
Riedesel, Freidrich Adol-phus, 213, 243, 247, 251
Rigal, Sieur, 129
Rigaud de Vaudreuil de Cavagnial, Pierre de (gov-ernor-general), 74, 77-79, 84-85, 93-94, 112-13, 138, 156

Rigaud de Vaudreuil, François-Pierre de, 77, 83, 86-87, 132

Rising Sun (sloop), 300

Riverside Cemetery, 322

Robbins, Ammi, 207

Roberts, Kenneth, 132, 143

Robertson, James, 313

Roche Regio, 361-62, 419

Rock Dunder, 364, 419

Rock Harbor, 418

Rockwell, Ell B., 408

Rogers, Elizabeth Brown, 157

Rogers, Platt, 178

Rogers, Richard, 147

Rogers, Robert, 79, 84, 108, 121, 126, 131-34, 142-44, 146-66, 291, 414, 424

Rogers, Thomas, 146

Rogers Island, 145-46

Rogers Rock, 88

Romans, Bernard, 190, 192

Roosevelt, Theodore, 295, 403, 423

Ross, Daniel, 178

Ross, Henry R., 352, 363

Rouses Point, 330, 368, 374, 378, 395, 424

Rouses Point Bridge, 395, 424

Row galleys (1758-1760), 106, 122, 127, 154-55, 162-63, 207-8, 210

Royal Edward (schooner), 289

Royal George (ship), 242-43, 245, 264, 291

Royal Savage (schooner), 195-96, 207, 209-10, 214-18, 220, 227, 302, 366, 405

Royce's Hotel, 363

Ruggles, Timothy, 110, 119, 135, 161

R. W. Sherman/America (steamboat), 351

Sabbath Day Point, 78-79, 118, 173

Sagard, Gabriel, 40

Sailly, Peter, 277, 285, 288-89, 302, 316

Sainte-Croix Island, 23-24

Salmon River, 181

Saranac River, 181-82, 305, 307, 314-15, 366-67, 405

Saranac (steamboat), 351

Saratoga, N. Y., 50, 52, 178, 238, 255

Saratoga (ship), 301, 304-5, 307-8, 310, 312-16, 318, 322-23, 340, 358

Sarrebource de Pontleroy, Nicolas, 79-80, 88

Scammell, Alexander, 259

Schank, John, 219

Schomberg, Alexander, 135

Schuyler, John, 47, 175, 179

Schuyler, Peter, 50, 119, 122, 136, 179

Schuyler, Philip, 159, 176-77, 179, 194-95, 206-7, 209, 219, 240-42, 245, 248, 251-52, 263, 277, 387

Schuyler (gunboat), 195-96

Schuyler Island, 67, 112, 154, 179, 219, 229, 231

Schuylerville, N. Y., 251-52, 256, 386

Scott, Thomas, 225

Seaman, Isaac, 209

Selkirk, Sibyl Blake, 385

Senezergues de La Rodde, Etienne-Guillaume de, 94

Seth G. Cowles (canal boat), 382

Sewall, Henry, 264

Shannon (sloop), 300

Shelburne Bay, 299

Shelburne Farms, 376

Shelburne Harbor, 300, 351, 358, 419

Shelburne Museum, 376

Shelburne Point, 419

Sheldon, Mary, 314-15

Sheridan, Philip H., 408-9

Shirley, William, 51, 57, 103, 120, 146

Shoreham, VT., 191-92, 360

Shute, Daniel, 93

Silliman, Benjamin, 329-30, 332, 340, 344

Silver Stream, 181

Simcoe (gunboat), 320

Simonds, Captain, 209, 211, 303-4, 309, 315

Sir George Prevost (gunboat), 320

Sir James Yeo (gunboat), 313, 320

Sir Sidney Beckwith (gunboat), 320

Sjöman, Anna Magaretha, 54

Skene, Philip, 172-73, 175, 192-93, 201, 208, 249, 251, 361

Skenesborough, 191-92, 208, 210, 248-50, 253, 265-66, 282

Skenesborough Museum, 358

Skinner, Henry, 106

Sloan, James, 310

Small, John, 120

Smith, Joseph, 95, 317

Smith, Sidney, 298-99

Smith, Stephen Keese, 311

Snedeker, Florence Watters, 376

Snow Shoe (transport vessel), 106, 173

South Bay, 249, 358, 393

South Hero Island, 110, 287, 322, 424-26

Specht, Johann Friedrich, 241, 251, 266

Spicer, Abel, 82

Spital, John, 95

Spitfire (gunboat), 209-11, 231

Split Rock, 50, 221, 231, 260, 288, 348, 361-62, 394-95

Split Rock Iron Mine, 418

Split Rock Mountain, 417-18

Squires' Spring House, 425

St. Albans, VT., 332, 368, 378, 426

St. Armand Bay, 213, 225-26

St. Clair, Arthur, 207, 245-48, 251, 262, 265, 285

St. Francis, 132, 151

St. Jean, 62, 64-65, 124, 128, 152-53, 156, 165-66, 193-97, 200, 206, 210, 212-13, 222, 242, 260, 278, 283, 290-91, 344, 349, 352, 385, 396

St. Leger, Barry, 252

St. Onge, Joseph Payant, 62, 65, 110, 112, 129, 137

Stanley, Edward, 340

Stansbury, John, 313, 322

Starbuck, David R., 207, 263

Stark, John, 127, 131, 144, 147, 250-51

Starke, John, 219

State University of New York at Plattsburgh, 423

Stephens, John, 192

Stevens, Ebenezer, 265

Stevens, Enos, 57

Stevens, Phineas, 57, 61, 120

Stevens, Samuel, 150-51

Stewart, Jahiel, 215, 217, 229

Stewart, Peter, 181

Stiles, Eli, 227

Stocker, James, 179

Stoddard, Benjamin, 59, 61

Stoddard, Emily Doty, 413

Stoddard, Helen Augusta Potter, 407, 412

Stoddard, Seneca Ray, 366, 374, 379-80

Stone, Enos, 245, 264-65,

Stoughton, John, 174

Strong, Samuel, 307

Stuart, James, 335, 342

Styles, R. S., 354

Sugar Loaf Hill, 245

Sullivan, John, 206, 264

Swanton, VT., 300

Sweetser, Charles H., 354

Tadoussac, 22, 26, 42

Taft, William Howard, 405-6

Taintor, Charles Newhall, 354

Talon de Boulay, Angéli-que-Louise, 73

Taylor, Nathan, 263

Tecumseh (gunboat), 320

Tercentenary Celebration, 17, 405-6

Terrot, Charles, 229

Thacher, James, 241, 251, 265-66

Thacher, John, 227

Thayendanagea (Joseph Brant), 252

The Twins (auto ferry), 424

Thomas, John, 161

Thompson, Robert Means, 404

Thompson, Zadock, 354, 360

Thornton, Arthur, 303, 362

Three Mile Point, 244-45, 264

Thunderer (radeau), 212-14, 229, 242, 245, 265, 291

Thwing, Samuel, 323

Ticonderoga, 37, 104, 106, 352, 359, 362, 378, 393, 416

Ticonderoga (schooner), 301, 303, 307-8, 310-11, 321-22, 358, 402, 405, 420

Tinkham, Seth, 79

Tocqueville, Alexis de, 335

Townshend, George, 102, 121

Townshend, Roger, 121

Treaty of Aix-la-Chappelle, 51, 74, 102-3

Treaty of Ghent, 317, 330

Treaty of Paris, 362

Treaty of Ryswick, 47

Treaty of Utrecht, 49, 362

Trembleau Hall, 374, 420

Trepezec, Sieur, 88-89

Trollope, Francis, 274, 284, 335

Trout Brook, 148

True, Henry, 118, 131

Trumbull, John, 222-23, 245, 265

Trumbull (row galley), 213-14, 217-21, 223, 226-27, 229, 242, 246, 256, 291

Turk, William, 318

Turner, George, 151

Tute, James, 158

Tweed, William Marcy, 418

Twiss, William, 245, 289

United States Hotel, 316, 360

United States (steamboat), 350, 358

University of Vermont, 330, 364

Valcour Island, 66, 173, 175, 181-83, 211, 213-14, 216, 226, 405, 421

Vanderbilt, William Henry, 376

Van Ness House, 365, 374

Vanstockum, Ken, 310

Vanstockum, William, 310

Vergennes, VT., 288, 301-7, 320, 341, 362-63, 378, 405, 418

Vermont (steamboat), 302, 323, 330, 419

Vermont II (steamboat), 350, 358, 378, 401, 408

Vermont III (steamboat), 401-2, 414, 417, 419, 424

Vermont Central Railroad, 365

Victor (steamboat), 417

Vigne, Godfrey, 345

Viper (galley), 308

Vose, Joseph, 206

Wadman, Arthur, 198, 200

Waggon (sloop), 130, 132, 155-56

Walker, Hovendon, 49

Wallace, Edwin R., 354, 367, 374

Warm, Jacobus de, 46, 287

Warner, Seth, 191-93, 195, 247

Warner, Seth A., 214, 226

Warren, Benjamin, 253

Warren, Joseph, 190

Warren County Agricultural Society, 355

Washington, George, 159, 206-7, 240, 242, 251, 257, 262-64, 282

Washington, Martha, 258

Washington (row galley), 82, 213, 217, 220-21, 223, 227, 229, 231, 244, 291

Washington (steamboat), 331

Wasmus, Julius Friedrich, 222-23, 225, 242-43, 252

Wasp (sloop), 300-301

Waterbury, David, 82, 196, 214, 218, 220-22, 227

Waterford, 332, 383-86, 403

Water Lily (steamboat), 378

Water Witch (steamboat/schooner), 331

Watson, Elkanah, 284-85, 288, 365

Watson, John, 177, 179

Watson, Winslow C., 216, 354, 365, 419

Wayne, Anthony, 94, 207, 224, 245

Wayside Inn, 357

Webb, Daniel, 74

Webb, Electra Havemeyer, 376

Webb, Eliza Vanderbilt, 376

Webb, J. Watson, 376

Webb, William Seward, 376

Webster-Ashburton Treaty, 330

Weld, Alexandria Home, 280

Weld, Charles Richard, 280

Weld, Isaac, 272-91

Welden House, 368

Wellington (gunboat), 320

Wells, Bayze, 205-6, 208-11, 213, 220, 222, 224, 227, 229, 231

Wentworth, Benning, 144

Western Inland Lock Navigation Company, 277

West Haven, 282

Weston, Richard, 335, 340

Westport, N.Y., 351, 353, 362, 378, 416

Westport Inn, 416-17

Whallon Bay, 361

Whitcomb, Benjamin, 211, 260

Whitehall, N.Y., 247, 276-79, 281-82, 298-99, 316, 329-31, 340, 345, 352, 358, 378, 390-92, 414

Whiting, Nathan, 117

Wickham Marsh, 180

Wigglesworth, Edward, 214, 218, 220-21, 229, 231

Wigwam Martinique, 154

Wilkinson, James, 248, 259, 302

Willard, Joseph, 260

Williams, Samuel, 354

Willsboro, N.Y., 173-78, 181, 211, 231, 303, 376, 418

Willsboro Bay, 243

Wilmer (gunboat), 301

Wilson, Commissary, 136, 179

Wilson, J. Arbuthnot, 15, 377

Wilson, John, 128,

Winans, James, 302, 419

Winans, John, 298, 302, 419

Windmill Point, 65, 134, 153-54, 175, 211, 227, 291

Winooski (steamboat), 331

Winslow, John, 78

Winthrop, Fitzjohn, 46-47

Witherbee, Sherman, and Co., 287, 361, 416

Witherill Hotel, 367, 374, 423

Woedtke, Frederick William, 206

Wolfe, James, 84-85, 102-4, 126, 135, 138

Wood, Lemuel, 108, 164

Wood Creek, 47, 54-55, 84, 149, 247-50, 266, 277-78, 281

Woolsey, Melancthon T., 298

Wooster, Colonel David, 122

Wright, Frances, 17

Wrightson, John, 122

Wurts, George, 354

Wynkoop, Jacobus, 208-9

Young Island, 110

Youngs, White, 323

Zarzynski, Joseph, 105

Purple Mountain Press, founded in 1973, is a publishing company committed to producing the best original books of regional interest as well as bringing back into print significant older works. For a free catalog of more than 300 hard-to-find books about New York State, write Purple Mountain Press, Ltd., P.O. Box E3, Fleischmanns, New York 12430-0378, or call 914-254-4062, or fax 914-254-4476, or email Purple@catskill.net.

http://www.catskill.net/purple